Modern Financial Accounting

Nelson Series in Accounting and Finance

Consulting editor
John Perrin, Professor and Director of the Centre for Industrial
Economic and Business Research, University of Warwick

J.M. Cope
Business Taxation

G.A. Lee
Modern Financial Accounting *Second edition*

T.A. Lee
Income and Value Measurement

T.A. Lee
Company Financial Reporting

J.M. Samuels and F.M. Wilkes
The Management of Company Finance *Second edition*

G A Lee

University of Nottingham

Modern Financial Accounting

Second Edition

Nelson

Thomas Nelson and Sons Ltd
Lincoln Way Windmill Road Sunbury-on-Thames Middlesex TW16 7HP
P.O. Box 73146 Nairobi Kenya

Thomas Nelson (Australia) Ltd
19–39 Jeffcott Street West Melbourne Victoria 3003

Thomas Nelson and Sons (Canada) Ltd
81 Curlew Drive Don Mills Ontario

Thomas Nelson (Nigeria) Ltd
8 Ilupeju Bypass PMB 1303 Ikeja Lagos

First published in Great Britain 1973
Reprinted 1974
Second edition 1975
Reprinted 1976
Copyright © G.A. Lee 1973, 1975

ISBN 0 17 761045 X (boards)
     0 17 771056 X (paper)

Printed in Great Britain by Butler & Tanner Ltd
Frome and London

To my wife

Contents

Preface to the first edition

The author's aim in writing this book has been to present to more advanced students of accountancy in universities, polytechnics, and establishments of further education, and in training for professional qualifications, a comprehensive view of financial accounting in Great Britain in the latter half of the twentieth century. In so doing he has sought to break away from the traditional technique-orientated approach and, on the foundation of an assumed knowledge of basic double entry book-keeping, to build up a solid understanding of the essential nature of the art—for it is not yet a science—and of the intellectual presuppositions upon which modern practice rests, before proceeding to expound the different forms of accounting which English law and business practice impose upon non-corporate and corporate enterprises.

In *Part 1*, Chapter 1 seeks to present the knowledge already possessed by most students in a new light, and to organize it more rigorously and coherently than heretofore, as well as to introduce something of the historical background to present day thinking and practice. Chapters 2 and 3 are designed to exhibit financial accounting in the wider context of accounting in general, and to show its connections with management accounting and data processing. Chapter 4, which the author believes to be an innovation in textbooks of this type (at least in Britain), is an attempt to guide the reader through the mazes of modern accounting theory—i.e. in general, that of the last dozen years—and to provide intellectual criteria against which may be evaluated the expositions, in Chapters 5, 6, and 7, of conventional methods of computing net asset valuations and periodic profits and losses, and of suggestions for reforming the procedures to allow, in particular, for the chronic inflation which now seems to be a permanent fact of economic life. Chapter 8 considers modern approaches to the use of financial accounting techniques in controlling the operations of subordinate managements, at home and abroad, and in providing them with goals against which their performance may be rationally evaluated by the principal management.

Part 2 is more orthodox in content, and perhaps calculated to appeal more directly to students for the final examinations of the main accountancy and allied professional bodies. The legal aspects of partnership and limited company accounting are exhaustively dealt with, and due weight given (as in Part 1) to the pronouncements of the Accounting Standards Steering Committee and the requirements of the London Stock Exchange and the Panel on Take-overs and Mergers. At the same time the interests of the student of financial management and of financial analysis have not been neglected, and the author has sought to build an adequate bridge between accountancy proper and these cognate disciplines as well as to connect the former with taxation studies. A full set of essay topics and exercises, including many questions from past professional examinations, is provided at the end of the book.

Acknowledgements are due to the Institute of Chartered Accountants in England and Wales, the Institute of Chartered Accountants of Scotland, the Association of Certified Accountants, the Institute of Cost and Management Accountants, and the Institute of Municipal Treasurers and Accountants, for permission to include questions from their past Final Examination papers; to Mr A. G. Piper, of the Department of Accounting, University of Birmingham, for most conscientious reading and criticism of the whole manuscript, and for many very helpful suggestions; to Mrs J. O. Tomkinson and Mrs M. Wass for typing the manuscript; and to the author's whole family, for their moral support, patience, and forbearance in the many months when he was able to give them so little of his time and attention.

G.A.L.

Preface to the second edition

The gratifying success of this work among lecturers and students in British and Irish universities, polytechnics and colleges, and its adoption as a prescribed text by the Institute of Chartered Accountants of Scotland, have made imperative a second edition within two years of the first. The urgency has been increased by the numerous changes in the accounting field since 1972, and their effects have been incorporated in the revised text.

Reform of the U.K. taxation system in 1973 has necessitated the rewriting of parts of Chapters 9 and 12, and minor changes elsewhere. No new company legislation has been passed, but the Accounting Standards Steering Committee has issued six new Statements of Standard Accounting Practice (with amendments to two earlier ones) and four unfinalized Exposure Drafts, while the Stock Exchange regulations, and the City Code on Take-overs and Mergers, have been revised. The U.K. and the Republic of Ireland have entered the EEC, and implementation of an eventual Fourth Directive of the Council looms in the background. The International Accounting Standards Committee has been formed, and to date has issued one Standard and two unfinalized Exposure Drafts.

In accounting theory, the most radical developments have been in accounting for inflation. The evil has grown rapidly worse since 1972, and accountancy has not stood still in face of it. The ASSC has acted in time, issuing first ED8 and then Provisional SSAP No. 7, while the government has set up the Sandilands Committee of Inquiry. All this has compelled the author to rewrite many pages of Chapter 7, and to attempt a new appraisal of the rival claims of current purchasing power, and replacement cost, accounting.

The essay topics and exercises in the Appendix have been thoroughly revised, and new matter added or substituted from professional examination papers since 1971. Some of the new questions have been taken from the examinations of the Institute of Chartered Accountants in Ireland, as some recognition of the very generous reception with which *Modern Financial Accounting* has met in both parts of the island; the Institute's courteous permission to do so is acknowledged, as well as the renewed permission to use such material from the Institute of Chartered Accountants in England and Wales. The Institute of Chartered Accountants of Scotland, the Association of Certified Accountants, the Institute of Cost and Management Accountants, and the Chartered Institute of Public Finance and Accountancy. The author also repeats his tribute to the moral support, patience and forbearance of his family in a trying period.

G.A.L.

Part 1 Accounting principles and practice

1
Nature, methodology, and development of accounting

Every human organization, however simple, requires written records of matters which the management or administration needs to keep in mind, as guides to routine action, the taking of decisions, the formulation of general rules, the making of policy, and the legal validation of the organization's status, procedures, and relationships with other organizations or with individuals. Among the most important matters of record are dealings in money or money's worth, and these are the province of *accounting,* or the keeping of accounts.

1.1 Nature of accounting

Accounts may thus be defined as the financial records of an organization, articulated to form an accounting system, and accounting as the activity of constructing and operating such a system. This in turn has two branches: i the making of routine records from day to day, in prescribed form and according to set rules, of all events which affect the financial state of the organization; and ii the summarization from time to time of the information contained in the records, its presentation in significant form to interested parties, and its interpretation as an aid to decision-making by these parties. Branch i is called *book-keeping,* or more generally *data processing*—especially where mechanical, electro-mechanical, or electronic devices are used to record, manipulate, and arrange the data, which in sophisticated modern systems include information of a statistical as well as financial nature. Branch ii is *accountancy,* the principal concern of this book.

All accounting information is a series of statements about a particular organization in terms of money, and normally in the currency of the country where the accounts are kept. The accounting system forms an arithmetical model of the organization's financial state at all times, and registers every change in that state over time—or rather, such changes as the system is designed to register. That is the nature of all such systems. Their usefulness for various purposes—internal control of the organization's money and other property, provision of management information, appraisal of the financial soundness or profitability of an undertaking, and so forth—is a function of the extent to which data entering the system are analysed, and of the manner in which they are classified and arranged within it.

The degree of elaboration depends on the nature and amount of financial information required by management, and sometimes extends to the setting-up of one or more accounting sub-systems within the main system, such as its division into financial and costing sub-systems, or the keeping of self-contained accounts at branches, as well as at head office. Sometimes, also, two or more self-contained accounting systems, or rather the summaries derived from them, are integrated to form a set of accounts of higher order, representing the financial position and recent history of a 'super-organization', such as a group of companies under common control. Finally, attempts have been made to construct 'social accounts' or 'macro-accounts' for a whole national economy and its various sectors; the techniques have great possibilities, but are limited as yet by the unsuitability as accounting data of many of the economic aggregates necessarily employed.[1]

1.2 Postulates of accounting

Accounting began, historically, as a purely practical discipline—a response by commercial men and public officials to the need to keep orderly and coherent financial records, and to 'render an account of their stewardship' to those who had entrusted them with money or goods to be employed on their behalf. Serious inquiry into the intellectual foundations of the subject hardly began before the present century, and nothing radical was done until the second half. One of the most vexed questions has been that of *accounting principles*—the fundamental notions upon which practice is based. Early attempts to clarify them—for example, by the Institute of Chartered Accountants in England and Wales, the American Institute of Certified Public Accountants, and individual academics on both sides of the Atlantic—tended, up to about 1960, to consist of mere rationalizations of existing practices, themselves not wholly rational in all respects, or abstractions from conditions obtaining in the accounting systems of capitalist business, not all of them relevant to accounting in other organizations. In the last fifteen years or so, however, closer attention has been paid to the field, by professional bodies and by academics, and endeavours made to distinguish what is common to all accounting from what is peculiar to certain forms of it, what is rational from what is arbitrary, and what takes account of economic reality from what ignores or overrides it. Several lists of 'accounting principles' have been drawn up, variously analysed and with varying terminology, and all have provoked more or less of controversy.

It is not the author's intention to reproduce any of these lists as they stand, nor to criticize overtly any particular one of his predecessors, but rather to distil the essence of their thinking, in so far as it agrees with his own approach. What follows should therefore be read with appropriate reservations, and in no sense regarded as final or authoritative.

In particular, there has been much discussion of the nature and content of the *postulates*—or, as some would say, the axioms—of accounting. These may be defined as the fundamental ideas upon which the entire intellectual structure of the discipline rests, and which are not susceptible of proof within the framework thereof. Some quite long lists of 'postulates' have been produced (a celebrated one, in 1962, contained fourteen propositions), but objections have been raised to them, that they include notions which are not essential to all types of accounting, or which are logically derivable from other propositions within the field. The author's own opinion is that the minimum set of postulates, for all financial accounting systems as at present understood, consists of three concepts, namely: **i** entity; **ii** money measurement; and **iii** time interval.

1.2.1 The entity postulate

An accounting system is a set of statements about the financial position of an entity at any point in time, and about changes in that position through time.

The word *entity* needs to be carefully defined. It is not the same thing as 'organization', or 'firm', or 'company', for these include many things not covered

---

[1] See: T. Gambling, *Societal Accounting*, George Allen & Unwin, 1974.

by an accounting system, such as the abilities of the owners, managers and workers, the structure of the managerial hierarchy, and the legal status of the undertaking. It is not synonymous with 'owners' or 'proprietors', since although entries may be made about them in the accounts they are not the exclusive concern of the system. An entity is best thought of as a set of resources (or *assets*) employed for a common purpose, and of obligations (or *liabilities*) incurred in furtherance of that purpose—such assets being owned, and liabilities owed, by one person, or by two or more persons associated for the common purpose aforesaid. The difference between the money values imputed to assets and to liabilities (see sub-section 1.2.2) is known as *equity*. In other words, an accounting system for an entity exhibits at any time the total values imputed to a set of assets uniquely included in that entity; to a set of liabilities uniquely payable out of those assets (at least in the first instance); and to a residual equity whose value at any time is determined by the values of the other components.

If assets, liabilities, and equity are denoted by their initial letters, the relationship may be stated algebraically as

$$E = A - L$$

or alternatively as

$$E + L = A$$

This, however, is valid only if A, L, and E are all taken as positive. In accounting theory it makes better sense to regard assets as positive and liabilities as negative, and to think of equity as numerically equal at all times to the algebraic sum of the other two but of opposite sign—being normally negative, since assets normally exceed liabilities in numerical value. Thus the *accounting identity* is better stated as

$$-E = A + L$$

or better still as

$$A + L + E = 0$$

This formulation emphasizes the fact that the entity has no legal personality—it cannot own assets or owe liabilities. It is a mere 'shell', containing a set of assets and liabilities which are legally those of one or more persons, either individuals or corporate bodies; and equity is most generally defined as the mere balance of the set. Hence, while an individual's wealth or 'net worth' (including his proprietary interest in his own business, if he has one) is normally positive (excess of assets over liabilities), since he legally owns the assets and owes the liabilities, the net worth of an accounting entity is zero at all times, since the entity is a mere abstraction, postulated in order to construct the accounting system.

The significance of equity varies with the type of organization. In unincorporated trading firms, where the assets are owned and liabilities owed individually by a sole trader or jointly by partners, equity is logically identified with the residual interest of the proprietors and, where there are more than one, needs to be partitioned among them according to agreed rules. A limited liability company, by contrast, is a body corporate, possessing legal personality and thus deemed to own its assets and owe its liabilities. Its personality, however, is a legal fiction, created to embody the interests of a large number of individuals (and/or corporate bodies, behind which stand other individuals) whose identities may change from time to time. Hence, the equity has to be partitioned into shares, of which a member of the company holds one or more, so that equity becomes identifiable with proprietary interests at one remove. The same applies to co-operative societies and building societies, and to unit trusts—with the difference, in the last-named, that there is no corporate status, and that the trustees, who legally own the trust's assets, stand in the place of the company in the foregoing analysis.

In capitalistic enterprises, then, all equity is ultimately ascribed to proprietors, individual or institutional, and subsumed under their private wealth. The private sector of the economy, though, includes a large number of bodies not conducted for profit, and generally unincorporated, such as trade unions, friendly societies, and clubs. These, too, are accounting entities, with assets and liabilities deemed to be owned, and owed, jointly by the members, and a residual equity, representing their joint interest. But this equity is not partitioned among them, since none has any identifiable share in it which can be reckoned as part of his private wealth—except for the (usually remote) possibility of a share-out in the event of liquidation of the association.

The public sector likewise contains many entities, usually incorporated, such as local authorities, government departments, and State corporations operating nationalized industries. Their main funds are raised in the form of loans (liabilities); but an element of equity, negative or positive in sign, appears as a result of under- or over-spending of revenues, or the making of profits or losses by trading concerns. To regard this as representing the 'interest' of any body of persons—even of the local community, or the whole nation—is dubious logic; there is no prospect of any distribution of surplus funds, and 'liquidation' of an entity of this kind generally means its replacement by, or merger with, one or more others which take over its assets and liabilities. These considerations illustrate the importance of defining equity more generally than is common in accounting textbooks.

Lastly, where a sub-system of accounts is set up within a main system (e.g. for a department or division of a firm), there is always the need for a control or total account, with balance equal, but of opposite sign, to the net balance of assets and liabilities. The accounts may then be regarded as those of a sub-entity within the main entity, and the net balance as its 'quasi-equity', subsumed under the main equity in the way that an individual's share in a business is subsumed under his total wealth. Conversely, it is possible (e.g. in a group of companies under common control) to consider a number of separate entities as component parts of one 'super-entity', and to combine their accounting summaries so as to exhibit a 'super-equity' for the group.

1.2.2 The money measurement postulate

All assets and liabilities of an entity can be quantified in terms of a single monetary unit, and the equity can be quantified as the algebraic sum, with sign reversed, of the assets and liabilities thus expressed.

In order to render assets and liabilities additive, and enable equity to be computed as a single number, it is necessary to reduce all these elements to a common measure. The only one applicable all round is money—i.e. the legal unit or sub-unit of currency in the country where the accounts are kept. Hence, all data entering the accounting system, if they do not consist already of sums of money in the appropriate currency, must be converted on some basis or other.

The application of money measurement to accounting data may seem obvious at first sight, but it involves many theoretical and practical difficulties which lie at the heart of all or most of the controversies that beset any deep discussion of modern accounting principles and practices. It is by no means self-evident that a non-monetary asset, such as a machine or an item of trading stock, can validly be represented by a particular sum of money at any given point in time—especially if there is no attempt, and no intent, to exchange the asset for money in the near future. Then, even granting the validity of the conversion, it is usually found that there is more than one reasonable basis for it, and that the reasonableness of the basis chosen depends on such factors as the purpose for which the accounts are prepared, management's assessment of future prospects, and changes in price levels, particular or general, since the asset was acquired. Further discussion of these matters will be found in Chapters 4 to 7. Here it suffices to point out that, since equity is merely the algebraic sum, with sign reversed, of a set of positive and negative money figures, variously derived, of varying validity or suitability, and subject to varying degrees of statistical error, it can seldom or never have an absolute value. It follows from this that changes in equity over time can rarely be accurately or unequivocally measured, and that virtually all accounting figures can only be approximations to truth, more or less valid for particular purposes and from particular standpoints. More elementary treatises tend to ignore these difficulties or assume them away; it is surely better to recognize them frankly from the outset.

1.2.3 The time interval postulate

Every change in the state of an entity can be recorded as occurring on a certain calendar day, and every statement of the position of the entity can be drawn up as at the end of one such day or the beginning of the next.

All that this amounts to is that, whereas changes of state of an entity occur continually, it is sufficient for normal purposes to divide up time into calendar days, and to record each change as occurring on the appropriate day.

It follows that an accounting period, if defined as the interval between the preparation of two position statements, must consist of one or more whole days. In practice such statements, and the accompanying summaries of changes of state since the previous position statement was prepared, are drawn up at longer intervals—four-weekly, monthly, or quarterly for reports to management, six-monthly or annually for statements to proprietors or persons external to the undertaking. Such periods are normally of equal length to facilitate comparison of one period's figures with another's, but there is no necessity for this in the nature of accounting itself, and periods of irregular length may be more suitable for particular purposes, such as reporting on the progress of a long-term project, stage by stage.

1.3 The dual aspect concept

To the three postulates enunciated in section 1.2 some authorities would add a dual aspect postulate, which might be formulated thus:

Every change in any one element of the assets, liabilities, or equity of an entity is accompanied by another change, numerically equal but of opposite sign, in another element.

This is, of course, the fundamental rule of double entry book-keeping, with which most readers of this work will already be familiar. The author, however, does not regard dual aspect as a postulate of accounting, but as a *corollary* of the three postulates already set out. Indeed, it rests principally upon the entity postulate, in that equity is so defined as to be always numerically equal, and of opposite sign, to the algebraic sum of assets and liabilities, in accordance with the accounting identity

$$A + L + E = 0$$

If the entity's position at the beginning of an accounting period is so formulated, then net numerical increments to the three components during that period may be represented by $(\Delta A, \Delta L, \Delta E)$. The position at the end of the period (when the algebraic sum of the new values of the components is still zero by definition) is thus

$$(A + \Delta A) + (L + \Delta L) + (E + \Delta E) = 0$$

Subtraction of the original identity leaves

$$\Delta A + \Delta L + \Delta E = 0,$$

i.e., the algebraic sum of the increments is also zero. This is true, whether the accounting period contains one set of changes or more than one; thus the analysis applies to a single set of changes. It follows that a change in one component must be accompanied by a numerically equal change, of opposite sign, in one of the others—or in both of them, their algebraic sum being likewise equal, and of opposite sign, to the first change. Similarly, if assets, liabilities, and equity are each partitioned into two or more elements, it can be shown that a change in any one element must be reflected by an equal and opposite change in one other, or in total in two or more others. (For the mathematically minded, formal proofs of these propositions are given in the Addendum to this chapter.)

The dual aspect concept may be fairly regarded as a tautology—a mere restatement of the three postulates in other terms. There is nothing magical about double entry, nor is it confined to accounts. Any set of variables able to take real positive, negative, or zero values, but not necessarily having a sum equal to zero, can be made into a double entry system (with zero sum at all times) by adding a further variable, so defined as to be always numerically equal, but of opposite sign, to the sum of the others. In accounting, equity is this variable.

1.4 Historical development

Accounting becomes practicable when its three postulates can be applied to human affairs. The time interval postulate is derived from the use of a calendar, and this in turn from observation of common astronomical phenomena; thus the concept has been recognized, at least implicitly, for thousands of years.

The other two postulates, though, are founded upon purely human conceptions. Entity stems from the legal ideas of personality and property, which lead to the possibility of exchange of goods and services in a community (initially by barter), and this again to the notions of rights and obligations (initially in terms of goods and services). All these notions, too, are of immense antiquity. Once they are accepted, records can be kept of holdings of, and transactions in, physical goods. Such records go back through many millenia, and specimens survive from ancient Mesopotamia, Egypt, Crete and Mycenae.

Money measurement, however, is possible only when a society begins to use money, and difficult until coinage is adopted. This was apparently invented in Lydia by 700 B.C., and fairly soon spread to other Mediterranean countries. Hence it is that accounting, in the true sense, first arose in classical Greece.

In Athens, the Parthenon building accounts were inscribed on marble tablets on the Acropolis, and portions still exist. More typical are the numerous sets of papyrus accounts from Ptolemaic and Roman Egypt. Greek and Roman accounts were mostly on the *charge and discharge* principle. A steward, public official, or other person entrusted with money or property rendered account periodically to his masters, by setting out in detail two lists of items, in money, weight, or measure, whose totals were always equal. The 'charge' consisted of the balance due to his masters at the beginning of the period, plus the money or goods which he was supposed to have received during it. The 'discharge' consisted of the sums disbursed, or goods sold and consumed, during the period, plus the balancing figure of money or goods due to the 'accountant's' masters at the end.[2]

Such a system could not serve the main purposes for which accounts are kept today, but only that of internal control—the use of a system of records and other checks to safeguard the property and revenues of an entity against waste or misappropriation. There was no way of finding the amount of equity at any time, nor that of income or profits (as distinct from cash flow) for a period.

1.4.1 Evolution of double entry book-keeping

Charge and discharge accounting survived, or was revived, in mediaeval Europe, and was imported into England by the Normans. The next major advance in technique occurred in Italy in the thirteenth and fourteenth centuries, when the growth of trade, manufactures, and banking, the increasing size of firms, the giving and receiving of credit, and the need to employ factors and agents who could not be personally supervised, made it imperative to devise more sophisticated accounting systems than those handed down from antiquity.

It would seem that the principles of charge and discharge accounting were extended to the cashier of a firm, who was charged with his receipts and discharged of his payments, and similarly to debtors, in relation to money borrowed or goods bought on credit (charge), and payments therefor (discharge). Creditors were accounted for likewise, with the firm charging itself with money deposited or goods sold on credit, and discharging itself of withdrawals or payments. Thus, although two-sided accounts were not used, an idea must have evolved that not only were receipts from, and payments to, the same person arithmetically opposite, but so were indebtedness to one person, and by another. By the second half of the thirteenth century, too, Italians had begun to notice that receipt of cash from a debtor necessitated two entries—a 'charge' in the cash record and a 'discharge' in the debtor's personal record—and had begun to cross-reference the two; and similarly for cash payments to creditors, in the reverse direction. By 1300 it was standard practice to distinguish 'positive' entries (cash receipts, loans or sales to customers, and payments to creditors) from 'negative' ones (cash payments, loans or purchases from depositors or suppliers, and receipts from debtors) by the conventional use in narrations of the Italian words *dare* [to give] and *avere* [to

[2] de Ste Croix, G. E. M., Greek and Roman Accounting. *In* Littleton, A. C. and B. S. Yamey, *Studies in the History of Accounting*, Sweet and Maxwell, 1956.

receive] –later rendered in English, for historical reasons, as *debit* (*Dr.*) and *credit* (*Cr.*). A further refinement, in the fourteenth century, was the use of the modern two-sided format, with debits on the left and credits on the right, visually emphasizing the dichotomy.

Goods were dealt with by debiting a separate account for each parcel purchased (crediting supplier, or cash), and crediting that account with each sale out of that parcel (debiting customer, or cash) until the whole was sold. The credits, at selling prices, normally exceeded the debits, at cost prices, and the account was closed by transferring the profit to the credit of a 'profit and loss account'. Observance of the debit–credit symmetry, in entries as described above, probably generated a feeling that every debit ought to have a credit, and vice versa; and, given the profit and loss account, it was a short step to debit to it any payments—rent, wages, proprietor's drawings, etc.—which had no other obvious home. When the proprietor introduced capital into the business, it was logical to open an account in his name and credit him with the sum debited to cash. Later it was seen that the credit balance (excess of profits over losses, expenses, and drawings) on the profit and loss account was really an augmentation of his equity, and the said balance was (occasionally) transferred to the proprietor's account.

Thus was evolved, by a series of innovations and probably without any conscious design or clear formulation of principles, the well-known system of *double entry book-keeping*. The revolution took place quietly between 1250 and 1350, in several cities at different dates, but with Florence, Venice, and Genoa in the lead. According to some authorities the earliest surviving double entry books date from 1296, but most contend for 1340, when the *massari*, or stewards, of the commune of Genoa produced the first extant set of completely balanced books. By 1400 the system was in general use among Italian firms at home and abroad.

The Italians, however, were slow to grasp the nature of double entry as providing, on certain assumptions, an arithmetical model of an entity's financial state at all times. Its main virtues for them were its coherence and consistency, the greater care and correctness which it demanded from clerical staff, the increased difficulty of falsifying the books to conceal fraud or theft (particularly where the book-keeping was divided among several clerks), and the automatic check provided by periodic balancing of the books and extraction of a 'trial balance' (see section 1.6) to prove the equality in total of the debits and credits. In other words, double entry was valued chiefly as a superior system of internal control.[3]

1.4.2 Luca Pacioli and the internationalization of double entry book-keeping

The dissemination of the technique over Europe was largely due to the publication in 1494 in Venice of *Summa de Arithmetica, Geometria, Proportione et Proportionalita* ('All About Arithmetic . . .'), a voluminous treatise in Italian, with Latin title and section-headings. It was the work of Luca Pacioli (*c.* 1445–*c.* 1515), a Franciscan friar, lecturer on mathematics, and friend of Piero della Francesca, Leon Battista Alberti, and Leonardo da Vinci. It contained a few chapters headed *Particularis de Computis et Scripturis* ('A Section on Accounts and Records'), and constituting the earliest published description of double entry book-keeping.

[3] de Roover, Raymond, The development of accounting prior to Luca Pacioli according to the account-books of mediaeval merchants. *In* Littleton and Yamey, *op. cit.*

Pacioli expounded the Venetian system, perhaps on the basis of manuscript manuals already available. He begins with the opening of a merchant's books, from an inventory of his assets and liabilities, business and private—for Pacioli takes the merchant's whole estate as the accounting entity, though he does not explain the latter concept. He then describes the three main books of account—the waste book, with rough notes of all transactions as they occur; the journal, in which the waste book entries are reduced into debit-and-credit form; and the ledger, containing the actual accounts, to which the journal entries are posted.

Pacioli was fully seized of the importance of money measurement, pointing out the need to convert all waste book items into (say) Venetian currency before entering them in the journal. He also stressed the need to date each entry, and to cross-reference all entries, debit to credit. But mercantile book-keeping in Venice was founded on a view of trade as a series of separate ventures, and on a conservative practice of reckoning the profit or loss on a venture only when it was fully wound up. Thus there was no place for accounting periods of fixed length, nor for regular balancing of the books as a whole, and hence no need for valuation of unsold stocks; nor does Pacioli discuss these matters, though he admits that in some other parts of Italy it was the custom to balance annually. *De Scripturis* deals with balancing of the ledger and extraction of a trial balance, but only on the closing of an old ledger when full and the transfer of its balances to a new volume. There is thus no provision for the regular ascertainment of overall profit or loss, or the closing of the profit and loss account to the proprietor's capital account; neither are there any instructions for drawing up a balance sheet, or statement of an entity's assets, liabilities, and equity at a given date—an established practice in Florence. There is no treatment of fixed assets, or of partnership (as distinct from joint venture) accounting—hence Pacioli's failure to grapple with the distinction between the proprietor as an individual and the business as an entity. Finally, his method of teaching the practice of double entry consists in giving examples of particular transactions as they are introduced, with no attempt to formulate a general rule; the student is expected to learn, by rote, which accounts to debit and credit in each case.[4]

For all that, Pacioli's treatise had many virtues—clarity, orderliness, a pleasant style, and a belief in the practical value of book-keeping. The *Summa* was reprinted in 1523, and during the sixteenth century *De Scripturis* was translated or imitated in many languages, the first English manual of double entry appearing in 1543. Partly as a result, the practice of this technique became widespread in Europe by the end of the seventeenth century, though older and cruder methods were by no means abolished.

Luca Pacioli's rôle as the 'father of accountancy' was assumed quite unintentionally. He was a mathematician, not a businessman, and book-keeping was merely a passing interest. Yet his work became the model, directly or at one or more removes, for English and other accounting texts until the eighteenth century. It was a long time, though, before any Englishman of comparable intellect became interested in the subject. The universities ignored it completely, and teaching and the writing of textbooks were left mainly to schoolmasters, without practical experience of office work. Most of them preferred to copy their predecessors rather than find out things for themselves, and their expositions thus tended to lag behind changes in counting-house procedure. Both their teaching and their writing

[4] Brown, R. G. and K. S. Johnston, *Paciolo on Accounting*, McGraw-Hill, 1963.

depended heavily on rote learning of a multiplicity of detailed rules designed to cover every eventuality, and attempts to enunciate a general rule of double entry were few and little regarded. Pacioli cannot be blamed for his successors' lack of imagination, but his failure to make clear the rationale of the system, or to provide it with a strong intellectual framework, sowed the seeds of stupefying dogmatism in his mediocre followers.[5]

1.4.3 Later developments in accounting

Accounting remained relatively stagnant from the sixteenth century to the early nineteenth, despite some refinements in book-keeping, such as subdivision of the journal and ledger, diminishing use of the waste book (which became redundant as it was replaced by files of primary documents, such as invoices and receipts), and the exclusion of household affairs from business books, enabling net profit to be determined directly. Goods accounts were classified more rationally, and a gross profit found for each line of merchandise dealt in. By 1800, too, it was fairly common for books to be balanced annually, and a profit and loss account and balance sheet extracted. But double entry was still regarded primarily as a system of internal control, and the annual accounts used merely as historical records.

The development of modern accounting, from about 1840 onwards, was conditioned by the interplay of five main factors, which are now discussed.

1 The growth of *large-scale corporate enterprises* began in earnest with the construction of the railway network after 1830. Railway companies were the first organizations in Britain to raise large amounts of capital from the middle classes by the issue of shares and debentures, on terms of limited liability. Higher management functions were delegated to the directors, while shareholders in general merely invested money in the hope of dividends and/or capital gains on sale of their shares. Ownership and effective control were thus divorced. Unable to participate in management, the investors were dependent for information upon the annual report and accounts rendered by the directors, who were legally obliged to pay dividends only out of profits. But accounting had still developed no coherent methods of computing profits, of distinguishing between capital expenditure (on additions to fixed assets) and revenue expenditure (incurred directly in earning revenue), or of amortizing expenditure on wasting assets. It was, therefore, easy for unscrupulous boards to manipulate the accounts so as to show any profit figure necessary to cover whatever dividend was thought sufficient to satisfy members. The results, in many cases, were concealment of the real position and the payment of dividends out of capital, with disastrous consequences.[6]

The possibilities of abuse, and even of fraud, were extended by the legalization from 1844 of joint stock companies for general commercial purposes, by registration with the Board of Trade. After the first comprehensive Joint Stock Companies Act, 1862, this type of organization became more and more common for large-scale business—a development which continues to this day.

2 The dangers inherent in joint stock enterprise, even with the protection of limited liability, were countered by *legal regulation,* though not until the 1860s was

[5] Jackson, J. G. C., The history of methods of exposition of double entry book-keeping in England. *In* Littleton and Yamey, *op. cit.*
[6] Pollins, H., Aspects of railway accounting before 1868. *In* Littleton and Yamey, *op. cit.*

anything very effective done. The Regulation of Railways Act, 1868, imposed upon railway companies proper accounting methods and a standard form of published accounts—the so-called 'double account system'; and later Acts regulated the accounts of other public utilities, such as gas, water, and electricity undertakings. For companies in general, however, reliance was placed mainly upon validation of the books and accounts, by auditors appointed by the shareholders. Even so, audits were not compulsory for banks until 1879, or for other companies until 1900. Until 1908 there was no obligation for registered companies to publish accounts, except to their own shareholders and debenture-holders; and not until 1948 did Parliament require the filing with the Board of Trade (for accessibility to inquirers) of really informative final accounts, including a summarized profit and loss account, and group accounts in the case of companies with subsidiaries.

3 Regulation by Parliament was built upon foundations laid by the *rise of the accountancy profession,* organized in Scotland from 1854 and in England from 1880. Beginning in a modest way before 1800, accountants had established, by 1860, a high reputation for competence and probity, and were increasingly employed as company auditors. In this capacity they gradually worked out ethically acceptable methods of computing profits available for dividend, distinguishing between capital and revenue expenditure, depreciating physical assets, and drawing up balance sheets. They enforced their standards by the sanction of refusing an unqualified audit report to those accounts which fell short of them. Indeed, it was accountants who led the way in raising standards of reporting of financial data by companies to their shareholders. Over the past century, and especially since 1918, legislation on the publication of accounts, and the matters to be disclosed in them, has tended to follow the practice of the most advanced and enlightened companies, and these in turn have grounded their practice upon the most up-to-date ideas current among professional accountants.

Until the Second World War the principles of accountancy constituted a somewhat arcane body of knowledge and beliefs, generally held by practitioners and by qualified accountants employed in industry, commerce, and the public services. These ideas were acquired by them during articled clerkship and afterwards, orally from their seniors and formally from the study of textbooks and correspondence courses, reinforced by more or less erudite articles in specialized professional journals. Only in 1942 did the Institute of Chartered Accountants in England and Wales begin to publish official *Recommendations on Accounting Principles,* which tended to be rationalizations of current practice rather than profound essays in accounting theory. The breaking down of this introverted attitude of the profession began in Britain in the 1960s, and was strongly, though belatedly, influenced by a fourth factor.

4 This was the infusion into accounting thinking of *economic and mathematical ideas.* The rise of modern accountancy in the nineteenth century was paralleled by the development of the science of economics, in which British thinkers, from Adam Smith onwards, played a leading rôle. But the two disciplines largely ignored each other; most economists were academics, and most accountants were 'practical' men of limited education, who had generally gone into the profession straight from school. Accountancy was not taught in any English university until 1902, and the first full-time chair in the subject was created in 1947.[7] In America, on the other

[7] Stacey, N.A.H., *English Accountancy 1800-1954,* Gee and Co., 1954. The first Scottish chair of accountancy was set up in 1919.

hand, the growth of university business schools from about 1910 had ensured the academic respectability of the subject, and laid a firm foundation for a largely graduate profession. It was only in 1944 that the main accountancy bodies in England did anything to encourage degree studies in economics as a preliminary to entry (the Scottish Institute has long required its 'apprentices' to attend a part-time course at a university for one year), and only in the later 1960s did graduates become a sizeable fraction of total entrants to articles in England and Wales—about one-third by 1972.[8]

It was during this period, too, that serious research into the economic foundations of accounting got under way in Britain (it had started earlier in America), and that a number of spectacular business collapses, and failures to meet widely-publicized profit forecasts, led to attacks on the accountancy profession for the insufficiency of its techniques in testing situations. Since 1970 the main British and Irish accountancy bodies, through their joint Accounting Standards Steering Committee, have begun in earnest to apply more rigorous thinking to accounting practice, with a view to tightening up standards through the sanction of a qualified audit report, mandatory upon all members in cases of serious deviation from recommended practice. The American Institute of Certified Public Accountants had an Accounting Principles Board, on similar lines, from 1959 to 1974, but there were complaints that it spent too much of its time 'putting out fires', instead of performing really deep research. This has been left mainly to academics, lacking the authority of an official body and with a constitutional tendency to disagree with one another!

Again, although the first writer on accounting was a mathematician, his successors (with one or two exceptions, such as Simon Stevin in Holland about 1600, and Sir Arthur Cayley at Cambridge in 1894) have generally ignored the subject. An algebraic exposition of double entry was published in England in 1818, but few took any notice, and the rote learning phase of book-keeping education was succeeded in the 1840s by the perverse and confusing method of teaching by 'personification' of accounts. This in turn gave place by 1900 to the concept of debit entries as denoting the 'receiving', and credit entries the 'giving', of value. It was only in the 1950s that teachers in this country began to use the 'balance sheet approach', explaining double entry as a record of movements in assets, liabilities, and equity—a technique established in American colleges since the early part of the century.[9]

The more direct impact of mathematics on accountancy occurred after the Second World War. Until then simple arithmetic was the only mathematical tool which a financial accountant was considered to need, and even management accounting depended mainly on arithmetical analysis, with a little algebra thrown in. The war stimulated the development of operational research—mathematical techniques designed to optimize the use of scarce military resources—and in peace-time this was applied to business management problems, with considerable success. Its spread was furthered by improvement of the electronic computer, able to perform rapidly the complicated and tedious calculations often required. This invention also familiarized the practitioner with the problems of mathematical logic and the design of complex information systems. Concomitantly, theories of financial management were worked out increasingly through the medium of vector and matrix algebra—a sore tax on the understanding of the older and less numerate accountant.

[8]D. Solomons, *Prospectus for a Profession*, Advisory Board of Accountancy Education, 1974.
[9]Jackson, J.G.C., *op. cit.*

5 The fifth main influence on accounting in modern times was *scientific management.* Originating in the United States in the late nineteenth century, this movement included close attention to costing and other forms of management accounting. Most British manufacturers neglected these until the First World War, when cost accounting was imposed by the government to control costs on munition contracts. The Institute of Cost and Works [now Management] Accountants was founded in 1919, and did much to promote the newer techniques in the ensuing decades. From the 1930s increasing importance was assumed by budgeting, forecasting, and standard costing–methods of accounting applied to the future instead of the past, and making much use of statistical devices for projecting economic trends. By the 1960s advanced British firms were adopting capital budgeting by discounted cash flow, and corporate planning of business strategy for several years ahead–both requiring considerable knowledge of economic theory and statistical probability–as well as operational research techniques, such as linear programming and the solution of transportation problems.

All these factors have interacted to produce the complex and many-sided pattern of modern accounting. In this book attention will be concentrated on financial accounting–the recording of historical data concerning the external transactions of an entity, their summarization from time to time, and the presentation of relevant information to management, proprietors, taxing authorities, regulatory agencies, and the general public. The task now is to outline a typical double entry system, and to present in a fresh way working methods already known, perhaps, to most readers.

1.5 Modern double entry book-keeping

All book-keeping is founded upon the three postulates set out in section 1.2, and double entry embodies the dual aspect concept in section 1.3. The construction of an actual system, however, requires the application of several additional principles. The commoner ones are set out below, together with a simple example based on them.

1.5.1 Assumptions

To begin with, it is necessary to make a number of *assumptions* about the entity's economic environment. In practice these tend to be vague, subjective notions, about which the average accountant would have to think rather hard, if asked to write them down. Here they are set forth explicitly, as they are applied to the generality of competitive businesses in the United Kingdom.

1 *The continuity assumption*
The entity will not be liquidated in the foreseeable future.

2 *The cost attachment assumption*
The amount of money paid, or the value of a liability assumed, or the money value imputed to any resource given up or transformed, necessarily in the provision of any asset other than money or a fixed claim thereto, may be regarded as the cost of such asset.

3 *The revenue-cost matching assumption*
The profit (or loss) of an entity for any period of time (i.e. the amount of growth (or decline) in equity, not attributable to the introduction or withdrawal of money

or other resources by the proprietors) may be regarded as equal to the excess (or deficiency) of the revenue arising during that period in return for the supply of goods or rendering of services on behalf of the proprietors, as compared with the imputed cost of the resources given up on behalf of the proprietors in the course of providing such goods or services.

4 *The stable monetary unit assumption*
Changes through time in the general purchasing power of money may be ignored.

5 *The constant time value of money assumption*
The present value of a given sum of money receivable or payable in the future may be taken as equal to that of the same sum receivable or payable immediately.

These propositions, especially the first three, are sometimes described as accounting postulates. This is not correct, however, since it is possible to keep accounts without making these assumptions, and there are situations in which they are not made.

The continuance of the entity, for at least as long as will enable all capital invested in existing non-monetary assets to be disinvested in the ordinary course of business (even if it is continuously reinvested in other such assets), is a rational assumption in the absence of evidence to the contrary. It breaks down only in the case of a business formed to carry out a single contract or venture in trade of short duration, or otherwise intended to have a short life, or of a business which has been put into bankruptcy or liquidation. In these situations the normal expectation as to disinvestment is defeated, and different treatment may have to be accorded in the accounts to 'long lived' expenditure.

The cost attachment assumption is necessary, if the expenditure of money or other using-up of an entity's assets is ever to be regarded as resulting in the acquisition of other assets to which money values can be imputed—normally on the basis of the costs incurred. The revenue-cost matching assumption is a necessary counterpart of the preceding one, since it covers the case where, through the operations of a trading concern, the excess of an entity's assets over its liabilities (both expressed in money terms) is increased or diminished over a period of time, by the making of a profit or loss on the said operations. In other words, the second and third assumptions have to be made in order to construct rational accounts for a business carried on for gain, and might be regarded as additional postulates of such accounts, as distinct from those of a non-trading concern.

The fourth and fifth assumptions are less rational—indeed they are contrary to observed fact. The purchasing power of any currency is never more than approximately constant at the best of times, and more often changes from year to year, with a long-term historical tendency to shrink, sometimes greatly accelerated in the short term. Disregard of this in accounting can have dire effects on the liquidity and solvency of a firm, and on its power to maintain its real level of investment; therefore, in modern times, the assumption of constant prices is sometimes abandoned and the accounts adjusted for inflation, as described in Chapter 7.

The present value of money, also, cannot be constant, regardless of deferment of receipt or payment, unless the current rate of interest on 'riskless' investments is zero. With any positive rate one always loses some actual or notional interest by postponing receipt of a sum of money, and gains some (or avoids paying it) by postponing a payment, even if the price level remains unchanged in the meantime. Hence, if debtors and creditors are stated at the amounts legally due, without regard to the periods of credit involved, then they are overstated in terms of current values, if no interest is charged to or by them. In practice it is rare to adjust for this factor in accounts, since the effect of ignoring it is seldom of much consequence in the long run.

1.5.2 Procedural rules and working rules

Subsumed under the dual aspect concept (see section 1.3) are the *procedural rules of double entry,* already familiar to most readers. These include the opening of separate ledger accounts for as many categories of assets, liabilities, and equity as need to be recognized (including accounts for individual debtors and creditors, either as part of the double entry itself or as memorandum records supporting total or control accounts in the main ledger). The 'equity' accounts will include a profit and loss account (or income and expenditure account, for a non-trading concern), with its supporting trading account, and sometimes manufacturing account also, where appropriate; and behind these will be a set of analytical accounts, designed to classify under suitable heads those entries which ultimately affect the profit and loss account, and through it equity. Within this framework are effected the two entries to record each transaction of the entity in money or money's worth—a *debit* (or positive) entry to denote an increase in an asset or a reduction in a liability, or in equity, and a *credit* (or negative) entry to denote a reduction in an asset, or an increase in a liability, or in equity. Entries affecting equity (other than cash or other assets introduced or withdrawn by the proprietor(s)) normally pass through the analytical accounts, whose balances are closed off to profit and loss (or allied) accounts at the end of the accounting period.

The mechanics of double entry are common to all fully articulated accounting systems, whether traditional two-sided accounts are used or not. The content of the system, and in particular the manner in which the values of assets, liabilities, and equity are altered over a particular accounting period, depend upon the definition of the *working rules,* properly so called; and these are conditioned by the assumptions already made. A typical set of such rules might be as follows.

a *The accounting period rule*

For the purposes of ascertaining from time to time the financial position of the entity and changes in it since it was last ascertained, the life of the entity shall be divided into accounting periods of one year in length, ending on such date in each calendar year as may be decided from time to time.

b *The historical-cost valuation rule*

The initial value imputed to any newly-acquired asset, other than money or a fixed claim thereto, shall be the amount of money paid or payable in exchange for it, or the money value imputed to the resources given up or transformed in producing it.

c *The lower realizable value/replacement price rule*

At the end of an accounting period any asset (other than money) which is expected to be realized in money in the ordinary course of business within the next accounting period shall be valued at the lowest of historical cost, current realizable value (less any further expenditure needed to effect realization), or current replacement price (on the terms on which it is usual for the firm to acquire such assets), or of such of these three values as may be applicable.

d *The fixed assets amortization rule*

The historical cost (less proceeds of final realization) of all wasting assets which are expected in the normal course of business to be retained for more than one year shall be amortized against the revenue of the entity over the period of time for which the said assets are held; such amortized amounts being apportioned to the intervening accounting periods in such manner as may be deemed appropriate.

e *The liabilities valuation rule*

All liabilities shall be valued at the amounts legally payable to the creditors concerned, irrespective of the due date of payment.

f *The revenue recognition rule*

Revenue shall be recognized as arising when a legally enforceable claim arises against the customer or other payee; except that money received from a customer, etc., in advance of the supply of goods or rendering of services shall be recognized as revenue when the goods are supplied or services rendered, and in the meantime shall be treated as a liability.

g *The cost recognition rule*

Costs shall be recognized as arising when they can reasonably be matched with revenue arising concomitantly, or, if they cannot be so matched because of their nature and incidence, when the benefit of the expenditure is received by the firm, or when it is clear that no such benefit is likely to be received.

h *The accruals and prepayments rule*

Costs recognized before the relevant expenditures have been incurred shall be treated as liabilities, and expenditures incurred before the relevant costs have been recognized shall be treated as assets.

These eight rules, it is submitted, give full effect to the five assumptions in section 1.5.1, and in conjunction with the procedural rules of double entry provide chapter and verse for all the operations of a conventional financial accounting system. Their effects will be traced in the example in section 1.6.

1.5.3 Conventions

In order to complete the edifice of theory, however, it is necessary to set forth a number of *conventions,* here defined as principles expressing the spirit in which the working rules are to be applied in practice. Three conventions may be distinguished:

1 *The consistency convention*

In case of doubt, a transaction shall be treated in the same manner as other transactions reasonably considered to belong to the same class; and working rules shall not be changed arbitrarily and without notice of the effects of the change to those who use the accounts.

2 *The prudence (conservatism) convention*

In case of doubt, that treatment shall be adopted which minimizes the reported figure of profit and/or asset valuation, or maximizes the reported figure of loss and/or liability valuation.

3 *The materiality convention*

Where minute analysis or the calculation of a precisely accurate figure would involve trouble, expense, or delay disproportionate to any advantage to be gained from such precision, a reasonable approximation shall be acceptable.

These are really 'sweeping-up' principles, designed to cover all cases where the working rules do not give clear answers as they stand. As to 2, it might be objected that prudence is one of the canons in accordance with which several of the working rules have been framed, notably, c, e, and f; but it still seems advisable to emphasize this fundamental attitude of the accountancy profession, although it has begun to be seriously questioned in recent years.

The application of the assumptions, working rules, and conventions is illustrated in the following example, which also provides a revision of the methods of double entry book-keeping and the preparation of simple final accounts.

1.6 A simple book-keeping example

Example 1 Below are the balance sheet of John Williams, a sole trader, as at 31 December 19.0, followed by his ledger accounts (summarized) for the year ended 31 December 19.1, trial balance as at that date (before closing the books), trading, and profit and loss, accounts for the year, and closing balance sheet. In the ledger each representative type of transaction is indicated by a 'block' entry, standing for the sum of all similar entries for the year. The closing entries are detailed after the trial balance, and made in the ledger accounts already set out. These are assumed to be all in one volume; the books of original entry are not shown.

John Williams

Balance Sheet, 31 December 19.0

	£	£		£	£	£
Capital			*Fixed assets*			
J. Williams		4,629	Fixtures			500
Loan			*Current assets*			
F. Smith		1,000	Stock		4,000	
			Debtors	2,740		
Current liabilities			*Less* Bad debts			
Creditors	1,500		provision	82		
Accruals	150			——	2,658	
	——	1,650	Bank balance		51	
			Prepayments		70	
					——	6,779
		£7,279				£7,279

Ledger

1 *Capital, J. Williams*

19.1		Fo.	£	19.1		Fo.	£
Dec 31	Drawings	2	1,200	Jan 1	Balance b/d	1	4,629
Dec 31	Balance c/d	1	4,704	Dec 31	Profit and loss a/c	—	1,275
			£5,904				£5,904
				19.2			
				Jan 1	Balance b/d	1	4,704

2 Drawings

19.1		Fo.	£	19.1		Fo.	£
Dec 31	Bank	11	£1,200	Dec 31	Capital, J. Williams	1	£1,200

3 Loan, F. Smith

		Fo.	£	19.1		Fo.	£
				Jan 1	Balance b/d	3	1,000

4 Creditors

19.1		Fo.	£	19.1		Fo.	£
Dec 31	Bank	11	15,300	Jan 1	Balance b/d	4	1,500
Dec 31	Discount received	22	200	Dec 31	Purchases	13	16,000
Dec 31	Returns outwards	14	300				
Dec 31	Balance c/d	4	1,700				
			£17,500				£17,500
				19.2			
				Jan 1	Balance b/d	4	1,700

5 Accruals

19.1		Fo.	£	19.1		Fo.	£
Jan 1	Wages	17	25	Jan 1	Balance b/d	5	150
Jan 1	Rent	18	125	Dec 31	Wages	17	30
Dec 31	Balance c/d	5	155	Dec 31	Rent	18	125
			£305				£305
				19.2			
				Jan 1	Balance b/d	5	155

6 Deposits

		Fo.	£	19.1		Fo.	£
				Dec 31	Bank	11	20

7 Fixtures

19.1		Fo.	£	19.1		Fo.	£
Jan 1	Balance b/d	7	500	Dec 31	Disposal of fixed assets	25	80
Dec 31	Bank	11	150	Dec 31	Depreciation	24	57
				Dec 31	Balance c/d	7	513
			£650				£650
19.2		Fo.					
Jan 1	Balance b/d	7	513				

8 Stock

19.1		Fo.	£	19.1		Fo.	£
Dec 31	Trading a/c	—	£4,000	Dec 31	Trading a/c	—	£4,000
19.1							
Dec 31	Trading a/c	—	4,200				

9 Debtors

19.1		Fo.	£	19.1		Fo.	£
Jan 1	Balance b/d	9	2,740	Dec 31	Bank	11	18,850
Dec 31	Sales	15	20,000	Dec 31	Discount allowed	21	350
				Dec 31	Returns inwards	16	500
				Dec 31	Bad debts	23	40
				Dec 31	Balance c/d	9	3,000
			£22,740				£22,740
19.2							
Jan 1	Balance b/d	9	3,000				

10 Bad Debts Provision

19.1		Fo.	£	19.1		Fo.	£
Dec 31	Balance c/d	10	90	Jan 1	Balance b/d	10	82
				Dec 31	Profit and loss a/c	—	8
			£90				£90
				19.2			
				Jan 1	Balance b/d	10	90

11 Bank

19.1		Fo.	£	19.1		Fo.	£
Jan 1	Balance b/d	11	51	Dec 31	Creditors	4	15,300
Dec 31	Debtors	9	18,850	Dec 31	Fixtures	7	150
Dec 31	Disposal of			Dec 31	Wages	17	1,195
	fixed assets	25	90	Dec 31	Rent	18	500
Dec 31	Deposit	6	20	Dec 31	Rates	19	300
Dec 31	Balance c/d	11	119	Dec 31	Sundry expenses	20	400
				Dec 31	Interest on loan, F. Smith	27	80
				Dec 31	Drawings	2	1,200
				Dec 31	Bank interest	26	5
			£19,130				£19,130
				19.2			
				Jan 1	Balance b/d	11	119

12 Prepayments

19.1		Fo.	£	19.1		Fo.	£
Jan 1	Balance b/d	12	70	Jan 1	Rates	19	70
Dec 31	Rates	19	75	Dec 31	Balance c/d	12	75
			£145				£145
19.2							
Jan 1	Balance b/d	12	75				

13 Purchases

19.1		Fo.	£	19.1		Fo.	£
Dec 31	Creditors	4	£16,000	Dec 31	Trading a/c	—	£16,000

14 Returns Outwards

19.1		Fo.	£	19.1		Fo.	£
Dec 31	Trading a/c	—	£300	Dec 31	Creditors	4	£300

15 *Sales*

19.1		Fo.	£	19.1		Fo.	£
Dec 31	Trading a/c	—	£20,000	Dec 31	Debtors	9	£20,000

16 *Returns Inwards*

19.1		Fo.	£	19.1		Fo.	£
Dec 31	Debtors	9	£500	Dec 31	Trading a/c	—	£500

17 *Wages*

19.1		Fo.	£	19.1		Fo.	£
Dec 31	Bank	11	1,195	Jan 1	Accruals	5	25
Dec 31	Accruals	5	30	Dec 31	Profit and loss a/c	—	1,200
			£1,225				£1,225

18 *Rent*

19.1		Fo.	£	19.1		Fo.	£
Dec 31	Bank	11	500	Jan 1	Accruals	5	125
Dec 31	Accruals	5	125	Dec 31	Profit and loss a/c	—	500
			£625				£625

19 *Rates*

19.1		Fo.	£	19.1		Fo.	£
Jan 1	Prepayments	12	70	Dec 31	Prepayments	12	75
Dec 31	Bank	11	300	Dec 31	Profit and loss a/c	—	295
			£370				£370

20 *Sundry Expenses*

19.1		Fo.	£	19.1		Fo.	£
Dec 31	Bank	11	£400	Dec 31	Profit and loss a/c	—	£400

21 *Discount Allowed*

19.1		Fo.	£	19.1		Fo.	£
Dec 31	Debtors	9	£350	Dec 31	Profit and loss a/c	—	£350

22 *Discount Received*

19.1		Fo.	£	19.1		Fo.	£
Dec 31	Profit and loss a/c	—	£200	Dec 31	Creditors		£200

23 *Bad Debts*

19.1		Fo.	£	19.1		Fo.	£
Dec 31	Debtors	9	£40	Dec 31	Profit and loss a/c	—	£40

24 Depreciation

19.1		Fo.	£	19.1		Fo.	£
Dec. 31	Fixtures	7	£57	Dec 31	Profit and loss a/c	–	£57

25 Disposal of Fixed Assets

19.1		Fo.	£	19.1		Fo.	£
Dec 31	Fixtures	7	80	Dec 31	Bank	11	90
Dec 31	Profit and loss a/c		10				
			£90				£90

26 Bank Interest

19.1		Fo.	£	19.1		Fo.	£
Dec 31	Bank	11	£5	Dec 31	Profit and loss a/c	–	£5

27 Interest on Loan, F. Smith

19.1		Fo.	£	19.1		Fo.	£
Dec. 31	Bank	11	£80	Dec 31	Profit and loss a/c	–	£80

Trial Balance, 31 December 19.1

	Fo.	Dr. £	Cr. £
Capital, J. Williams	1		4,629
Drawings	2	1,200	
Loan, F. Smith	3		1,000
Creditors	4		1,700
Deposits	6		20
Fixtures	7	570	
Stock	8	4,000	
Debtors	9	3,000	
Bad debts provision	10		82
Bank	11		119
Purchases	13	16,000	
Returns outwards	14		300
Sales	15		20,000
Returns inwards	16	500	
Wages	17	1,170	
Rent	18	375	
Rates	19	370	
Sundry expenses	20	400	
Discount allowed	21	350	
Discount received	22		200
Bad debts	23	40	
Disposal of fixed assets	25		10
Bank interest	26	5	
Interest on loan, F. Smith	27	80	
		£28,060	£28,060

Notes on adjustments The entries up to the trial balance stage are all explicable in terms of the procedural rules of double entry. The accounts numbered 1–12 (omitting number 2, *Drawings*) could have been used, albeit clumsily, to record all the transactions for the year, by the fundamental rule of debiting changes of positive sign and crediting those of negative sign, as between the elements of assets, liabilities, and equity. Such accounts are customarily classified as *real* (numbers 7 and 8), denoting the position with regard to assets other than claims to money against persons, or as *personal* (numbers 1–6, 9–12), denoting the position with regard to assets and liabilities in the form of money claims in favour of, or against, the legal owners of the entity, plus the residual equity of those owners. Note that the Bad Debts Provision Account is really a 'contra-asset' (an account whose credit balance represents, not a liability or equity, but a reduction in the value of an asset); note also that separate Accruals, Deposits, and Prepayments Accounts are used. Accruals and prepayments of expenditure are transferred to the accounts so named from the expense accounts at the end of a year, and transferred back again at the beginning of the next year; this is preferable, on the grounds of coherence and consistency, to the alternative of carrying down balances on the expense accounts themselves. Deposits are credited to their account as received, and transferred to Debtors when the goods are sold, thus reducing the customers' liability for the price.

In order to provide an effective analysis of all changes in equity due to the trading operations, and to strike the balances of gross, and net, profit for the year, it is necessary to make use of additional accounts (numbers 13–27). These fall into two classes. Numbers 13–16, together with number 8, are essentially 'real' in nature, (as dealing with movements in stock, a physical asset), but Sales has also an element of gross profit, which is isolated *en bloc* for a year's turnover, by bringing together all the balances of the said accounts in the Trading Account (see below). Accounts numbers 17–27, though, are *nominal* accounts, in which debits in appropriate accounts denote reductions in the value imputed to equity, and credits denote increases therein. Balances of this type, along with the gross profit (credit balance of the Trading Account), are brought together in the Profit and Loss Account, whose balance (net profit, or loss) is used to adjust the Capital Account (equity).

The post-trial balance adjustments, and the principles by which they are individually justified, are:

i Stock, 31 December 19.1, £4,200, was taken physically at the close of business on that day, and valued on the 'first in, first out' (FIFO) basis. Certain items were revalued downwards, to replacement price; realizable value was higher than cost in all cases.
(Rules b and c; Convention 3.)

ii Rent, £500 per annum, was outstanding for one quarter (£125) at 31 December 19.0 and 19.1. Part of a week's wages was also outstanding at both these dates (£25, £30). Adjustments were made through Accruals. In 19.1 two half-years' rates were paid in advance, for the year to 31 March 19.2. Hence, £75—one-fourth of the year's charge, £300—was treated as a prepayment at 31 December 19.1, and £70—paid in 19.0 for the three months to 31 March 19.1—was brought into charge.
(Rules g and h.)

iii Bad Debts Provision, £82 at 31 December 19.0, was adjusted to £90, being 3 per cent of Debtors at 31 December 19.1, £3,000.
(Rule c; Convention 2.)

iv Depreciation of Fixtures, £57, represents 10 per cent per annum, reducing balance, on £570 (£650 − £80).

(Rules **b, d** and **g**.)

John Williams

Trading Account for the Year ended 31 December 19.1

	£	£		£	£
Opening stock		4,000	Sales	20,000	
Purchases	16,000		*Less* Returns		
Less Returns			inwards	500	
outwards	300				
		15,700			19,500
		19,700			
Less Closing stock		4,200			
Cost of sales		15,500			
Gross profit		4,000			
		£19,500			£19,500

Profit and Loss Account for the Year ended 31 December 19.1

	£		£
Wages	1,200	Gross profit	4,000
Rent	500		
Rates	295	Discount received	200
Sundry expenses	400		
Discount allowed	350	Surplus on disposal of	
Bad debts	40	fixed assets	10
Increase in bad debts provision	8		
Depreciation—fixtures	57		
Bank interest	5		
Interest on loan, F. Smith	80		
	2,935		
Net Profit	1,275		
	£4,210		£4,210

Balance Sheet, 31 December 19.1

	£	£		£	£	£
Capital			**Fixed Assets**			
J. Williams		4,704	Fixtures			513
Loan			**Current Assets**			
F. Smith		1,000	Stock		4,200	
			Debtors	3,000		
Current Liabilities			*Less* Bad debts			
Bank overdraft	119		provision	90		
Creditors	1,700				2,910	
Accruals	155		Prepayments		75	
Deposits	20					7,185
		1,994				
		£7,698				£7,698

1.7 Preparation of accounts from incomplete records

Although double entry is applicable to the accounts of all entities without exception, not all businesses maintain a full set of books. Many small traders keep only a cash record, with notes of annual stocktakings, but preserve their cheque counterfoils, suppliers' invoices, receipted statements, etc., and other documentation. From these, and from the closing balance sheet of the previous year (or a balance sheet specially drawn up as at the beginning of the current year), it is usually possible to construct fairly accurate accounts, sufficient for presentation to the proprietor and the inspector of taxes (in support of the income tax computation).

The first step is to analyse the cash record or, if there is none, the bank statements, using the cheque counterfoils to ascertain the actual dates of payments. A cash (or bank) account is then drawn up in debit and credit form, and postings made from it to the opposite sides of a memorandum set of accounts. Entries are made in these in respect of non-cash items—opening and closing stocks, debtors and creditors, depreciation of fixed assets, bad debts provisions, etc.—to derive correct figures of purchases, sales, gross profit, expenses, and hence net profit. Thus, it is feasible to draw up final accounts adequate for the modest purposes of the business. Sometimes a firm keeps proper cash books, and debtors' and creditors' ledgers, but leaves the writing-up of the nominal and private accounts to a professional accountant-cum-auditor, whose task is correspondingly eased except that he now has to check the personal ledger postings and lists of balances, or extract the latter himself, as well as prepare a trial balance of the system.

At the other extreme, there is the theoretical case of a firm which keeps no books at all, and whose opening and closing balance sheets for a year must be compiled according to the best evidence available, with the proprietor's capital, at both dates, inserted as balancing figures. The excess of the closing, over the opening, capital, less any fresh moneys introduced by the proprietor during the year, is the retained profit for the year; addition to it of the proprietor's drawings, known or estimated, gives the net profit—but with no details as to how it was achieved (*mutatis mutandis* for a net loss). Such a situation is mercifully rare.

Example 2 J. Bloggs's balance sheet as at 1 January 19.1 was:

J. Bloggs

Balance Sheet, 1 January 19.1

	£		£	£
Capital		*Fixed assets*		
J. Bloggs	1,000	Fixtures		200
Current liabilities		*Current assets*		
Creditors	500	Stock	1,000	
		Debtors	200	
		Bank balance	100	
				1,300
	£1,500			£1,500

Bloggs kept no proper books, but analysis of his bank statements and cheque counterfoils allowed the following summary Bank Account to be prepared for the year ended 31 December 19.1:

Bank

19.1		£	19.1		£
Jan 1	Balance b/f	100	Dec 31	Suppliers	5,800
Dec 31	Customers	8,200	Dec 31	Wages	500
Dec 31	Sale of fixtures	40	Dec 31	Rent	300
			Dec 31	Sundry expenses	150
			Dec 31	Purchase of fixtures	100
			Dec 31	Drawings	1,200
			Dec 31	Balance c/f	290
		£8,340			£8,340

Stock, 31 December 19.1, was valued at £1,100. Debtors (from Bloggs's rough records) were £250, and creditors (from outstanding invoices) £600. The fixtures sold had been written down to £30; those on hand were to be depreciated by 10 per cent.

Key figures, not otherwise obvious, are computed thus:

Purchases

	£
Payments to suppliers	5,800
Less Opening creditors	500
	5,300
Add Closing creditors	600
	£5,900

Sales

	£
Receipts from customers	8,200
Less Opening debtors	200
	8,000
Add Closing debtors	250
	£8,250

Fixtures

	£
Opening balance	200
Additions	100
	300
Less Disposals (written down value)	30
	270
Less Depreciation, 10 per cent	27
	£243

The final accounts were:

J. Bloggs

Trading Account for the year ended 31 December 19.1

	£		£
Opening stock	1,000	Sales	8,250
Purchases	5,900		
	6,900		
Less Closing stock	1,100		
Cost of sales	5,800		
Gross profit	2,450		
	£8,250		£8,250

Profit and Loss Account for the Year ended 31 December 19.1

	£		£
Wages	500	Gross profit	2,450
Rent	300	Surplus on disposal of	
Sundry expenses	150	fixed assets	10
Depreciation—fixtures	27		
	977		
Net profit	1,483		
	£2,460		£2,460

Balance Sheet, 31 December 19.1

	£	£		£	£
Capital			*Fixed assets*		
J. Bloggs, as at			Fixtures		243
1 January 19.1	1,000				
Add Net profit	1,483		*Current assets*		
			Stock	1,100	
	2,483		Debtors	250	
Less Drawings	1,200		Bank balance	290	
					1,640
		1,283			
Current liabilities					
Creditors		600			
		£1,883			£1,883

Addendum: *mathematical proof of the dual aspect concept*

Let $(A_1, A_2, \ldots A_n)$ be the assets of an entity,

and $(L_1, L_2, \ldots L_p)$ be its liabilities,

and $(E_1, E_2, \ldots E_q)$ be its equity.

Let $(\Delta A_1^t, \Delta A_2^t, \ldots \Delta A_n^t)$

$(\Delta L_1^t, \Delta L_2^t, \ldots \Delta L_p^t)$

$(\Delta E_1^t, \Delta E_2^t, \ldots \Delta E_q^t)$

be the respective increments in the said elements over any period t.

Let $(A_1, A_2, \ldots A_n) \geqslant 0,$

and $(L_1, L_2, \ldots L_p) \leqslant 0$

If
$$\sum_{x=1}^{n} \Delta A_x^{t-1} + \sum_{y=1}^{p} \Delta L_y^{t-1} + \sum_{z=1}^{q} \Delta E_z^{t-1} = 0 \qquad 1$$

and
$$\sum_{x=1}^{n} (A_x^{t-1} + \Delta A_x^t) + \sum_{y=1}^{p} (L_y^{t-1} + \Delta L_y^t) + \sum_{z=1}^{q} (E_z^{t-1} + \Delta E_z^t) = 0 \qquad 2$$

then
$$\sum_{x=1}^{n} \Delta A_x^t + \sum_{y=1}^{p} \Delta L_y^t + \sum_{z=1}^{q} \Delta E_z^t = 0 \qquad 3$$

If
$$(\Delta L_1, \Delta L_2, \ldots \Delta L_p) = (\Delta E_1, \Delta E_2, \ldots \Delta E_q) = 0 \qquad 4$$

then
$$\sum_{x=1}^{n} \Delta A_x^t = 0 \qquad 5$$

and similarly for ΔL and ΔE. $\qquad$ 6, 7

If
$$(\Delta E_1, \Delta E_2, \ldots \Delta E_q) = 0 \qquad 8$$

then
$$\sum_{x=1}^{n} \Delta A_x^t + \sum_{y=1}^{p} \Delta L_y^t = 0 \qquad 9$$

and similarly for ΔA and ΔE, and for ΔL and ΔE. $\qquad$ 10, 11

2

Accounting: its utility to management

Discussion of accounting has been largely confined thus far to its function as an arithmetical model of the financial state of an entity from day to day, in terms of assets, liabilities, and equity. This is indeed its primary function, from which all others stem. It is now necessary to consider the other functions of an accounting system, and to show how it may be expanded and elaborated in order to fulfil them.

2.1 Organization of an accounting system

Every fully-articulated accounting system is essentially a unity, in relation to the single entity for which it is designed. Its ultimate concern is always with money values created by exchanges of economic goods and services, or their equivalents in current money, between the entity and other entities (including individual human beings, or rather their personal estates), and manifesting themselves in the shorter or longer run as flows of cash into or out of the entity. Over the whole life of an entity all its transactions reduce to cash flows, and the opening and closing values imputed to its assets, liabilities, and equity are all zero. During the operation of the entity, however, they take non-zero values as a result of time-lags between acquiring resources and paying for them, between acquiring resources and utilizing them, between providing goods or services to outsiders and obtaining payment for them, and (in a capitalistic business) between obtaining capital from proprietors, and/or accumulating profits, and distributing those profits and/or repaying that capital.

All these values are generated, in the first instance, at the interface between the entity and the outside world—normally through the process of exchange in the market, and with an immediate cash flow, or one which is only briefly delayed in most cases. The time-lags referred to in the previous paragraph, however, include several of longer duration, and it is these which create most of the difficulties and uncertainties of accounting in practice, with its need to ascertain the entity's financial position at arbitrary intervals of one year or less, and to measure changes in it since the last position statement was drawn up. Those difficulties and uncertainties become especially acute where value-transformations occur as a regular part of the activities of the entity's business, as in the manufacture or processing of goods for sale, or the use of materials, labour, and capital equipment to render intangible services, such as the transport of passengers or goods. Such internal movements of resources, not involving transactions across the boundary between the entity and the rest of the economic system, call for assumptions about the manner in which the costs of resources attach to the activities in which they are used up, or to the tangible goods in which they are deemed to be embodied, so as to enable profit or loss to be intelligently computed—with special reference to the valuation of unused raw materials, components or fuel, work in progress, and unsold stocks of finished goods as at the beginning and end of the accounting period.

Thus it is that even for the purposes of rational periodic accounting in financial terms some form of *cost accounting* (or *costing*) is essential, for all but the simplest operations of buying and reselling goods without change of form, or of rendering personal services without employing hired labour. In other words, there is usually a need to partition the accounting system into a minimum of two sub-systems— *financial accounts* and *cost accounts*. The first are normally in double entry; the second may be incorporated in the main system, or set up as a semi-autonomous double entry sub-system linked to, or periodically reconciled with, the financial sub-system, or exist merely as a set of separate calculations using figures extracted from the financial books of account. Whatever the technique adopted, the costing sub-system is always subordinate to the financial one, and all the values used in the former are derived from those arising in the latter, through the application of whatever rules are in force for recognizing the incurrence of the relevant expenditures, and for imputing to revenue the expiry of the benefits obtained from them.

A historical costing sub-system, then, is fundamentally intended to account for internal movements of values, having no explicit market price. The ascertainment of average costs per unit of output or service results from the division of total costs for a period by the number of such units of output produced, or units of service rendered, during that period. It does not arise directly from recording the total costs, whether by double entry methods or otherwise, but from analysing the totals by reference to non-monetary information, arising from outside the accounting system. Similarly, the amount of detailed information yielded by the financial accounting sub-system depends, not upon following the operative rules of double entry, nor upon the establishment of a set of working rules and conventions such as those set out in Chapter 1, but upon the degree of analysis built into the sub-system (and into the accounting system as a whole) in the process of designing its detailed layout.

It follows, not only that the accounting system must contain, for example, all the nominal accounts required for the dissection of expenditure under all the heads considered significant for appraisal of the results of any period, all the cost accounts needed to ascertain on the basis chosen the unit cost of each line of product or service, and separate accounts to show the turnover of each line of product or the gross receipts for each type of service, but also that the arrangements for collecting basic data from day to day must be so designed as to provide all the detail needed to ensure that every item is correctly analysed within the system. In other words, the accountant should not start with the availability of given data and then decide how much of them he can use with advantage; he should begin by deciding what information he requires to meet the needs of management, and then set out to design a system of accounts that will provide it, *and* a system of data collection and recognition which will enable the accounting system to operate properly.

2.1.1 Financial and cost accounts in a manufacturing business

There are several ways in which the accounting records of a manufacturing business can be arranged so as to account for the cost of goods produced by the firm. The simplest is an adaptation of the procedure by which an orthodox trading account is produced, but involving, in addition, the use of a *Manufacturing Account,* to which are transferred the net debits for materials consumed, direct labour cost, and manufacturing overheads, including depreciation of fixed assets employed in manufacture. The total costs incurred for the year are then adjusted by debiting the value imputed to opening work in progress, and crediting the closing amount thereof. The resulting figure is the estimated total cost of all work completed during the year and transferred to finished goods stock. In order to complete the double entry it is credited to manufacturing account (thus closing it) and debited to trading account, where it takes the place of the cost of purchased goods in a wholesale or retail business. Opening and closing stocks of finished goods are dealt with, through the trading account, in the manner illustrated in Chapter 1. Alternatively, manufacturing account may be credited, and trading account debited, with the amount of production for the year valued at what it would have cost to purchase in the open market. The difference on the manufacturing account represents profit or loss on manufacture as against outside purchase, and is transferred to the credit or debit of profit and loss account, separately from the gross profit on trading account, which is reduced or increased *pro tanto,* the total profit remaining unchanged.

    Example 1 Below are the (simplified) ledger accounts and final accounts of Steamage Products Ltd, kept on the principles outlined above, and using the average market price for the year of the single product as a transfer price between manufacturing and trading accounts. The entries are otherwise self-explanatory.

Steamage Products Ltd

Share Capital

			19.1		£
			Apr 1	Balance b/d	500,000

Creditors

19.1		£	19.0		£
Mar 31	Bank	370,000	Apr 1	Balance b/d	20,000
Mar 31	Balance c/d	25,000	19.1		
			Mar 31	Raw materials stock	375,000
		£395,000			£395,000
			19.1		
			Apr 1	Balance b/d	25,000

Corporation Tax

19.1		£	19.0		£
Jan 1	Bank	30,000	Apr 1	Balance b/d	30,000
Mar 31	Balance c/d	40,000	19.1		
			Mar 31	Profit and loss a/c	40,000
		£70,000			£70,000
			19.1		
			Apr 1	Balance b/d	40,000

Dividend

19.1		£	19.0		£
Mar 31	Bank	50,000	Apr 1	Balance b/d	50,000
Mar 31	Balance c/d	50,000	19.1		
			Mar 31	Profit and loss a/c	50,000
		£100,000			£100,000
			19.1		
			Apr 1	Balance b/d	50,000

Plant

19.0		£	19.1		£
Apr 1	Balance b/d	400,000	Mar 31	Depreciation	40,000
			Mar 31	Balance c/d	360,000
		£400,000			£400,000
19.1					
Apr 1	Balance b/d	360,000			

Raw Materials Stock

19.0		£	19.1		£
Apr 1	Balance b/d	35,000	Mar 31	Manufacturing a/c	370,000
19.1			Mar 31	Balance c/d	40,000
Mar 31	Creditors	375,000			
		£410,000			£410,000
19.1					
Apr 1	Balance b/d	40,000			

Work In Progress

19.0		£	19.1		£
Apr 1	Balance b/d	60,000	Mar 31	Manufacturing a/c	60,000
19.1			Mar 31	Balance c/d	80,000
Mar 31	Manufacturing a/c	80,000			
		£140,000			£140,000
19.1					
Apr 1	Balance b/d	80,000			

Finished Goods Stock

19.0		£	19.1		£
Apr 1	Balance b/d	130,000	Mar 31	Trading a/c	130,000
19.1			Mar 31	Balance c/d	150,000
Mar 31	Trading a/c	150,000			
		£280,000			£280,000
19.1					
Apr 1	Balance b/d	150,000			

Debtors

19.0		£	19.1		£
Apr 1	Balance b/d	90,000	Mar 31	Bank	990,000
19.1			Mar 31	Balance c/d	100,000
Mar 31	Sales	1,000,000			
		£1,090,000			£1,090,000
19.1					
Apr 1	Balance b/d	100,000			

Bank

19.0		£	19.1		£
Apr 1	Balance b/d	10,000	Jan 1	Corporation tax	30,000
19.1			Mar 31	Dividend	50,000
Mar 31	Debtors	990,000	Mar 31	Creditors	370,000
			Mar 31	Direct labour	330,000
			Mar 31	Manufacturing overheads	130,000
			Mar 31	Selling & administrative overheads	70,000
			Mar 31	Balance c/d	20,000
		£1,000,000			£1,000,000
19.1					
Apr 1	Balance b/d	20,000			

Direct Labour

19.1		£	19.1		£
Mar 31	Bank	330,000	Mar 31	Manufacturing a/c	330,000

Manufacturing Overheads

19.1		£	19.1		£
Mar 31	Bank	130,000	Mar 31	Manufacturing a/c	130,000

Depreciation—Plant

19.1		£	19.1		£
Mar 31	Plant	40,000	Mar 31	Manufacturing a/c	40,000

Sales

19.1		£	19.1		£
Mar 31	Trading a/c	1,000,000	Mar 31	Debtors	1,000,000

Selling & Administrative Overheads

19.1		£	19.1		£
Mar 31	Bank	70,000	Mar 31	Profit and loss a/c	70,000

Manufacturing Account for the Year ended 31 March 19.1

	£		£
Raw materials consumed	370,000	**Trading Account**	
Direct labour	330,000	30,000 tons produced, at	
Manufacturing overheads	130,000	£30 per ton (average	
Depreciation—Plant	40,000	market price for year)	900,000
	870,000		
Add Work in progress,			
1 April 19.0	60,000		
	930,000		
Less Work in progress			
31 March 19.1	80,000		
Cost of production	850,000		
Profit & Loss Account			
Manufacturing profit	50,000		
	£900,000		£900,000

Trading Account for the Year ended 31 March 19.1

	£		£
Manufacturing Account		Sales	1,000,000
Total production at			
market price	900,000		
Add Finished goods			
stock, 1 April 19.0	130,000		
	1,030,000		
Less Finished goods			
stock, 31 March 19.1	150,000		
Cost of sales	880,000		
Profit & Loss Account			
Trading profit	120,000		
	£1,000,000		£1,000,000

Profit and Loss Account for the Year ended 31 March 19.1

	£		£
Selling & administrative		Manufacturing profit	50,000
overheads	70,000	Trading profit	120,000
Net profit before taxation	100,000		
	£170,000		£170,000
Corporation tax	40,000	Net profit before taxation	100,000
Net profit after taxation	60,000		
	£100,000		£100,000
Dividend	50,000	Net profit after taxation	60,000
Balance carried forward to			
next year	135,000	Balance brought forward from	
		previous year	125,000
	£185,000		£185,000

Balance Sheet, 31 March 19.1

	£	£		£	£
Share Capital		500,000	Fixed Assets		
			Plant		360,000
Profit and Loss Account		135,000			
		———	Current Assets		
		635,000	Raw materials stock	40,000	
Current Liabilities			Work in progress	80,000	
Creditors	25,000		Finished goods stock	150,000	
Corporation tax	40,000			———	
Proposed dividend	50,000			270,000	
	———	115,000	Debtors	100,000	
			Bank	20,000	
				———	390,000
		£750,000			£750,000

The manufacturing account method has the merit of simplicity, but no other; indeed, it has no real use except in single-product undertakings, such as the one in Example 1, and these are rare today. The year's results are shown as a whole, with no record in the books of the weekly, monthly, or quarterly flows of cost through the system, and with no clue to variations in unit costs during periods of less than a year—the annual average alone being ascertainable by dividing total units of output into total costs, and the components thereof. Materials consumption is taken as the residual figure after adjustment of purchases for opening and closing stocks, and the effects of waste, spoilage, and pilfering are concealed. Direct labour is shown as total wages paid, including payments for time on abortive work, idle time, and wasted time, without differentiation; and works overheads are simply stated as incurred (with more or less of analysis under different heads) and with, again, no indication as to whether they are inflated by extravagance or inefficiency. Without a proper costing system, too, the amounts of work in progress can only be estimates, based on assessment of the value of the materials and labour content up to the stage reached at the year-end, with or without an addition (necessarily arbitrary) for imputed works overheads; and errors in the estimates may seriously distort total reported costs from one year to the next. The only cost comparisons possible are between the totals, and the unit averages, of each element from year to year, with no sort of guarantee that any of the figures are anywhere near optimal—they are in any case distorted by failure to allow for the corresponding elements in the work in progress figures.

Clearly, such a system is of little use for purposes of management control, and breaks down completely in a multi-product firm. It needs to be supplemented or replaced by a regular sub-system of cost accounts, either outside the double entry books on suitably-ruled analysis sheets (for each week's, month's, etc. production or each batch of each product-line, or for each individual job or contract), or in a separate set of books periodically reconciled with the financial ones (with a total or control account to render the cost accounts self-balancing), or linked to the financial books by control accounts in both sets, or incorporated within (or integrated with) the main books of account. This is not a treatise on cost accounting, and space allows only of the illustration of a linked set of cost accounts using the same data as in Example 1.

Example 2 If Steamage Products Ltd had kept two linked set of books, financial and costing, for the year ended 31 March 19.1, they might have appeared thus (simplified):

Steamage Products Ltd
General Ledger

Share Capital

	£	19.0		£
		Apr 1	Balance b/d	500,000

Creditors

19.1		£	19.1		£
Mar 31	Bank	370,000	Apr 1	Balance b/d	20,000
Mar 31	Balance c/d	25,000	19.1		
			Mar 31	Cost ledger control a/c	375,000
		£395,000			£395,000
			19.1		
			Apr 1	Balance b/d	25,000

Corporation Tax

19.1		£	19.1		£
Jan 1	Bank	30,000	Apr 1	Balance b/d	30,000
Mar 31	Balance c/d	40,000	19.1		
			Mar 31	Profit and loss a/c	40,000
		£70,000			£70,000
			19.1		
			Apr 1	Balance b/d	40,000

Dividend

19.1		£	19.0		£
Mar 31	Bank	50,000	Apr 1	Balance b/d	50,000
Mar 31	Balance c/d	50,000	19.1		
			Mar 31	Profit and loss a/c	50,000
		£100,000			£100,000
			19.1		
			Apr 1	Balance b/d	50,000

	£	19.1		£
	90,000	Mar 31	Bank	990,000
	1,000,000	Mar 31	Balance c/d	100,000
	£1,090,000			£1,090,000
	100,000			

Bank

19.0		£	19.1		£
Apr 1	Balance b/d	10,000	Jan 1	Corporation tax	30,000
19.1			Mar 31	Dividend	50,000
Mar 31	Debtors	990,000	Mar 31	Creditors	370,000
			Mar 31	*Cost Ledger Control A/c*	
				Direct labour	330,000
				Manufacturing overheads	130,000
			Mar 31	Selling & administrative overheads	70,000
			Mar 31	Balance c/d	20,000
		£1,000,000			£1,000,000
19.1					
Apr 1	Balance b/d	20,000			

Finished Goods Stock

19.0		£	19.1		£
Apr 1	Balance b/d	130,000	Mar 31	Cost of sales	880,000
19.1			Mar 31	Balance c/d	150,000
Mar 31	Cost ledger control a/c	900,000			
		£1,030,000			£1,030,000
19.1					
Apr 1	Balance b/d	150,000			

Cost of Sales

19.1		£	19.1		£
Mar 31	Finished goods stock	880,000	Mar 31	Trading a/c	880,000

Sales

19.1		£	19.1		£
Mar 31	Trading a/c	1,000,000	Mar 31	Debtors	1,000,000

Selling & Administrative Overheads

19.1		£	19.1		£
Mar 31	Bank	70,000	Mar 31	Profit and loss a/c	70,000

Manufacturing Profit

19.1		£	19.1		£
Mar 31	Profit and loss a/c	50,000	Mar 31	General ledger control a/c	50,000

Cost Ledger Control Account

19.0		£	19.1		£
Apr 1	Balance b/d	495,000	Mar 31	Finished goods	
19.1				stock	900,000
Mar 31	Creditors—raw		Mar 31	Balance c/d	480,000
	materials stock	375,000			
Mar 31	Bank—				
	Direct labour	330,000			
	Manufacturing				
	overheads	130,000			
Mar 31	Manufacturing				
	profit	50,000			
		£1,380,000			£1,380,000

19.1					
Apr 1	Balance b/d	480,000			

Cost Ledger

General Ledger Control Account

19.1		£	19.0		£
Mar 31	Work in progress	900,000	Apr 1	Balance b/d	495,000
Mar 31	Balance c/d	480,000	*19.1*		
			Mar 31	Raw materials stock	375,000
			Mar 31	Direct labour	330,000
			Mar 31	Manufacturing	
				overheads	130,000
			Mar 31	Work in progress—	
				Manufacturing profit	50,000
		£1,380,000			£1,380,000
			19.1		
			Apr 1	Balance b/d	480,000

Plant

19.0		£	19.1		£
Apr 1	Balance b/d	400,000	Mar 31	*Depreciation*	
				Plant	40,000
			Mar 31	Balance c/d	360,000
		£400,000			£400,000

19.1					
Apr 1	Balance b/d	360,000			

Raw Materials Stock

19.0		£	19.1		£
Apr 1	Balance b/d	35,000	Mar 31	Work in progress	370,000
19.1			Mar 31	Balance c/d	40,000
Mar 31	General ledger				
	control A/c	375,000			
		£410,000			£410,000

19.1					
Apr 1	Balance b/d	40,000			

Direct Labour

19.1		£	19.1		£
Mar 31	General ledger control a/c	330,000	Mar 31	Work in progress	330,000

Manufacturing Overheads

19.1		£	19.1		£
Mar 31	General ledger control a/c	130,000	Mar 31	Work in progress	130,000

Depreciation—Plant

19.1		£	19.1		£
Mar 31	Plant	40,000	Mar 31	Work in progress	40,000

Work In Progress

19.0		£	19.1		£
Apr 1	Balance b/d	60,000	Mar 31	*General Ledger Control A/c* Finished goods at market price	900,000
19.1			Mar 31	Balance c/d	80,000
Mar 31	Raw materials stock	370,000			
Mar 31	Direct labour	330,000			
Mar 31	Manufacturing overheads	130,000			
Mar 31	*Depreciation* Plant	40,000			
Mar 31	*General Ledger Control A/c* Manufacturing profit	50,000			
		£980,000			£980,000
19.1					
Apr 1	Balance b/d	80,000			

Trading Account for the Year ended 31 March 19.1

	£		£
Cost of sales	880,000	Sales	1,000,000
Profit & Loss Account Trading profit	120,000		
	£1,000,000		£1,000,000

[Profit and Loss Account, and Balance sheet, as before.]

It will be noted that the general ledger contains the accounts for the financial assets, liabilities, and equity of the company, and the finished goods stocks, as well as those nominal accounts which affect the profit and loss account, while the cost ledger deals with the productive assets (plant, raw material stocks, and work in progress), and the nominal accounts which in Example 1 were closed off to the manufacturing account. Hiving-off of the 'cost' accounts necessitates the opening in the general ledger of a Cost Ledger Control Account, and the transfer to it of the balances on the excluded accounts, so as to eliminate them from the general ledger. The same accounts are then opened in the cost ledger, and *its* double entry completed by the opening of a General Ledger Control Account, whose balance, after due adjustment, is at all times equal and opposite to that of its counterpart. At the balancing date, trial balances may be extracted from both sets of books, and final accounts for the company prepared from both sets combined—the control account balances cancelling out. In day to day operation, any debit in the general ledger whose corresponding credit lies in the cost ledger will require two further entries—*Cr.* Cost Ledger Control Account and *Dr.* General Ledger Control Account—to connect the two ledgers and keep them both in balance; and similarly for entries in the reverse direction. In the language of Chapter 1, the two sub-systems are the accounts of sub-entities, with the control account balance in the cost ledger (credit) as the 'quasi-equity' of the costing section, and the countervailing debit balance in the general ledger as the financial sub-entity's 'investment' in the costing sub-entity.

In an integrated set of financial and cost accounts there is a single set of books, with the two control accounts omitted, but the other accounts much as in Example 2—the double entry being effected in the usual way. The format is illustrated, in relation to standard costing, in Example 3 (see sub-section **2.1.2**).

A double entry historical costing sub-system, even when presented in the summary form shown above, has the advantage of exhibiting the flow of values through the business, with work in progress as the key account. In its fully developed form, with (say) monthly balancing of the cost accounts and estimation of the month-end stock and work in progress figures, it enables management to estimate average costs (through division by the number of appropriate units) much more frequently than with an annual manufacturing account and, in the case of a firm with more than one product, to compile separate costing information for each product, by multiplying work in progress accounts. The same arrangements can, however, be applied to the manufacturing account; indeed, the work in progress account is, fairly obviously, the manufacturing account in a slightly different format. In order to control costs effectively in a business whose operations are to any extent repetitive (as opposed to one where each job or contract is unique, as in civil engineering), it is necessary to install some form of *standard costing,* preferably incorporated in the books of account.

2.1.2 Double entry standard costing

The essence of standard costing is that unit costs are pre-determined—most rationally, on the basis of what is consistently attainable at a high, but not super-human, level of efficiency, with existing facilities utilized to their maximum sustainable extent rather than their full theoretical capacity. The resulting *standards,* revised annually or more often and adjusted in detail whenever there is a major change in the cost factors assumed as the basis for the original standard, are intended to provide management with a series of goals which can be reached with reasonable effort and good fortune, and thus offer, to managers at all levels on the production side, such incentives as they need to make them give of their best.

An accounting system is then set up to calculate the standard cost of production-units (or service-units) as they emerge from the production (or service-rendering) process, to separate off the *variances,* or differences between standard and actual costs, as soon as they can be recognized, and to analyse those variances according to their presumed causes. It is then the job of higher management to consider the variances of significant size, and to apportion praise or blame to subordinates where that is appropriate—an example of a process commonly known as 'management by exception'. In the financial accounts output is shown at standard cost (as most recently revised), as are stocks and work in progress, and the variances appear as separate adjustments to reconcile total standard cost with total actual cost; or, less satisfactorily, the financial figures are adjusted to an actual-cost basis by writing back the variances, once they have served their main purpose of showing up the nature and extent of deviations of performance from plan.

In accordance with the general scheme of this chapter it is proposed not to go into all the details of the subject but to illustrate a simple sub-system of standard costs, incorporated in the financial books, and comment briefly on the significance of the variances.

Example 3 Suppose that Steamage Products Ltd, in Examples 1 and 2, had installed an integrated set of financial and standard cost accounts. For the year ended 31 March 19.1, the standard cost of one ton of the product was computed thus:

	£
Direct materials: 1.25 tons at £9.00 per ton	£11.25
Direct wages: 15 hours at £0.70 per hour	10.50
Manufacturing overheads (detailed, in practice):	
£120,000 per annum for an output of 28,000 tons	4.29
Depreciation—Plant:	
£40,000 per annum for an output of 28,000 tons	1.43
	£27.47

At 1 April 19.0 the inventories, all valued at standard cost for the year ended 31 March 19.0, were as follows, on the assumptions that all raw materials entered into process at the outset, and that all work was on average half finished at the balancing date:

	£
Raw materials stock	33,000
Work in progress	54,525
Finished goods stock	128,000
	£215,525

The profit and loss account balance at 1 April 19.0 was £115,525; all other balances as at that date were as previously assumed. Forecast sales for the year ended 31 March 19.0 were 27,000 tons at £33.00 per ton, or £891,000.

The first six accounts in Example 2, and that for Plant, are substantially unchanged. The rest of the ledger, and the final accounts, would appear thus (simplified):

Steamage Products Ltd

Raw Materials Stock

19.0		£	19.1		£
Apr 1	Balance b/d	33,000	Mar 31	Raw materials	
Apr 1	Raw materials			price variance	18,000
	price variance	2,000	Mar 31	Work in progress	354,000
19.1			Mar 31	Balance c/d	38,000
Mar 31	Creditors	375,000			
		£410,000			£410,000
19.1					
Apr 1	Balance b/d	38,000			

Direct Labour

19.1		£	19.1		£
Mar 31	Bank	330,000	Mar 31	Direct labour	
				rate variance	14,000
			Mar 31	Work in progress	316,000
		£330,000			£330,000

Manufacturing Overheads

19.1		£	19.1		£
Mar 31	Bank	130,000	Mar 31	Mfg overheads	
				price variance	5,000
			Mar 31	Work in progress	125,000
		£130,000			£130,000

Depreciation—Plant

19.1		£	19.1		£
Mar 31	Plant	40,000	Mar 31	Work in progress	40,000

Work in progress

19.0		£	19.1		£
Apr 1	*Balance b/d*		Mar 31	*Finished Goods Stock*	
	Raw materials			Raw materials,	
	3,000 x £10.75	32,250		30,000 x £11.25	337,500
	Direct labour,			Direct labour,	
	1,500 x £9.50	14,250		30,000 x £10.50	315,000
	Mfg overheads,			Mfg overheads,	
	1,500 x £4.00	6,000		30,000 x £4.29	128,700
	Depreciation—plant,			Depreciation—plant,	
	1,500 x £1.35	2,025		30,000 x £1.43	42,900
		54,525			824,100
Apr 1	Raw materials		Mar 31	Raw materials	
	price variance,			usage variance	5,250
	3,000 x £0.50	1,500	Mar 31	*Balance c/d*	
Apr 1	Direct labour			Raw materials,	
	rate variance,			4,000 x £11.25	45,000
	1,500 x £1.00	1,500		Direct labour,	
Apr 1	Mfg overheads			2,000 x £10.50	21,000
	price variance,			Mfg overheads,	
	1,500 x £0.29	435		2,000 x £4.29	8,580
Apr 1	Depreciation—plant—			Depreciation—plant,	
	rate variance,			2,000 x £1.43	2,860
	1,500 x £0.08	120			

19.1					
Mar 31	Raw materials				
	stock	354,000			
Mar 31	Direct labour	316,000			
Mar 31	Mfg overheads	125,000			
Mar 31	Depreciation—plant	40,000			
Mar 31	Direct labour				
	efficiency				
	variance	4,250			
Mar 31	Mfg overheads				
	activity variance	5,845			
Mar 31	Depreciation—plant—				
	activity variance	3,615			
		£906,790			£906,790

19.1		£
Apr 1	*Balance b/d*	
	Raw materials,	
	4,000 x £11.25	45,000
	Direct labour,	
	2,000 x £10.50	21,000
	Mfg overheads,	
	2,000 x £4.29	8,580
	Depreciation—plant,	
	2,000 x £1.43	2,860
		77,440

Finished Goods Stock

19.0		£	19.1		£
Apr 1	Balance b/d 5,000 x £25.60	128,000	Mar 31	Standard Cost of Sales 29,800 x £27.47	818,606
Apr 1	Raw materials price variance, 5,000 x £0.50	2,500	Mar 31	Balance c/d 5,200 x £27.47	142,844
Apr 1	Direct labour rate variance, 5,000 x £1.00	5,000			
Apr 1	Mfg overheads price variance, 5,000 x £0.29	1,450			
Apr 1	Depreciation—plant— rate variance, 5,000 x £0.08	400			
19.1					
Mar 31	Work in progress— 30,000 x £27.47	824,100			
		£961,450			£961,450
19.1					
Apr 1	Balance b/d 5,200 x £27.47	142,844			

Standard Cost of Sales

19.1		£	19.1		£
Mar 31	Finished goods stock	818,606	Mar 31	Trading a/c	818,606

Sales

19.1		£	19.1		£
Mar 31	Sales price variance 29,000 x £0.56	16,600	Mar 31	Debtors	1,000,000
Mar 31	Trading A/c— 29,800 x £33.00	983,400			
		£1,000,000			£1,000,000

Selling and Administrative Overheads

19.1		£	19.1		£
Mar 31	Bank	70,000	Mar 31	Profit and loss a/c	70,000

Raw Materials Price Variance

19.1		£	19.0		£
Mar 31	Raw materials stock	18,000	Apr 1	Raw materials stock	2,000
			Apr 1	Work in progress	1,500
			Apr 1	Finished goods stock	2,500
			19.1		
			Mar 31	Trading a/c	12,000
		£18,000			£18,000

Raw Materials Usage Variance

19.1		£	19.1		£
Mar 31	Work in progress	5,250	Mar 31	Trading a/c	5,250

Direct Labour Rate Variance

19.1		£	19.0		£
Mar 31	Direct labour	14,000	Apr 1	Work in progress	1,500
			Apr 1	Finished goods stock	5,000
			19.1		
			Mar 31	Trading a/c	7,500
		£14,000			£14,000

Direct Labour Efficiency Variance

19.1		£	19.1		£
Mar 31	Trading a/c	4,250	Mar 31	Work in progress	4,250

Manufacturing Overheads Price Variance

19.1		£	19.1		£
Mar 31	Mfg overheads	5,000	Apr 1	Work in progress	435
			Apr 1	Finished goods stock	1,450
			19.1		
			Mar 31	Trading a/c	3,115
		£5,000			£5,000

Manufacturing Overheads Activity Variance

19.1		£	19.1		£
Mar 31	Trading a/c	5,845	Mar 31	Work in progress	5,845

Depreciation—Plant—Rate Variance

19.1		£	19.0		£
Mar 31	Trading a/c	520	Apr 1	Work in progress	120
			Apr 1	Finished goods stock	400
		£520			£520

Depreciation—Plant—Activity Variance

19.1		£	19.1		£
Mar 31	Trading a/c	3,615	Mar 31	Work in progress	3,615

Sales Price Variance

19.1		£	19.1		£
Mar 31	Trading a/c	16,600	Mar 31	Sales	16,600

Trading Account for the Year ended 31 March 19.1

	£		£
Standard cost of sales	818,606	Sales at standard price	983,400
Standard gross profit			
c/d	164,794		
	£983,400		£983,400
Adverse Variances		Standard gross profit	
Raw materials price	12,000	b/d	164,794
Raw materials usage	5,250	*Favourable Variances*	
Direct labour rate	7,500	Direct labour efficiency	4,250
Manufacturing overheads price	3,115	Manufacturing overheads activity	5,845
Profit & Loss Account		Depreciation—plant—rate	520
Actual gross profit	167,759	Depreciation—plant—activity	3,615
		Sales price	16,600
	£195,624		£195,624

Profit and Loss Account for the Year ended 31 March 19.1

	£		£
Selling and administrative		*Trading Account*	
overheads	70,000	Actual gross profit	167,759
Net profit before taxation	97,759		
	£167,759		£167,759
Corporation tax	40,000	Net profit before taxation	97,759
Net profit after taxation	57,759		
	£97,759		£97,759
Dividend	50,000	Net profit after taxation	57,759
Balance carried forward to next		Balance brought forward from	
year	123,284	previous year	115,525
	£173,284		£173,284

Balance Sheet, 31 March 19.1

	£	£		£	£
Share Capital		500,000	*Fixed assets*		
			Plant		360,000
Profit and Loss Account		123,284			
		623,284	*Current assets*		
			Raw materials		
Current Liabilities			stock	38,000	
Creditors	25,000		Work in progress	77,440	
Corporation			Finished goods		
tax	40,000		stock	142,844	
Proposed					258,284
dividend	50,000		Debtors	100,000	
		115,000	Bank	20,000	
					378,284
		£738,284			£738,284

The mechanics of this over-simplified system of combined financial and standard cost accounts should be fairly familiar to most readers, and the arithmetic whereby the work in progress variances are computed is made explicit. It will be noted that price or equivalent variances are isolated in the accounts which 'feed' the work in progress account, while efficiency-type variances emerge there in the course of ascertaining the standard cost of finished goods and of unfinished work at the year-end. The opening work in progress and finished goods stock are brought up to standard cost for the current year by taking favourable price variances and this, while making no difference to the actual profit reported, makes it easier to calculate the truly significant—because controllable—usage, efficiency, and activity variances.

From these it appears that higher labour productivity than was assumed in setting the standards (a favourable efficiency variance) has been more than offset by higher consumption of raw material—perhaps due to less careful work and more waste and/or spoilage, as might be clearer from a more refined system, with further analysis of variances. A somewhat higher volume of production than was planned, though it has increased total overheads to some extent, has spread the total over more units and caused an over-recovery (favourable activity variance)—and similarly with depreciation, where the rate variance is nil, except for the work in progress and finished stock adjustments at the beginning of the year. This, indeed, has been the main factor in maintaining gross profit at approximately the standard percentage on sales—16.8 per cent—since the increased selling price, giving a favourable variance of £16,600, was inadequate to cover inflation of input prices totalling £22,095 net (£12,000 + £7,500 + £3,115 − £520). In this respect then, the company has been running hard to stay in the same place.

Building standard costing into the accounting system, even at a relatively unsophisticated level, immensely increases the amount of valuable information which the system affords to management, and at the same time ensures the internal consistency of that information, provided the rules are followed. The full implications cannot be gone into here, but enough has been said, it is hoped, to indicate how progressive expansion of the double entry framework enables it to accommodate more functions in one set of books than the mere recording of external transactions of the entity. Commonly the process stops at the point of integrating financial accounts and standard costs, but can be carried further, at least in theory.

2.2 Accounting and forward planning

Every firm or undertaking whose business is to any extent stable and predictable in its operations, which has a forecastable demand for its outputs, and/or which requires the commitment of large amounts of capital for long periods of time, has need of some kind of forward planning, in greater or less detail. The basic device is the *budget,* prepared for up to one year ahead at a time, and regularly compared with the achieved results by a system of *budgetary control.*

A budget consists of a series of interlocking statements containing the planned financial results, in total, for the forthcoming year or shorter period, all broken down to sub-periods (quarters, months, four-week or four/five-week periods, as appropriate) and integrated to produce, in effect, the planned profit and loss account and ending balance sheet for the budget period. As each sub-period passes the corresponding figures from the accounts are compared with the budgeted figures, and variances found by difference as in standard costing. These are then analysed for causes, and praise or blame apportioned where relevant, as already shown.

The budgetary control system, so far as the flow of profits is concerned, may be incorporated in the financial/cost accounting system, by adding variance accounts relative to differences between achieved, and budgeted, volumes of sales (and the cost thereof), and between achieved, and budgeted, totals of items which do not enter into the cost of sales. A comprehensive budgetary system, however, is concerned also with flows of funds not directly affecting the profit and loss account—issue and redemption of share and loan capital, purchases and sales of fixed assets, increases and decreases in credit given or taken, etc.—and these are generally accommodated by means of analyses outside the books. It is theoretically possible to provide a set of self-balancing variance accounts for such movements, and use them to adjust all asset, liability, and equity balances at monthly or other intervals to the budgeted amounts, while summarizing the variances in a Funds Flow Variance Account, adjusted for depreciation charges and other revenue flows which do not represent movements of funds into or out of the entity. This is seldom, if ever, done in practice, but is illustrated in sub-section 2.2.1 in order to emphasize the double entry nature of such variances, and the need to make them internally consistent.

2.2.1 An integrated accounting/budgetary control system

Example 4 The accounting system of Steamage Products Ltd, as shown in Example 3, is now extended to incorporate a double entry sub-system of budgetary control, as outlined above. In the budget for the year ended 31 March 19.1, sales were forecast as 27,000 tons at £33.00 per ton, and selling and administrative overheads as £65,000. The budgeted trading and profit and loss account, and year-end balance sheet (with all amounts rounded to the nearest £1,000), were as follows:

Steamage Products Ltd

Budgeted Trading and Profit and Loss Account for the Year ended 31 March 19.1

	£		£
Standard cost of sales	742,000	Sales at standard price—	
Standard gross profit	149,000	27,000 tons at £33.00	891,000
	£891,000		£891,000
Selling and administrative		Standard gross profit	149,000
overheads	65,000		
Net profit before taxation	84,000		
	£149,000		£149,000
Corporation tax	34,000	Net profit before taxation	84,000
Net profit after taxation	50,000		
	£84,000		£84,000
Dividend	50,000	Net profit after taxation	50,000
Balance carried forward to next		Balance brought forward from	
year	116,000	previous year	116,000
	£166,000		£166,000

Budgeted Balance Sheet 31 March 19.1

	£	£		£	£
Share Capital		500,000	*Fixed Assets*		
Profit and Loss			Plant		360,000
Account		116,000			
		616,000			
			Current Assets		
			Raw materials		
			stock	35,000	
Current Liabilities			Work in progress	58,000	
Creditors	24,000		Finished goods		
Corporation			stock	165,000	
tax	34,000				
Proposed					258,000
dividend	50,000		Debtors		90,000
		108,000	Bank		16,000
					364,000
		£724,000			£724,000

The accounts (simplified), insofar as they differ materially from those in Example 3, might appear thus:

Steamage Products Ltd

Standard Cost of Sales

19.1		£	19.1		£
Mar 31	Finished goods		Mar 31	Cost of sales	
	stock	818,606		volume variance	76,606
			Mar 31	Trading a/c	742,000
		£818,606			£818,606

Sales

19.1		£	19.1		£
Mar 31	Sales price		Mar 31	Debtors	1,000,000
	variance				
	29,800 x £0.56	16,600			
Mar 31	Sales volume				
	variance	92,400			
Mar 31	Trading a/c	891,000			
		£1,000,000			£1,000,000

Selling and Administrative Overheads

19.1		£	19.1		£
Mar 31	Bank	70,000	Mar 31	Selling and administrative	
				overheads	
				price variance	5,000
			Mar 31	Profit and loss a/c	65,000
		£70,000			£70,000

* * *

Sales Volume Variance

19.1		£	19.1		£
Mar 31	Trading a/c	92,400	Mar 31	Sales	92,400

Selling and Administrative Overheads Price Variance

19.1		£	19.1		£
Mar 31	Selling and administrative overheads	5,000	Mar 31	Profit and loss a/c	5,000

Retained Profit Variance

19.1		£			£
Mar 31	Funds flow variance	7,759			

Creditors Variance

19.1		£			£
Mar 31	Funds flow variance	1,000			

Corporation Tax Variance

19.1		£			£
Mar 31	Funds flow variance	6,000			

Plant Cost Variance

		£	19.1		£
			Mar 31	Funds flow variance	—

Plant Accumulated Depreciation Variance

19.1		£			£
Mar 31	Funds flow variance	—			

Raw Materials Stock Total Variance

		£	19.1		£
			Mar 31	Funds flow variance	3,000

Work in Progress Total Variance

		£	19.1		£
			Mar 31	Funds flow variance	19,440

Finished Goods Stock Total Variance

19.1		£			£
Mar 31	Funds flow variance	22,156			

Debtors Variance

	£	19.1		£
		Mar 31	Funds flow variance	10,000

Bank Variance

	£	19.1		£
		Mar 31	Funds flow variance	4,000

Funds Flow Variance

19.1		£	19.1		£
Mar 31	Plant cost variance	–	Mar 31	Retained profit variance	7,284
Mar 31	Raw materials stock total variance	3,000	Mar 31	Plant accumulated depreciation variance	–
Mar 31	Work in progress total variance	19,440			7,284
Mar 31	Finished goods stock total variance	(22,156)	Mar 31	Creditors variance	1,000
		284	Mar 31	Corporation tax variance	6,000
Mar 31	Debtors variance	10,000			
Mar 31	Bank variance	4,000			
		£14,284			£14,284

Trading Account for the Year ended 31 March 19.1

		£			£
Cost of sales			Sales		
Budgeted		742,000	Budgeted		891,000
Volume variance		76,606	Volume variance		92,400
At standard cost		818,606	At standard price		983,400
Standard gross profit c/d		164,794			
		£983, 400			£983,400
Cost of sales variances			Standard gross profit		
Raw materials	Price	12,000	b/d		164,794
do	Usage	5,250	Sales variance		
Direct labour	Rate	7,500	Price		16,600
do	Efficiency	(4,250)			
Manufacturing overheads					
Price		3,115			
Activity		(5,845)			
Depreciation—plant					
Rate		(520)			
Activity		(3,615)			
		13,635			
Profit and Loss Account					
Actual gross profit		167,759			
		£181,394			£181,394

Profit and Loss Account for the Year ended 31 March 19.1

	£	£		£
Selling and Administrative Overheads			*Trading Account*	
			Actual gross profit	167,759
Budgeted	65,000			
Price variance	5,000			
		70,000		
Net profit before Taxation		97,759		
		£167,759		£167,759
Corporation tax		40,000	Net profit before taxation	97,759
Net profit after taxation		57,759		
		£97,759		£97,759
Dividend		50,000	Net profit after taxation	57,759
Balance carried forward to next year		123,284	Balance brought forward from previous year	115,525
		£173,284		£173,284

Balance Sheet, 31 March 19.1

	Budget		Actual		Variances
£	£	£	£	£	£
Share Capital	500,000		500,000		—
Profit and Loss a/c	116,000		123,284		7,284
	616,000		623,284		7,284
Current Liabilities					
Creditors	24,000		25,000	1,000	
Corporation tax	34,000		40,000	6,000	
Proposed dividend	50,000		50,000	—	
		108,000		115,000	7,000
		£724,000		£738,284	£14,284
Fixed Assets					
Plant	360,000		360,000		—
Current Assets					
Raw materials stock	35,000		38,000	3,000	
Work in progress	58,000		77,440	19,440	
Finished goods stock	165,000		142,844	(22,156)	
	258,000		258,284	284	
Debtors	90,000		100,000	10,000	
Bank	16,000		20,000	4,000	
		364,000		378,284	14,284
		£724,000		£738,284	£14,284

The additional and rearranged variances make clear the part played by the increased volume of sales in augmenting the gross profit, and show how the increased 'cash flow' from trading (retained profit plus depreciation added back), £7,284, has been applied almost entirely in improving the liquidity position by £7,000 (£10,000 + £4,000 − £1,000 − £6,000) as compared with the budget. The liquidity ratio, £120,000/£115,000 or 1.04, now seems just adequate, whereas the budget provided for a ratio of only £106,000/£108,000, or 0.98—below the bare minimum of 1. The large excess of debtors over the budgeted amount requires investigation, and analysis as between increased sales, in volume and in price, and changes in the speed of collection of receivables. The funds flow variance account, and the detailed variances which accompany it, may be treated as memorandum entries—in which case the detailed accounts might be omitted and the main one used alone. For theoretical correctness, these variances should be written back to the funds flow variance account as on 1 April 19.1, thus closing all the accounts.

2.2.2 Further development of the accounting system

Integration of the financial, costing and budgetary functions of the firm, on lines indicated above, exploits the full possibilities of double entry book-keeping in the present state of the art. In large modern businesses the planning function extends beyond traditional budgetary control, with its time-horizon of one year at most, and embraces capital budgeting and corporate planning. *Capital budgeting* endeavours to lay down a programme of capital expenditure for several years ahead—about five years is the usual horizon—on the basis of major projects selected, most scientifically, by discounted cash flow analysis, in which the incremental cash flows from the project (estimated with the aid of the statistical techniques of risk analysis and sensitivity analysis) are evaluated by time-discounting to a base date at a rate of interest derived from the estimated cost of raising capital for the firm (see Chapter 5). These operations cannot initially be brought within the double entry system, but as time overtakes the plans for capital expenditure they are progressively incorporated into the annual budgets, and thence into the financial and costing records. *Corporate planning*, developed in America in the 1950s and adopted by many large British companies from the 1960s, seeks to lay down in quantitative terms the fundamental business strategies to be pursued by the company over the next ten to twenty years—basically, by forecasting the probable economic evolution of the relevant and allied industries over the period, and devising developments which are calculated to enable the company to earn for its equity shareholders a long-term rate of return on their investment which shall be at least equal to the expected average for investments with a similar degree of risk. It is within the framework of the corporate plan (if any) that the capital budget is drawn up.

From what has been said, it is apparent that the accounting system forms the core of the firm's system of *management information* in general. Every scrap of information which is quantifiable in terms of money is either derived from the accounting system or related to it in some way, and if it appears in any other records of the firm, these must be consistent with the accounts. Obvious examples are the stores and stock records, generally in the form of memorandum ledger accounts of quantities and values received, and issued or despatched, and of balances on hand at any time. It is from monthly or more frequent summaries of such movements that the entries in the cost accounts are built up, on the basis of assumptions about the sequence in which raw materials purchased at different times enter production, and of the quantities of finished goods transferred to the warehouse; while the detailed incidence of costs in the productive processes is followed in memorandum work in progress records which, again, form the basis of monthly or more frequent costing entries. Even such non-accounting papers as salesmen's reports, personnel records, legal documents, and minutes of directors' and shareholders' meetings are ultimately related to the raising and disbursement of money, and to controls thereover, and cannot be wholly neglected by a company accountant who takes a broad view of his responsibilities, or by an external auditor who endeavours conscientiously to satisfy himself that the accounts give the 'true and fair view' required by law.

All this applies, still more cogently, to the firm's system of *management reports.* These are furnished daily, weekly, four-weekly or monthly, or at longer intervals by those responsible for processing information to those who are to act or take decisions upon it, at all levels of management from foremen to directors. Reports to the junior grades are primarily in non-monetary terms, such as physical quantities of output of a single machine-shop or section of the works; but as one moves up the hierarchy the reports contain a larger and larger amount of financial data, until at board level they take the form, for the most part, of monthly or four-weekly profit and loss statements and balance sheets. Such information comes mainly from the accounting system, which must be so arranged as to allow the figures to be promptly ascertained and extracted, if the information is to be available in time to be of any use for rapid decision-making. For example, the works manager will require monthly or four-weekly summaries of the standard costs of all finished production, with variances and work in progress (quantities and values). Not only must the particulars of raw materials consumed, wages earned, and overheads incurred be entered as soon as possible after the events, and reach the work in progress account by the month-end or very soon after, but the month-end work in progress must be calculated as accurately as is practicable, before reliable variances can be extracted. Speed is more vital than meticulous precision, since all work in progress valuations can only be approximations; but the accounting function must take note of the shop-floor position, and is dependent upon production records, punctually written up in as much detail as is needed to denote the numbers of units in process, and the stage which each one or each batch has reached. Hence the chief accountant, and the cost accountant, must be consulted in the design of the routine records in the works, and approve the time-table for keeping them up to date.

To sum up, then, the information system of any undertaking is a unity whose various parts must be logically related, and their contents mutually consistent. The accounting system, in its widest sense, is the nerve-centre of the business, and all other information sub-systems must be articulated with it to a greater or lesser degree. How far this ideal is attained depends largely, however, upon the organization of the *data processing system* which collects, transmits, and operates upon the vast mass of information which continually presents itself to the firm; and this is the subject of Chapter 3.

3 Data processing systems

Every accounting system, simple or complex, needs a mechanism for collecting economic data at the point in time when they impinge upon the accounting entity, translating them where necessary into money terms, and ordering them into the most significant form for incorporation in the double entry records as expeditiously as possible. This mechanism is the *data processing system,* in its widest sense and regardless of the detailed methods used—hand-written journals, document files, or mechanical, electro-mechanical, or electronic apparatus of greater or less sophistication. The more advanced applications may produce few records recognizable as 'books of account' in the format commonly visualized, but the principles of double entry book-keeping underlie them all, and the figures can always be reduced conceptually to debit-and-credit accounts. The content of these accounts depends upon the chosen set of rules employed to recognize and quantify changes of state in the entity, and is independent of the means adopted to collect and order the basic data.

3.1 Principles of data processing

At least seven functions can be distinguished in any data processing system:

1 the *recognition* of relevant data;
2 its *classification* according to its nature and relation to the system;
3 the *recording* of it in prescribed form;
4 its *monetization,* or conversion (where necessary) into the currency in which the accounts are kept;
5 its *summarization,* or grouping with other data of a similar nature;
6 its *translation into double entry*; and
7 its *manipulation* according to the rules of the accounting system.

Planning must take account of all these factors, but more fundamental still are the purpose of the system, and the kind of information it is intended to provide. Many systems have been constructed haphazardly, beginning with simple book-keeping and expanding as the firm grew, by means of unco-ordinated *ad hoc* additions. There is then no guarantee that the most useful data will always be collected, or that they will be analysed in the most significant ways, or communicated in the most suitable form to those who are to make decisions or take action on them. The installation of mechanized or electronic data processing equipment is often the first occasion on which the system is looked at comprehensively and critically, and a new one consciously designed to attain chosen objectives. Even so, every system needs to be continuously reviewed and kept up to date, if it is to meet the changing requirements of management for significant information.

Design, then, begins with the construction of a set of double entry accounts, on lines described in Chapter 2. Apart from standard accounts common to all business firms, or to all manufacturing firms (if relevant), there must be nominal accounts so arranged as to analyse revenue and expenditure in the manner most significant for costing, internal control, and profit planning purposes—e.g. so as to separate fixed and variable costs, and/or the fixed and variable elements in costs which increase or decrease with total output or sales, but not proportionately; to allocate overhead expenditure to 'cost centres', such as departments, machine shops, or individual machines, and obtain a standard rate of charge per hour for work passing through the cost centre; and to throw up the required variances for standard costing and budgetary control. Besides all this, there must be set up all the non-accounting records, especially those which make use of financial information, or provide non-financial data for use in the accounts (such as hours of work and wage-rates of individual employees, or daily or weekly volumes of finished production). There must also be designed, concurrently, the system of internal management reports, integrating the information which is to be furnished to each level of responsibility in the organization. Only when all this is done is it really possible to decide just what inputs of information are required, how they may be most efficiently processed, and how the accuracy of the records may best be guaranteed.

Of the seven steps in data processing set out at the beginning of this section, the first three may be taken together. *Recognition* of data should take place as soon as possible after an economic event occurs which changes the financial state of the entity concerned, or which is a necessary preliminary to such a change—e.g. the receipt of an order from a customer, or the engagement of a new employee. Normally the event is signalled by the presentation of a document, either from outside the firm (such as a delivery note or an invoice for goods supplied), or from within it (such as a time card or a sales dispatch note). *Classification* assigns the document to the member of staff responsible for dealing with all similar documents, and he or she must then *record* the information according to the rules prescribed in the firm's data processing manual (prepared by the chief accountant or by a specialist data processing manager).

The first step in recording is to assign to an 'outside' document, such as a supplier's invoice, a serial number, usually impressed by a stamp which advances the number after each use. Each number, or the first and last numbers for each day for each kind of document, is/are entered in a register, so that it is always known how many such documents are in the system, and so that they may be followed up, by serial number, in due course. At the point of entry, too, an outside document will be stamped with a 'grid' of rectangular spaces, containing words indicating the nature of the further operations to be performed upon the document, and places for the initials of those who perform them. An 'inside' document, such as a sales invoice, already has a printed serial number and spaces for initialling as operations are performed, and normally two or more copies are prepared at once. Documents of either kind are then passed in order to all the persons whose duty it is to make a permanent record of all or some of the data, their tasks being so arranged that every item considered to be significant is set down for processing. When a document has gone through every process it is filed away with all like items in serial number order, within its proper batch (of serial numbers) and/or its proper accounting sub-period (week, month, etc.), and the fact noted, preferably on the register of such documents.

Thus are generated all the original entries, consistency being assured as far as practicable by the use of one document for many purposes—a different person making each type of entry, and initialling for it. Some entries are made directly in the double entry books (e.g. the cash book, or, in mechanized systems, the personal ledgers), others in intermediate books, such as purchases or sales journals, where they are subjected to such analysis as the accounting system requires. *Monetization* often occurs simultaneously with recording, where data are originally presented in sterling; otherwise quantitative information must be converted into money—labour-hours multiplied by each man's hourly rate of wages, stores requisition notes priced out for the costing records, sales dispatch notes priced and extended to produce sales invoices, etc.—by reference to properly authorized schedules of rates or prices, before being incorporated in the accounts. The further stages of *summarization, translation into double entry,* and *manipulation* within it, vary considerably according to the type of data processing system in force, as explained in section **3.2.**

3.1.1 Internal control

One of the most important functions of management is *internal control* of the undertaking. This comprises all arrangements intended to control the raising of the firm's funds, safeguard its assets, ensure that both are raised or applied only for properly authorized purposes, and maintain accurate and reliable records of all matters concerning the firm.

Internal control rests upon a coherent management structure, with clear separation of functions between different sections of the staff, proper definition of authority and accountability between different levels of 'line' management, and precise assignment of responsibilities to individuals. Insofar as this ideal is approximated, an effective system can be devised to make sure, e.g. that the raising of substantial amounts of capital is always sanctioned by the board of directors; that all major capital expenditure is similarly sanctioned, with smaller projects and minor replacement of assets controlled by senior executives; that physical assets and cash are properly protected, and adequately insured, against fire, theft, accidental damage, and other casualties, and that the firm has full insurance cover for liability in respect of injury to the persons or property of employees and the public; that there is a proper system of books of account, for financial, costing, budgetary, and internal reporting purposes, and adequate records otherwise; and that adequate precautions are taken against error and fraud.

To begin with, in a business of any size it is desirable that all the ledger accounts, especially those in the general ledger, should be denoted by a set of code numbers, according to some consistent plan—preferably a form of decimal coding, analogous to the Dewey system used to classify books in libraries. In such a system one or more digits to the left of the decimal point stand for a general class of accounts—fixed assets, current liabilities, manufacturing expenses, etc.—and the digits to the right of the point denote finer and finer subdivisions of the class, the more places that are taken. Thus, as a hypothetical example: '105.4125' might mean 'manufacturing overheads (105.)—repairs and renewals (0.4)—to plant and machinery (0.01)—at the Birmingham factory (0.002)—in machine-shop No. 5 (0.0005)'. Such a scheme may be laid down by the senior management, as to the first few places of figures and applied to the most obviously-required accounts, leaving middle management to extend the codes to further places (rightwards), so as to meet their own needs for detailed analysis.

In some countries, indeed, such 'charts of accounts' have been laid down officially as standard classifications, recommended, or required, for use by all taxpaying businesses.[1] The British government is not concerned to regulate book-keeping methods in detail, in a country where accounting and the accountancy profession are highly developed; but every large company, and group of companies in particular, must find it advantageous to devise an accounts code which allows the ledgers to be structured on the lines indicated. The technique may be further refined, especially in the cost accounts, by establishing a hierarchy of ledger accounts, associated with the system of internal reports. Thus (to continue the previous example), an invoice coded 105.4125 would be credited to the suppliers' personal account, and debited to Account 105.4125—Manufacturing Overheads—Repairs and Renewals—Plant and Machinery—Birmingham Factory—Machine-Shop No. 5. At the end of the month or four-week period concerned, the debit balance of the account might be incorporated in a report to the foreman of that shop, then transferred to the debit of Account 105.412—Manufacturing Overheads—Repairs and Renewals—Plant and Machinery—Birmingham Factory. The balance for the month, etc., could then be incorporated in a report to the works manager at Birmingham, after which it would be transferred to the debit of Account 105.41—Manufacturing Overheads—Repairs and Renewals—Plant and Machinery, and so on upwards to Account 105—Manufacturing Overheads, whose balance would be taken into the monthly manufacturing account, presented to the board of directors. Alternatively, the detail account balances might be channelled to accounts for cost centres, from which a charge, at a standard rate, would be made to Work in Progress Account.

The coherence of the accounting system having been secured by some such procedure, it is also necessary to build in arrangements for *sectional balancing*. The annual trial balance, though useful as a prima facie proof of the double entry before preparing the final accounts, is not enough. In a complex system it is necessary to balance the books, at least at the end of each sub-period, or even oftener—in extreme cases, every day, as in a branch of a bank. The great number of personal (particularly, debtors') accounts in many firms makes it imperative to be able to balance each set of ledgers, and each individual ledger, separately, and so localize errors revealed by failure to agree the totals of debit, and credit, balances. Accordingly, each set of accounts not included in the general ledger is represented therein by a *Control Account,* or *Total Account,* for the other ledger. By the use of suitable analysis in the books of original entry or other auxiliary records, the entries in each personal ledger or division thereof for a month or other sub-period are summarized, type by type, and the totals entered in the control account, on the *same* sides as in the personal ledgers (where they appear as detail entries in individual customers' or suppliers' accounts). The opening balance of a control account is equal to, and of the same sign as, the algebraic sum of all opening balances in the relevant ledger, and it follows that, if there have been no errors, the closing balance of the control account will similarly correspond with the total of the closing balances on the personal ledger. Any differences between the two figures will denote one or more errors in the control account, or in the personal ledger, or both, and these must be searched for and corrected in a methodical manner. The same system may be applied to the cash and/or bank accounts, particularly where separate cash receipts and cash payments books are kept, and

[1] See: Mattessich, R. *Accounting and Analytical Methods,* Irwin, 1964.

analyses of them brought into a Cash (and/or Bank) Control Account in the general ledger—with receipts on the debit, and payments on the credit, sides as in an ordinary cash book.

Example 1 A typical Sales Ledger Control Account might appear as under:

Sales Ledger Control Account

19.1		£	19.1		£
May 1	Balance b/d	30,000	May 31	Bank control a/c	26,000
May 31	Sales	40,000	May 31	Discounts allowed	700
			May 31	Returns inwards	1,200
			May 31	Purchases ledger control a/c	800
			May 31	Bad debts	1,100
			May 31	Balance c/d	40,200
		£70,000			£70,000
19.1					
Jun 1	Balance b/d	40,200			

In such a system the control account is regarded as part of the double entry while the personal ledger is treated as a memorandum record, outside the double entry and providing detailed analysis, by customers or suppliers, of the summary entries in the account. This approach is adequate in simpler cases, but where there is a large number of personal ledgers, subdivided alphabetically, geographically, or otherwise, it is better policy to make each of them self-balancing, as well as the main book-keeping system. This is done by opening in each volume of each ledger a General Ledger Control Account, summarizing the total balances and entries for each month, etc., on the opposite sides to those in which they appear in the body of the ledger; for example, the Control Account in Sales Ledger A–D will open with a credit balance equal and opposite to the total opening debit balances in the ledger, and be credited with sales to customers A–D for the month, and debited with cash, etc., received from them. The single Debtors Control Account in the general ledger, whose debit balance represents the total debtors of the firm, thus has its counterparts in the several control accounts in the sales ledgers, whose total credit balances should be equal and opposite. The supervisor of each sales ledger section is then responsible for agreeing the control account balances in his own ledgers with the total of the month-end list of customers' balances therein, and for searching for errors causing discrepancies. When all ledgers are balanced, the control account balances are totalled and the amount furnished to the general ledger section, for comparison with the independently prepared control account therein—with more error investigation if the two balances do not agree. Similarly, the Bank Control Account balance must be reconciled with that reported by the bank at a given date, and the inventory account balances with the physical stocks and work in progress, or (during the year) with the 'perpetual inventories' in the memorandum stores, and stock, ledgers. If a balanced trial balance cannot then be extracted from the general ledger, the source of the discrepancy must be sought there, or in the books which are posted to it.

The financial accounts, then, are often divided into several double entry sub-systems, linked together by control accounts (cf. Example 2 in Chapter 2, where the financial and costing sub-systems were so linked). The final accounts are prepared exclusively from the general ledger.

3.1.2 Internal check and internal audit

An important aspect of internal control is *internal check*–the arrangement of the book-keeping and other records so as to ensure as far as practicable that every entry is checked, in the ordinary course of duty, by at least one person other than the one who made it, and that every original entry is properly supported by a document made out or checked by some other person. The objects are to make each part of the records provide independent confirmation of some other part; to bring errors to light as early as possible, and to correct them with minimum trouble; and to make fraud or theft as difficult as possible to perpetrate, or conceal by false entries in the records, without securing the co-operation of some other person in the organization or outside it, and thus exposing the criminal to a greater risk of detection or denunciation, as well as forcing him to share his ill-gotten gains.

Apart from the obvious devices of causing each book of original entry to be kept by a different person, and the ledgers by different persons again, internal check consists very largely of dividing the various steps in a transaction between several persons, none of them under the authority or influence of any other in that group. Thus, raw materials or bought-out goods are requisitioned by the storekeeper or warehouse manager, ordered by the purchasing officer, checked on to the premises by the gatekeeper, received into the stores or warehouse by, again, the storekeeper or warehouse manager, and released only on the authority of a foreman or engineer, or of the dispatch department. Each person concerned makes his own record–storekeeper's, etc., requisition form, copy of order form, goods inwards book at the gate, bin cards, stores requisition note–on consecutively numbered stationery where applicable, and related records should be compared from time to time. A delivery note is presented to the storekeeper by the driver; one copy is signed and returned as a receipt (after the load has been checked), the other is retained as the basis of the bin card entries, then sent to the stores ledger keeper, who enters the quantities, and to the purchasing officer, who checks that the goods are as ordered and attaches the note to his copy order. When the supplier's invoice arrives it is passed through the control procedure (see section 3.1), then goes to the purchasing officer, who checks it with the delivery note; to the stores ledger keeper (with the delivery note), who prices out the entry previously made, and retains the delivery note; to the keeper of the purchases journal or equivalent record, who enters it; to the purchasing officer again, who agrees it with the supplier's statement and passes the statement for payment (or directly to the cashier, who draws a cheque against it and obtains the signature of, say, a director and the chief accountant); and finally to the purchases journal keeper, etc., who files it in sequence.

This is a fairly straightforward illustration of internal check in relation to transactions evidenced by documents originating outside the firm, where the main danger of fraud lies in the making of fictitious entries, supported by forged or altered documents–in the case of purchases, intended to cover up fictitious payments entered in the cash book, or payments to outside accomplices for goods or services which have not been supplied. Where the evidential documents (or 'vouchers') are made out within the firm, as with receipts for cash and invoices to customers, internal check includes consecutive numbering by the printers and rigorous control of custody and issue, by persons unconnected with the book-keeping. The danger here is that misappropriation of cash (for which genuine receipts are given) may be covered up by omission of the amounts from the cash book—the wrongdoer using a 'spare' receipt book. The fraud may be extended, if there is collusion with someone in the sales ledger section, by the suppression of sales invoices to genuine customers, whose payments are misappropriated as above. Again, the main defences are separation of tasks and frequent comparison of related records—e.g. goods outwards book with sales invoices, to see whether any goods have gone out and not apparently been charged to anyone.

Worse dangers arise where cheques are received and no formal receipts given, as is general today; or where large sums in wages are paid out weekly without receipts from the employees. The first situation is covered, for example, by the making of a record of all cheques coming in through the post, and the stamping of them with the crossing 'account payee only' by a responsible person independent of the cashier; the latter by rigorous joining and leaving procedures, maximum subdivision of the labour of preparing the payroll, and rotation of tasks among the clerks at short intervals, with a foreman present at the pay-out to ensure that strangers do not collect wages, and a strict rule that no packet is given except to the worker named or to someone bringing a note signed by him/her, together with strict control over the disposal of unclaimed packets.

Internal check, like internal control in general, thus goes well outside formal book-keeping. In larger organizations (particularly in the public sector of the economy) it is reinforced by *internal audit*, conducted by a specialized staff entirely separate from those who maintain the accounts and other records, but responsible to the chief accounting executive. The internal auditor keeps under continuous review the various systems of internal control and internal check, watching for weaknesses and lapses of vigilance, recommending their eradication where they are found, and generally endeavouring continually to improve the accuracy and efficiency of the data processing. His subordinates conduct continuous test-checks upon the detailed operations of the record-keepers, including, for example, regular spot-checks on stores and stock to satisfy themselves that the 'perpetual inventory' in the stores and stock ledgers is reasonably in line with the physical quantities on hand, and the following-up of all significant divergencies which appear.

Internal check, whether or not supplemented by internal audit, is most valuable as a mechanism for bringing clerical errors to light quickly, before they run right through the accounting system, and as a moral deterrent to employees of weak character who might otherwise be tempted to defraud the firm. The really dishonest employee is compelled to exercise more ingenuity, and ideally to obtain one or more confederates; the gain to him is reduced and the risk of detection multiplied. Yet internal check, and audit, can restrain only relatively junior employees; senior staff, if fraudulent, are commonly able to circumvent such devices. The main defence is the *external audit* by independent professional accountants, appointed by the proprietors or shareholders and given full powers to investigate annually or more frequently all aspects of the business which bear upon the accounts, and to report to their principals thereon. (See Chapter 14.)

3.2 Design of data processing systems

The variety of business recording systems is immense, being governed by variations in the size and complexity of businesses, and the degree of sophistication of the management and its consequent demand for information. Four main types may be distinguished:

a hand-written systems;
b keyboard machine systems;
c punched-card systems; and
d electronic or computerized systems.

Only broad outlines can be given here.

3.2.1 Hand-written systems

The conventional two- or three-column cash-book (for cash and bank accounts, and sometimes discounts allowed and received) is still common enough in smaller firms. In medium-sized and larger firms its two sides generally become separate receipts and payments books (dealing with bank transactions only), whose weekly or other totals are posted to the debit and credit of a Bank Control (or Total) Account in the general ledger, or summarized in a separate cash book, without details. All cash received is banked intact, preferably the same, or next, business day so as to prevent the 'borrowing' of one or more days' receipts by the cashier ('teeming and lading'). All payments of any size are made by cheque, and small cash items pass through a separate petty cash book kept on the 'imprest' system.

The purchases, sales, and returns outwards and inwards journals (or day books), described in elementary textbooks, are now relatively rare. They are either reduced to mere registers of invoices and credit notes, with monthly totals, or replaced by the documents themselves, filed in numerically-ordered batches, analysed on their faces by means of the stamped 'grid' mentioned earlier, and accompanied by adding-machine listings, totalled by analysis categories and overall. It is these figures which enter the purchases, sales, returns, and personal ledger control accounts, via the journal proper. In some systems even the creditors' ledger is dispensed with. Purchase invoices, as they are passed correct, are placed in an accounts payable file and, at the month-end, are used to prepare cheques to suppliers, and then transferred to an accounts paid file. The double entry consists of credits to Bank, duly analysed and totalled, and a single debit to Purchases (or Raw Materials, or Stock) for the total amount. At the year-end, creditors are computed from unpaid invoices; the amount is treated as an 'accrual' on Purchases or other appropriate account(s). Often, too, batches of invoices (less credit notes) are paid net of cash discount and purchases valued thus. If discount is forfeited for late payment, a Discount Receivable Forfeited Account is debited with the extra amount paid, and the year's total transferred to the debit of Profit and Loss Account, as a species of financing charge—a form of interest at a penal rate. (This system also provides a check on the efficiency of the cashier's department—a form of management by exception.)

Further savings of labour, without using any machinery, can be effected by means of a pegboard—a substantial base-board with metal pegs down the left-hand side. These pegs fit into perforations in the special stationery supplied, and enable a carbon-backed original document, such as a receipt form or a cheque, to be so positioned over, e.g. a cash received or cash paid sheet that the entry thereon is made as the document is written, without the possibility of any unintended discrepancy. With the use of a special typewriter, allowing documents to be inserted in front of, and correctly aligned with, the record-sheet as it is moved up line by line, the process can be further speeded up. The ledgers are still hand-written, but flexibility is attained by using loose-leaf binders.

3.2.2 Keyboard machine systems

Real mechanization normally begins with the ledgers, especially the debtors' or sales ledgers, which are generally the most bulky. The accounts are kept on cards, filed in trays, and having three money columns—for debit, credit, and balance. Entries are made from original documents by means of a keyboard machine, like an expanded typewriter, which has adding devices, providing periodic totals of similar items, and which also calculates and prints out a revised balance in the third column of the card after each entry in either of the other two. (The same machine can be used, without resetting, for the creditors' ledger by using cards with the debit and credit columns reversed, and reading positive balances as credit instead of debit.)

The keyboard-operator works at high speed in a quasi-mechanical fashion, the documents being previously inserted before the relevant accounts, or the cards extracted, or offset in the trays. The documents are also batched and pre-listed on an adding machine, and the totals noted beforehand by the supervisor, who compares them with the keyboard machine totals, reported by the operators from registers or from printed paper tape automatically produced during posting. As a further check on accuracy, 'hash totals' are calculated before and during posting, and compared—i.e. the document serial numbers are added up, and/or each customer's account number is added to the amount posted each time (taking the number as pounds) and the whole added—producing totals which, though meaningless in themselves, are almost certain to disagree as between pre-list and machine-operator if any posting error is made, and so constitute a rigorous test of the correctness of each batch. One source of weakness is the need for the operator, before posting an item, to pick up the previous balance, if the machine is to calculate and print out the new one correctly. Some systems require her to pick up the old balance both before and after posting, the machine subtracting the second figure from the first and locking if the answer is not zero. More sophisticated machines require pick-up of double the old balance (printed on the card at the same time as the balance) before posting and of the single old balance after, the machine doubling the latter and subtracting, and printing out the revised, doubled balance. Finally, it is essential to have a control account (see sub-section 3.1.1) for each tray, and to balance it at least monthly, against a machine-list of account-card balances.

3.2.3 Punched-card systems

The oldest form of total mechanization of the data processing system (introduced before the Second World War) involves the use of electro-mechanical devices actuated by holes punched in small cards. The position of each hole denotes one digit, or one letter or other sign, and the commonest size of card is 80 columns. Thus, up to 80 characters per card can theoretically be accommodated; the actual number is less, as gaps have to be left between the various 'fields'—serial number of document, supplier/customer number, description, expense analysis code, amount in pounds and pence, etc.

Every original document, after passing through a control procedure and entering the system of internal check as already described, is represented by a card (or several cards, one to each item), into which is punched all the information on the document, in numerical form as far as possible. A second machine-operator then passes the cards through a verifier, operating its keyboard from the same documents. In some systems the first punching makes round holes in the card, and the verifier makes them oval, so that later machines reject a card which shows a round hole anywhere. In others, the punch makes rectangular holes and the verifier senses them; it locks if the second key-depression does not agree with the first, and the cause of the discrepancy must then be investigated. A further development is the use of a gang-punch to insert the same constants on a large number of cards; the variables are added by the hand-punch operator, but the whole of each card has to be verified (in case the wrong gang-punched cards are selected), or some consistency check provided in a later machine. Several copies of a series of cards can also be made by a reproducer.

Each card is normally used for several purposes before being filed away. Since cards can only be processed one at a time, they must be sorted into an appropriate sequence (according to the numbers or letters in one field) for each operation, by means of a sorter, which orders them by one 'place' at a time, beginning with the digits of highest order (on the left). The cards are then fed into a tabulator, which by changing the permutations of its internal electrical connections can be 'programmed' to print out on a continuous roll or sheet the information on each card or selected parts of it; a sub-total or balance (algebraic total) of each sub-section or account, as the relevant number changes; and a grand total where necessary. In a ledger application a series of opening balance cards for all accounts must be collated, by another machine, with the new data cards, and the tabulator automatically punches out a new balance card for each account—to be used as the old balance card next time.

Such arrangements, with heavy overheads in depreciation and maintenance, or rental, or expensive equipment, require intensive usage to make them economic. Not only are the conventional financial and cost accounts produced in recognizable double entry form, albeit with 'plus and minus' instead of 'left-hand and right-hand' layout, but the stores and stock ledgers can also be kept in this way, utilizing the same data inputs, and customers' statements and other documents prepared at the same time. (Payroll still has to be made out manually, owing to the limitations of the tabulators.) The gains are not only the handling of an increased bulk of data with (often) fewer staff, but greater accuracy through diminished possibility of human error, and assured consistency between related records, since the same punched cards provide the original entries in both or all. On the other hand, there is greater danger than in a manual system that an error made at the outset (e.g. a card on which both punch operator and verifier make the same mistake) will run right through to the final accounts, since the processing machines have no discretion and no judgement. It is therefore advisable to make use of hash totals derived from batches of original documents, and to feed them into the tabulators by means of special cards, one at the end of each batch of data cards—the tabulator being set to produce corresponding hash totals and to subtract the ones on the special cards, and the supervisor checking that the answers are all zero. Control accounts will also be employed as on manual or keyboard systems, but will normally be compiled by hand, from the totals of the analysis sheets and ledger balance lists produced by the tabulators. The trial balance will generally be hand-written also.

3.2.4 Electronic or computerized systems

The first digital computers suitable for commercial use became available in the early 1950s. Technological improvements since then have enormously amplified their storage capacity and calculating speed, while spectacularly reducing their physical bulk, and their costs of operation in real terms. In its early days electronic data processing (EDP) was regarded as the next step after punched cards—the last word in sophistication for a giant organization. Today the range of installation capacity is very wide, and companies of quite modest size find it economic to computerize an information system previously based on keyboard machinery, while still smaller firms may obtain the benefits of EDP, without installing their own equipment, by sending work to a computer service bureau.

The distinctive features of EDP, as compared with other information processing systems, are comprehensiveness and versatility. In principle the entire management information system can be computerized, while still leaving capacity for other purposes, such as engineering and operational research calculations; and the computer can be programmed, not merely to keep the records but to perform many routine control and decision-making functions, such as determining optimum levels of stock and directing middle management when and how much to re-order as each line runs down—or even making out the orders itself. Again, unlike conventional punched-card equipment, a computer can store vast quantities of numerical information, in the form of magnetic charges, both temporarily in its immediate access store and more permanently on magnetic tape or disks, transfer information from one location to another, compare two figures and, according to whether the difference is positive, negative, or zero and/or whether it does or does not fall within given limits, execute one set of instructions rather than another ('branching'). The computer has the further advantage over electro-mechanical devices that it not only works much more swiftly and silently, but does so without the need to print out anything save the information which is actually wanted for management purposes, and with the ability to print it in any form reasonably required and simultaneously with any other documents required—e.g. customers' statements *and* a list of debtors' balances, or a complete payroll *and* employees' pay slips.

More than any other kind of data processing, EDP compels management, before deciding whether to install it, to make a complete and thorough appraisal of its existing information system, of the types of information which it produces, and of the uses to which they are put. The preliminary feasibility study, even if it results in a decision against computerization, is never a wasted exercise, for it subjects the whole system, often for the first time in the firm's history, to minute examination in every part, and calls in question the necessity of every operation concerned with the gathering, recording, and manipulation of data and its communication to those who use it. Improvement and simplification of the old system may alone suffice to pay for the feasibility study; if a decision to install EDP results, the benefits are greater still. The next step is a detailed systems study, by systems analysts, concentrating on each of the main data flows and deciding how it will be handled by the computer. Each flow is first worked out schematically in a *flow chart,* using standard symbols to show the main data processing steps in a general way. The computing operations are then set down in a *block diagram,* followed by a detailed diagram of computing steps. When the computer and its peripheral equipment are installed, each detailed diagram must be translated into a *program,* normally written in a programming language such as COBOL—the manufacturers supplying a 'compiler' or 'translator' program, permanently stored in the computer, which converts the written program into the appropriate machine language (entirely in numerical form). Before any program can be put into regular operation it must be exhaustively tested and freed of faults ('debugged'); even then, it is usual for the old hand or mechanical system to be run for a short experimental period in parallel with the new electronic one, until the latter is working reliably.

EDP, too, is in the highest degree output-orientated—there is no room for the production of information without a clear idea as to its practical usefulness to management, nor for print-outs which do not provide either objective, or control, information. The computer imposes a need to treat the information system as a unity, in which the financial accounting records are but one element, and in which it is more important to process all related figures together than to observe the conventional divisions between different 'books of account', or between these and non-accounting records. Finally, EDP shows up mercilessly the true cost of unnecessary exception routines, in complicating the programming of a job and wasting very expensive computing time every week or every day that the job is run. The systems analyst has not only to produce an integrated information system, or set of sub-systems, but to press the management to simplify and streamline its requirements—to consider, for example, whether it is really necessary to have fifteen different rates of trade discount to customers of various standings, when three rates would be so much easier for the computer to deal with.

Again, EDP is unique in the degree of centralization which it imposes on the information system. The equipment is delicate and requires special air-conditioned accommodation, accessible only to the computing staff. These personnel form a self-contained department, to which the 'user' departments supply properly batched data documents, supported by pre-calculated hash totals and other control figures. Within the EDP department, the data are translated into punched cards or punched paper tape, duly verified. In the case of tape, the verifier repunches the original and, if the second punching agrees with the first, punches a second tape of a different colour, which is fed into the central processing unit (the actual computer). Standing data—debtors' or creditors' balances, standard costs of raw materials and components, selling prices of products, etc.—are input at the same time on magnetic disks, or on magnetic tape with the program for the job written at the head, and read into the immediate access store at the outset. The output consists of print-outs on special stationery, and/or magnetic tape providing input for the next stage of the job, or for the same job the next time round—the latter carrying the program, read out from the internal storage. Magnetic tapes go back into the library at the end of the job; output in visible form, after careful editing, is dispatched to the user department.

Such centralization requires a system of internal control within the EDP department, to compensate for diminution in the potency of orthodox internal check based on wide dispersion of clerical tasks; this is not wholly eliminated, but still applies to movements of cash and goods, and to documents before they are handed over to the EDP department. Within the latter, there is distinction of tasks between the sections devoted to input preparation, computer operation, editing of output, and custody of programs and tape-files; programming, systems analysis and development; and overall control. Physical security of both 'hardware' (computing equipment) and 'software' (programs, magnetic files, special stationery, etc.) must be provided for. In particular, written master copies of all proved programs should be stored under lock and key at a location remote from the installation, so that a fire or other catastrophe does not destroy many man-years of work on them, while all magnetic files, such as ledger balances, which are constantly updated by rewriting on to a new tape should be kept intact until, at least, the next two tapes in the sequence have been proved correct (the 'grandfather–father–son' system). All computing work needs to be tightly scheduled, with each regular job done on a set day at a set time; materials required for the job, including the program, are to be signed out of the library when the job commences, and signed in again when it finishes; and the computer console operator must enter details in his log, including times of starting and finishing. In addition, there is often an automatic typewriter log, locked away from the operator and examined periodically by the computer manager, which records every manipulation of the console controls.

Precautions against error are more important than in any other system, because of the absence of human intervention, once the data have been rendered into machine-sensible form. Hash totals and counts of the number of items must be pre-calculated by the user departments for each batch of data, and fed into the computer, programmed to calculate them independently, subtract from the given figures and test that the answers are zero. Each separate number, of every kind, may be subjected to a parity check by having an extra digit added, such that the sum of the digits always possesses some arithmetical peculiarity (e.g. exact divisibility by a particular prime number), for which the computer is programmed to test each time—rejecting any item which does not conform. Other validity checks include tests to detect meaningless code numbers, and limit checks to query amounts which appear absurdly large or small in their context—the latter being usually processed, but printed out separately for examination. Any errors that do arise are normally corrected by hand at the stage of editing output. A proper set of error routines should be laid down in the EDP manual, and scrupulously followed.

Computerization makes fraud at once more difficult to perpetrate and more difficult to detect. The interdependence of the whole information system, and the elaborate numerical checks imposed on all data, make simple invention or suppression of entries almost impossible within the system, without affecting the question of fabrication of external documents or suppression of internally-generated ones. Successful fraud is most likely to be perpetrated by an ingenious programmer who writes in sub-routines designed to transfer moneys, in very small sums, from a large number of accounts to one—e.g., by rounding all wages calculations downwards, and transferring the resulting overall difference to his own or an accomplice's pay packet, or abstracting trivial sums from a great number of bank accounts for the benefit of one in a false name—as has been done. The main safeguards are vetting of all programs by senior systems analysts, the retention of master copies inaccessible to the programmers, the need for senior approval (or at least knowledge) of all alterations, the occasional printing-out of working programs for comparison with the master copies—preferably by surprise, when the programs are about to be run—and the running of test-packs of punched cards containing pre-calculated data which are checked with the print-out.

The use of a computer service bureau, or the hiring of time on another company's computer, places the problems of EDP departmental security and control outside the competence of the user company, while making it less likely that anyone in the bureau, etc., will have the motivation or ability to commit a fraud. Control is concentrated on the preparation of data for the bureau, and on the vetting of the computer output returned by it.[2]

[2] See further, Thomas, A. J., *The Accountant and Computers,* Pitman, 1967.

4 Modern accounting thought

Thus far this book has been concerned primarily with the mechanics of accounting systems, and the manner in which inputs of financial data are identified and processed. The principal subjects of Chapter 4 are the way in which present-day academic accountants (and the more thoughtful members of the profession on its commercial and practising sides) regard accounting as an intellectual discipline, and as one of the applied social sciences, and the endeavours which have been and are being made to give its theoretical structures greater coherence and consistency, as sure foundations for improved techniques of financial measurement and reporting

4.1 The modern accounting revolution

As Chapter 1 explains, accounting has passed in history through two periods of far-reaching change—the evolution of double entry book-keeping in mediaeval Italy, and the great developments of the nineteenth and early twentieth centuries in analytical and reporting techniques. The pace of innovation has quickened since 1945, and has now begun seriously to affect the patterns of thought about the fundamentals of the subject; indeed, it was said by one American professor that 'there has been more development of accounting theory in the 'sixties than in the previous 500 years'.[1] This third revolution in the discipline is still in progress and its outcome cannot yet be seen, but it is certain that neither thinking nor practice can ever be the same as before.

Up to about 1960 no great attention was paid to theory. Most textbooks of financial accounting contained a perfunctory list of 'principles' or 'concepts', such as entity, dual aspect, prudence, and the like, with no attempt at structuring and no distinction between basic ideas and derived notions; after which the writers hastened to expound the mechanics of double entry. Academic teaching consisted mainly of descriptive and technique-orientated courses, centring on the preparation of final accounts for different kinds of business enterprise, with a little analysis thrown in. In universities the subject was generally taught as an option in economics degrees, or (in America) as part of the curriculum in schools of business administration. The bulk of writing by academics was concerned with management accounting, operational research, electronic data processing and financial theory, with the problems of changing price levels as the most lively issue in the field of financial accounting. These problems became acute as inflation accelerated after 1945; the deficiencies of historical-cost accounting were mercilessly exposed, and many proposals were made for improvement. Orthodox opinion, however, was little

[1] Wheeler, John T. Accounting Theory and Research in Perspective. *The Accounting Review,* January 1970.

moved, either in Britain or America, and the discussions had little effect on practice; the accountancy institutions poured cold water on the new ideas, and in Britain the Royal Commission on Taxation, in its 1955 Report, was unable to recommend any adjustment for inflation in computing profits for tax purposes. After that the controversy subsided.

The climate began to change in 1959, when the American Institute of Certified Public Accountants replaced its Committee on Accounting Procedure (which had concerned itself mainly with codifying existing practice) with an Accounting Principles Board, empowered to issue, by a two-thirds majority, *Opinions* on major questions of theory and practice which were to be binding, as 'generally accepted accounting principles', upon all members of the AICPA reporting as auditors upon the published accounts of client corporations. One of the APB's first acts was to commission Professor Maurice Moonitz to inquire into the fundamentals of the discipline; in 1961 he produced *Accounting Research Study No. 1,* 'The Basic Postulates of Accounting', and in 1962 (with Robert T. Sprouse) *No. 3,* 'A Tentative Set of Broad Accounting Principles for Business Enterprises'. Neither set really satisfied academic accountants or the profession, and the next few years saw the appearance of several other suggestions for a comprehensive set of accounting principles, notably those of Richard Mattessich (1964)[2] in America, and of Raymond J. Chambers (1966)[3] in Australia, followed (1967) by the Japanese-American Yuji Ijiri's study of accounting as a science of measurement.[4] Meanwhile the Accounting Principles Board has issued (to date) thirty-one *Opinions* on various aspects of practice, some welcomed as genuine clarifications of the position, others attacked as unsatisfactory compromises between conflicting views—such as, in 1970, Opinions No. 16, 'Business Combinations', and No. 17, 'Intangible Assets', which were passed by majorities of 12 to 6, and 13 to 5, respectively, after the field had been divided into two in order to get any two-thirds majority at all. From 1974 the APB has been replaced by a small full-time Financial Accounting Standards Board, independent of practising accountants and engaged in much more fundamental research.

In Britain progress was slower. Valuable theoretical work has been and is being done in our universities (as by W. T. Baxter, L. R. Amey and T. Gambling), but not much of it has been widely circulated as yet, and no writers as influential as Mattessich, Chambers or Ijiri have emerged. It was only in 1970 that the three Institutes of Chartered Accountants set up their Accounting Standards Steering Committee, to which were later added representatives of the Association of Certified Accountants and the Institute of Cost and Management Accountants. The work of the ASSC has been similar to that of the American APB, but on a more restricted scale—i.e. it has concerned itself with 'putting out bush fires' rather than with fundamental research. All in all, while the 1960s have been the seminal period of the new accounting revolution, it is in the years to come that the fruits may be expected, in the shape of greater intellectual coherence in the many as well as the few, and codes of practice firmly and rigorously based upon a solid theoretical foundation.

[2] Mattessich, Richard. *Accounting and Analytical Methods,* Irwin, 1964.
[3] Chambers, Raymond J. *Accounting, Evaluation and Economic Behavior,* Prentice-Hall, 1966.
[4] Ijiri, Yuji. *The Foundations of Accounting Measurement,* Prentice-Hall, 1967.

4.2 The search for a general theory of accounting

The construction of lists of accounting 'principles', by whatever names called, has been popular among adepts for half a century, but activity has greatly increased since 1960. The result has been a large number of schemes, mutually inconsistent or at any rate hard to reconcile, sometimes faulty in their premises or in their logical structure, and whose influence on accounting practice has been minimal.

If any progress is to be made it is necessary to determine, not merely the structure of the formal accounting system, but the nature of the required *outputs* from it, and thence the types of *inputs* to it. If, for the purpose of the present discussion, attention is restricted to financial accounting reports—the outputs of the main accounting system—then the first step is to ascertain the object of preparing them. This is, fairly obviously, to give information of some kind to one or more classes of persons interested in receiving it, and intending to take action of some kind in response to it. When the receivers of information have been identified, it is not sufficient to adopt a purely psychological approach to their information requirements to discover what information they think they need, and what effects it has upon their behaviour, for there is no guarantee that the users of the accounts are the best judges of the types of information which they need, or that they are responding rationally to it, without conditioning, or that what they are receiving is information and not misinformation. Rather is it necessary to ascertain what *decision theories* they are using, consciously or unconsciously, to motivate them to action, how sound these theories are for their intended purposes and, given sound decision theories, what information inputs are needed to enable the most appropriate decisions to be taken. Accounting reports should thus be designed as efficient inputs to rational decision theories—say, to allow investors in a company consistently to decide rationally (if not always 'correctly') whether to sell, hold, or add to their shareholdings. When it is known what outputs are needed from the accounting systems (including the format which is most effective for communication with the decision-makers), it becomes the responsibility of the accountant to design the system so as to produce the requisite material; and this includes correct specification of the data inputs needed to operate it. In short, accounting is to be seen as a process of *measurement* and *communication*.[5]

Such a conception links the discipline, not only with its traditional sister-science of economics, but also with the newer field of the behavioural sciences—information and communication theory, management science, human relations, psychology, sociology, etc. Accounting gives quantitative substance to the theory of the firm, and sets bounds to abstract speculation, tending to ignore the extent to which the factors alleged to influence economic behaviour are either perceptible or measurable by those supposedly affected. As a system of economic measurement, however, accounting is limited by the fact that the key figures which it produces—profit, asset valuations, equity, etc.—are the bases of economic judgements, while themselves being insusceptible of objective validation outside the system. The auditor may assure himself that the proper data have entered it and been correctly processed according to consistent rules, and that the published accounts accurately reflect the results of such processing, but there is no directly observable phenomenon called 'profit' with which the measurement of it can be

[5] See: Sterling, Robert R. On Theory Construction and Verification. *The Accounting Review,* July 1970.

compared, as the alleged height or weight of a man can be checked with a measuring-standard or scales. When the sphere of accounting is extended to embrace the communication of economic information, the need to provide efficient inputs to the decision theories of external decision-makers furnishes the accountant with a set of standards against which to determine the validity of his reports, and applies to their contents a test of their correspondence with reality, such as direct observation cannot carry out. Research along these lines is in its early stages, but it offers the strongest hope of a real break-through in the next few years.

4.2.1 Construction of accounting theories

Definition of the objectives of accounting is a necessary first step in the construction of any sound theory of it, and the foregoing discussion has suggested the most promising approach in the eyes of many modern thinkers. The next stage is *induction*—the process of making generalizations from a sufficient number of particular instances, applied in this context to identification of the salient features of actual accounting systems, and orderly listing of their common characteristics. Induction continues with the isolation of what the researcher sees as the *postulates* of accounting, rigorously defined as those propositions which belong to the system of thought in question, imply further propositions thereof, do not contradict one another, and are not logically derivable, one from another. The theorist next proceeds to *deduction*—the logical derivation of additional propositions from the postulates, within the constraints of the defined objectives; after which he *structures* his model accounting system accordingly, carefully defining both the contents of the reports (output) and the data to be collected (input). The follow-up to all this is the *testing of the model system* in a real-life organization, arranging for proper 'feedback' from the users of the reports, and analysis of their comments with a view to modifications to the accounts, so as to make the reports more efficient as bases for economic decisions (i.e. to correct for deviations of the real situation from the decision-theory assumptions on which the original model was predicated).

Up to now there has not been a deal of work done on these lines. Much theory-spinning suffers from failure to define objectives properly, and/or from lack of clarity as to the *scope* of the theory—either because the perspective is confined to business accounting, so that too many accepted ideas are designated as 'postulates' (when they are not so in relation to other types of organization), or because over-ambitious attempts are made to produce a unified theory covering the whole field, a procedure which is no more valuable than it would be in economics or any other science. Such an all-purpose theory can have little operational effectiveness if it ignores the utility of accounting reports to users in different areas of financial activity, and it would be far better (some think) if a number of special theories were to be hammered out by different research-workers, on the foundation of such postulates as are truly common ground.[6]

Even at this level, the sets of 'postulates', 'axioms', 'basic concepts', 'assumptions', and so forth which have been put forward in recent years are legion, and often wildly inconsistent with one another. The concepts appear to fall into three classes: 1 ethical values; 2 assumptions about the economic environment; and

[6] See: Buckley, J. W., P. Kircher and R. L. Mathews, Methodology in Accounting Theory. *The Accounting Review,* April 1968.

3 inductions from existing practices. (Many sets combine more than one of these types.)

Thus, at the one extreme there is L. Spacek (1961),[7] who asserts that accounting has but one postulate—fairness. Others of the 'ethical' school are disposed to add a few more, such as H. R. Givens (1966)[8]—usefulness, fairness and legality. Many thinkers, though—and the author agrees with them—reject this approach as too vague and subjective; such notions are not confined to accounting, and it is hard to deduce convincingly from them any directly useful principles. The second class of postulates offers more promise. It includes concepts such as quantification, exchange, entities, time period, and unit of measurement (the first five of M. Moonitz's fourteen 'basic postulates' (1961)[9]), or private property, exchange, and market prices (the first three of P. Kircher's seventeen 'coded concepts' (1965)[10]—some of Moonitz's appearing under other heads). The author's own position, as set out in Chapter 1, is close to that of such thinkers, and his three suggested postulates (entity, money measurement, and time interval) are at least defensible in their company. The third approach is more questionable, as it often leads to the classification as postulates of accounting of concepts which are at best postulates of particular varieties of it, and at worst are logical inferences from other propositions within the field—i.e. not postulates at all. Such are Moonitz's last five—continuity, objectivity, consistency, stable monetary unit (!), and disclosure. (It is only fair to state that most reputable writers no longer regard double entry, or dual aspect, as a postulate; the present author has already demonstrated that it cannot be one.)

As to fully developed theories of accounting, these are set out in books at considerable length, and cannot easily be summarized shortly. R. Mattessich (1964)[11] has adopted a mathematical approach, proving the validity of double entry from set theory, and conceiving of the accounting process as an input—output system, expressible in terms of matrix and vector algebra; while his logical structure rests upon eighteen 'assumptions' (they are not called postulates), including (at random) structure, economic objectives, entities, realization, and allocation. His work, though most stimulating and thought-provoking, is nevertheless difficult reading for the less-than-moderately numerate.

The same cannot be said of the most ambitious treatment of modern times, perhaps—that of R. J. Chambers (1966).[12] The Professor of Accounting at Sydney has set out to construct a comprehensive theory, in syllogistic terms with a minimum of mathematical exposition. His chosen field of study is a wide one, for he bases his arguments upon the conception of the organization as a *homeostatic* system—one which continuously adapts itself to changes in its environment, in order to survive and preserve its well-being, or (more literally) one which endeavours to maintain itself in a steady state. This goal of homeostasis is in reality that of the individuals who compose the organization. They seek constantly to relieve the manifold strains to which they are subject, among which is the need to employ scarce means to promote various personal ends, which are

[7] Spacek, L. *The Single Postulate of Accounting,* Arthur Andersen & Co., 1961.
[8] Givens, H. R. Basic Accounting Postulates. *The Accounting Review,* July 1966.
[9] Moonitz, M. *The Basic Postulates of Accounting,* American Institute of Certified Public Accountants, 1961.
[10] Kircher, P. Coding Accounting Principles. *The Accounting Review,* October 1965.
[11] See: Footnote 2.
[12] See: Footnote 3.

incommensurable, and inscrutable by the economist. In order to promote certain ends not realizable by individual action, human beings form associations, among which are entities to promote economic ends, such as the production of goods or services in the expectation of selling them in the market at prices (in standard monetary units) yielding greater utilities than those yielded by the resources sacrificed in the process. These are measured, in turn, by the current equivalents, as at the date of the sales, of the moneys expended in procuring those resources. Investments are made in such entities in the expectation that a better rate of return (in terms of purchasing power) can be obtained than by other means.

Accounting is necessary as a device for measuring rationally that rate of return, and in particular the income of the entity, defined as the growth of its 'residual equity' over time after allowing for investment and disinvestment by 'constituents' (proprietors)—such growth being measured by comparing opening and closing equity, both valued in terms of the general price level as at the end of the period. Detailed rules for keeping accounting records and summarizing them from time to time in reports are then derived from these propositions, and others, for both profit-making and non-profit-making entities. Accounting is further recognized as a system of information processing, distinct from the 'actors' (executive management), serving them with numerical data not directly apprehensible, and designed to correspond at all times with the entity's objective financial state. For this reason it requires constant feedback from both environment and management to counteract the *entropy* of all complex systems operating in isolation (i.e. their continual tendency to break down into disorder and randomness)—in this case, the tendency of the accounting records, though always internally consistent, to become less and less relevant to economic realities. Finally, the importance of communication is recognized, in terms which will reduce misunderstanding to a minimum; the decision theory approach is not explicitly set forth, but may be regarded as implicit in Chambers's conclusions.

The full statement of the theory, in *Accounting, Evaluation and Economic Behavior,* is made in English of crystalline purity, and each of the fourteen main chapters is summarized in an 'Argument' in syllogistic form, as well as by a diagram. The total number of propositions is no less than 403, of which 115 are classed as 'postulates or definitions', and 288 as 'inferences', and it is obviously impracticable to reproduce them here. The book should be regarded as indispensable reading for all advanced students of accountancy.

Lastly, it should be made clear that the present author has not anywhere in this work attempted to put forward a complete theory of his own—that would require a book to itself. The scheme in Chapter 1, apart from the postulates and their corollary, dual aspect, is purely a summary of the principles on which most conventional systems of business accounts appear to be constructed and operated, and in subsequent chapters many of these principles will be weighed in the balance and found wanting.

4.3 The concept of measurement in accounting

Accounting, it has been said, is a system of measurement and communication. The place of communication in accounting theory has been outlined in a way which avoids the outdated assumptions that all entrepreneurs, managers, and investors, if rational, are motivated solely, or even mainly, by desire to maximize profit in the shorter or longer run, or to maximize or optimize the rate of return on capital, having regard to the risks of the enterprise—the aims seem rather to be to 'satisfice' these parameters. Modern management theory recognizes that an organization itself, being inanimate, has no goals—only those who work in it or invest in it can have them, and they do not all have a single goal, either individually or collectively. Nor are the efforts of the managers necessarily directed to maximizing the wealth of the investors, especially where the two classes are distinct, as they are for the most part in public companies. The behavioural approach emphasizes these facts, in relation to both management and financial accounting, and offers possibilities of constructing systems better adapted than the existing ones to promote the effective working of the economic institutions which they serve.

The aspect of measurement has also received much attention from modern theorists. Conventional accounting translates all entries into the units of a given currency, with the object of rendering them additive and thus allowing equity to be expressed as a single number, as well as the net change in it over a period. To many thinkers this process and its end-products are unconvincing when applied to items other than cash and fixed claims thereto, and increasingly prone to error and misunderstanding the further one moves away from these relative certainties; while changes in the purchasing power of money compound the inaccuracies. The response of some theorists is to devise systems of accounting which avoid the necessity for such controversial measurements, or which replace the allegedly spurious objectivity of traditional procedures with subjective estimates based on expectations about the future. Others, however, meet the difficulties head on and seek more relevant, yet still objective, measures, and these will be considered first.

If the figures in accounting reports are to be used with confidence by those who make decisions on the basis thereof, these persons must have some idea as to the *reliability* of the figures for the purposes of decision-making; but this is not the same thing as their *objectivity*—the degree of probability that different measurers (accountants) will agree on the figures to be reported. Thus, all competent accountants could be expected to report the same amount as the cash balance of a firm at a given date, but there might well be differences between them as to the proper figure for receivables (some writing off bad debts more rigorously than others, and/or making larger or smaller provision for doubtful items), and still larger differences as to inventories (FIFO *v.* LIFO, absorption-cost *v.* variable-cost pricing, etc.) and physical fixed assets (historical cost *v.* revaluation, different bases and rates of depreciation, etc.). These differences are compounded in the measurement of equity, and hence of profit for a period. An auditor's report that the accounts show a 'true and fair view' merely means that in his opinion reasonable rules of measurement have been correctly and consistently applied to all figures; if the accountant had chosen other rules, now and in the past, the auditor might have approved with as little qualification any one of millions of permissible figure-combinations!

There is thus no such thing as absolute objectivity in accounting (except in the counting of the discrete money-tokens which constitute the cash balance); there are only different degrees of it. A suggested measure of objectivity, in relation to the calculation of a given item (such as profit), is the *variance* of the distribution of measurements made (actually or hypothetically) by several different accountants of the same order of expertise—i.e. the arithmetic mean of the squares of the deviations of the given measurements from the arithmetic mean of them all. Thus, if one supposes the same item (x) in a set of accounts to be computed by n accountants, the mean of their figures is $\bar{x}$, and the variance is

$$V = \frac{1}{n} \sum_{i=1}^{n} (x_i - \bar{x})^2$$

Hence, the smaller is V ($\geqslant 0$), the more objective is the system of measurement ($V = 0$ denotes perfect objectivity—all measurers agree).

The *reliability* of an accounting measure is subjective to a user of the information, as distinct from an accountant. It is postulated that each decision-maker regards a piece of accounting information as having some value for predicting another figure not in the same accounts, and connects the two by means of a decision formula—e.g. an investor may expect a company's ordinary dividend to be about half its reported after-tax profit for the relevant year. When the dividend is declared, it may be significantly more or less than half the profit; but by reversing the formula the investor, if he still retains confidence in it, may assert that the profit ought to have been twice the dividend, and that there must be some irregularity in the profit calculation. The subjective 'proper' figure (the alleged value) may be denoted by x^*, and a measure of reliability derived by finding the mean of the squared deviations from it of the (actual or hypothetical) measurements made by n accountants, as for the objectivity measure V. The new measure is

$$R = \frac{1}{n} \sum_{i=1}^{n} (x_i - x^*)^2$$

As before, the smaller is R ($\geqslant 0$), the more confidence may the user repose in the reported figure as a basis for decision-making ($R = 0$ denotes perfect reliability). It is easily shown that

$$R = \frac{1}{n} \sum_{i=1}^{n} (x_i - \bar{x})^2 + (\bar{x} - x^*)^2$$

or $\qquad R = V + B$

where $B = (\bar{x} - x^*)^2$—the squared difference between the mean of the measurements and the 'alleged value' of the reported figure to the particular user.

Since B cannot be negative, it follows that R can never be less than V, and is usually greater—i.e. the reliability coefficient is the sum of the objectivity coefficient and a subjective 'bias' in the user's mind. This suggests (leaving aside the difficulties of computing V and B in practice) that, if the *usefulness* of accounting information is to be improved, the accountancy profession needs not only to define its measurement rules more precisely and to leave open fewer opportunities for unnecessary variation (i.e. to reduce V), but to educate managers, investors, and other users of accounting information as to its real significance and usefulness for different purposes—thus helping to reduce B, by promoting the use of more rational decision theories.

4.3.1 Measurement and the structure of accounting

The foregoing analysis forms part of a much-discussed work, *The Foundations of Accounting Measurement: A Mathematical, Economic and Behavioral Inquiry*, by Yuji Ijiri (1967)[13]—shorter than Mattessich or Chambers, and intermediate between

[13] See: Footnote 4. The relevant chapter is substantially a reprint of Ijiri, Y. and R. K. Jaedicke, Reliability and Objectivity of Accounting Measurements, *The Accounting Review*, July 1966.

them in difficulty. Like Chambers, Ijiri builds upon the foundations of economics and the behavioural sciences, but emphasizes the rôle of accounting as a system of measurement of economic data, founded upon three 'axioms'—control (i.e. entity), quantities, and exchanges. Double entry book-keeping is seen as predominantly a set of rules by which an increment in net assets is connected with its corresponding decrement (and where necessary with the balancing increment/decrement in equity). In other words, double entry is *causal,* rather than merely *classificational* (treating each increment or decrement independently, and achieving duality by classifying the same set of objects, the resources of the entity, twice—by physical characteristics, and by the claims upon the resources). Resting, as it does, primarily upon the recording of exchanges, the system has a propensity to value assets at historical cost, and would seem to have evolved around this concept. It is, in fact, the most 'objective' method of measurement, in the sense of the analysis in section **4.3**, in that the amount of the increment to any asset is determined by the amount of the decrement incurred in procuring it. Yet Ijiri is careful not to assert that historical cost is the most 'reliable' measure (as above defined); indeed, a sophisticated investor is likely to attach a large bias to it, which will more than outweigh the relatively small variance of the measure.

Ijiri recognizes that double entry, though usually operated in money terms, is from the causal point of view independent of any single measure. He suggests that, instead of valuing non-monetary assets, one might keep the accounts for them in appropriate units, e.g. of service potential, and make transfers to and from 'activity' accounts in these units by the rules of double entry. The activity accounts (such as sales and work in progress) would be in a mixture of units, and would not 'balance', but the hash totals of all debits and all credits would agree at all times (with the addition, in lieu of equity, of a control account in mixed units, which Ijiri does not illustrate). The non-monetary items might then be converted to money outside the books, on different bases for different purposes. This novel idea is not developed at any length, but certainly seems to have possibilities, especially in non-commercial entities such as local authorities; and present-day developments in electronic data processing seem to point in the same direction.[14]

Chambers is less radical, in that he does not advocate any giving up of monetary measurement, nor does he oppose the use of historical cost in historical records, made at the time of acquiring the assets. These are rational as of that time, and must not be tampered with, lest the record of what really happened should be obliterated. At the same time, though, he is adamant that at any later date cost is irrelevant to economic decision-making, which must be based on the opportunity cost (see Chapter 7, sub-section **7.2.1**) of assets held. The accounting system, too, must at all times be 'isomorphic' to the real entity—i.e. be an accurate model of it, in terms of money of current purchasing power; and this necessitates the preparation of periodical accounts, in which all figures from dates significantly earlier than the year-end are converted to current monetary units by the application of price level index adjustments—of which more in Chapter 7.

Those who are disposed to reject the conventional balance sheet and profit and loss account, as hopelessly unrealistic and quite useless as a guide to economic decision-making, tend to go to one of two extremes. On the one hand, there are those who assert that it is impossible to measure profit, in any meaningful way,

---

[14]The author is indebted, for some of these suggestions, to an unpublished MA thesis by J. Etor: *Capital Accounting for Local Authority Housing: a Study in Economic Theory,* University of Nottingham, 1971.

over periods shorter than the whole life of an enterprise, and wish to replace the profit and loss account by a flow of funds statement, showing changes in net liquid assets—the only transaction statement for the period which is, in their eyes, truly objective and in current moneys throughout. Year-end position statements (they cannot be called 'balance sheets', as they do not balance) would show in monetary terms only the components of net liquid assets, while non-monetary assets would be measured in physical units, or (better) in units of service potential. The affinities with Ijiri's 'multi-dimensional book-keeping' are obvious, but so far little progress has been made.

The other alternative to conventional accounts is some form of 'economic' accounting, designed to value the entity as a whole, at any point in time, in terms of its net liquid assets plus the net present value (NPV) of its expected future cash flows, discounted at the marginal rate of interest (or its equivalent) on the capital raised to finance the relevant activities. Calculations would be made in terms of the year-end price level, and 'economic' income measured as the cash flow for the year (exclusive of capital introduced and withdrawn), plus or minus changes over the year in the NPV of future expectations. More will be said of this in Chapter 7, but it is as well to state here that to most accountants, and many theorists, such procedures are anathema—to Chambers, they are not accounting at all, since one cannot render an account of what has not yet happened! If such methods ever are adopted, even experimentally, it would almost certainly have to be done by way of supplements to conventional 'stewardship' accounts; and the same applies to proposals for price-level-adjusted final accounts.

All in all, then, the academic scene is a lively one, and no treatise on modern financial accounting can be complete without some appraisal of it. Which of the more radical ideas now current will stand the test of experience and come to influence practice, it is impossible to say at this stage; but revolutionary trends in thought are already permeating many aspects of professional life, from final account preparation to the education and training of future accountants, and some of the more advanced ideas will be developed in Chapters 5 to 8.

5

Asset valuation and income measurement: historical-cost accounting (1)

Chapter 4 was mainly devoted to modern accounting theory as it relates to the nature, objects, and methodology of the art. One of the most important areas of controversy, however, is concerned with the related topics of *asset valuation* at various points of time during an accounting period (especially at the beginning and end of it), and of *income measurement* over that period. Conventional practice has come under very heavy fire since the Second World War, and Chapter 7 will set forth the criticisms made, followed by suggestions for reforming accountancy so as to furnish more realistic and reliable information to those who use the accounts. Yet traditional methods are very far from defunct, and Chapters 5 and 6 summarize them, as the foundation upon which any new system is likely to be built.

5.1 Historical-cost basis of accounting

The principles set out in Chapter 1, except for the generalized postulates and their corollary, are those of orthodox accounting for the results of business enterprises in a capitalist economy, and the remainder of this book is confined to such entities, since space does not permit further discussion of non-business accounts, or those of public bodies.

In a business entity the whole of the equity is at all times identical with the residual interest of the proprietor(s) or, in the case where a corporate body is the legal proprietor, that of the members of the corporation. Over the whole life of the entity the proprietors, as a body, contribute the initial fund of capital with which the enterprise is to trade, make additional contributions from time to time, receive periodic dividends on their investment (or withdraw moneys directly), and finally liquidate the enterprise and withdraw the remaining assets. The entity thus begins and ends with zero equity, and the *money* income from the enterprise of the proprietors collectively is the excess of the moneys withdrawn from the entity, over those put into it. This is an objective fact, which cannot be altered by any manipulations of the accounting system. What such manipulations can do, though, is to alter the pattern of *business* income as between different accounting periods, and hence as between successive members of the proprietorial body, since, for a member who does not invest in the entity for its whole life, his money income is affected by the incidence of dividends while he holds the investment, and by the agreed amount of capital which he is able to withdraw—or the price at which he is able to sell his interest to another, or its market value when it passes to the investor's heirs at his death. Again, over the whole life of an entity, changes in the general price level, interacting with the amount of business income to produce the entity's *real* income in constant pounds of any particular vintage, are independent of the accounting conventions used; but the real income of individual proprietors may be affected by the differential incidence through time of their disposable money incomes, as calculated on the basis of the accounts produced, since pounds distributed in years of lower prices have higher purchasing power than pounds made available in years more subject to inflation; and similarly with capital contributions (sacrifices) and realizations (benefits). Furthermore, the quality of the information provided to management by the accounting system is itself a factor influencing decisions on which the achieved level of business income partly depends. The quality of accounting reports to investors also influences the degree to which their financial policy can be optimized in the matter of putting their money into, and taking it out of, one investment or another at the right times.

Accounting methods, then, are not neutral or passive in relation to the operations of a firm through time. If the output of the system is faulty as input to the decision theories of managers or investors or both, then at worst the decision-makers, if sufficiently naïve, may make wrong decisions on the basis of misleading data taken at face value; at best, if sophisticated enough to realize the limitations of the data, they will have to make subjective corrections before using them. It has also been explained, in Chapter 4, that the reliability of information is not the same thing as its objectivity, since the degree to which a user of information can rely upon its accuracy is compounded of the degree to which there is agreement upon that accuracy, *and* the user's belief as to how closely the information squares with his own (subjective) opinion as to what it ought to be—i.e. unreliability = subjectivity + bias; and the relative importance of the two elements varies in different contexts.

Few types of information exemplify this notion better than accounts prepared on the historical-cost basis, as set out in Chapter 1, with special reference to the 'working rules' in sub-section 1.5.2. Historical-cost accounting rests on two concepts:

1 *acquisition cost*—all assets are taken on to the books on acquisition from other entities, at values equal to those imputed to the assets given up, or obligations assumed, in return (cf. working rule b); and
2 *realization*—the historical costs thus generated remain on the books, regardless of changes in the market prices of similar assets or in the general purchasing power of money, until the assets are realized, when the historical costs are matched with the corresponding revenue and the difference taken as profit or loss in the accounting period when the revenues are deemed to be earned (cf. working rules f and g).

'Realization' in this context means i the sale of goods or services to other entities in return for cash, payable immediately or at a later date, or (rarely) in exchange for non-monetary assets of an agreed value, or ii the loss or destruction of assets, or other casualty rendering them worthless or greatly impairing their value—whether or not any money is recovered by way of insurance or scrap value. In relation to tangible fixed assets, held for more than one accounting period and disposed of, normally, only when it is considered necessary to replace them, the realization concept is extended to include iii the presumed embodiment of part of their service potential in the costs of production or service of a given accounting period, by way of depreciation. A similar principle is invoked when raw materials are incorporated in work in progress, or the latter in finished goods for sale. In both these cases, though, it is assumed that one asset has been transformed into another within the same entity, and that the transfer price is equal to the underlying historical cost, so that there is no net increase in the book value of the net assets until goods or services pass out of the entity at a price in excess of their cost (less depreciation, in the case of fixed assets).

Such a system of imputing money values to non-monetary assets (so as to render them additive class by class, and overall so as to impute a money value to equity) has several advantages. It arises naturally from double entry book-keeping, which seems indeed to have been founded upon it (see Chapter 1, sub-section 1.4.1). The rules are relatively easy to specify, and enable a data processing system to be operated by persons without a high degree of accounting knowledge, with no need for them to exercise any great skill or judgement in determining either entry or exit values for assets. Most of all, historical-cost accounting allegedly minimizes the sphere of subjective estimation, and avoids the recognition in accounts of profits not yet realized in cash received or receivable, and not certain ever to be so realized. It is these attributes, particularly the second and third, which cause it to be regarded as the most 'objective' accounting method available. In fact, there are areas where it is necessary for the accountant to make a choice from a wide range of possible valuation rules, and where different choices can, in the short run, make a considerable difference to reported profits (income of the entity). Objectivity, as previously defined, is thus materially reduced. Apart from that, historical-cost-based accounts are in many ways defective as guides to business or investment decision, as Chapter 7 will make clear. An informed decision-maker will have to make large allowance for this, and so add to the relative subjectivity of the measurements a sizeable personal bias—thus further diminishing their 'reliability' for him.

For all its shortcomings, though, historical cost has played an important part in the development of accounting. As explained in Chapter 1, sub-section 1.4.2, the vagaries of early nineteenth century practice were curbed by the evolution of logical principles for matching the revenues and costs of each accounting period, and discouraging the arbitrary carrying forward, as additions to assets, of expenditures whose benefit had wholly expired in the period—in other words, for making rational distinctions between capital expenditure and revenue expenditure. The next campaign was for the recognition of adequate depreciation charges as a cost of operation, and not as a voluntary appropriation of profits for asset replacement; by 1920 this was generally accepted. Then came the practice, particularly rife in America in the 'twenties, of writing up the book values of fixed assets, and of goodwill, in accordance with subjective estimates of market value, based on optimistic forecasts of future profits—often with the dubious motive of raising the market price of the corporation's stock and allowing 'insiders' to make large capital gains before the trading results justified them. Frequently the results failed to do so, and the assets had to be heavily written down. The stock market crash of 1929 and the subsequent depression helped to discredit revaluation accounting, and from 1934 the Securities and Exchange Commission refused to countenance it. American accountants regarded historical cost as the only legitimate basis for financial statements, and British practitioners followed them—the abuses of revaluation had in any case been much less prevalent here, partly because this country did not see very much of the prosperity which America enjoyed up to 1929. It was the rapid and continuous rise in prices after 1945 which revealed the limitations of the system, and led to the quest for a more sophisticated one; while orthodox accounting had become riddled with exceptions and compromises, and had largely lost what intellectual coherence it had.

5.2 Valuation of short-term monetary assets and liabilities

For the purposes of this section the current or short-term assets and liabilities of a typical business may be divided into two parts: a monetary assets and their countervailing liabilities; and b short-term physical assets—raw material stocks, work in progress, and finished goods stocks—or 'inventories' as they are termed in America.

The treatment of short-term monetary assets and liabilities is not a major area of controversy. Cash and bank balances in sterling, including overdrafts and advances, can have only one value at any time, so long as the bank is solvent. Balances in other currencies require conversion into sterling, at the market rate of exchange for the balancing date (see Chapter 8, section 8.2).

Quoted securities, held as temporary investments of cash which is, for the time being, surplus to immediate requirements, but likely to be needed before very long, are customarily valued at cost, including dealing expenses (brokerage, stamp duties, etc.). No profit is taken until sale, when the proceeds, net of dealing expenses, are credited to the investments account and the balance written off to Profits and Losses on Sale of Investments Account, and thence in due course to Profit and Loss Account. In the event of partial realization, the proceeds should be compared with their rateable proportion of the cost of the holding, and the average cost of the remaining securities carried down as a debit balance.

On the other hand, if at the year-end the market price is lower than average unit cost, the convention of 'prudence' requires that a provision be made for the notional loss, on the ground that, whereas unrealized profits may not be anticipated, all likely losses arising from events which have already occurred before the balancing date must be taken into account in computing the year's profit. The usual procedure is to take as market price the mean of the selling and buying prices in the *Stock Exchange List* for the day ('middle market price'), as representing an approximation to the price which a keen stockbroker might have been able to secure for a selling client in an active market. It would surely be more logical to use selling price (the lower figure quoted) less an allowance for dealing costs—or at most, quoted selling price *tout court,* reckoning that the broker ought to be able to raise it enough to cover his costs. Apart from this, the 'one-way option' involved appears irrational, if the guiding principle is to show the net monetary resources of the firm at the balancing date. A small holding of any stock which is actively traded—especially in the gilt-edged market—is only one remove from money in the bank, and should appear at market value, whether above or below cost—any resulting credit to profit and loss account being regarded as a gain 'virtually realized'. The difference between historical cost and market value will then be represented by the debit, or credit, balance on (say) a Quoted Investments Adjustment Account, which for balance sheet purposes will be added algebraically to the debit balance on Quoted Investments Account.

Bills of exchange, both receivable and payable, are commonly taken at face value, less a provision for any doubtful bills receivable. Since, however, collection is often postponed for several months, and immediate cash could be obtained only at a discount in the case of receivables, there is a case for reducing bills, in both directions, to present discounted value. In practice this is rarely done, since the two opposite adjustments would often nearly offset one another, and even if they did not, the writing back, at the beginning of the year, of last year's interest adjustments (*Dr.* Provision for Discount on Bills Receivable, *Cr.* Profit and Loss Account—and in the opposite direction for bills payable) would usually offset most of the year-end adjustment. The amending entries, therefore, are normally omitted, as infringing the convention of materiality.

Similar considerations apply to debtors (accounts receivable) and creditors (accounts payable), because of the shortness of the credit terms in most cases, and the tendency of the two totals to offset one another to a large extent. As to receivables, it is common practice, after writing off through the Bad Debts Account (and thence to profit and loss account) all accounts judged to be uncollectible, to raise a small provision—say, 3 per cent of year-end debtors—for bad and doubtful debts, writing it up or down at each balancing date. Cash discounts from creditors, if regularly earned, are best dealt with by deducting them in the original entries for purchases, so that the year-end payables appear net; otherwise it is perhaps best to leave the latter gross. Discounts allowed to debtors are less predictable; customers are always debited with the full amount invoiced, and credited with discount when they earn it. In the balance sheet it is, however, desirable to raise a small percentage provision for discount—calculated on debtors, net of any provision for bad and doubtful debts. Accounting for accruals, prepayments, and advance receipts or deposits, is straightforward, on the lines laid down in Chapter 1; it is desirable to credit/debit a single Accruals/Prepayments/Income Received in Advance/Deposits Account in each case, and to write back the entries on the first day of the following year, to the other accounts affected.

Complications arise with hire purchase and credit sale transactions, where there is an element of implicit interest, and it is considered best practice to equalize the effective rate over the term of each contract. The effective rate is that which, used as a discounting rate, serves to reduce the present value of all instalments to equality with the cash price of the goods supplied, less the deposit (received at the outset). In general

$$P - D = I_1/(1+r) + I_2/(1+r)^2 + \ldots + I_n/(1+r)^n$$

or

$$P - D = \sum_{i=1}^{n} I_i/(1+r)^i$$

where

P = cash price of the goods;
D = amount of deposit;
I = amount of each instalment; and
r = effective rate of interest per period between each two instalments.

Example 1 If a motor-vehicle with a cash price of £2,000 is sold on hire purchase on 30 June 19.1 for a deposit of £500 and twelve monthly instalments of £144 each (commencing one month after delivery), then

$$2,000 - 500 = 1,500 = 144/(1+r) + 144/(1+r)^2 \ldots + 144/(1+r)^{12}$$

and r is evaluated (by the use of discounting tables, or by iteration on a computer) at 2.25 per cent per month approximately. The initial balance of £1,500 is then deemed to decline month by month as follows:

Month		£
0	(cash price – deposit)	1,500.00
1	(interest thereon at 2.25 per cent)	33.75
		1,533.75
1	(instalment)	−144.00
1	(closing balance)	1,389.75
2	(interest thereon at 2.25 per cent)	31.32
		1,421.07
2	(instalment)	−144.00
2	(closing balance)	1,277.02
	* * *	
5	(closing balance)	923.38
6	(interest)	20.78
		944.16
6	(instalment)	−144.00
6	(closing balance)	800.16
	* * *	
11	(closing balance)	141.19
12	(interest, adjusted for cumulative error of +£0.36)	2.81
		144.00
12	(instalment)	−144.00
12	(closing balance)	0.00

The 'closing balances' are the amounts deemed to be outstanding at the end of each month, so that at the year-end each hirer's debt may be evaluated according to the number of instalments paid. His account is debited with the cash price, and credited with the deposit and instalments to the year-end; the computed balance is carried down, and included in the balance sheet total of debtors, while the difference (interest) is transferred to the credit of Hire Purchase Interest Earned Account, and thence to profit and loss account. (The trading account matches the sale at cash price with the historical cost of the goods.) Thus, for the transactions illustrated, the principal entries (assuming that the books are balanced on 31 December) are:

Hire Purchase Debtors Ledger

X.Y.

19.1		£	19.1			£
Jun 30	Sales	2,000.00	Jun 30	Bank	(Deposit)	500.00
Dec 31	Hire purchase		Jul 31	do	(Instalment)	144.00
	interest earned	164.16	Aug 31	do	do	144.00
			Sep 30	do	do	144.00
			Oct 31	do	do	144.00
			Nov 30	do	do	144.00
			Dec 31	do	do	144.00
			Dec 31	Balance c/d		800.16
		£2,164.16				£2,164.16

19.2			19.2			
Jan 1	Balance b/d	800.16	Jan 31	Bank (Instalment)		144.00
Dec 31	Hire purchase		Feb 28	do	do	144.00
	interest earned	63.84	Mar 31	do	do	144.00
			Apr 30	do	do	144.00
			May 31	do	do	144.00
			Jun 30	do	do	144.00
		£864.00				£864.00

No adjustment is normally made for the value of the goods in the hirer's hands, which legally belong to the seller until the last instalment is paid. If they are repossessed on the hirer's default, the estimated second-hand value should be debited to Stock and credited to the hirer, and the balance of his account written off to Losses on Default. Before this stage is reached, adequate provision should be made for accounts with payments in arrears.

Where the firm purchases fixed assets on hire purchase, the seller's, or finance company's, claim should be evaluated as described (with the sides of his account reversed). The credit balance should not, however, be shown as a current liability, but be deducted inset from the depreciated cash price (entered separately in the balance sheet) of the relevant assets—to make it clear to unsecured creditors that the said assets are not available to them in the event of bankruptcy or liquidation.

Outstanding instalments receivable or payable on a credit sale agreement extending over several months should, it is suggested, be discounted back to the present, not at the internal rate of return (which is zero, unless a lower cash-sale price is assumed), but at some approximation to the firm's *cost of capital*—i.e., the rate at which it is able to raise equity capital, or (as a surrogate) the rate of return expected on it, after tax. In the personal account the full amount of the outstanding instalments should be debited/credited, and the discount credited/debited to an Instalment Credit Discount Account, with adjusting entries in profit and loss account—the ledger balances being offset, personal account against discount, in the balance sheet. A credit balance (less discount) in respect of assets purchased by instalments should appear among the liabilities, as the creditor has no specific charge over the said assets.

5.3 Valuation of inventories

The valuation of unsold inventories, including work in progress, is one of the crucial areas of controversy, in relation to the determination of periodic profit. As shown in Chapter 1, gross profit for a period is the excess of sales revenue over the imputed historical cost of the goods sold, and the latter is found by adding purchases in the period to the opening stock and deducting the closing stock from the total. Opening stock is identical with the closing stock in the previous period's accounts, but closing stock for the current period has to be valued on a basis or bases consistent with that or those used last time—or the opening stock must be revalued in accordance with any new basis/bases chosen, and the opening figure of equity adjusted by the amount of the revaluation.

In the U.K. the position has been complicated by the issue of the Accounting Standards Steering Committee's Exposure Draft 6 *Stocks and work in progress,* (1972). Its recommendations do not differ widely from the author's tentative conclusions, and the general line taken in ED6 is indicated, where appropriate, in sub-sections **5.3.1** to **5.3.4**. Nevertheless, it is considered that the arguments in the text are valid and supported by reputable authorities, and they have not been rewritten to harmonize with the draft, which is summarized in sub-section **5.3.5**. What follows should be read in the light of these remarks.

5.3.1 Historical cost in relation to inventories

The general rule is, that end-of-period inventories shall be valued in the first place at some approximation to their cost to the firm, in order to match period cost of sales with period sales, and avoid anticipating profit on unsold goods. Insofar as this rule is adhered to, profit is taken entirely in the period of sale, regardless of the time pattern of stock acquisition and holding, and of price movements during the holding interval. The argument is, that in most trades and industries there is no guarantee that goods or services made available in advance of specific orders will be sold profitably, or in some cases at all; and that profit is made by selling goods, not by producing and holding them. The realization concept is paramount. Its symmetry is marred, however, by the 'prudent' rule that ending inventories be valued at 'market price', if this is *lower* than cost—on the ground that expected losses must be provided for as soon as events occur which make the losses probable. The usual definition of market price is net realizable value—current selling price, less estimated costs to be incurred before sale can be effected; stock may never be valued higher than this, or a break-even may be shown in the current period, and a loss in the next one.

It is sometimes contended, though, that market price should be more rigorously defined, as the lower of net realizable value and replacement price (of goods in the quantities usually purchased, and on the usual terms). The argument is, that over time most prices tend to move in sympathy, particularly in the same trade. If inputs become cheaper, competition will induce or compel firms to reduce output prices. Those firms which hold inventories bought at higher prices than those prevailing currently will thus be unable to achieve their expected profit margins, if they do not actually make losses. They ought, therefore, to reduce the carrying values of stocks to current cost levels, thus recognizing the effects of sub-optimal buying and showing normal profit margins when the goods are sold.

Recognition of net realizable value as the maximum carrying value is rational, and forms part of all reputable systems of inventory valuation, as Chapter 7 makes clear. Replacement price is proved, in the same context, to be more significant than historical cost in the determination of operating profit—partly because of the output pricing effect just noted. But this applies whether replacement price is below or above historical cost; it is illogical to make the adjustment in one direction only. If historical cost is to be the norm, though, it seems more sensible to write down inventory only when *total* replacement cost, taking all current prices as they stand, is less than *total* historical cost; such a situation is more clearly indicative of an actual or potential reduction in selling prices (or failure to increase them, relatively to rises in other costs) than one in which, though some current prices may be lower than those recently paid, total replacement cost of the inventory is higher than its acquisition cost.

The force of the three governing figures varies in different industries, and as between raw materials, work in progress, and finished goods. In retailing, the case for writing down to replacement price is strongest where a fall results from reductions in import duty or excise duty, which must be promptly passed on to consumers. The same arguments do not apply to value added tax, as it does not enter into costs. In any case replacement price, and its surrogate 'adjusted selling price' (current selling price less normal profit margin), have taken a knock from the law in Britain. In *BSC Footwear Ltd. v. Ridgway* (1972) it was held that for income tax and corporation tax purposes retail inventories must be valued at the lower of cost or market price—now interpreted as meaning net realizable value, *not* replacement price or adjusted selling price. In wholesaling of industrial goods the position is similar. Where bulk commodities are dealt in, the risks of price movements in stocks on hand are generally covered by sales of futures, so that there is no need for writing down to replacement price, especially if there is to be no writing up to it—a gain on holding stocks is always offset, at least in part, by a loss on futures, and vice versa, and a one-way adjustment is distorting and confusing. Finally, the ASSC has now pronounced against the recognition of replacement cost, in Exposure Draft 6 (see sub-section **5.3.5**).

In manufacturing it is seldom necessary to value raw materials otherwise than at cost, as long as orthodox accounting practice is upheld. Net realizable value (except of obsolescent items) is scarcely ever lower if the materials are considered as realized, not by hypothetical sales on a possibly falling market but by incorporation in products, whose eventual selling price may be expected to cover all costs, including historical cost of the materials. Lower replacement price is relevant only in industries, such as flour-milling or cotton-spinning, where the price of output is closely tied to that of physical input; as in commodity wholesaling, sales of futures can be used to protect profit margins, rendering one-way stock price adjustments otiose. Similar arguments apply to work in progress, where current costs of production are surrogates for replacement price, and there is normally no market for unfinished work—it can be realized only by completion. In relation to finished goods, historical cost and replacement cost are represented by the actual, and the estimated current, costs of production; the latter lacks the objectivity of an external buying price, and the choice is usually cost or lower selling price (less any specific selling and distribution costs).

5.3.2 Inventory valuation other than at historical cost

There are sectors of the economy in which net realizable value is more than a mere upper limit to inventory valuation. In industries where two or more products are made from a single physical input, as in oil-refining and the manufacture of meat products, the incidence of joint costs defeats any rational attempt to allocate raw material costs to units of output. Selling price then becomes the starting-point; it is desirable to find the average margin between sale proceeds and allocable costs of a representative 'mix' of products made from a given unit of physical input—say, 1,000 tons of crude oil—and then scale down the selling prices, by deducting either the same percentage from each, or different percentages according to management's assessment of such factors as relative importance of their markets to the firm's business (e.g. petrol and diesel oil are the leading products of a refinery, and may be assigned the lion's share of the profit margin), parameters common to all products (e.g. weight of meat products, with some adjustment for quality), or somewhat arbitrary transfer prices, fixed as between one division of the company and another (see Chapter 8, section **8.4**). Such devices are intended to reduce selling prices, in total, to somewhere near the cost of production of the selected mix of outputs. By-products are a special case of joint outputs; stocks may be valued, either on the basis of selling prices, or at some arbitrary cost estimate, or at zero if by-products are merely sold for what they will fetch and the proceeds treated as a partial recovery of the cost of the main product.

Where the period of production is long (over one year), as in shipbuilding and civil engineering, a compromise has to be made with the realization principle if profits are not to be unacceptably irregular—high when several profitable contracts are completed in a year, low or non-existent when there are few completions, regardless of the general level of activity. It is therefore accepted practice to add to the cost of work in progress on each contract an allowance for profit deemed to have been earned to date, so that the excess of this over the previous year's allowance may enter into the total profit of the firm for the year, with a final adjustment in the year of completion of the contract—an account for the contract profit or loss being debited, and profit and loss account credited, via a Profits/Losses on Contracts Account. As work is certified as completed, by a qualified architect, civil engineer, naval architect, etc., the customer becomes liable for progress payments, usually 90 per cent of the (contract) value of the work completed since the last certificate; the other 10 per cent is 'retention moneys', payable (say) six months after the contract is finished—less allowances for any defective work discovered by then. This system, from the accountant's point of view, simplifies the problems of measuring profit accrued, as well as furnishing a theoretical justification of the 'partially realized' profit taken. ED 6, also, favours the taking of profit on uncompleted contracts, under certain conditions (see sub-section 5.3.5).

To avoid obscuring the total cost to date, the Contract Account is debited with expenditure as it is incurred, while the value of work certified is debited to the customer's account and credited to a Work Certified Account for the contract. Progress payments are credited to the customer as received; retention moneys remain as a debit balance on his account, and it is desirable in the balance sheet to show them as a non-current asset, discounted for time like other deferred receivables. In principle, the debit balances on the Contract No... Account (cost to date) and the Contract No... Profit/Loss Account are offset against the credit balance on the Contract No... Work Certified Account, and the net debit balance reported as the value of work in progress on Contract No.... Optimally the three balances should cancel out, except for the cost of uncertified work at the year-end; the excess of certified work over relevant cost is the maximum imputed profit. In practice the cost may be running ahead of the estimates and, even after allowing for the effect of any 'escalator clauses' to cover rises in material prices and wage rates, a heavy loss may be in prospect; the excess cost should then be offset by a credit to Contract No...Profit/Loss Account, with a debit to Profits and Losses on Contracts Account—work in progress being zero, except for the cost of uncertified work. In addition, a separate Provision for Anticipated Losses on Contracts (credit balance) will be raised out of the profit and loss account, to cover future losses (including any penalties in the contract) arising out of the decision, made *before* the year-end, to accept the contract.

Example 2 In a civil engineering firm, the accounts below exhibit the position as at the year-end (31 December 19.1) on a contract commenced in July 19.1 and expected to take two years to complete, at a price of £100,000 (subject to escalator clauses). The estimated cost (before allowing for price/wage escalation) was £80,000. At 31 December 19.1 work certified, and 90 per cent paid for, was £20,000 at original rates plus 2 per cent escalation (total £20,400). Cost (after an average of 2 per cent escalation) had reached £18,870 on work certified, and £1,020 uncertified. In preparing the accounts for the year ended 31 December 19.1 it is forecast that, if there is no further rate escalation, it will cost a total of £96,900 to complete the contract, against an escalated price of £102,000.

Contract No. 317

19.1		£
Jul 1		
to		
Dec 31	Creditors and bank	19,890

Contract No. 317 Work Certified

19.1		£
Jul 1		
to		
Dec 31	A. Customer	20,400

Contract No. 317 Profit/Loss

19.1		£
Dec 31	Profits/Losses on contracts	1,530

A. Customer

19.1		£	19.1		£
Jul 1			Jul 1		
to			to		
Dec 31	Contract No. 317 work certified	20,400	Dec 31	Bank	18,360
			Dec 31	Balance c/d	2,040
		£20,400			£20,400
19.2					
Jan 1	Balance b/d	2,040			

Time Discount on Non-Current Receivables

			19.1		£
			Dec 31	Profit and loss a/c	354

Notes

1 The profit to date on the contract is computed thus:

	£	£
Work certified to 31 December 19.1		20,400
Less Cost to that date	19,890	
Less Cost of uncertified work	1,020	
		18,870
Profit earned to 31 December 19.1		£1,530

88 Asset valuation and income measurement: historical-cost accounting (1)

2 Time discount on the retention moneys (assumed payable at 31 December 19.3, six months after scheduled date of finishing the contract (30 June 19.3) is computed thus:

	£
Retention moneys accrued to 31 December 19.1	2,040
Less Present value of that sum, discounted at 10 per cent per annum for two years—	
£2,040/(1.10)^2 =	1,686
Time discount	£354

10 per cent per annum is assumed to be the firm's cost of capital. (In practice, this adjustment is usually omitted.)

3 Work in progress on Contract No. 317 is shown in the balance sheet, 31 December 19.1, at £1,020—the cost of uncertified work. This is the net debit balance of the first three accounts illustrated

$$(£19,890 - £20,400 + £1,530 = £1,020).$$

4 On the best estimates available, management expects a final profit on the contract of £102,000 − £96,900 = £5,100—only 5 per cent on the escalated price, as against a planned 20 per cent (£20,000 on £100,000). The expected profit, poor as it is, still exceeds the profit to date, £1,530, by £3,570, and no provision for a loss seems called for at this stage. The position will need to be watched carefully during the year 19.2.

Similar principles apply to businesses in which the period of stockholding is very long, and in which the stock tends to appreciate in value over time, such as those of timber-merchants, wine-merchants, and whisky-distillers. As with civil engineering contracts, the normal rule of recognizing revenue only on sale is modified, and it is usual to write up the values of the stocks annually, as they mature—by direct appraisal, or the addition of interest on moneys presumed to finance stockholdings, or the application of rule-of-thumb percentages on cost or on the increasing balance—a species of 'depreciation in reverse'. The result is to take some profit in each year of (say) a seven-year period of maturation of whisky in bond instead of taking it all on sale, either as mature spirit or (earlier) as immature, but still at a higher price than was paid for it.

Finally, there are cases in which the pricing of inventories at net realizable value is not merely respectable, but well-nigh unavoidable. In agriculture and horti-culture, production is seasonal and it is highly desirable to match the sale proceeds of a crop with the costs of growing and harvesting it. If unsold produce were carried forward to next year at cost of production—even supposing that that could be estimated with any accuracy from the average farmer's accounts—then next year's profit would include an element relating to this year's harvest. Valuation at net realizable value is the only sensible procedure, on grounds of practicality and of matching revenues and costs of the same season; it may also be justified on the realization criterion, in that agricultural produce has a guaranteed market at some known price, unless it is unsaleable because of a glut, in which case its inventory value is zero. The opening and closing inventories of a farm will also include the market value of livestock (profit being recognized as accruing from the maturing or fattening of animals which, if born on the farm, may have no obvious cost of acquisition) and the 'tenantright' value of tillage—work done on ploughing, harrowing, fertilizer-spreading, sowing, etc., for next season's crops. In mining and oil-drilling, too, it is general to value stocks of ore or crude oil at selling prices, there being normally a ready market and difficulty in costing output with much accuracy. Once more, profit determination is orientated towards production, rather than sales as with manufacturing industry.

5.3.3 Concepts of cost in inventory pricing

Up to this point 'historical cost' has been taken very much for granted in relation to inventory valuation. It is, in fact, neither a simple nor an unambiguous concept.

Historical cost is found by ascertaining the physical quantity on hand of each line of stock, or work in progress, multiplying it by an appropriate unit price, and totalling the products of the multiplications. The quantities may be discovered, either by 'taking stock' at the year-end, or by maintaining a 'perpetual inventory' in a memorandum stock ledger, with a running record of items delivered and consumed or sold, frequent balancing, and continuous checks to keep the stock ledger in line with the factual position.

One of the main problems, under either system, is the identification of the goods or work in progress on hand with particular items acquired during the year, or on hand at the beginning of it. When large, durable, and expensive items are dealt in, wholesale or retail (e.g. motor cars or furniture), it is relatively simple to keep records enabling each article to be traced into and out of the entity, and allowing precise identification of each one in stock at the balancing date. It can then be priced at its actual cost to the firm. In most firms, however, the goods handled are too numerous, too similar to one another within each line, and/or of too low unit value, to make identification of each item either practicable or economic. In industrial processes, also, raw materials lose their identity very quickly, and other costs, such as labour and overheads, have to be taken into account as well, in evaluating work in progress. It follows that, even within the framework of historical cost, the pricing of inventories generally depends upon the adoption of some set of conventions for imputing cost to individual items.

The most common convention, for discrete items of raw material or finished goods, is *first in, first out* (FIFO). This is based on the assumption that goods flow continuously through the processes of production (if any) and sales, with raw materials entering the works in the order in which they were delivered, work in progress being completed in the order in which it was put in hand, and finished goods being sold in the order in which they were delivered from the works or from outside. Such an assumption appears the most rational one in the absence of evidence as to the real pattern of movements, but should not be accepted (at any rate in large firms) without some attempt to discover how raw materials or goods are in fact selected for processing or sale—they may be taken from the front of the shelves, or the top of the pile, each time, so that it is the latest, not the earliest, deliveries which are most often moved first. To many accountants, though, such factors are subsidiary ones. The virtues of the FIFO system are firstly, that it is easy to operate with or without a perpetual inventory—the year-end stock can be priced by taking the latest invoice price for each line and, if the stock exceeds the last delivery, going back to the previous one to find a price for the excess, and so on (see Example 3). Secondly, it tends to give recent prices, approaching replacement cost, for the closing stocks. Thirdly, it is approved by the British Inland Revenue for use in accounts presented as a basis for income tax or corporation tax computations, and there is no need to adjust the regular financial accounts in this respect. The drawbacks are, that identically-similar goods may be priced at two or more different rates, because they are deemed to belong to different parcels—hence complications in costing—and, more seriously, that unless turnover of stock is very rapid the matching of purchases with sales takes place after a considerable interval, during which both buying and selling prices may have changed appreciably, so that (usually) purchases at a lower level of prices are matched with sales at a higher one, and the reported profit is inflated as compared with the figure which would result from the use of current costs. This objection really arises, though, from the nature of historical-cost accounting itself; FIFO merely fails to disguise the problem.

In dealing with raw materials consisting of liquid, viscous, or granular substances, which are continually delivered into, and drawn from, tanks, silos, dumps, etc. which are seldom or never empty, it is reasonable to assume (particularly with liquids) that the stock at any time contains elements of all quantities which have ever been delivered to the 'pool'. The FIFO assumption thus gives place to an 'averaging' one, and pricing is conducted (through the medium of a perpetual inventory) by using a weighted mean of the prices of all deliveries to date, or at least all those since the system started, and recalculating it after each delivery (see Example 3). The result is a moving average price, applied for both costing and annual reporting purposes. Over time the effect on profits is much the same as with FIFO, since the latest delivered prices are dominant in the average, but without the sudden jumps as one parcel is deemed to be exhausted, and with only one price in use at any given time. Against this there is the more complex and tedious arithmetic (easily handled, though, by a computer). The *average cost* system, like FIFO, is acceptable to the Inland Revenue in this country.

The third main inventory pricing system based on historical-cost is *last in, first out* (LIFO). The assumption here is that outflows of goods come always from the latest, not the earliest, deliveries; it was suggested above that this might be the case in many firms. To establish it as a fact might not be easy, though it is likely enough as regards, say, stocks of coal, where the bottom of the heap is seldom reached and is largely rubbish anyway. The proper tracing of costs in a LIFO system calls for a perpetual inventory, but if this is not maintained an approximation can be arrived at for ending inventory by assuming, for each line of stock, that the final quantity represents the opening inventory (priced as in last year's accounts) plus the whole or part of the earliest delivery in the current year—and so on forward; or, if stock has been run down, the previous year's total, less the fall in quantity valued at the latest prices paid in that year. The main advantages over FIFO are that LIFO tends to match sales with more recent purchase prices, and so report profit margins closer to those maintainable over time; and that in a period of rising prices total profit for the year is stated conservatively, at a figure closer than otherwise to what is truly distributable (but vice versa, if prices fall). This also minimizes tax assessments under inflation, where the revenue authorities recognize the method. The United States federal tax code has permitted the use of LIFO, under certain conditions, since 1954,[1] and many companies there have taken advantage of it; but in Britain the Inland Revenue, and the courts, insist firmly upon FIFO or average cost in accounts for tax purposes, and this has largely inhibited the adoption of LIFO over here. It has, in any case, the effect of postponing the

[1] Edwards, E. O. and P. W. Bell. *The Theory and Measurement of Business Income,* University of California, 1961.

incidence of reported profits only as long as the physical inventory remains stable or grows in an inflationary period. If it declines, then older and lower purchase prices begin to be matched with current sales, and profits are inflated as compared with FIFO; indeed, over the whole life of a business total money profits are equal by both methods, as was shown in section 5.1. Further, the LIFO system usually results in unrealistic valuation of ending inventories, as compared with current replacement cost.

A few companies in the non-ferrous metals industries make use of the *base stock* method of valuation, in which the minimum physical quantities held over time are regarded as a quasi-fixed asset, and priced permanently at the cost of acquiring the original stocks, which are thought of as continually renewed. One or more of the three previous methods is applied to the rest. The base stock method, too, is not countenanced by the British Inland Revenue, and those companies which use it must adjust their profits for tax purposes. Further, both the LIFO and base stock methods are now condemned by ED6.

Example 3 Below is a comparison, in tabular form, of the gross profits and ending inventories reported under the FIFO, average cost, and LIFO systems, given certain assumptions as to opening inventories, purchases and sales (pence rounded off).

	FIFO			Average cost			LIFO		
	Quantity	Price £	Value £	Quantity	Price £	Value £	Quantity	Price £	Value £
Stock	50	10.00	500	100	10.10	1,010	30	9.00	270
Jan 1	50	10.25	513				70	9.80	686
	100		£1,013	100		£1,010	100		£ 956
Purchases									
Jan 31	50	10.25	512						
Feb 28	70	10.50	735						
Mar 31	80	10.60	848						
Apr 30	100	10.60	1,060						
May 31	100	10.70	1,070						
Jun 30	80	10.75	860						
	480		£5,085	480		£5,085	480		£5,085
	580		£6,098	580		£6,095	580		£6,041
Cost of Sales									
Jan 15	50	10.00	500	75	10.10	757	70	9.80	686
	25	10.25	256				5	9.00	45
Feb 14	25	10.25	257	60	10.20	612	50	10.25	512
	35	10.25	358				10	9.00	90
Mar 15	15	10.25	154	70	10.45	731	70	10.50	735
	55	10.50	578						
Apr 15	15	10.50	157	70	10.58	741	70	10.60	742
	55	10.60	583						
May 15	25	10.60	265	90	10.60	954	90	10.60	954
	65	10.60	689						
Jun 15	35	10.60	371	95	10.67	1,014	95	10.70	1,017
	60	10.70	642						
	460		£4,810	460		£4,809	460		£4,781

Stock									
Jun 30	40	10.70	428	120	10.72	1,286	15	9.00	135
	80	10.75	860				10	10.60	106
							10	10.60	106
							5	10.70	53
							80	10.75	860
	120		£1,288	120		£1,286	120		£1,260
	580		£6,098	580		£6,095	580		£6,041

Sales									
Jan 15	75	12.80	960						
Feb 14	60	12.80	768						
Mar 15	70	12.80	896						
Apr 15	70	13.50	945						
May 15	90	13.50	1,215						
Jun 15	95	13.50	1,283						
	460		£6,067	460		£6,067	460		£6,067
Cost of sales	460		4,810	460		4,809	460		4,781
Gross profit			£1,257			£1,258			£1,286

In the 'average cost' columns, the first cost of sales price is that of the opening stock, since there were no deliveries in the meantime. The second price (applied to the February sales) is computed thus:

	£	£
Stock, Jan 1	100 x 10.10 =	1,010.00
Less Sales, Jan 15	75 x 10.10 =	757.50
	25	252.50
Add Purchases, Jan 31	50 x 10.25 =	512.50
Stock before sales, Feb 14	75 x 10.20* =	£765.00

* Derived from the other two figures—i.e. £765.00/75.

The same principle is applied in deriving the other prices, as moving averages.

It will be observed that, while there is no significant difference between the results for FIFO and average cost, LIFO gives a lower closing stock value, yet a lower cost of sales and higher gross profit, though prices were rising all the time and physical stock increased over the period. This occurred because, early in the half-year, much of the opening stock which was valued at old prices was drawn upon, so that very little of it entered into the closing inventory, made up mainly of stock at recent prices. Had there been no continuous stock record the average cost method would have been inapplicable, but under FIFO the same answers, in respect of the half-year as a whole, could have been obtained by valuing closing stock directly. Under LIFO, though, it would have been necessary to resort to the expedient of assuming the closing stock to be the opening stock, plus the net increase over the period priced as for the earliest delivery, thus:

	£	£
Stock, Jan 1	30 x 9.00 =	270
	70 x 9.80 =	686
	100	956
Add Increase over half-year	20 x 10.25 =	205
Estimated stock, June 30	120	£1,161

Application of this estimate would have increased cost of sales to £4,880 and reduced gross profit to £1,187—appreciably lower than by FIFO or average cost. The situation envisaged is therefore a salutary warning as to the pitfalls of LIFO, for which exaggerated claims are often made.

In manufacturing, raw materials, work in progress and finished goods are frequently priced at *standard cost.* If raw material prices and wage rates change during the accounting period, by percentages greater than those allowed for when setting the standards, the material and labour contents of the closing stock and work in progress should be totalled separately and uplifted by the appropriate percentages, and the price and rate variances reduced accordingly. Calculation of the works overhead element is dealt with below.

5.3.4 Problem of overhead costs

The costing of industrial inventories of work in progress and finished goods, however identified, always involves a decision as to the treatment of manufacturing overheads; it is not normal to take account of overheads relating to selling or general administration. The controversial issue concerns the inclusion or exclusion of manufacturing overheads—i.e. the choice lies between full cost (or, better, absorption cost) and marginal cost (or, more accurately, variable cost).

Absorption costing adds to the cost of direct materials and direct labour, deemed to be embodied in work in progress, an allowance for manufacturing overheads—power, light and heat, rent (or equivalent) and rates of the factory, salaries of supervisory and managerial staff in the works ('indirect labour'), welfare facilities, maintenance and depreciation of building and plant, etc. Sophisticated standard costing systems usually channel these expenses to cost centres within the works—departments, shops, production-lines, or individual machines—and compute for each centre a time rate (such as a machine-hour rate for each piece of plant), charged for the number of minutes for which a piece of work (or batch of articles, etc.) makes use of the facilities of the cost centre. This means that elements of overhead are incorporated at several different stages of a job's progress through the factory, making it a tedious and unprofitable exercise to 'unscramble' the total cost and separate out the overheads. The firm is then committed to the use of absorption cost in the inventories.

Very often, though, standard (or other) costing traces only direct materials and labour to particular cost units, and works overheads are 'absorbed' by means of a general addition to the variable cost—most commonly, in the form of a percentage on direct labour cost, since both labour and (most) overheads are functions of time devoted to production, or the provision of facilities therefor. The most rational method of calculating the percentage is to estimate *ex ante* (before the event) total overheads for a period, on the basis of normal utilization of capacity, and then divide by the estimated total direct wages for the period, at that level of utilization, multiplying by 100 to express the answer as a percentage. This is then applied to direct labour cost to find the estimated total cost of each unit of production, and inventories of work in progress and finished goods are valued accordingly. There is, of course, no guarantee or likelihood that the total absorption will coincide with the total overheads for the year—there is certain to be an under- or over-recovery, appearing as an activity variance in a standard costing system. With or without standard costing, an under- or over-recovery of overheads means under- or over-estimation (respectively) of the historical cost of inventories, and the absorption percentage may need to be recalculated *ex post* (after the event).

In the view of many accountants, however, such refinements are all beside the point. The computation of an overhead absorption rate is essentially arbitrary, since there is no direct connection between the incurring of many overhead items, and a decision to produce one more unit, or batch of units. This is especially true of those costs which, over a wide range of possible volumes of output, are largely fixed in total, since they can be changed to a material extent only by abandoning or adding very large and expensive installations, such as a whole factory. Also, any attempt to fix an absorption rate is subject to a wide margin of error, so that a figure of annual profit so found is highly suspect and, if taken at its face value by managers or investors, may induce them to take wrong decisions. In other words, it is a very 'unreliable' measurement in the sense defined in Chapter 4, section 4.3.

The remedy, in the eyes of those who reason thus, is the substitution of what is loosely called marginal costing, but which is better described as *variable costing*. Marginal cost has a definite, and distinct, meaning in economic theory—as the increment to total costs of a firm which results from the production of one more unit of output, or the decrement resulting from the production of one fewer, than the actual volume over any particular period. This is not very relevant to practical problems of cost accounting, and is not measured by so-called 'marginal costing'. 'Variable costing' (the proper term) seeks to measure only those costs of output whose total can be said to vary closely with the quantity produced—i.e. direct materials and direct labour. The unit cost of these items, being deducted from the sales revenue per unit of output, leaves the *contribution* of each unit to total overheads (by this hypothesis, unallocable to individual units) and, hopefully, to operating profit, which can arise only when total contributions exceed total overheads. Total profit is maximized, in the short run, by concentrating production on those lines whose unit contributions are largest, and the system of management accounts should be so designed as to make it clear which these are. Arbitrary allocations of overhead are irrelevant, and may be misleading.

As to the financial accounts, it is urged that inventories should be priced at the historical cost (however defined) of direct materials and labour only, and that each year should be left to bear its own overheads, with no part of them carried over in inventory from one year to the next. Net profit for the year will then consist of (sales *less* direct cost of sales =) contribution *less* overheads. This profit will be primarily determined by the level of sales, and there will be no distortions caused by variations in the physical quantity of stocks from one year-end to another, as the following over-simplified, and extreme, example illustrates.

Example 4 Two firms in the same industry commence business on 1 January 19.1, and for the calendar years 19.1 and 19.2 their production (30,000, and 10,000, units), sales and cost structures are precisely similar. Inventories are in both cases zero at 1 January 19.1, 10,000 units at 31 December of that year, and zero again at 31 December 19.2. Firm A prices its inventories at absorption cost, and Firm B at variable cost. Total sales, in both years for both firms, are 20,000 units at £5 per unit, with variable costs £3 per unit, and overheads £30,000 per annum. The reported results are as follows:

Firm A		19.1		19.2	
	£	£	£	£	£
Sales (20,000 x £5)			100,000		100,000
Raw Materials Purchases and Direct Wages					
30,000 x £3		90,000			
10,000 x £3				30,000	
Overheads		30,000		30,000	
		120,000		60,000	
Add Opening stock		0		40,000	
		120,000		100,000	
Less Closing stock (19.1)—					
Variable cost,					
10,000 x £3	30,000				
Overheads, £30,000 x 10,000/30,000	10,000				
		40,000		0	
Cost of sales			80,000		100,000
Operating profit			£20,000		£0

Firm B		19.1		19.2	
	£	£	£	£	£
Sales (20,000 x £5)			100,000		100,000
Raw materials purchases and direct wages		90,000		30,000	
Add Opening stock		0		30,000	
		90,000		60,000	
Less Closing stock (19.1)—					
Variable cost,					
10,000 x £3	30,000			0	
			60,000		60,000
Contribution			40,000		40,000
Overheads			30,000		30,000
Operating profit			£10,000		£10,000

Everything about the two firms is similar except their inventory valuation methods; yet, though they both make £20,000 operating profit in two years, Firm A is shown as making £20,000 in the first year and nothing in the second, while Firm B makes £10,000 in each year! The reason is that A has carried £10,000 of its first-year overheads across to the second year, by assuming that, since ending inventory for 19.1 was one-third of total production, it ought to bear one-third of the overheads. Addition of these to the costs for 19.2, when none of that year's own overheads were carried forward because there was no ending inventory, was enough to wipe out all profit. Firm B, on the other hand, makes each year bear its own overheads, irrespective of the level of production or sales.

Variable costing makes profit depend primarily on the level of sales, irrespective of that of production, and avoids inflation/deflation of a year's profits through build-up/run-down of stocks over the year (causing more/less overhead to be carried forward to the following year than has been brought forward from the previous one). Its main drawback is that inventory values in the balance sheet bear little relation to the long-run cost of producing goods—they could not be produced at all without the facilities whose costs are included in overheads. A mode of valuation which excludes these costs is fundamentally unsound, in the eyes of opponents of variable costing, and ED6 supports them. No real reconciliation of the two viewpoints has yet been reached, and there is reason to suppose that none is possible within the framework of historical costing.[2] The same applies to several other contentious issues in the field of inventory valuation, as will be brought out in Chapter 7.

5.3.5 Exposure draft 6 (1972): Stocks and work in progress

As is explained more fully in Chapter 14, section **14.6**, an *Exposure Draft* is a proposed *Statement of Standard Accounting Practice* which, when finalized, becomes mandatory upon all companies whose accounts are audited by chartered or certified accountants. The published accounts must normally comply with the terms of the SSAP, or else the auditors must qualify their report in respect of any deviation which in their opinion is unjustified, and prejudicial to the 'true and fair view' required by the Companies Acts.

ED6 attempts to reduce the diversity of practice in inventory valuation, within the conventional framework of company accounting. If it becomes a SSAP it is to apply to accounts for any period beginning on or after 1 January 1973. The actual Statement is short—one page only—but the accompanying explanations and definitions are somewhat longer.

The basic propositions are two:

1 stocks and work in progress should be valued at the lower of cost and net realizable value; but
2 work in progress on a long-term contract should be valued at cost, plus attributable profit to date, less anticipated losses.

The accounting policies followed in arriving at the stated amounts should be disclosed. The methods used to calculate cost (including overheads) and to arrive at net realizable value should be stated if they are material for an understanding of the accounts.

As to 1, 'cost' is defined as all expenditure incurred in bringing the product or service to its present location and condition. This comprises *cost of purchase* (including import duties, transport and handling costs, and any other directly attributable costs, less trade discounts, rebates, and subsidies), and *cost of conversion,* where applicable. The latter is defined as the total of: i costs specifically attributable to units of production (direct labour, direct expenses including depreciation, and sub-contracted work); ii production overheads based on

---

[2] One suggestion is 'relevant costing'—the inclusion in inventory cost of production overheads related to *activity* and the exclusion of those related purely to *time*. This, too, is rejected by ED 6. See: Sorter, G. H. and C. T. Horngren, Asset recognition and economic attributes: the relevant costing approach. *The Accounting Review,* July 1962.

the normal level of activity, taking one year with another; and **iii** other overheads attributable in the particular circumstances of the business to bringing the product or service to its present location and condition (such as overheads relating to the custody of maturing stocks, and design and selling costs relating to products manufactured to customer's specification).

The ASSC has thus plainly rejected variable-cost pricing. In its eyes, all normal production overheads, whatever their nature, are part of the cost of 'bringing the product to its present location and condition', and may not be left out of account, or selectively omitted on the ground that they relate to time rather than to directly productive activities. In large and complex organizations it is fairly easy to distinguish production overheads from those relative to marketing, selling, or administration, though even there it is often necessary to make some arbitrary division of the costs of central service departments, such as the accounting function. In smaller businesses, where there is less division of labour, especially in general management, even the remuneration of directors may have to be treated in part as a production overhead. Once the allocations have been made, though, the overhead element in total conversion costs should be calculated on the basis of the company's normal level of activity, taking one year with another and having regard to the volume of production which the facilities are intended by their designers and by management to produce under the working conditions prevailing during the year, the budgeted level of activity during the current and the ensuing year, and the level of activity achieved in the current year and in previous years.

As to particular methods of cost determination, that or those should be used which give(s) the nearest approximation to actual cost. This in turn involves the selection of appropriate methods: **a** for relating costs to stocks and work in progress (e.g. job, batch, or processs costing); and **b** for calculating the related cost where a number of identical items have been purchased or made at different times (e.g. unit cost, average cost, or FIFO). Where standard costs are used they need to be reviewed frequently to ensure that they bear a reasonable relationship to actual costs obtaining during the period. Methods such as base stock and LIFO do not usually bear such a relationship (and are, by implication, condemned by the ASSC as they already are by the Inland Revenue). It is unacceptable to arrive at cost by applying the latest purchase price to all items in stock, or to use selling price less an estimated profit margin (unless it can be demonstrated that the latter method gives a reasonable approximation of the actual cost of each item). In industries where by-products cannot be separately costed, stocks of such by-products may be stated at their net realizable value, and the cost of the main products calculated after deducting the net realizable value of the by-products.

Net realizable value is to be substituted for cost where the first figure is lower than the second. The comparison is to be made item by item, and the lower amount taken for each. If this is impracticable, groups or categories of similar items should be taken together. Comparison of total realizable value with total cost of stocks is unacceptable, as involving a setting-off of foreseeable losses against unrealized profits.

Net realizable value is defined as the estimated selling price (net of trade discounts, but gross of cash discounts), less all further costs to completion and less all costs to be incurred in marketing, distribution, and selling, but without deduction for administration—i.e. the amount at which it is expected that an item can be carried forward without creating either profit or loss in the year of sale. Special considerations apply to the employment of formulae to compute net realizable value (taking account, e.g. of the age, past movements, expected future movements, and estimated scrap value of the stock); this is useful as a consistent basis for a provision, but the results must be reviewed in the light of any special circumstances not anticipated in the formula, such as changes in the state of the order book. It is also necessary to consider the values of stocks of parts and sub-assemblies, and of stocks on order, where the main product has been written down; and of stocks of spares held for sale, having regard to the number of whole units sold, the estimated frequency of replacement of a spare part, and the expected life of the whole unit. It is not necessary to write down the cost of material stocks, provided that the product in which they are to be incorporated can still be sold at a profit after incorporating the materials at cost price.

The treatment of replacement cost is very brief. As an alternative to cost and net realizable value it can arise only if it is lower than both. The ASSC rejects its use when it is below net realizable value, on the ground that the effect is to take account of a loss greater than that which is expected to be incurred—irrespective of whether cost or net realizable value is the highest of the three. Such a position has the merit of consistency, and by-passes arguments about the distortions caused by the traditional one-way adjustment—down to replacement cost, but not up to it—as well as the question of whether individual items, or the overall position, should be considered. The trend of accounting thought has for some time been moving towards the ASSC's position, but it is a pity that the arguments for and against it are not set out at length—e.g. the contention that replacement cost belongs to a different conception of accounting from the conventional one, or (contrarily) that it is doubtfully realistic to show stock at historical cost when that is above replacement cost, even if net realizable value is higher than both.

The most controversial aspect of ED6 is its recommendations as to valuation of work in progress on a long-term contract. Many companies in the relevant fields do not take any profit until a contract is finished, or nearing completion, and the proposals have already caused an outcry, mainly because of fears that liability for corporation tax will be brought forward in time, and the cash flow position worsened without any countervailing advantage. This is irrelevant in determining the most rational theory of valuation, but the views of industrialists can scarcely be ignored, where compulsion by a non-statutory body may injure their financial interests.

A long-term contract is defined as one for the manufacture or building of a single entity or the provision of a service, where the time taken to manufacture, build, or provide is such that a substantial proportion of all such contract work will normally extend for a period exceeding a year. It is pointed out that in arriving at the cost of work in progress on such contracts it is normally inappropriate to include interest payable on borrowed money, except possibly in the few cases where sums borrowed can be identified as financing specific contracts, in which case the facts should be clearly stated. Where long-term contracts exist for the supply of services, or the manufacture and supply of goods, which are invoiced according to separate parts of the contract, it is best to treat each separable part as a separate contract for the purposes of profit determination, but to compare future revenues from the contract with future estimated costs and make provision for any foreseen loss.

The ASSC does not lay down any general rules for finding the proportion of prospective profit to be taken, when valuing work in progress on a long-term contract; the type of business concerned must always be taken into account. It is normal, though, to define the earliest point which must be reached before a profit is taken up—in principle, the point at which the outcome can first be reasonably foreseen. Of the profit which in the light of all the circumstances can be reasonably foreseen to arise on completion of the contract, it is essential to regard as earned to date only that proportion which prudently reflects the amount of work carried out to date; the method adopted for taking up profits needs to be consistently aplied.

The total estimated profit on the contract is to be calculated by taking into account, not only total costs to date and total estimated further costs to completion (on the same basis), but also estimated future costs of rectification and guarantee work, and any other future work to be undertaken under the contract terms. Future costs must be computed with regard to likely increases in wages and salaries, raw material prices, and general overheads, insofar as such increases are not recoverable from the customer under the terms of the contract. The total costs, so ascertained, are then to be compared with the total sales value of the contract. In respect of the latter, an addition, known or conservatively estimated, is to be made for the value of any variations made during the course of the contract. On the other hand, provision needs to be made for foreseen claims or penalties arising out of delays in completion or from other causes. In view of such uncertainties estimates need to be prudently made, so that the total estimated profit on the contract is not inflated.

The amount to be reflected in the current year's profit and loss account will be the appropriate proportion of total profit by reference to the work done to date, less any profit already taken up in prior years. This is not necessarily the proportion of total profit which is appropriate to the amount of work carried out in the year, as there may be variations over time in profit expectations.

Finally, additional information relative to long-term contracts should be disclosed in the published accounts. The profit and loss account should show separately the amount of profit or loss arising from such contracts, distinguishing between:

i the net amount provided in the year for anticipated losses;
ii the profits, less losses, relating to contracts which had been treated as completed at the close of the preceding financial year; and
iii other profits and losses on long-term contracts.

In the balance sheet (or in notes, thereon) the following amounts should be distinguished:

a the separate amounts included in respect of cost and attributable profit;
b the amount deducted in respect of anticipated losses;
c the further amount provided for anticipated losses on those contracts where the total anticipated losses exceed the costs to date; and
d cash received and receivable at the accounting date as progress payments on account of contracts.

The value of the work in progress on long-term contracts will be made up of a minus b minus d, with c appearing among the liabilities as a separate provision.

On the whole, ED6 does not go beyond the practice of the most progressive British companies. Like other pronouncements of the ASSC to date, it fails to go deeply into the underlying theory or to set out in any detail the arguments for and against different treatments of the subject-matter, but concentrates on laying down what is considered best practice within the canons of historical-cost accounting.

This is better than the previous permissive system of *Recommendations on Accounting Principles*, but a truly authoritative formulation of the principles of inventory valuation, and of many other matters, is still awaited. (See also Exposure Draft 2 of the International Accounting Standards Committee, in Chapter 14, sub-section **14.7.2.**)[3]

5.4 Voyage accounting in the shipping industry

One peculiar form of 'work in progress' merits passing mention. In the shipping industry, each voyage is separately accounted for, and the profit or loss on it transferred in due course to the profit and loss account for the business as a whole—there is no trading or operating account. A Voyage Account is opened each time a ship sails, and is debited with all expenditure ascribed to the voyage—salaries and wages of officers and crew, fuel and stores purchased, insurance, dock and harbour dues, etc.—but not depreciation of the vessel, which is charged in the profit and loss account as an overhead. The voyage account is credited with freight and/or passage moneys earned, and a balance of profit or loss struck at the end of the voyage (after adjustment for any balances of fuel or stores, etc., carried over to another voyage). The profit or loss is transferred to an Earnings Account in the name of the ship, and *its* balance is in turn transferred annually to the profit and loss account.

An anomaly arises in respect of voyages still in progress at the year-end. These should have been charged with all expenditure up to that point, but may or may not have been credited with freight, according to whether this is payable in advance, or only on safe arrival of the cargo. Passage moneys are always payable in advance, and will have been credited at an early stage. The conventional solution to the problem of apportioning revenue and costs on uncompleted voyages is simply to ignore it. Each voyage account is balanced as it stands, and the debit, and credit, balances totalled separately and entered on opposite sides of the balance sheet, as current assets and current liabilities respectively, and both captioned as 'open voyage accounts'. When a voyage is completed the whole profit or loss is taken to profit and loss account in the year of completion, irrespective of the period of accrual.

These procedures are a relic of the 'venture accounting' familiar to Luca Pacioli, and cut right across the accrual principle which underlies modern business accounting. The year-end figures have no real meaning in a present-day balance sheet, being mere cash flow balances, neither true assets nor true liabilities—the credit balances normally contain an element of profit earned, and ought to belong to equity, at least in part. There does not seem to be much pressure for reform, among either shipowners or accountants, but the adoption of some kind of accruals basis for voyage accounts, analogous to the treatment of long-term contracts in shore-based industries, appears long overdue.

[3]ED6 is now superseded by SSAP No. 9: *Stocks and work in progress* (1975), in force for accounting periods starting on or after 1 January 1976. Work in progress on long-term contracts is now to be stated at 'cost plus any attributable profit, less any foreseeable losses and progress payments received and receivable.' If anticipated losses on individual contracts exceed cost less progress payments, such excesses should be shown as provisions. Accounting policies used in calculating cost, net realizable value, attributable profit, and foreseeable losses should be stated. Inventory should be sub-classified in balance sheets or notes 'in a manner which is appropriate to the business and so as to indicate the amounts held in each of the main categories.' Statements of long-term contract work in progress should distinguish between a work in progress at cost plus attributable profit, less foreseeable losses; and b progress payments received and receivable.

6
Asset valuation and income measurement: historical-cost accounting (2)

Chapter 5 having dealt with current assets and liabilities, it is now necessary to consider the valuation of non-current items in the balance sheet, and their connection with the determination of periodic profit within the principles of historical-cost accounting. As compared with current items the effect, on the profit reported in any one year, of differences in valuation methods is generally less, but by their nature long-lived assets (and, to a less extent, liabilities) affect the profits of several years, and a faulty method of determining their stated values at each year-end may have an insidious influence which takes longer to correct itself than, say, an error in valuing the ending inventory of one year.

6.1 Non-current liabilities and provisions

There is no hard and fast distinction between current and other liabilities in the continuous life of an entity, since they all fall due for payment sooner or later. The division of that life into accounting periods of arbitrary length—normally one year—creates a need to distinguish between the short run, with a time-horizon limited at farthest to the length of one accounting period, and the medium to long run, with a time-horizon of greater extent. A further distinction is sometimes made between the medium term (one to three, four, or five years) and the long term (after that), but it is vague and subjective, and of little practical value. In this book it appears sufficient to classify liabilities as: *current,* payable within twelve months of the balance sheet date; and *non-current,* payable after that. Similarly, assets are commonly divided into: *current,* expected to be liquidated (turned into cash) within twelve months; and *fixed,* expected to be retained for more than twelve months (in the ordinary course of business).

Most liabilities for goods or services purchased are current in the sense defined; as stated in Chapter 5, section 5.2, they are normally retained on the books at the legal amount due until they are paid, with exceptions for hire purchase and instalment credit liabilities, which should be discounted in the manner described, and the implicit interest allowed for in computing profit for the periods covered. Bank overdrafts are best regarded as short-term loans, continually repaid and re-advanced, with interest charged explicitly from day to day; they are 'current' even if they go on for years, as the bank is always at liberty to call them in at short notice. Bank advances, repayable by fixed monthly instalments, should be treated similarly to hire purchase, the implicit rate of interest (higher than the nominal rate stated in the agreement with the bank, to determine the total sum due) being taken into account.

Non-current liabilities include loans for a term of years, with interest paid annually or more frequently (most often, half-yearly). If the principal is repaid at par, with no element of premium or discount, then discounting of the future payments (interest and principal) at the contractual rate of interest will at all times, and over any term of years, reduce them to the precise amount of the advance, which is, by this reasoning, the correct amount to be shown in the balance sheet. Thus, if £100 is borrowed at 10 per cent per annum (payable at the end of each year), and the principal is repaid after three years, then

$$P = £10/(1.10) + £10/(1.10)^2 + £10/(1.10)^3 + £100/(1.10)^3$$
$$= £(9.0909 + 8.2645 + 7.5131 + 75.1315)$$
$$= £100$$

and so for any number of years. Hence (it is argued) it is consistent with the canons of historical-cost accounting to show the loan at par. Company debentures, though, are generally issued at a discount and repaid at par, making the effective rate of interest higher; if this is applied as the discounting rate, the future payments reduce to the principal less the discount, as at the date of issue. At later dates the outstanding payments will discount to a higher amount, and the book amount of issue discount must be written down progressively, as explained fully in Chapter 12, sub-section 12.4.1.

6.1.1 Provisions for taxation

In addition to liabilities presently incurred, by purchasing goods or services or borrowing money, an entity must take into account certain obligations not currently enforceable as money payments. For these it is necessary to make *provisions* out of current revenue, by debiting profit and loss account and crediting an account for each provision—thus reducing the reported profit for the year. When (or if) the liability matures, it is debited to the provision and credited to the creditor concerned (or to cash), and any remaining debit or credit balance (under- or over-provision) transferred from the provision account to the debit or credit of profit and loss account, so as to adjust the equity to its 'correct' amount.

One of the commonest types of provision (in this sense) is for *taxation on profits*—income tax on unincorporated businesses, and corporation tax on bodies corporate, including limited companies. Such taxes arise, potentially, as the profits are made, and proper provisions need to be raised for them in the annual accounts where the profits are computed—generally speaking, on a historical-cost basis. The actual payments, though, are normally deferred, by as much as one year or more, and assessment of them takes place some considerable time after the accounts are prepared. It is thus necessary to make a provision for the tax, as an estimated sum rounded up to, say, the next £1,000, and then adjust it, as indicated in the previous paragraph, when an accurate assessment is agreed with the tax authorities. However, in view of the close connection of accounting methods with legal complications in this field, detailed discussion is postponed to *Part 2*—income tax being treated in Chapter 9, section 9.4., and corporation tax in Chapter 12, section 12.3. Something may nevertheless be said in this place about the accounting treatment of other U.K. taxes and dues, which are normally regarded as current liabilities.

Income tax deducted at source from employees' wages and salaries, under the *Pay As You Earn* (PAYE) system, is in the first place debited to Wages and/or Salaries Accounts additionally to *net* remuneration, and credited to the PAYE Account, as a sum due to the Inland Revenue, having been withheld from the employees' *gross* remuneration (the amount to be charged for labour costs, with some additions described hereunder). The sum due (net of refunds to individuals who have overpaid tax to date) is paid over monthly to the local Collector of Taxes, and the PAYE Account debited. *National Insurance contributions* are collected through the same machinery, part of the sum due each week being deducted from remuneration, and part paid by the firm; the full amount should be debited to wages and/or salaries (so that the employer's proportion is a cost, additional to gross remuneration), and credited to National Insurance Account, which is debited with the monthly payments (made to the Collector with the PAYE deductions). The total charge is therefore gross remuneration plus employer's proportion of national insurance contributions.

As to indirect taxes on goods, *import duties* are paid to the customs officers at the port of importation, before the goods are released, and in the books are added to the price. If the goods are put into bond, payment of duty and its recording in the books are postponed until the goods leave bond. Import duties thus enter directly into the cost of manufacture of sale. *Excise duties* (on hydrocarbon oils, beer, spirits, etc.) are levied on the manufacturer. They are payable every three months during the calendar year, and should be provided for, at least every month, in respect of production or sales during the month, by debiting Excise Duty Account and crediting Customs and Excise Account, which is debited with payments and its balance in the meantime treated as a current liability. The duty is passed on in the selling price of the goods. It is best to debit it separately to the customer and credit the duty account, whose debit balance outstanding at the year-end is shown as a current asset, or added to the value of inventory, calculated net of duty. This procedure avoids inflating both cost of sales and turnover by the amount of the impost, which does not properly form part of either. A firm at a later stage in the distribution process, however, will normally treat excise duty as part of its cost of sales, and pass it on in sales, as well as including unrecovered duty in its inventory cost. This is because it may not be able to pass on all the duty, if the rates should be lowered in the annual Finance Act; there is no refund of duty in the purchase price of stock on hand, charged at higher rates.

From April 1973 the U.K., having entered the European Economic Community, has imposed a *value added tax* (VAT) on most goods and services. VAT is paid by all manufacturers and wholesalers, and most retailers and suppliers of personal services, currently at the rate of 8 per cent, with some items, such as food and books, at a zero rate, while many durable goods, and petrol, are charged at a 25 per cent. Each seller charges the tax to his immediate customers, on the price of the goods or services, but pays to the customs and excise department only the difference between tax charged to his customers, and tax charged by his suppliers (as evidenced by invoices showing VAT separately in all cases). Settlements are made every three months, but 'staggered' so that different firms begin the payments cycle in January, February, or March in each year.

A Value Added Tax Account must be opened, and debited with tax in suppliers' invoices, the full value of an invoice being credited to the supplier. Customers (or cash) are debited with the selling price of goods or services, inclusive of VAT, and the tax credited to VAT account. At the settlement date the firm pays over the credit balance on the account (debiting it). Thus each firm, from manufacturer to retailer, accounts for the tax on 'value added' by it — i.e. labour costs plus profit margin—and the whole burden falls upon the final consumer. If the rate of tax is reduced there will be no loss on stocks, as the firm holding them will pay only the difference between the lower-rated charge to the customer and the higher-rated charge by the supplier; while firms in zero-rated trades are able to reclaim all VAT on purchased inputs (the debit balance on the VAT account at the end of the settlement period). 'Exempt' firms (generally speaking, those with a turnover not exceeding £5,000 per annum) are unable to recover any VAT on inputs, and the tax must be charged under the appropriate heads of cost, no VAT Account being opened. If some activities are exempt, and others not, VAT on inputs must be apportioned between costs and the VAT Account. All traders must bear VAT on non-deductible inputs, such as motor cars (not for resale) and certain business entertaining expenses.

Statement of Standard Accounting Practice No. 5: *Accounting for value added tax* (1974) is effective for accounting periods beginning on or after 1 January 1974. Besides explaining the points made above, it emphasizes that no recoverable VAT should enter into a company's costs, nor payable VAT into its revenues, and that a year-end balance on the VAT Account should be included among debtors or creditors, as the case may be. In the published accounts, turnover should be shown net of VAT; or, if it is desired to show the gross amount, the tax should be deducted explicitly to give the net sum. Irrecoverable VAT allocated to fixed assets and to other items disclosed separately should be included in their cost where practicable and material.

Finally, *excise licences* on motor vehicles are simply treated in the accounts as costs of the period covered, a rateable proportion of the fee for each unexpired licence being carried forward at the year-end as a prepayment.

6.1.2 Provisions for other liabilities and losses

Most outstanding taxes, other than on profits, thus appear as current liabilities, rather than as provisions in the true sense. The latter more often represent known liabilities which are uncertain or problematical in amount, and/or deferred in time—such as the said taxes on profits. More generally, provisions are made in respect of net sums of money expected to become payable, in the shorter or longer run, wholly or partly as a result of decisions which have already been taken by management, or events which have already occurred, as at the balancing date. They are not made, or should not be made, in respect of expenses or losses calculated to arise entirely from hypothetical happenings in the future, for historical-cost accounting has no concern with these unless and until they in fact come about, and are seen to have an actual or potential effect on the fortunes of the entity.

For example, a contract may have been entered into, in civil engineering or shipbuilding, at a certain price, with or without escalation clauses to cover inflation of material prices and wage rates. By the year-end it is apparent that work is behind schedule, that unexpected technical difficulties have arisen, that there is no prospect of completion by the agreed date (meaning that heavy penalties will become payable), and/or that for other reasons the contract is likely to cause the firm serious loss, instead of the planned profit. In that case it is a normal practice to raise a provision for the maximum loss which can reasonably be foreseen as a result of the present situation and its probable consequences. A second situation which should normally give rise to a provision is the existence of guarantees or maintenance agreements in respect of durable goods sold before the year-end. If any of the buyers complain of faults or malfunctioning of the equipment within the guarantee or maintenance periods, the firm will have to incur expense in rectifying the trouble. In a third type of situation, the firm faces two alternatives: a considerable gain, or no loss, on the one hand, and a moderate, or heavy, loss on the other—as when litigation is pending, in which the firm is plaintiff or defendant, and the outcome is unforeseeable. In this case it is common to make no provision, but merely to report the situation in a note on the accounts, with some estimate of the maximum loss likely to be suffered if the firm loses the action—a 'contingent liability'.

Conventional practice shows little consistency in such matters. In the first situation (a *probable loss or expense* of uncertain amount, often deferred in time), a 'blanket' provision tends to be made in accordance with the convention of prudence—that, although profits may not be anticipated, expected losses must be taken into account as soon as they are reasonably foreseen. It is more rational, if future events are to be taken into consideration at all, to attempt an assessment, both of their probability and of their timing, and then to find the *present value of the expected outcome.* Given the expected timing of the net cash flows on an unprofitable contract, their 'expected' amounts may be computed by the use of Bayesian[1] probability coefficients—subjective estimates of various possible outcomes as decimals of 1, and totalling to 1, which represents certainty that one or other of the possibilities will materialize. The amount of each possible outcome is multiplied by its probability coefficient, the products are summed and divided by the sum of the coefficients (which, as that is 1, leaves the sum of products unchanged), and the answer is the average of all outcomes, weighted for probability—the 'expected outcome'. (This is not the same as the 'most probable outcome'—the one to which the highest probability coefficient is attached.) The expected outcomes of the various cash flows are then discounted for time, using the firm's *marginal cost of capital*—the rate at which it could expect to raise additional amounts of equity, or (as a surrogate) the rate of return expected, over time, by the proprietors. The result is the theoretically correct amount of the provision for the loss.

Example 1 On 1 January 19.1, a building contract is commenced for a price of £100,000, payable as to 90 per cent on work as certified, over an estimated two years to completion, and 10 per cent as retention moneys, six months after completion. At 31 December 19.1, £50,000 of work has been certified (there is none uncertified) and £45,000 received in progress payments, with £5,000 retention moneys accrued; total costs to date are £40,000. It is now estimated that, while the contract should be completed on time (on 31 December 19.2), technical difficulties are likely to arise, and on three different assumptions as to future progress the costs to completion are estimated at, respectively, £40,000, £70,000, and £100,000 (being in each case the mid-point of a range of possible costs). The Bayesian probability coefficients assigned by management to the three outcomes are respectively 0.2, 0.5, and 0.3. The marginal cost of capital to the firm is estimated at 10 per cent per annum.

On the principles laid down in section 5.3, the position shown by the books, as at 31 December 19.1, is as follows.

[1] From Thomas Bayes, an eighteenth-century mathematician.

Contract No. . . .

19.1		£	19.1		£
Jan 1 to Dec 31	Bank and creditors	40,000	Jan 1 to Dec 31	Customer	50,000
Dec 31	Profit/Loss on Contract No. . . .	10,000			
		£50,000			£50,000

Profit/Loss on Contract No. . . .

19.1		£	19.1		£
Dec 31	Profit and loss a/c	£10,000	Dec 31	Contract No. . . .	£10,000

Customer

19.1		£	19.1		£
Jan 1 to Dec 31	Contract No. . . .	50,000	Jan 1 to Dec 31 Dec 31	Bank Balance c/d	45,000 5,000
		£50,000			£50,000
19.2 Jan 1	Balance b/d	5,000			

Time Discount on Retention Moneys

			19.1		£
			Dec 31	Profit and loss a/c	666

The time discount on the retention moneys (with 18 months to go to expected date of receipt) is

$$D = £5,000\{1 - 1/(1.10)^{3/2}\}$$
$$= £5,000 - £5,000/1.1537$$
$$= £(5,000 - 4,334)$$
$$= £666$$

The provision for expected loss on the contract as at 31 December 19.1 is computed as the difference between the present value of the further amounts receivable, and that of the further amounts payable, in 19.2 and 19.3. The first amount is

$$R = £45,000/(1.10)^{1/2} + £5,000/(1.10)^{3/2}$$
$$= £(45,000/1.0488 + 5,000/1.1537)$$
$$= £(42,906 + 4,334)$$
$$= £47,240$$

The present value of the expected cost to completion is computed thus

Possible outcomes	Cost estimates £	Probability coefficients	Probability products £
Best	40,000	0.2	8,000
Most probable	70,000	0.5	35,000
Worst	100,000	0.3	30,000
Expected		1.0	£73,000

$$C = £73,000/(1.10)^{1/2}$$
$$= £73,000/1.0488$$
$$= £69,603$$

Hence, the present value of the expected loss is

$$L = £(69,603 - 47,240)$$
$$= £22,363$$

and this is the amount of the provision as at 31 December 19.1. It compares with the provision of £20,000 (70,000 − £50,000) which a less sophisticated management might have made on the basis of the most probable outcome, or the £50,000 (£100,000 − £50,000) which a 'conservative' management might have provided, in case the worst happened—in both cases, without time-discounting.

If the actual outcome were that the costs in 19.2 amounted to £68,000, and that the work was finished on schedule, the accounts would appear thus (with the provision for loss written back on completion):

Contract No. ...

19.2		£	19.2		£
Jan 1 to Dec 31	Bank and creditors	68,000	Jan 1 to Dec 31 Dec 31	Customer Profit/Loss on Contract No. ...	50,000 18,000
		£68,000			£68,000

Profit/Loss on Contract No. ...

19.2		£	19.2		£
Dec 31	Contract No. ...	£18,000	Dec 31	Provision for loss on Contract No. ...	£18,000

Customer

19.2		£	19.2		£
Jan 1 Jan 1 to Dec 31	Balance b/d Contract No. ...	5,000 50,000	Jan 1 to Dec 31 Dec 31	 Bank Balance c/d	 45,000 10,000
		£55,000			£55,000
19.3 Jan 1	Balance b/d	£10,000	19.3 Jun 30	Bank	£10,000

19.2		£	19.1		£
Dec 31	Profit and loss a/c	200	Dec 31	Profit and loss a/c	666
Dec 31	Balance c/d	466*			
		£666			£666
19.3			19.3		
Dec 31	Profit and loss a/c	£466	Jan 1	Balance b/d	£466

Provision for Loss on Contract No. ....

19.2		£	19.1		£
Dec 31	Profit/Loss on Contract No. ...	18,000	Dec 31	Profit and loss a/c	22,363
Dec 31	Profit and loss a/c	4,363			
		£22,363			£22,363

* £10,000 $\left\{1 - 1/(1.10)^{1/2}\right\}$

Calculation of profits over the three years, by the method described and by a simplistic comparison of costs with work certified, would be as follows.

	19.1 £	19.2 £	19.3 £
Work certified	50,000	50,000	—
Costs incurred	(40,000)	(68,000)	—
'Simple' profit/(loss)	10,000	(18,000)	—
Time discount on retention moneys	(666)	200	466
Provision for loss	(22,363)	22,363	—
'Present value' profit/(loss)	(£13,029)	£4,563	£466

The net loss over the whole commitment is £8,000 by either method, but the more scientific one throws into the first year the result (or rather more) of the mistake then made, of taking on an unprofitable contract. Had the costs in 19.2 been £73,000 as forecast, there would have been a loss of £437 in that year, because of the interest adjustments involved. As it is, the effect is masked by the over-provision—it is in practice impossible to foresee exactly what will happen.

The case of *guarantees or maintenance agreements* raises similar questions of future burdens upon the firm's finances, arising from actions taken in the past. The incidence of faults in goods under guarantees given on sale, or subject to maintenance agreements for which an annual fee is receivable, is random or stochastic, and Bayesian methods, applicable to a single set of chances, cannot be used. Instead of making subjective probability estimates it is necessary, either to analyse past records over many years and endeavour to see patterns of failures which can be extrapolated into the future as bases for cost estimates, such that reasonable approximations to reality can be derived from some formula in which the year's sales are a variable; or else to employ a computer, suitably programmed, to simulate (by so-called 'Monte Carlo' methods) a likely pattern of troubles, on the basis of data on the current and previous years' sales, and other factors. The techniques for these procedures cannot be described here, but should be studied in manuals of operational research. Without such devices the accountant is reduced to rule-of-thumb or blanket provisions for future liabilities in this field, such as a fixed percentage on each year's sales, varied occasionally in the light of experience.

With 'win or lose' situations, such as law-suits, it appears best to make some forecast, rather than merely note a contingent liability at the year-end. Whether the firm is plaintiff or defendant, a set of Bayesian estimates should be made, if only on the assumption that success and failure are equally probable. Since a plaintiff has more to gain from victory than to lose from defeat if his damages exceed the costs of both parties, the firm will more often than not make no provision when it is in this position; the case is opposite for a defendant, and a provision will generally be made.

One other common type of contingent liability is in respect of bills receivable, discounted before the year-end but not yet presented for payment by the holders. Should the acceptor dishonour a bill at maturity the firm may become liable to the holder, as a drawer or indorser. In most cases it is sufficient merely to note in the final accounts that such a situation exists, and to state the total amount of the bills involved. A provision need be made only if there is reason to suspect that particular bills are likely to be dishonoured (e.g. because the acceptor is bankrupt). Such a provision must appear on the liabilities side of the balance sheet; it cannot be deducted from the value of the bills, as they no longer appear in the books as assets.

6.2 Long-term investments

The position regarding short-term or temporary investments was discussed in Chapter 5, section 5.2. A firm (particularly a limited company) may also hold quoted or unquoted securities as a long-term investment to secure an income, or to exercise control over another undertaking, or both.

Such investments are regarded as of the nature of fixed assets, and appear as such in the balance sheet, though under a separate heading, after the physical fixed assets. The usual rule in historical-cost accounting is to retain long-term investments on the books at cost, regardless of fluctuations in the market value, if any—though with quoted investments the market value at the year-end should be noted on the balance sheet. Provision is made only for a heavy and permanent fall in market value, whether determined by the stock exchange price or by subjective valuation of unquoted shares—e.g. because of the loss of a large part of the other company's business, or its actual failure. Writing up, on account of increased profitability of the other company, is discouraged (but see Chapter 16, section 16.7, with regard to holdings of 20 per cent or more of the other's equity).

In financial institutions such as investment trusts and unit trusts, however, where the realization of capital gains on the holding of investments is a normal expectation of management and investors, it is accepted practice to revalue the portfolio on the basis of market prices as at the balance sheet date. Write-ups are credited, and write-downs debited, to a Reserve for Unrealized Capital Gains less Losses, which appears as part of the equity. From the reserve a transfer of the potential liability for capital gains tax (currently 30 per cent) should be made to the credit of the Deferred Taxation Account—a provision, whose operation is described in Chapter 12, sub-section 12.3.2.[2]

[2] See further: The Institute of Chartered Accountants in England and Wales, *Recommendation N28. The Accounts of Investment Trust Companies* (1968).

Dividends and interest from all investments, long-term or short-term, are normally passed through the profit and loss account for the year in which they are received. Complications arise on the purchase, or sale, of securities *cum div.* or *ex div.* With fixed-interest stocks the *cum div.* price, paid or received, is deemed to include accrued interest to the date of purchase or sale; the amount of the accrual (taken as less income tax) should theoretically be transferred to the debit, or credit, of Investment Income, but in practice this is not done, because of complications with income tax. With Treasury bills, accrued interest should be included in the year-end valuation and credited to investment income, so that on redemption only the interest accrued after the year-end is included in next year's profits. Such adjustments are not usual with equity securities (e.g. ordinary shares); the dividends are simply taken as income for the accounting periods in which they are actually received. Interest, both received and paid, under deduction of income tax should be written up to its gross amount, and the tax debited, or credited, to the Income Tax Account, as is described more fully in Chapters 9 and 12.

For the special position of companies holding shares in subsidiary or associated companies, reference should be made to Chapters 15 and 16.

6.3 Tangible fixed assets

Major problems, in valuation and in profit determination, arise from the existence of *tangible fixed assets*, such as land and buildings, plant, vehicles, etc., which are retained for several accounting periods, give services to the business during them, and are disposed of eventually—usually at lower prices than were paid initially.

Expenditure on acquisition of such assets is regarded as *capital* expenditure, to be carried forward to future periods, while expenditure on their repair, maintenance, rearrangement, or demolition is treated as *revenue* expenditure, to be charged to profit and loss account in the period when it is incurred. The distinction is usually clear, but a few borderline cases need to be noted. The cost of freehold or leasehold land is generally held to include the legal costs of acquisition (though some firms write them off immediately to revenue); effect must be given to the apportionments of prepaid or outstanding rates, gas, electricity, water, or kindred charges, and the revenue accounts adjusted accordingly. The cost of plant includes the charges for delivering and installing it, but not for removing old plant, to another place or altogether. An invoice for a motor vehicle requires capitalization only of the basic price, VAT, cost of registration plates and other fitments, and delivery charges, with other items charged to revenue. Additions and alterations are treated on their merits, by capitalizing the (significant) cost of adding anything which was not previously there, and writing off, as disposed of, the current book value assigned to anything of a different nature which is removed or destroyed (such as a wall which is demolished in extending a factory).

In the case of freehold property the land content has an indefinite economic life while the building content has a finite one, and for accounting purposes the costs of the two need to be distinguished. This is easy when the firm erects the buildings on a vacant site, but if it purchases derelict property and demolishes it to make way for the new buildings, it should capitalize the demolition costs as part of the cost of the site, since it may be argued that the same site, unencumbered, would have cost about that much more to buy. Costs of levelling or otherwise preparing the site, before commencing to build, should likewise be capitalized as site cost, if it is considered that they add value to the site, irrespective of what may be erected on it now or in the future. (Where buildings with an economic value are purchased and demolished, part of the total cost will have to be written off, as well as the expenses of demolition, since they cannot be said to add value to the site.) When freehold land and buildings are purchased for use substantially as they stand, the price has to be apportioned between land and buildings—most rationally, by treating the fire insurance replacement value of the buildings, less estimated depreciation for age, as their cost, and regarding the residual price as that of the land. If the buildings are in a dilapidated state when acquired, the cost of reconditioning them, or such part of it as represents the difference between their estimated market value when reconditioned and their acquisition cost, should be capitalized.

The finding of the historical cost of fixed assets is not usually very controversial; neither is the finding of the proceeds on disposal at the end of their economic lives, so far as the entity is concerned. All that is normally involved is a sum of money receivable, sometimes net of disposal costs, and of apportionments of revenue items in the case of land. Sometimes an asset is worth nothing, or its 'junk' value is less than the cost of demolition or removal, which has to be charged to revenue.

Over the time during which an entity holds it, then, a fixed asset's book value falls from historical cost of acquisition to proceeds of disposal, if any. The difference is its *depreciation,* which under historical-cost accounting must be absorbed into the entity's costs over the holding period, and assigned in some equitable manner to all the accounting periods affected. It is in relation to annual charges for depreciation that controversy rages most fiercely, and that so many conflicting solutions have been proposed.

6.3.1 Amortization, depreciation, obsolescence, and optimum life

Before considering the accounting problems involved, it is well to clarify the meanings of certain terms. *Amortization* is the generic name for all accounting processes by which a fixed asset's book value is progressively reduced from its entry value (normally historical cost) to its exit value (scrap or resale price), and the difference charged to profit and loss account (or some division thereof) over the intervening accounting periods. Where the asset consists of a contractual right to possess and use a physical property for a determinate number of years, as in the case of a lease of land, the term 'amortization' is most properly applied, without further analysis.

Where, however, a tangible asset is purchased with an indeterminate working life, the length of which is limited at least in part by physical deterioration, loss of efficiency, and/or rising maintenance costs, due to ageing, wear and tear, exposure to the elements, or damage commonly sustained during use, it is more usual to describe the effect of such factors, and the accounting measure of it, as *depreciation* proper. This may occur predominantly through: *use,* as where a motor vehicle becomes unreliable after running for so many tens of thousands of miles; *depletion,* as through the extraction of ore from a mine, which hastens the day when the deposit will be worked out; or *time,* where there is no physical depletion, and the asset deteriorates from causes independent of reasonable usage, such as crumbling, warping, or rusting of the fabric.

Apart from physical deterioration, an asset may decline in market value through causes external to itself, collectively known as *obsolescence.* There may be *technical* obsolescence, through the invention of an improved model, or a quite different machine able to render the existing asset's services at lower cost per unit; or *economic* obsolescence, through a fall in market demand for the products or services of the asset, as when a railway line becomes unprofitable through diversion of traffic to a parallel road, or the closing down of a mine whose output it was built to carry away. The first situation tends to accelerate replacement of the asset or, to the extent that obsolescence is reasonably foreseeable on account of the march of technology in the industry, to shorten the planned life, so that the amortization provision in the accounts is compounded of elements of depreciation and obsolescence—as in the case of aircraft. The second type of obsolescence is generally unforeseeable when the asset is acquired, and its effect is to inhibit replacement altogether, or in extreme cases to close down the business. In the accounts it is necessary to superimpose an additional provision on that already made for depreciation.

From the foregoing it is apparent that it is the exception, not the rule, for a physical asset to be retained until it is no longer serviceable. Apart from obsolescence, there is usually a trade-off between spreading the initial cost over more years of active life (or postponing payment for a replacement), and incurring rising charges for maintenance in later years, as well as reducing resale value, the longer disposal is postponed. Regard must also be had to the time value of money. The rate of interest to be used is normally the cost of capital, except in a 'capital rationing' situation (inability to raise fresh funds from outside the entity), when moneys must be diverted from other uses. The existing return achieved on such funds within the business (their 'opportunity cost') is then the measure of the sacrifice to be made, and determines the discounting rate instead of the cost of capital (which it normally exceeds). It is by taking these factors into account that management determines the *optimum life* of an asset—the number of years for which it should be retained, if the average cost of using it is to be at a minimum.

The method of computation consists firstly of forecasting the cash flows arising from holding the asset for several different numbers of years, from one upwards, to the extent that they vary from one year to another. The flows are the initial cost (at the end of Year 0), maintenance costs in excess of the basic minimum (as a rule, the first year's charge), and resale proceeds—together with any falls in the sale value of the products in later years. These flows are all discounted to Year 0 at the cost of capital (or higher opportunity cost of internal funds, if applicable), and the net present values (NPV) found by summation. The NPVs are then each converted into an annual rate, by dividing the NPV by the present value of an annuity of 1 for the required number of years at the proper rate of interest. The lowest annual rate so found indicates the optimum number of years for which the asset should be held before replacement, on the assumption that the new asset will exhibit the same pattern of cash flows as the old one. If that is expected to be different the calculation becomes more complex, and reference should be made to specialized works on management accounting.[3]

Example 2 A machine is to be purchased for £10,000, and will work efficiently for five years, before the value of its annual products begins to fall off. Its maintenance costs are £2,000 in the first year, but rise by £300 in each of the next three years, and £500 in the fifth. The second-hand values of the machine, at the ends of Years 1 to 5, are respectively £7,000, £5,000, £4,000, £2,400, and £800.

[3] See: Baxter, W. T., *Depreciation*, Sweet & Maxwell, 1971—from which many of the arguments in this section are derived. All students are strongly recommended to read it.

The cost of capital to the firm is 10 per cent per annum. The optimum life (where average cost per annum is at a minimum) is to be calculated to the nearest year.

The cash flows if the machine is held for 1, 2, ... 5 years are as follows:

Years of Life	1	2	3	4	5
	£	£	£	£	£
Purchase at 0	10,000	10,000	10,000	10,000	10,000
Maintenance (excess over £2,000)					
Year 2		300	300	300	300
Year 3			600	600	600
Year 4				900	900
Year 5					1,400
	10,000	10,300	10,900	11,800	13,200
Resale value	−7,000	−5,000	−4,000	−2,400	−800
Total net outlay	£3,000	£5,300	£6,900	£9,400	£12,400
Annual average	£3,000	£2,650	£2,300	£2,350	£2,480

On this simplistic calculation, which ignores the time value of money, replacement every three years would appear to give the lowest average cost per annum (£2,300). If, now, all the components of total net outlay are discounted back to 0 at 10 per cent per annum (assuming for simplicity that all moneys are paid or received at the year-end), and the discounted net outlays converted to annual equivalents by dividing them by the present values of 1 per annum for 1, 2, ... 5 years (0.9091, 1.7355, 2.4869, 3.1699, 3.7908), the results are (to the nearest £)

Years of Life	1	2	3	4	5
	£	£	£	£	£
Purchase at 0	10,000	10,000	10,000	10,000	10,000
Maintenance (excess over £2,000)					
Year 2		248	248	248	248
Year 3			451	451	451
Year 4				615	615
Year 5					869
	10,000	10,248	10,699	11,314	12,183
Resale value	−6,364	−4,132	−3,005	−1,639	− 497
Total net outlay	£3,636	£6,116	£7,694	£9,675	£11,686
Annual equivalent	£4,000	£3,524	£3,094	£3,052	£3,083

This time, replacement every four years gives the lowest annual 'rental' (£3,052), and this is the correct decision on the assumptions as stated—i.e. the optimum life is four years.

Had there been a fall in the sale value of annual production after Year 3, the amount of the drop (below the level of Years 1 to 3) would have been added cumulatively in Years 4 and 5, and duly discounted. This would have worsened the annual equivalents in those years, and might have made them both higher than in Year 3, which would then have been the optimum time for replacement.

6.3.2 Depreciation in annual accounts: simpler methods

Given a fixed asset's historical cost, optimum life, and resale value at the end thereof, conventional accounting is concerned to allocate the difference between the two amounts to revenue over the chosen number of years, on some plausible assumption as to the services rendered by the asset to the business, and in a manner which makes for consistent, and fairly easy, calculations from year to year. The book values resulting at intermediate year-ends are mere by-products of this process—unallocated historical costs, nothing more; they are not, and do not pretend to be, approximations to either replacement cost or realizable value, nor yet attempts to estimate 'value in use'. Some describe them as 'fair value to a going concern', but to most theorists this phrase has no meaning beyond itself—it is a term of art invented purely to denote the result of what accountants choose to do in this respect.

Further, accountants in modern times no longer regard depreciation as primarily a means of providing for the replacement of fixed assets—the usual view in the nineteenth century. Given a stable price level, or at any rate no change in the prices of the replacement assets, the charging of depreciation on historical cost (by whatever formula) over the whole life of the assets causes the reported net profits to fall short, by the amount of the depreciation, of the total flow of funds from current trading. If the reported profits are all withdrawn or distributed and no fresh capital is raised, then the net current assets of the entity will increase by the amount of the total depreciation charge, and the increased amount (to the extent that it represents, or can be turned easily into, cash), together with the sale proceeds of the old assets, is then just sufficient to purchase new fixed assets at the old prices. In reality this theoretical equilibrium is seldom or never achieved, owing to retention of reported profits, changes in the general price level and in the particular price levels of the fixed assets, and the fact that in an age of technological progress it is the exception rather than the rule for one asset to be replaced by an identically-similar one. Hence, the conservation of the 'physical' capital of the entity is no longer postulated, even as an ideal, by most accountants today. Emphasis has shifted, in a period of inflation and rapid changes in technology, to conservation of the 'real' capital in terms of purchasing power—a subject to be considered more fully in Chapter 7; and to this problem historical-cost accounting, with its accent on conserving 'money' capital only, is impotent to contribute a full solution.

The common methods of computing depreciation are rule-of-thumb cost allocations, ignoring the time value of money, and often paying scant regard to the way in which replacement prices, and resale values, decline as assets age. The main aim is to write down the asset to its estimated resale or scrap value over its economic life (whether scientifically estimated, or merely guessed at on the basis of experience and/or the advice of engineers or other technical experts). Any difference between the written-down amount (it is hardly a 'value') at disposal and the proceeds thereof is adjusted into the profit and loss account, as depreciation under- or over-provided to date. In some countries (notably in the U.S.A. since 1954) the choice of depreciation method is influenced by the tax laws. The charge in the accounts is accepted for the purposes of tax computation, provided that the method used is a recognized one, consistently applied, whose effect is to write off in total the difference between historical cost and resale proceeds. There is then an incentive to adopt a formula which writes off as much as the revenue authorities will allow in the early years of an asset's life, and so postpones tax thereon for as long as possible—a gain to the business, because of the very time value of money which is ignored in depreciation accounting! In the U.K., accounting depreciation and tax allowances on fixed assets are divorced, as explained more fully in Chapter 12, sub-section 12.3.2. The tax allowances are in most cases strongly biased towards giving large reliefs in the early years, and from 1972 most industrial plant (except motor cars) may be entirely written off in the first year ('free depreciation').

1 *The equal instalment, or straight line, method*
This is probably the most common method in the U.K., because of its simplicity. Historical cost, less scrap value as estimated, is written off in equal instalments over the estimated life of the asset, the required percentage of cost being

$$D = 100(C-S)/CN$$

where D = annual depreciation as a percentage on cost;

C = historical cost;

S = scrap or resale value at disposal; and

N = number of years of economic life.

Thus, if a machine costs £1,000, and is expected to be sold for £100 after five years, its straight-line depreciation in each those years is

$$D = 100(1,000-100)/(1,000 \times 5)$$
$$= 18 \text{ per cent, or } £180.$$

The underlying assumption is that the asset's efficiency remains constant throughout its life, and that it renders an approximately equal number of units of service in each year; or alternatively, that its economic life is unaffected by the intensity with which its service potential is exploited (within reason), so that its depreciation is a function of time, not use. This makes for easier cost calculations in respect of overheads, since there is no variation through the use on a job of older or newer plant. In the financial accounts there is a constant charge for depreciation from year to year, and (*ceteris paribus*) a constant operating profit; but the accumulation of funds representing the depreciation provision, and the additional profits normally earned from their utilization in the business, will tend to increase the net profit while the total capital employed remains static, and thus inflate the rate of return, which will appear to increase annually—until the accumulated funds are used to replace the asset, when the profit, and the rate of return, will drop abruptly to their original level. This lack of stability is a consequence of ignoring the interest element in the depreciation computation. In practice there is generally an offsetting factor, in that repair and maintenance charges tend to rise as an asset grows older, and thus cut into the additional profits obtained from use in the meantime of the 'depreciation' funds; but there can be no expectation that the two irregularities will wholly neutralize each other.

2 *The reducing balance, or reducing instalment, method*
This, too, is widely used in the U.K., but is more popular in the U.S.A., because of the tax advantages noted above. Historical cost is written down in the first year by a certain percentage; in the second year the same percentage is applied to the

written-down amount, and so on. Given the three factors C, S, and N, noted above, the correct depreciation percentage D is computed as

$$D = 100\{1 - (S/C)^{1/N}\}$$

or in logarithmic form, to avoid the inconvenience of using roots higher than the square, and with $d = D/100$

$$N \log (1-d) = \log S - \log C$$

For the example in 1 the calculation is

$$5 \log (1-d) = \log 100 - \log 1,000$$

which works out as $d = 0.3690$, or $D = 36.90$ per cent. The successive annual charges (to the nearest £) are

Year	1	2	3	4	5
	£	£	£	£	£
Opening balance	1,000	631	398	251	158
Depreciation (36.90 per cent)	−369	−233	−147	−93	−58
Closing balance	£631	£398	£251	£158	100
Scrap value					−100

If S is small relative to C, and N is also small, the last term of the original formula may become very small, so that D works out as a percentage much higher than under the straight line method. If S is zero, the last term vanishes and $D = 100$ per cent—thus defeating the object of a depreciation formula. Because of this, and for easier calculation, many American accountants substitute

3 The double-rate declining balance method
This proceeds as 2, but uses twice the percentage rate which would be appropriate for the straight line method. In the example it would be 36 per cent, which as it happens is very close to the true reducing balance rate. In most cases the 'double' rate would be inadequate to write the asset down to scrap value at the end of its life, and in an extreme case would be quite wide of the mark. If an asset costing £1,000 were to be written off in five years with zero scrap value, a 20 per cent straight line rate would do it exactly, but a 40 per cent declining rate would leave a residue of about £78 to be disposed of by a terminal adjustment. Another form of accelerated depreciation is

4 The sum of the years' digits method
This is, again, popular in America, but seldom met with here. The integers from 1 to the number of years of life (N) are added together to form the denominator of a fraction whose numerator, in the first year, is N, in the second ($N - 1$), and so on; and this is multiplied, year by year, by ($C - S$). Thus, in the basic example, $1 + 2 + 3 + 4 + 5 = 15$; depreciation in Year 1 is £(1,000 − 100) × 5/15 = £300; in Year 2, £900 × 4/15 = £240; etc., down to £60 in Year 5, leaving £100 precisely (since the sum of the numerators is the same as the denominator). The method gives higher intermediate year-end amounts than either 2 or 3, though lower than 1, but it is commended by its precision and ease of working.

An argument often used in favour of all three 'accelerated' methods is, that by showing declining amounts of depreciation the firm offsets rising charges for maintenance, thus levelling out total costs of using the asset from year to year. There is something in this, though exact compensation is unlikely; but the effect is counter-balanced by increased retentions of funds in early years, so that earnings on these 'secondary' assets, no longer offset by rising total costs as under the straight line method, inflate profits and progressively increase the rate of return on an unchanged capital employed—until the asset needs replacement.

Apart from this, the main defence of accelerated methods rests upon their supposed ability to mirror the decline in market values of certain assets, such as motor vehicles, which are observed to lose resale, and replacement, value rapidly in early years, and more slowly later on. It is very doubtful, however, whether this phenomenon applies to the generality of durable assets, and there are some reasons for believing that it does not. Even where the analysis is valid, neglect of the interest factor is bound to give faulty and misleading results.

A few firms take maintenance directly into account, and seek to smooth out fluctuations both in it and in depreciation charges by means of

5 The composite provision for depreciation and maintenance method

Total maintenance costs are estimated for the whole life of an asset, and added to its capital cost (less scrap value) to produce a composite figure, which is then averaged over the asset's life, usually though not necessarily by the straight line method. The stated amount is provided annually, and repairs, etc., as incurred are debited to the provision, instead of to profit and loss account. The remaining credit balance on the provision account is treated as depreciation to date and set off against the historical cost. Hence, the book amount tends to fall more rapidly in periods of low expenditure on maintenance, and more slowly when much is being spent under this head; it is unlikely to rise, but if it does the annual provision may be increased. Thus, if as before $C = £1,000$, $S = £100$, and $N = 5$, but there are estimated maintenance costs in the five years as shown below, totalling £300, then a total of £$(1,000 - 100 + 300) = £1,200$ will be provided, at £240 per annum. The results, if the forecasts turn out exactly right, will be

Year	1	2	3	4	5
	£	£	£	£	£
Opening balance	1,000	770	570	400	240
Maintenance cost	10	40	70	80	100
	1,010	810	640	480	340
Composite provision	−240	−240	−240	−240	−240
Closing balance	£770	£570	£400	£240	100
Scrap value					−100

The economic lives of some assets are determined by use, or physical depletion, rather than by time. Many firms, for instance, change the representatives' cars when they have run, say, 25,000 miles or so and are beginning to look shabby—even though average running costs might be lower if the cars were kept longer. The capital cost of a mine, quarry or oil-field is most logically written off on the basis of a period's production, as a fraction of the geologist's estimate of reserves as at the date of purchase; while freehold land, though normally not depreciated (as being theoretically everlasting) may, if used as a cemetery, be reasonably written off in proportion as it is filled up with graves. These are examples of—

6 *The unit of service method*
The number of service-units (as appropriate) which an asset is estimated to be capable of rendering is divided into the historical cost, to find an average depreciation cost per unit. This is applied to the actual production or services of each year, so that annual depreciation varies with intensity of exploitation. Sometimes a 'tapered' rate is applied, as in mining, where a high unit charge is made per ton of ore from the levels nearest the surface, and progressively lower ones for ore from deeper levels, where direct costs of winning it rise continuously. Such a procedure, as with accelerated time depreciation, helps to stabilize the total unit cost of production of all output.

It may be remarked in passing that some mining and kindred enterprises, and firms operated to exploit a foreign concession for a limited term, have a policy of not charging depreciation on the principal asset, constituting the 'substratum' of the business. It is not to be replaced when it is of no more value, but the firm will then be wound up. In the meantime (the reasoning runs) it is pointless to restrict proprietors' dividends by charging depreciation, merely to keep their money capital intact to give back to them at the end; they might just as well—indeed, better—withdraw it piecemeal in the form of higher distributions, as long as they are aware of the position, and do not expect to receive much on liquidation. This practice has legal sanctions (see Chapter 12, sub-section **12.2.3**), and the overt writing-down of the main asset out of profits, however desirable as a matter of accounting principle, might well inhibit rational distribution of surplus cash, or compel a company to make formal repayments of share capital, requiring the permission of the High Court.

Lastly, there are certain long-lived assets of substantial construction, which are thought to be virtually 'immortal' as long as they are regularly maintained; or rather, their physical lives are often much longer than their economic lives. Such are railway lines, bridges, tunnels, earthworks, dock basins, and blast-furnaces (whose brick linings need periodic renewal as they burn out). These, too, are not normally depreciated, but all expenditure on maintenance and renewals of parts is charged to revenue, or to a maintenance equalization provision, credited with constant annual transfers from profit and loss account. Write-offs of construction cost take place only on demolition or abandonment, or in anticipation thereof, by way of obsolescence provisions. Such a policy used to be common with industrial and commercial buildings in general, but today these are normally depreciated; the land, if freehold, should not be written down, but less conscientious accountants sometimes depreciate the entire property without distinction, albeit at a lower rate than is usual for the buildings only.

6.3.3 Depreciation in annual accounts: allowing for the time value of money

Traditional modes of allowing for depreciation tend to treat a fixed asset as though it were a bundle of services, all available at once if desired, and all of equal present value. They ignore the fact that the said services are inevitably spread out in time, usually over several years, and that the later ones cannot as of the date of payment in advance (on acquisition of the asset) have the same value as those available immediately, unless the cost of capital is assumed to be zero. Further, as the charging of depreciation, on any basis, causes net current assets to be accumulated until they are used to purchase other fixed assets, these secondary assets must be expected to earn a rate of return at least equal to the cost of capital; otherwise it would pay the firm to utilize them in redeeming capital or distribute them to proprietors, and then raise fresh capital to replace the fixed assets when their time comes.

It follows that for each of the simplistic methods of charging depreciation, explained in sub-section 6.3.2, there is at least one further one which allows for interest. In practice this additional sophistication is usually applied only to the straight line method, and discussion here will be confined to that; but in principle interest may be allowed for in adaptations of the accelerated methods also, and those in which the charge varies irregularly.

The most straightforward treatment, though little used in the U.K., is what may be called

7 The rising charges method[4]

The first step here is to find the annual sum which, accumulated at a compound rate of interest equal to the cost of capital, will amount over the asset's life to its cost less scrap value. This is done by dividing cost, etc., by the amount of an annuity of 1, accumulating at the required rate for the required number of years. This gives the first year's quota of depreciation. The second year's quota is the first year's plus one year's interest thereon at the agreed rate; the third year's is the basic amount plus one year's interest on the accumulated depreciation of the first two years (or rather, on the secondary assets deemed to represent it); and so on, the depreciation charges becoming larger each year.

Reverting to the basic example, with $C = £1,000$, $S = £100$, and $N = 5$, and setting the cost of capital, $R = 15$ per cent per annum; the amount to which an annuity of 1 accumulates in five years at 15 per cent interest is 6.74238, and $£(1,000 - 100)/6.74238 = £133.48$. This is the first year's depreciation, and the computation proceeds thus

Year	Basic quota £	Interest (15 per cent p.a.) £	Total for year £	Cumulative £	Closing balance £
1	133.48	–	133.48	133.48	866.52
2	133.48	20.02	153.50	286.98	713.02
3	133.48	43.05	176.53	463.51	536.49
4	133.48	69.53	203.01	666.52	333.48
5	133.48	99.98 ⎫	233.46 ⎫	899.98 ⎫	100.00
Adjust-ment (rounding error)	–	0.02 ⎭	0.02 ⎭	0.02 ⎭	
				900.00	
Scrap value				100.00	0.00
				£1,000.00	

The figures in the third column are those of annual depreciation, and the **cumulative figures in the fourth column** are deducted at each year-end from £1,000 to arrive at the balance sheet amount. In the final accounts the full depreciation

[4] See: Baxter, W. T., *op. cit.*

charge is shown (e.g. in the manufacturing account, if any), and the earnings on the secondary assets are credited separately in the body of the profit and loss account. The reported net profit will then (*ceteris paribus*) be level for all five years, and a level rate of return will be shown on a constant capital employed.

It is more common in this country, insofar as interest is considered at all, to use

8 *The annuity method*

This is sometimes applied to the amortization of leasehold properties, to write off the premium over the term of the lease, leaving no residue. The length of the term involved is perhaps thought to make interest a significant factor and to justify the more complex arithmetic, as compared with the obvious alternative, the straight line method. In fact, the annuity method (like the rising charges method) is perfectly general in its application to any asset which can fairly be deemed to render services of equal value in each year of life.

The difference between 7 and 8 lies in equalization of the annual charges by the annuity method. The cost of the asset, less the present value of its expected scrap value, is divided by the *present value* of an annuity of 1 under the conditions specified, and the result is the annual charge for depreciation. Interest at the specified rate is computed annually on the opening balance of the asset; it is debited to the depreciation provision and credited to profit and loss account. The depreciation charge is much heavier than under the rising charges method, but there is a correspondingly larger credit of interest, falling from year to year as the income from the secondary assets rises.

Repeating the figures for 7, one divides £$\{1,000 - 100/(1.15)^5\}$ by the present value of an annuity of 1 for five years at 15 per cent per annum—i.e. £950.2823/3.35216 = £283.48. The answer is the depreciation charge, and the computation proceeds

Year	1	2	3	4	5
	£	£	£	£	£
Opening balance	1,000.00	866.52	713.02	536.49	333.48
Interest (15 per cent p.a.)	150.00	129.98	106.95	80.47	50.00*
	1,150.00	996.50	819.97	616.96	383.48
Depreciation	−283.48	−283.48	−283.48	−283.48	−283.48
Closing balance	£866.52	£713.02	£536.49	£333.48	100.00
Proceeds on disposal					100.00

* Adjusted by £0.02, for rounding errors.

It will be noted that the closing balances are identical with those under 7, and that, as will be demonstrated presently, the total reported profits are also the same in all years.

Another variant is

9 *The depreciation fund method*

This is a version of 7, in which the basic quota (in the illustration, £133.48 per annum) is shown as the depreciation charge, and the accruing interest debited separately in the profit and loss account, as an appropriation to the 'depreciation fund' of income deemed to arise on the secondary assets. Both amounts are credited annually to an account for the said 'fund', whose balance may be either deducted from the historical cost of the fixed asset on the balance sheet, or segregated as a provision on the opposite side, as being notionally represented by the (undifferentiated) secondary assets. This method is, on the whole, the most informative one of its genre.

10 *The sinking fund method*
Here method **9** is formalized by segregating in the balance sheet both the fund and the secondary assets which represent it—the latter being shown as an intermediate class of asset, between fixed and current, under a separate heading. Only the basic quota appears in the final accounts, as a sinking fund instalment; income, as it is received on the secondary assets, is credited directly to the fund, and the actual moneys segregated in the countervailing class of assets. In practice, the secondary assets—the moneys earmarked for the fund by the above process—are invested in gilt-edged or other stock exchange securities, whose book cost is at all times equal to the credit balance on the sinking fund. The rate of return on such investments is, as a rule, markedly below the firm's cost of capital, and the annual instalments must be correspondingly larger.

When the fixed asset needs replacing, the fund investments are sold; any profit or loss as compared with cost is written off to profit and loss account, and a new asset is bought. The credit balance of the fund is transferred to the credit of the account for the old asset, as are the proceeds of sale, and any difference is written off. The term 'sinking fund', originally applied to a similar device for redemption of loan stocks by the central government, indicates the intention of 'sinking' the debt, or the burden of replacing the asset, by means of cash set aside in advance to avoid any strain upon liquidity when the time comes. In view, though, of the low rate of return on sinking fund investments as compared with secondary assets employed in the business, the advantages of having liquidity when needed seem dearly bought, and the method is not widely used in practice.

11 *The endowment policy method*
This is another device to ensure liquid funds for fixed asset replacement. The sinking fund is renamed 'endowment policy fund', and the place of the investments is taken by an endowment policy, issued by an insurance company upon the asset to be replaced, in the amount of its estimated replacement price. The premiums as paid are debited to an account for the policy, while equal sums are debited to profit and loss account in lieu of depreciation, and credited to the policy fund. At the year-end, either there is an equal write-up of both fund and policy by the amount of interest allowed by the insurance company in its calculations, or (more conservatively) an adjustment of both balances to the amount of the surrender value as notified by the insurers—downwards in earlier years, upwards in later. When the policy matures the agreed sum is received from the insurers and used to replace the fixed asset, and the credit balance of the fund is written off against the cost of the old asset.

The endowment policy method has the advantage over the sinking fund of protecting the firm against loss on realization, as well as against loss or destruction of the asset, but, since the insurance company's allowance for interest is less generous than with gilt-edged securities, the premiums are higher than the sinking fund instalments. As a result, no great use is made of this device.

6.3.4 Comparison of different depreciation methods

To sum up the foregoing discussion, the effects of different modes of providing for depreciation, on the accounts of six firms in which all else is held constant, are exhibited in simplified form.

Example 3 The data relative to the single fixed asset of an imaginary firm are those specified in sub-sections **6.3.2** and **6.3.3**; other figures are assumed as necessary, and changes in them should be fairly obvious from what has been said in those sub-sections. The opening balance sheet, as at the end of Year 0, shows Capital, £1,500, represented by Fixed Asset (cost), £1,000, and Current Assets (initial), £500.

Straight Line Method

Year	1	2	3	4	5
	£	£	£	£	£
Profit and Loss Account					
Operating cash flow	433.48	433.48	433.48	433.48	433.48
Depreciation	(180.00)	(180.00)	(180.00)	(180.00)	(180.00)
Operating profit	253.48	253.48	253.48	253.48	253.48
Income from secondary assets (15 per cent)	0.00	27.00	54.00	81.00	108.00
Net profit (all withdrawn)	£ 253.48	£ 280.48	£ 307.48	£ 334.48	£ 361.48
Balance Sheet (ending)					
Capital	£1,500.00	£1,500.00	£1,500.00	£1,500.00	£1,500.00
Fixed asset—					
Cost	1,000.00	1,000.00	1,000.00	1,000.00	1,000.00
Depreciation	(180.00)	(360.00)	(540.00)	(720.00)	(900.00)
	820.00	640.00	460.00	280.00	100.00
Current assets—					
Original	500.00	500.00	500.00	500.00	500.00
Secondary	180.00	360.00	540.00	720.00	900.00
	£1,500.00	£1,500.00	£1,500.00	£1,500.00	£1,500.00
	Per cent p.a.	Per cent p.a.	Per cent p.a.	Per cent p.a.	Per cent p.a.
Rate of Return on Opening Capital	16.9	18.7	20.5	22.3	24.1

Reducing Balance Method

Year	1	2	3	4	5
	£	£	£	£	£
Profit and Loss Account					
Operating cash flow	433.48	433.48	433.48	433.48	433.48
Depreciation	(369.00)	(233.00)	(147.00)	(93.00)	(58.00)
Operating profit	64.48	200.48	286.48	340.48	375.48
Income from secondary assets (15 per cent)	0.00	55.35	90.30	112.35	126.30
Net profit (all withdrawn)	£64.48	£255.83	£376.78	£452.83	£501.78
Balance Sheet (ending)					
Capital	£1,500.00	£1,500.00	£1,500.00	£1,500.00	£1,500.00
Fixed Asset					
Cost	1,000.00	1,000.00	1,000.00	1,000.00	1,000.00
Depreciation	(369.00)	(602.00)	(749.00)	(842.00)	(900.00)
	631.00	398.00	251.00	158.00	100.00
Current Assets					
Original	500.00	500.00	500.00	500.00	500.00
Secondary	369.00	602.00	749.00	842.00	900.00
	£1,500.00	£1,500.00	£1,500.00	£1,500.00	£1,500.00
	Per cent p.a.	Per cent p.a.	Per cent p.a.	Per cent p.a.	Per cent p.a.
Rate of Return on Opening Capital	4.3	17.1	25.1	30.2	33.5

Sum of Years' Digits Method

Year	1	2	3	4	5
	£	£	£	£	£
Profit and Loss Account					
Operating cash flow	433.48	433.48	433.48	433.48	433.48
Depreciation	(300.00)	(240.00)	(180.00)	(120.00)	(60.00)
Operating profit	133.48	193.48	253.48	313.48	373.48
Income from secondary assets (15 per cent)	0.00	45.00	81.00	108.00	126.00
Net profit (all withdrawn)	£133.48	£238.48	£334.48	£421.48	£499.48
Balance Sheet (ending)					
Capital	£1,500.00	£1,500.00	£1,500.00	£1,500.00	£1,500.00
Fixed Asset					
Cost	1,000.00	1,000.00	1,000.00	1,000.00	1,000.00
Depreciation	(300.00)	(540.00)	(720.00)	(840.00)	(900.00)
	700.00	460.00	280.00	160.00	100.00
Current Assets					
Original	500.00	500.00	500.00	500.00	500.00
Secondary	300.00	540.00	720.00	840.00	900.00
	£1,500.00	£1,500.00	£1,500.00	£1,500.00	£1,500.00

	Per cent p.a.	Per cent p.a.	Per cent p.a.	Per cent p.a.	Per cent p.a.
Rate of Return on Opening Capital	8.9	15.9	22.3	28.1	33.3

Rising Charges Method

Year	1	2	3	4	5
	£	£	£	£	£
Profit and Loss Account					
Operating cash flow	433.48	433.48	433.48	433.48	433.48
Depreciation	(133.48)	(153.50)	(176.53)	(203.01)	(233.48)
Operating profit	300.00	279.98	256.95	230.47	200.00
Income from secondary assets (15 per cent)	0.00	20.02	43.05	69.53	100.00
Net profit (all withdrawn)	£300.00	£300.00	£300.00	£300.00	£300.00
Balance Sheet (ending)					
Capital	£1,500.00	£1,500.00	£1,500.00	£1,500.00	£1,500.00
Fixed Asset					
Cost	1,000.00	1,000.00	1,000.00	1,000.00	1,000.00
Depreciation	(133.48)	(286.98)	(463.51)	(666.52)	(900.00)
	866.52	713.02	536.49	333.48	100.00
Current Assets					
Original	500.00	500.00	500.00	500.00	500.00
Secondary	133.48	286.98	463.51	666.52	900.00
	£1,500.00	£1,500.00	£1,500.00	£1,500.00	£1,500.00
	Per cent p.a.	Per cent p.a.	Per cent p.a.	Per cent p.a.	Per cent p.a.
Rate of Return on Opening Capital	20.0	20.0	20.0	20.0	20.0

Annuity Method

Year	1	2	3	4	5
	£	£	£	£	£
Profit and Loss Account					
Operating cash flow	433.48	433.48	433.48	433.48	433.48
Depreciation	(283.48)	(283.48)	(283.48)	(283.48)	(283.48)
Operating profit	150.00	150.00	150.00	150.00	150.00
Income from secondary assets (15 per cent)	0.00	20.02	43.05	69.53	100.00
Interest element in depreciation charge	150.00	129.98	106.95	80.47	50.00
Net profit (all withdrawn)	£300.00	£300.00	£300.00	£300.00	£300.00

(Balance sheets, and rates of return, similar to those for rising charges method.)

Depreciation Fund Method

Year	1	2	3	4	5
	£	£	£	£	£
Profit and Loss Account					
Operating cash flow	433.48	433.48	433.48	433.48	433.48
Depreciation	(133.48)	(133.48)	(133.48)	(133.48)	(133.48)
Operating profit	300.00	300.00	300.00	300.00	300.00
Income from secondary assets (15 per cent)	0.00	20.02	43.05	69.53	100.00
Interest on depreciation fund (15 per cent)	(0.00)	(20.02)	(43.05)	(69.53)	(100.00)
Net profit (all withdrawn)	£300.00	£300.00	£300.00	£300.00	£300.00

(Balance sheets, and rates of return, similar to those for rising charges method.)

It will be noticed at once that, although operating efficiency, volume of business, year-end capital, and price level were the same in all years, only the three methods which recognize the cost of capital give equal profit, and rate of return, figures throughout. The 'simpler' methods all show increasing profits and rates of return, year by year to the end of the cycle; after which, in the conditions postulated, the secondary assets must be realized, the main asset be replaced, and the whole cycle begin again. It is also to be observed that the 'accelerated' depreciation methods are the worst offenders in this respect. If the reported profits are added up, the totals also are found to vary considerably; for the 'simple' methods they are respectively £1,537.40, £1,651.70, and £1,627.40, while for the 'sophisticated' ones they are consistently £1,500.00. The differences arise solely from the different timings of the withdrawals. If all profit-series are discounted back to end-Year 0 at 15 per cent per annum, all have the same present value, £1,005.65. Straightforward averaging over the five years would have suggested that the firm using the reducing balance method was the most profitable of all six!

The figures chosen are highly artificial—in particular, it has been assumed that secondary assets earn precisely the cost of capital, which is very unlikely—but the message is clear. With rates of interest at modern levels serious errors, leading to major mistakes by managers and investors, can ensue if the time value of money is disregarded. It may not be possible to estimate the cost of capital with great accuracy, but a rate which is 2 or 3 per cent out is surely better than one which is assumed to be zero.

6.3.5 Exposure Draft 15 (1975): Accounting for depreciation

This proposed Statement of Standard Accounting Practice contains few surprises, but serves to clarify some points.

Depreciation is defined as 'the measure of the wearing out, consumption or other loss of value of a fixed asset whether arising from use, effluxion of time or obsolescence through technology [sic] and market changes'. It should be allocated to accounting periods so as to charge a fair proportion to each period during the expected useful life of the asset. Depreciation includes amortization of fixed assets whose useful life is pre-determined (e.g. leases), and depletion of wasting assets (e.g. mines).

Three factors are to be considered, viz.:

a cost (or valuation when an asset has been revalued in the books);

b the nature of the asset and the length of its expected useful life to the business, having regard to the incidence of obsolescence; and

c estimated residual value.

Useful life may be pre-determined (as in leaseholds), governed by extraction or consumption, dependent on the extent of use, or reduced by obsolescence or physical deterioration. Residual value is normally difficult to determine; where it is likely to be small in relation to cost, it is convenient to regard it as nil and make an adjustment for it on disposal.

No specific guidance is offered on allocation of depreciation to accounting periods—it is a matter of judgement in the light of technical, commercial and accounting considerations, and requires annual review. If revision of the estimate of remaining useful life is called for, the unamortized cost should be written off over the revised remaining useful life. If at any time the unamortized cost is seen not to be recoverable in full (e.g. through obsolescence) it should be immediately written down to the estimated recoverable amount, which should be written off over the remaining useful life. Any difference on disposal, between book value and sale proceeds, should be reflected in the year's profit and shown separately, if material; differences arising on discontinuance of a significant part of the business should be dealt with as extraordinary items (see sub-section **14.6.3**).

The management has a duty to allocate depreciation as fairly as possible to the periods expected to benefit from use of the asset, and should select the method regarded as most appropriate to the type of asset and its use in the business. A change of method is permissible only on the ground that the new method will give a fairer presentation of the results and financial position; the unamortized cost should still be written off over the remaining useful life. Where assets are revalued in the books, the depreciation charge should be based on the revalued amount, and in the year of change there should be shown, in a note to the accounts, the subdivision of the charge between depreciation on the old value, and on the amount of the change in value. Depreciation should not be omitted on the ground that the market value of an asset is higher than its net book value.

Freehold land, unless depleted by, e.g., extraction of minerals or otherwise reduced in value, will not normally require a depreciation provision, since its life is extended indefinitely. It should, nevertheless, be written down if its value has been adversely affected by changes in the desirability of its location, either social or economic. All buildings, however, have a limited life and should be depreciated. Accordingly, freehold land and buildings should be regarded as separate assets—the separate costs or revaluations, if not known, being estimated. As with fixed assets in general, a rise in the value of land or buildings does not remove the necessity of charging depreciation on the buildings, and if they are revalued in the books the charge must be increased proportionately.

The proposed SSAP itself incorporates most of the above recommendations, and is summarized in sub-section **14.6.9**. It also recommends that the accounts should disclose the method by which depreciation is calculated for each category of assets, together with the effective useful lives assumed. Where existing buildings are depreciated for the first time, this will represent a change in accounting policy; depreciation for prior years should therefore be treated as a prior year adjustment and charged against the opening balance of retained profits, in accordance with SSAP No. 6 (see sub-section 14.6.3).

6.3.6 Government grants towards the cost of fixed assets

Under the Industry Act, 1972, the British Government may make cash *grants* to firms in respect of certain expenditures. Revenue-based grants should be credited to accounts for the relevant costs, reducing the charge to profit and loss account. Capital-based grants, however, may be treated in several ways—credited to revenue, or to a special reserve, or offset against the relevant capital expenditure.

Statement of Standard Accounting Practice No. 4; *The accounting treatment of government grants* (1974) is effective for accounting periods beginning on or after 1 January 1974. It rejects the immediate crediting of capital-based grants to revenue or to a special reserve, as inconsistent with the principle of revenue-cost matching, and requires them to be credited to revenue over the expected useful life of the asset. This may be achieved by: **a** reducing the cost of acquisition by the amount of the grant (and reducing annual depreciation charges in proportion); or **b** treating the amount of the grant as a deferred credit, a portion of which is transferred to revenue annually (*pari passu*, as a rule, with depreciation charges on the full cost). The unamortized credit should appear separately in the balance sheet, but not be included in equity. Both methods have the same arithmetical effect, but **b** appears preferable, as keeping distinct the elements of cost and grant, and allowing comparability with fixed assets not attracting grant.

6.4 Intangible assets

Finally, historical-cost accounting is concerned with assigning values to, and amortizing expenditure on, assets having no underlying physical content, and representing no legally-enforceable claim to money, in any direct way. These are *intangible assets* and, in view of the considerable differences between them, are best treated under individual headings.

6.4.1 Research and development expenditure; patents, know-how, designs, copyrights, and trade marks.

In many industries, particularly the 'science-based' ones, such as electronics and pharmaceuticals, a large part of the resources of the firm must be devoted to applied scientific research, and in some cases pure research, if the firm is to continue to produce new lines, competitive with the products of rivals. With research is linked the development of new products—the building and testing of prototypes, field tests of new brands, etc.—and the two sets of expenditures are generally lumped together in the books of account, as *research and development expenditure*, or 'R & D'.

Guidance as to its proper treatment in accounts is hard to find. Very many firms, particularly in the U.K., adopt an ultra-conservative approach and write off all such expenditure to revenue in the period when it is incurred, recognizing no asset at any stage. Others capitalize expenditure clearly attributable to particular projects, including a proportion of overheads, and carry it forward as an asset until such time as the prospects of success or failure become clearer. If a project is unlikely to result in any valuable discovery or, although technically sound, it is so expensive that there seems no prospect of its ever being paid for out of relevant profits, it should be written off at once. In the aircraft industry, many millions of pounds may have gone into developing a new and revolutionary model (such as the Concorde) with government backing; if it is seen that costs have escalated far beyond anything foreseeable at the outset, and that demand for the aircraft is never likely to cover them in full, a subsidy will be sought from the government, to be credited to the R & D Account when received. If none is forthcoming, or it does not meet all the cost, a heavy write-off is inevitable, perhaps causing a net loss for the year.

If, more fortunately, a project pays off handsomely, even after meeting all R & D costs, the question arises as to how they should be expensed. Some accountants are inclined to write them off rapidly, in the early years when the new product is leading the field and still, perhaps, protected by a patent, and when the large profits being made can easily absorb the write-off. This procedure, though, appears to violate the basic principles of revenue-cost matching, as well as being very subjective in its calculations. If R & D is a cost, then it is a cost of production and should be related to output volume in some way—e.g. by writing off such proportion as output for the current year bears to the most pessimistic estimate of total sales over, say, the first three, four, or five years, or such other time as it may take for competing products to render the one in question obsolescent. (The tooling costs of the year's models in a motor factory are normally written off in the year of production of the model.) Failure to adopt consistent policies in such matters can severely accentuate profit fluctuations from year to year, and make rational inter-firm comparison almost impossible.

Very many successful research and development projects result in the taking out of *patents*. A patent is the legal right to exploit a new invention in any lawful manner, and to restrain all others from doing so except on the patentee's terms, including the payment of royalties to him, based on the number of units of output or sales of a product incorporating the invention. Such protection is obtained by the inventor's registering the specification with the Department of Trade, and lasts for a maximum of sixteen years—renewal fees being payable for its continuance over each year beyond the fourth. A patent may be assigned to others at any time during its currency.

R & D expenditure relevant to a patent should be capitalized as part of its cost. Too often, though, it has been expensed as incurred, and the book value of the patent consists mainly of fees paid to the Patent Office and to a patent agent, plus incidental expenses, as for preparing the specification—a total of a few hundred pounds at most. The capitalized cost must be written off in sixteen years at most—often sooner, if renewal is not considered worth while—and generally by the straight line method (though the annuity method is theoretically preferable). The purchase price of an assigned patent is written off over its remaining years of life.

In many manufacturing industries a firm may develop a specially efficient method of carrying out some process, but be unable to patent it, as it is insufficiently original. The process, whether 'secret' or not, may be communicated to other firms in return for large sums of money, and there is then said to be a sale of *know-how.* This is purely revenue to the firm, as there is normally no cost that can be matched with it. The purchaser may write off the cost of the know-how at once, or he may amortize it over a few years; the Inland Revenue allows straight line write-off in six years for tax purposes, and this may be taken as a guide. (Secret processes and formulae may never be patented, because of the fear that competitors may use them after sixteen years, or imitate them earlier, if publicity is given to them by registration; the above remarks apply to their treatment in accounts.)

Designs, copyrights, and trade marks may be shortly dealt with. A registered design is protected in the same manner as a patent (for five to fifteen years), and the accounting treatment is similar. Copyright in a literary, artistic, or musical work arises automatically upon creation, and does not have to be formally registered; it lasts during the lifetime of the author, artist, or composer, and to the end of the fiftieth calendar year after his death. Copyrights held by the author, etc., seldom have an imputed cost, but purchased ones may have a high book value. Very few copyrights are worth much in royalty expectations after the first few years, and the cost, if any, should be written off by then; even if the work is very successful, or has become a classic, it is prudent to amortize its copyright in, say, twenty years at most. Trade marks, if registered, are protected indefinitely; those originating with the firm seldom have a significant cost, yet may be among its most valuable properties, if the product has become a household name—acquisition of the right to use it may even be the main object of a take-over bid! A purchased trade mark or brand name is quite often carried indefinitely on the books without any write-off; if demand for the product declines, though, amortization will have to be considered on the merits of the case, as with goodwill.

6.4.2 Exposure Draft 14 (1975): Accounting for research and development

ED14 is more conservative in its conclusions than the first part of sub-section **6.4.1**, but the author has preferred to let his text stand.

The definition of research and development expenditure is based on that used by the Organization for Economic Co-operation and Development (OECD). It does not include expenditure on locating and exploiting mineral deposits, or on market research; nor does it cover development work carried out under a contract by which third parties are to reimburse the whole cost, or one by which goods are to be developed and manufactured at an agreed price, calculated to cover costs of both development and manufacture. R & D expenditure proper falls into three categories:

a *pure* (or *basic*) *research,* undertaken in order to gain new scientific or technical knowledge and understanding, and not primarily directed towards any specific practical aim or application;

b *applied research,* undertaken as above, but directed towards a specific practical aim or objective; and

c *development,* being the use of scientific or technical knowledge to produce new or substantially improved materials, devices, products, processes, systems, or services.

Accounting treatment of R & D expenditure (it is argued) must have regard to the 'fundamental accounting concepts' of SSAP No. 2 (see sub-section **14.6.1**), and in particular to the 'accruals' and 'prudence' concepts. Costs must be matched with revenues of the periods to which the costs relate; but revenue and profits must not be anticipated, and expenditure should be written off in the period in which it arises, unless its relationship to the revenue of a future period can be established with reasonable certainty. Expenditure on pure and applied research is part of a continuing operation to maintain a company's business and its competitive position. In general, one particular period rather than another will not be expected to benefit, and therefore such costs should be written off as incurred. Development expenditure, however, is normally undertaken with a reasonable expectation of specific commercial success and of future benefits, from increased revenue and profits or reduced costs. Thus it may be argued that such expenditure should be deferred and matched against future revenue.

In the ASSC's opinion, the future potential benefits of development expenditure can only be evaluated if there is a clearly defined project and the related expenditure is separately identifiable. In that case the project would then need to be examined for technical feasbility, and ultimate commercial viability in the light of (e.g.) likely market conditions, public opinion, and consumer and environmental legislation. Furthermore, such a project will only be of value if all related future costs to be incurred on it will be more than covered by related future revenues, and there are, or are reasonably expected to be, adequate resources to enable the project to be completed and to provide any consequential increase in working capital. In view of all these considerable uncertainties, of the need for different persons with different levels of judgement to assess the technical, commercial and financial viability of the project, and of the widely differing assessments which might emerge, it does not seem that many development projects would be judged to have sufficient certainty of producing future benefits to justify carrying them forward. Such uncertainties are considered to make an insecure foundation for a practical standard. Accordingly, it is proposed that research and development expenditure should be written off in the year in which it is incurred.

Fixed assets acquired or constructed to provide facilities for research and/or development activities will usually provide them over a number of accounting periods. They should therefore be capitalized and written off over their useful life. Depreciation thus charged should be included as part of the R & D expenditure.

Expenditure on market research, though not classed as R & D expenditure, should (it is considered) be written off as incurred, on similar principles.

The total amount of expenditure incurred in a year on R & D should be separately disclosed in the published accounts.

The proposed SSAP itself embodies briefly the above recommendations, and is summarized in sub-section **14.6.8**.

6.4.3 Goodwill

The assets considered in sub-section **6.4.1**, though intangible by nature, are yet *separable* from the enterprise as a whole, and have a cost of acquisition, however hard to find in some instances, and (usually) a determinate life, though their economic lives are often difficult to assess and generally shorter. Goodwill is different in all these respects, and its treatment in accounts highly controversial.

Goodwill is most usefully defined, perhaps, as the excess of the going-concern realizable value of an entity as a whole, over the sum of the replacement or realizable values of its separable assets, less liabilities. It bears no relation to the cost of the separable assets, individually or collectively, and hence must fit very awkwardly into a conception of accounting based on the primacy of historical cost. Most of the time it is possible to side-step the problems by ignoring goodwill, but there are situations where its existence must be recognized and a book value placed upon it.

Non-purchased goodwill is that which arises in the course of building up a business from scratch. If through enterprise, foresight, efficiency, and good fortune a firm becomes more profitable than the average for firms whose businesses are subject to a comparable degree of commercial risk, it must be presumed (and is sometimes confirmed by events) that a purchaser of the undertaking would be willing to pay a price exceeding the total which he would pay for the separate tangible assets, less liabilities. He would do so because he is primarily interested in acquiring a going concern—a business already organized and in working order, with commercial connections, regular customers, an established reputation for good workmanship or service, and efficient management. He would be saved the toil, risk, expense, and delay of setting up and developing the business himself, and hence would gladly pay for the ready provision of those intangible elements, inseparable from the entity, as well as for the chance to earn as proprietor of the firm a super-normal rate of return on the net tangible assets. The value placed upon all these advantages is the goodwill of the business.

Because this value depends upon a hypothetical future sale of the concern, its present amount can only be subjectively estimated. No historical cost can be assigned to it, since goodwill has been built up incidentally to the general development of the business, and there is no expenditure which can be directly ascribed to its creation. There is thus no case within the framework of conventional accounting for bringing non-purchased goodwill on to the books, even in a situation where it is obviously valuable if sold: to do so is to anticipate gains which have yet to be realized, and which might never be made. The same arguments apply to values which appear without cost or effort, such as valuable minerals discovered under a farm, purchased at a price appropriate to agricultural land pure and simple; but there are both legal authority and economic considerations in favour of writing up the land on the basis of the present value of the cash flows to be expected from exploiting the minerals.

The situation changes where there is an actual or prospective sale of the business, or of a controlling interest in it, or where the existing owners admit an outsider to partnership, or where an existing partner retires or dies and he or his executors or administrators wish to withdraw his capital. These are all events significant enough to call for a general revaluation of the entity's assets and liabilities, to establish its present financial position irrespective of historical costs. The seller(s) of an entire going concern will normally make a sizeable capital gain, by which their equity will be augmented, since the asset acquired (cash, or a debt due from the purchaser) will exceed the book values of the assets given up, less any liabilities taken over by the purchaser. The difference will be credited to equity in one sum, but no attempt is usually made to analyse it as gains (less losses) on specific tangibles, and as a receipt for unrecorded goodwill (see Chapter 10, section 10.5, for the accounting entries). The purchaser, on the other hand, although he has paid a single agreed price for the business, must apportion it among the assets which he has acquired, in some more or less arbitrary manner. The basis which makes most sense is the replacement price of each tangible asset—what he would have expected to pay for it, or for something able to render him equivalent services, in isolation—with the residue of the purchase price regarded as the cost of goodwill.

Similarly, as explained in Chapter 10, section 10.1, a sole trader, or partners, who admit a new partner to the business will normally revalue all the assets as at the date of the change, on the basis of replacement prices (or realizable value, in the case of land). They will also have to place a value on non-purchased (and therefore unrecorded) goodwill, or to revise the value placed on goodwill on some such occasion in the past. The benefit of the revaluation goes to the old partners as an increase in the book value of their equity, thus ensuring that if any capital gain is made after the admission of the new partner, he gets only his share of any part of the gain which accrued since his admission (and conversely for a capital loss). For similar reasons a revaluation is also needed when the profit-sharing ratio is revised. Again, when a partner retires or dies a general revaluation (including goodwill) should be made in order to establish the fair value of his interest in the firm, to be withdrawn, or purchased from him (or his executors or administrators) by the other partners. Finally, when one company acquires all, or a majority, of the shares in another company, so as to make that other its 'subsidiary', the price paid, whether in cash, or new shares of the 'holding' company, or both, will generally include an element for the subsidiary's goodwill. This appears when the annual accounts of the two companies are 'consolidated' to produce statements for the group as a whole, and the investment in the holding company's books is replaced by the underlying assets, less liabilities, of the subsidiary; a figure for goodwill must be inserted in order to complete the consolidated balance sheet, as described in Chapter 16, sub-section **16.4.2**.

Where there is no sale of the business at arm's length, but merely a change of partners or of profit-sharing ratio, a goodwill valuation can only be subjective, with the need for agreement by all parties setting maximum and minimum limits to the possible amount. Often (especially in professional practices) there is an attempt at objectivity, by agreeing (then or in the partnership agreement made years before) to base the valuation upon past events. Thus, goodwill may be taken as two years' gross fees averaged over the last four years, or the total profits of the last three or four years. The obvious objection, that such a procedure does not discriminate between a rising and a falling trend, may be countered by weighting the most recent years' figures more heavily than earlier ones—e.g. if four years' average profits are to be taken, by multiplying the last four years' figures respectively, and in chronological order, by 1, 2, 3, and 4, summing the products, and dividing by 10 (the sum of the weights). A rising series will then show a higher weighted average than a static or falling one, and multiplication by 4 gives the goodwill value.

This refinement cannot remove the fundamental disadvantage of such allegedly 'objective' valuations—that they are unrelated to what they are supposed to measure. The existence of goodwill arises, not from the making of profits in the past, but from the expectation of profits in the future; past profits are no more than an aid in making projections. It is unwise merely to extrapolate recent net profits without analysis; the main factors which have determined them—sales, variable and fixed costs of production or service, general overheads, financial charges, etc.—should all be examined, any trends or cycles noted and allowed for, and adjustments made for any anticipated changes of circumstances (e.g. the expiry of a lease, or the redemption of a loan). Rising prices are on the whole best disregarded, the projected sums being taken as the real equivalents in terms of today's purchasing power of the, probably higher, money amounts which will actually apply. In a partnership, too, an adequate allowance should be deducted annually, for working partners' managerial salaries—irrespective of any token 'salaries' used in the accounts to adjust the profit-sharing ratio. Profit projections on these lines should be made for at least five years into the future, using Bayesian or other probability calculations to allow for uncertainties. For years beyond the 'horizon' it is necessary to make assumptions, the simplest of which is that the fifth year's figures repeat themselves indefinitely—often as rational a supposition as any other!

Given reasonable projections of future profits, there are two goodwill valuation methods in common use, both improvements on the averaging of past results, but both open to the objection that they ignore the time value of money. The first consists of averaging (say) the next five years' estimated profits (net of partners' remuneration), assuming the average to be a perpetual annuity, and capitalizing it at the rate of return expected on an investment of that character. The capital sum is deemed to be the global value of the business, and the goodwill found by elimination of the tangible items at replacement or other suitable values. Thus, if the average profits over the next five years are £20,000 per annum, partners' salaries of £5,000 per annum are deducted to leave £15,000, and the expected rate of return before tax is 15 per cent per annum, then the global sum is £15,000 × 100/15 = £100,000. If tangible assets are valued at £75,000, goodwill is £25,000.

The second approach is by way of the concept of 'super-profits'. The tangible assets are valued as above, and a suitable rate of return applied, giving an annual figure of 'normal' profit. This is compared with the average projected profit, and the excess of the latter over the former regarded as a super-profit, justifying the assumption that a goodwill exists. The super-profit is then capitalized, at a rate of interest somewhat higher than the basic rate because of the greater uncertainty involved, and the capital sum is the goodwill value. Thus, in the previous example, a 15 per cent 'accounting' rate of return on £75,000 tangible assets is £11,250 per annum, compared with £15,000 average profits after partners' remuneration. The difference of £3,750 is the super-profit—and if this is capitalized at, say, 20 per cent the goodwill is valued at £18,750.

Such are the common methods of goodwill valuation, in partnership agreements and as guide-lines in negotiation for the sale of a business. They are unsound in their assumptions that all future profits have an undiminished present value regardless of their time pattern, and that super-profits are receivable in perpetuity. In the majority of cases purchased goodwill must be supposed to have a limited life, during which the effects of the old management wear off and are replaced by those of the new one. A more scientific means of deriving a goodwill valuation is to take (say) the first five years' projected profits (if that is the period over which the goodwill is held to expire), deduct from all of them the average 'maintainable' profit (normal rate of return on tangibles), and discount the remaining 'super-profits' back to the present at the firm's cost of capital, to give the goodwill valuation. Thus, if as before the tangible assets are valued at £75,000, the cost of capital (and expected rate of return) 15 per cent per annum, and the projected profits net of remuneration for the next five years are £21,000, £16,000, £14,000, £12,000, and £12,000 (average: £15,000); the maintainable profit is £75,000 × 15/100, or £11,250 per annum, the super-profits are £9,750, £4,750, £2,750, £750, and £750, and their present value is £14,680—the goodwill value, on these assumptions.

Since purchased goodwill (however arrived at) normally has a limited life, it should be written down out of profits over that life. This is commonly done by the use of the straight line method of amortization; a better approach—particularly when goodwill has been estimated by discounting future super-profits—is to debit the Goodwill Account with interest on the balance equal to the cost of capital assumed in the previous computation, and credit it with the amount of super-profit arising in the year, debiting the net of the two figures to profit and loss account. Any balance of goodwill unamortized at the end of the agreed life will be written off then. Thus is goodwill written off against the profits which constitute its *raison d'être*. 'Revaluation' goodwill in a partnership should not be written down, on the assumption that, so long as some continuity of management is maintained between the 'old' and 'new' firms, there is no reason to suppose that goodwill has declined in value.

It is argued by some American accountants[5] (especially in relation to goodwill arising on a merger of two companies) that goodwill is not an asset, but merely the price paid for future super-profits out of the equity of the purchasing firm. Only the tangible assets should be valued (at replacement cost, etc.), and the balance of the purchase price should be written off the company's capital surplus, and then, if necessary, off its retained profits (see Chapters 14 and 16). The depletion should be temporary only, and be restored out of the super-profits when they come in. These arguments were put to the Accounting Principles Board in 1970, but in its Opinion No. 17, 'Intangible Assets', the Board rejected them, and came to much more orthodox conclusions—that purchased goodwill should be recognized as an asset, and that it should be amortized against profits over a period of not more than forty years—less, if appropriate. The main weakness in the opposing view seems to be that it rests on assumptions alien to historical-cost accounting—e.g. the assertions that it is the function of the balance sheet to show the values of the entity's separable resources, and that goodwill is an asset of the proprietors, rather than of the entity itself. Where there is such division among eminent authorities it is imprudent to reject either contention out of hand; much fundamental research remains to be done before the question is settled. It should, though, be clear to the reader that the whole subject of goodwill is a perplexed one, and that it is very doubtful whether any coherent solution is possible within the canons of historical-cost accounting.

[5] See, e.g.: Catlett, George R. and Norman O. Olson, *Accounting Research Study No. 10: Accounting for Goodwill,* American Institute of Certified Public Accountants, 1968.

7

Accounting for price level changes; funds flow and cash flow

Chapters 5 and 6 have been devoted to an outline of present-day historical-cost accounting in relation to businesses conducted for gain in the private sector of the economy. The concept has been set forth as a necessary stage in the development of accounting in an industrial society—a means of bringing some consistency into the valuation of assets and liabilities (and hence of equity) and the determination of business income, and, through the machinery of audit by professional accountants, of restraining businessmen from indulging in over-optimism, fantasy, manipulation of profits and values, or sheer fraud. Furthermore, since in most countries historical-cost-based accounts are still the norm, it has been necessary to expound in considerable detail the principles on which they are conventionally prepared, and the many complexities which result from their practical application in varying circumstances. Some suggestions, too, have been incorporated for refining the system and enabling it to perform its functions more efficiently—without departing from its fundamental assumptions. Yet it is these very refinements which emphasize the inadequacy of historical-cost accounting as an intellectual concept and as a practical methodology of economic measurement, and it is to its shortcomings that attention must now be given.

7.1 Modern criticisms of historical-cost accounting

On its intellectual side, the most telling objection to historical-cost accounting is its lack of coherence. It is not really a system at all, but a compendium of practices slowly evolved by accountants over the past six or seven centuries, and clearly formulated only within the last fifty years. Those moderns who tried to make sense of them were faced with a series of *faits accomplis*—of usages adopted in order to deal with problems arising at various periods, particularly during the nineteenth and twentieth centuries as a result of industrialization, the growth of joint-stock enterprise, and the heavy taxation of profits since 1914. All that accountants could do was to codify practice for the guidance of practitioners and students, and to abstract from existing usages a series of 'principles'—revenue-cost matching, non-anticipation of income, full provision for losses, etc.—which essentially were nothing more than rationalizations of those usages, and did nothing to justify them philosophically. Some of the practices are logical enough, such as the use of historical costs as entry values for assets, and amounts realized on sale (or insurance compensation, or nothing, on destruction) as exit values, in an economy based upon exchanges of values expressed in terms of money. The weaknesses lie in the methods of establishing asset values, and profits for successive accounting periods, and stem primarily from the lack of thought given in the past to the nature of value and of profit, by accountants as opposed to economists. In fact, most conventional accounting practice solidified before the formulation of modern theories on these matters, and the general dearth of accountants with a sound academic training in economics, and the will or ability to keep up with current developments in the science, made it hard until recent years to secure widespread acceptance of the need to rethink the time-honoured assumptions in accordance with those developments.

As to practice, the most bewildering variety of rules grew up in the matter of determining the degree to which historical costs might be said to expire, and need matching with revenues for a given period. There was general agreement on the adjustment of cash flows for end-of-period indebtedness to or by the entity, and on the distinction between capital and revenue expenditure in relation to physical assets and investments. The main areas of uncertainty, as the reader will have gathered from Chapters 5 and 6, were and are in the fields of inventory valuation, fixed asset amortization, and the treatment of intangibles. The freedom of choice allowed, and the want of consistency between one firm and another, cause possible figures of reported profit in a large-scale business for any particular period to vary over a wide range, and make accounting profit impossible to define, except as the result of what accountants do to measure it. The position is equally chaotic as to asset valuation and the determination of equity—indeed, many balance sheet amounts are mere residuals of past expenditure, after the making of arbitrary allocations to revenue, and bear little relation to economic value, in exchange or in use.

A further, and more fundamental, objection is levelled at the whole concept of historical cost as a reliable basis for accounting. Its general principles were worked out mainly in the nineteenth century, when price levels changed only slowly, and not always in the same direction. Its rigorous application began in the 1930s, when, also, the price level was relatively stable in developed countries. The distortions through ignoring price changes over the economic lives of most assets except land were not large, and were not considered sufficient reason for departing from asset values established by acts of exchange between the entity and the outside world, or connected therewith by chosen rules consistently followed. (The same applied to neglect of the time value of money, owing to the low rates of interest current in the 1930s and 'forties.) The picture changed after 1945, when prices rose steadily, year by year, with a brief burst of rapid inflation early in the Korean War (1950–53), and a more violent and sustained one in the 1970s. The pent-up need to replace capital equipment after the Second World War, at prices double or treble the·amounts accumulated in depreciation provisions on the old assets, aggravated the problems, and occasioned bitter criticism of an accounting system which failed to conserve either the physical, or the real, capital of a business unless a large proportion of the reported profits were ploughed back, and which caused income taxes to be levied upon profits which, to an economist, were not income at all.

As mentioned in Chapter 4, immediately post-war discussions of 'price level' accounting finally came to very little in America and Britain. On the continent of Europe, where inflation was much more severe, the revenue systems of many countries permitted adjustment of profits for price level changes in arriving at the base for income taxes, and in the Netherlands there has been some acceptance of replacement-cost accounting, pioneered by the Philips electrical group. In Anglo-Saxon lands a renewed interest arose after the publication in 1961 of *The Theory and Measurement of Business Income*, by the American economists (not accountants) Edgar O. Edwards and Philip W. Bell,[1] and was further stimulated by

[1] Edwards, E. O. and Bell, P. W. *The Theory and Measurement of Business Income*, University of California Press, 1961.

R.J. Chambers's *Accounting, Evaluation and Economic Behavior* (1966).[2]

From 1970 the (British/Irish) Accounting Standards Steering Committee applied itself to the question of inflation accounting, and in 1973 produced Exposure Draft 8: *Accounting for changes in the purchasing power of money*. Soon afterwards the (then) Department of Trade and Industry set up the Sandilands Committee on Accounting for Inflation, to consider the applications of the new techniques to company accounting within the framework of existing or future Companies Acts. This annoyed the U.K. accountancy profession, which saw the Sandilands Committee as a governmental device to stifle discussion of a politically sensitive issue—endorsement of accounting for inflation might be seen as to minimize its effects. The Committee is expected to report in 1975; in the meantime the ASSC has published (1974) Statement of Standard Accounting Practice No. 7: *Accounting for changes in the purchasing power of money*, while making it clear that this is provisional until further notice, and hence *money*, while making it clear that this is provisional until further notice, and hence of persuasive force only. Its advocacy of the current purchasing power method of inflation accounting contrasts sharply with the replacement-cost approach of Edwards and Bell, and latterly of Lawrence Revsine (1973),[3] and keen controversy now rages in the accountancy and financial press.

7.2 Replacement-cost accounting

In considering methods of allowing for price level changes in accounts, it is necessary to distinguish clearly between: **a** movements in the *market prices of a particular firm's inputs* during an accounting period; and **b** changes in the *general level of prices* in the relevant country during the same period. **a** is the concern of replacement-cost accounting, and **b** of current purchasing power accounting. These will be discussed in turn—it being first assumed that, though there are changes in the price of goods and services bought by the firm, the average price level does not alter significantly during the accounting period.

7.2.1 Economic arguments for replacement-cost accounting

It has already been intimated that accounting and economics offer different definitions of 'income'. To the economist the usual starting-point of a discussion on the nature of income is the well-known statement of J.R. Hicks, that a person's income is 'the maximum value which he can consume during a week, and still expect to be as well off at the end of the week as he was at the beginning'.[4] To the accountant the normal definition of income (or profit) is the excess of revenues over historical cost (however measured) of inputs consumed in earning them, plus/minus capital gains/losses realized, in a given accounting period. Neither of these, as they stand, provides a sound basis for the rational measurement of income arising from business operations.

Economic income is essentially a subjective concept, since it depends upon a comparison of an individual's sense of 'well-offness' at the beginning and end of a period, plus his actual consumption during it, all evaluated in

[2] Chambers, R. J. *Accounting, Evaluation and Economic Behavior,* Prentice-Hall, 1966.
[3] Revsine, L. *Replacement Cost Accounting,* Prentice-Hall, 1973.
[4] Hicks, J. R. *Value and Capital* (2nd edn), Clarendon Press, 1946.

money terms. To adapt the notion to business enterprise, the sense of well-offness must be imputed to the managers or working proprietors, since the entity itself has no feelings. Also, in order to provide a basis for objective measurement in the accounts, it must be quantified as the present value at any time of the expected future net receipts from business operations. Thus, if at a given date a firm is set up to earn net receipts of £10,000 in each of the next five years, and then to be liquidated with no residual value, and the expected rate of return is 10 per cent per annum, the present value of management's expectations is at end-Year 0 $£\{10,000/1.10 + 10,000/(1.10)^2 + \ldots + 10,000/(1.10)^5\} = £37,908$. If £10,000 is indeed earned in Year 1, and the other expectations are unchanged at the end of that year, the present value of them is now £31,699. The income for the year is this sum, plus the cash flow, minus the opening value of expectations, or $£\{(31,699 + 10,000) - 37,908\} = £3,791$, which is 10 per cent on £37,908—the expected rate of return; the remaining £6,209 of the cash flow represents capital disinvested. Similarly, in Year 2 (if the first year's £10,000 is entirely withdrawn) the present value of expectations falls to £24,869—i.e. by £6,830, leaving the other £3,170 of cash flow as income of 10 per cent on £31,699; etc.

In a stationary society, in which the level of economic activity in all fields did not vary significantly over time, such a system would be practicable, and it would be possible for a firm to assure its proprietors of the going rate of return on their original capital in perpetuity, by reinvesting at that rate the part of the annual cash flow which exceeded the said rate of return on their initial capital. Thus, in the previous illustration, £6,209 reinvested at the end of Year 1 would have earned £621 in Year 2, which, with the £3,170 on the original project, would have enabled proprietors to withdraw £3,791 as in Year 1. It is easy to compute that, by proceeding thus to the end of Year 5, they could take out £3,791 every year, and end with all the initial capital of £37,908 disinvested, and reinvested to produce £3,791 per annum in perpetuity.

In a dynamic economy these assumptions do not hold. Expectations about the future change continually, and a mere deduction of expected present value of future cash flows at end-Year 0 from those at end-Year 1 would not yield a figure which, when added algebraically to Year 1's cash flow, gave a reliable estimate of the year's income. It would be necessary to recalculate the opening present value, as though management has *then* had its end-year expectations about future cash flows, plus expectations about the flows of Year 1, perhaps corresponding with what actually happened! This somewhat tortuous procedure would cause repeated revisions, year by year, of the 'target' profit and, joined with variations in the expected rate of return, differences between expected and actual cash flows, and differential risks between investment outlets, would make it impossible to assure a steady income to investors. This would vary, not according to current activity, but according to changes in the subjective expectations of management, which could not be validated in advance and would give ample scope for anything from unjustified optimism to downright fraud.

An approximation to such a situation would arise from an accounting system which valued opening and closing assets at their *opportunity cost*—their economic value to the firm in their most profitable use. This is the higher of the (subjective) present value of future net receipts, or the (objective) net realizable value on immediate disposal. Again, opening present values would have to be revised in the light of year-end expectations, and opening equity adjusted; a more serious objection would be the impossibility in many cases of assigning present values of receipts to assets used jointly to produce them. From the standpoint of management policy, such accounting would be inadequate as a guide to the success of management in making the most profitable use of assets in the past, and of little help in adapting past plans to take cognizance of changed expectations.

The next alternative is to value opening and closing assets at *net realizable value*. This, at least, eliminates the element of 'subjective goodwill' (present value of future expected net receipts from using an asset, less net realizable value) inevitably entering into pure opportunity-cost valuations, and relates reported profit to the verifiable activities of the firm during an accounting period, without considering changes in management's expectations of future cash flow. It has also the advantage of by-passing the problems of historical cost determination and depreciation calculations. The main weakness is that in a manufacturing or trading business profit is imputed when goods are made ready for sale, and amended if selling price is raised or lowered; actual sale adds nothing, and it makes no difference whether goods are sold or held (unless they become shop-soiled and have to be marked down). With fixed assets, resale price valuation is often much lower than current buying prices, even at the moment of acquisition, and in extreme cases (of large, immobile, and unique assets) there may be a very limited market, and no discoverable selling price above scrap value; so that rigorous application of the method could result in the writing off of most of the asset's cost in the year of acquisition. It can be argued that such a procedure would disclose the true position as to the entity's short-term ability to adapt itself to changes in demand for the products of the fixed assets concerned, and R. J. Chambers[5] inclines to this view. Yet even he recoils from such logic, and suggests replacement cost as a surrogate for resale value in all cases, on the ground that the latter often cannot be reliably ascertained, and that the difference between it and replacement cost is due to market imperfections; and there seems little prospect of any great number of accountants' agreeing to dispose of large fixed asset values by 'burying them alive'.

Replacement cost is thus the third solution to be proposed. In economic theory, historical cost is irrelevant except at acquisition of the asset, when it coincides with replacement cost. After that the two usually diverge, and the economic cost of using up or selling an asset, or its services, is its replacement cost at that point in time—what the input would have cost to buy or make, if it had not been on hand just then. If it has been purchased or produced some time before, at lower cost, then by holding it until now the firm has effected a *cost saving* equal to replacement cost less historical cost (if interest on the historical cost over the time interval be ignored). The *current cost of sales*, so far as it affects the asset consumed, is the replacement cost. Thus, if goods costing £100 are sold for £130, at a time when their replacement cost is £120, conventional accounting computes the gross profit as £$(130 - 100)$ = £30. The above analysis shows that this is made up of *current trading profit*, £$(130 - 120)$ = £10, and *holding gain*, £$(120 - 100)$ = £20. Both elements are realized profit, to be added to equity, but only the current trading profit, £10, can be regarded as withdrawable by the proprietors. The other £20, together with the recovered historical cost of £100, is needed to replace the depleted stock, and cannot be taken out if the business is to continue on the same scale. It must be retained in order to conserve the *physical* capital intact, whereas withdrawal of the whole £30 of accounting profit would merely maintain the

[5] See: Footnote 2.

money capital intact, regardless of its reduced power (*ceteris paribus*) to command resources of the kind needed to operate the business.

In the normal case the replacement cost of inventory is below its opportunity cost (defined as net resale value), except for work in progress, whose resale value as it stands may be very low, or zero. *Its* opportunity cost, though, is the higher alternative, the present value of expected future net receipts—i.e. the sale value of the product in which it is to be incorporated, less future costs (at replacement prices) to be incurred to complete it, all suitably discounted; and this is normally higher than replacement cost of the work in progress (or, more precisely, its *present cost*—the replacement costs of all the inputs needed to reproduce it as of now). The opportunity cost of a stock of raw materials is, on the same argument, almost always higher than its replacement cost. With fixed assets, the cost input to be matched with sales is the depreciation charge, by whatever formula computed. If consistency is to be observed, the charge must be computed on the replacement cost of the asset, not the historical cost as is usual. Once more, the opportunity cost of the fixed asset is normally the present value of the expected future cash flow from its services—almost always above resale value, or it would pay to sell the asset instead of holding and using it. Replacement cost (less depreciation) is normally related to opportunity cost, though tending as a rule to be lower, by reason of market imperfections.

If, then, historical cost is relevant only as an entry value to the accounting system of an entity, synonymous with replacement cost at that point in time, it follows that it ought to be superseded by replacement cost proper whenever that changes, or at least whenever an asset gives up its services as inputs to the cost of production or of sales. The difference between replacement cost, so arising, and underlying historical cost is a *realized cost saving*, to be credited to a special division of equity distinct from both contributed capital and retained profit. Further, if all assets are valued for balance sheet purposes at the lower of replacement cost and opportunity cost, then the difference between whichever is used and historical cost (of assets acquired in the period) or opening balance sheet value (of assets held throughout the period) is a *realizable costing saving*—one expected to be realized, wholly or partly, in the next period—also taken to equity, separately from the current operating profit. Finally, if a fixed asset is sold in the period for a price different from its depreciated replacement cost, the difference is a *realized capital gain/loss,* credited/debited to profit and loss account and entering into retained profit. To sum up: if opening and closing assets are valued at, or on the basis of, replacement cost at the two dates, and allowance made for proprietary capital introduced or withdrawn during the period, the net growth in equity may be called *business profit* (as by Edwards and Bell[6]), and must be expected to differ from accounting profit, already defined.

Accounting profit consists of four elements:

1 current operating profit (sales revenue less replacement cost of inputs used during year);
2 realized cost savings (replacement cost less historical cost of the said inputs);
3 realized capital gains/losses (sale proceeds of fixed assets disposed of less depreciated replacement cost thereof); and
4 capital holding gains/losses (depreciated replacement cost less depreciated historical cost, of the said fixed assets disposed of).

[6] See: Footnote 1.

In conventional accounting, **1** and **2** are not distinguished, neither are **3** and **4**, respectively. It would be a first step towards reform if they were; but merely to do so would still mean showing balance sheet assets at historical-cost-based values.

Business profit, on the other hand, consists of three elements—**1** and **3** above, plus **5** realizable cost savings (replacement cost [simple or depreciated] of ending assets less historical cost in the period, or value at which they were brought forward from the previous period). Realizable cost savings result from using replacement cost, instead of historical cost, as the basis for terminal valuations, and represent the price gain on assets held to the end of the period, not recognized in conventional accounting.

7.2.2 A practical system of replacement-cost accounting

Perhaps the most highly developed system of replacement-cost accounting currently in use is that of the great Philips international electrical manufacturing group, based in the Netherlands. Founded on the ideas of Professor Th. Limperg, before the Second World War, it includes a complete set of standard cost accounts based on replacement cost, and updated every month to current prices. The financial books are on the same basis, and the published accounts are drawn up in replacement-cost terms. It is not here proposed to describe the Philips system in any detail, but to illustrate the principles fairly simply.

The books are arranged in the first place on conventional lines, so that it is possible to extract historical-cost final accounts from them for legal and taxation purposes. To them are added an array of adjustment accounts, to implement replacement-cost accounting at all other levels, including final accounts; these may be published on the replacement-cost basis only, or on the historical-cost basis as well, for comparison. The two main areas of adjustment are inventories and fixed assets, where there is inevitable delay before expenditures incurred find their way into costs. With expenditure on intangible services (not entering into inventory costs) there is no such delay, and historical and replacement costs are one.

As to *inventories,* raw material stocks should be kept on the FIFO or average-cost basis, as appropriate, being simplest to calculate and in line with taxation requirements. To the ordinary Raw Materials Stock Account is added a Raw Materials Stock Valuation Adjustment Account. Both of these are total or summary accounts, backed by memorandum perpetual inventories in FIFO/ average-cost terms. Purchases are debited to Raw Materials Stock at cost, and credits for issues to production (*Dr.* Work In Progress Account) are on the same basis. The raw materials stock valuation adjustment account has an opening balance (normally debit) for each month, equal to the difference between replacement cost and historical cost of the opening stock. There is also a Stock Revaluation Reserve Account, forming part of the equity of the firm, with a credit balance at the outset, equal to the total holding gains which have accrued to date on inventories.

At the end of the month, the debits in the Raw Materials Stock Account (opening balance and purchases) are revalued at closing replacement cost. The amount of the net gain on the opening stock, over the historical cost plus last month's revaluation adjustment (opening debit balance on the valuation adjustment account), is debited to the last-named account and credited to a Realizable Cost Savings Account. The excess of replacement cost, over historical cost, of purchases during the month is treated similarly. The credit to realizable cost savings represents the price gain during the month on raw materials, whether embodied in work in progress or still in stores at the end; it is then transferred to the credit of Stock Revaluation Reserve, closing the realizable cost savings account for the month.

The issues to production are evaluated, also, at closing replacement cost. The amount of gain on the 'old' replacement cost of the opening stock, and that on the historical cost of the purchases used up in the month, are both credited to the Stock Valuation Adjustment Account and debited to a Work In Progress Material Cost Adjustment Account. The first account is balanced, its debit balance representing the price gain on closing stock; it is added to the debit balance on Stock Account to find the balance sheet valuation of raw materials inventory, at replacement cost (see *Example 1,* below).

Work in progress is thus charged with the replacement cost of raw material inputs, month by month, and also, as explained below, with depreciation of fixed assets, where relevant, on a replacement-cost basis. Labour inputs need no adjustment, since their historical and replacement costs are identical at the time of consumption, and the same may be said of overheads. If the production process lasts no more than one month, there seems to be no strong case for any further adjustment in respect of price gains on inputs during that time; if it lasts much longer, adjustments should be made on the lines indicated above. Subject to this, transfers from work in progress to Finished Goods Stock Account should be made at book value. Transfers to Cost of Sales, on the other hand, should be uplifted to current cost of production (or purchase, if lower), by devices similar to those described for raw materials; but the amount of the uplift should be credited to Finished Goods Stock Valuation Adjustment Account and debited to a Realized Cost Savings Account (and transferred thence to Cost of Sales), since it represents past savings by buying or making below present replacement cost, now matched with sales.

With regard to *fixed assets,* the conventional cost, and depreciation provision, accounts should be kept, on a historical-cost basis, for each class of assets. To them should be added, for each class, a Valuation Adjustment Account and a Depreciation Provision Adjustment Account. Their opening debit and credit balances respectively represent the excesses of replacement cost over historical cost, and of accumulated depreciation based on the one over that based on the other. A Fixed Assets Revaluation Reserve Account forms part of the firm's equity, its credit balance consisting of past price adjustments (net of depreciation adjustments) on fixed assets.

Replacement cost of fixed assets may be ascertained, say, monthly in the case of machinery, motor vehicles, and the like. For land and buildings, and large, complex structures, it is necessary as a rule to use specific price indices, such as the Department of Trade's *Index of Building Costs,* or to compute such indices internally (as at Philips). The historical cost is multiplied by the index number as at the date of revaluation, and divided by the number as at the date of acquisition—e.g. if the index has risen from 150 to 250 over the life to date of an asset which cost £100,000, its estimated replacement cost is £100,000 x 250/150 = £166,667. With long-lived assets such estimates should be corrected every few years by a professional revaluation. Apart from all this, it may not be necessary to revalue every month—every quarter, or half-year, may be enough to ensure reasonable accuracy.

The amount of an upward revaluation is debited to the relevant Valuation Adjustment Account and credited to Realizable Cost Savings, whence it is transferred to Fixed Assets Revaluation Reserve. The accumulated depreciation is then uplifted proportionately, by crediting the Depreciation Provision Adjustment Account and debiting Realizable Cost Savings, whence the amount is transferred to the debit of the Revaluation Reserve. The Depreciation Account for the month or longer period is debited, for each class of assets, with depreciation calculated on a historical-cost basis, and a Depreciation Adjustment Account with an additional charge to bring it up to a period-end replacement-cost basis, or a mean for the period (particularly if it is longer than one month). The respective credits are made in the Depreciation Provision, and Depreciation Provision Adjustment, Accounts. Transfers are then made from Depreciation, and Depreciation Adjustment, to Work In Progress and its Valuation Adjustment Account, or directly to Profit and Loss Account; in the latter case the element of uplift to replacement-cost basis should pass through the Realized Cost Savings Account. If replacement cost continues to rise the total amount charged to revenue over the working life of a fixed asset, plus its proceeds of sale if any, will not equal its final replacement price, and some accountants argue that the deficiency should be made up out of revenue at each revaluation. Against this it may be argued that the replacement costs of the asset's various services have been properly priced as they were rendered, and that the assets in which the depreciation provisions have been reinvested should have shown some growth in value in the meantime. In any case a progressive firm seldom, if ever, replaces any fixed asset with a precisely similar one, and this must be allowed for as the calculations proceed, by using the prices of assets calculated to render equivalent services. With obsolescent assets, not to be replaced, the two adjustment account balances may have to be written *down*, to the asset's opportunity cost (higher of use value or exchange value) as the net difference. Such a write-down should be charged to profit and loss account, not to the revaluation reserve, as it is the result of technological change, not of price movements as such.

On disposal of a fixed asset, the historical cost, and the accumulated depreciation based thereon, are transferred to the debit and credit sides of a Disposal of Fixed Assets Account, which is credited with the sale proceeds if any, and the surplus or deficit transferred to profit and loss account. The relevant portions of the balances on the Fixed Assets Valuation Adjustment, and Depreciation Provision Adjustment, Accounts are transferred to the debit and credit of a Disposal of Fixed Assets Adjustment Account, and the difference written off separately to profit and loss account.

From the accounts produced by the above operations are compiled a trading account and profit and loss account, showing current operational profit plus realized capital gains, or minus realized capital losses, on a replacement-cost basis. In the opening and closing balance sheets all assets will be valued at replacement cost (depreciated where necessary), and the difference between opening and closing equity, after allowing for capital introduced and withdrawn, will be the business profit—the figure shown by the profit and loss account, plus realizable cost savings, as represented by the changes on the Fixed Assets, and Inventory, Revaluation Reserves. In the books, however, the realizable, and realized, cost savings have both been highlighted in special accounts, and memorandum accounts can be prepared on a historical-cost basis, if desired. This can be done for taxation purposes, and in the case of companies the replacement-cost profit and loss account will be adjusted by adding back the realized cost savings element, so as to show the base upon which corporation tax is computed, and deducting it again to show the distributable profit after tax. In companies, too, the element of deferred corporation tax in the revaluation reserves (past realizable cost savings) should be transferred (via the Realizable Cost Savings Account) to the credit of a Deferred Taxation Account (see further in Chapter 12, sub-section **12.3.2**), and released into the profit and loss account when realized cost savings accrue, as an offset to corporation tax payable on historical-cost-based profits. This adjustment is shown in *Example 1* for reference, though the reader is unlikely to understand it fully before he has read Chapter 12.[7]

7.2.3 Replacement-cost accounting illustrated

To consolidate and clarify the explanations in sub-section **7.2.2**, there is now exhibited a set of accounts for an imaginary manufacturing company for one month, in which historical costs are adjusted to a replacement-cost basis. The system is based on that of the Philips organization[8] (which, however, uses standard costing as a basis), and incorporates some ideas from Edwards and Bell, whose proposed layout is rather different, and less easily adapted to British accounting requirements. The question of adjustments for movements in the general price level is deferred to section **7.3**.

Example 1 Below are shown the accounts, on a replacement-cost basis, of Modern Manufacturers Ltd, a single-product company, for the first month of 19.1. In the case of raw materials and finished goods, the FIFO system is used for historical cost, and the convention is to revalue opening stocks to the average replacement cost for the month, and additions to the closing replacement cost (also opening stock, so far as still on hand). Completed work is transferred to finished goods stock at replacement cost of production for the current month. Corporation tax is at 52 per cent; it is assumed that capital allowances coincide with historical-cost depreciation in the books. Replacement costs of inventories were as follows.

	Raw materials (per ton)	Work in progress (per unit)	Finished goods (per unit)
1 Jan 19.1	£10.00	£15.00	£15.00
Average for Jan 19.1	£10.50	£16.20	£16.20
31 Jan 19.1	£10.70	£16.20	£16.20

Depreciation is at the rate of 1½ per cent per month on cost of fixed assets, adjusted to month-end replacement-cost basis. During the month a fixed asset was disposed of for £240; its historical and replacement costs were respectively £1,000 and £1,250, and the relevant depreciation provisions were £800 and £1,000.

---

[7] The Philips group, as from 1971, has begun to write back deferred taxation, on fixed assets revaluations, to profit and loss account, *pari passu* with the provision of depreciation on the write-up, as well as to make a similar adjustment in respect of realized cost savings on stocks.

[8] See, e.g.: Holmes, G. Replacement Value Accounting, *Accountancy,* March 1972.

Modern Manufacturers Limited

Balance Sheet, 1 January 19.1

	£	£		£	£
Share Capital		6,000	*Fixed Assets*		
			Valuation	5,000	
			Depreciation	2,000	
					3,000
Reserves					
Fixed assets revaluation reserve	600				
Inventory revaluation reserve	120		*Net Current Assets*		
Retained profit	300		Inventory—		
		1,020	Raw materials	600	
			Work in progress	400	
			Finished goods	3,000	
		7,020		4,000	
			Net monetary assets	700	
Deferred Taxation		480			4,700
Corporation Tax		200			
		£7,700			£7,700

Share Capital

			19.1		£
			Jan 1	Balance b/d	6,000

Fixed Assets Revaluation Reserve

19.1		£	19.1		£
Jan 31	Balance c/d	744	Jan 1	Balance b/d	600
			Jan 31	Realizable cost savings	144
		£744			£744
			19.1		
			Feb 1	Balance b/d	744

Inventory Revaluation Reserve

19.1		£	19.1		£
Jan 1	Balance c/d	254	Jan 1	Balance b/d	120
			Jan 31	Realizable cost savings	134
		£254			£254
			19.1		
			Feb 1	Balance b/d	254

Retained Profit

19.1		£	19.1		£
Jan 31	Balance c/d	372	Jan 1	Balance b/d	300
			Jan 31	Profit and loss a/c	72
		£372			£372
			19.1		
			Feb 1	Balance b/d	372

Deferred Taxation

19.1		£	19.1		£
Jan 31	Profit and loss a/c	86	Jan 1	Balance b/d	480
Jan 31	do	26	Jan 31	Realizable cost savings	302
Jan 31	Balance c/d	670			
		£782			£782
			19.1		
			Feb 1	Balance b/d	670

Corporation Tax

19.1		£	19.1		£
Jan 31	Balance c/d	390	Jan 1	Balance b/d	200
			Jan 31	Profit and loss a/c	190
		£390			£390
			19.1		
			Feb 1	Balance b/d	390

Fixed Assets

19.1		£	19.1		£
Jan 1	Balance b/d	4,000	Jan 1	Disposal of fixed assets	1,000
			Jan 31	Balance c/d	3,000
		£4,000			£4,000
19.1					
Feb 1	Balance b/d	3,000			

Depreciation Provision

19.1		£	19.1		£
Jan 1	Disposal of fixed assets	800	Jan 1	Balance b/d	1,600
Jan 31	Balance c/d	845	Jan 31	Depreciation	45
		£1,645			£1,645
			19.1		
			Feb 1	Balance b/d	845

Fixed Assets Valuation Adjustment

19.1		£	19.1		£
Jan 1	Balance b/d	1,000	Jan 1	Disposal of fixed assets adjustment	250
Jan 31	Realizable cost savings	400	Jan 31	Balance c/d	1,150
		£1,400			£1,400
19.1					
Feb 1	Balance b/d	1,150			

Depreciation Provision Adjustment

19.1		£	19.1		£
Jan 1	Disposal of fixed assets adjustment	200	Jan 1	Balance b/d	400
Jan 31	Balance c/d	317	Jan 31	Realizable cost savings	100
			Jan 31	Depreciation adjustment	17
		£517			£517
			19.1		
			Feb 1	Balance b/d	317

Raw Materials Stock

19.1		£	19.1		£
Jan 1	Balance b/d— 60 x £9.00	540	Jan 31	Work in progress— 60 x £9.00	540
Jan 31	Net monetary assets— 50 x £10.50	525		10 x £10.50	105
			Jan 31	Balance c/d— 40 x £10.50	420
		£1,065			£1,065
19.1					
Feb 1	Balance b/d— 40 x £10.50	420			

Raw Materials Stock Valuation Adjustment

19.1		£	19.1		£
Jan 1	Balance b/d— 60 x £1.00	60	Jan 31	Work in progress valuation adjustment— 60 x £1.50	90
Jan 31	Realizable cost savings— 60 x £0.50	30		10 x £0.20	2
	50 x £0.20	10	Jan 31	Balance c/d— 40 x £0.20	8
		£100			£100
19.1					
Feb 1	Balance b/d— 40 x £0.20	8			

Work In Progress

19.1		£	19.1		£
Jan 1	Balance b/d	380	Jan 31	Finished goods stock— 80 x £15.00	1,200
Jan 31	Raw materials stock	645	Jan 31	Balance c/d	390
Jan 31	Wages	400			
Jan 31	Works overheads	120			
Jan 31	Depreciation	45			
		£1,590			£1,590
19.1					
Feb 1	Balance b/d	390			

Work In Progress Valuation Adjustment

19.1		£	19.1		£
Jan 1	Balance b/d	20	Jan 31	Finished goods stock	
Jan 31	Raw materials stock			valuation adjustment—	
	valuation adjustment	92		80 × £1.20	96
Jan 31	Depreciation adjustment	17	Jan 31	Balance c/d	33
		£129			£129
19.1					
Feb 1	Balance b/d	33			

Finished Goods Stock

19.1		£	19.1		£
Jan 1	Balance b/d—		Jan 31	Cost of sales—	
	200 × £14.00	2,800		75 × £14.00	1,050
Jan 31	Work in progress—		Jan 31	Balance c/d—	
	80 × £15.00	1,200		125 × £14.00	1,750
				80 × £15.00	1,200
		£4,000			£4,000
19.1					
Feb 1	Balance b/d—				
	125 × £14.00	1,750			
	80 × £15.00	1,200			

Finished Goods Stock Valuation Adjustment

19.1		£	19.1		£
Jan 1	Balance b/d—		Jan 31	Realized cost savings—	
	200 × £1.00	200		75 × £2.20	165
Jan 31	Work in progress		Jan 31	Balance c/d—	
	valuation adjustment—			125 × £2.20	275
	80 × £1.20	96		80 × £1.20	96
Jan 31	Realizable cost savings—				
	200 × £1.20	240			
		£536			£536
19.1					
Feb 1	Balance b/d—				
	125 × £2.20	275			
	80 × £1.20	96			

Net Monetary Assets

19.1		£	19.1		£
Jan 1	Balance b/d	700	Jan 31	Raw materials stock	525
Jan 31	Sales	1,575	Jan 31	Wages	400
Jan 31	Disposal of fixed assets	240	Jan 31	Works overheads	120
			Jan 31	General overheads	200
			Jan 31	Balance c/d	1,270
		£2,515			£2,515
19.1					
Feb 1	Balance b/d	1,270			

Realizable Cost Savings

19.1		£	19.1		£
Jan 31	Depreciation provision adjustment	100	Jan 31	Fixed assets valuation adjustment	400
Jan 31	Fixed assets valuation reserve	144	Jan 31	Raw materials stock valuation adjustment	40
Jan 31	Inventory revaluation reserve	134	Jan 31	Finished goods stock valuation adjustment	240
Jan 31	Deferred taxation	302			
		£680			£680

Realized Cost Savings

19.1		£	19.1		£
Jan 31	Finished goods stock valuation adjustment	165	Jan 31	Cost of sales	165

Wages

19.1		£	19.1		£
Jan 31	Net monetary assets	400	Jan 31	Work in progress	400

Works Overheads

19.1		£	19.1		£
Jan 31	Net monetary assets	120	Jan 31	Work in progress	120

General Overheads

19.1		£	19.1		£
Jan 31	Net monetary assets	200	Jan 31	Profit and loss a/c	200

Depreciation

19.1		£	19.1		£
Jan 31	Depreciation provision	45	Jan 31	Work in progress	45

Depreciation Adjustment

19.1		£	19.1		£
Jan 31	Depreciation provision adjustment	17	Jan 31	Work in progress valuation adjustment	17

Sales

19.1		£	19.1		£
Jan 31	Trading a/c	1,575	Jan 31	Net monetary assets	1,575

Cost of Sales

19.1		£	19.1		£
Jan 31	Finished goods stock	1,050	Jan 31	Trading a/c	1,215
Jan 31	Realized cost savings	165			
		£1,215			£1,215

Disposal of Fixed Assets

19.1		£	19.1		£
Jan 1	Fixed assets	1,000	Jan 1	Depreciation provision	800
Jan 31	Profit and loss a/c	40	Jan 31	Net monetary assets	240
		£1,040			£1,040

Disposal of Fixed Assets Adjustment

19.1		£	19.1		£
Jan 1	Fixed assets valuation adjustment	250	Jan 1	Depreciation provision adjustment	200
			Jan 31	Profit and loss a/c	50
		£250			£250

Trading Account for the Month of January 19.1

	£		£
Cost of sales (at replacement cost)	1,215	Sales	1,575
Current gross profit	360		
	£1,575		£1,575

Profit and Loss Account for the Month of January 19.1

	£		£
General overheads	200	Current gross profit	360
Current operating profit	160		
	£360		£360
Deficit on disposal of fixed assets (at replacement cost)	10	Current operating profit	160
Current net profit	150		
	£160		£160
Conventional net profit before taxation	365	Current net profit	150
		Realized cost savings	165
		Excess of surplus on disposal of fixed assets (at historical cost) over deficit on disposal (at replacement cost)	50
	£365		£365

Corporation tax (52 per cent)	190	Conventional net profit before	
Conventional net profit after		taxation	365
taxation	175		
	£365		£365

Realized cost savings	165	Conventional net profit after	
Excess of surplus on disposal of		taxation	175
fixed assets (at historical cost)		Deferred taxation now assessed—	
over deficit on disposal (at		On realized cost savings	86
replacement cost)	50	On excess of surplus on disposal	
Retained profit	72	of fixed assets over deficit, as	
		aforesaid	26
	£287		£287

Balance Sheet, 31 January 19.1

	£	£		£	£
Share Capital		6,000	**Fixed Assets**		
			Valuation	4,150	
			Depreciation	1,162	
					2,988
Reserves					
Fixed assets revaluation					
reserve	744				
Inventory revaluation			**Net Current Assets**		
reserve	254		Inventory—		
Retained profit	372		Raw materials	428	
	—	1,370	Work in progress	423	
		—	Finished goods	3,321	
		7,370		——	
Deferred Taxation		670		4,172	
			Net monetary assets	1,270	
				——	5,442
Corporation Tax		390			
		£8,430			£8,430

A comparison of the two balance sheets reveals a growth in equity of £(7,370 − 7,020) = £350, with no capital introduced or withdrawn. This is made up as follows:

	£	£
Current operating profit		160
Deficit on disposal of fixed assets (at replacement cost)		(10)
Realizable cost savings		580
Business profit before taxation		730
Less Corporation tax—		
Current, on accounting profit (£365)		190
Deferred, on realizable cost savings	£302	
Less Written back, on realized cost savings, etc. (£215)	112	
	—	190
		—
		380
Business profit after taxation		£350

This is £175 more than the conventional net profit after taxation (coinc
dentally, twice as much), because of the allowance for growth in replacement cost
of assets held over the month. The addition to retained profit, though, is only £72,
as this is all that is distributable (on the assumptions made), if the physical capital
of the business is to be maintained. Conventional accounts would show a net profit
after taxation of £175, with no indication that £103 of it could not prudently be
distributed to shareholders.

7.2.4 Further points on replacement-cost accounting

Other aspects of replacement-cost accounting may be quickly dealt with, and need
not be illustrated. *Quoted investments* are naturally valued at market price at all
balancing dates, and the net gain or loss over any period credited or debited to an
Investments Revaluation Reserve, and to Deferred Taxation Account, in due
proportions. As to *long-term fixed-interest borrowings,* such as debentures of a
company, where these are quoted on the stock exchange the price movements over
time (ignoring minor day-to-day fluctuations) reflect changes in the company's cost
of borrowing—a rise in price denoting a proportionate fall in the rate of interest
payable, and vice versa. It is therefore advocated by many (including Edwards and
Bell) that when the price of a company's debentures rises the company is the loser,
since by committing itself to the loan when prices were lower (and interest rates
higher) it has forgone the chance to borrow a larger amount now, for the same
burden of interest, or the same amount for a lesser interest charge. It follows that
the difference between the ending and beginning market values of the debentures
ought to be credited to a Debenture Valuation Adjustment Account (a provision,
not a reserve—i.e. included in liabilities, not in equity), and debited to profit and
loss account; and the reverse for a fall in the price (the company has gained by
having had the money when rates of interest were lower, and can now write back to
equity part of the provision raised before). Should market value fall below book
value, the debenture valuation adjustment account will have a debit balance, and
should be deducted inset from the debentures.

    Intangible assets raise many problems in relation to the finding of a
replacement cost, or an acceptable surrogate therefor. Specific intangibles, such as
research and development expenditure and patents, tend to be unique, and
replacement cost has no meaning. It is best, perhaps, to estimate the maximum
price which the firm would pay now to have the advantages of the assets in
question, and this means, in effect, the opportunity cost—normally the present
value of expected cash flows attributable to the intangibles in the future. Goodwill,
if acquired in the past at a price still not wholly written off, is perhaps most
correctly left alone, and not adjusted up or down to any supposed opportunity
cost. Subjective goodwill should, by the same token, be ignored as in historical-cost
accounting.

Despite the manifest virtues of replacement-cost accounting, the only applications of it which are widespread in the U.K. consist in the making, from about 1960
onwards, of additional depreciation charges (credited to a fixed assets replacement
reserve), or of periodic (not annual) revaluations of long-lived physical assets to a
replacement-cost basis—or in the case of land to a realizable-value basis—with
countervailing credits to a revaluation reserve and to deferred taxation account, in
proper proportions. Either practice is better than nothing at all, but inadequate in

that inventories are ignored, despite their major importance in most industrial and commercial enterprises—though FIFO valuation brings them nearer to replacement cost than any other conventional method. The depreciation charges after the revaluation are adjusted upwards in proportion, and make the reported profit somewhat more realistic, but tend to lag behind changes in replacement cost. It is still necessary, for reasons of financial prudence, to restrain dividends well within the accounting profits, to avoid depleting working capital in a time of generally rising input prices. General inflation makes the problems worse, and it is to this matter that attention must now be given.

7.3 Current purchasing power accounting

The principles of adjusting historical-cost accounts so as to allow for movements in a country's general price level were worked out in the U.S.A. by Henry W. Sweeney in 1936.[9] The aftermath of the depression, and the insistence on strict historical-cost accounting by the newly-established SEC, made American accountants unreceptive to such ideas, and Sweeney's book attracted little attention. After the Second World War replacement-cost accounting was seen as the answer to the problems of adjusting for inflation; but its complexity, and the unsympathetic attitude of the tax authorities, militated against its widespread adoption, even in the Netherlands where its following was strongest. Sweeney's *Stabilized Accounting* was reissued in 1964, and it was about then that current purchasing power accounting began to be seen as a simpler solution to the enigma. After one or two preliminary studies, the ASSC in the U.K. brought out its ED8 in 1973, and (despite the setting-up of the Sandilands Committee) its Provisional SSAP No. 7: *Accounting for changes in the purchasing power of money* in 1974. The rest of section 7.3 is mainly based on the latter.

The basic conception is the restatement of the final accounts of an entity in terms of the purchasing power of money as at the end of the accounting period. This causes less disturbance than replacement-cost accounting, since it is based on conventional books of account; there is no need for the array of additional adjustment accounts, continually posted up during the year, which is required by a fully developed system such as the (imaginary) one described in section 7.2. Ordinary historical-cost final accounts are produced from the conventional books, and price-level-adjusted accounts constructed from the former as supplementary statements giving additional information to the investor, for whose benefit the technique is principally designed. Initiation of the system involves much time-consuming research and calculation, especially in a large and complex enterprise, but after the first year the current price level accounts can be produced quite easily. It is this relative simplicity which commends the method to the manager and the accountant, and ought to make it easier to 'sell' to the industrial and commercial world than the much more complicated alternative of replacement-cost accounting—despite the latter's greater subtlety and closer attention to the needs of management for continuous, relevant and up-to-date information about the financing requirements of the business. In fact, a fully developed replacement-cost system such as that of the Philips organization does incorporate adjustments to allow for general price level changes, and this aspect of the matter is considered later.

[9]Sweeney, H.W. *Stabilized Accounting,* 1st edition Harper & Bros., 1936; 2nd edition Holt, Rinehart & Winston, 1964.

7.3.1 Provisional Statement of Standard Accounting Practice No. 7 (1974): Accounting for changes in the purchasing power of money

Beside laying down standard practice in presenting current purchasing power (CPP) statements as part of the published accounts of a company (see Chapter 14, sub-section **14.6.4**), PSSAP No. 7 offers guidance on their preparation. In this it is supplemented by *Accounting for Inflation: A working guide to the accounting procedures,* a book in two parts *(Part 1: Text; Part 2: Tables)* published in 1973 under the auspices of the Institute of Chartered Accountants in England and Wales.[10] The main points of the Statement are now summarized.

PSSAP No. 7 (in Part 1—Explanatory Note) makes it clear that the intention is not to abandon historical-cost accounting, nor to adopt replacement-cost methods, but to provide supplementary accounting statements in which all historical costs are converted to their current purchasing power equivalents, by the application of a suitable index of general price level changes. These supplementary accounts, though recommended for all companies, are initially to be regarded as standard practice only for the annual accounts of companies listed on a British or Irish stock exchange. Later, as experience is gained, the practice may be extended to other financial statements, such as interim accounts, preliminary announcements of figures for the year, ten year summaries, profit forecasts, and prospectuses (see Chapters 11 to 15).

The historical cost convention has the advantages that figures are derived from factual monetary transactions, and that its use helps to limit the number of matters within the accounts which are subject to the exercise of judgement. These advantages, are however, impaired by the incidence of significant change in the purchasing power of money over a period of years, and the accelerated inflation of recent years makes the problem of pressing importance. Subjective mental adjustments by readers of annual accounts do not meet the case, as they can be no more than crude estimates, vitiated by lack of, or failure to appreciate, the relevant data on inflation and its effects on a particular company. Only the directors are in a position to provide suitable information to enable users of accounts to understand the effects of inflation on the results and financial position.

The main requirements of the PSSAP are:

a   that companies will continue to keep their records, and present their basic annual accounts, in historical pounds (as of the time of each transaction or revaluation);

b   that in addition all listed companies should present to their shareholders a *supplementary statement* in terms of the value of the pound at the end of the relevant accounting period;

c   that the conversion of 'basic' to 'supplementary' figures should be by means of a general index of the purchasing power of the pound; and

d   that the directors should provide, in a note to the supplementary statement, an explanation of the basis on which it has been prepared, and that it is desirable that directors should comment on the significance of the figures.

---

[10]*Accounting for Inflation: A working guide to the accounting procedures,* The Trustees of Chartered Accountants' Trust for Education and Research of The Institute of Chartered Accountants in England and Wales, 1973.

The form of the supplementary statement is a matter for the directors to decide, provided that they conform to the standard. The amount of detail is not specified, but the standard itself makes it clear that it is not necessary to provide a converted figure for every item in the basic accounts. The form in *Example 2* (suc-section **7.3.2**) follows the examples in *Accounting for Inflation*, and in Appendix 2 to PSSAP No. 7.

In the conversion process a distinction is made between historical figures for monetary, and non-monetary, items. *Monetary items* are assets, liabilities, or capital whose amounts are fixed by contract or statute in terms of numbers of pounds, regardless of changes in the purchasing power of the pound (e.g. cash, debtors, creditors, and loan capital). The year-end values are not adjusted for inflation, since the fixed money amounts are unaltered by it; but a calculation is made of the loss (or gain) through holding net monetary assets (or being subject to net monetary liabilities) in a period of inflation, and the CPP accounts are adjusted for this amount. *Non-monetary items* are all items which are not monetary items (e.g. stock, plant and buildings), with the exception of the *total equity interest* (i.e. share capital, reserves, and retained profits). The historical amounts of non-monetary items are adjusted for changes in the *general* price level, between acquisition and the end of the year under review, on the (very heroic) assumption that their prices have moved, on average, in step with the general level; no notice is taken of movements in the replacement cost or realizable value of the actual assets. The converted figures must, however, be compared in each category with net realizable value in the case of current assets, and with 'value to the business' (presumably the lower of replacement cost and opportunity cost) in the case of fixed assets, and the lower of the two amounts (converted historical cost or net realizable value, etc.) is to be used in the supplementary statement. It may also be necessary to consider the adequacy of the depreciation charge on freehold and long leasehold properties, and whether to include in the deferred taxation account on the supplementary balance sheet an amount for corporation tax on any chargeable gain which would arise if the assets were sold at the balance sheet date at the amount shown in the supplementary statement. Finally, the total equity interest is neither a monetary nor a non-monetary item; it is a mixed figure, being the algebraic total, with sign reversed, of converted non-monetary assets and unconverted monetary assets and liabilities.

PSSAP No. 7 points out that, in applying the above tests and during the whole process of conversion, it is important to balance the effort involved against the materiality of the figures concerned. The supplementary CPP statement can be no more than an approximation, and it is pointless to strive for over-elaborate precision. With overseas subsidiaries and associated companies there may be particular difficulties in obtaining the information necessary to produce the supplementary statements; in such cases directors will have to weigh the materiality of the items concerned against the cost of obtaining the necessary information. The reasons for the treatment adopted, and the magnitude of the items involved, should be disclosed in a note to the supplementary statements.

The choice of a suitable index of changes in the general purchasing power of the pound is something of a problem. The most relevant indices are those measuring changes in the price level of goods and services for personal consumption, as being the ones of most interest to shareholders as distinct from business managers. In the U.K. there are two strong candidates—the *Consumers' Expenditure Deflator* (CED) (formerly the Consumer Price Index), and the *General Index of Retail*

Prices (RPI). The CED is broader in its coverage, and at first sight more appropriate in this context; but it has the great drawback of appearing only once a year, in March as an average for the previous calendar year. The RPI covers a narrower range of goods and services, but is published monthly, with an average for the previous calendar year. Hence ED8 proposed the CED as the basis of conversion from historical to year-end pounds, with the RPI as a monthly interpolator; but PSSAP No. 7 adopts the simpler device of using the RPI directly—on the ground that greater ease of calculation outweighs a slight loss of precision. The RPI began only in January 1962; for the years 1939–61 the CED is to be used, and for 1914–38 (if relevant) the Ministry of Labour Cost of Living Index. In PSSAP No. 7, Appendix 4, all these indices have been spliced together to form a continuous series of annual averages, 1914–73 (excepting the war years 1939–45), with a figure for December 1973—all to the base January 1974 = 100.[11] From January 1974 the RPI number is published in the *Monthly Digest of Statistics* (HMSO) and in *Trade and Industry* (HMSO for the Departments of Trade and Industry). Monthly figures and annual averages from January 1954 appear also at intervals in *Accountancy,* beginning with the issue for November 1974. The latest known figure as this edition goes to press is for April 1975. (See sub-section 7.3.2). In the Republic of Ireland the quarterly *Consumer Price Index* (CPI) is to be used for conversion of figures; a continuous series has been constructed from 1922 to date, to the base January 1974 = 100. Where an Irish company's year-end falls between two index dates, an approximate relative for the year-end must be computed by interpolation or extrapolation.

The actual Standard Accounting Practice is summarized in Chapter 14, sub-section **14.6.4**, where its requirements as to published information are stressed. Here it is necessary to explain more fully the process of constructing a supplementary CPP statement from conventional published accounts, utilizing information available to the directors but not necessarily disclosed to shareholders.

7.3.2 Preparation of CPP supplementary statements

On inception of a system of CPP supplementary statements it is necessary to take the *opening balance sheet* of the first year (the closing one of the previous year) and establish the ages of all non-monetary items—fixed assets, stocks, investments in ordinary shares, and deferred taxation provisions (deferral method—see Chapter 12, sub-section **12.3.2**). The accountant must find out when each item was acquired and for what price (or when it was last revalued) and, where relevant, how much depreciation has been provided on each item. All non-monetary items must then be converted to current purchasing power equivalents as at the date of the balance sheet, and updated thence to the *end* of the accounting year; this is done in practice in one operation, by multiplying each item by the year-end RPI number and dividing by that for the date of acquisition. All monetary items (loans, creditors, debtors, fixed-interest investment, and cash), are left unconverted as at the balance sheet date, but updated to the year-end, by multiplying by the year-end RPI number and dividing by the beginning-of-year number. Total equity interest (share capital and reserves) is not converted or updated directly, but

---

[11]For a monthly series, with annual averages, see P.D. Reynolds, *United Kingdom Indices and Inflation Factors (1914 to 1974)* (Accountants Digest No. 8), Institute of Chartered Accountants in England and Wales, 1974.

entered as the balance of the other items. The figures thus derived are used as corresponding figures in the published CPP balance sheet as at the year-end. In the second and subsequent years after installation of the system this part of the work is greatly eased; all the accountant needs to do is to take the previous year's CPP balance sheet and update all the figures (including equity) by one year.

The *CPP closing balance sheet* for the year is similarly prepared, only the non-monetary items being converted to year-end CPP equivalents; in 'ageing' the fixed assets and depreciation provisions, information gathered for the opening balance sheet conversion and updating may be utilized. Monetary items are unchanged, and total equity interest is found by difference. Using the 'net change method', it is possible to arrive at a CPP net profit (or loss) for the year, by noting the difference between opening and closing CPP equity interest and adding back the CPP equivalent of dividends, while deducting (adding) the CPP equivalent of capital raised (redeemed) during the year. It is better, however, to prepare a *CPP profit and loss account* for the year, whose retained profit agrees with the change in total equity interest after allowance for capital changes.

All conversions and updatings are carried out by multiplying the amount in historical pounds by the RPI index number for the year-end, and dividing by the number for the (known or estimated) date of the item. Thus, if at the year-end the index number was 100, and at the date of purchase of an asset for £100,000 it was 80, then the CPP equivalent of the historical £100,000 (which may be called £H100,000) is £100,000 x 100/80 = £125,000 (or, by this convention, £C125,000). Where an item is some years old—say, earlier than the previous year—it is usually sufficient to divide by the RPI number for the 'middle' month of the relevant accounting year; for anything more recent it is better to use the index number for the appropriate month.

With *fixed assets,* the depreciation provisions, and the year's depreciation charges, are 'aged' according to the ages of the corresponding assets, so that the net book values are computed consistently. Thus, if a machine was bought four years ago (RPI mid-year number 80) for £100,000, and it has been depreciated at 10 per cent per annum straight line (making the beginning-of-year provision £40,000), both figures, and the current year's charge (£10,000), are brought to end-of-year CPP equivalents (closing RPI number assumed 100) by applying the factor 100/80. Hence, for the cost, £H100,000 x 100/80 = £C125,000; for the closing depreciation provision, £H50,000 x 100/80 = £C62,500; and for the year's charge, £H10,000 x 100/80 = £C12,500. *Inventories* are aged according to the mid-point of the period over which they are deemed to have accumulated; if a stock of goods is considered to represent four months' consumption or sales, it is treated as two months old at the year-end—or 14 months in the case of the opening inventory. *Cash flow items* (turnover, purchases, overheads, etc.) in the profit and loss account are normally regarded as occurring, on average, at the mid-point of the accounting year; if they are known to vary seasonally, though, it may be more realistic to use a weighted average—e.g. by using the RPI average for the year, instead of the index number for the middle month, as the denominator.

The *loss on holding net monetary assets* (or *gains on being subject to net monetary liabilities*) in a period of rising prices (vice versa in a period of falling prices) is computed separately and passed through the CPP profit and loss account. The closing net balance (unchanged) is compared with the total of net opening balance and net cash flow (both updated), and the difference recorded as an inflation loss (*Dr.*) or gain (*Cr.*), as appropriate. Thus, if the RPI numbers for the beginning, middle, and end of the year are 100, 110, and 120, the opening net monetary assets are £50,000, the net cash flows (positive, and assumed even over the year) £30,000, and the closing net monetary assets (therefore) £80,000, the calculation proceeds as follows:

	£H	Updating Factors	£C
Opening net monetary assets	50,000	120/100	60,000
Net cash flows (positive)	30,000	120/110	32,727
	80,000		92,727
Closing net monetary assets	80,000	120/120	80,000
Loss on holding net monetary assets			£12,727

Had the company started with net monetary *liabilities* of £50,000 and ended with them reduced to £20,000, the calculation would have been:

	£H	Updating Factors	£C
Opening net monetary liabilities	(50,000)	120/100	(60,000)
Net cash flows (positive)	30,000	120/110	32,727
	(20,000)		(27,273)
Closing net monetary liabilities	(20,000)	120/120	(20,000)
Gain on being subject to net monetary liabilities			(£7,273)

Example 2 The Withit Trading Co. Ltd, whose accounting date is 30 June, decides as from 1 July 1973 to comply with PSSAP No. 7. The historical balance sheet as at that date, the adjustments required (on stated assumptions), and the CPP draft balance sheet (in pounds of 30 June 1974 purchasing power), are shown below. Fixed assets and unquoted (equity) investments were acquired mid-year (or evenly over the year) as indicated, and stock during the last four months of the year.

Conversion or Updating Factors for preparing CPP Accounts

Year		ASSC Price Index, based on General Index of Retail Prices (January 1974 = 100)	Conversion or Updating Factors (108.7/ASSC index number)
1968	December	66.9	1.625
1969	December	70.1	1.551
1970	December	75.6	1.438
1971	December	82.4	1.319
1972	June	85.3	1.239
	December	88.7	1.225
1973	April	92.1	1.180
	June	93.3	1.165
	December	98.1	1.108
1974	April	106.1	1.025
	June	108.7	1.000

Withit Trading Company Ltd.
Conventional Balance Sheet, 30 June 1973

	£	£		Cost £	Depreciation £	£
Share Capital			*Fixed Assets*			
Ordinary shares		500,000	Sundries	640,000	370,000	270,000
Reserves			*Unquoted Investments,*			
Share premium			at cost			150,000
account	50,000					
Profit and loss			*Current Assets*			
account	80,000		Stock	400,000		
		130,000	Debtors	240,000		
		630,000	Quoted investments	30,000		
			(market value £32,000)			
12 per cent Debentures		200,000	Bank and cash			
			balances	50,000		
*Deferred Taxation**		7,143				720,000
Corporation Tax—						
Current Year		40,000				
Current Liabilities						
Creditors	185,000					
Corporation tax—						
previous year	35,000					
Proposed dividend	30,000					
ACT on proposed						
dividend*	12,857					
		262,857				
		£1,140,000				£1,140,000

*For an explanation of these items, see Chapter 12, sub-section **12.3.2**; on a first reading the adjustments may be taken on trust, and looked at again when Chapter 12 has been covered. For the present purpose, deferred taxation (by the so-called 'deferral method', as assumed here) is a non-monetary item, except for the offset of ACT (advance corporation tax) on proposed dividend (the double entry counterpart of the current liability therefore), which is monetary.*

Conversion/Updating of Fixed Assets, 30 June 1973 (Depreciation 20 per cent per annum, straight line)

	Historical £'s			30 June 1974 £'s	
Year ended 30 June	Cost £	Depreciation to 30 June 1973 £	Conversion/ Updating Factors	Cost £	Depreciation to 30 June 1973 £
1969	180,000	170,000	1.625	292,500	276,250
1970	120,000	90,000	1.551	186,120	139,590
1971	90,000	50,000	1.438	129,420	71,900
1972	50,000	20,000	1.319	65,950	26,380
1973	200,000	40,000	1.225	245,000	49,000
	£640,000	£370,000		£918,990	£563,120

Conversion/Updating of Balance Sheet, 30 June 1973

Item	Year	Historical £'s £	Conversion/ Updating £	30 June 1974 £'s £
Fixed Assets				
Cost	See above	640,000	Various	918,990
Depreciation	do	(370,000)	do	(563,120)
		270,000		355,870
Unquoted Investments	1968 December	150,000	1.625	243,750
Current Assets				
Stock	1973 April	400,000	1.180	472,000
Debtors	1973 June	240,000	1.165	279,600
Quoted investments (market value £32,000)	1973 June	30,000	1.165	34,950
Bank and cash balances	1973 June	50,000	1.165	58,250
		720,000		844,800
Less Current Liabilities				
Creditors	1973 June	185,000	1.165	215,525
Corporation tax— previous year	1973 June	35,000	1.165	40,775
Proposed dividend	1973 June	30,000	1.165	34,950
ACT on proposed dividend	1973 June	12,857	1.165	14,978
		262,857		306,228
Net Current Assets		457,143		538,572
Total Net Assets		£877,143		£1,138,192
12% Debentures	1973 June	200,000	1.165	233,000
Deferred Taxation				
Tax 30.6.1972	1972 June	8,000	1.239	9,912
Tax 30.6.1973	1973 June	12,000	1.165	13,980
		20,000		23,892
Less ACT recoverable	1973 June	12,857	1.165	14,978
		7,143		8,914
Corporation Tax— Current Year	1973 June	40,000	1.165	46,600
Total Non-Current Liabilities		£247,143		£288,514
Total Equity Interest		£630,000		£849,678

Withit Trading Company Ltd
*Conventional Trading and Profit and Loss Accounts (unpublished) for the Year ended
30 June 1974*

	£	£		£	£
Opening stock		400,000	Sales		2,000,000
Purchases		1,600,000			
		2,000,000			
Less Closing stock		600,000			
Cost of Sales		1,400,000			
Gross profit		600,000			
		£2,000,000			£2,000,000
General overheads		314,000	Gross profit		600,000
Depreciation	106,000		Income from		
Less Surplus on disposal of			investments—		
fixed assets	10,000		Unquoted	27,000	
		96,000	Quoted	3,000	30,000
Provision to reduce quoted					
investments to market value		5,000			
Interest on 12% debentures		24,000			
		439,000			
Net profit before taxation		191,000			
		£630,000			£630,000
Corporation tax		90,000	Net profit before		
Net Profit after taxation		101,000	taxation		191,000
		£191,000			£191,000
Dividends—			Net profit after		
Paid	30,000		taxation		101,000
Proposed	30,000		Balance brought		
		60,000	forward from		
Balance carried forward to			previous year		80,000
next year		121,000			
		£181,000			£181,000

Conversion of Trading and Profit and Loss Accounts for the Year ended 30 June 1974

	Historical £'s			30 June 1974 £'s	
	£	£	Conversion Factors	£	£
Sales		2,000,000	1.108		2,216,000
Opening stock	400,000		1.180	472,000	
Purchases	1,600,000		1.108	1,772,800	
	2,000,000			2,244,800	
Less Closing stock	600,000		1.025	615,000	
		1,400,000			1,629,800
Gross profit		600,000			586,200
General overheads	314,000		1.108	347,912	
Depreciation	106,000		See below	140,810	
(Surplus on disposal of fixed assets)	(10,000)		do	(5,910)	
Provision to reduce quoted investments to market value	5,000		1.000	5,000	
Interest on 12% debentures—					
31.12.1973	12,000		1.108	13,296	
30.6.1974	12,000		1.000	12,000	
		439,000			513,108
		161,000			73,092
Income from investments		30,000	1.108		33,240
		191,000			106,332
Gain on being subject to net monetary liabilities		—	See below		33,018
Net profit before taxation		191,000			139,350
Corporation tax		90,000	1.000		90,000
Net profit after taxation		101,000			49,350
Dividends—					
Paid	30,000		1.108	33,240	
Proposed	30,000		1.000	30,000	
		60,000			63,240
Retained profit (over-distribution)		£41,000			£13,890

Conversion of Movements on Fixed Assets during the Year ended 30 June 1974

	Historical £'s				30 June 1974 £'s		
	Cost	Depreci-ation	Net	Conversion	Cost	Depreci-ation	Net
	£	£	£	Factors	£	£	£
Balances at 1.7.1973	640,000	370,000	270,000	Various	918,990	563,120	355,870
Disposal of 30.6.1969 items	(100,000)	(90,000)	(10,000)	1.625	(162,500)	(146,250)	(16,250)
	540,000	280,000	260,000		756,490	416,870	339,620
Additions, December 1973	140,000	—	140,000	1.108	155,120	—	155,120
Depreciation for year ended 30.6.1974— 20% on old items not written off*	—	92,000	(92,000)	Various	—	125,298	(125,298)
10% on additions	—	14,000	(14,000)	1.108	—	15,512	(15,512)
Balances at 30.6.1974	£680,000	£386,000	£294,000		£911,610	£557,680	£353,930
Disposals during year ended 40.6.1974— Balances at 1.7.1973	100,000	90,000	10,000	1.625	162,500	146,250	16,250
Proceeds of sale			20,000	1.108			22,160
Surplus on disposal			£10,000				£5,910
*Items from year ended 30.6.1969	180,000	170,000	10,000	1.625	292,500	276,250	16,250
Less Disposals	100,000	90,000	10,000	1.625	162,500	146,250	16,250
	80,000	80,000	—		130,000	130,000	—
Items 1.7.1969 to 30.6.1973	460,000	200,000	260,000	Various	626,490	286,870	339,620
Depreciation for year ended 30.6.1974— 20% on latter	—	92,000	(92,000)	do	—	125,298	(125,298)

Computation of Gain on being subject to Net Monetary Liabilities

	Historical £'s		Conversion Factors	30 June 1974 £'s
	£	£		£
Net Monetary Liabilities at 1.7.1973—				
12% debentures		200,000		
Corporation tax—current year		40,000		
Current liabilities	262,857			
Less ACT recoverable (offset against deferred taxation)	12,857			
		250,000		
		490,000		
Less Current assets	720,000			
Less Stock	400,000			
		320,000		
		170,000	1.165	198,050
Add Increases in net monetary liabilities—				
Purchases		1,600,000	1.108	1,772,800
General overheads		314,000	1.108	347,912
Provision to reduce quoted investments to market value		5,000	1.000	5,000
Interest on 12% debentures—				
31.12.1973		12,000	1.108	13,296
30.6.1974		12,000	1.000	12,000
Corporation tax-year ended 30.6.1974	90,000			
Less Deferred taxation	6,000			
		84,000	1.000	84,000
Dividends—				
Paid		30,000	1.108	33,240
Proposed		30,000	1.000	30,000
Additions to fixed assets		140,000	1.108	155,120
		£2,397,000		£2,651,418
Less Reductions in net monetary liabilities—				
Sales		2,000,000	1.108	2,216,000
Income from investments		30,000	1.108	33,240
Proceeds of sale of fixed assets		20,000	1.108	22,160
		2,050,000		2,271,400
Net Monetary Liabilities at 30.6.1974—				
12% debentures		200,000		
Corporation tax—current year		48,979		
Current liabilities	515,185			
Less ACT recoverable (as above)	22,164			
		493,021		
		742,000		
Less Current assets	995,000			
Less Stock	600,000			
		395,000		
			Theoretical	
Actual Net Monetary Liabilities, 30.6.1974		£347,000	*N.M.L.*	£380,018
Net Monetary Liabilities at 30.6.1974—				
Theoretical		380,018		
Less Actual		347,000		
Gain through Inflation		£33,018		

Conventional Balance Sheet, 30 June 1974

	£	£		Cost £	Depreciation £	£
Share Capital			*Fixed Assets*			
Ordinary shares		500,000	Sundries	680,000	386,000	294,000
Reserves			*Unquoted Investments,*			
Share premium account	50,000		at cost			150,000
Profit and loss account	121,000		*Current Assets*			
		171,000	Stock		600,000	
			Debtors		300,000	
		671,000	Quoted investments (market value)		25,000	
			Bank and cash balances		70,000	
12% Debentures		200,000				995,000
Deferred Taxation		3,836				
Corporation Tax—						
Current Year		48,979				
Current Liabilities						
Creditors	423,021					
Corporation tax— previous year	40,000					
Proposed dividend	30,000					
ACT on proposed dividend	22,164					
		515,185				
		£1,439,000				£1,439,000

Conversion of Balance Sheet, 30 June 1974

Item	Year	Historical £'s £	Conversion Factors	30 June 1974 £'s £
Fixed Assets				
Cost	See above	680,000	Various	911,610
Depreciation	do	(386,000)	do	(557,680)
		294,000		353,930
Unquoted Investments	1968 December	150,000	1.625	243,750
Current Assets				
Stock	1974 April	600,000	1.025	615,000
Debtors	1974 June	300,000	1.000	300,000
Quoted investments (market value)	1974 June	25,000	1.000	25,000
Bank and cash balances	1974 June	70,000	1.000	70,000
		995,000		1,010,000
Less Current Liabilities				
Creditors	1974 June	423,021	1.000	423,021
Corporation tax— previous year	1974 June	40,000	1.000	40,000
Proposed dividend	1974 June	30,000	1.000	30,000
ACT on proposed dividend	1974 June	22,164	1.000	22,164
		515,185		515,185
Net Current Assets		479,815		494,815
Total Net Assets		£923,815		£1,092,495
12% Debentures	1974 June	200,000	1.000	200,000
Deferred Taxation				
Tax 30.6.1972	1972 June	8,000	1.239	9,912
Tax 30.6.1973	1973 June	12,000	1.165	13,980
Tax 30.6.1974	1974 June	6,000	1.000	6,000
		26,000		29,892
Less ACT recoverable	1974 June	22,164	1.000	22,164
		3,836		7,728
Corporation Tax — Current Year	1974 June	48,979	1.000	48,979
Total Non-Current Liabilities		£252,815		£256,707
Total Equity Interest		£671,000		£835,788

Withit Trading Company Ltd
Summary of Results and Financial Position adjusted for the Effects of Inflation (Note 1)
Year ended 30 June 1974

	Historical Basis				Current Purchasing Power Basis			
	Year ended 30.6.1973 £000 £000		Year ended 30.6.1974 £000 £000		Year ended 30.6.1974 £000 £000		Year ended 30.6.1973 £000 £000	
Results for the Year								
Sales				2,000		2,216		
Profit before taxation (see Note 2)				191		139		
Taxation	[Not given in first year]			90		90 [Not given in first year]		
Profit after taxation				101		49		
Dividends				60		63		
Retained profit (over-distribution) for the year				41		(14)		
Financial Position at End of Year								
Net current assets		457		480		495		538
Long-term investments		150		150		244		244
Fixed assets less depreciation		270		294		354		356
		877		924		1,093		1,138
Less Loan capital (see Note 3)	200		200		200		233	
Deferred taxation	7		4		8		9	
Current year's taxation	40		49		49		46	
		247		253		257		288
Total equity interest		630		671		836		850
Ratios								
Earnings per share (p) (based on 500,000 shares in issue)				20.2		9.8		
Dividend cover (times)				1.7		0.8		
Return on total equity interest (%)				15.1		5.9		
Net assets per share (£)		1.3		1.3		1.7		1.7

Notes

1 The figures in the current purchasing power basis columns were arrived at by converting the corresponding figures in the historical basis columns by reference to the changes in a general price index between the dates of the original transactions and 30 June 1974. The current purchasing power basis figures for both this and last year are measured in pounds of purchasing power at 30 June 1974. The general price index used was that specified in Provisional Statement of Standard Accounting Practice No. 7. The Retail Price Index at 30 June 1974 was 108.7 and at 30 June 1973 was 93.3. Both figures are based on January 1974 = 100.

As the Inland Revenue do not at present accept CPP basis accounting, taxation liabilities are calculated by reference to profits on the historical basis and no adjustment therefore is made to the tax charge in the CPP basis column.

2 Profit before taxation
How the difference between profit on a historical basis and on a current purchasing power basis is made up.

	Year ended 30 June 1974	
	£000	£000
Profit Before Taxation (historical basis)		191

Adjustment to convert to current purchasing power basis—

Stock Additional charge based on restating the cost of stock at the beginning and end of the year in pounds of current purchasing power, thus taking the inflationary element out of the profit on the sale of stocks	(57)	
Depreciation Additional depreciation based on cost, measured in pounds of current purchasing power, of fixed assets	(39)	
Monetary Items Net gain in purchasing power resulting from the effects of inflation on the Company's net monetary liabilities	33	
Sales, Purchases and all other costs These are increased by the change in the index between the average date at which they occurred and the end of the year. This adjustment increases profit as sales exceed the costs included in this heading	11	
		(52)
Profit Before Taxation (Current purchasing power basis at 30 June 1974)		139

3 The loan capital at 1 July 1973 amounted to £200,000. £200,000 at that date is equivalent in purchasing power to £233,000 at 30 June 1974 (because inflation has been 16.5 per cent during the year). As the Company's liability to the providers of loan capital is fixed in money terms this liability has declined during the year in real terms from £233,000 to £200,000. This reduction of £33,000 in the Company's obligation in terms of current purchasing power is included in the net gain on monetary items of £33,000 shown in Note 2.

In subsequent years details will be given of the previous year's profit and loss account figures, on the historical basis, and on the CPP basis as at the end of the *current* year. In the table to Note 2 the corresponding CPP profit and loss figures will be those used in the 'current year' column the previous year, with a single-figure adjustment to raise the adjusted profit before taxation to its CPP equivalent at the end of the current year (see Chapter 14, section **14.12**, and Chapter 18, section **18.3**).

The salient features of the CPP accounts are:

a the over-distribution, in CPP terms, of £14,000, as against a retained profit in historical terms of £41,000. Comparison of the opening and closing equity amounts, on both bases, tells the same tale—the company has failed even to maintain its capital in real terms (on the assumption that non-monetary asset prices moved in step with the general price level);

b the major roles played by stock appreciation and inadequate depreciation, charges, in producing an inflated pre-tax figure on the historical, as compared with the CPP, basis; and

c the fact that the inflation gain (£33,000) on assets financed by debentures—an effect purely attributable to the company's capital structure—prevented a much worse result from being shown. Inflation at 16.5 per cent over the year was greater than the rate of interest on the debentures, 12.0 per cent, so that the cost of borrowing was negative in real terms—the inflation gain, £33,000, being nearly £8,000 more than the (undisclosed) interest in CPP terms. (The residual gain on net current monetary liabilities plus corporation tax liability was only £18 as computed—too small to register on the CPP summary of results).

7.3.3. Replacement-cost and current purchasing power accounting compared

At first sight, then, replacement-cost and current purchasing power accounting appear to have divergent aims—the one, to maintain the purchasing power of the firm's capital in relation to the inputs which it requires to purchase, and the other, to maintain its purchasing power in relation to the general price level. In other words, replacement-cost accounting considers the purchasing power of the firm as an entity, while current purchasing power accounting considers that of the proprietors as individuals.

In practice the dichotomy is not so absolute, since systems of replacement-cost accounting include an allowance for loss in purchasing power, over a period, of the average net monetary assets, by debiting profit and loss account and crediting a special reserve. (The Philips system incorporates such a reserve, for subsidiaries abroad whose net monetary assets are positive—the group as a whole has a consistent excess of *total* liabilities over monetary assets). Even so, the two methods are bound to give different answers to the question: 'What is the distributable profit for any particular year?'

It is as an indicator of distributable profit that the replacement-cost system is, in the author's view, superior from the investor's standpoint, as well as that of management. The rate of return on his investment in a company, even in money terms, is determined by the price paid for the shares, the amount and timing of dividends, and the price, and date, of sale of the shares. As explained more fully in Chapter 18, sub-section **18.2.3**, the effective (discounted cash flow) rate of return is that rate of compound interest which discounts the actual cash flows, negative (purchase of shares) and positive (dividends and sale of shares), to an algebraic sum of zero as at the date of purchase. Hence the rational investor is most immediately concerned with short-term forecasting of dividends, and more remotely with forecasting of the eventual selling price. Dividends are generally thought, with some reason, to be determined primarily by equity earnings—profits net of interest, tax and preference dividends. In a world of unstable (especially rising) prices historical-cost-based accounts become unreliable as indicators of distributable earnings, which they tend on the whole to overstate. Replacement-cost accounting, by eliminating holding gains from profit, makes precisely and objectively the corrections which management, using historical accounts, tends to make vaguely and subjectively. The method thus produces an earnings figure which gives a much better indicator of maximum dividends payable.[12]

Current purchasing power accounting, on the other hand, is more conservative, in that it seeks to preserve the essential elements of historical-cost accounting, while abandoning the traditional assumption of a stable monetary unit. The object is to match revenues and costs within an accounting period, using inflation-adjusted end-of-period equivalents of the historical cash flows, instead of the historical

[12]See: Revsine, L., *Replacement Cost Accounting*, Prentice-Hall, 1973

pounds of conventional accounting. Such a procedure is more realistic than what it supersedes, but it is difficult to interpret the resulting profit figures in terms of distributable earnings. In particular, a company with a highly-geared financial structure (a high proportion of loan and/or preference capital to equity) is sure to make a large paper gain in a period of rapid inflation such as the present, and this may well cause the accounts to show much higher earnings than can by any stretch of imagination be regarded as distributable. Deduction of this 'gain on long money' will reduce reported earnings to somewhere nearer the distributable amount—indeed, it might be an improvement if such gains were taken directly to reserves, and not passed through the profit and loss account. Even so, if the test of an accounting system is the provision of efficient inputs to rational decision theories, and if the decision theories of investors are considered paramount (as suggested in Chapter 4, section 4.3), then current purchasing power is inferior to replacement-cost accounting in this respect. The main advantages of CPP are simplicity and rapidity in preparing the adjusted final accounts, and greater objectivity of measurements in the sense of Chapter 4, section 4.3—i.e. closer agreement among different accountants as to what the figures should be.

A further argument often advanced in favour of CPP accounting (e.g. in Appendix 1 to PSSAP No. 7) is that it shows assets, liabilities and equity revalued in terms of changes in the general purchasing power of money in, for example, the U.K., and that this general purchasing power is of most interest to the investor, as distinct from management. (The validity of the General Index of Retail Prices as a surrogate for each investor's individual price index is a separate, and smaller, issue.) While admitting the force of this contention as regards the investor's own income and expenditure, the author for one is unable to see any close connection between revaluation of the *company's* assets, etc., in CPP terms and the current purchasing power of the *shareholder's* cash flows from his investment over time. The investor in equities is concerned, as stated above, with the money amounts of his dividends and the 'entry' and 'exit' prices of his shares; with their timing; and with the general price index at the dates of receipt of payment. Given these, he is able to reduce the cash flows to a common measure of purchasing power at a chosen date—e.g. that of sale of the shares—and to compute a DCF rate to represent his *real* rate of return on the investment. He is unconcerned with any method of valuing the company's equity, and earnings, which does not also act as an indicator of future dividends, and through them as a (less reliable) indicator of future share price movements. Replacement cost provides such an indicator; current purchasing power does not. More fundamentally, CPP accounting appears to rest upon the 'proprietary' theory of accounting (which views the entity as an extension of the proprietors' private wealth), and replacement-cost accounting upon the 'entity' theory (which treats the entity as a semi-autonomous collection of net assets, in which the proprietors have a residual interest). The author's preference for the latter approach has already been made clear; but, even if the other concept is preferred, current purchasing power seems a less adequate surrogate for net realizable value in the ordinary course of business (the most relevant measure here) than replacement cost. The fact that the contention between proponents of the two systems is so heated, and still unresolved, arises in large part from failure to rationalize accounting theory at any really deep level.

To be fair, there are proposals to reconcile the two approaches to accounting for price level changes. One is a system (such as that suggested by R.J. Chambers[13])

[13] See footnote 2.

which, while revaluing contributed capital in terms of year-end purchasing power, and allowing for inflation losses (or deflation gains) on holdings of net monetary assets, values non-monetary assets on a replacement-cost basis (with opportunity cost as an upper limit), and determines profits on the same basis, subject to the aforesaid adjustments and to a further one to maintain the purchasing power of the accumulated reserves. Something of this nature would seem to provide the most hopeful solution, but academic and professional thought is today in such a state of turmoil that it would be premature to speculate further.

For the same reason, only passing mention can be made of yet more radical proposals for 'economic' accounting on the basis of opportunity cost—normally the present value of expected future cash flows, with resale value as an upper bound. Such systems would necessarily involve much subjective valuation *ex ante*, with correction *ex post* and, despite the strong theoretical arguments in favour, there seems no prospect of the accountancy profession accepting any such technique in the foreseeable future, for reporting purposes (as distinct from investment decision-making, as at present). By taking non-purchased goodwill into account, such systems would be at the opposite pole to that of, again, Chambers who, somewhat dogmatically, rejects the notion that even purchased goodwill can be truly an asset, since it is not severable from the entity as a whole, and since the benefit of the expenditure runs to the proprietors, rather than the firm as such. He advocates the immediate writing-off against reserves of any goodwill element in the acquisition cost of a going concern; but, as stated in Chapter 6, sub-section **6.4.2** the sense of the majority of accountants is adamantly opposed to this, and the controversy has yet to be resolved (otherwise than by fiat of the leading accountancy bodies).

7.3.4 Depreciation and price level adjustment

In the analysis in this chapter, depreciation calculations have thus far been taken for granted, with the straight line method used in illustrations for simplicity. It remains to relate both replacement-cost and current purchasing power accounting to modern depreciation theory.

In Chapter 6, sub-section **6.3.2**, it was suggested that in a time of changing prices the problem of computing depreciation rationally is insoluble within the confines of historical-cost accounting. Not only is there inadequate allowance for the real consumption of values through use of an asset over its whole life; there is also, under conventional modes of calculation, no guarantee that the accounting pattern of charges, year by year, corresponds at all closely to the progressive reductions in the asset's resale value, or (what amounts to the same thing) that the successive year-end written-down amounts bear any close relation to current resale values—surely the most defensible basis of intermediate valuation, since the object of charging depreciation is to write down the asset from cost to ultimate resale price, as accurately as possible. With stable prices this can theoretically be achieved by any of the accepted methods of charge, in a more or less mechanistic manner and without checking intermediate resale prices; and as long as there is no need for premature replacement no great harm is done by using an inappropriate time-pattern. Also, if the firm has many fixed assets of each class, of many different vintages and regularly replaced at stable prices, it makes little difference to the total reported cost per annum, whether one uses straight line or accelerated charges, since in the latter case high charges on new assets will tend to be compensated by low charges on older items. All the same, the more accelerated the method the lower will be the average reported year-end values, even though the firm's stock of fixed assets is neither expanding nor contracting; for in the past, while the present stock of fixed assets (or their predecessors) was being built up, total depreciation charges were heavier than if the straight line method had been used, and the same effect will appear in any future expansion (vice versa in a period of contraction).

Whichever pattern of resale price decline is assumed, it is important to take the cost of capital into account, e.g. by the annuity method. This is customarily applied to the straight line pattern, and has the effect of retarding the book rate of decline in the earlier years, and increasing it in the later ones, so that on a graph the curve of successive year-end values is concave to the origin—that is, it lies entirely above the linear curve representing the result of equal-instalment depreciation, except at the two ends, where all possible curves coincide at historical cost, and resale proceeds. The sum of years' digits method gives a curve, or rather a series of straight lines, convex to the origin (i.e. lying entirely below the 'straight line' curve, except at the ends), and the declining balance method a smooth curve of sharper convexity still. If the two latter methods are modified by reference to the cost of capital, their curves become less convex, and closer to the straight line; and if, in the absence of reliable market quotations for old assets of the type in question, it is uncertain whether the pattern of decline is linear or accelerated, the simple straight line write-off may be an acceptable compromise, if interest is taken into account in both alternatives.[14] (See Fig. 7.1 relating to a fixed asset bought for £10,000 and sold five years later for £1,000, the price level being stable in the meantime.)

The introduction of replacement-cost accounting makes it possible to fit the depreciation curve of a fixed asset more closely to the facts in a period of considerable change in the prices of similar assets. At the end the resale price is likely to correspond more precisely to the final written-down amount, and during the asset's life the charges will bear a closer relationship to the current cost of similar inputs—i.e. the services which would be rendered in the period by similar assets bought new at the average replacement cost ruling in that period—provided that the time-pattern of depreciation is a suitable one.

With current purchasing power accounting the fixed assets, and the depreciation charges, are recalculated as though their prices moved in step with the general price level throughout the year. Most probably they did not, and the revised depreciation charge is either excessive or inadequate as a replacement provision, even in relation only to the services rendered by the asset in the year. Indeed, the proponents of the system deny any intention of providing for replacement of any existing assets; but this does not answer the objection, since it is the service-potential, not the particular piece of hardware, which is to be replaced in some form in due course. A sounder defence is, that current purchasing power accounting is concerned with ascertaining whether and to what extent the contributed capital of the proprietors has been maintained or augmented in real terms, and that the particular form in which it has been invested is immaterial, except as touching the distinction between non-monetary assets, whose opportunity cost is deemed on the whole to keep pace with inflation, and monetary ones, whose values are eroded by rising prices in general. The underlying assumption appears to be, that in a reasonably long time all prices rise or fall by about the same percentage; but this is not in accordance with

[14]See Baxter, W.T. *Depreciation*, Sweet & Maxwell, 1971.

observation, especially when obsolescence supervenes in some instances. These weaknesses appear greatly to reinforce the case for replacement-cost accounting, adjusted for changes in the general price level.

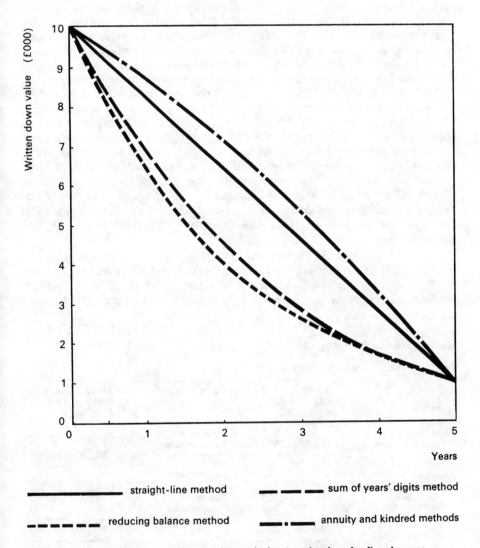

Fig 7.1 Book values, by different depreciation methods, of a fixed asset purchased for £10,000 and sold 5 years later for £1,000

7.4 Funds flow and cash flow accounting

Before leaving the subject of accounting reform, it is convenient to examine briefly a topic which has received a good deal of attention in recent years, though its principles have been known for much longer—namely, the measurement of an entity's *flow of funds* over a year or other period. Connected with this is the subordinate *flow of cash* over the same period.

From basic accounting theory, any increase (or decrease) in the numerical amount of equity or liabilities is exactly counterbalanced by an equal and opposite increase (or decrease) in the numerical amount of assets. Any transaction causing such a movement constitutes a flow of funds relative to the entity, by changing both the total amount of investments in the business (from all sources) and the total amount of resources representing those investments. Conversions of one asset into another are not true flows of funds in this sense, except where a profit or loss arises, which alters both total assets and total equity; nor are transfers between equity and liabilities, in the form of provisions for non-current losses and expenses.

The simplest form of *Statement of Source and Application of Funds* for a period (there are alternative titles) is derived from a straightforward comparison of the opening and closing balance sheets; it is not taken directly from the books of account, and lies outside the double entry system. It describes on the one hand, as the *Source of Funds,* net increases in equity or liabilities over the period, plus net decreases in assets—i.e. net additional funds provided, plus existing funds released from their former employments and made available for other uses. On the other hand the *Application of Funds* is shown as net increases in assets, plus net decreases in liabilities and equity—i.e. total funds invested in resources or used to discharge the claims of investors and creditors—the totals of source and application being equal.

Example 3 The opening and closing balance sheets (simplified) of the General Trading Company Ltd, for the year ended 31 December 19.1, are shown below, together with a statement of source and application of funds for the year, derived from an item by item comparison of the opening and closing positions.

General Trading Company Ltd

Balance Sheets, 31 December 19.0 and 19.1

	31. 12. 19.0 £	31. 12. 19.1 £		31. 12. 19.0 £	31. 12. 19.1 £
Share Capital			*Fixed Assets*		
Ordinary shares	100,000	150,000	Sundries (book amounts)	148,000	180,000
Reserves			*Current Assets*		
Share premium account	–	10,000	Stock	50,000	52,000
Profit and loss account	20,000	25,000	Debtors	30,000	28,000
			Bank balance	–	20,500
	20,000	35,000		80,000	100,500
	120,000	185,000			
8 Per Cent Debentures	50,000	50,000			
Corporation Tax—					
Current Year	10,000	12,000			

Current Liabilities		
Bank overdraft	20,000	—
Creditors	10,000	11,000
Corporation tax—		
previous year	8,000	10,000
Proposed dividend	10,000	12,500
	48,000	33,500
	£228,000	£280,500

Right-side totals: £228,000 £280,500

Statement of Source and Application of Funds for the Year ended 31 December 19.1

	£	£
Source		
Increases in equity of shareholders—		
Ordinary shares	50,000	
Share premium account	10,000	
Profit and loss account (retained profits)	5,000	
		65,000
Increases in liabilities—		
Corporation tax—current year	2,000	
Creditors	1,000	
Corporation tax—previous year	2,000	
Proposed dividend	2,500	
		7,500
Reduction in assets—		
Debtors		2,000
		£74,500
Application		
Increases in assets—		
Fixed assets	32,000	
Stock	2,000	
Bank balance	20,500	
		54,500
Reduction in liabilities—		
Bank overdraft		20,000
		£74,500

The main limitation of such a statement is that it groups together, as single items, several movements of different natures. For instance, the net change in fixed assets is compounded of new assets purchased (additions), depreciation charges (reductions), and possibly disposals (reductions). The charging of depreciation, in particular, cannot properly be regarded as either a source or application of funds, since it is an internal book entry, representing no movement of resources into or out of the firm. As it stands, the funds statement adds little to the information which could be gleaned from a simple comparison of the two balance sheets.

It is therefore desirable to produce a more analytical statement, incorporating detailed information about fixed asset movements and funds generated by trading operations during the year. This involves a more exact definition of sources of funds, as activities which draw additional *net current assets* into the entity, or liberate moneys invested in other forms within it, and of applications of funds, as activities which reduce net current assets, by reinvesting them in more permanent form or dispersing them outside the entity. Thus, the prime sources are subscriptions of new capital, retained profits before charging depreciation (which has to be added back to the retained profit as reported in the profit and loss account), increased taxation provisions, and sale proceeds of fixed assets; while the prime applications are purchases of fixed assets, redemption of loans, and trading losses (before charging depreciation), with the year's increase (decrease) in net current assets inserted under 'application' ('source'), or shown separately as the difference of the totals of source and application.

Example 4 Given the following additional information, the funds statement in *Example 3* may be redrafted on the lines just set out.

Profit and Loss Account for the Year ended 31 December 19.1

	£	£
Net profit before charging depreciation, etc.		65,000
Depreciation		(30,000)
Surplus on disposal of fixed assets		2,500
Net profit before taxation		37,500
Corporation tax		(15,000)
Net profit after taxation		22,500
Dividends—		
Paid	(5,000)	
Proposed	(12,500)	
		(17,500)
Retained profit		£5,000

Movements on Fixed Assets

	Cost £	Depreciation £	Net £
Balances, 1 January 19.1	300,000	152,000	148,000
Disposals (proceeds £12,500)	(80,000)	(70,000)	(10,000)
	220,000	82,000	138,000
Additions	72,000	—	72,000
Depreciation for year	—	30,000	(30,000)
Balances, 31 December 19.1	£292,000	£112,000	£180,000

Statement of Source and Application of Funds for the Year ended 31 December 19.1

	£	£
Source		
Capital subscribed—		
Ordinary shares (nominal value)	50,000	
Share premium account	10,000	
		60,000
Retained profits—		
Per profit and loss account	5,000	
Add back Depreciation	30,000	
	35,000	
Less Surplus on disposal of fixed assets	2,500	
		32,500

Increase in non-current liabilities		
Corporation tax—current year		2,000
Proceeds of sale of fixed assets		12,500
		£107,000

Application

Purchases of fixed assets		72,000
Increase in current assets—		
Stock	2,000	
Debtors	(2,000)	
Bank balance (as compared with overdraft)	40,500	
	40,500	
Less Increase in current liabilities—		
Creditors	1,000	
Corporation tax—previous year	2,000	
Proposed dividend	2,500	
	5,500	
Increase in net current assets		35,000
		£107,000

This is a much more informative statement than the previous one. It can be seen that trading operations added £34,500 to net current assets, while another £60,000 of funds was raised by a capital issue. £59,500 (£72,000 – £12,500) of 'new' money was invested in fixed assets, while there was a 'turn-round' in the cash position of £40,500 (£20,000 overdraft changed to £20,500 positive balance), offset by a worsening of £5,500 in the other net current assets. All the same, working capital has more than doubled, from £32,000 (£80,000 – £48,000) to £67,000 (£100,500 – £33,500), and the liquidity position (short-term monetary assets compared with current liabilities) has greatly improved, with net liquid assets now £15,000, against a deficiency of £18,000 last year.

There is, indeed, a strong case for drafting the funds statement so as to show directly the effect of the year's transactions on net short-term monetary assets—the movement on stock being grouped with that on other physical assets, since the amounts invested in them cannot normally be regarded as easily disinvestible in the short run, if the present scale of business operations is to be maintained. The statement may then be considered as a *cash flow* statement—'cash flow' meaning, in its broader sense, the change in net liquid assets over a period, though some accountants prefer to treat it as the change in cash-type assets (cash and bank balances, bills receivable, and short-term quoted investments), and this approach is now favoured by the Accounting Standards Steering Committee in its Exposure Draft 13 (see sub-section **7.4.1**). In fact, the majority of British companies which currently publish funds statements adopt the 'flow of liquid funds' form, as against the overwhelming majority of American ones, which show movements in working capital (net current assets).[14]

[14]See: Lee, T.A., *The Funds Statement,* Institute of Chartered Accountants of Scotland, 1974.

Example 5 The Statement of Cash Flow for the General Trading Company Ltd for the year ended 31 December 19.1 might appear as follows.

General Trading Company Ltd

Statement of Cash Flow for the Year ended 31 December 19.1

	£	£
Source of Liquid Funds		
Retained profits—		
Per profit and loss account	5,000	
Add back Depreciation	30,000	
	35,000	
Less Surplus on disposal of fixed assets	2,500	
		32,500
Increase in provision for current year's taxation		2,000
Capital subscribed—		
Ordinary shares (nominal value)	50,000	
Share premium account	10,000	
		60,000
		£94,500
Application of Liquid Funds		
Purchases of fixed assets	72,000	
Less Proceeds of sale of old assets	12,500	
		59,500
Increased investment in stock		2,000
		£61,500
Net Increase in Liquid Funds		
Non-cash items (decrease)—		
Decrease in debtors	(2,000)	
Increase in creditors	(1,000)	
do in corporation tax—previous year	(2,000)	
do in proposed dividend	(2,500)	
		(7,500)
Cash items (increase)		40,500
		£33,000

7.4.1 Funds and cash flow and accounting theory

The presentation of some form of funds flow, or cash flow, statement as part of the published financial accounts has long been general in North America, and in the U.S.A. is now obligatory under the SEC regulations. In the U.K. the practice has grown rapidly in recent years, being followed in 1972–73 by 39 per cent of the 300 largest British companies. The ASSC has now (1974) issued Exposure Draft 13: *Statements of source and application of funds,* recommending that the publication of a funds statement be made standard practice in the U.K. and the Republic of Ireland (see Chapter 14, sub-section **14.6.7**).

Some theorists in Britain[15] have suggested that, since accounting for non-monetary asset values contains such a large element of arbitrariness, making balance sheet amounts largely meaningless as guides to investment decisions, and since the success of a business is measured ultimately by its ability to maximize its cash flow through time, a statement of changes in liquid funds would be more significant to the investor than a conventional profit and loss account. It would be supplemented by a position statement as at the year-end, showing only the components of liquid funds, and 'legal' items such as share capital, in money terms. No money values would be placed upon physical assets, but they would be described in terms of such technical or other measures (horse-power of machines, floor-area of buildings, etc.) as were thought most appropriate to give the reader an adequate idea of their nature and capacity for rendering service to the firm. No value would be imputed to equity as a whole, nor would the statement 'balance' in any normal sense. (Double entry book-keeping might still be used to maintain the accounting records—or it might give place to multi-dimensional book-keeping, as suggested by Y. Ijiri (see Chapter 4, sub-section 4.3.1).)

The proposals have a certain attractiveness, as a means of short-circuiting the many knotty problems attending the construction of rational accounts as now understood, and still defying real solution. But the whole idea of pure cash-flow accounting has a rather defeatist ring about it, and savours to many accountants of throwing out the baby with the bath-water. The most likely developments now seem to be concerned with the improvement, and incorporation into law, of current purchasing power accounting, and its eventual supersession by replacement-cost accounting, or by some hybrid of the two, revealing the 'real' gain or loss on non-monetary assets at replacement cost, as compared with the CPP equivalents of their historical cost. Further speculation is unprofitable, but enough has been said to indicate that accounting may well be in the midst of a turbulent, yet fruitful, period of its history.

[15] See, e.g.: Rayman, R. A. Is Conventional Accounting Obsolete? *Accountancy*, June 1970; and Is Double-Entry Really Necessary? *Accountancy*, October 1970.

8
Accounting for sub-entities; foreign exchange transactions

Part I is rounded off by an extension of the principles and practice of accounting from the transactions of an entity as a whole to those of various types of *sub-entity*, as defined in Chapter 1, sub-section **1.2.1.** Each has a sub-system of accounts within the main system, and the layout of each sub-system, and its relation to the whole, will be demonstrated. It is also necessary to consider the uses of sub-entity accounting in controlling the subordinate managements, and in appraising their success or otherwise in reaching appropriate business objectives.

8.1 Branch accounting

The first sub-entity to be dealt with is the *branch*. A branch may be defined as a section of an undertaking, geographically separated from the rest, and carrying on the same productive or selling activities as the undertaking generally. Some businesses, such as multiple retailing, consist principally of branch establishments, controlled by a central organization; in others, branches are a peripheral and subordinate part of the entity. The degree of autonomy accorded to branch managements also varies a good deal, and is reflected in the design of the accounts relating to each branch.

8.1.1 Accounting control of non-autonomous branches

In many multiple retailing organizations all or most of the merchandise is bought in bulk by a central purchasing department, and distributed to branches from a central or district warehouse. Prices in the shops are fixed nationally or on a local basis by the head office, and branch managers have generally no discretion in the matter. An individual manager orders goods from the warehouse as his stocks near exhaustion, and they are sent to him with a pro forma invoice, stating all items at selling price. He does not know the cost or the mark-up, nor does he keep accounts showing the branch profit for any period; and, though he has discretion to engage and dismiss staff, he must pay the company rates of wages, while most other branch overheads are fixed within narrow limits and paid as far as possible from head office. All cash taken in the shop must be banked intact, the same or next day, for the benefit of head office, and the granting of credit is usually forbidden.

The branch manager does not keep a full set of double entry books, but only memorandum records of cash, sales and stocks (and debtors, if he is allowed to give credit), from which he writes up weekly *returns* in prescribed form—a cash account, summarizing his receipts and payments, with opening and closing balances; a stock account, with opening and closing stocks, deliveries and sales, all at selling prices and thus showing neither profit nor loss (though there is usually a small difference, debit or credit, to balance the account); sometimes a detailed weekly stock return;

and a short report on the week's trading. The return goes to head office, and is used as a basis for entries in the main books of account. The accuracy of managers' returns is checked by internal auditors, who visit all branches from time to time without warning, count the manager's cash and test-check his stock, check his records for consistency therewith, and with recent returns, and report any unusual circumstances to head office for further investigation.

The special entries for the branch in the head office books are entirely for the purposes of internal control. The only significant parameter which emerges for each individual branch is its turnover—profit can be found only for the firm as a whole. Each manager is motivated to maximize his sales, by being set a sales target for each month or quarter and compelled to keep cumulative records, to show him how well he is succeeding—the target being in money terms, and revised whenever there is a significant change in selling prices, as fixed by head office. Since selling prices are related to cost, and overheads do not move in proportion to turnover, this policy ensures that profit is maximized, so far as lies in the branch managers' power. Maximization of the firm's overall profit is a matter of head office planning—siting of branches, skill in purchasing and stock control, marketing and sales promotion efforts, financial management and control, and so on.

The method requires the keeping, for each branch, of four accounts—Goods Sent to ... Branch Account, ... Branch Stock Account, ... Branch Expenses Account, and ... Branch Sales Account, with a fifth, ... Branch Total Debtors Account, if the manager is authorized to allow credit to customers. When goods are sent to the branch from the warehouse they are debited to Branch Stock Account and credited to Goods Sent to Branch Account at *selling* price as on the pro forma invoice; they cannot be credited to Sales, as they have not yet passed out of the firm's hands. When they are sold, Cash, or Branch Total Debtors Account, is debited and Branch Stock credited. Goods returned to warehouse, or transferred to another branch, or lost or stolen, are debited to Goods Sent to Branch and credited to Branch Stock, still at selling price; any loss or theft of cash is credited to the latter account and debited to Branch Expenses Account (or some appropriate subdivision of it). Branch overheads are debited to this account (or these accounts), and cash received from branch debtors, with discounts and bad debt write-offs, pass through Branch Total Debtors in the usual way. At each year-end the branch stock is taken physically by the branch, valued at both cost and selling prices by head office, and the latter figure reconciled with the debit balance on the Branch Stock Account, any difference being written off to Goods Sent to Branch—without question, if it is within the normal range of error due to breaking bulk, or mistakes in ringing up on the till or giving change, and so forth; differences due to deterioration and/or mark-downs should be separately authorized or explained. On Goods Sent to Branch Account, a *credit* balance is carried down, equal and opposite to the debit balance on Branch Stock Account; the remainder of the credit side represents the total sales of the branch, and the account is closed by debiting it and crediting Branch Sales Account, whose credit balance is transferred annually to Total Sales Account (for the business as a whole). In preparing the Trading Account, closing stock for the whole firm is entered at cost or lower net realizable value in the usual manner; the debit and credit balances on Branch Stock, and Goods Sent to Branch, Accounts respectively cancel out, and are ignored in the final accounts for the year.

Example 1 Entries on these lines are shown below for the Middletown branch of Northern Groceries Ltd, in summary form for the year ended 31 December 19.1.

Northern Groceries Ltd

Goods Sent to Middletown Branch

19.1		£	19.1		£
Dec 31	Middletown branch stock—returns	1,000	Jan 1	Balance b/d	25,000
Dec 31	Middletown branch sales	148,200	Dec 31	Middletown branch stock—deliveries stock difference	150,000 200
Dec 31	Balance c/d	26,000			
		£175,200			£175,200
			19.2		
			Jan 1	Balance b/d	26,000

Middletown Branch Stock

19.1		£	19.1		£
Jan 1	Balance b/d	25,000	Dec 31	Goods sent to Middletown branch—returns	1,000
Dec 31	Goods sent to Middletown branch—deliveries stock difference	150,000 200	Dec 31	Bank	109,950
			Dec 31	Middletown branch expenses—cash difference	50
			Dec 31	Middletown branch total debtors	38,200
			Dec 31	Balance c/d	26,000
		£175,200			£175,200
19.2					
Jan 1	Balance b/d	26,000			

Middletown Branch Expenses

19.1		£	19.1		£
Dec 31	Bank—salaries and wages general expenses	12,000 4,000	Dec 31	Profit and loss a/c	16,050
Dec 31	Middletown branch stock—cash difference	50			
		£16,050			£16,050

Middletown Branch Sales

19.1		£	19.1		£
			Dec 31	Goods sent to Middletown branch	148,200
Dec 31	Total sales	148,200			

Middletown Branch Total Debtors

19.1		£	19.1		£
Jan 1	Balance b/d	6,000	Dec 31	Bank	37,700
Dec 31	Middletown branch stock	38,200	Dec 31	Bad debts	100
			Dec 31	Balance c/d	6,400
		£44,200			£44,200
19.2					
Jan 1	Balance b/d	6,400			

Such a system is appropriate where the branch manager's discretion is minimal. In some trades, though, such as furniture and household durables generally, goods are bought in bulk but selling prices cannot be rigidly laid down at head office—the branch manager must use his judgement, within limits, when fixing prices in the light of local conditions, including competition from rival firms. He is then set two targets—total gross sales, and a percentage of gross profit thereon (that is, he must not achieve one by disregarding the other, as by recklessly cutting prices to secure business in a competitive situation). If he has funds to spend on sales promotion, these should be brought into the calculation, and the manager should be called upon to attain a minimum profit margin on sales after charging such expenditure. In this type of business goods are invoiced pro forma at cost plus a percentage mark-up corresponding to the target rate of gross profit—e.g. if 25 per cent is the target gross profit on turnover, then the mark-up is $33\frac{1}{3}$ per cent on cost, i.e. $100 \times 25/(100 - 25)$. The branch manager thus has an average selling price given to him; if he charges less in some cases, he must charge more in others. The weekly returns should be modified to include a 'trading account', with pro forma prices in lieu of cost of sales, and stocks priced on the same basis; the 'gross profit' will be low, and sometimes negative, but the branch must come out on the right side over time, or the manager may be in trouble.

The head office book-keeping is somewhat similar to that already described, except that the Goods Sent to Branch Account is kept in terms of cost only, and the element of mark-up dealt with in a Branch Stock Adjustment Account. The Branch Stock Account is kept, as before, in terms of internally invoiced prices, and actual sales are credited to it; but as these are not necessarily at the pro forma price a difference normally arises, which is transferred to Branch Stock Adjustment Account, as (say) 'apparent profit (or loss)'. The closing stock is carried down at marked-up price, and a countervailing credit balance on the Adjustment Account represents the mark-up element, so that the two, being offset, enter into the firm's balance sheet as stock at cost. The credit balance on the Goods Sent to Branch Account is transferred to the credit of Purchases (closing the former account), and the profit element in the Adjustment Account is transferred to the credit of Profit and Loss Account. Such a system thus shows not only the turnover but the gross profit on the branch's trading, and the extent to which it deviates from the target percentage. Branch overheads are written off to the general profit and loss account.

Example 2 Below are the relevant entries for the activities of the Tynecastle branch of the Midland Furnishing Company Ltd, for the year ended 31 December 19.1. Goods are invoiced pro forma to the branch at a mark-up of $33\frac{1}{3}$ per cent on cost.

Midland Furnishing Company Ltd
Goods Sent to Tynecastle Branch

19.1		£	19.1		£
Dec 31	Tynecastle branch stock—returns (cost)	9,000	Dec 31	Tynecastle branch stock—deliveries (cost)	204,000
Dec 31	Purchases	195,000			
		£204,000			£204,000

Tynecastle Branch Stock Adjustment Account

19.1		£	19.1		£
Dec 31	Tynecastle branch stock—returns (mark-up)	3,000	Jan 1	Balance c/d	20,000
Dec 31	Tynecastle branch stock—apparent loss	1,000	Dec 31	Tynecastle branch stock—deliveries (mark-up)	68,000
Dec 31	Profit and loss a/c— gross profit	63,000			
Dec 31	Balance c/d— stock mark-up	21,000			
		£88,000			£88,000
			19.2		
			Jan 1	Balance b/d	21,000

Tynecastle Branch Stock

19.1		£	19.1		£
Jan 1	Balance b/d	80,000	Dec 31	Sundries—returns (cost plus mark-up)	12,000
Dec 31	Sundries—deliveries (cost plus mark-up)	272,000	Dec 31	Tynecastle branch total debtors	205,000
			Dec 31	Bank	50,000
			Dec 31	Tynecastle branch stock adjustment a/c—apparent loss	1,000
			Dec 31	Balance c/d—stock (cost plus mark-up)	84,000
		£352,000			£352,000
19.2					
Jan 1	Balance b/d	84,000			

Tynecastle Branch Expenses

19.1		£	19.1		£
Dec 31	Bank—sundries	40,000	Dec 31	Profit and loss a/c	40,000

Tynecastle Branch Total Debtors

19.1		£	19.1		£
Jan 1	Balance b/d	45,000	Dec 31	Bank	197,000
Dec 31	Tynecastle branch stock	205,000	Dec 31	Bad debts	3,000
			Dec 31	Balance c/d	50,000
		£250,000			£250,000
19.2					
Jan 1	Balance b/d	50,000			

Closing stock for the branch will be included in the final balance sheet at cost, £63,000—the net amount of the Branch Stock and Branch Stock Adjustment Account Balances. (The opening stock was £60,000, or 80,000 − 20,000). Actual sales for the year were £(205,000 + 50,000 =) £255,000. The apparent loss, £1,000, is the balancing figure of the Stock Account, indicating that the quantity of goods sold ought to have been charged out at £256,000; 25 per cent gross profit on this would be £64,000, and this is represented in the Stock Adjustment Account by the actual gross profit, £63,000, plus the apparent loss, £1,000. The manager has thus achieved a gross profit of $100 \times 63,000/255,000 = 24.7$ per cent, which is very close, and acceptable if the sales target has been equalled or exceeded.

In the third situation, the goods sold by the branch are perishables, such as fruit, vegetables or fish, and cannot be stored in bulk. The manager must buy every day in the local market, or arrange for daily deliveries by wholesalers, and endeavour to set his prices at levels which will maximize his gross profit each day—often varying them during the day, to take advantage of brisk demand or stimulate lagging sales. Head office must, therefore, require him to make weekly returns incorporating a branch trading account, and see that over a period he is making a reasonable percentage of gross profit on turnover, as well as meeting his sales target in money terms, as adjusted for the average prices prevailing. The same applies to 'semi-manufacturing' branches, as in multiple tailoring.

In the head office books the branch stock account is replaced by a Branch Trading Account, with opening and closing stocks brought in at cost, deliveries to the branch debited at cost (and credited, either to Goods Sent to Branch Account, or to the suppliers' accounts where the manager does the buying locally), and sales credited at actual amounts, with gross profit, as realized, transferred to the credit of the firm's profit and loss account. Branch expenses are debited to an appropriate account or accounts, and transferred to the debit of the general profit and loss account. Any goods sent from head office are closed off to the credit of Purchases Account, and thus excluded from head office cost of sales, if any. The closing stock, brought down as a debit balance on the Branch Trading Account, is included in the balance sheet amount. This series of entries appears obvious and easy to visualize from what has gone before, and is not illustrated.

8.1.2 Accounting control of autonomous branches

In discussing non-autonomous, or at best semi-autonomous, branches the author has deliberately proceeded from tighter to looser systems of internal control over branch managers' activities, as more discretion is given to the managers because of the nature of the trades. A further stage is reached when the branch is so large in relation to the firm as a whole, and its functions so complex, that it is treated as autonomous, with the manager taking more responsibility, and being given more freedom of action, than is usual in a true multiple retail enterprise. This normally comes about when manufacturing activities are carried on at the branch, and/or a wholesaling, or specialized retailing, business is conducted at a few establishments strategically situated in large centres of population, so that none is clearly dominant over the others, though one of them is constituted as the head office of the organization.

In such circumstances each branch keeps its own set of double entry books, from which it prepares an annual trading account, profit and loss account, and balance sheet, as though it were an independent firm, but with one important difference. As it is not in fact independent, its books contain no accounts for proprietary capital or retained profits as such. Instead there is a Head Office Control Account, whose credit balance at any balancing date represents the net difference between total assets and total external liabilities in the branch books. In other words, it is an account for the *quasi-equity* of a sub-entity, the branch.

The entries in the control account are all derived from transactions between branch and head office—transfers of physical assets, and payments of cash, mainly from branch to head office—and the accrual of profits or losses, which must be imputed to head office as a surrogate proprietor of the branch. In the head office books there is a counterpart Branch Control Account, with corresponding entries on the opposite sides, and a debit balance equal and opposite at all times (subject to time-lags in receiving information) to the credit balance of the Head Office Control Account. The final accounts of the firm are constructed by consolidation of those of the head office and all branches—the adding together of all like items, and cancelling out of the control account balances as a species of internal indebtedness. In order to facilitate such consolidation, the management will arrange for all branches and the head office to keep books and prepare final accounts on the same accounting principles, and in the same format, and for the year-end balances on each control account in a branch's books, and on its counterpart in the head office books, to agree, credit to debit. If, for example, cash has been forwarded from branch to head office just before the year-end, but does not arrive until just after it, the control account at the branch will have been debited but the one at head office will not have been credited, and its debit balance will exceed the counterpart credit balance. It is then necessary to credit the amount to Branch Control Account and debit it to Cash in Transit Account, whose balance is included as an asset in the firm's balance sheet. When the cash arrives it is debited to Bank and credited to Cash in Transit Account, which is closed. Similar treatment is accorded to any goods, or other physical assets, in transit at the year-end between head office and branch, or between two branches (which record such matters in Current Accounts in each other's name).

Example 3 Technical Books Ltd has two establishments, in London (the head office) and Birmingham, each keeping its own books of account, and preparing final accounts for years ended December 31, which are consolidated to produce the firm's accounts. The two control accounts are shown below, in summary form, for the year ended 31 December 19.1. At that date, £2,000 was in transit from the Birmingham branch to the London head office.

Technical Books Ltd
Birmingham Branch Books
London Head Office Control Account

19.1		£	19.1		£
Dec 31	Bank	45,000	Jan 1	Balance b/d	200,000
Dec 31	Balance c/d	225,000	Dec 31	Goods received from Head Office	50,000
			Dec 31	Profit and loss a/c—net profit	20,000
		£270,000			£270,000
			19.2		
			Jan 1	Balance b/d	225,000

London Head Office Books
Birmingham Branch Control Account

19.1		£	19.1		£
Jan 1	Balance b/d	200,000	Dec 31	Bank	43,000
Dec 31	Goods sent to		Dec 31	Cash in transit	2,000
	Birmingham branch	50,000	Dec 31	Balance c/d	225,000
Dec 31	Profit and loss a/c–net profit, Birmingham branch	20,000			
		£270,000			£270,000
19.2					
Jan 1	Balance b/d	225,000			

Cash in Transit

19.1		£	19.2		£
Dec 31	Birmingham branch control a/c	2,000	Jan 2	Bank	2,000

Alternatively, the control accounts may each be subdivided into a Capital Account and a Current Account, with equal and opposite balances as between head office and branch. The Capital Accounts then contain details of initial assets and liabilities taken over by branch from head office, and of any further fixed assets transferred or loans made. The Current Accounts deal with stock and cash transfers, and accruals of profit or loss. Further subdivision is possible as desired, but the principle is not affected; the sub-entities are still part of the main entity, and their quasi-equities are in one way or another subsumed under the equity of that entity.

8.2 Overseas branches and foreign exchange

An overseas branch of a British firm must of necessity keep its own set of books, connected with the main books in Britain by control accounts, or by capital and current accounts, as described. Frequently, a subsidiary company is set up in the foreign country under its laws, with all its shares held by the British company; but the laws of some countries insist that a certain minority, or even a small majority, of the shares be held by their own nationals. In either case there is the need for consolidation of the branch or subsidiary's accounts, at least annually, with those of the British head office or holding company. The main complication is that the overseas books are kept in the currency of the other country, and that their balances must be converted to sterling before consolidation can take place.

All national currencies fluctuate continually in relation to others, and in particular to sterling, which in the accounts of British firms or groups is taken as the fixed currency, against which all others move. Up to 1972 most currencies were 'pegged' to the U.S. dollar, but free to vary a few points either side of the official parity. Since then the system has broken down, and currencies have been left to 'float', in groups or separately, in relation to the dollar and to each other; but the difference, from an accounting point of view, is one of degree only. Occasionally, a currency is 'devalued' or 'revalued' against the dollar (its official parity is adjusted downwards or upwards in one step), and a special adjustment must be made in the accounts. All these matters have affected sterling, as well as most other currencies, in recent years.

There are two principal methods in use for converting the accounts of an overseas branch or subsidiary to sterling for the purposes of consolidation with the home accounts—the historic rate, and closing rate, methods. Each is considered in turn.

8.2.1 The historic rate method of conversion

The *historic rate* method is the more traditional one, dating from the nineteenth century when Britain was economically dominant in the world, and overseas branches, particularly in 'underdeveloped' countries, were largely financed from Britain. Sterling, before 1914, was a highly stable currency, and it was quite reasonable to make it the standard for evaluating an overseas investment on a historical-cost basis.

Accordingly, each figure in a balance sheet, other than short-term monetary items, is converted at the rate ruling when the relevant item was acquired or arose. The cost of fixed assets is converted as at the date of purchase, and depreciation accumulated to date is converted at corresponding rates, regardless of those in force when it was provided. Contributed capital, and long-term liabilities, are similarly taken at historical rates. Stocks are evaluated at the rates ruling when they are estimated to have been acquired—normally, an average taken over the latter part of the year; if purchased out of sterling funds, they are taken at actual sterling cost. Short-term monetary assets, and current liabilities, are converted at the rate as on the last day of the year, since realizable amounts are the criterion. As to retained profits, the opening balance for the year is taken at the actual sterling amount arrived at last year. All 'cash flow' items for the year (excluding depreciation) are converted at the average rate for the year, on the assumption that they arose evenly over the year. Depreciation is inserted at its historical-cost-based rate, to arrive at the sterling amount of net profit or loss, while remittances of profits (including dividends from a subsidiary) during the year are taken at the actual amounts realized in sterling, and deducted to leave the balance sheet amount of retained profit as at the year-end. All these varying rates mean that the resulting sterling balance sheet does not 'balance', and the difference has to be inserted on the smaller side, as a special item below all others. (The process should be compared with the production of current purchasing power accounts, as described in Chapter 7, section 7.3).

Example 4 Below are trading and profit and loss accounts, and closing balance sheet, for the year ended 31 March 19.1, of General Trading (Gombovia) Ltd, a wholly-owned subsidiary of General Trading Ltd, of London. The accounts are drawn up in Gombovian reals (*Rl*), whose official parity with sterling is currently £1 = *Rl*. 20.00. The relevant historical rates were:

	Rl to £
1 January 19-6 (issue of ordinary shares)	16.00
1 April 19-6 (purchase of land and buildings)	16.20
1 January 19-7 (issue of 8% debentures, at par)	16.50
1 September 19-8 (purchase of fixtures, etc.)	18.00
31 March 19.0 (end of previous year)	19.80
Average for January-March 19.0 (when opening stocks acquired)	19.70
31 March 19.1 (end of current year)	20.10
Average for January-March 19.1 (when closing stocks acquired)	20.05
Average for year ended 31 March 19.1	20.00

General Trading (Gombovia) Ltd

Trading and Profit and Loss Accounts for the Year ended 31 March 19.1

	RI.000	RI.000		RI.000
Opening stock		1,800	Sales	10,000
Purchases		7,700		
		9,500		
Less Closing stock		2,000		
Cost of sales		7,500		
Gross profit		2,500		
		10,000		10,000
Wages and salaries		600	Gross Profit	2,500
Sundry expenses		380		
Depreciation—				
Buildings	100			
Fixtures, etc.	100			
		200		
Interest on 8% debentures		120		
		1,300		
Net profit before taxation		1,200		
		2,500		2,500
Corporation tax (Gombovian)		600	Net profit before taxation	1,200
Net profit after taxation		600		
		1,200		1,200
Dividends paid	150		Net profit after taxation	600
Proposed	300		Balance brought forward from	
		450	previous year	200
Balance carried forward to				
next year		350		
		800		800

Balance Sheet, 31 March 19.1

	RI.000	RI.000		Cost RI.000	Dep'n RI.000	Net RI.000
Share Capital			Fixed Assets			
Ordinary shares		3,000	Land and buildings	2,500	500	2,000
(RI.10)			Fixtures, etc.	500	250	250
Reserves						
Profit and loss account		350		3,000	750	2,250
		3,350				
			Current Assets			
			Stock		2,000	
8% Debentures		1,500	Debtors		2,000	
			Bank and cash		1,500	
						5,500
Current Liabilities						
Creditors	2,000					
Corporation tax						
(Gombovian)	600					
Proposed dividend	300					
		2,900				
		7,750				7,750

The conversion to sterling proceeds as follows:

General Trading (Gombovia) Ltd

Trading and Profit and Loss Accounts for the Year ended 31 March 19.1

	Gombovian		Exchange Rate	Sterling	
	Rl.000	Rl.000		£	£
Sales		10,000	20.00		500,000
Less Cost of sales—					
Opening stock	1,800		19.70	91,371	
Purchases	7,700		20.00	385,000	
	9,500			476,371	
Less Closing stock	2,000		20.05	99,751	
		7,500			376,620
Gross profit		2,500			123,380
Less Wages and salaries	600		20.00	30,000	
Sundry expenses	380		20.00	19,000	
Depreciation—					
Buildings	100		16.20	6,173	
Fixtures, etc.	100		18.00	5,556	
	200			11,729	
Interest on 8% debentures	120		20.00	6,000	
		1,300			66,729
Net profit before taxation		1,200			56,651
Corporation tax (Gombovian)		600	20.00		30,000
Net profit after taxation		600			26,651
Balance brought forward from previous year		200	Calculated		10,240
		800			36,891
Less Dividends (remitted to Britain)—					
Paid	150		Actual	7,543	
Proposed	300		20.10	14,925	
		450			22,468
Adjustment of last year's proposed—					
As last year	300		19.80	15,152	
Amount realized	300		Actual	15,003	
		–			(149)
Balance carried forward to next year		350			£14,572

Balance Sheet, 31 March 19.1

	Gombovian		Exchange Rate	Sterling	
	RI.000	RI.000		£	£
Share Capital					
Ordinary shares (RI. 10)		3,000	16.00		187,500
Reserves					
Profit and loss account		350	Calculated		14,572
		3,350			202,072
8% Debentures		1,500	16.50		90,909
Current Liabilities					
Creditors	2,000		20.10	99,502	
Corporation tax					
(Gombovian)	600		20.10	29,851	
Proposed dividend	300		20.10	14,925	
		2,900			144,278
		7,750			£437,259
Fixed Assets					
Land and buildings—					
Cost	2,500		16.20	154,321	
Depreciation	500		16.20	30,864	
		2,000			123,457
Fixtures, etc.—					
Cost	500		18.00	27,778	
Depreciation	250		18.00	13,889	
		250			13,889
		2,250			137,346
Current Assets					
Stock	2,000		20.05	99,751	
Debtors	2,000		20.10	99,502	
Bank and cash	1,500		20.10	74,627	
		5,500			273,880
		7,750			411,226
Difference on Conversion					
of Gombovian Currency			Balancing		
into Sterling		—	figure		26,033
		7,750			£437,259

The last figure is significant, as indicating the extent to which the holding company's investment in the subsidiary has failed to hold its value in sterling, owing to the progressive depreciation of the Gombovian real as against the pound. Indeed, the equity may properly be valued at £(202,072 − 26,033 =) £176,039. It should be noted that in the conversion of the profit and loss account the balance brought forward is taken at the amount calculated last year, here assumed to be £10,240, and that last year's proposed dividend is adjusted retrospectively to the actual sum realized in sterling, as this represents an actual conversion across the exchanges. There is no revaluation of other 31 March 19.0 balances, as they have not moved out of Gombovian currency, and thus there has been no *realized* gain or loss on exchange.

8.2.2 The closing rate method of conversion

The *closing rate* method appears more appropriate to modern conditions, as well as being much simpler to operate. It is recognized that most overseas branches and subsidiaries, after the early days, are self-financing out of retained profits, which tend to be used to acquire assets in the foreign country, and which sometimes cannot be freely remitted to Britain, owing to currency restrictions, or heavy withholding taxes on dividends paid to non-nationals of the country concerned.

Instead of using different historic rates, therefore, the accountant converts the items in the overseas final accounts into sterling at the rate ruling on the balancing day. The only exceptions are for stocks purchased with sterling funds (at actual sterling cost), and for remittances during the year (at actual sterling amounts realized). It follows that the difference on conversion is usually small.

Example 5 If the conversion to sterling of the accounts of General Trading (Gombovia) Ltd had been made by the closing rate method, the calculations would have proceeded thus (the closing rate being £1 = *Rl.* 20.10, as stated above)

General Trading (Gombovia) Ltd

Trading and Profit and Loss Accounts for the Year ended 31 March 19.1

	Gombovian		Exchange Rate	Sterling	
	Rl.000	Rl.000		£	£
Sales		10,000	20.10		497,512
Less Cost of sales—					
Opening stock	1,800		20.10	89,552	
Purchases	7,700		20.10	383,085	
	9,500			472,637	
Less Closing stock	2,000		20.10	99,502	
		7,500			373,135
Gross Profit		2,500			124,377
Less Wages and salaries	600		20.10	29,851	
Sundry expenses	380		20.10	18,905	
Depreciation—					
Buildings	100		20.10	4,975	
Fixtures, etc.	100		20.10	4,975	
	200			9,950	
Interest on 8% debentures	120		20.10	5,970	
		1,300			64,676
Net profit before taxation		1,200			59,701
Corporation tax (Gombovian)		600	20.10		29,851
Net profit after taxation		600			29,850
Balance brought forward					
from previous year		200	20.10		9,950
		800			39,800
Less Dividends (remitted to Britain)—					
Paid	150		Actual	7,543	
Proposed	300		20.10	14,925	
		450			22,468
Adjustment of last year's proposed dividend—					
As last year	300		20.10	14,925	
Amount realized	300		Actual	15,003	
		—			78
Balance carried forward to next year		350			£17,254

	Gombovian		Exchange Rate	Sterling	
	RI.000	RI.000		£	£
Share Capital					
Ordinary shares (*RI.* 10)		3,000	20.10		149,254
Reserves					
Profit and loss account		350	Calculated		17,254
		3,350			166,508
8% Debentures		1,500	20.10		74,627
Current Liabilities					
Creditors	2,000		20.10	99,502	
Corporation tax (Gombovian)	600		20.10	29,851	
Proposed dividend	300		20.10	14,925	
		2,900			144,278
		7,750			385,413
Difference on Conversion of Gombovian Currency into Sterling		—	Balancing figure		158
		7,750			£385,571
Fixed Assets					
Land and buildings—					
Cost	2,500		20.10	124,378	
Depreciation	500		20.10	24,876	
		2,000			99,502
Fixtures, etc.					
Cost	500		20.10	24,876	
Depreciation	250		20.10	12,438	
		250			12,438
		2,250			111,940
Current Assets					
Stock	2,000		20.10	99,502	
Debtors	2,000		20.10	99,502	
Bank and cash	1,500		20.10	74,627	
		5,500			273,631
		7,750			£385,571

The method converts in effect the opening, as well as the closing, balance sheet on the basis of the year-end exchange rate, so that the trading and profit and loss accounts need converting also on that basis. Exceptions are made for actual transfers across the exchanges, in order to harmonize with the sterling entries in the holding company's books, and these occasion the difference of £158, i.e. £80 on the interim dividend paid during the year (£7,543 actual, against £7,463 for *Rl.* 150,000 converted at 20.10 to the pound), and £78 for the excess of last year's final dividend over its end-year conversion. In other words, the past is 'written off' every year, and modern exchange rates used where possible. This is not necessarily more realistic, though. In the illustration the Gombovian real is assumed to have declined continuously in the foreign exchange market, and this phenomenon normally accompanies a rate of internal inflation higher than that in Britain. The physical assets could be expected, at least, to hold their own in resale values stated in Gombovian currency, and rigid application of the closing rate method is almost certain to undervalue them, even in current sterling, as well as to understate the depreciation charges in the profit and loss account in current sterling terms. It is such considerations which lead to modification of both methods of conversion, to take account of abrupt changes in the rate by devaluation or revaluation, and some parallel treatment seems called for in the case of creeping depreciation of the currency over a lengthy period.

As regards consolidation of a branch's or subsidiary's accounts with those of the parent organization (the branch's control or similar account(s) with head office taking the place of the subsidiary's share capital and reserves in *Examples 4* and *5*), the historic rate method produces an exact match between the 'internal' balances in the two sets of books, while leaving the (often rather large) difference on conversion in the foreign accounts to be brought into the home ones. The closing rate method, on the other hand, can cause a wide discrepancy between the corresponding balances in the two sets of books, so that a large one-sided adjustment has to be made in the consolidated balance sheet, even though the difference on the converted balance sheet itself is small. Thus, if General Trading Ltd's investment in its Gombovian subsidiary has been confined to putting up the share capital of *Rl. 3m.*, and these shares are carried on its books at their original sterling cost of £187,500, then if the historic rate method of conversion is used, the share capital in the Gombovian balance sheet will exactly cancel out in consolidation, and the subsidiary's converted reserves, liabilities and assets will be added to their home equivalents (except that the proposed dividend, being internal indebtedness, will be added back to profit and loss account). The whole of the conversion difference will then have to come on to the assets side of the group balance sheet, at £26,033. If, on the other hand, the closing rate method is adopted, there will be a discrepancy of £38,246 (i.e. £187,500 − £149,254) between the two 'share capital' balances which, with deduction of the contrary conversion difference of £158, will leave £38,088 as a difference on the assets side of the consolidated balance sheet—£12,055 more!

The existence of two equally respectable and equally arguable techniques for currency conversion, giving such different answers, cannot be regarded with equanimity by the accounting theorist. Here is yet another area where the profession needs to carry out fundamental research, to seek one or more approaches which will reconcile, if possible, the conflicting aims of the present methods.

8.2.3 Accounting for changes in parity

The above discussions have been concerned with normal and gradual alterations in exchange rates. When there is an abrupt change of parity, through devaluation or revaluation of sterling or another currency against the U.S. dollar, or when as in 1971 the dollar itself is devalued in terms of gold, it is necessary to make special adjustments in recognition of the exceptional gains or losses which accrue to a British firm with overseas interests. For this purpose it is immaterial which currency is actually devalued or revalued—sterling is considered as remaining fixed, and the other currency as changing in value.

With foreign assets and liabilities, other than investments in branches and subsidiaries, the book amount will be expressed in sterling, at the cost of the currency used to acquire a physical asset or investment, or at the currency amount of cash, a bank balance, or indebtedness in either direction, converted at the historic rate or closing rate method. These assets and liabilities should first be converted from currency amounts to sterling at the rate ruling just before the parity change, their book amounts adjusted upwards or downwards, and the changes debited or credited to Profits and Losses on Exchange Fluctuations Account, whose balance is written off at the year-end to Profit and Loss Account, in the main body of it as a debit or credit in arriving at net profit before taxation. Then all the 'foreign' balances should be revalued in sterling in terms of the new parity, and the gains and losses credited or debited to a Profits and Losses on Devaluation of Sterling Account (or whatever title is appropriate), whose balance at the year-end is transferred to Profit and Loss Account, *after* the determination of net profit after taxation, and with adjustment, where necessary, for the tax effect. In other words it is treated as an extraordinary item, on the lines set out in Chapter 14, sub-section 14.6.3).

As for branches and subsidiaries abroad, the historic rate method automatically involves conversion of the profit and loss account items, except depreciation, at the average rate for the year, but it is better to allow specifically for the parity change, by dealing separately with the items (apportioned, generally, on a time basis) up to, and after, the change, using different averages. The closing rate method does not normally require this, and a special apportionment should be made, the earlier items being converted at the old rate just before the change, and the later ones at the closing rate for the year. By either method, a special valuation of all assets and liabilities should be made as at the relevant date, as though it were the year-end (including the profits accrued up to then), and then there should be a revaluation at the new rate, with a net adjustment to profit and loss account 'below the line'. The closing balance sheet will be drawn up as usual, including a difference on conversion; with the historic rate method, fixed assets (and depreciation provisions), and long-term liabilities, should be converted at the new rate, or (in the case of fixed assets) revalued in terms of sterling, and the revised amounts used in conversion instead of the original currency amounts taken at the historic rates.[1]

8.3 Departmental accounting

After branch accounting it is necessary to consider, more briefly, the methods used to account for the operations of different *departments* of a business, particularly where they are engaged in selling goods, as in a departmental store.

A department is, perhaps, best thought of as a section of the undertaking with distinct functions, or selling distinct lines of merchandise, but normally without geographical separation from the rest of the business. In a factory different departments carry out various production processes, so that the output of one is the input of another, until the goods are completed and transferred to the warehouse, and their records thus lie rather in the realm of cost or management, than in that of financial, accounting. In a departmental store, on the other hand, most of the departments are sellers of different lines of goods, and have a large measure of autonomy—much more than most branches of multiple undertakings. Each departmental manager, or buyer, has his own allocation of funds with which to buy goods at his discretion, either direct from the manufacturers or through a central purchasing department (in the case of chains of stores), ordering in bulk to minimize costs. He fixes his own prices, indents for staff from a special section

[1] See, in particular: The Institute of Chartered Accountants in England and Wales. *Recommendation N 25:* The Accounting Treatment of Major Changes in the Sterling Parity of Overseas Currencies, 1968.

concerned with recruitment and training, and often has some say as to which floor his department shall be sited on, and as to how much space he shall take up. In return he is required to reach targets set by the senior management—sales, gross profit (in money and as a percentage on sales), and (sometimes) sales and/or gross profit per square foot of floor-space.

It is not usual for each department to have its own books of account, other than in memorandum form. All accounting information passes to a central accounting department, which keeps books for the store as a whole, so analysed that the results for each selling department for a period can be extracted and summarized for comparison with that department's budget. For this reason it is not strictly correct to call a department a sub-entity; but the term has already been stretched to cover branches without a distinct accounting sub-system, and in both cases it is possible in principle for separate double entry books to be kept, and linked to the main system by control accounts. Whether or not this is done is a matter of convenience.

8.3.1 Contents of departmental accounts

At a minimum it is practicable, and necessary for control and appraisal, to produce an analysed trading account, in which turnover, cost of sales, and gross profit are allocated to each selling department, and the ratio or percentage of gross profit to turnover computed in each case. The more contentious issue is the extent to which the analysis can be carried out in the profit and loss account, in relation to departmental overheads.

Some overheads, such as wages and salaries of department staff, depreciation and maintenance of special equipment such as racks for suits and dresses, and bad debts, are easily apportioned on the facts. The difficulties arise with costs relating to the store as a whole, such as wages of maintenance staff, rates, depreciation of the building, and operating expenses of service departments such as accounts and advertising. If apportionment is made of all costs some of the allocations are bound to be arbitrary, and the net profit or loss computed for each department to be meaningless as a guide to the manager's performance. The object of a departmental accounting system must be to credit each department with its achieved revenues, and to charge it with all costs over which the departmental manager has any control. The difference is his controllable net profit, or *contribution,* and this is the severest test of his effectiveness as a manager.

Some systems produce an analysed trading account, followed by a set of departmental profit and loss accounts in which each department's gross profit is reduced by the overheads peculiar to it, leaving its contribution, which may be expressed as a percentage on turnover. The total contributions are carried down to a general profit and loss account, which includes general overheads and miscellaneous revenue, to arrive at the total net profit before taxation—and so on. There is no division among departments of the running costs or depreciation of the building—the main fixed asset, whose optimal or sub-optimal use is one of the main determinants of overall profit.

The fact is that the success of a department depends to a large extent upon its position in the building, its position relative to other departments, its floor-space, and its layout. Some departments need a ground-floor or first-floor position, others can make do with the basement or the higher floors. Some need a larger area, some a smaller. Some flourish better when they are close to departments attracting a similar class of customer (housewives, teenagers, sportsmen, etc.), others sell much the same (*ceteris paribus*) wherever they are. Allocation of space is the prerogative of the senior management, as is the provision of finance to departmental heads; but the latter are usually consulted at intervals (of not more than one year) on both aspects, and can, within limits, have more or less, better or worse, floor-space, as well as more or less cash.

Hence, it is only just that the manager should be required to earn a minimum rate of return on the funds invested in his department (whether or not he is formally charged 'interest' thereon—usually he is not), *after* paying an equitable 'rent' for the space which he takes up, and which thus becomes unavailable to other departments. An annual estimate will be made of the total costs of operating the building (including depreciation), and divided by the total floor-area to produce a rent per square foot per annum, duly charged out to the selling departments (and to the non-selling ones, to the extent that they use space suitable for selling). The rents are credited to (e.g.) an Establishment Charges Account, to which the actual costs are debited—any difference at the year-end, and/or any uncharged overheads, being transferred to profit and loss account. A further refinement is to work out differential rents for space on different floors—the highest on the ground floor, and the lowest on the top floor, with the basement charged less than the ground floor. This is done by assigning weights to the various levels, on the basis of subjective estimates of their attractiveness to customers, to determine what proportion of the budgeted cost is to be attributed to each floor, and then dividing by the number of square feet. Thus a selling manager, if he thinks he needs a better position, must weigh against this the obligation to secure a higher gross profit, if he is to satisfy his superiors.

Finally, it is quite unsound to allocate overheads in proportion to turnover, as is sometimes done by less sophisticated firms. This penalizes the manager who by hard work and acumen expands his sales by a greater percentage than the average, and if the gross margin on his goods is low, may actually cause him to show less profit over the year, or even a loss. Use of scarce resources, of cash and of floor-space, is the criterion, if he is to be charged the fair value of the inputs consumed in producing his output—sales to customers.

Example 6 Below is the internal trading and profit and loss account (simplified) of Super Stores Ltd for the year ended 31 January 19.2, with details of three of the departments. The company requires each manager to earn a minimum of 15 per cent per annum on funds advanced to him at the beginning of each year, after charging a floor-space rental which varies according to the level used, and according to the number of square feet taken. The funds made available to the departments shown were as follows.

	Electrical Goods £	Soft Furnishings £	Books and Stationery £
Stock	8,000	12,000	7,000
Debtors	5,000	14,000	3,000
Bank and cash	1,000	2,000	500
	14,000	28,000	10,500
Less Creditors	4,000	8,000	2,000
	£10,000	£20,000	£8,500

Super Stores Ltd

Departmental Trading and Profit and Loss Accounts for the Year ended 31 January 19.2

	Electrical Goods £	Soft Furnishings £	Books and Stationery £	[etc.]	Total £
Sales	50,000	70,000	30,000		1,600,000
Opening stock	8,000	12,000	7,000		200,000
Purchases	40,000	50,000	22,500		1,300,000
	48,000	62,000	29,500		1,500,000
Less Closing stock	9,000	13,000	7,500		220,000
Cost of Sales	39,000	49,000	22,000		1,280,000
Gross Profit	11,000	21,000	8,000		320,000
Wages, salaries and commission	7,000	13,000	5,500		200,000
Floor-space rental	1,500	3,000	800		40,000
Sundry departmental expenses	500	1,000	200		14,000
	9,000	17,000	6,500		254,000
Contribution	2,000	4,000	1,500		66,000
General overheads					14,000
Net Trading Profit					52,000
Interest on debentures					10,000
Net Profit Before Taxation					42,000
Corporation tax					21,000
Net Profit After Taxation					21,000
Dividends					15,000
Retained Profit					£6,000

It will be noted that each of the three departments achieved its target percentage of contribution upon opening net current assets—the most useful measure of the funds invested in the department; the actual rates were respectively 20.0 per cent, 20.0 per cent, and 17.6 per cent per annum.

8.4 Divisional accounting

The last topic to be considered is that of accounting for the periodic results of distinct *divisions* of a large organization—a division being defined as a major, autonomous section of a complex enterprise, usually in extractive or manufacturing industry, producing a range of products which may be either sold to other firms, or to the general public, or transferred to other divisions of the same group at internally-fixed prices. A division is often organized as a separate company, a subsidiary of the group, but may equally well be a part of the parent company, as in Imperial Chemical Industries Ltd.

Where the division is a subsidiary its accounting system is entirely self-contained, only its final accounts being consolidated with those of the parent (and of fellow-subsidiaries), on the principles laid down in Chapter 16. Where the division is not a separate legal entity its accounting records form a complete double entry sub-system, connected with the main system by control accounts—the credit balance of the one in the divisional books constituting the division's quasi-equity. Segregation of revenues and costs is thus achieved quite easily; but a few major problems still arise, and need to be dealt with as a conclusion to this chapter, and to *Part I* of this book.

8.4.1 Framework of divisional accounts

In a truly divisionalized (not merely departmentalized) undertaking the divisional management is given real responsibility for both production and sales, and expected to run the division as an autonomous business. Some divisions of ICI, indeed, are much larger than many independent companies in the same fields, and their senior managers wield quite as much authority as the latter companies' directors. Hence every division keeps its own books, fixes its own prices, controls its own costs, and is called upon to make a budgeted profit, and/or to earn a target rate of return upon its capital employed. The great questions in divisional management are as to how far autonomy should extend *vis-à-vis* the corporate management, how the performance of divisions is to be measured, and how divisions should be restrained from pursuing policies which increase their apparent commercial success while diminishing the real success of the enterprise as a whole.

The consensus of recognized authorities on the subject, such as David Solomons[2] and L. R. Amey,[3] is that, while a division should have as much discretion as possible in its profit-making policies, it should not be allowed to determine its own investment policies, except for plant disposals, and minor expenditure on replacements and additions. All major capital expenditure should be authorized by the corporate board of directors. This follows from the fact that a division has no independent capital-raising powers; even if it is a subsidiary company, it cannot issue shares or debentures without the consent of the holding company's directors, who control all appointments to the subsidiary's board and frequently sit thereon. Since such long- and medium-term funds are mainly invested in fixed asets, few corporate boards are disposed to hand the money over to divisional managements without a strict account of the purposes for which it is to be spent. Again, although a division must have working capital as well as fixed capital, it is not normally allowed to retain the cash which accumulates as a result of making profits and providing for depreciation; this is siphoned off by the central management, so as to optimize its use and prevent the growth of idle bank balances. Many companies have a central purchasing department, through which must pass all orders for bulk materials required in quantity by more than one division—thus maximizing trade and cash discounts; in such cases the accounts payable function will also be centralized. Finally, all companies have centralized service functions, such as research and data processing, whose costs are either charged out to divisions, or deducted from the total of divisional profits to arrive at the company profit. Taxation, also, is best dealt with on this basis, with no attempt to allocate it divisionally.

The second question concerns the definition of divisional profit, in the way most meaningful as a measure of managerial efficiency. The basic concept is that of a division's contribution to the overall profit of the company (before taxation). At

[2] David Solomons, *Divisional Performance: Measurement and Control* (Irwin, 1965).
[3] L. R. Amey, *The Efficiency of Business Enterprises* (George Allen & Unwin, 1969).

least three significant figures can be extracted from a division's profit and loss account, as shown in the annexed table, and they can all be calculated in more than one way. A well-designed set of internal accounts should reveal all of them, thus:

British Chemicals Ltd

Plastics Division

Profit and Loss Statement of the Year ended 31 December 19.1

	£000	£000
Sales Revenue		
Sales to third parties		5,000
Transfers to other divisions		800
		5,800
Less Variable costs (including cost of goods transferred to other divisions)		4,200
Variable Profit (or *Contribution*)		1,600
Less Controllable divisional overheads	750	
Depreciation, etc., on controllable fixed assets	50	
		800
Controllable Net Profit Before Taxation		800
Less Non-controllable divisional overheads	300	
Separable general overheads	50	
		350
Divisional Net Profit Before Taxation		450

The above categories may be regarded as the minimum number needed to provide an adequate analysis; they can, of course, be broken down to any desired extent. *Variable profit* (sometimes called, rather misleadingly, 'contribution') answers to gross profit in the enterprise as a whole, but not perfectly, since the turnover figure includes goods 'sold' internally to other divisions of the company, and appearing as inputs in their accounts. The division may also have 'bought' goods from other divisions, and included them in variable costs; they could be shown separately, inset. The proper pricing of such transfers poses many problems, which are considered further in sub-section 8.4.2.

From variable profit are deducted the fixed or semi-fixed costs which are under the division's control, including depreciation on the (generally rather small) amount of fixed assets whose purchase is at divisional management's discretion. This deduction leaves what is probably the most significant figure from the standpoint of appraisal of divisional results for the year—*controllable net profit before taxation*. Controllable divisional overheads include staffing, warehousing, selling, and transport costs, etc. Then are deducted overheads fairly attributable to the division, but not variable at the will of its management, such as rentals for company buildings assigned to the division's use. Separable general overheads (often omitted here) are non-allocable expenses which, it is estimated, would be saved if the division were closed down—a very debatable item, since logically it ought, if all divisions are taken together, precisely to absorb all general overheads—there would be no business left if all divisions went! In fact, if the estimated savings are added together, on the separate assumptions that each individual division was removed, but no other, the total might come to more or less than the full overheads. If it is less, the charge is defensible; if more, it is very questionable—there would have to be a negative charge in the full profit and loss account of the company. The final residue, *divisional net profit before taxation,* is more interesting to the financial accountant, as being the net contribution (in the true sense) made by the division to the overall pre-tax profit.

8.4.2 The pricing of inter-divisional transfers

All the above 'profit' figures are affected by the prices assigned to inter-divisional transfers of goods, and by charges made for inter-divisional services. These are not matters which can safely be left to the discretion of the divisional managements, especially when transfers form a major part of the outputs and/or inputs of any division—or constitute substantially the whole of either, as in a vertically-integrated concern such as a steelworks. Unless transfer prices are carefully set, by persons independent of the divisional managements—i.e. by members of the central administration—there may be grave danger of exploitation of one division by another. This will cause, not merely an unfair allocation of profit between them, with consequent misjudgement of the two managements' relative competence, but an actual diminution of the total profit of the company or group. If one division is able grossly to overcharge another, the seller will show inflated profits on lower physical production, and the buyer may be induced to restrict his own production to avoid making a loss on his later output—particularly if he is faced with a highly competitive market, in which he can expand sales only by progressively cutting prices and/or increasing selling costs, even though his own unit production costs may not be rising much. Thus the gain to the selling division (as compared with the position if internal prices had been more equitable) will be less than the reduction in the buying division's profit, and the seller's behaviour, though successful from its own point of view, is sub-optimal from the company's. (The reverse will occur if a buying division is able unfairly to keep down the price it pays to a selling division which may have no other outlet for its production.)

In practice several different methods are used to fix transfer prices—variable cost, average cost, standard cost (on either of the preceding bases), any of these plus a margin of profit, market price, a price negotiated between the divisional managers, etc. None of these is satisfactory in all circumstances, and some are unsuitable in any. The theory of internal pricing has been much discussed in the literature, notably by Solomons and Amey, and the consensus is, that the ideal price is the opportunity cost to the firm *as a whole*—not necessarily the opportunity cost to either division.

In the most straightforward case there is a wide market for the transferred product, so that a single price, or a narrow range of prices, can be easily discovered at any time. Market price then provides an equitable basis for transfer pricing; the supplying division is indifferent (*ceteris paribus*) between selling to outsiders and to the consuming division, the latter is indifferent (*ceteris paribus*) as to whence it obtains its supply, and the actions of neither can affect the market price to any noticeable extent. Market price is thus the opportunity cost, to the firm as a whole *and* to the supplying division, which will have an incentive to expand its output to the point where marginal revenue equals marginal cost—the point of maximum absolute profit, and the optimum position for division and firm. In fact, transfer price needs to be a shade lower than market price, to pass on to the consuming division the savings on selling and transport costs, bad debts, etc., realized by the supplying division, and to give the consuming division an incentive to prefer the internal supplier to external ones, only buying from the latter if the former cannot keep up with demand. Both divisions will then tend to expand to the point where marginal revenue equals marginal cost, and the firm's profit is maximized as well, in the same way as it would be if both divisions constituted one profit centre, with materials flowing through it on a cost basis; i.e. any profit made by the supplying division is exactly offset by a reduction in that of the other, as compared with transfers at cost. (In year-end inventories, any internal profit must be eliminated in arriving at the balance sheet value.)

This idyllic situation is rather rare in practice. There may be no competitive market for the transfer products, to which both divisions may freely resort—e.g. in the case of partly-finished or intermediate goods; or the firm may be so large relative to the market that its policies materially affect prices. If the volume of transfers is not important, either presently or potentially, no great harm is likely to come of allowing the two parties to negotiate a price from time to time, on such bases as seem fair to both of them—not below marginal cost to the supplier, nor above opportunity cost to the consumer. If, though, the quantities involved are important, or likely to become so in the foreseeable future, more scientific criteria must be used if sub-optimal policies are to be avoided.

In general, where there are no physical constraints on production of the intermediate good (the supplying division can make all that the consuming one can reasonably require), the *volume* of transfers should be so fixed that the supplying division's marginal cost is equal to the consuming one's opportunity cost, as aforesaid, and the transfer price should be set at that level. If the supplier sends all or most of its output to the consumer (as in vertical integration of processes), *and* there is no outside price, it is best to price transfers at standard variable cost, and to make a periodic charge to the consumer to cover fixed costs of the supplier division—which becomes a service centre, making no profit, so that the object of divisionalization is rather defeated, and non-profit criteria of efficiency must be applied.

Where, however, the supplying division's capacity to produce intermediates is limited, and there is no outside source of supply to make up for this, an optimal solution (to maximize the two divisions' total contribution to the firm's profit) must be sought by techniques of mathematical programming, linear or otherwise. The solution will indicate that some facilities be used to capacity, and others to less than capacity, because of imbalances between the several facilities. Where a facility is not fully utilized, the transfer price of its product will be variable cost; if it is fully stretched, then in the programming solution a 'shadow price' will be indicated—i.e. the reduction in overall profit which will occur if that facility produces one unit less than capacity. The shadow price is thus considered as an internal opportunity cost, per output unit, of using the 'stretched' facility, and is added to the variable cost to find the optimal transfer price. (Where there is spare capacity in a facility the shadow price is zero.)[4] In practice this approach is not commonly used, perhaps because of the complex calculations involved; but a computer can be used to solve rapidly the vast number of equations required in a case where many variables must be considered, and the practical objections then have little weight beside the increased profits which can be earned.

[4] See: Solomons, D. *op cit.*, for a full and lucid illustration.

8.4.3 Interest on capital in divisional accounting

Finally, one of the thorniest problems in divisional accounting is that of making, or not making, a charge to divisions for notional interest on capital supplied to them by central management. Solomons and Amey disagree strongly on this, and the author has been guided by some suggestions of J. M. Samuels,[5] reconciling the two viewpoints.

Where a divisional management has little control over the amount of capital which it uses, its profit target (i.e. its budgeted controllable net profit before taxation) will be set in absolute terms, and nothing is added, as an incentive *ex ante* or as a measure of performance *ex post,* by expressing the net profit as a rate of return on divisional capital employed, however defined. It follows that there is no point either in charging the division interest on capital, or in setting a target rate of return on that capital.

Where, on the other hand, a division is able to determine, within limits, its own capital investment policy, and to ask central management to supply more or less capital in a given year, it makes better sense to charge the division interest at a rate as close as possible to the company's cost of capital, to show such interest in the divisional profit and loss account as a deduction from controllable net profit before taxation, and to set a profit target in terms of *controllable residual income before taxation* (the excess after charging such interest, but before charging non-controllable overheads—now extended to include an interest charge on non-controllable investment). If this is not done, there is an incentive for divisional management to expand absolute controllable net profit by employing more and more capital as long as any return at all can be secured on it, and regardless of whether the overall return is satisfactory. With an interest charge such a policy pays only so long as the rate of return on incremental capital exceeds the company's cost thereof, so that the return on equity is maximized. It is a matter for research as to which of these two situations is the more common; one sincerely hopes that the first one is, for it is the sounder policy to keep authorization of major investment projects in the hands of the corporate board.

So concludes the survey of modern financial accounting theory and practice, on the side of asset and liability valuation and profit determination, and the organization of business accounting systems. *Part II* is concerned with the influence of English law and British financial institutions upon accounting, with special reference to the equity of different forms of enterprise.

[5] Samuels, J. M. Divisional performance measurement and interest on capital: a contributed note. *Journal of Business Finance,* Autumn 1969.

Part **2** Financial accounting in modern Britain

9
Accounting for unincorporated businesses (1)

In *Part I* of this book have been set forth the principles on which all financial accounting is based—those relating to the construction of accounting systems, valuation of assets and liabilities, and measurement of profits, funds, and cash flows. These principles are of international application, and are accepted and operated, to a greater or less degree, in all countries of the non-communist world.

Part 2, is devoted to the modifications and constraints imposed on accounting practice by the laws, customs, and business conditions of one particular state, i.e. the U.K., and especially England. These modifications arise from the recognition by English law of different types of entity, and appear chiefly in four areas of accounting. These are: i *equity structure*; ii *loan capital*; iii *division of profits and losses*; and iv *taxation of profits*.

9.1 Accounts of a sole trader

The oldest and simplest form of business entity is that of a *sole trader*. The business has no corporate status, and the law does not recognize it as having any existence apart from its proprietor. The physical assets and cash belong to him personally, and all receivables and payables are owed to and by him, respectively. The equity represents that part of his personal wealth which is invested in the business, and needs no partitioning. In the books it is indicated by the credit balance of the owner's *capital account*, made up of all sums of money and any physical assets transferred from his private estate, plus all profits (less losses) accrued since the business commenced, less all drawings thereout in cash or kind. Income tax is imposed on the annual profits, and losses are set off, normally against later profits, thus relieving them of taxation to that extent; but tax assessments are regarded as personal liabilities of the proprietor, and not passed through the books. If taxes are paid out of business funds, they are treated as drawings. Finally, the trader has *unlimited liability* for all his debts. In the event of his bankruptcy the whole of his assets, business and private, form a single fund, out of which all his creditors, business and private, are paid according to the legal ranking of their claims—or *pro rata*, if assets are insufficient to pay any class of liabilities in full.

The customary forms of book-keeping and accounts for a sole trader have been illustrated in Chapter 1, and adequately exhibit the legal position, and the movements on capital account during the year covered by the profit and loss account. From a managerial point of view, though, the method is uninformative. Net profit is shown as a single sum, in which are lumped together all its economic elements: *rent* (of any land owned by the proprietor, and used for business purposes); *wages* (remuneration of the working proprietor's services to the business, at a fair rate); *interest* (at a fair rate, on the equity funds employed, less any land to which a rent is imputed); and *profit* (in the economic sense of a residue over and above the other three amounts) or *loss* (a shortfall in accounting profit, as compared with the total of the three amounts aforesaid). Only if there is, over time, a margin of profit in this sense (after full allowance for price level changes, as described in Chapter 7), can the business be considered an economic success, justifying the owner's efforts and the locking up in it of resources which might be otherwise employed.

It is therefore submitted that, first, a sole trader's books should contain both a *capital account* and a *current account* for the proprietor. The capital account should be credited, as now, with all capital introduced by the owner, in cash or in kind, and credited/debited with the amount of any upward/downward revaluation of assets still held, as well as with capital gains/losses (less taxation thereof) arising on sale of a substantial section of the undertaking, or of fixed assets for more than their historical cost or later revaluation. The current account should be debited with drawings (including tax payments), either directly or through the medium of a drawings account, closed off annually to the current account; and credited/debited with the net profit/loss for the year (before tax), divided as follows:

1 A fair open market rent for any freehold property owned and used for business purposes, *less* any charge already made in the profit and loss account for maintenance and depreciation of buildings comprised in the property.
2 A salary in respect of the fair value of the proprietor's services as a self-employed manager, executive, technologist, or clerical or manual worker.
3 Interest at a fair market rate on, at least, the credit balance of his capital account *less* the value of any property for which a notional rent charge is made and, more scientifically, on the credit balance of the current account also—weight being given in both cases to the timing of increments and decrements of the balance during the year, with profits/losses normally deemed to accrue evenly. The rate of interest should be, approximately, the yield currently obtainable on dated gilt-edged securities (computed on a 'discounted cash flow' basis), plus an addition for the higher risk and lower liquidity of an investment in an unincorporated business. Allowance for prospective inflation is already built into the gilt-edged rate, unless the pace of inflation has materially quickened and the market has not yet adjusted to it, in which case some addition should be made.
4 The residual, economic profit or loss.

The profit and loss account should be in two sections: a the *profit and loss account proper,* ending with the net profit/loss, as conventionally calculated by crediting gross profit and other income, and debiting the cost of all factors purchased (except those charged in the manufacturing and/or trading accounts), including amortization of fixed assets; and b the *appropriation accounts* credited/debited with the net profit/loss aforesaid, and debited with items 1 to 4 above—with 4 credited, if negative. If the 'accounting' profit is to be adjusted for price level changes (see Chapter 7), this should be done in a third section, intermediate between a and b.

Example 1 Prudent owns a grocery business whose net profit for the year ended 31 December 19.1 was £3,000. The credit balances of Prudent's capital and current accounts, as at 1 January 19.1, were £5,000 and £2,000. Additional capital of £1,000 was introduced on 1 April 19.1. Drawings for the year were £2,500. The assets included a freehold shop valued at £3,000, the rental value of which was estimated at £500 per annum; £100 had already been charged for its maintenance. Prudent's services to the business were considered to be worth £1,500 per annum. The fair rate of return on capital employed was estimated to be 12 per cent per annum for the type of business concerned.

The economic elements in the accounting profit of £3,000 may be computed thus:

	£	£
Net profit per accounts		3,000
Add Maintenance of shop		100
		3,100
Less Rent charge	500	
Salary, Prudent	1,500	
Interest on capital (12% on £4,850)	582	
		2,582
Residual profit		£518

N.B. Interest on capital computed thus:	Actual	Weighted
	£	£
Capital account balance, 1.1.19.1	5,000	5,000
Additional capital, 1.4.19.1	1,000	750
	6,000	5,750
Less Freehold property	3,000	3,000
	3,000	2,750
Current account balance, 1.1.19.1	2,000	2,000
Net profit per accounts	3,000	1,500
	5,000	3,500
Less Drawings	2,800	1,400
	2,200	2,100
Total capital employed (less property)	£5,200	£4,850

On the most rigorous criteria, then, Prudent's business is profitable, and if the year 19.1 is typical he is amply justified in continuing it.

The above calculation may be made in memorandum form only, as a supplement to the conventional accounts prepared in support of the income tax computation for the tax year 19.2-.3. If it is desired to incorporate it in the accounts, as described earlier, the relevant entries will be as follows.

Prefudent

Profit and Loss Appropriation Account for the Year ended 31 December 19.1

	£		£
Rent charge	500	Net profit b/d	3,100
Salary, Prudent	1,500		
Interest on capital	582		
Residual profit	518		
	£3,100		£3,100

Balance Sheet, 31 December 19.1 (extract)

	£		£
Equity of Proprietor	£		
Capital account	6,000		
Current account	2,200		
	———	8,200	

Capital Account

19.1	£	19.1	£
Dec 31 Balance c/d	6,000	Jan 1 Balance b/d	5,000
		Apr 1 Bank	1,000
	£6,000		£6,000
		19.2	
		Jan 1 Balance b/d	6,000

Current Account

	£		£
19.1		19.1	
Dec 31 Drawings	2,800	Jan 1 Balance b/d	2,000
Dec 31 Maintenance of shop	100	Dec 31 Rent charge	500
Dec 31 Balance c/d	2,200	Dec 31 Salary	1,500
		Dec 31 Interest on capital	582
		Dec 31 Residual profit	518
	£5,100		£5,100
		19.2	
		Jan 1 Balance b/d	2,200

9.2 Partnership

Partnership, the owning of a business by two or more persons jointly, is the logical extension of sole trader operation. As mentioned in Chapter 1, it existed in mediaeval Italy, principally in the form of joint ventures between merchants to finance single voyages. Profit calculations (by 'single entry' methods) exist in respect of three such ventures by two Genoese merchants in 1156-58.[1] From the thirteenth century, however, permanent partnerships became common, particularly among bankers, whose business was more continuous and less easily thought of as a series of ventures. The earliest known ledger accounts are those of a Florentine banking firm in 1211, and mention the christian names of several partners.[2] It is arguable that the development of partnerships, and the consequent need to ascertain and divide profits regularly, or at least consistently, helped to promote the use of double entry, and to clarify the idea of the accounting entity, in the fourteenth and fifteenth centuries.

In England joint ventures were more common during the early days of double entry book-keeping, in the sixteenth and seventeenth centuries. Regular partnerships became frequent during the eighteenth and nineteenth centuries, especially as

[1] de Roover, Florence Edler, Partnership accounts in twelfth-century Genoa (1941), reprinted in Littleton, A. C. and Yamey, B. S., *Studies in the History of Accounting,* Sweet and Maxwell, 1956.

[2] Lee, G. A., The oldest European account book: a Florentine bank ledger of 1211, *Nottingham Mediaeval Studies,* vol. XVI, 1972; Lee, G.A. The development of Italian book-keeping 1211-1300, *Abacus,* vol. 9, No. 2, December 1973.

the industrial revolution gathered momentum and the size of business units increased. The situation was complicated by the Bubble Act, 1719, which required every business firm of more than six partners to be incorporated by Royal Charter or private Act of Parliament—a restriction lifted only in 1825, when the maximum number of partners was twenty generally, or six (later ten) in banking. But the legalization in 1855 of limited liability companies, registered with the Board of Trade, offered a type of organization more suited to large-scale enterprises, and by 1900 it was becoming popular among industrialists, even for businesses of quite modest size. The authorization in 1907 of 'limited partnerships' on the French and German model, in which some of the partners were registered with limited liability but could not then take part in the management, came too late to reverse the trend. It was immediately followed, in 1908, by the relaxation of requirements for the formation and operation of 'private' limited companies, whereby it became easy to obtain limited liability for *all* participants in a business. Today partnerships (almost all 'general', with all partners subject to unlimited liability) are found mainly in the fields of small-scale enterprise, farming, merchant banking, and the professions (except for barristers, who are compelled to practise singly).

9.2.1 Legal framework of partnership accounting

The law of partnership in England developed mainly in the field of equity, as distinct from common law. The Partnership Act, 1890, codified the relevant equitable principles and, with the Limited Partnerships Act, 1907, and the Registration of Business Names Act, 1916, constitutes the legal foundation of this branch of business. Some important provisions, though, are found in the Companies Act, 1967.

The 1890 Act is fairly brief (50 sections and one schedule), and extremely lucid. The policy behind it is to regulate relations between partners and the outside world (especially their creditors), while leaving the partners themselves to regulate their relations with one another by agreement, express or implied. The Act does, however, provide a number of 'fall-back' rules to apply in cases where the partners have failed to agree, or have omitted to consider a matter before it arose. The 1907 Act has very little application in practice, though the 1916 one is still effective. There are also a number of leading cases, concerned mainly with interpretation of the principal Act.

This is not the place for a comprehensive survey of partnership law, and details should be sought in legal works; but some important principles are here stated, as bearing upon the structure of partnership accounting. References are to the 1890 Act unless otherwise indicated.

Partnership is succinctly defined as 'the relation which subsists between persons carrying on business in common with a view of profit' (s. 1), and it is made clear that joint ownership of property, or even participation in profits, do not of themselves constitute partnership; there must be an intention by two or more persons to act in concert, and to become one another's agents within the scope of their business, each binding the others by his lawful and properly authorized acts. But a person who holds himself out, or allows himself to be held out, as a partner in a firm may be made liable as a partner to anyone who grants credit to the firm on the faith of such a representation (s. 14); while a third party who deals with a partner in good faith and in the ordinary course of the type of business concerned is able to hold all the partners bound by the acts of the one, even if he was acting beyond the scope of his authority—provided that the third party had no reason to suspect this (s. 10). More than that: even unlawful acts by a partner (such as fraudulent misappropriation of clients' moneys entrusted to a solicitor) will make the others jointly and severally liable, if carried out apparently in the ordinary course of business (s. 11).

Everyone who enters into partnership with another thus assumes the grave risk of being financially ruined through that other's negligence, incompetence, bad faith, or dishonesty. Accordingly, a partnership agreement is a contract *uberrimae fidei* (of the utmost good faith), in which each party has an absolute obligation to disclose to the others, before they enter into the agreement, all facts known to him which are calculated to affect their willingness to become his partners. Concealment of any such fact entitles the other partners to rescission of the agreement, if they subsequently discover the true position.

Once constituted by agreement (to be discussed in more detail below), the *firm* becomes an unincorporated association in England, a body corporate in Scotland. The maximum permitted number of partners is normally twenty (the same figure now applies to banks, with permission of the Department of Trade if there are to be more than ten), but firms of solicitors, accountants qualified to audit limited companies (chiefly chartered, and certified, accountants), or members of stock exchanges may have any desired number (Companies Act, 1967, ss. 119-121). Firms trading for gain which exceed the permitted number of partners must register under the Companies Acts, or become incorporated in some other manner; otherwise they are illegal associations, and cannot enforce at law any claims against third parties.

If the name of the firm does not consist strictly of the surnames of all the partners, with no additions except their christian names or initials, it is necessary to register the name with the Department of Trade, through its *Registrar of Business Names* (identical with the Registrar of Companies); the same applies to a sole trader, trading under any name other than his own, without addition. Particulars must be given in prescribed form of the firm name, general nature of the business, principal place of business, and date of commencement of business, together with particulars of each partner—his present names in full, any former names in full, nationality (present and former, if different), usual residence, and other occupation(s) if any; and the corporate name and registered or principal office of any body corporate which is a partner. Any change in these particulars must be notified to the Registrar. The register is open to inspection at Companies House, so that anyone may discover the identities of the proprietors of any English firm. Firms required to register must disclose legibly the surnames, and christian names or initials, present and former, of all the partners, on all trade catalogues, trade circulars, showcards and business letters (Registration of Business Names Act, 1916).

Most firms are *general partnerships,* in which all the partners have unlimited liability for the debts of the firm. These can be constituted with few legal formalities, and do not need to be registered, except under the Business Names Act where applicable. A few firms, though, are *limited partnerships,* and must be registered with the Department of Trade (Registrar of Companies). Particulars must be given as to the firm name, general nature of the business, principal place of business, full names of all partners, the term of the partnership, a statement that the partnership is limited, and a description of every limited partner, with the amount of capital to be contributed by him, in cash or otherwise. Changes must be notified. Stamp duty is payable on a limited partner's registered capital, at the rate of 50p per £100 of capital, or part thereof. The limited partner then enjoys limited liability, in that he cannot be compelled to contribute to the liabilities of the firm beyond the amount of his registered capital, which he may not wilfully withdraw, directly or by overdrawing his share of profits. If he inadvertently does so he is obliged to replace it, and in the meantime remains liable to the same extent as before. The limited partner is prohibited from taking any part in the management of the firm, beyond giving advice to the active (general) partners; failure to observe this restriction will make him a general partner with unlimited liability (Limited Partnerships Act, 1907.)

Lastly, it is possible to invest in a partnership, and share the profits, other than as a partner. A person may lend money to a firm at a rate of interest varying with the profits, or in return for an actual share of profit; or he may sell his business to the firm, and be paid for the goodwill by means of such a share of profits. Provided there is an agreement in writing in the first case, signed by all the partners, then the lender (or vendor) does not become liable as a partner; but if the firm is dissolved his claim for repayment of the principal (if any) is postponed to the claims of all external creditors, and he can receive nothing until they have been paid in full (Partnership Act, 1890, ss. 2, 3.)

9.2.2 The partnership agreement

Every partnership is constituted by *agreement* between the partners, except in the rare case of 'holding out' (see sub-section 9.2.1). The agreement may be written, oral, or merely implied from conduct; if two or more persons act as though they were partners in a business, the law will presume them to be such, even if no actual agreement can be proved. An agreement, once made, subsists only as long as the partners wish it to subsist; if all agree to change it, then it is changed. A written or oral agreement can be altered, in either case, by a later written or oral amendment, or even by a 'course of conduct', inconsistent with the agreement and pursued for a considerable time by all partners, without protest from any of them (s. 19).

Permissive as the law is with regard to what concerns only the partners themselves, it is prudent to reduce every partnership agreement to writing, and have all partners sign it; and similarly with all amendments. The terms should cover all important matters, and be clearly and unambiguously worded. Among the matters normally dealt with are:

1 The firm name.
2 The term of the partnership—whether for a specific venture, or a fixed period, or indefinitely ('partnership at will').
3 The nature of the business to be carried on.
4 The principal place of business.
5 Whether the partners are to devote the whole of their time and attention to the business.
6 The amount of capital to be contributed by each partner.
7 The manner in which profits and losses are to be divided between the partners.
8 Provision for the regular preparation of accounts, and for audit.
9 The types of decision to be taken by majority vote of the partners, and those requiring unanimity.
10 Provision for admission of new partners, and for the taking of accounts, and revaluation of assets, on such occasions.

11 Procedure on death or retirement of partners, including restrictions on withdrawal of the outgoing partner's capital.

In cases where the partners have failed to agree on any point, the 1890 Act applies certain rules. These, however, are most conveniently dealt with after consideration of the accounting methods peculiar to partnerships.

9.3 Accounts of a partnership

As compared with a sole trader's business, a partnership requires modification of its accounting system in the four areas denoted in the introduction to this chapter: equity, loan capital, division of profits and losses, and taxation.

First, the equity needs to be partitioned among the proprietors, with distinction between *contributed capital* and *retained profits.* Hence, each partner has opened in his name a *capital account* and a *current account,* with, preferably, a *drawings account* also. Capital introduced, in cash or kind, according to the partnership agreement or any modification of it, is debited to cash or other asset accounts affected, and credited to capital; while current account is credited with the partner's shares of profit, ascertained annually or more frequently, and debited with his share of losses. Drawings, in cash or kind, are debited in the first instance to drawings account, whose debit balance is then transferred at the year-end to the debit of current account—a procedure which avoids encumbering the latter account with detail. In the balance sheet the closing balances of the capital and current accounts are arranged in two separate blocks, distinguishing each partner's balance by name; two sub-totals are made, then added to produce the total value of the equity. It is advisable, also, to annex to the accounts a columnar schedule exhibiting for each partner the opening balances of his capital and current accounts, movements on the accounts during the year, and the closing balances, agreeing with those on the balance sheet.

Secondly, loan capital may take the form, either of borrowings from third parties, or of *advances by partners* over and above their agreed capital contributions. Credit balances on the appropriate accounts appear in the balance sheet as long- or medium-term liabilities, partners' advances being entered immediately after the sub-total of equity, and external loans, if any, next. Interest allowed or paid for the year is debited to interest payable and credited to the current account of the partner concerned, or to cash/bank. At the year-end the interest payable account is closed off to the profit and loss account proper (see below).

Thirdly, the profit and loss account is divided into a *profit and loss account proper,* ending with net profit or loss, and an *appropriation account,* to which the net profit/loss is credited/debited (cf. the suggested form for a sole trader, in section 9.1). Division of the amount among the partners is then performed according to the partnership agreement, by means of debit or credit entries, with opposite ones in the current accounts—thus closing the profit and loss account for the year. The various methods of division are now considered in detail.

9.3.1 Division of profits and losses among partners

The simplest mode of apportionment of profits or losses is according to some arithmetical ratio. Shares may be: **a** equal between all partners; **b** proportionate to partners' capitals (i.e. to the credit balances of their capital accounts); or c unequal and different from the proportions in which capital is contributed. Division is not necessarily proportionate to capital, since a partner's value to his firm is affected also by other factors, such as his business experience and acumen, energy, qualifications, specialized knowledge, and time devoted to the business. Hence some partners may have larger, and others smaller, shares of profit than their capitals appear to warrant—the actual proportions being arrived at by hard bargaining.

The objection to rewarding a partner's merit in this way lies, apart from its imprecision, in the fact that a larger share of profit in good times means a larger share of loss in bad ones, even though the loss may be smaller than it might have been, but for the partner's exertions. It is therefore better to recognize virtue directly by means of *partnership salaries*—fixed sums out of profits and regardless of losses, credited to the current accounts of partners, and sometimes drawn regularly by them in cash. In practice the salaries agreed on are usually much less than the fair values of the recipients' services to the business, even at the time of the partnership agreement, and represent only partial adjustments of the profit-sharing ratios.

Again, it is common, where profits are not divided in proportion to capitals, to allow each partner *interest on capital*—so much per cent per annum on the credit balance of his capital account, weighted for any changes during a year. Like salaries, such interest comes out of net profit, and after charging either or both a residue remains, which has to be divided arithmetically. The object of allowing interest on capital is supposedly to give each partner a fair rate of return on his original investment (current account balances are generally ignored), before ascertaining the extra amounts due to the partners' energy, enterprise and assumption of the risks of competitive business. As with salaries, rates of interest tend to be fixed for many years at a time, at conventional levels which are unrealistically low, even as rates of return on 'riskless' investments—especially today, when gilt-edged securities produce about 15 per cent per annum. The common rates of interest on capital, 5—6 per cent or so, really need revising upwards, to a figure reflecting present expected returns on investments of the degree of riskiness and illiquidity found in unincorporated businesses with unlimited liability, and should then be reviewed every year.

In some firms it is agreed to charge the partners *interest on drawings*, at some rate per cent per annum on each amount drawn, from the date of withdrawal to the end of the year. Each current account is debited with the total charge to that partner, and appropriation account credited. This procedure augments the residual profit (or reduces the residual loss), so that each partner receives back part, or all, or more than all, of the interest charged on his drawings. Some partners thus lose and others gain, on balance, accordingly as they draw heavily or sparingly, and so deplete the firm's working capital more or less. But the net effects are usually quite small, relative to the trouble of making the adjustments, and few firms bother to carry out the procedure. Much the same effect can be obtained in practice by agreeing that the partners shall make regular drawings of fixed amounts, roughly proportioned to their normally expected shares of profit.

Such are the lines on which profits and losses are commonly apportioned, whether in general or limited partnerships—there is no difference in the accounting, except on dissolution of the firm. The following example illustrates the methods comprehensively.

Example 2 Brick, Stone, and Tile are partners in a building business. Their capital account credit balances at 1 January 19.1, were respectively £5,000, £3,000, and £2,000, and their current account balances £800 *Cr.*, £300 *Cr.*, and £200 *Dr.* Their drawings, upon which interest is charged at 8 per cent per annum, are made quarterly on the 1st day of January, April, July, and October, at fixed amounts per quarter of £750 for Brick, £600 for Stone, and £500 for Tile. Interest at 20 per cent per annum is allowed on the balances of the partners' capital accounts; they are allowed annual salaries—Brick, £2,000; Stone, £1,800; and Tile, £1,600; and residual profits or losses are divided—Brick, one-half; Stone, one-third; and Tile, one-sixth. The net profit for the year ended 31 December 19.1 (after allowing interest at 20 per cent per annum on an advance of £1,000 made by Stone on 1 July 19.1) was £9,000. At 31 December 19.1 fixed assets of the firm were £10,000, current assets £6,100, and current liabilities £2,500.

The profit and loss appropriation account of Brick, Stone, and Tile for the year ended 31 December 19.1, the balance sheet as at that date, and the partners' capital, current, drawings, and advance accounts for the year (in columnar form) are as follows (ignoring taxation):

Brick, Stone, and Tile

Profit and Loss Appropriation Account for the Year ended 31 December 19.1

	£	£		£	£
Interest on Capital			Net profit b/d		9,000
Brick	1,000				
Stone	600		**Interest on Drawings**		
Tile	400		Brick	150	
		2,000	Stone	120	
			Tile	100	
					370
Partners' Salaries					
Brick	2,000				
Stone	1,800				
Tile	1,600				
		5,400			
Division of Residue					
Brick, 1/2	985				
Stone, 1/3	657				
Tile, 1/6	328				
		1,970			
		£9,370			£9,370

Balance Sheet, 31 December 19.1

	£	£		£	£
Equity of Partners			**Fixed Assets**		10,000
Capital Accounts			**Current Assets**		6,100
Brick	5,000				
Stone	3,000				
Tile	2,000				
		10,000			
Current Accounts					
Brick	1,635				
Stone	937				
Tile	28				
		2,600			
		12,600			
Partner's Advance					
Stone		1,000			
Current Liabilities		2,500			
		£16,100			£16,100

Capital Accounts

	Brick £	Stone £	Tile £		Brick £	Stone £	Tile £
				19.1			
				Jan 1 Balance			
				b/d	5,000	3,000	2,000

Current Accounts

19.1	Brick £	Stone £	Tile £	19.1	Brick £	Stone £	Tile £
Jan 1 Balance				Jan 1 Balances			
b/d	–	–	200	b/d	800	300	–
Dec 31				Dec 31 Interest			
Drawings	3,000	2,400	2,000	on advance	–	100	–
Dec 31 Interest				Dec 31 Interest			
on drawings	150	120	100	on capital	1,000	600	400
Dec 31 Balance				Dec 31 Salaries	2,000	1,800	1,600
c/d	1,635	937	28	Dec 31 Division			
				of residue	985	657	328
	£4,785	£3,457	£2,328		£4,785	£3,457	£2,328
				19.2			
				Jan 1 Balance			
				b/d	1,635	937	28

Drawings Accounts

19.1	Brick £	Stone £	Tile £	19.1	Brick £	Stone £	Tile £
Jan 1 Bank	750	600	500	Dec 31 Current			
Apr 1 do	750	600	500	a/c	3,000	2,400	2,000
July 1 do	750	600	500				
Oct 1 do	750	600	500				
	£3,000	£2,400	£2,000		£3,000	£2,400	£2,000

Stone £		19.1		Stone £
		July 1 Bank		1,000

N.B. Interest on drawings is computed thus:
Brick
19.1

```
Jan  1 £750 @ 8% for 12 months = £60
Apr  1 £750 @ 8% for  9 months =  45
July 1 £750 @ 8% for  6 months =  30
Oct  1 £750 @ 8% for  3 months =  15
                                 ____
                                 £150
                                 ____
```

etc.

Without the entries for interest on drawings the residual profit would have been £370 less, and the credits to the current accounts of Brick, Stone, and Tile would have been less by, respectively, £185, £123, and £62 (to the nearest £). Thus, Brick would have been worse off by £35, and Stone by £3, while Tile would have been better off by £38. The balance of advantage is small in relation to the total sums involved, and might not be in the same directions every year. Hence, though the calculations were included in the illustration to show the method, they would probably be dispensed with in practice.

9.3.2 Provisions of the Partnership Act, 1890, in the event of the partners' failure to agree

The profit-sharing and other arrangements of a business firm are normally derived from the partnership agreement. The existence of the partnership proves in itself the existence of an agreement, if only in the shape of a tacit understanding; but the agreement may not have been reduced to writing, and some of its terms may be in dispute, or it may have omitted to provide for some contingency which arises, and the partners cannot agree on what to do. Ss. 24 and 25 of the Partnership Act, 1890, therefore lay down rules to be applied in cases where there is no agreement to the contrary, and these are set out below, with a commentary.

Section 24

The interests of partners in the partnership property, and their rights and duties in relation to the partnership shall be determined, subject to any agreement, express or implied, between the partners by the following rules:—

1 All the partners are entitled to share equally in the capital and profits of the business, and must contribute equally towards the losses, whether of capital or otherwise, sustained by the firm.

This rule has little application in practice, since partners are almost certain to agree on the amounts of capital to be contributed, and proportions in which profits and losses are to be shared, if on nothing else. The contribution of different amounts of capital would be taken as an agreement that capital, at least, should not be shared equally. Where the law imposes equality under rule 1 it does so on the ground that, though equality may not be equity, it cannot be shown that any particular degree of inequality is more equitable.

2 The firm must indemnify every partner in respect of payments made and personal liabilities incurred by him –

    a in the ordinary and proper conduct of the business of the firm; or

    b in or about anything necessarily done for the preservation of the business or property of the firm.

3 A partner making, for the purpose of the partnership, any payment or advance beyond the amount of capital which he has agreed to subscribe, is entitled to interest at the rate of 5 per cent per annum from the date of the payment or advance.

These two rules may be read together. A partner may not only make a formal loan to the firm, but may in an emergency (such as a temporary shortage of cash) pay some of the firm's expenses, or discharge its liabilities, out of his own pocket. In such a case the appropriate expense, or creditor's, account should be debited and an advance account for the partner credited. The partner is then entitled to interest at 5 per cent per annum on the balance of the advance account, or such other rate as may be agreed, until the advance is repaid by the firm. Such interest, as explained in sub-section 9.3.1, should be debited at the year-end to the profit and loss account proper, and credited to the partner's current account.

4 A partner is not entitled, before the ascertainment of profits, to interest on the capital subscribed by him.

Any agreement to allow interest should make it clear that the intention is to allow the full rate of interest, irrespective of the level of profits. Thus, if in the example in 9.3.1 there had been only £800 of profit left after meeting partners' salaries, then prima facie only 8 per cent interest would have been available, and there would have been no residue to divide. If full interest were insisted on, there would have been a notional loss of £200, divided between Brick, Stone, and Tile in the proportions £100; £67: £33. This would have left Brick's position unchanged, but worsened Stone's, and bettered Tile's, by £7 in either case.

5 Every partner may take part in the management of the partnership business.

6 No partner shall be entitled to remuneration for acting in the partnership business.

All partners are 'active' unless stipulated to be part-time, 'sleeping' or 'dormant' (acting as investors only, and not as managers), or limited (when the Limited Partnerships Act, 1907, forbids them to take part in the management). Salaries, however, are allowed only if specifically agreed on—partners are normally remunerated by sharing in the profits, if any.

7 No person may be introduced as a partner without the consent of all existing partners.

8 Any difference arising as to ordinary matters connected with the partnership business may be decided by a majority of the partners, but no change may be made in the nature of the partnership business without the consent of all existing partners.

9 The partnership books are to be kept at the place of business of the partnership (or the principal place, if there is more than one), and every partner may, when he thinks fit, have access to and inspect and copy any of them.

These rules are self-explanatory. It should be noted, though, that a partner who takes a copy of any part of the books is not entitled to communicate the copy, or any information about the contents, to unauthorized persons, to the detriment of his partners' interests.

Section 25

No majority of the partners can expel any partner unless a power to do so has been conferred by express agreement between the partners.

This again, is self-explanatory.

Finally, the Partnership Act, 1890, imposes certain *duties* on all partners. In particular, a partner must account to the firm for any benefit derived by him without the consent of the other partners from any transaction concerning the partnership, or from any use by him of the partnership property, name or business connection (s. 29); and if a partner, without the consent of the other partners, carries on a business which competes with that of the firm, he must account for and pay over to the firm all profits made by him in that business (s. 30).

9.4 Treatment of taxation in partnership accounts

The taxation of the profits of a sole trader is entirely a personal matter, and there seems to be no case for his making any special provision for income tax or surtax in his business accounts—he will merely debit any tax payments out of business funds to drawings account or directly to capital, with a credit to bank, at the dates of the actual payments. With a partnership the position is more complex.

9.4.1 Assessment and collection of income tax on partnerships

Income tax assessments on business profits, under Schedule D, Case 1 (trades and businesses) or Case Ii (professions and vocations), are normally made on a 'previous year' basis. The assessment is made for a *tax year* ended 5 April—e.g. 1974-75, the tax year ended 5 April 1975. It is based, however, on profits made by the business according to the latest annual profit and loss account, prepared up to a date within the *previous* tax year; e.g. an assessment for 1974-75 might be based on profits for an *accounting* year ended on any date between 6 April 1973 and 5 April 1974 inclusive—provided that it is the only account prepared in 1973-74, covers one year, and continues from the date at which the previous account ended, or from the commencement of the business. This is the normal position, and it is not here proposed to discuss the complications which ensue in the earliest and latest years of a business's life, or on a change of accounting date.

The assessable profit having been computed from the appropriate annual accounts according to the legal rules for adjusting the net profit shown thereby, it is apportioned among the partners in accordance with the partnership agreement, as though it were an actual net profit—i.e. taking account of interest on advances, interest on capital, partners' salaries, interest on drawings, and arithmetical division of the residue. The basis of division is not, however, that in force for the period when the profits were earned, but for the *tax year* (with apportionment on a time basis, if there is a change of rules during the tax year). The next step is to deduct, from each partner's share of the assessable profit less capital allowances (granted in lieu of depreciation), the income tax reliefs due to him—personal relief, child reliefs, etc. (These are set off first against other income taxable by assessment, to extinguish the liability thereon, and the residue is set against partnership profit, so that all tax not deducted at source may be collected through the firm.)

The balance for each partner is his total income, on which tax is computed at basic rate (for 1974-75, 33 per cent on the first £4,500) and, where applicable, at higher rates. The tax payable by the partners is then aggregated to produce the assessment on the firm for the tax year. The firm pays it in two instalments: on 1 January in the tax year, and on the following 1 July (e.g. for 1974-75, on 1 January and 1 July 1975), and debits the partners' current accounts in the proportions indicated by the notice of assessment. The firm thus acts as a collector of income tax from the partners.

Example 3 The adjusted profit, for income tax purposes, of Tappitt & Bangitt, engineers, for the year ended 31 December 1973 was £10,000. Capital allowances for the year 1974-75 are £1,000. The partnership agreement, in force during the whole of the year ended 5 April 1975, provides for interest on capital at 20 per cent per annum. Tappitt's capital is £10,000, and Bangitt's, £5,000; Tappitt's salary is £1,500 per annum, and Bangitt's £1,000. The residual profit or loss is to be divided equally.

The income tax computation of Tappitt & Bangitt for 1974-75 is as follows; the partners' allowances are as assumed below.

	Total		Tappitt		Bangitt	
	£	£	£	£	£	£
Adjusted profit for year ended 31 December 1973		10,000				
Less Capital allowances 1974-75		1,000				
Assessment		£9,000				
Apportionment						
Interest on capital, 20%		3,000		2,000		1,000
Salaries		2,500		1,500		1,000
Residue (divided equally)		3,500		1,750		1,750
		9,000		5,250		3,750
Less Reliefs						
Personal	1,730		865		865	
Child	825		550		275	
Life assurance	35		25		10	
Retirement annuity payments	600		400		200	
	3,190		1,840		1,350	
Less Family allowance deduction	52		52		—	
Family allowance	47		47		—	
		3,091		1,741		1,350
Total income		£5,909		£3,509		£2,400
Income Tax 1974-75 @ 33%		£1,949.97		£1,157.97		£792.00
Payable						
1 January 1975		£974.99		£578.99		£396.00
1 July 1975		£974.98		£578.98		£396.00

Conventionally, no entry is made in Tappitt & Bangitt's books until 1 January 1975 (or whenever the first instalment is actually paid), when bank is credited £974.99 and Tappitt's current account is debited £578.99 and Bangitt's, £396.00. Similar entries (allowing for the odd 1p) are made at 1 July 1975, or later date of payment of the second instalment. (If any of the reliefs had been set off against unearned income taxed by assessment, such as bank interest, all the tax relative to that income would have been payable on 1 January 1975, thus making the first instalment larger than the second.)

9.4.2 Adjustment on a change of profit-sharing ratios

The common method of accounting for income tax in partnerships recognizes the tax payments purely as partners' drawings, the firm being a mere collector for the Inland Revenue. This is reasonable, as long as the partners' shares of the assessment are in the same proportions as their shares of the profits on which the assessment is based; since the law regards any amount paid or credited to a partner, out of the profits of a firm, as part of his share of those profits. Inequity may occur, though, if there is a change of profit-sharing ratio, or the admission or departure of one or more partners, between the earning of profits and their assessment to tax. If no adjustments are made some partners will pay more tax, and others less, than is warranted by their shares of the underlying profits.

The simplest way to allow for the position is to insert in the partnership agreement, and in every agreement to vary the profit-sharing ratio, or to admit new partners, a clause requiring adjustment of partners' income tax liabilities in such manner as is fair and equitable, by means of debits and credits to their current accounts.

Example 4 Primus and Secundus, who share profits equally, admit to partnership Tertius, as from 1 July 1974, giving him one-fifth of the profits and continuing to share equally between themselves. The business year-end is 31 December. Income tax assessments, on a 'previous year' basis throughout, were: 1973-74, £6,000; 1974-75, £10,000; and 1975-76, £15,000. The partners elect for assessment on a 'continuing' basis, instead of the normal 'cessation and commencement' basis.

The legal division of assessments (before deducting allowances personal to the partners) is:

	Total £	Primus £	Secundus £	Tertius £
1973-74				
12 months ended 5 April 1974—				
Primus: Secundus = 1: 1	£6,000	£3,000	£3,000	–
1974-75				
2-5/6ths months ended 30 June 1974—				
Primus: Secundus = 1: 1	2,361	1,181	1,180	–
9-1/6th months ended 5 April 1975—				
Primus: Secundus: Tertius = 2: 2: 1	7,639	3,055	3,056	1,528
	£10,000	£4,236	£4,236	£1,528
1975-76				
12 months ended 5 April 1976—				
Primus: Secundus: Tertius = 2: 2: 1	£15,000	£6,000	£6,000	£3,000
Total for 3 years	£31,000	£13,236	£13,236	£4,528

The division of the relevant profits (for the years ended 31 December 1972, 1973, and 1974) in the books of the firm, had they been identical with the assessed profits, would have been:

	Total	Primus	Secundus	Tertius
	£	£	£	£
Year ended 31 December 1972—				
12 months ended 31 December				
1972—Primus: Secundus = 1 : 1	£6,000	£3,000	£3,000	–
Year ended 31 December 1973				
(Similarly)	£10,000	£5,000	£5,000	–
Year ended 31 December 1974				
6 months ended 30 June 1974—				
Primus: Secundus = 1: 1	7,500	3,750	3,750	–
6 months ended 31 December				
1974– Primus: Secundus:				
Tertius = 2: 2: 1	7,500	3,000	3,000	1,500
	£15,000	£6,750	£6,750	£1,500
Total for 3 years	£31,000	£14,750	£14,750	£1,500

Such a situation is obviously unfair to Tertius—his current account will be debited with income tax on £3,028 more profit than has been credited to the account, while the other partners are correspondingly relieved of tax! (After 1975, profits and tax assessments will be divided in the same ratios).

The position may be rectified by crediting Tertius's current account, and debiting those of Primus and Secundus in equal shares, with the marginal tax on £3,028—ie.. £3,028 x 33/100 = £999.24. This is correct if the marginal rates of tax are the same for all three partners. It is acceptable if Primus and /or Secundus have higher marginal rates than Tertius, as seems probable—he is no worse off than if tax had been assessed on an 'actual year' basis, and they are somewhat better off. But if such an adjustment involved a transfer from a partner with a lower marginal tax rate to one with a higher, the second partner would be worse off than if 'actual year' assessment had applied. In such cases some formula will have to be agreed on, so that all share equitably the additional tax burden; and the same formula may be used in the converse case also, to enable all to share in any overall relief.

9.4.3 The income tax account

A more formal method of securing equitable treatment of partners' tax liabilities is based on a change in the underlying accounting assumption. Conventionally, income tax is treated as a personal liability of each partner; the firm, as an entity, discharges it for him, and his current account is debited, thus registering a diminution in his share of the equity. The contrary assumption is, that liability of the partners for income tax accrues as profits are earned, and proportionately to the partners' shares in these profits—though the liability is not legally enforceable by the Inland Revenue until some time later. It is therefore argued that, as soon as a partner's share of profit is ascertained for an accounting year, and credited to his current account, the same account should be debited with the best estimate that can be made of his tax liability thereon, and the total liability, so found, for all partners should be credited to an Income Tax Account. When the actual liability falling on the firm is agreed with the Inland Revenue, the balance on the income tax account is adjusted to the total amount due, and the partners' current accounts adjusted, in the same proportions as before—with such additional adjustments as may be agreed for any difference in the total sum due, because of differences in partners' marginal tax rates (see sub-section **9.4.2**). Tax payments are then debited to the income tax account.

In many firms the income tax account at the financial year-end will have a credit balance representing two years' tax—e.g. at year-end 31 December 1973, the balance on income tax account will normally represent agreed income tax for 1973-74 (based on 1972 profits), plus estimated tax for 1974-75 (based on 1973 profits). The two elements need to be distinguished in the balance sheet. The earlier year's tax (payable, in the example, half on 1 January 1974 and half on 1 July 1974) should be shown as a current liability, and the later year's tax—for a tax year which has not yet begun—as Future Income Tax Reserve, placed immediately after the total of partners' equity, and before all liabilities proper. During the following accounting year, the current liability will be extinguished by debiting tax payments to the income tax account; the future income tax will be adjusted to actual, and become a current liability in next year's balance sheet; and a new future income tax reserve will be raised in respect of the second year's profits. By this procedure the partners will be insulated from the effects on income tax of future changes in profit-sharing ratios.

Example 5 At 1 January 1974, the income tax account of Williams & Evans showed a credit balance of £7,000, made up of income tax for 1973-74 (actual), £3,000, and for 1974-75 (estimated), £4,000. The 1973-74 tax was paid on the due dates. The 1974-75 liability was agreed during the year at £3,800, Williams's share of it being reduced by £120 and Evans's by £80. At the year-end the 1975-76 liability was estimated at £5,500, of which £3,500 was apportioned to Williams and £2,000 to Evans.

The income tax account for the year ended 31 December 1974, and year-end balance sheet, with other figures assumed as necessary, appear thus.

Williams and Evans

Income Tax

1974		£	1974		£
Jan 1	Bank (1973-74)	1,500	Jan 1	Balance b/d—	
July 1	do (1973-74)	1,500		Tax 1973-74	3,000
Sept 1	Current a/cs (1973-74)—			do 1974-75	4,000
	Williams	120	Dec 31	Current a/cs (1975-76)	
	Evans	80		Williams	3,500
Dec 31	Balance c/d—			Evans	2,000
	Tax 1974-75	3,800			
	do 1975-76	5,500			
		£12,500			£12,500
			1975		
			Jan 1	Balance b/d—	
				Tax 1974-75	3,800
				do 1975-76	5,500

Balance Sheet, 31 December 1974

	£	£		£
Equity of Partners			*Fixed Assets*	20,000
Capital accounts —			*Current Assets*	12,800
Williams	10,000			
Evans	6,000			
		16,000		
Current accounts—				
Williams	3,000			
Evans	2,000			
		5,000		
		21,000		
Future Income Tax				
Reserve		5,500		
Current Liabilities				
Creditors	2,500			
Current income tax	3,800			
		6,300		
		£32,800		£32,800

The main obstacle to the adoption of this system is the need, when changing over from the 'cash' system of accounting for tax, to provide or reserve for two years' income tax in one year, in addition to accounting for the tax payments during that year. Thus the partners' current accounts are debited with three years' tax at once, and may appear overdrawn at the year-end. This inconvenience may be mitigated by providing in the first year (e.g. the year ended 31 December 1973) for current taxation (1973-74) only (in addition to debiting to current accounts the payments for 1972-73), making a note on the balance sheet as to the position. In the second year (ended 31 December 1974) the tax for 1973-74 is paid (*Dr.* income tax), and provision made, out of current accounts, for current tax (1974-75) and future tax (1975-76) —thus phasing in the new system, which thereafter requires only one year's tax to be debited to current accounts in each accounting year. (Four years' income tax has been charged against two years' profits, instead of three years' tax against one year's profits.) All the same, unless the method of keeping a separate income tax account is used from the inception of the business, partners' objections to the temporary restriction of their drawing rights may militate against its introduction. In that event it is better to use the cash system, with *ad hoc* adjustments for changes in partners or in profit-sharing.

10 Accounting for unincorporated businesses (2)

The mechanics of everyday accounting for partnerships having been dealt with in Chapter 9, it is now necessary to consider the problems which arise when partners enter or leave the firm, when the basis of profit-sharing changes, and when the business ceases to exist as a partnership, or at all.

10.1 Admission of a partner

As already stated (see Chapter 9, sub-section 9.3.2), the admission of a new partner requires, as a rule, the consent of all existing (general) partners; and the terms of admission—capital to be introduced, share of profits, duties, etc.—are normally the subject of much bargaining.

When a new partner enters he automatically takes a share in the net assets, and prospective future profits, of the business built up by the existing partners. If the latter have used the historical-cost basis of accounting, the current replacement or realizable values of the physical assets and investments will almost certainly be different from the book amounts, and there will be no value placed on goodwill generated by the old partners' entrepreneurial and managerial efforts to date, or by external factors beyond their control. The equity of the old partners will thus be overvalued or undervalued—generally the latter; and the incoming partner will buy a share, not of the out-of-date figure in the books, but of the underlying current value.

It follows that, when any undervalued asset (such as land) is subsequently sold, or the whole business disposed of at a price including an element for non-purchased goodwill, a capital gain will have to be recognized in the partnership books, and credited to all the partners' capital accounts in profit-sharing ratio. The late-entering partner will thus take his agreed share of the entire book profit as realized, irrespective of the fact that some it may have accrued before he joined the firm, and ought therefore to be ascribed entirely to the old partners. (*Mutatis mutandis* for a capital loss.) Again, the admission of a new partner constitutes a disposal by the old partners of a portion of their equity. An act of exchange therefore occurs, justifying, and indeed demanding, recognition in the accounts of the new valuation which is thus placed, at least implicitly, upon the set of assets, less liabilities, which underlie the said equity—including the expectation of future super-profits (if any). Lastly, the admission of a partner is, in the eyes of the law, a winding-up of the old firm, followed immediately by the commencement of a new one. All these arguments apply equally to the admission of a partner by a sole trader.

10.1.1 Accounting for admission of a partner

In practice the books are not formally closed and reopened, but entries are made which produce the same effect. To begin with, the net profit or loss is ascertained by conventional methods for the period from the taking of the last regular account up to the eve of the new partner's entry, and divided between the old partners as previously agreed; the nominal accounts being closed off in the process.

A Revaluation Account is then opened. All assets (except cash), and (where applicable) liabilities, are appraised at current values, as at the eve of the change of partners, in such manner as all the partners may agree upon—either by subjective assessment in the light of such evidence as is available, or by employing an independent valuer. A value is also placed upon goodwill, on such basis as is agreed, and preferably with reference to bona fide forecasts of future profits or cash flows, discounted at a suitable rate of interest (see Chapter 6, sub-section 6.4.2). The amount of any upward revaluation of an asset is debited to the asset account, and credited to revaluation account—the reverse for any downward revaluation. (Vice versa for increases, and decreases, in liabilities.) The net upward revaluation of total equity then appears as the credit balance of the revaluation account, and is transferred in profit-sharing ratio to the credit of the old partners' capital accounts. (Vice versa for a net downward revaluation.) On the following day the new partner pays in his agreed capital contribution (*Dr.* Cash, *Cr.* his Capital Account), and the new firm starts fair, with all assets and liabilities at current values. These provide base-lines from which to measure all subsequent capital gains and losses, so that the new partner shares only in that part of each one which is deemed to have accrued since his admission.

Example 1 Major and Minor are partners in a retail firm, sharing profits and losses 3:2. Their balance sheet at 30 June 19.0 was as follows:

Major and Minor

Balance Sheet, 30 June 19.0

	£	£		£	£
Equity of Partners			*Fixed Assets*		
Capital accounts			Freehold property	5,000	
Major	4,000		Fixtures	2,000	
Minor	3,000			——	7,000
	——	7,000			
Current accounts			*Current Assets*		
Major	900		Stock	1,500	
Minor	600		Debtors	1,000	
	——	1,500	Cash	500	
		8,500		——	3,000
Current Liabilities					
Creditors		1,500			
		£10,000			£10,000

On 1 July 19.0 Minimus is admitted to a one-sixth share in the firm, for a capital contribution of £2,500 in cash. As at 30 June, freehold property is revalued at £8,000, fixtures at £1,800, and stock at £1,400, and goodwill is agreed to be worth £4,000. The relevant book entries are:

Freehold Property

19.0		£	19.0		£
June 30	Balance b/d	5,000	June 30	Balance c/d	8,000
June 30	Revaluation a/c	3,000			
		£8,000			£8,000
19.0					
July 1	Balance b/d	8,000			

Fixtures

19.0		£	19.0		£
June 30	Balance b/d	2,000	June 30	Revaluation a/c	200
			June 30	Balance c/d	1,800
		£2,000			£2,000
19.0					
July 1	Balance b/d	1,800			

Stock

19.0		£	19.0		£
June 30	Balance b/d	1,500	June 30	Revaluation a/c	100
			June 30	Balance c/d	1,400
		£1,500			£1,500
19.0					
July 1	Balance b/d	1,400			

Goodwill

19.0		£
June 30	Revaluation a/c	4,000

Revaluation Account

19.0		£	19.0		£
June 30	Fixtures	200	June 30	Freehold property	3,000
June 30	Stock	100	June 30	Goodwill	4,000
June 30	Capital a/cs—				
	Major (3/5ths)	4,020			
	Minor (2/5ths)	2,680			
		£7,000			£7,000

Capital Accounts

19.0		Major	Minor	19.0		Major	Minor
June 30	Balances c/d	8,020	5,680	June 30	Balances b/d	4,000	3,000
				June 30	Revaluation a/c	4,020	2,680
		£8,020	£5,680			£8,020	£5,680
				19.0			
				July 1	Balance b/d	8,020	5,680

If interest on capital is to be allowed, the revaluation will increase the amounts due to Major and Minor. If, on the other hand, it is not desired to produce this effect to the degree implied, and/or not desired to change the book values of the assets permanently (with consequent effect on the depreciation charges for the future), the revaluation entries may be written back to the capital accounts of *all* the partners in the new profit-sharing ratio (3 : 2 : 1), thus:

Revaluation Account

19.0		£	19.0		£
July 1	Freehold property	3,000	July 1	Fixtures	200
July 1	Goodwill	4,000	July 1	Stock	100
			July 1	Capital a/cs—	
				Major (1/2)	3,350
				Minor (1/3rd)	2,233
				Minimus (1/6th)	1,117
		£7,000			£7,000

Capital Accounts

19.0	Major £	Minor £	Minimus £	19.0	Major £	Minor £	Minim £
July 1 Revaluation a/c	3,350	2,233	1,117	July 1 Balances b/d	8,020	5,680	—
July 1 Balance c/d	4,670	3,447	1,383	July 1 Cash	—	—	2,500
	£8,020	£5,680	£2,500		£8,020	£5,680	£2,500
				19.0			
				July 2 Balances b/d	4,670	3,447	1,383

The total of the three capital account balances is now £9,500 *Cr.*—i.e. the old £7,000 plus the £2,500 newly contributed by Minimus. But the main effect of the original adjustment—to prevent Minimus from sharing in the £6,700 capital surplus to 30 June 19.0—is not undone. Without any adjustment he would have taken, eventually, one-sixth of the surplus, or £1,117 (to the nearest £). As it is, this sum has been transferred from his capital to the capitals of Major and Minor, in the old profit-sharing ratio 3 : 2 (£670, £447), and they have thus been compensated in advance.

Instead of the above procedure, the effect of the two sets of adjustments may be computed in memorandum form, outside the books of account, and a single set of entries made to adjust the capitals, thus:

19.0		Dr. £	Cr. £
July 1	Capital account—Minimus	1,117	
	Capital account—Major		670
	Capital account—Minor		447
		£1,117	£1,117

This has the advantages of leaving the asset accounts unaltered, and of dispensing with a formal revaluation account. For all that, though, the original operation, leaving the assets permanently revalued, appears the correct one from the theoretical viewpoint.

10.1.2 Alternative treatment of goodwill on admission of a new partner

The procedure described in sub-section **10.1.1**, in one or other of its variants, is normal when dealing with an industrial or commercial business. Goodwill is treated as an asset to be revalued (often from a zero base) like the others, since it inheres in the enterprise as a whole, rather than in individual partners, whose personal qualities tend to be less important than such factors as product quality and reputation, trade connections, know-how or secret processes, local monopoly, difficulty of entry to the trade, etc.

In professional practices, though, goodwill inheres rather in the partners as individuals. Clients are gained, kept or lost, to a large extent, according to their opinion of the service which they receive from the partner who looks after their affairs. Loyalty is to him, rather than to the firm, and if a successful partner moves to another practice, or sets up independently, in the same area, many of 'his' clients will often follow him. Again, if (e.g.) a solicitor or accountant is taken into partnership from outside, or is promoted from the status of managing clerk, some of the existing clients will usually have to be assigned to him, to ease the work-load of the other partners; so that goodwill tends to be transferred from them to him, if he is as acceptable to the clients as the old partners were.

On the admission of a new partner to a practice, therefore, only the tangible assets are revalued, if of significant amount. The incoming partner, besides contributing an agreed sum as capital (whether in cash down, or by instalments charged, over a term of years, against his share of profits), has to pay the other partners in some way for his share of goodwill, which is not valued in the firm's books. There are basically two methods of so doing: a by paying cash to the other partners; and b by transferring part of his equity in the firm to them. Both alternatives, and their variants, are now illustrated.

Example 2 Deeds and Tape are in practice as solicitors, sharing profits equally. On 1 January 19.1, they admit Parchment to a one-fifth share in the practice; he introduces capital of £3,000. The goodwill of the old firm is valued at £5,000, but no entry for it appears in the books, and it is not desired to bring it in as an asset. Parchment is thus obliged to pay Deeds and Tape for his one-fifth share of the £5,000–i.e. £1,000. If he pays in cash, he may:

1 give Deeds and Tape £500 each, privately and without any entry in the books of the firm;
2 pay £1,000 into the firm's bank account, for Deeds and Tape to withdraw £500 each—achieving the same result as in 1, but making a record in the books; or
3 pay £1,000 into the firm as in 2, but stipulate that it be retained in the business as additional capital—being credited to the capital accounts of Deeds and Tape in equal shares.

Alternative 3 is preferable, provided that the £1,000 can be profitably employed in the practice; otherwise, 2 is marginally better than 1. If, on the other hand, Parchment is unable to pay £1,000 in addition to his £3,000 capital, he will be obliged to transfer £1,000 of the £3,000, in the books, to his partners in equal shares (*Dr.* Capital—Parchment, £1,000; *Cr.* Capital—Deeds, and Tape, £500 each). This is tantamount to raising a debit of £5,000 on Goodwill Account, with credits of £2,500 each to Deeds and Tape's capital accounts, and then reversing the entry, debiting the partners in the proportions Deeds : Tape : Parchment = 2 : 2 : 1 (*cf.* the last variant of *Example 1*).

Sometimes, where the last-mentioned procedure has been adopted or where an explicit account for goodwill has been retained on the books, the new partner is allowed to 'earn' his share of the goodwill. As he proves his worth to the firm, a proportion of the said goodwill is transferred from the other partners' capital accounts (in their profit-sharing ratio) to his, over a period of years, until the new partner's account has been credited with his full share of the asset's value. Thus, to continue *Example 2*, Deeds and Tape might agree to give back to Parchment the £1,000 debited to him, by equal instalments over four years of satisfactory work. The entry at the end of each year will be: *Dr.* Capital—Deeds and Tape, £125 each; *Cr.* Capital—Parchment, £250.

10.2 Changes in profit-sharing ratio

An agreed change in the ratio in which profits or losses are shared (after deducting interest on capital and/or salaries, and adding interest on drawings), though not an act of exchange, is yet an event sufficiently significant to require a general revaluation of partnership assets including goodwill. The change of ratio will affect the division of any capital gain or loss recognized in the accounts in the future and, to the extent that any part of the gain/loss accrued before the change, will increase the shares of some partners therein, and diminish the shares of others. To avoid this inequity it is necessary to make a revaluation as on the eve of the change, and thus ascertain the gains/losses to date. They are then divided between the partners in the old profit-sharing ratio. Any gains/losses subsequently realized will then be measured from the new base-lines, and the amounts so found subjected to division by the new ratio.

10.3 Assurances on partners' lives

The retirement or death of a partner legally dissolves the firm, though in practice the remaining partners usually agree to continue business, and so bring a new firm into existence immediately. More significantly, the retiring partner, or the executors or administrators of the deceased one (generically, his 'personal representatives'), has/have the right to demand repayment of his capital. If they insist on this being done quickly the continuing partners may have great difficulty in raising the money without a forced sale of assets, damaging, and possibly ruinous, to the business.

One way to guard against this possibility is for each partner to take out assurances on the lives of the others, or for each to assure his own life for the benefit of the firm. Endowment policies, maturing at 65 years or other expected retiring age, may be used instead of whole-life assurance, and health insurance policies may also be taken out by individual partners. The premiums, in all these cases, are paid out of partnership funds, and the benefits, when received, become partnership moneys and are credited to all the partners' capital accounts in profit-sharing ratio when they fall due. The effect is thus to augment to some extent the sum needed to discharge the firm's liability, but the remainder of the cash becomes available to repay the rest of the sum due. The trouble is, that the more senior the partner who dies or retires, the smaller is the proportion of the insurance moneys which goes to alleviate the firm's financial position. Thus, if the deceased, etc., is entitled to one-fifth of the profits, then four-fifths of the policy proceeds will go towards repaying his capital before reckoning his share of those proceeds. If, however, his share of profits is one-half, then only half the policy proceeds are available for use as stated. Furthermore, partners with larger shares of profit tend also to have larger capitals, so that the disparity is aggravated. It follows that, unless a very heavy burden of premiums is shouldered, the taking out of life assurance can only partially solve the problem of cash depletion in the case of senior partners.

10.3.1 Accounting for partnership assurance policies

There are three basic methods of accounting for premiums on partnership assurance policies, and they are set out here in ascending order of desirability.

1 Premiums, as paid, are debited to a Life Assurance Policies Account (shown as an asset in the balance sheet), and thus capitalized. There is no charge to partners' current accounts, directly or through the profit and loss account, and if they withdraw all or most of their profits as stated, the firm's cash will be doubly depleted. On the other hand, when the policies mature the proceeds will be credited to the policy account, and only the excess over premiums paid falls to be transferred to partners' current accounts in profit-sharing ratio; the distortion noted in section 10.2 is thus minimized.

  A variant of this procedure involves the writing of the capitalized total premiums to date, down or up to surrender value of the policies at each year-end— the corresponding debit or credit being made to profit and loss account, or directly to current accounts in profit-sharing ratio. The write-downs in the earlier years of the policies, when surrender values are low, help to restrain partners' drawings, but the write-ups later on, as interest accumulates in the hands of the insurers, may have the opposite effect, unless the partners exercise self-discipline. Failing this, the danger that the amount of the total premiums will be paid out twice over the currency of the policies is still a real one.

2 Premiums, as paid, are charged to revenue, and no value is placed on the policies in the books. On maturity the whole proceeds are credited to capital accounts in profit-sharing ratio. This plan has the merit of conservatism, since partners' current accounts bear their rateable shares of premiums paid, and the money cannot unwittingly be paid out twice; but it also has the demerit of conservatism, in that the balance sheets understate the financial strength of the firm by the amounts of the surrender values at successive dates. On maturity, too, the problem outlined in section 10.2 arises in full measure, mitigated though it may be by the fact that each partner has borne his full share of the relevant premiums to date.

3 Premiums, as paid, are capitalized as in 1. At each year-end a sum equal to the premiums for the year is debited to profit and loss account and credited to a Life Assurance Policies Fund Account. Both the policies account and the policies fund account balances (*Dr.* and *Cr.* respectively) are written down or up to surrender value (by debiting one and crediting the other), and their equal and opposite balances appear on opposite sides of the balance sheet—the policies as an asset and the fund as a reserve, immediately after partners' equity. On maturity, the proceeds are credited to policies account. Any excess credit is written off to policies fund (making its balance equal to the proceeds, but of opposite sign), and the fund balance is then transferred to capital or current accounts in profit-sharing ratio. The final effect of this system is the same as in 2, but in the meantime the financial position is more accurately stated.

The treatment of partners' life policies should be compared with that of endowment policies to provide funds for replacement of fixed assets (see Chapter 6, sub-section **6.3.3**).

Example 3 Check, Vouch, and Cast are in practice as chartered accountants, sharing profits 2 : 2 : 1, and making up accounts to 31 December in each year. In 19.1 they take out whole-life policies on their own lives, with benefits of £10,000 each to Check and Vouch, and £5,000 to Cast (all with profits), and annual premium (payable 1 July) £1,500. Check dies on 29 June 19.9; the profits on his policy are £3,000. The surrender values are: 31 December 19.1, £700; . . . 31 December 19.8, £9,500; after settlement re Check's death (10 December 19.9), £6,000.

The relevant accounts (under method **3**) are:

Life Assurance Policies

19.1		£	19.1		£
July 1	Bank	1,500	Dec 31	Life assurance policies fund	800
			Dec 31	Balance c/d	700
		£1,500			£1,500
19.2					
Jan 1	Balance b/d	700			
		. . .			
19.9			**19.9**		
Jan 1	Balance b/d	9,500	Dec 10	Bank (Check)	13,000
July 1	Bank	1,500	Dec 31	Life assurance policies fund	5,000
Dec 31	Life assurance policies fund	13,000	Dec 31	Balance c/d	6,000
		£24,000			£24,000
19.1					
Jan 1	Balance b/d	6,000			

Life Assurance Policies Fund

19.1		£	19.1		£
Dec 31	Life assurance policies	800	Dec 31	Profit and loss a/c	1,500
Dec 31	Balance c/d	700			
		£1,500			£1,500
			19.2		
			Jan 1	Balance b/d	700
			. . .		
19.9			**19.9**		
Dec 10	Capital a/cs		Jan 1	Balance b/d	9,500
	Check	5,200	Dec 10	Life assurance policies	13,000
	Vouch	5,200	Dec 31	Profit and loss a/c	1,500
	Cast	2,600			
Dec 31	Life assurance policies	5,000			
Dec 31	Balance c/d	6,000			
		£24,000			£24,000
			19:0		
			Jan 1	Balance b/d	6,000

10.4 Death or retirement of a partner

A partner who retires from a firm is entitled to repayment of the amount of capital due to him as at the date of retirement, and the personal representatives of a deceased partner are similarly entitled to repayment of his capital as at the date of death (Partnership Act, 1890, s. 43). In either case settlement is made on the basis of current values, ascertained, as on the entry of a partner, by the preparation of conventional accounts for the period since the date of the last regular ones, followed by a general revaluation of assets (including non-purchased goodwill) and liabilities, and consequent adjustment of the partners' capital accounts—thus giving them all the benefit of any capital gains, and imposing on them all the burden of any capital losses, accrued to date but not yet realized.

The balance of an outgoing partner's current account should be transferred to his capital account, thus showing, in one figure, his equity as revalued. The credit balance of his capital account now represents a debt due to him or his personal representatives from the firm—i.e. from the other partners jointly. Payment of this liability may be facilitated by the use of life or endowment assurance (see section 10.3), or by the introduction of new capital by surviving or continuing partners; or one or more of the latter may exercise an option to purchase the outgoing partner's share. Frequently, though, this is not the case, and it is necessary to make some arrangement to defer payment, if the business is not to be damaged by sudden withdrawal of a large proportion of its assets.

Two forms of arrangement are in common use:

a the outgoing partner's capital is left with the firm as a loan; or
b it is made over to the firm in return for an annuity, payable to the partner and/or his widow, or other dependants, for his life.

10.4.1 Accounting for an outgoing partner's loan

Under arrangement a, the credit balance of the outgoing partner's capital account is transferred to the credit of a Loan Account in his name. The principal is usually repaid by regular instalments over a period of years, together with interest at an agreed rate on the outstanding balance from time to time.

S. 42 of the Partnership Act, 1890, provides that, where the surviving or continuing partners carry on business with the firm's capital or assets, without any final settlement of accounts with the outgoing partner or his estate, then, in the absence of any agreement to the contrary, the outgoing partner or his estate is entitled at the option of himself or his representatives to such share of the profits made since the dissolution as the court may find to be attributable to the use of his share of the partnership assets, or to interest at 5 per cent per annum on the amount of such share.

It is no simple matter to ascertain the share of profits attributable to the use of an outgoing partner's share of assets. His share of profits as an active partner is not significant, since it was designed to remunerate his work for the firm, and compensate him for the risks of trading with unlimited liability, as well as provide a return upon his (decidedly illiquid) investment. To isolate the last element is likely to be a complex task, and in the context of litigation an expensive one; and until fairly recently it was more usual to accept the alternative of 5 per cent interest. Today, however, this is a grossly inadequate return, in a period when gilt-edged securities produce some 15 per cent (the rate in 1890 was about 2½ per cent), and a higher rate is normally negotiated—say, 20 per cent—with an action for a share of profits as the ultimate weapon of a dissatisfied lender.

Example 4 Peters, Jameson, and Johnson are partners, sharing profits 3 : 2 : 1. Jameson dies on 17 May 19.1. His capital, and current, account credit balances at 31 December 19.0 (the last accounting date) were £4,000 and £1,340, and his drawings since then are £1,350. Accounts for the period 1 January to 17 May 19.1 show a net profit of £4,200, and a revaluation of assets at the latter date produces a surplus of £3,600. It is agreed with Jameson's executors to repay his capital by five annual instalments at the anniversaries of his death, and to allow interest at 20 per cent per annum on the declining balance in lieu of his share of profits.

The relevant accounts (assuming income tax of 33 per cent throughout) are:

Capital Account—Jameson

19.1		£	19.1		£
May 18	Loan a/c—Exors. of Jameson	6,590	Jan 1	Balance b/d	4,000
			May 17	Revaluation a/c	1,200
			May 17	Current a/c—Jameson	1,390
		£6,590			£6,590

Current Account—Jameson

19.1		£	19.1		£
May 17	Drawings—Jameson	1,350	Jan 1	Balance b/d	1,340
May 17	Capital a/c—Jameson	1,390	May 17	Profit and loss a/c	1,400
		£2,740			£2,740

Loan Account—Exors. of Jameson

19.1		£	19.1		£
Dec 31	Balance c/d	7,413	May 18	Capital a/c—Jameson	6,590
			Dec 31	Interest (228 days)	823
		£7,413			£7,413
19.2			19.2		
May 17	Bank—principal	1,318	Jan 1	Balance b/d	7,413
May 17	do—interest (net)	883	May 17	Interest (balance)	495
May 17	Income tax	435	Dec 31	do— (228 days)	659
Dec 31	Balance c/d	5,931			
		£8,567			£8,567
19.3			19.3		
May 17	Bank—principal	1,318	Jan 1	Balance b/d	5,931
May 17	do—interest (net)	706	May 17	Interest (balance)	395
May 17	Income tax	348	Dec 31	do— (228 days)	494
Dec 31	Balance c/d	4,448			
		£6,820			£6,820
			19.4		
			Jan 1	Balance b/d	4,448
					(etc.,)

Note

1 Interest paid at each 17 May (20 per cent on £6,590 less instalments to date) is subject to deduction of income tax at basic rate, which is accounted for to the Inland Revenue in due course.

2 As Jameson has not been so considerate as to die on the firm's accounting date (31 December), it is necessary, at each year-end, to allow for 228 days' interest accrued since 17 May (all debits of this kind are made to Interest Account, whose balance is transferred annually to profit and loss account).

10.4.2 Accounting for an outgoing partner's annuity

Under arrangement **b** above, the final credit balance of the outgoing partner's capital account is transferred to the credit of an Annuity Suspense Account in his name. The partner and/or his widow (or other nominated dependant) is/are then granted a (joint) annuity for life, paid quarterly as a rule, in an amount bearing some close relation to what could be purchased from an insurance company with the amount of capital available. The annuity payments are debited to the suspense account, which is credited, from profit and loss account, with notional interest, at a fair rate, on the declining balance—thus accounting for net profit on the same basis as if the annuity suspense were a loan being redeemed by the payments. The credit balance of the suspense account, at each year-end, is shown in the balance sheet as a deferred liability, before current liabilities; no attempt is usually made to revalue it actuarially, since a single life cannot be expected to conform closely to the average experience for a large number of lives—the basis of standard actuarial calculations.

If the annuitant, or the survivor of two joint annuitants, dies before the credit balance of the suspense account is exhausted, the deferred liability ceases to exist and is apportioned to the continuing partners' capital accounts in profit-sharing ratio. If the annuity continues after the credit balance is reduced to nil, further payments should be debited to the continuing partners' capital accounts in profit-sharing ratio.

Example 5 Evans, Richards, and Edwards are in partnership, sharing profits 2 : 1 : 1 : accounts to 31 December. Evans retires on 30 June 19.1; his capital is finally ascertained at £10,000. The other partners continue the business, sharing profits equally. It is agreed that Evans shall receive from the firm an annuity of £2,000 per annum for life, paid half-yearly in advance, in lieu of repayment of his capital. Interest is to be credited to the annuity suspense account at the rate of 20 per cent per annum on the declining balance. Evans dies on 6 August 19.4.

The annuity suspense account appears as follows:

19.1		£	19.1		£
July 1	Bank	1,000	June 30	Capital a/c—Evans	10,000
Dec 31	Balance c/d	9,900	Dec 31	Interest	900
		£10,900			£10,900
19.2			19.2		
Jan 1	Bank	1,000	Jan 1	Balance b/d	9,900
July 1	do	1,000	Dec 31	Interest	1,769
Dec 31	Balance c/d	9,669			
		£11,669			£11,669
19.3			19.3		
Jan 1	Bank	1,000	Jan 1	Balance b/d	9,669
July 1	do	1,000	Dec 31	Interest	1,721
Dec 31	Balance c/d	9,390			
		£11,390			£11,390
19.4			19.4		
Jan 1	Bank	1,000	Jan 1	Balance b/d	9,390
July 1	do	1,000	Aug 6	Interest	1,004
Aug 6	Capital a/cs—				
	Richards	4,197			
	Edwards	4,197			
		£10,394			£10.394

10.4.3 Purchase of an outgoing partner's share

The partnership agreement often gives the surviving or continuing partners, or any of them, an option to purchase an outgoing partner's share, at its fair valuation, within a limited period of time (with interest from the date of retirement or death). Even without such a clause, it is always open to partners to negotiate a sale. The purchaser pays the vendor, or his personal representatives, privately, without entries in the firm's books; the vendor's capital account balance is transferred to the purchaser's capital account, and he obtains in future the share of profits previously enjoyed by the vendor. The present value of the share of profits normally exceeds the value of the net tangible assets underlying the vendor's share of capital, and the transfer price should take this into account.

10.5 Dissolution of partnership

Businesses conducted as partnerships may come to an end for various reasons. Sometimes the firm was founded for a temporary and limited purpose, and is wound up when this is achieved. More often the firm is intended to continue indefinitely, and is liquidated, either through bankruptcy, or because the partners die or retire and can find no successors, or because their products have become obsolescent, the market for them is vanishing, and the partners feel disinclined, or too old, to make a fresh start. On the other hand, an industrial or commercial business owned by a sole trader or partners may prosper and expand to such an extent that unincorporated status becomes inappropriate, and unlimited liability too dangerous. The firm will then have to be converted into a limited liability company. Lastly, the firm's business may be absorbed by a larger organization which buys out the partners, for cash or by issuing some of its own shares to them.

The common feature is, that the assets (except cash and debtors) are all disposed of for a consideration whose value generally differs from the book values of the assets. A capital gain or loss thus arises, which has to be divided between the partners in profit-sharing ratio and adjusted into their capital accounts. If all these still show credit balances, the cash (including that collected from debtors) will suffice to pay all external creditors in full, leaving a surplus to be divided among the partners according to the balances on their capital accounts. All accounts will then show nil balances, and the books are closed. If any capital account, after adjustment, shows a debit balance, then that partner owes money to the firm and must pay it in, producing just enough cash to pay creditors *and* repay the partners with credit balances. Inability of a partner to pay off his debit balance leads to complications, in that the deficit must be borne by the other partners; while inability to pay the creditors in full normally leads to bankruptcy proceedings.

The law concerning the contribution of partners to losses and deficiencies of capital on dissolution, and the distribution of the firm's assets, is enunciated in Partnership Act 1890, s. 44, as follows.

In settling accounts between the partners after a dissolution of partnership, the following rules shall, subject to any agreement, be observed:

a Losses, including losses and deficiencies of capital, shall be paid first out of profits, next out of capital, and lastly, if necessary, by the partners individually in the proportion in which they were entitled to share profits:
b The assets of the firm including the sums, if any, contributed by the partners to make up losses or deficiencies of capital, shall be applied in the following manner and order:

1 In paying the debts and liabilities of the firm to persons who are not partners therein:
2 In paying to each partner rateably what is due from the firm to him for advances as distinguished from capital:
3 In paying to each partner rateably what is due from the firm to him in respect of capital:
4 The ultimate residue, if any, shall be divided among the partners in the proportion in which the profits are divisible.

The significance of the various provisions will be brought out in the ensuing exposition.

10.5.1 Accounting for dissolution of a solvent partnership

Accounts should be made up to the date of cessation of business, and the books balanced. A Realization Account should then be opened, in order to ascertain the net gain or loss on realization of the assets, and divide it among the partners. This is the accepted method of giving effect to s. 44(a) of the Act. Losses on realization are first set off against profits thereon, in the realization account ('paid first out of profits'). Any net loss is paid 'next out of capital' by being charged to partners' (amalgamated) capital and current accounts in profit-sharing ratio, while if any partner's capital is inadequate to cover his agreed share of the loss, he is due to pay in the excess. When he has done so, s. 44(b) can be complied with, by paying or repaying: 1 the creditors; 2 partners' advances, if any; and 3 and 4 the partners' capitals, duly adjusted for net profit or loss 'in the proportion in which the profits are divisable'.

There are two standard methods of dealing with gains and losses on realization:

i to credit the proceeds of sale to each individual asset account until all the assets of a class have been disposed of, and then transfer the net (book) profit or loss to realization account, which is adjusted for any savings on settling accounts payable; or

ii to transfer all physical and intangible assets to the debit of realization account, write off thereto any losses on collection of receivables and any gains on payment of creditors (discounts, etc.), and credit all proceeds of sale to the account, in order to arrive at the net gain or loss overall.

Method i is more appropriate when a business is closed down and its assets realized piecemeal, while ii is preferable when the business is disposed of as a going concern. In either case the net gain or loss on realization is transferred to the partners' capital accounts in profit-sharing ratio.

Sometimes, instead of selling an asset, the partners allow one of them to take it over at a fair valuation. The amount thereof is credited to the asset account and debited to the partner's capital account, and the net gain or loss, as compared with the book amount, is transferred to the credit or debit of realization account. This procedure is equivalent to revaluing the asset, with adjustment of all capital accounts, and then permitting the partner to withdraw part of his capital in kind.

Example 6 Player and Wills, partners in a retail firm, share profits 3 : 2. They decide to discontinue business and dissolve partnership on 30 September 19.1, and their balance sheet as at that date appears thus:

Player and Wills

Balance Sheet, 30 September 19.1

	£	£		£	£
Equity of Partners			*Fixed Assets*		
Capital accounts			Fixtures		2,000
Player	2,000				
Wills	1,000		*Current Assets*		
		3,000	Stock	2,000	
			Debtors	3,000	
Current accounts			Cash	500	
Player	50				5,500
Wills	(750)				
		(700)			
		2,300			
Partner's Advance					
Player		1,000			
Current Liabilities					
Creditors		4,200			
		£7,500			£7,500

Over the following three months the fixtures are sold for £1,700, and the stock for £1,200, except for certain items, book value £400, which are taken over by Player at a valuation of £300. £250 of debtors proved bad; discounts allowed to debtors, and received from creditors, total £50 and £30 respectively. All creditors are paid, and settlement made with the partners, on 31 December 19.1. The accounts appear as follows:

Player and Wills

Fixtures

19.1		£	19.1		£
Oct 1	Balance b/d	2,000	Nov 16	Cash	1,700
			Nov 16	Realization a/c	300
		£2,000			£2,000

Stock

19.1		£	19.1		£
Oct 1	Balance b/d	2,000	Oct 31	Cash	1,200
			Oct 31	Capital a/c	
				Player	300
			Oct 31	Realization a/c	500
		£2,000			£2,000

Debtors

19.1		£	19.1		£
Oct 1	Balances b/d	3,000	Oct 1 to Dec 31	Cash (sundries)	2,700
			Dec 31	Realization a/c	
				Discounts	50
				Bad debts	250
		£3,000			£3,000

Creditors

19.1		£	19.1		£
Oct 1 to Dec 31	Cash	4,170	Oct 1	Balances b/d	4,200
Dec 31	Realization a/c				
	Discounts	30			
		£4,200			£4,200

Realization Account

19.1		£	19.1		£
Oct 31	Stock (loss)	500	Dec 31	*Creditors*	
Nov 16	Fixtures (loss)	300		Discounts	30
Dec 31	Debtors—		Dec 31	Capital a/cs—	
	Discounts	50		Player, 3/5ths	642
	Bad debts	250		Wills, 2/5ths	428
		£1,100			£1,100

Current Accounts

19.1		Player	Wills	19.1		Player	Wills
Oct 1	Balance b/d	–	750	Oct 1	Balance b/d	50	–
Oct 1	Capital a/c	50	–	Oct 1	Capital a/c	–	750
		£50	£750			£50	£750

Capital Accounts

19.1		Player £	Wills £	19.1		Player £	Wills £
Oct 1	Current a/c	–	750	Oct 1	Balances b/d	2,000	1,000
Oct 31	Stock	300		Oct 1	Current a/c	50	–
Dec 31	Realization a/c	642	428	Dec 31	Cash	–	178
Dec 31	Cash	1,108	–				
		£2,050	£1,178			£2,050	£1,178

Partner's Advance

19.1		Player £	19.1		Player £
Dec 31	Cash	1,000	Oct 1	Balance b/d	1,000

Cash

19.1		£	19.1		£
Oct 1	Balance b/d	500	Oct 1 to ⎱ Creditors		4,170
Oct 31	Stock	1,200	Dec 31 ⎰ (Sundries)		
Nov 16	Fixtures	1,700	Dec 31	Partner's advance	
Oct 1 to ⎱ Debtors		2,700		Player	1,000
Dec 31 ⎰ (Sundries)			Dec 31	Capital a/c	
Dec 31	Capital a/c			Player	1,108
	Wills	178			
		£6,278			£6,278

Sometimes, as liquidation of a firm proceeds, the partners withdraw cash as it comes in, debiting it to their capital accounts. The danger here is that profits realized in the early stages, and withdrawn, may be more than swallowed by losses later on, so that some partners are compelled to refund. To avoid this, the device is often adopted of distributing cash in such a way as to bring the capital account balances, as soon as possible, into the same ratio as that in which profits are shared. Any subsequent losses on realization will reduce all capitals by the same percentage all round, and can at worst eliminate them; but none will go into debit, and there will be no refunds.

Example 7 Crash, Bang, and Wallop are partners, sharing profits 3 : 2 : 1. Prior to dissolution of the firm and disposal of the assets, their capitals are respectively £4,000, £3,000, and £2,000. They intend to realize the assets piecemeal and to make interim distributions, but in such a way as to avoid any risk of over-distributions.

The technique to be used requires adjustment, first of the partner's capital which is largest in proportion to his share of profits, and then of the next largest in proportion; and so on for any number of partners. The measure adopted is 'capital per unit of profit'—i.e. the partner's capital divided by the number of shares of profit ascribed to him, the appropriate denominator in this case being $6 (= 3 + 2 + 1)$. The partner with the smallest capital per unit of profit is the one whose capital is most in line with his profit-sharing ratio, and it is most convenient to reduce the other partners' capitals to conformity with his, by paying first to them whatever cash is not needed to meet creditors' claims—as the following calculation makes clear:

	Crash £	Bang £	Wallop £
Opening capitals	4,000	3,000	2,000
Number of shares of profit (out of 6)	3	2	1
	£	£	£
Capital per unit of profit	1,333	1,500	2,000
Opening capitals	4,000	3,000	2,000
In profit-sharing ratio based on Crash	4,000	2,667	1,333
Surplus capital	–	333	667
Number of shares of profit (out of 3) (Bang and Wallop only)	–	2	1
	£	£	£
Capital per unit of profit	–	167	667
Surplus capital	–	333	667
In profit-sharing ratio based on Bang	–	333	167
Surplus capital	–	–	500

Order of priority for distributions (after providing for creditors' claims)				Adjusted capitals Crash £	Bang £	Wallop £
First £500	–	–	500	4,000	3,000	1,500
Next £500	–	333	167	4,000	2,667	1,333

(Subsequent distributions in profit-sharing ratio—3 : 2 : 1.)

Thus, the first £500 (the final amount of surplus capital of Wallop) is paid to him, to bring his capital into a 1 : 2 ratio with Bang's. Payment of the next £500 to them in that ratio brings them into a 1 : 2 : 3 ratio with Crash, as required.

10.5.2 Disposal for a consideration other than cash

When a business is sold as a going concern, the consideration sometimes includes a non-cash element. In particular, when a company takes over a partnership's undertaking, it often does so by issuing to the partners shares in the company, with or without a further sum in cash.

Such shares should be valued in the partnership books at market price—i.e. the middle market price, as defined in Chapter 5, section 5.2—as being the most significant value to a holder at the date of acquisition. As a rule, only physical and intangible assets are taken over by the company, so as to save stamp duty on the transfer deed. The vendors retain cash, collect receivables, pay creditors, and wind up the firm when the process is complete. In the final settlement the consideration shares, in terms of market value, are apportioned between the partners according to the credit balances on their capital accounts, and similarly with any cash element in the consideration.

Example 8 Super Stores Ltd takes over the physical assets and goodwill of the grocery business of Box and Cox, who share profits equally, on 1 January 19.2. The consideration is 8,000 shares in Super Stores Ltd (market price on 1 January 19.2, £1.23-£1.27). Box and Cox's balance sheet as at 31 December 19.1 was:

Box and Cox

Balance Sheet, 31 December 19.1

	£	£		£	£
Equity of Partners			*Fixed Assets*		
Capital accounts—			Motor vehicles	1,500	
Box	3,500		Fixtures	1,000	
Cox	2,500			———	2,500
	———	6,000			
Current accounts—			*Current Assets*		
Box	800		Stock	5,000	
Cox	700		Debtors	500	
	———	1,500	Cash	2,500	
		———		———	8,000
		7,500			
Current Liabilities					
Creditors		3,000			
		———			———
		£10,500			£10,500

Box and Cox close their books on 31 March 19.2; bad debts £40, discounts received from creditors, £20. It is agreed to divide the shares proportionately to capitals before collecting and paying debts, and to settle the balances in cash. The most significant accounts appear thus:

Realization Account

19.2			£	19.2		£
Jan	1	Motor vehicles	1,500	Jan 1	Shares in Super Stores	
Jan	1	Fixtures	1,000		Ltd:	
Jan	1	Stock	5,000		8,000 x £1.25	10,000
Jan	1	Capital a/cs—				
		Box	1,250			
		Cox	1,250			
			———			———
			£10,000			£10,000
19.2				*19.2*		
Mar 31	Debtors—			Mar 31	Creditors—	
		Bad debts	40		Discounts	20
				Mar 31	Capital a/cs—	
					Box	10
					Cox	10
			——			——
			40			40

Shares in Super Stores Ltd

19.2		£	19.2			£
Jan 1	Realization a/c: 8,000 x £1.25	10,000	Mar 31	Capital a/cs— Box 4,440 x £1.25 Cox 3,560 x £1.25		5,550 4,450
		£10,000				£10,000

Capital Accounts

19.2		Box £	Cox £	19.2		Box £	Cox £
Mar 31	Shares in Super Stores Ltd— 4,440 x £1.25 3,560 x £1.25	5,550 —	 4,450	Jan 1 Jan 1 Jan 1 Mar 31	Balances b/d Current a/cs Realization a/c Cash	3,500 800 1,250 10	2,500 700 1,250 10
Mar 31	Realization a/c	10	10				
		£5,560	£4,460			£5,560	£4,460

Cash

19.1		£	19.2		£
Jan 1	Balance b/d	2,500	Jan 1 to ⎫ Mar 31 ⎬	Creditors (Sundries)	2,980
Jan 31 to ⎫ Mar 31 ⎬ Mar 31	Debtors (Sundries) Capital a/cs— Box Cox	460 10 10			
		£2,980			£2,980

10.5.3 Conversion of a partnership into a limited company

The entries in the partnership books do not differ in principle when the firm is converted into a private limited company. The company is registered by the partners, who transfer to it all the assets and liabilities of the firm, including cash, debtors, and creditors. The consideration takes the form entirely of shares, divided among the partners, who appoint themselves directors. Two main problems arise—valuation of the shares in the partnership books, and apportionment of the shares among the partners.

The shares, being unquoted, have no easily-determined market value. Hence, since it is difficult to value directly the consideration received for the net assets of the firm, and so determine the book gain or loss to the partners, the alternative is taken of stating the consideration at the value imputed to the net assets given up. Revaluation of assets, including goodwill, has to be carried out in order to establish the commencing values in the company's books, and determine the number of shares to be issued to the old partners, preferably at par. It follows that the par value of the shares is the acceptable one for the realization account or, if the shares are issued at a premium, the par value plus the premium—though this seems an unnecessary complication.

The second problem has a less obvious solution. It is rational to allocate the shares proportionally to the final balances on the capital accounts—exactly pound for pound in terms of par values, in the normal case. A difficulty is that future earnings of the company will accrue to the former partners precisely in proportion to (ordinary) shareholdings, whereas the partnership profits may not have been divided proportionately to capitals. This, however, does not seem a good reason for departing from the above-stated basis for allocating shares. Company earnings are net of directors' remuneration, and the old partners, as controlling shareholders, can fix their remuneration as directors at whatever level the company's profits will allow, and apportion it between themselves, and vary it from time to time, in any way which satisfies their sense of fairness. Alternatively, some part of the consideration for the sale of the firm's business may take the form of debentures and/or preference shares.

A more fundamental problem is that of control. Partners normally agree on management decisions, or the firm could not hold together for very long; but any differences that do arise, and are not sufficiently serious to break up the firm, are generally settled by majority vote. In a company voting power is normally proportionate to shareholdings (one vote per ordinary share), so that something less than a numerical majority of the former partners may be able to overrule the others (e.g. the senior of two partners, whose votes previously had equal weight). In an extreme case it becomes possible to remove a director from office if he disagrees with his colleagues, and make it very hard for him to sell his shares at a fair price without resort to litigation. A system of weighted voting, and other legal safeguards, may therefore have to be written into the articles of association at the outset.

10.5.4 Amalgamation of partnerships

The union of a small partnership, or a sole trader's business, with an appreciably larger firm may conveniently be treated as an absorption, or as the admission of one or more partners whose contributed capital consists partly of assets other than cash. Where two or more fairly large firms merge, however, it is better to treat both or all of them as being dissolved at the same date, and to set up a new firm as on the following day.

Revaluation of physical assets, and corresponding book entries, can be effected in accordance with the principles already explained. Goodwill, also, may be valued for each component firm separately, and the total carried forward as the goodwill of the new firm—being regarded as the cost of goodwill acquired by the new firm at its inception, without regard to any higher value expected to accrue as a result of the reorganization. Each partner's share in the new firm will be equal to the adjusted value of his share in his old firm, but the profit-sharing ratios may have to be renegotiated in the light of the expected contributions of the new partners to the success of the new undertaking, as well as of their reasonable expectations if they had continued on the old bases.

Accounting in each old firm, after preparation of final accounts to the date of the change, requires a revaluation account, to revise all non-cash assets and liabilities to the agreed figures and adjust the capital accounts in profit-sharing ratio; and a realization account, to which the revised values (including cash) are all transferred. The net balance of the account is then transferred to the debit of an account in the name of the new firm, as at the date of the amalgamation—thus dealing formally with the consideration, in the form of shares of capital in the new firm. On the same day the said shares are treated as conveyed to the old partners—being credited separately to the new firm's account and debited to the individual capital accounts; the books are thus closed. In the new firm's books, as on the day of the merger, the assets, liabilities, and capitals as agreed are all brought into the ledgers.

10.5.5 Insolvency

A firm, like an individual, is *insolvent* when its assets, at current values, amount in total to less than its legally-enforceable liabilities—or, in other words, when owners' equity exhibits a debit, instead of a credit, balance. Either an individual or a firm is *bankrupt* when it has been declared, by legal process, to be unable to pay its debts as they fall due, and its assets have been vested in the court's Official Receiver, who hands them over in due course to a Trustee in Bankruptcy, appointed by the creditors and controlled by a Committee of Inspection, representative of them. The trustee's duties are to realize the assets (other than cash) to best advantage; to attach any earnings or other receipts of the bankrupt subsequent to his failure, after allowing him reasonable living expenses; and to distribute the moneys received, from time to time, to the creditors in due order of priority and proportionately to their claims—until all are paid in full with interest at the rate allowed by law, or until the court decides for other reasons to discharge the bankrupt and remit all outstanding claims against him, thus enabling him to make a fresh start in life.

It is not intended here to expound the general law relating to insolvency, contained principally in the Bankruptcy Acts, 1914 and 1926, but only to describe the accounting treatment of insolvent firms, whether the proprietors have or have not been made bankrupt.

The most significant date is that of the *receiving order,* by which the court declares the debtor(s) bankrupt and vests the assets in the Official Receiver. The firm's books must be balanced at that date, and the assets revalued at estimated realizable value, with adjustment to the capital account(s); thus providing figures for the statement of affairs—presented to the Official Receiver within seven days, unless extension of time is granted. If the trustee in bankruptcy (successor to the Official Receiver) continues the business, it must be solely for the purpose of beneficial realization. Once that is achieved he will close its books, having already entered the assets and liabilities in his own accounts, kept in prescribed form.

The assets of a bankrupt sole trader, business and private, form a single fund out of which all his creditors, business and private, are paid, class by class; all the creditors of a prior class being paid 100p in the pound before those of the class next in order can receive anything. The classes recognized by law are:

1 *Secured debts*—charged by contract upon particular assets (e.g., mortgages on land), and paid out of the sale proceeds thereof as far as possible, with any surplus going to unsecured creditors.
2 *Pre-preferential debts*—moneys which do not really belong to the debtor, such as funds of a friendly society or trustee savings bank in the hands of a bankrupt officer.
3 *Preferential debts*—notably unpaid rates, PAYE deductions, VAT or national insurance contributions accrued within twelve months before the receiving order; income tax for any *one* year of assessment, assessed up to 5 April next before the receiving order; wages and salaries of employees up to four

months in arrear and up to £200 per individual; and accrued holiday remuneration of employees.

4 *Ordinary debts*—all not included in the other classes, as well as secured debts to the extent that the security proves insufficient.

5 *Deferred debts*—including money lent by a wife to her husband for the purposes of his trade or business, or by a husband to his wife for use in *any* business; money lent to a firm in return for a share of the profits, or for a rate of interest varying with the profits; money due to a vendor of goodwill, compensated by an annuity or share of profits; and accrued interest on moneylenders' loans in excess of 5 per cent per annum (up to the date of the receiving order).

If there are insufficient funds to pay any class in full, then all claims of that class are abated proportionately and later classes receive nothing. If there are enough funds to pay all classes in full, they are all then entitled to interest at 4 per cent per annum (free of income tax) from the date of the receiving order to the actual dates of payment; only then will the debtor be entitled to discharge from bankruptcy on the ground of payment in full.

When a partnership goes bankrupt, all the partners are made bankrupt simultaneously, and one trustee in bankruptcy is appointed for them all, and the firm. The assets of the firm, and of each individual partner (excluding his interest in the firm), are treated initially as distinct estates, out of which the 'joint' creditors (of the firm), and the 'separate' creditors of each partner, are first paid as far as possible. If there is a deficiency on the joint estate (represented by a net debit balance on partners' total equity, as adjusted), it must be made up by the partners out of the surpluses, if any, on their separate estates (i.e. they must pay in the amount of their debit balances), while if there is a deficiency on a partner's separate estate, and he has a credit balance finally on his capital account, he must withdraw it for his own creditors' benefit.

10.5.6 The rule in *Garner* v. *Murray*

Complications arise when a partner has *both* a deficiency on his separate estate *and* a final debit balance on his capital account, while one or more other partners have surpluses on their separate estates and either credit balances on their capital accounts, or debit balances which they can meet in full. In that case, by the rule of unlimited liability, the solvent partners must make up the deficiency on the joint estate between them as far as they are able, claiming the amount advanced from the insolvent partner if he is ever in a position to repay them.

The question then arises, as to the proportions in which two or more solvent partners are to contribute to, or bear, a final debit balance on capital account which another partner is unable to pay in. (This problem is not restricted to bankrupt firms, but may arise even if all creditors have been paid in full.) At one time it was thought that the deficit should be borne in profit-sharing ratio, but the leading case of *Garner* v. *Murray* (1904) produced a different rule.

Garner, Murray, and Wilkins were briefly in partnership in 1900—contributing unequally to capital, but sharing equally in profits. After realizing all assets and repaying creditors and partners' advances, the final cash balance was £634 short of the amount needed to repay the *original* capitals of Garner and Murray, and the deficit was augmented by an irrecoverable debit balance on Wilkins's current account of £263 (he had no original capital). It was decided that s. 44(b) of the

Partnership Act, 1890, did not require a solvent partner to contribute for an insolvent one, but assumed that partners were actually to pay in the amount of any losses of their original capitals, and then withdraw the original amounts—a result normally achieved in practice by refunding the written-down balances of the capital accounts. The profit-sharing ratio applied to losses sustained by the firm—not by partners as individuals. Hence, 'the assets must be applied in paying to each partner rateably what is due from the firm to him in respect of capital, account being taken of the equal contribution to be made by him towards the deficiency of capital'. These words of the learned judge were interpreted as meaning that the £634 loss was to be apportioned equally to the three partners (increasing Wilkins's deficiency to some £474), and that that amount was then to be debited proportionately to the capital accounts of Garner and Murray, after which the cash was paid out to them.

The rule in *Garner* v. *Murray* is commonly supposed to state that an irrecoverable debit balance on a partner's capital account (after taking account of all other losses) is to be borne by the other partners in proportion to the balances of their capital accounts before dissolution commenced. This is indeed the effect of a strict application of s. 44 if, as in the leading case, all partners' advances are repaid in full (or non-existent).

Example 9 The balance sheet of Good, Indifferent, and Bad (sharing profits equally) appears thus, after realizing all non-cash assets and paying off all external liabilities, but before closing off the realization account:

Good, Indifferent, and Bad

Balance Sheet, 30 June 19.1

	£	£		£
Capital Accounts			Cash	1,150
Good	1,000			
Indifferent	500		Realization Account—	
Bad	(600)		Deficiency	750
		900		
Partner's Advance				
Good		1,000		
		£1,900		£1,900

Bad is insolvent and unable to contribute anything. The rule in *Garner* v. *Murray*, by either the conventional procedure or by a literal following of s. 44 of the Act, produces the same final result—Good receives £1,183, and Indifferent pays in £33, thus:

a Conventional procedure:

	Advance Good £	Good £	Capital Indifferent £	Bad £
Opening balances	1,000	1,000	500	(600)
Shares of deficiency	—	(250)	(250)	(250)
	1,000	750	250	(850)
Apportionment of Bad's deficit, 1,000:500	—	(567)	(283)	850
	£1,000	£183	(£33)	—

b Strict observance of Partnership Act, 1890, s. 44:

	Advance Good £	Good £	Capital Indifferent £	Bad £
Opening balances, less deficiency	1,000	750	250	(850)
Contributions to restore original capitals	–	250	250	–
	1,000	1,000	500	(850)
Repayment of advance, then of capitals, *pro rata*	(1,000)	(433)	(217)	–
Closing deficiencies	–	£567	£283	(£850)

If, however, the final assets (after the solvent partners have paid in their shares of the deficiency) are insufficient to repay advances in full, the conventional procedure will not work justice. S. 44 must then be strictly observed, as the next illustration makes clear.

Example 10 Suppose that the position of Good, Indifferent, and Bad had been

Good, Indifferent, and Bad

Balance Sheet, 30 June 19.1

	£	£		£
Capital Accounts			Cash	200
Good	600			
Indifferent	400		*Realization Account–*	
Bad	(1,000)		Deficiency	1,800
		–		
Partner's Advance				
Good		2,000		
		£2,000		£2,000

a Conventional procedure:

	Advance Good £	Good £	Capital Indifferent £	Bad £
Opening balances	2,000	600	400	(1,000)
Shares of deficiency	–	(600)	(600)	(600)
	2,000	–	(200)	(1,600)
Apportionment of Bad's deficit, 600 : 400	–	(960)	(640)	1,600
Amounts repaid	£2,000	(£960)	(£840)	–

i.e. Good receives £1,040, and Indifferent pays in £840.

	Advance Good £	Good £	Capital Indifferent £	Bad £
Opening balances, less deficiency	2,000	–	(200)	(1,600)
Contributions to restore original capitals	–	600	600	–
	2,000	600	400	(1,600)
Repayment of advance, then of capitals, *pro rata*	(1,400)	–	–	–
Closing deficiencies	£600	£600	£400	(£1,600)

I.e. Good receives £800 net, and Indifferent pays in £600. This is the correct legal position, and the rule in *Garner* v. *Murray*, as usually stated, is inapplicable, being merely a convenient working procedure for the normal situation, where the advances can be repaid in full. The rarity of the converse case is perhaps the reason why the misunderstanding has persisted for so long.[1]

---

[1] See: Gibson, C. J., Partner's liability. *Accountancy*, September 1970.

11

Accounting for limited liability companies (1)

The fluid structure of an unincorporated firm, and the absence of a stable fund of permanent, non-withdrawable capital, militate against the continuous growth of a large industrial or commercial enterprise, in which massive sums must be invested in long-lived physical assets; nor can the requisite amounts of money be raised, except by subscription from an extensive body of investors, reluctant to participate on a footing of unlimited liability. For these reasons the laws of England, and most other countries, have in modern times made available the privileges of corporate status and limited liability, through the machinery of the *limited liability company*.

In England, incorporation of overseas trading companies began in the sixteenth century, by means of Royal Charters (the Hudson's Bay Company, chartered in 1670, is still a going concern). From about 1760 the industrialization of Britain led to the construction of canals, docks, water and gas works, and later railways, by large companies incorporated with limited liability by private Acts of Parliament. Such Acts also granted extensive powers not normally possessed by individuals—to purchase land compulsorily, to operate the undertaking in spite of disturbance to local amenities, etc.—besides regulating the charges made to users, and other matters in which there was danger of abuse of monopoly power. In modern times, special Acts have been passed to create the State corporations (such as the British Railways Board) which own and operate the nationalized industries.

In 1844 came the first Joint Stock Companies Act, allowing any business firm to be registered with the Board of Trade as a body corporate. A further Act (1855) permitted such a company to be registered with limited liability for the members (proprietors), and in 1862 came the first statute providing a comprehensive code of law for joint-stock enterprises. Current legislation consists of the Companies Acts, 1948 and 1967, the second amending and partially repealing the first. The 1967 Act was based largely on the recommendations of the Jenkins Committee on Company Law, which reported in 1962; a further Act, to consolidate the two existing ones and enact many of the remaining proposals of the Jenkins Report, is expected in the 1970s.

11.1 Formation of a registered company

The Companies Act, 1948, s. 1, permits any seven (or, in certain circumstances, two) or more persons, associated for any lawful purpose, to form, by registration under the Act, an incorporated company, with or without limited liability. Three types of company are recognized: a the *company limited by shares*; b the *company limited by guarantee*; and c the *unlimited company*.

In a, the proprietors' capital is divided into a number of shares, the original holders of which are required to subscribe a certain 'nominal' amount per share (e.g. £1) to the company. When the full amount has been paid the holder has no further liability for the company's debts. The creditors must claim from the company, not from individual shareholders, and the latter are not obliged to make up any deficiency if the company becomes insolvent, or fails altogether. At worst, they lose the money invested, either as original subscribers or as purchasers of shares from existing holders. This is the ordinary form of business company, and the only type to be considered here at length.

In **b**, each member undertakes to contribute, while a member or within one year after ceasing to be one, a fixed sum to the company's assets in the event of winding up, for payment of the company's debts and liabilities contracted before he ceased to be a member, and of the costs, charges, and expenses of winding up, and for adjustment of the rights of the contributories among themselves; or such lesser sum as may be required. There is no need to have a share capital. This type of company is not used commercially, but is suitable for non-profit-making bodies (such as prestigious London clubs and learned societies) for which a more formal and continuing organization is required than that of an unincorporated association.

The name of a company limited by shares, or by guarantee, must end with the word 'limited', unless the Department of Trade licences it to dispense with the word—as being a company formed to promote commerce, art, science, religion, charity, or any other useful object, and intending to apply its profits or other income in promoting its objects, and to prohibit the payment of any dividend to its members (1948, s. 19).

The unlimited company **c** has corporate status, but does not limit its members' liability. Members are liable to contribute to its debts, if necessary, to the full extent of their resources, while members and up to one year after ceasing to be such. As with **b**, there is no need for a share capital. The form is generally used to incorporate large landed estates, especially if settled or entailed within a family, and provide continuing management, separate and distinct from successive life-tenants. Under the 1967 Act, the unlimited company alone is exempt from filing its accounts with the Department of Trade, and may thus have some attraction for the small business. Indeed, the 1967 Act (s. 43) lays down a procedure for re-registering a limited company as unlimited.

11.1.1 Registration of a limited company

Registration of a limited company is effected by delivering certain documents, and paying certain fees and duties to the Department of Trade's Registrar of Companies (in London for English companies and in Edinburgh for Scottish ones). The documents are:

1 The memorandum of association.
2 The articles of association.
3 A statement of nominal capital.
4 A statutory declaration of compliance with the requirements of the 1948 Act.
   In addition there is:
5 Notice of situation of the registered office—legally required within fourteen days after incorporation but usually delivered with 1 to 4 above.

The *memorandum of association* (1948 Act, ss. 2-5) is, in effect, the company's charter, defining its basic constitution and the objects for which it is formed. It contains six clauses, as a rule, thus:

 i The name of the company, ending with 'limited';

ii The country (England or Scotland) in which the registered office is to be situate (England includes Wales);

iii The objects of the company—very long and comprehensive, with many standard sub-clauses as well as those peculiar to the business concerned. Since the company cannot do anything not covered by the objects clause, and since the procedure for altering the clause later on is somewhat cumbrous, the objects tend to be made as wide as the foreseeable needs of the undertaking could possibly demand—though they must be definite ones, such as the running of a given business enterprise and the various subsidiary activities necessary to effect this purpose, and to broaden or alter the scope of the main business from time to time;

iv A statement that the liability of the members is limited;

v The amount of share capital with which the company proposes to be registered, and its division into shares of a fixed amount; and

vi A formal declaration that the subscribers are desirous of being formed into a company, in pursuance of the memorandum, and respectively agree to take the number of shares in the company, set opposite their names.

There follow the names, addresses, and descriptions of seven (or two) persons, with the number of shares which each agrees to take if the company is formed, and the signature of a witness.

The memorandum must be printed and stamped as a deed for 50p, and with a registration fee stamp, varying with the amount of the nominal or authorized capital—£20 for the first £2,000; £1 for each of the next three £1,000 steps; 25p for each additional £1,000 up to £100,000 in total, and 5p for each further £1,000—maximum £68 (1967 Act, Schedule 3). Additional fees must be paid on any subsequent increase of capital, unless the maximum has already been paid.

The *articles of association* (1948 Act, ss. 6-10) are the internal regulations of the company, which all members are legally bound to observe. They usually adopt most of the model set of 136 articles (1948 Act, First Schedule, Table A), with some articles peculiar to the company. If Table A is adopted *in toto,* no special articles need be registered; otherwise, Table A applies to the extent that it is not specifically excluded or modified. The articles must be printed and divided into numbered paragraphs, bear a deed stamp (50p), and be signed by all the subscribers to the memorandum, with the signature of one witness.

Table A, and most special articles, deal with such matters as share and loan capital and the holders' rights, meetings and voting rights, the powers, duties, appointment, and removal of directors, accounts and audit. Alteration of the articles requires a special resolution of the members, with twenty-one days' notice to them and a three-fourths majority of votes cast at the meeting.

The *statement of nominal capital* repeats the information in clause v of the memorandum. It is required by the Finance Act, 1933, which imposes a capital duty of 50p per £100 of nominal (authorized) capital on registration, and on the amount of any increase from time to time. As this is easily effected by ordinary resolution (needing a simple majority only, of votes cast at the meeting), and as there are no refunds of duty, it is inadvisable to fix the initial capital greatly in excess of foreseeable requirements.

The *statutory declaration* (1948 Act, s. 15) is made by a solicitor engaged in the formation of the company, or by a person named in the articles as a director or secretary of the company, to the effect that all the requirements of the Acts regarding registration have been complied with. The Jenkins Committee considered that this declaration serves no useful purpose, but Parliament has not yet abolished it.

The *notice of situation of the registered office* states the company's official address, to which all communications will be sent. Notice must be given of changes in it from time to time.

11.1.2 Public and private companies

Any company may be registered as a 'private company' by inserting certain restrictions in its articles of association, in return for exemption from certain requirements of the Companies Acts. If it does not do so it is registered as a 'public company'. Machinery is provided for changing from one status to the other. The articles of a private company must:

a restrict the right to transfer its shares;
b limit the number of members to 50, excluding the company's employees, and its ex-employees who have been its members since a date prior to the termination of their employment; and
c prohibit any invitation to the public to subscribe for any shares or debentures of the company (1948 Act, s. 28).

The distinction between the two classes was first authorized in 1908. Private company status was devised for the small- to medium-sized business, owned and operated by a small number of closely associated persons, with no present intention of admitting outsiders or seeking a stock exchange quotation; while large-scale enterprises, raising capital from the general public, having their securities quoted and dealt in on a stock exchange, and being operated by an inner group of 'professional' directors, continued to be public companies, subject to provisions designed to safeguard outside investors from misinformation or malpractice. The most important difference between the two classes was that private companies' annual accounts needed to be circulated only to those financially interested in the company, whereas those of public companies had also to be filed with the Registrar of Companies, and made available for inspection by members of the public. Abuse of the exemption—by registering as private companies the subsidiaries of large public companies—led in 1948 to its being restricted, in effect, to those private companies which were genuinely independent of outside control ('exempt private companies'). The Companies Act, 1967, now requires all limited companies, without exception, to file their accounts with the Registrar, though small companies are excused from giving certain information (see Chapter 14, sub-section 14.4.1).

The residual advantages of private company status are:

i the memorandum of association need have only two subscribers, whereas a public company requires seven (1948, s.1);
ii the company may operate with two members, as against the minimum of seven for a public company (s. 31);
iii it may commence business immediately on incorporation, without the further steps required of a public company (s. 109);
iv it need not issue a prospectus or deliver a statement in lieu of prospectus (s. 48—see sub-section 11.2.1);
v it need not hold a statutory meeting, or circulate a statutory report (s. 130—see sub-section 11.4.2.); and

vi it need have only one director, against a minimum of two for most public companies (s. 176), and is exempt from certain restrictions on directors' appointment and tenure of office.

In addition to the documents (1 to 5 in sub-section 11.1.1) required on registration of any company, the applicants for registration of a public company must deliver a *list of persons who have consented to be its directors.* If a director is named as such in the articles he must, on registration, deliver to the Registrar a *written consent to act,* and a *declaration,* or other proof, *that he has taken,* or will take, *his qualification shares;* otherwise he need not do so until the issue of a prospectus, or delivery of a statement in lieu thereof (s. 181).

11.1.3 Commencement of business

On delivery to the Registrar of the prescribed documents, and payment of the proper fees and duty, a *certificate of incorporation* is issued, constituting the subscribers of the memorandum, and any other future members of the company, a body corporate under the name of the company, with perpetual succession and a common seal, and with limited liability (1948 Act, s. 13).

A private company is then free to commence business—usually by taking over the promoters' existing business, issuing shares to them, and enabling them to appoint themselves directors. A public company, likewise, is seldom or never started from scratch in modern times. An existing private company is often re-registered (the special restrictions in the articles being deleted), because the needs of its expanding business for fresh capital have outrun the resources of the present shareholder-directors and it is necessary to offer shares to the investing public, or because it is desired to render marketable the somewhat illiquid investments of its existing members.

Sometimes a new public company is formed in order to merge two or more existing ones, or as part of the reconstruction of an unsuccessful enterprise. It is then necessary to obtain from the Registrar a *certificate of entitlement to commence business.* This is granted when a share issue for cash to the public, involving the issue of a prospectus, has been finalized or, where there is no such issue, a statement in lieu of prospectus has been delivered (see section 11.2), all the directors have paid the amounts due so far on their shares, and a statutory declaration of compliance with these conditions, signed by the secretary or any director, has been delivered to the Registrar (s. 109).

11.2 Issue of shares

A private company usually issues shares informally, by personal contact between the directors and the prospective—often existing—shareholders. A contract is executed, consideration passes, share certificates are made out, and records made in the company's books. The only notice to the Registrar is the *return of allotments,* delivered within one month after allotment. It states the number and nominal amount of the shares, particulars of the allottees, and the amount paid, or due and payable, on each share. It is accompanied, in the case of allotment for a consideration other than cash, by the relevant contract, or a written memorandum thereof, with a return of the number and nominal amount of the shares so allotted, the extent to which they are treated as paid up, and details of the consideration (1948 Act, s. 52).

11.2.1 Prospectuses and offers for sale

When it first re-registers as a public company, a former private company normally seeks a stock exchange quotation[1] on a provincial exchange or, if the company is sufficiently large and well-known, on the London Stock Exchange. (To be considered for a London quotation, the company must have an expected market value of at least £250,000, and the class of shares concerned, one of at least £100,000.) In London, applications are submitted, at least fourteen days in advance, to the Quotations Department, and investigated, most rigorously, by the Committee on Quotations. A draft *prospectus,* advertising the shares for subscription and having an application form attached, must be submitted, and must comply, both with the requirements of the Stock Exchange (as set out in its regulations on 'Admission of Securities to Quotation') and with those of the Companies Act, 1948, ss. 37 and 38 and Fourth Schedule. If approved, the prospectus must be published as directed (including advertisement in two leading London newspapers), and application for a quotation made formally after two days; it is usually granted unless new facts, adverse to the company's reputation, have come to light in the meantime.

The above business is conducted by an issuing house, which prepares all the documents. Sometimes the issuing house receives a commission out of the proceeds of an issue directly to the public; otherwise, the issuing house contracts to purchase the entire issue from the company at a fixed price, and then resells the shares to the public, at a profit to itself, by means of an *offer for sale,* similar in form to a prospectus and subject to similar legal and Stock Exchange requirements (1948 Act, s. 45). The company must, however, deliver to the Registrar of Companies a *statement in lieu of prospectus* (1948 Act, s. 48 and Fifth Schedule), giving much the same information. Small issues are sometimes handled by the issuing house's 'placing' the shares with financial institutions, without a public offer for sale; a statement in lieu of prospectus is still required, but compliance with the 1948 Act regarding prospectuses is generally waived, by obtaining from the Stock Exchange a *certificate of exemption* (s. 39). (Most of the rules of the Stock Exchange have still to be observed, though, as for an issue by prospectus or offer for sale.) Lastly, shares already quoted on a provincial exchange may be 'introduced' to London, and granted a quotation, without any new ones being issued at the time.

The detailed requirements of the 1948 Act and of the London Stock Exchange as to the contents of a prospectus or offer for sale are long and complicated, and cannot be reproduced here; those of the Stock Exchange are the more exacting, but do not completely comprehend those of the Act. Between them they demand full particulars of the company, its business, past history, future prospects, directors, officers, and professional advisers, as well as of the securities to be issued; the penalties for giving false or misleading information are severe. The accountant is most directly interested in the mandatory report by the company's auditors, covering, in the London Stock Exchange's regulations:

i the company's profits or losses for the last ten financial years (or such shorter period as the company has existed), with a note if no accounts have been made up to a date within the last three months (the Fourth Schedule requires the report to cover five years only, but this is virtually a dead letter today); *or*

---

[1] References in the 1948 Act to 'permission to deal' in securities are obsolete; today a quotation automatically includes such permission, and vice versa.

ii in the case of an issue by a holding company, the profits or losses for ten years or less as above, of the holding company and its subsidiaries, so far as they concern members of the holding company, with a note as aforesaid;

iii the rates of dividend for the last five years, with details of any waivers in that time;

iv the assets and liabilities of the company, and of its subsidiaries (if any) in so far as such assets can properly be attributed to the holding company's interests; including an explanation of the bases of valuation of the fixed assets and a reasonably detailed indication of the nature of the tangible assets;

v the aggregate directors' emoluments for the latest accounting period, and the amount (if any) by which they differ from the amounts which would have been payable under the arrangements in force at the date of the prospectus; and

vi any other matters which the auditors consider relevant for the purpose of the report.

In making their report the auditors shall make such adjustments as are in their opinion appropriate for the purposes of the prospectus.

If the company, or any of its subsidiaries, has acquired, or agreed to acquire, or is proposing to acquire, any business, or shares in any company (none of whose securities are quoted), so as to make it a subsidiary, the prospectus must include a report by named qualified accountants, covering:

i the profits or losses of the business, or those attributable to the interests (to be) acquired, for its last ten financial years (or such shorter period as the business, etc., has existed), with a note if no accounts have been made up to a date within the last three months; the report being extended to the subsidiaries, if any, of the company whose shares have been/are to be acquired, as in **ii** above;

ii the assets and liabilities of the business or subsidiary, as in **iv** above;

iii any other matters which the accountants consider relevant for the purpose of the report.

In making their report the accountants shall make such adjustments as are in their opinion appropriate for the purpose of the prospectus.

(The Fourth Schedule of the 1948 Act requires an accountants' report, for the last five years only, on the profits, etc., of any business, etc., to be acquired out of the proceeds of the issue in question. Once more, the Stock Exchange regulations go beyond the law's demands, and largely supersede them.)[2]

11.2.2 Application and allotment

After the publication of a prospectus or offer for sale, at least three days (excluding Saturdays, Sundays, and Bank Holidays) must be allowed for applications to come in. Only at the beginning of the third day ('the time of opening of the subscription lists') is it permitted to proceed further (1948 Act, s. 50).

In the case of a company's *first* public issue, the prospectus, etc., must specify the 'minimum subscription'—the minimum amount of share capital necessary to be raised, in order to provide for:

a payment of the purchase price of any property (to be) purchased out of the proceeds of the issue;

---

[2] Briston, R. J., *The Stock Exchange and Investment Analysis,* George Allen & Unwin, 2nd edition, 1973.

b payment of any preliminary expenses payable by the company, and any commission payable to any person for agreeing to subscribe for, or for procuring or agreeing to procure subscribers for, any shares in the company;

c repayment of any moneys borrowed by the company for the above purposes; and

d working capital.

It must also state, where applicable, how the balance of the total sums thus required is to be provided, otherwise than out of the issue proceeds (s. 47 and Fourth Schedule, para. 4).

If shares to the required amount have not been applied for, and the sums due on application paid to the company, within 40 days after issue of the prospectus, then no shares can be allotted, and the moneys received must be refunded to the applicants, with interest at 5 per cent per annum from the expiry of the 48th day, if refund is not made before then (s. 47).

The minimum subscription rule does not apply to the second and subsequent public issues by a company, but under-subscription of an issue, though it does not normally invalidate it, is damaging to the company's reputation and that of the issuing house concerned. The latter is therefore careful to set the issue price at a level calculated to make the shares attractive to the market, even if somewhat below the price at which they are expected to settle once dealings commence. As an additional insurance against failure, the issuing house arranges for 'underwriting' of the shares by a syndicate of merchant bankers, discount houses or the like. The underwriters agree to take and pay for any shares not subscribed for by the public, and are remunerated by a commission from the company on the total value of the issue (usually between 0.25 and 3 per cent), payable in any event. Underwriting commissions tend to be easily earned, since most issues are over-subscribed many times.

This situation is apparent to the promoters or the issuing house before the opening of the subscription lists—which are usually closed a few minutes later. The shares are then 'allotted' to applicants, normally by eliminating multiple applications from the same person (where they can be detected), satisfying larger, genuine applications wholly or partly, and rejecting smaller ones, or allocating a small part of the issue to a few of them, selected by ballot. Those fortunate enough to receive any shares are sent *letters of allotment*, making them members of the company from the date of posting; those wholly unlucky receive *letters of regret*, together with refunds of their application moneys.

The prospectus or offer for sale always states the amounts per share payable on application, on allotment, and on subsequent call(s)—e.g., for £1 shares, 25p on application, 50p (including 25p premium) on allotment, and 50p on first and final call—say, one month later. Shares cannot normally be issued below their 'par' (nominal) value (at a discount), but those of an established undertaking usually command a 'premium' over and above par—a kind of entrance fee to the company. The application moneys must be sent with the application form; they may not be fixed at less than 5 per cent of the nominal value (s. 47). Moneys from a successful applicant are retained; those relating to shares in excess of his allotment are regarded as allotment moneys in advance, and only the balance is demanded. An allotment letter is a temporary document of title; it may be sold in the market and the outstanding allotment moneys paid by the purchaser. All such letters are exchanged within two months for regularly sealed *share certificates.* The company must also, within one month of any allotment, deliver to the Registrar a return of allotments, as described in section **11.2**.

Shares are occasionally offered for subscription or sale by 'tender'. The prospectus or offer for sale states a minimum figure, at or above which investors are invited to price their applications. A 'striking price' is then fixed, somewhere in the middle of the range of offers, and shares allotted to all who offered as much or more—at the fixed price, regardless of their actual offers. At a maximum, the price is just low enough to absorb all equal or higher offers. More often, it is pitched lower to create a wider spread of shareholdings and a more active market, and successful applications are scaled down accordingly. The advantages of this system are that it enables market demand to be more accurately judged, and that the company (or the issuing house) obtains some part of the profit otherwise made by 'stags'—speculators who apply for newly-issued shares with intent to sell them as soon as dealings begin. The strongest objection to tenders—that investors are deterred by uncertainty as to the final price payable—may even be a gain, if it is stags who are mainly frightened off. Adoption of the method, however, has been retarded, more than anything else, by the conservatism of the City and an irrational feeling that this kind of higgling is undignified.[3]

11.2.3 Accounting for issue of securities

In the books of a limited company the contributed capital of the shareholders (members) is represented by the credit balances on two or more accounts—the Share Capital Account(s) and the Share Premium Account. All accretions to these balances appear as single block amounts, without distinction as to the persons who contribute the capital, while the partitioning of the share capital (but not the premium) is shown in a Share Ledger, outside the books of account. The consideration for the shares issued (including the premium) is debited to appropriate asset accounts.

In the illustrations which follow, it is assumed that the company has only one class of share capital—the basic 'ordinary' shares, representing aliquot parts of the total equity of members.

When a private company is formed it usually takes on to its books the revalued assets, and liabilities, of the business to which it succeeds. Shares of a nominal value equal to the net assets are issued to the proprietors, and divided between them as they agree—generally on the basis of their shares in the old partnership.

Example 1 Brown and Wilson Ltd is registered as a private company (authorized capital, £80,000) to acquire the partnership business of Brown and Wilson as from 1 January 19.2. The firm having previously paid the expenses of incorporation, £500, its balance sheet as at 31 December 19.1 (after revaluation of all assets) was:

[3] Briston, R. J., *op. cit.*

Brown and Wilson

Balance Sheet, 31 December 19.1

	£	£		£	£
Equity of Partners			*Fixed Assets*		
Capital accounts—			Freehold property	10,000	
Brown	40,000		Plant	20,000	
Wilson	23,000		Fixtures	5,000	
		63,000			35,000
			Goodwill		6,000
					41,000
Current Liabilities					
Creditors		10,000			
			Current Assets		
			Stock and work in		
			progress	9,000	
			Debtors	16,000	
			Bank balance	6,500	
					31,500
			Other Assets		
			Company formation		
			expenses		500
		£73,000			£73,000

In the books of Brown and Wilson Ltd, the assets as stated are debited, and the liabilities credited, to appropriate accounts, as at 1 January 19.2. The opening journal entry is completed by a credit of £63,000 to Ordinary Share Capital, representing the issue to Brown and Wilson, respectively, of 40,000, and 23,000, ordinary shares of £1 each. The books of the partnership are closed by bringing all assets and liabilities to the debit and credit sides of the realization account (see 1948 Act, s. 5 and *passim*), crediting the latter with Shares in Brown and Wilson Ltd, £63,000, and debiting their capital accounts as indicated, via an account for the shares.

The opening balance sheet of the company appears as follows. Note the treatment of the authorized, and issued, share capitals—the first being merely a note, unrepresented by a balance in the books—and of the 'preliminary expenses', as they, are usually described.

Brown and Wilson Ltd

Balance Sheet, 1 January 19.2

	£	£		£	£
Share Capital			*Fixed Assets*		
Authorized			Freehold property	10,000	
80,000 ordinary			Plant	20,000	
shares of £1 each £80,000			Fixtures	5,000	
					35,000
Issued			Goodwill		6,000
63,000 ordinary					
shares of £1 each,					41,000
fully paid		63,000	*Current Assets*		
			Stock and work in		
Current Liabilities			progress	9,000	
Creditors		10,000	Debtors	16,000	
			Bank balance	6,500	
					31,500
			Other Assets		
			Preliminary expenses		500
		£73,000			£73,000

When a public company makes an issue for cash it is advisable to open a special bank account, and pay into it all cheques for application moneys which arrive before the closing of the subscription lists—any late ones being returned to the senders, with a stereotyped covering letter. The application forms are then considered by employees of the issuing house, assisted by the promoters of the company. As the fate of each application is decided it is processed manually, mechanically, or electronically and key totals accumulated for entry in the company's books.

In the ledger, an Application and Allotment Account is opened for the particular issue. The total application moneys received are debited in one sum to the special bank account, suitably identified, and credited to application and allotment account, as representing deposits potentially returnable. When all shares have been allotted, either a letter of allotment or a letter of regret is made out for each applicant. The moneys from rejected applicants are returned with their letters of regret, and the total debited to application and allotment account and credited to bank—thus discharging the contingent liabilities which have now crystallized.

The shares comprised in the letters of allotment must total to the precise number available for issue, and each letter must demand the allotment moneys for the shares allotted, less excess application moneys retained. This operation constitutes issue of the shares. The Ordinary Share Capital Account, and (where applicable) the Share Premium Account, are credited with the total application and allotment moneys due according to the prospectus or offer for sale, with the corresponding debit(s) in the application and allotment account. Allotment moneys as they come in are debited to bank and credited to application and allotment account, until the latter account is closed. The bank balance is then transferred to the normal current account.

When the balance outstanding on shares is called up, in one or more instalments, a *call letter* is sent to each holder, demanding the sum due. A Call Account is opened, and debited with the total amount called up, credited to ordinary share capital—which thus shows eventually a credit balance equal to the full nominal value of the shares. Call moneys received are debited to bank and credited to call account—hopefully until the latter's balance is cleared.

It occasionally happens, however, that one or more shareholders fail to pay their calls. If the requisite power is conferred by the articles of association (as it is by Table A), a defaulter may, after due warning, be adjudged by the directors to have forfeited his shares. His title is extinguished, but the amount paid to date is not refunded, and the shares are not cancelled. The full nominal amount is transferred from the share capital account to the credit of a Forfeited Shares Account, to the debit of which is transferred the debit balance on the call account. The share premium account is unaffected. On the balance sheet the net credit balance (amount paid up on the forfeited shares) is shown separately, after issued capital.

The forfeited shares may be reissued to anyone who is prepared to pay the company at least the amount of the unpaid call. The credit balance of the forfeited shares account is transferred to the credit of a Forfeited Shares Reissued Account, which is credited with the further amount received. The nominal value is then transferred back to the credit of share capital account, and the remaining credit balance to the share premium account as an additional premium obtained.

Example 2 The Reliant Engineering Co. Ltd, with an authorized capital of £1,500,000 and issued capital of £1,000,000, all in £1 ordinary shares, issues the remaining shares for cash at a price of £1.80 – 30p on application, £1.00 on allotment (including the 80p premium), and 50p on first and final call. (Accounts to 31 December.)

The subscription lists open, and close, on 1 April 19.1. Applications are received for 2,500,000 shares; small applications for 1,000,000 shares are rejected, and the application moneys returned on 8 April. On the same day the whole issue is allotted to the remaining applicants, all of whom receive at least one-fourth of their requirements, and the allotment moneys are all received by 30 April. The first and final call is made on 1 June 19.1, and the call moneys received by 30 June, except those on 800 shares. These are forfeited on 31 December 19.1; on 28 February 19.2 they are reissued at a price of 75p.

The accounts, other than Bank, and the relevant part of the balance sheet at 31 December 19.1 are as follows:

Ordinary Share Capital

19.1		£	19.1		£
Dec 31	Forfeited shares	800	Jan 1	Balance b/d	1,000,000
Dec 31	Balance c/d	1,499,200	Apr 8	Application and allotment a/c	250,000
			Jun 1	First and final call	250,000
		£1,500,000			£1,500,000
			19.2		
			Jan 1	Balance b/d	1,499,200
			Feb 28	Forfeited shares reissued	800
					1,500,000

Share Premium Account

			19.1		£
			Apr 8	Application and allotment a/c	400,000
			19.2		
			Feb 28	Forfeited shares reissued	200
					400,200

Application and Allotment Account

19.1		£	19.1		£
Apr 8	Bank	300,000	Apr 1	Bank	750,000
Apr 8	Ordinary share capital	250,000	Apr 30	Bank	200,000
Apr 8	Share premium account	400,000			
		£950,000			£950,000

First and Final Call

19.1		£	19.1		£
Jun 1	Ordinary share capital	250,000	Jun 30	Bank	249,600
			Dec 31	Forfeited shares	400
		£250,000			£250,000

Forfeited Shares

19.1	£	19.1	£
Dec 31 First and final call	400	Dec 31 Ordinary share capital	800
Dec 31 Balance c/d	400		
	£800		£800
19.2		19.2	
Feb 28 Forfeited shares reissued	400	Jan 1 Balance b/d	400
	£400		£400

Forfeited Shares Reissued

19.2	£	19.2	£
Feb 28 Ordinary share capital	800	Feb 28 Forfeited shares	400
Feb 28 Share premium account	200	Feb 28 Bank	600
	£1,000		£1,000

Reliant Engineering Company Ltd

Balance Sheet, 31 December 19.1

	£	£
Share Capital		
Authorized		
1,500,000 ordinary shares of £1 each	£1,500,000	
Issued		
1,499,200 ordinary shares of £1 each, fully paid		1,499,200
Forfeited		
800 ordinary shares of £1 each, 50p paid		400
		1,499,600
Reserves		
Share premium account	400,000	
	[etc.]	

Note that payments for Share Issue Expenses (including the issuing house's commission and fees), and for Commissions on Issue of Shares (usually underwriting commission), are debited to separate accounts, and appear in the balance sheet as 'Other Assets'.

If the shares are sold *en bloc* to the issuing house, which pays the usual instalments as it collects them from investors, the said instalments will be credited to ordinary share capital, and to share premium account, and debited to the issuing house, as they arise—being credited to the latter's account as settlement is made in cash. Account will be taken of the total amount payable by the issuing house to the company, not of the higher amount at which the shares are marketed. If the shares are issued by tender, the amount of the final call is determined only when the striking price has been decided.

11.3 Share and loan capital

The variety of investment arrangements in a partnership is restricted by the rule of unlimited liability, which must be compensated for by absence of formal limitation on the amount of profit receivable by a partner in good times. Limited liability, similar to that of an ordinary shareholder, can be obtained only at the price of non-participation in management. Partners' advances are analogous to preference capital, and loans to a firm by non-partners usually require mortgage or hypothecation of specific assets of the business, or of individual partners. Further, investments in unincorporated firms are highly illiquid, and disposal of them, without withdrawal of cash, is impracticable unless the prospective purchaser is acceptable to the other partners, or the latter are themselves prepared to purchase the interest of the outgoing one.

A high degree of marketability without noticeably adverse effect, through entering the market, on the price paid or received, is attained only in the quoted securities of a large limited company, or of a public body or the government. But limited liability, by setting a floor to financial disaster without inhibiting the energies of the entrepreneur, allows much more trade-off in business investment between security from loss and prospect of gain, and offers the investor a great variety of risk-opportunity situations to choose from, according to his needs, circumstances, and temperament.

11.3.1 Further provisions concerning share capital

All types of proprietary capital of a company must, initially, be divided into shares of fixed nominal amount. Only whole shares may be subscribed for, or transferred by sale, gift, inheritance, or operation of law. Transferability of shares must, in the case of a private company, be restricted by the articles in some way. Usually the shares must be offered first to other members at a price mutually agreed, or fixed by arbitration or independent valuation; or the directors have power to refuse to register a transfer, without giving a reason. In quoted public companies, though, free transferability of shares is generally obligatory by stock exchange rules. A deed of transfer, bearing stamp duty (paid by the transferee) equal to 1 per cent of the market value, is lodged with the company together with the old share certificate for cancellation; the change of ownership is recorded in the company's share ledger, and a new certificate issued to the transferee. A fee of 12½p may legally be charged to the transferee; the policy of the London Stock Exchange is to abolish it by degrees, in respect of all quoted securities.

Some companies issue share warrants to bearer, in lieu of share certificates. The warrants are transferable by delivery without notice to the company, but the Exchange Control Act, 1947, requires them to be deposited with a stockbroker, banker, or solicitor, and to be transferred by deed. Since the holders' names and addresses are unknown to the company, dividends must be collected by sending in the coupons attached to the warrants.

By the Companies Act, 1948, s. 61, a company's articles may give it power to alter its memorandum so as to increase its authorized capital, cancel unissued shares, consolidate its capital into shares of larger denomination or subdivide it into shares of smaller denomination (without altering the proportion paid up on each share), or convert its *fully-paid* shares into stock (or vice versa). Notice of the change must be given to the Registrar within one month (s. 62).

Stock may be regarded as shares melted down into one mass, and transferable in fractional parts, theoretically of 1p. Most companies, though, impose a minimum unit of transfer, such as 5p. Stock conversions used to be popular as a means of evading the obligation to number shares consecutively, but since that was abolished by the 1948 Act, the *raison d'être* of the operation has largely disappeared.

Most shares are fully called, and paid, within a short time after issue. Partly-paid shares are unpopular with investors, on account of the contingent liability attached, though this may be mitigated by a special resolution to the effect that the 'reserve liability' shall not be called up, except on liquidation of the company (s. 60). Any alteration of the articles of association, purporting to impose additional liability on existing shareholders or to compel them to contribute additional capital, is void.

All shares must bear a fixed nominal amount, and any excess subscription proceeds must be treated as a premium (see Chapter 12, sub-section 12.1.2). In North America it is permitted to issue 'shares of no par value', and credit the whole proceeds to share capital account—each share representing simply a fraction of the company's equity. (Dividends must be expressed as so many cents per share.) The Jenkins Report (1962) recommended the legalization of no par value shares in Great Britain, for both equity and preference capital, but no such change has yet been effected (see Chapter 13, section 13.3).

No British company is permitted to purchase its own shares. In the U.S.A. this practice is sanctioned—the shares appearing in the books as an asset, 'stock in treasury' or 'treasury stock'. They may subsequently be reissued, or cancelled against the nominal value, or issue price, of the shares. Such a system is patently open to abuse; the Jenkins Committee could see no strong arguments for it, and there are no official proposals to introduce it in this country.

The issue of shares at a discount was first permitted in Great Britain by the 1948 Act (s. 57). The shares must be of a class already issued; the issue must be sanctioned by the High Court; and the company must have been entitled to commence business at least one year before. Such issues are extremely rare—if they ever occur at all—and would usually be made in connection with the 'reconstruction' of a company in financial trouble (see Chapter 13, sub-section 13.2.4). In the books of account the full nominal value of the shares is credited to share capital, and the discount debited to Discount on Shares Account.

11.3.2 Types of share capital

The conventional classification of shares or stock, in descending order of priority for payment of dividends and return of capital on liquidation, is threefold:

1 preference; 2 ordinary; and 3 deferred.

Only class 2 is indispensable, as being normally entitled to residual profits and net assets after satisfying prior claims to limited sums out of these funds—which claims may be zero, and generally are, in small private companies.

Preference shares (or stock) always carry the right to a fixed annual dividend—usually a percentage on the nominal amount—payable in priority to the ordinary dividend, which cannot be paid at all unless the preference dividend is met in full. Most preference shares are 'cumulative'—unpaid dividends must be carried forward and made up out of future profits, together with the current dividends, before any further distributions can be made to ordinary shareholders. Indeed, all preference shares are deemed to be cumulative unless the contrary is specified. Most preference shares are also given priority of repayment of nominal capital on liquidation—a right which has, however, to be specifically granted. The legal presumption, though, is that such priority, together with the right to any outstanding cumulative dividends, exhausts the shareholders' rights; they cannot claim any share in surplus assets, unless the articles or the terms of issue clearly grant this (*Re Isle of Thanet Electricity Supply Co. Ltd* (1950)).

A few preference shares are 'participating'—entitled to an additional dividend in certain contingencies, such as the declaration of an ordinary dividend at or above a certain percentage. They are most commonly issued as part of a scheme of reconstruction (see Chapter 13, sub-section **13.2.4**).

Since 1929, it has been legal to issue 'redeemable' preference shares—the sole exception to the rule that, unless special leave is given by the High Court in a capital reduction scheme, no share capital may be repaid or withdrawn until liquidation of the company. The shares are declared, from the beginning, to be redeemable at par or at a small premium, on a given date, or between two dates or at the company's option. On redemption, however, either the capital must be replaced by the proceeds of a new issue for cash, or an equivalent amount of distributable profits must be transferred to a special reserve, from which they cannot then be distributed (1948 Act, s.58) (see Chapter 12, sub-section **12.1.2**).

Most preference shares, of all varieties, carry no votes at general meetings. Because of their entrenched rights and the limited risk assumed, the holders are not deemed to merit the additional protection of a voice in management. Some preference shares, though, are given votes while the dividends are in arrear, particularly if these are non-cumulative.

Two or more classes of preference share (first, second, etc.) may be issued, ranking in order for dividend and capital repayment.

Ordinary shares constitute the majority of a normal company's share capital—often the whole of it. They have no right to any fixed dividend, but are entitled, as a rule, to the whole of the profits, after corporation tax, and after paying preference dividends to date. Out of these 'equity earnings' the company pays such dividends as the directors think fit, but usually retains a large part of the earnings as additions to reserves—hopefully to generate more earnings in the future, and enable the ordinary dividend to be progressively raised. The market value of ordinary shares is determined to a large extent by the current and expected level of dividends and of earnings; their prices are much more volatile than those of preference shares, and afford much more chance of capital gains, and losses. On liquidation, ordinary shareholders are the last to be paid out; if lucky they take all surplus assets, if unlucky they are likely to receive nothing.

Ordinary (or equity) shares thus form the 'risk capital' of the undertaking, and their holders are its proprietors in the full sense. They accordingly exercise voting rights—normally one vote per share, or one vote per (say) £10 of stock—and a majority holding confers control of company policy, through the power it gives to appoint and remove directors at will. Some companies, nevertheless, have 'non-voting' ordinary shares (for issue to the public), as well as voting ones (held by an inner circle, of the directors and their relatives); they are uniform in other respects, except that the voting shares always command a higher market price.

Occasionally the ordinary shares are divided into a 'preferred' and a 'deferred' class, the first being entitled to a certain minimum dividend, then the second similarly, then both to the same excess over the minimum, if profits permit. The same priority may or may not obtain on repayment of capital.

Deferred shares (not the same as 'deferred ordinary' shares) are not common today. They rank after ordinaries, whose rights must therefore be restricted to accommodate them; e.g. the ordinary shares are entitled to a maximum dividend of (say) 10 per cent per annum, with all surplus profits going to the deferred shares, or being apportioned between the two classes on a formula which gives very large percentage dividends to the deferreds, if the profits are more than mediocre. Deferred shares are generally of small nominal value, but with one vote per share all the same. On liquidation they take all, or a goodly proportion, of any surplus assets after repaying the ordinaries at par. They are sometimes issued as 'founders' shares to the original backers of a highly speculative undertaking (as were. the independent television companies in their early days), or as 'management' shares to the vendors of the goodwill of an acquired undertaking—a dubious procedure, since they are enabled to retain the very super-profits from which the value of the goodwill is derived! Deferred shares may also be used to strengthen family holdings in a private company when it goes public. As 'super-risk' capital, such shares may be very valuable if a speculation pays off, virtually worthless if it does not.

11.3.3 Loan capital

Besides its proprietary capital, a company is usually given power by its memorandum to borrow money, although the articles may restrict the exercise of this power by the directors—e.g. by forbidding them to borrow more than the amount of the authorized share capital at any time, except for short-term bank loans. Borrowings for more than one year are regarded as loan capital, and normally evidenced by *debentures* (in fixed units of, e.g., £100) or *debenture stock* (in fractional parts, say 5p at a minimum). They are issued, and transferred, in the same manner as shares.

Debentures (including debenture stock) always carry interest at a fixed rate, payable regardless of profit or loss. This is one factor which distinguishes them from preference shares, whose dividends, though fixed, are conditional on the earning of sufficient profits. Another is, that debentures are almost always redeemable—they are loans for a term of years only. Again, unlike shares, debentures may be freely issued at a discount—the normal procedure today—and a company may purchase its own debentures, for cancellation or reissue, if so authorized by the articles or terms of issue.

Virtually all debentures are formally secured, so that the holders have priority of repayment over the ordinary trade creditors. The two usual forms of security (sometimes combined) are the 'fixed charge' (a mortgage or hypothecation of specific tangible assets, especially land) and the 'floating charge' (granted over the general assets at all times). Since debentures carry no voting power (though the holders have the right to attend general meetings), a body of trustees is appointed to enforce the security, should the company default on the interest or principal, or in any way jeopardize the debenture-holders' position. A fixed charge is enforced by the trustees' seizing and selling the charged assets, and paying off the debentures, with arrears of interest and all costs of the operation, out of the proceeds—any surplus being handed back to the company. A floating charge is less effective, since it is deferred to the claims of preferential creditors (see Chapter 10, sub-section **10.5.4**). The trustees appoint a receiver (or a receiver and manager, who supplants the directors and takes over the management of the business), and he realizes enough of the assets to pay the preferential creditors, the debenture-holders, and his own costs and charges—after which he concludes the receivership and returns the company to the directors and shareholders (see Chapter 17, section 17.3).

A company's bank overdraft is frequently secured by a single debenture of indefinite amount, giving the bank a fixed and/or floating charge to cover the total overdraft (including accrued interest) at any time.

Some large undertakings issue *unsecured notes* for short terms of years. They are covered many times over by net assets, and formal security is unnecessary to attract lenders.

Today, 'convertible' debentures are often issued. They are loans, typically at a somewhat lower rate of interest than usual, but carrying an option to convert them into ordinary shares of the company after a certain time. The option remains open for some years, but the number of shares issued, per £100-worth of debentures surrendered, usually falls progressively as given dates are passed without exercising the option. The holder thus has a choice between switching into equity if the market value and prospects of the ordinary shares are advantageous at a conversion date, and holding on to the loan if they are not.

11.4 Books of account, statutory books and returns

Every company must keep proper books of account, as prescribed in the 1948 Act, ss. 147 and 331. These provisions are more conveniently dealt with in Chapter 14, sub-section 14.2.1; here it suffices to say that a normal double entry system, whether manual, mechanical, or electronic, with suitable internal controls, will fulfil the requirements of the law.

11.4.1 Statutory books

The 1948 and 1967 Acts compel a company to keep certain 'statutory' books, outside the accounting system. These books are the concern of the company secretary, rather than the accountant, but they need to be examined and verified by the auditor, as sources of evidence supporting some of the entries in the books of account. The statutory books are:

a the *register of members*, containing the members' names and addresses, numbers of shares held, with serial numbers if any, amounts paid or deemed to be paid on each member's shares, and dates of entry on the register, and of ceasing to be a member (1948 Act, s. 110). A company with more than fifty members must also provide an index, unless the register is in such a form as to constitute in itself an index (s. 111). The register of members is usually combined, in practice, with the *share ledger*, a voluntary 'statistical' book, showing changes in each member's shareholding in debit-and-credit form; a debenture register/ledger is also kept, where applicable;

b the *register of charges*, containing details of all charges created by the company upon its assets (including fixed and floating charges to secure debentures), and required to be registered with the Registrar of Companies (s. 95). The register must give in each case a short description of the property charged, the amount of the charge, and (except in the case of bearer securities) the names of the persons entitled thereto (s. 104);

c *minute books* of all proceedings at general meetings, meetings of directors, and meetings of managers (if any) (s. 145);

d the *register of directors and secretaries,* giving for each person his name, any former names, and usual residential address (or, for a corporation, its corporate name and registered or principal office), together with, for a director, his nationality, business occupation (if any), particulars of any other directorships held, and, in the case of a public company or any subsidiary thereof, the director's date of birth (s. 200);

e the *register of directors' interests* (widely defined and including those of his/her spouse and children under eighteen, as well as in connection with any trust) in any shares or debentures of the company, its holding company, subsidiaries or fellow-subsidiaries, together with particulars of the grant to any director of any option to subscribe for shares or debentures of the company, and of any exercise of that option. The entries for each director must be in chronological order, and an index must be provided unless the register is in such a form as to constitute in itself an index (1967 Act, s. 29); and

f the *register of shareholders' '10 per cent' interests,* showing all interests (defined as in e) of any one person in any voting share capital of the company, amounting to 10 per cent or more of the nominal value of all such capital; with an index as in e above (1967 Act, s. 34).

All the above books must be available for inspection by any persons, normally at the company's registered office, for at least two hours a day during business hours.

In addition, the company must keep at the registered office copies of all *instruments creating charges* (1948 Act, s. 103), available for inspection as above; and copies or memoranda of all *directors' service contracts,* available for inspection by members only—except for contracts having less than one year to run, or terminable within one year without compensation, or relating to a director whose duties are discharged wholly or mainly outside the U.K. (1967 Act, s. 26).

11.4.2 Statutory returns

The few public companies which do not start life as private ones must hold a general meeting of members, known as the 'statutory meeting', between one and three months after becoming entitled to commence business. The main purpose is to discuss the *statutory report,* which must be forwarded by the directors to every member, at least fourteen days before the meeting, and filed with the Registrar of Companies.

The report, certified by at least two directors, must state the total number of shares allotted, and the total cash received for all such shares, with certain other details; an abstract of receipts and payments of the company, analysed as prescribed, up to a date within seven days before the date of the report; particulars of the directors, auditors (if any), managers (if any), and secretary; and particulars of any contract whose modification is to be submitted to the meeting for approval, with details of the modification. The statements relating to allotments, cash received for shares, and receipts and payments on capital account, must be certified by the auditors (1948 Act, s. 130).

This rather pointless procedure is virtually obsolete today, and the Jenkins Report recommended its abolition; but no change was made by the 1967 Act.

Of much more importance is the *annual return,* which must be forwarded to the Registrar by every company, within 42 days after the annual general meeting for each year. The return must be made up to the fourteenth day after the AGM, in the form prescribed by the 1948 Act, Sixth Schedule, and be signed by a director and the secretary (1948 Act, ss. 124-126). It must be accompanied, in all cases, by a copy, certified as a true copy by a director and the secretary, of the latest *annual accounts,* and all reports attached thereto, as laid before the AGM (s. 127) (see Chapter 14). The fee for filing each annual return is £3.

The annual return states: the address of the registered office; the situation of the registers of members and of debenture-holders, if different; full particulars, duly tabulated, of share and loan capital as issued and outstanding at the date of the return; the total indebtedness of the company in respect of all charges required to be registered under the 1948 Act, s. 95 (see sub-section **11.4.1**); a list of names, addresses and shareholdings of all persons who have been members at any time since the date of the last annual return, and of all changes in their holdings in the intervening period (with an index, if the names are not in alphabetical order); and full particulars of the directors and secretary as at the date of the return, as given in the register of directors and secretary. If desired, a full list of members may be given every third year, with details of changes only, in the two intervening years.

The annual return of a private company must have annexed to it a certificate, signed by a director and the secretary, to the effect that the company has not, since the incorporation of the company or the last annual return (as the case may be), issued any invitation to the public to subscribe for its shares or debentures. If the number of members as stated in the return exceeds fifty, a further certificate, signed as above, must be annexed to the effect that the excess consists wholly of members who, by the 1948 Act, s. 28, are not to be reckoned in the number of fifty (i.e. employees and certain ex-employees).

12

Accounting for limited liability companies (2)

The great size and complexity of many public companies' businesses makes their choice of accounting principles crucially important in view of the very large sums involved, the immense scope for manipulation of published figures, even within the bounds of legality and accepted accounting practices, and the effects of the published information upon the market prices of the company's securities. These issues have been discussed in *Part 1,* and only occasional reference need be made to them at this stage. The main peculiarities of limited company accounting, as of the accounting of other types of organization, lie in the four fields of owners' equity, loan capital, division of profits and losses, and taxation of profits.

12.1 Share capital, reserves, and provisions

Accounting for the owners' equity of a company is based on the legal distinction between contributed capital and accumulated profits. Contributed capital (share capital and premiums) is the permanent capital fund of the enterprise and may not, as a rule, be returned to the shareholders, except on liquidation of the company or by special permission of the High Court; nor may the company's funds be used to purchase its own shares (*Trevor* v. *Whitworth* (1887)). These legal restrictions give the share capital of a company a stability and continuity which do not exist to the same extent in a partnership, and are a necessary concomitant of the rule of limited liability, as preventing the withdrawal by investors of funds required to pay creditors.

Accumulated profits arise from the use in the business of the funds entrusted to the company, and represent a surplus accruing to the shareholders, out of which dividends may be paid to them, and which, if not so distributed, is ultimately attributable to those entitled to surplus assets on liquidation—in general, to the ordinary shareholders. In the books of account such accumulated profits are kept separate and distinct from the share capital and premium, and constitute the company's *reserves*, as commonly understood—though, legally, the term includes also the share premium account, and unrealized capital surpluses. There are arrangements for converting reserves into share capital, but not vice versa (see Chapter 13, sub-section 13.2.1).

12.1.1 Reserves, reserve funds, and provisions

Reserves, then, may arise in three ways:

i by the contribution of capital moneys by shareholders, over and above the nominal amount of their shares;

ii by the accumulation of profits, initially in the profit and loss account; and

iii by upward revaluation of assets, with a countervailing adjustment to owners' equity.

All reserves are represented in the books by credit balances, and appear in the balance sheet as amounts added to share capital to produce a sub-total of owners' equity.

Such reserves are normally regarded as invested in the business generally. Sometimes, though, a reserve is invested specifically in quoted securities, or in a life or endowment assurance poliçy, which are/is to be converted into cash at a future date, and the cash used for some specific purpose. A reserve so represented by 'earmarked' assets is known as a *reserve fund.* (The strict use of the term was enjoined by the Institute of Chartered Accountants in England and Wales, in an opinion issued in 1948; previously, 'reserve' and 'reserve fund' were virtually interchangeable.)

Reserves (including reserve funds) are alternatively classified as *capital reserves* and *revenue reserves.* A capital reserve is one which as a matter of law, prudence, or business policy cannot or will not be distributed in dividend to shareholders through the profit and loss account; a revenue reserve is one free for distribution as aforesaid. The first category comprises types **i** and **iii** above, since neither a share premium nor an unrealized surplus is legally distributable, but a reserve of type **ii**, though initially of a revenue nature, may become capital by operation of law or through company policy.

The principal revenue reserve is the profit and loss account, whose credit balance at any time represents net profits (less losses) after tax, accrued since the inception of the company, and not distributed in dividend or otherwise appropriated. The profit and loss account of a company is not closed off annually to capital, but runs on from year to year, and its balance appears separately in the balance sheet. The net profit enures to the company in its corporate capacity, and in that capacity the company pays *corporation tax* on the profits. The amount of the tax is debited to the profit and loss account, as being legally an appropriation of them. Out of the post-tax profit for the year, plus the unappropriated balance brought forward from the previous year, the company declares and pays one or more *dividends* on the shares. These are analogous to the drawings of a partnership, but, whereas the latter are informal transfers of cash from the joint fund to the separate estates of the partners, and thus debited separately to their current accounts, the dividends of a company are formal payments out of corporate assets to the members of the corporation. They are therefore debited to profit and loss account, as reductions in the fund of undistributed profits. If it is thought necessary to create more specific reserves out of profits, either capital or revenue by nature, this is done by debiting profit and loss account and crediting the other reserve accounts.

Provisions are also credit balances raised in the books by debiting profit and loss account and crediting the provision account. Their purpose is:

a to amortize the cost of fixed assets of a wasting nature,
b to reduce the book value of current assets or investments from cost or amount legally receivable to some lower figure, such as market value or amount estimated to be recoverable;
c to provide for a known liability, presently accrued due, whose amount cannot as yet be estimated with substantial accuracy; or
d to provide for a deferred or future liability, certain or likely to arise from events which have already happened as at the date of the final accounts.

Provisions of types **a** and **b** are deducted, in the balance sheet, from the cost or other base value of the assets concerned; those of types **c** and **d** appear among the liabilities, after loan capital. They are shown as current, or as non-current, liabilities according to the due dates of payment. Type c and d provisions are distinguished from reserves in that they represent amounts which, on immediate liquidation, would go to outsiders, as distinct from shareholders, and from creditors or accruals in that the amounts are uncertain, instead of certain or closely calculable, or payable more than one year ahead, instead of within the next year. If any provision, of whatever type, is considered by the directors to be in excess of the amount reasonably required for its purpose the excess must, legally, be transferred to reserves.

Secret, or *hidden, reserves* are amounts by which the fair value of the owners' equity is understated in the accounts, by reason of failure to observe the rule last mentioned—e.g. by deliberately depreciating fixed assets more rapidly than is justified by their time-patterns of earning-power deterioration; writing down current assets or investments below all reasonable estimates of current realizable value; writing off capital expenditure to revenue; making unreasonably pessimistic estimates of unquantified liabilities, or making provisions for future losses unrelated to any events which have yet happened, or can reasonably be expected to happen in the foreseeable future. As is made clear in Chapter 14, the Companies Act, 1967, forbids a company to understate its equity deliberately, by practices which violate generally accepted principles of historical-cost accounting; but it does not limit the accountant's choice of valuation or income-determination practices within the ambit of those principles, nor require him to depart from them, or to introduce different ones, where his own judgement of the situation does not suggest that he should.

A more sinister connotation of the term 'secret reserves' is that of actual reserves whose true nature is concealed, and which are or can be manipulated in ways considered unethical. The most celebrated example of such practices came to light in *Rex* v. *Kylsant and Morland* (1931), in which the chairman and auditor of the Royal Mail Steam Packet Company were acquitted on charges of fraud and falsification of accounts, but the chairman was later imprisoned for using the same figures in a prospectus. During a period of unsuccessful trading the profit figures were bolstered by undisclosed transfers from undisclosed reserves for taxation, accumulated during the First World War and no longer required for their original purpose, and dividends were paid, although the company was making losses. Such misrepresentation was not illegal at that time, though strongly condemned by the aceountancy profession afterwards; it was forbidden by the Companies Act, 1948, which required all movements on reserves to be disclosed.

12.1.2 Some examples of capital reserves

i *Share premium account*

The Companies Act, 1948, s. 56, requires any premium received on shares issued, for cash or otherwise, to be credited to a special 'share premium account', and generally to be treated as additional share capital. This means, in particular, that no part of it may be returned to shareholders, except on liquidation, or under a scheme of capital reduction authorized by the High Court. It is, however, permitted to capitalize the share premium account, by using the balance to pay up unissued shares for distribution to the members as bonus shares (see Chapter 13, sub-section 13.2.1); to write off against it the preliminary expenses of forming the company, share and debenture issue expenses and commissions, and discounts on shares or deben- and to debit to the account any premium paid on redemption of redeemable preference shares or debentures.

The function of a share premium is to secure for the company, on a new issue of ordinary shares in particular, some part at least of the premium ascribed by the market to existing shares of the same class. A side-effect is to reduce the prospective rate of return on an investment in the new shares to something near that obtainable by purchasing existing ones at the current price and, to the extent that the full market premium is not exacted, to reduce the price of all shares of the class concerned, old and new, to (*ceteris paribus*) a weighted average of the old market price and the new issue price (cf. Chapter 13, sub-section 13.2.2, on rights issues). Even so, those who took up the old shares when the company's prospects of success were less clear, and the risk of capital loss greater, are still rewarded for their boldness by a higher rate of return on their money than those who came in later, though the nominal rate of dividend (on the par value) is the same all round. On liquidation the premium, if still intact, becomes an undifferentiated part of the ordinary shareholders' equity, and is divided between them all, regardless of who contributed it, so that the earlier entrants, if they still hold their shares, make a capital gain at the expense of the later ones—or, if they have sold out earlier, should have made one then.

ii *Capital redemption reserve fund*

This is the second of the two 'statutory' capital reserves. When redeemable preference shares (see Chapter 11, sub-section 11.3.2) are redeemed the 1948 Act, s. 58, requires replacement of the par value of the shares by the proceeds of a fresh issue of shares[1] (of any class—but not by debentures); or, alternatively, the transfer of an equivalent amount of distributable profits from the profit and loss account, or other revenue reserve, to the credit of a capital reserve, misleadingly entitled the 'capital redemption reserve *fund*', though it is seldom represented by earmarked assets. Profits so dealt with are for ever undistributable, except on liquidation or in a capital reduction scheme. The balance may be capitalized by a bonus issue of shares, but no other debits against it are permitted. A combination of the two methods of redemption is allowable.

The effect of creating the 'fund' is to capitalize profits which might otherwise have been paid out in dividend. If the procedure is intended from the outset, it is best to spread the burden on distributable earnings over the whole currency of the preference shares, or the maximum term if there is flexibility, by transferring equal instalments of the nominal value of the shares (plus redemption premium if there is no share premium account) annually from profit and loss account to a Preference Share Redemption Reserve. At maturity the shares are redeemed, either at par (*Dr*. Redeemable Preference Share Capital, *Cr*. Bank) or at a premium (*Dr*. Redeemable Preference Share Capital, and Share Premium Account or other available reserve, *Cr*. Bank), and the credit balance of the preference share redemption reserve is transferred to capital redemption reserve fund. If separate investment of the latter is desired, one or other of the procedures outlined below, as for debenture redemption, should be followed.

[1] Such shares are exempt from stamp duty, provided that the issue is made after, or within one month before, the redemption of the old shares. Redemption does not constitute a reduction of capital.

Example 1 A company issues 10,000 10 per cent redeemable preference shares of £1 each, at par, on 1 January 19.1, and redeems them out of profits, at a premium of 1 per cent, on 1 January 19.6. Accounts are made up to 31 December in each year. Share premium account balance, £5,000 *Cr.* at 1 January 19.1.

The relevant entries (other than in the cash book) are:

10% Redeemable Preference Share Capital

19.6		£	19.1		£
Jan 1 Bank		10,000	Jan 1 Bank		10,000

10% Redeemable Preference Shares—Premium on Redemption

19.6		£	19.6		£
Jan 1 Bank		100	Jan 1 Share premium a/c		100

Share Premium Account

19.6		£	19.1		£
Jan 1 10% redeemable preference shares— premium on redemption		100	Jan 1 Balance b/d		5,000
Dec 31 Balance c/d		4,900			
		£5,000			£5,000
			19.7		
			Jan 1 Balance b/d		4,900

Preference Share Redemption Reserve

19.6		£	19.1		£
			Dec 31 Profit and loss a/c		2,000
			19.2		
			Dec 31 Profit and loss a/c		2,000
					4,000
			* * *		
					8,000
			19.5		
			Dec 31 Profit and loss a/c		2,000
					10,000
19.6					
Jan 1 Capital redemption reserve fund		10,000			
		£10,000			£10,000

Capital Redemption Reserve Fund

		£	19.6		£
			Jan 1 Preference share redemption reserve		10,000

Profit and Loss Account for the Year ended 31 December 19.1 (extract)

	£	£		£
Transfer to preference share			Net profit after taxation b/d	20,000
redemption reserve		2,000		
Dividends				
Paid—				
Redeemable preference, 10%	1,000			
		[etc.]		

iii *Debenture redemption reserve (fund)*

There are no statutory provisions concerning redemption of debentures. The law treats the holders as creditors, not as providers of capital, and does not require the company to conserve or replace the funds. Debenture-holders generally rank ahead of unsecured creditors, while redeemable preference shareholders always rank after them. Thus redemption of secured debentures, even by an insolvent company, cannot worsen the position of unsecured creditors (unless the debenture-holders' security is inadequate), whereas redemption of preference shares could result in their holders' being unfairly preferred before *all* creditors—hence the legal restrictions in the latter case.

A company, therefore, may elect to make no provision for conserving its loan capital, with the intention of re-borrowing, if necessary, when the debentures come to be redeemed. Without re-borrowing, though, redemption will deplete the company's working capital at the time, and may injure its financial stability, unless steps have been taken to build up cash by restraining distributions, through the creation of a capital reserve—with or without separate investment of the moneys representing it. Such a reserve (or reserve fund) is truly such, and not a provision—a provision, in such a context, is a liability, and the liability already exists, in the shape of the debentures themselves. A debenture redemption reserve (fund) is a voluntary appropriation of profits, available on liquidation to ordinary share-holders, and thus properly shown as part of owners' equity.

Some debentures are stated on issue to be redeemable by annual drawings; i.e. a fixed proportion of them is repaid annually, the serial numbers of debentures to be redeemed being selected each year by lot—e.g. for a ten-year period, by repaying each year those ending with a different digit, drawn at random. In that case a sum equal to (say) one-tenth of the total nominal value of the debentures is transferred from profit and loss account to debenture redemption reserve. When redemption is complete the balance of the reserve is transferred to a General Capital Reserve, since the original title is now obsolete, but the sum involved is unlikely to be regarded as free for distribution, even though there is no legal prohibition.

Where redemption takes place in one sum, at a fixed or flexible date in the future, it is most prudent to create some form of sinking fund, as is obligatory for gilt-edged securities, and for local authority and public corporation loan stocks. The most common method used is to transfer annually, from profit and loss account to debenture redemption reserve fund, such constant sum as, being accumulated at a relevant rate of compound interest over the term of the debentures, will amount at the end to the sum needed to repay them. The relevant rate is the average return expected on gilt-edged securities over the period—gross of income tax, since the company will obtain refunds, but net of corporation tax, charged on the interest. A sum in cash equal to the annual appropriation is invested each year in gilts. Interest received on them, adjusted for taxes, is credited to the reserve fund, and an equal sum reinvested in gilts—thus keeping the historical cost of the fund investments (a debit balance) equal and opposite to the credit balance of the fund at all times, the two balances appearing on opposite sides of the balance sheet. When the debentures mature, the investments are realized (any profit or loss being written off to revenue) and the proceeds used to redeem the debentures. The debenture redemption reserve fund balance is then transferred to general capital reserve, as for redemption by annual drawings. Any major change in the gilt-edged rate of return will necessitate recalculation of the annual instalments; otherwise it is to be noted that a fall in the rate is offset, though not precisely, by a capital gain on maturity—a rise in the rate leading to a capital loss.

The annual appropriation is found by taking the nominal value of the debentures and dividing it by the sum (found from annuity tables) to which an annuity of £1 (received at the end of each year and reinvested at the average gilt-edged rate less tax) amounts at the end of the number of years for which the debentures will be current. Thus, if the relevant figures are £10,000, 16.67 per cent per annum gross less 52 per cent corporation tax (= 8.0 per cent per annum net), and 10 years, the amount of an annuity of £1 for 10 years, accumulated at 8 per cent per annum compound, is £14.4866. Division of this into £10,000 gives, to the nearest 1p, £690.29, and this will be used in the following illustration. (In practice, gilt-edged interest is normally received half-yearly, and it is necessary to compute a half-yearly appropriation, using half the interest rate for twice the number of periods; eg.. in the case supposed, the amount of £1 per half-year for 20 half-years at 4 per cent per half-year (net) is £29.7781, and division of this into £10,000 gives £335.82 as the half-yearly appropriation.)

Example 2 Given the figures as above, and assuming a constant rate of return on gilt-edged securities of 16.67 per cent per annum gross, received at the end of each accounting year (31 December), with income tax at 33 per cent and corporation tax 52 per cent, the redemption at par of £10,000 18 per cent debentures, issued on 1 January 19.1 for 10 years, proceeds in the books as follows (omitting the obvious entries):

18% Debentures

19x1		£	19.1		£
Jan 1	Bank	10,000.00	Jan 1	Application and allotment a/c	10,000.00

Debenture Redemption Reserve Fund

		£	19.1		£
			Dec 31	Profit and loss a/c	690.29
19.2			*19.2*		
Dec 31	Corporation tax [adjustment of		Dec 31	Bank [16.67% interest less income tax]	77.08
	total charge]	59.53	Dec 31	Income tax [recoverable]	37.97
Dec 31	Balance c/d	1,436.10	Dec 31	Profit and loss a/c	690.29
		£1,495.63			£1,495.63

19.3			19.3		
Dec 31	Corporation tax	124.46	Jan 1	Balance b/d	1,436.10
Dec 31	Balance c/d	2,241.28	Dec 31	Bank	160.36
			Dec 31	Income tax	78.99
			Dec 31	Profit and loss a/c	690.29
		£2,365.74			£2,365.74
			19.4		
			Jan 1	Balance b/d	2,241.28

*   *   *

19x0			19x0		
Dec 31	Corporation tax	747.08	Jan 1	Balance b/d	8,620.10
Dec 31	Balance c/d	10,000.00	Dec 31	Bank	962.58
			Dec 31	Income tax	474.11
			Dec 31	Profit and loss a/c	690.29
		£10,747.08			£10,747.08
19x1			19x1		
Jan 1	General capital reserve	10,000.00	Jan 1	Balance b/d	10,000.00

Investments on Debenture Redemption Reserve Fund

19.1		£	19.1		£
Dec 31	Bank	690.29			
19.2			19.2		
Dec 31	Bank [net interest reinvested]	55.52	Dec 31	Balance c/d	1,436.10
Dec 31	Bank [annual instalment]	690.29			
		£1,436.10			£1,436.10
19.3			19.3		
Jan 1	Balance b/d	1,436.10	Dec 31	Balance c/d	2,241.28
Dec 31	Bank	114.89			
Dec 31	do	690.29			
		£2,241.28			£2,241.28
19.4					
Jan 1	Balance b/d	2,241.28			

*   *   *

19x0			19x0		
Jan 1	Balance b/d	8,620.10	Dec 31	Balance c/d	10,000.00
Dec 31	Bank	689.61*			
Dec 31	do	690.29*			
		£10,000.00			£10,000.00
19x1			19x1		
Jan 1	Balance b/d	10,000.00	Jan 1	Bank	9,950.00
			Jan 1	Profits and losses on sale of investments	50.00
		£10,000.00			£10,000.00

* These sums would not in practice be invested so close to the date of redemption.

General Capital Reserve

			19x1		£
			Jan 1	Debenture redemption reserve fund	10,000.00

Share capital, reserves, and provisions   281

If it is objected that the above method involves the investment of large sums of money outside the business at a lower rate of return than could normally be obtained by using the funds within it, then the investments may be dispensed with. A suitable rate of interest having been agreed upon—say, 8 per cent per annum net, as in *Example 2*—the profit and loss account (appropriation section) is debited, and the debenture redemption reserve credited, annually with a notional sinking fund instalment as above, and with one year's notional interest on the balance of the reserve as at the beginning of the year. The reserve thus grows at a compound rate, instead of linearly by 'straight line' appropriations as in *Example 1,* and the total burden on equity earnings increases from year to year as the date of redemption of the debentures draws nearer, instead of remaining constant. The growth of the reserve thus mirrors that of the reserve fund under the sinking fund system, and proportions the burden on earnings to the presumed growth of them, as retained profits accumulate and are employed in the business, instead of being invested outside it. But the rate of interest used is necessarily arbitrary, and tends to bear little relation to the underlying rate of return upon the capital employed in the business, while the effect on the total equity is no different from that of the straight line method. For these reasons the 'uninvested sinking fund', despite greater theoretical correctness, is seldom preferred to the more simplistic approach.

Example 3 On the system outlined above, the debenture redemption reserve fund in *Example 2* would become:

Debenture Redemption Reserve

	£	19.1		£
		Dec 31 Profit and loss a/c		690.29
19.2		**19.2**		
Dec 31 Balance c/d	1,436.10	Dec 31 Profit and loss a/c		55.52
		Dec 31	do	690.29
	£1,436.10			£1,436.10
		19.3		
		Jan 1 Balance b/d		£1,436.10
			[etc.]	

Where external investment is used, an alternative method to that of *Example 2* consists in the use of *dated* gilt-edged securities with maturity dates close to that of the debentures to be redeemed. Bonds of the required redemption value are purchased by equal instalments at the going prices (which increase as maturity approaches), and the interest is credited to profit and loss account—the rise of the securities to redemption value sufficing to produce cash to pay off the debentures. Meanwhile the reserve fund is built up by transfer from profit and loss account, on either the straight line or the sinking fund system. These entries are thus divorced from those in the investment account, and the two balances are not equal—the investment account showing the smaller one, since the securities purchased earlier are not written up as they appreciate. Thus, at maturity, there is always a (tax-free) gain to be transferred to revenue.

The terms of issue of some debentures allow the company to redeem them by purchase in the open market—a procedure which is good business only when the market price is less than the future interest plus the redemption value, discounted back to the present at the company's cost of capital (see Chapter 6, sub-section

6.1.2). The purchased debentures appear first as an asset, at cost, and the company saves the interest on them. If they are cancelled, the nominal value is offset against them (*Dr.* Debentures, *Cr.* Debentures Purchased), a proportionate part of the outstanding discount is written off to the *debit* of the same debentures purchased account, and the difference (profit) transferred to revenue. A proportion of the debenture redemption reserve (fund) is transferred to general capital reserve (since normal redemption has been anticipated), with adjustment to the investment account (if any), when the next purchase of investments takes place. If the purchased debentures are reissued instead, the sale price is credited to the appropriate account and the profit written off to revenue—the debenture, discount, and redemption accounts being undisturbed.

Example 4 At 1 January 19.1 the balances on the books of X Ltd, relative to its debentures, are as shown below. On 30 June debentures of a nominal value of £500 are purchased in the open market for £400. On 31 July £200-worth are cancelled, and the other £300-worth reissued on 31 August for £280. The relevant entries (other than Bank) are:

15% Debentures

19.1	£	19.1	£
Jul 31 Company's debentures purchased	200	Jan 1 Balance b/d	20,000

Discount on Debentures

19.1	£	19.1	£
Jan 1 Balance b/d	300	Jul 31 Company's debentures purchased	3

Debenture Redemption Reserve Fund

19.1	£	19.1	£
Jul 31 General capital reserve	15	Jan 1 Balance b/d	1,500

Investments on Debenture Redemption Reserve Fund

19.1	£		
Jan 1 Balance b/d	1,500		

Company's Debentures Purchased

19.1	£	19.1	£
Jun 30 Bank	400	Jul 31 15% Debentures	200
Jul 31 Discount on debentures	3	Aug 31 Bank	280
Dec 31 Profit and loss a/c	77		
	£480		£480

General Capital Reserve

		19.1	£
		Jul 31 Debenture redemption reserve fund	15

Share capital, reserves, and provisions 283

iv *General capital reserve*

As already indicated, this is a repository for capital reserves created out of profits for specific purposes, after those purposes have become obsolete without rendering it prudent to distribute the profits so impounded.

v *Assets revaluation reserve*

A credit to this reserve is necessary to balance the ledger when there is a net upward revaluation of fixed assets (see Chapter 7, sub-section 7.2.4). It represents an un-realised accretion to owners' equity, and is normally regarded as undistributable, despite the controversial *Dimbula Valley* decision of 1961 (see sub-section 12.2.3).

12.1.3 Some examples of revenue reserves

i *Profit and loss account*

This is dealt with at length in section 12.2; here it is treated from the standpoint of its character as the 'original' revenue reserve, from which all others are derived. Its credit balance at any given time represents the maximum fund out of which the directors presently *intend* to declare dividends, while the total revenue reserves constitute the maximum fund presently *available* for that purpose.

The profit and loss account is the only reserve which can become negative (or in strict theory 'positive') by going into debit. This is legal only if the excess debits arise from causes beyond the directors' control—i.e. losses of one kind or another. If there are credit balances on other reserves free for distribution, they should be utilized to eliminate the debit balance on profit and loss account. Only when all such reserves are exhausted should a debit balance be shown on the account in the balance sheet; it should be deducted inset from the total of other reserves or, if this is inadequate, from the total of share capital and other reserves.

ii *General (revenue) reserve*

A general revenue reserve—usually called simply 'general reserve' where there is no non-specific capital reserve—represents nothing more than retained earnings which the directors have no present intention of distributing.

Modern practice is averse to the needless multiplication of revenue reserve accounts. In particular, contingency reserves (against losses arising from possible future events) are now very much out of favour. Normally, the only non-specific reserves required are the profit and loss account and the general reserve, under whatever name.

iii *Dividend equalization reserve*

This is really an alternative name for a general reserve, but implying an intention, in a company whose trade follows a cyclical pattern over time, to maintain a moderate level of ordinary dividend throughout by transferring surplus profits in good years to the equalization reserve, and back to profit and loss account in bad ones. A true general reserve, on the other hand, normally experiences transfers in one direction only.

12.1.4 Presentation of reserves in the balance sheet

The share capital and reserves of a limited company are set out at the top of the left-hand side, or the 'capital employed' section, of the balance sheet, in two blocks with a sub-total of owners' equity. Debentures follow immediately, after which come provisions and current liabilities.

Reserves are arranged in order of non-distributability, with capital ones first. The Companies Act, 1948, in relation to published accounts, required capital, and revenue, reserves to be distinguished, but the 1967 Act has repealed this obligation, and merely requires reserves to be classified under appropriate heads. This method has been observed in the illustration.

Example 5. The owners' equity and loan capital sections of a typical company balance sheet appear thus:

XYZ Company Ltd

Balance Sheet, 31 December 19.1 (extract)

	£	£
Share Capital—Authorized, Issued and Fully Paid		
10,000 8% cumulative preference shares of £1 each	10,000	
50,000 ordinary shares of £1 each	50,000	
		60,000
Reserves		
Share premium account	8,000	
Debenture redemption reserve fund	12,000	
General reserve	10,000	
Profit and loss a/c	4,000	
		34,000
		94,000
15% Debentures		40,000
		[etc.]

12.2 The profit and loss account

The profit and loss account of a company is made up in two forms—the complete version, presented to the board of directors, and the abridged one, furnished to the shareholders and debenture-holders and filed with the Registrar of Companies, along with the balance sheet. The second version is considered in Chapter 14, section 14.4, and the first one below.

12.2.1 Layout of the profit and loss account

In a partnership, division of the net profit is effected in an appropriation section. The same arrangement, suitably modified, is adopted in a company's profit and loss account; but an additional complication arises from the fact that a company is a body corporate, and taxed as such.

The net profit, as ascertained in the first section of the account, is arrived at after debiting all revenue expenditure for the year, including the remuneration of directors. They are officers of the company, not proprietors, and receive emoluments out of its funds, by way of fees as directors, and/or salaries, commissions, bonuses, etc. for acting as managers, executives, technologists or the like. Retired directors may be awarded pensions (though these are normally paid today out of separate superannuation funds), and occasionally a dismissed director may receive compensation for loss of office. In a public company, where directors' remuneration is negotiated at arm's length in a competitive market, there is thus a clear statement in the accounts of the 'wages of management', which in a non-corporate enterprise form an undifferentiated part of the accounting profit. In an independent private company controlled by the directors, however, the fixing of emoluments tends to be arbitrary. The directors regard their salaries in the light of drawings, or set them at levels designed to minimize the combined burden of corporation tax and income tax, rather than attempt genuinely to evaluate the services rendered to the company. The distinction between economic profit and managerial remuneration is thus blurred.

Interest on borrowed moneys (debentures, bank loans, etc.) is also charged in the first part of the profit and loss account, which is credited with interest and dividends received on investments (except where the interest is accumulated in a sinking fund, and reinvested). Debenture, and most gilt-edged, interest, payable or receivable, is subject to deduction of *income tax* at the basic rate (in 1974-75, 33 per cent). The company pays, and receives, the moneys net of tax—then, at the following fifth day of the month, makes a monthly settlement with the Inland Revenue. Income tax deducted from payments is demanded from the company, tax deducted from receipts is reclaimed by it; and the net difference is paid or received by the company on or before the nineteenth day of the month. A final settlement is effected at every 5 April, the end of the income tax year.

In the books, the net sums paid/received are debited/credited to the proper accounts for interest. These are then debited/credited with the income tax payable/reclaimable, thus bringing the payments/receipts up to the gross figures, which are in due course transferred to the profit and loss account. The corresponding credits/debits are made in the Income Tax Account, as representing sums due to/from the Inland Revenue, which receives/pays the net balance of the account each tax-month.

Example 6 On 30 June 1974 a company pays £10,000 (gross) in debenture interest, and receives £4,000 (gross) interest on debentures held in another company (income tax, 33 per cent). The book entries (other than Bank) are:

Interest on Debentures

1974	£
Jun 30 Bank [net]	6,700
Jun 30 Income tax	3,300

Income from Investments

		1974	£
		Jun 30 Bank [net]	2,680
		Jun 30 Income tax	1,320

Income Tax

1974	£	1974	£
Jun 30 Income from investments	1,320	Jun 30 Interest on debentures	3,300
Jul 19 Bank	1,980		
	£3,300		£3,300

The balance of the first section of the profit and loss account is the *net profit* (or *loss*) *before taxation.* This is carried, and brought, down to the credit (or debit) of the second section, which is debited (in the normal case of a net profit) with the estimated corporation tax charge for the year, related to the said profit; the corresponding credit, in a simple case, being made in the Corporation Tax Account (but see sub-section **12.3.1** for the complications which usually arise). If dividends (not interest) have been received from another company, the credit in the first section of the profit and loss account should be grossed up by the amount of the underlying tax credit (the income tax notionally deducted by the other company), thus increasing the net profit before taxation; i.e. the actual sums received are multiplied by the factor $1/(1 - c)$, where c is the basic rate of income tax as a decimal — the factor for a 33 per cent basic rate being $1/(1 - 0.33) = 1/(0.67)$. A sum equal to the tax credit added back is then debited in the second section of the profit and loss account, leaving the net profit after taxation unchanged (see sub-section **12.3.2**). A separate adjustment is made to reduce last year's corporation tax provision to the agreed assessment since made by the inspector of taxes. The balance of the second section is the net *profit (*or *loss) after taxation,* which in turn is carried, and brought down, to the credit (or debit) of the third, or appropriation, section (sometimes called the 'appropriation account').

The section is credited further with: extraordinary profits; retrospective credit adjustments to the results of previous years; the credit balance brought forward from the previous year (i.e. the amount of the reserve labelled 'profit and loss account' in last year's balance sheet); and any reductions in, or write-backs of, other special provisions, or reserves. The total of the credit side of the appropriation section represents the total fund of profit available to shareholders of all classes, and the actual appropriation appear on the debit side—extraordinary losses and write-offs; retrospective debit adjustments to previous years' results; increases in, or transfers to, other special provisions, or reserves; dividends declared, or to be declared, upon all classes of share capital in respect of the current year (actual sums payable to shareholders—see **12.2.2.**), and the balance carried forward to the next year (i.e. the sum captioned as 'profit and loss account' in the current balance sheet). Thus is the continuity of the account maintained from year to year.

Example 7 A typical profit and loss account, as prepared for internal use, appears thus, in summary form:

	£		£	£
Selling and distribution		Gross profit		103,000
expenses	10,000	Income from		
Administrative expenses	8,000	investments—		
Directors' emoluments	20,000	Interest	2,000	
Depreciation	15,000	Dividends	10,000*	
Interest on bank loans	1,000			12,000
Interest on debentures	5,000	Reduction in bad		
		debts provision		1,000
	59,000			
Net profit before taxation	57,000			
	£116,000			£116,000
Corporation tax based on		Net profit before taxation		57,000
current year's profits	24,000	Corporation tax provision		
Tax credit on dividends		for previous year no		
received	3,300	longer required		2,000
Net profit after taxation	31,700			
	£59,000			£59,000
Adjustment to stock valuation		Net profit after taxation		31,700
at beginning of year, less		Profit on sale of invest-		
corporation tax	3,000	ments, less corporation		
Transfer to general reserve	20,000	tax		6,000
Dividends—		Balance brought forward		
Preference, 7%	3,500	from previous year		10,100
Ordinary—				
Interim, 5%	5,000			
Final, 10%	10,000			
	18,500			
Balance carried forward				
to next year	6,300			
	£47,800			£47,800

* Actual cash, £6,700, multiplied by factor 1/(0.67) (i.e. increased by £3,300).

It should be noted that all 'below the line' adjustments which affect the company's corporation tax liability must be adjusted for this factor, before being transferred to the appropriation section of the profit and loss account.

12.2.2 Dividends and income tax

All dividends on share capital must be declared in general meeting; normally this is done by ordinary resolution at the annual general meeting. The articles of most companies, as well as Table A, arts. 114-117, require that no dividend shall exceed the amount recommended by the directors; that interim dividends may be paid at their discretion; that no dividend shall be paid otherwise than out of profits; and that the directors may, before recommending any dividend, set aside such sums to reserve out of profits as they think fit (either employing them in the business or investing them externally), and carry forward any other sums which they think it prudent not to divide.

Preference dividends are usually paid half-yearly at fixed dates, and authorized retrospectively by resolution at the AGM. They may, however, be 'passed' (omitted) if the directors consider that profits are inadequate to cover them. In that case there can be no declaration of any dividends for that year. Ordinary (and deferred) dividends are declared purely at the directors' discretion. The articles, as stated above, normally permit them to pay one or more interim dividends during the year; at the AGM these are retrospectively declared, together with a final dividend if profits permit, making up the total equity dividend for the year. The final dividend is paid after the meeting.

Under the old 'classical' system of corporation tax (1965-73) all dividends were paid, like debenture interest, after deduction of standard rate income tax by the company, which paid over the tax monthly to the Inland Revenue (offsetting any tax deducted from dividends received). Now, under the 'imputation' system (see section 12.3), as from 1973-74 all dividends are declared and paid as net sums, and appear as such in the profit and loss account. In the shareholder's hands, however, a dividend must be grossed up at the basic rate of income tax (t), using the factor $1/(1 - t)$; i.e. for 1974-75 (basic rate 33 per cent) a net dividend of £100 grosses to £100 x $1/(0.67)$ = £149.25. The shareholder returns the grossed-up amount as his income, and is taxed thereon, but sets against his liability a *tax credit* equal to basic rate on the gross sum; e.g. 33 per cent of £149.25 is £49.25. Thus, if he is liable only to basic rate on his dividend the shareholder pays no further tax; whereas if he is liable at, say, 38 per cent he pays £149.25 x $38/100$ − £49.25 = £7.91 (i.e. 5 per cent on £149.25). No adjustments are required in the company's books but, as explained in section 12.3, a dividend payment has other consequences, relative to the corporation tax liability.

Preference dividends, fixed before 6 April 1973 as gross sums subject to deduction of income tax, have as from that date to be restated as net sums equal to 7/10ths of the old rate—an adjustment designed to offset the effect of changing to the new system at a basic rate (1973-74) of 30 per cent. Thus, old preference shares issued at 10 per cent per annum less tax now carry a dividend of 7 per cent per annum net. The tax credit for 1973-74 was 3 per cent on the capital sum. From 1974-75 the basic rate is 33 per cent, but no further adjustment is made to the dividend rate; the shareholder still receives 7 per cent net, but his tax credit rises to 33/67ths thereof, or 3.45 per cent, making the grossed-up sum 10.45 per cent. If his marginal rate is 33 per cent he has the same post-tax dividend as before; if the marginal rate is higher he is slightly worse off, as the excess tax is computed on a larger base.

A dividend paid during the company's accounting year is debited to the appropriate Dividend Account, and transferred at the year-end to profit and loss account. A final dividend, payable after the year-end, is debited to profit and loss account and credited to Proposed Dividend Account, to which the payment is eventually debited. In the year-end balance sheet the proposed dividend appears among the current liabilities, though strictly there is no liability until the dividend is declared in general meeting. Under the imputation system, however, further entries are required in respect of advance corporation tax (ACT), as described in sub-section 12.3.2.

12.2.3 Availability of profits for dividend

Theoretically, a company is at liberty to pay out in dividend the whole amount of the revenue reserves, as shown by accounts properly drawn up in accordance with generally accepted accounting principles. These include, in particular, a proper distinction between capital and revenue expenditure, rational and consistent valuation of all assets, reasonable provision for depreciation of fixed assets, and full allowance for all known liabilities. In an inflationary period such as the present it is necessary also to make adequate adjustments for falls in the purchasing power of money, especially as they affect major items of capital expenditure in the foreseeable future, and to take care at all times to maintain working capital and cash at safe, but not wastefully high, levels. It is within such constraints that a prudent board of directors must decide on the rate of dividend which the company can sustain without embarrassment, while endeavouring to keep the market value of the shares at a height which minimizes the company's marginal cost of capital.

A company's dividend policy, then, is governed primarily by considerations of good accounting and sound finance. The legal position on the availability of profits for dividend is more equivocal. It is a settled rule that dividends must not be paid out of capital, in the sense that they must not exceed the legally-distributable reserves, and thus constitute an illegal return of capital to the shareholders. This is plainly a fraud on the creditors, and cannot be allowed in any circumstances. But it is by no means established that it is unlawful in all circumstances to pay dividends in excess of accounting profits. For example, a number of judicial decisions from 1889 onwards appear to absolve directors of the need to make provision for depreciation of fixed assets—or, at any rate, of those constituting the substratum of the business—in arriving at divisible profits; though losses of 'circulating capital' (current assets, and fixed assets subsidiary to the main business) must always be allowed for in full.[2] There is no obligation to make up past losses, either of capital or of revenue, before distributing current profits. The accountant regards the profit and loss account as a continuous one, but the directors, if it suits them, may take each year on its own.[3] A genuine revaluation of assets may be used to wipe out an accumulated loss on revenue account;[4] and goodwill 'prudently' written off in the past may be brought back on to the books, at a reasonable valuation, if it still exists—and, again, be used to extinguish revenue losses.[5]

As regards capital gains, it is accepted that a realized gain may be distributed if the articles so permit,[6] but that such a gain must still exist after a general bona fide appraisal of all assets, setting off any net downward revaluation against the realized surplus.[7] Doubt has, however, been thrown on the matter by the controversial decision in *Dimbula Valley (Ceylon) Tea Co. Ltd* v. *Laurie* (1961), that a dividend may legitimately be paid out of an *unrealized* capital surplus, provided that the company has 'fluid assets' available for the purpose, and that it retains assets enough to cover its liabilities.

All in all, the law seems more permissive with regard to distributions than the accountancy profession or the weight of business opinion. Pending a further Companies Act, which (following the Jenkins Report) may compel proper provision for depreciation of wasting assets, prohibit dividends out of current profits while past revenue losses are not made up, and restrain distribution of unrealized capital

---

[2] *Lee* v. *Neuchatel Asphalte Co. Ltd* (1889); *Verner* v. *General and Commercial Investment Trust Ltd* (1894); *Wilmer* v. *McNamara & Co. Ltd* (1895); *Bond* v. *Barrow Haematite Steel Co. Ltd* (1902).

[3] *Ammonia Soda Co.* v. *Chamberlain* (1918).

[4] *Ibid.*

[5] *Stapley* v. *Read Bros. Ltd* (1924).

[6] *Lubbock* v. *British Bank of South America* (1892).

[7] *Foster* v. *New Trinidad Lake Asphalte Co. Ltd* (1902).

gains, it is safe to say that good accounting and prudent management will never be bad law in these respects.

12.2.4 Interest out of capital

The Companies Act, 1948, s. 65, allows a company, in certain circumstances, to pay interest on its share capital, out of capital. The shares must be issued in order to pay for works, buildings, or plant which cannot become profitable for a lengthened period, and the interest may be capitalized as part of the cost of such works, etc. Payment must be authorized by the company's articles and sanctioned by the Department of Trade, which may first conduct an inquiry at the company's expense. The interest may be paid only for so long as the Department permits, and in no case beyond the end of the half-year (ending, presumably, on 30 June or 31 December) after the half-year in which the works, etc., are completed or provided. The rate payable may not exceed 4 per cent per annum, or such higher rate as the Treasury may prescribe from time to time by statutory instrument. In fact, the Companies (Interest Out of Capital) Order, 1929, allows 6 per cent.

Interest of this nature is paid under deduction of income tax, and in the books it must be adjusted to the gross amount, through the income tax account, before being debited to the asset account(s) concerned. It does not pass through the profit and loss account directly, but subsequent depreciation charges will be so computed as to write off the interest along with other elements of the assets' cost.

12.3 Corporation tax in company accounts

Since the Finance Act, 1965, all bodies corporate, except local authorities and with the addition of unit trusts, have been subject to corporation tax on their profits. The rate of tax is normally fixed by each year's Finance Act, retrospectively for the previous 'financial year', ended 31 March and denoted by the calendar year in which it begins—e.g. the financial year 1974 runs from 1 April 1974 to 31 March 1975. In company accounts corporation tax calculations for the current financial year, or any part of it, are made on the assumption that the rate will be the same as for the previous year, unless the government has announced a different intention.

Corporation tax computations relate to the company's profits for 'accounting periods', not exceeding 12 months and normally coinciding with the accounting year. (If this is, exceptionally, longer than 12 months owing to a change of year-end, it is divided into two periods—the first 12 months, and the rest—and the profits apportioned on a time basis.) Since the accounting period does not necessarily correspond with any financial year, a period spanning parts of two years with different tax-rates requires division at 31 March, with time apportionment of profits, and the taxing of the two segments at different rates. The latest rate known at the time of going to press is 52 per cent for the year 1974, and this is assumed in all illustrations. Small companies (with profits not exceeding £25,000) pay 42 per cent, while those with profits between £25,000 and £40,000 pay 52 per cent, less an abatement equal to one-sixth of the amount by which profits fall short of £40,000.

The tax for an accounting period is payable nine months after the end of the period, if the company commenced business on or after 1 April 1965. For companies which were already in business at that date, and thus paid income tax on their profits under the old system, corporation tax is payable on the same date on which income tax would have been payable, had it continued in force—i.e. on 1 January in the income tax year relative to the accounting year, on the 'previous year' basis generally applicable to business profits (companies did not defer half the tax to the following 1 July, as do sole traders and partnerships). Thus, if a company's year ends on 31 December 1974, it would, under the old system, have been assessed to income tax on those profits for 1975-76, and would have paid it on 1 January 1976; and this is the date on which corporation tax is due. Hence, 'old' companies with year-ends between 1 January and 1 April inclusive pay corporation tax on the following 1 January, those (if any) between 2 April and 5 April nine months later (the minimum period of grace), and those between 6 April and 31 December on the 1 January next but one. The period of deferment thus varies from 9, to nearly 21, months from the year-end; the average time between earning profits and paying tax on them therefore ranges from 15, to nearly 27, months. (If assessment is delayed, tax is due one month thereafter, should this be later than the normal date.)

The U.K. originally adopted the 'classical' system of corporation tax, modelled on that of the U.S.A. A moderate rate of tax (finally, 40 per cent for the financial year 1972) was imposed on company profits generally, but distributed profits were then subjected to income tax at standard rate (finally, 38.75 per cent for 1972-73), deducted at source by the company and paid over to the Inland Revenue; i.e. dividends gross of income tax were paid out of profits net of corporation tax, causing double taxation of distributions. From 1 April 1973 the U.K., having entered the European Economic Community, changed over to the 'imputation' system, based on French practice (in preference to the West German 'two-rate' system). Corporation tax is levied on profits at a higher rate (for 1973, 52 per cent), but distributions are relieved of income tax in the recipients' hands up to the basic rate (1974-75, 33 per cent); as explained in sub-section **12.2.2**, the shareholder is assessed on the grossed-up amount, but given a tax credit, leaving him liable only for any tax in excess of the basic rate. The Company pays out the net sum only, and does not (as in the classical system) account to the Inland Revenue for the income tax; but that is not quite the end of the matter.

During a quarter (ending on the last day of March, June, September or December) a company may receive *franked investment income* and/or make *franked payments.* Franked investment income consists of dividends or bonuses on shares in other companies; having been paid out of profits charged to corporation tax in the payer's hands, they are exempt from tax in those of the recipient. Franked payments are dividends, etc., paid to the company's own shareholders out of its own profits after tax. If at the end of the quarter franked payments exceed franked investment income, then within 14 days the company must pay to the Inland Revenue a proportion of the excess, *as advance corporation tax* (ACT). This goes to reduce the corporation tax liability at the normal due date (see above), the company losing the interest which it might have earned by withholding payment for the full term. If franked investment income exceeds franked payments for the quarter, the excess is carried forward and offset in the next quarter, and so on. For 1973-74 the ACT was the amount of the tax credit relative to the excess payments, i.e. 3/7ths of them, or 30 per cent (the then basic rate) on the grossed-up amount. For 1974-75, however, not only has the basic rate (tax credit) risen to 33 per cent, but the ACT is subject to a 50 per cent surcharge, making 49½ per cent on a net 67 per cent, or 99/134ths (73.9 per cent) of the net sum—

thus putting a heavier strain upon the company's liquidity. (For 1975-76 the basic rate is 35 per cent (ACT 35/65ths, or 7/13ths), but the surcharge is lifted.)

12.3.1 Computation of corporation tax

It is not proposed to deal here with the very complex rules for computing corporation tax, except to the extent that they affect accounting practice. The net profit before tax is the starting-point of any computation, but it has to be adjusted by disallowing some debits in the profit and loss account, and exempting some credits from taxation (including franked investment income—see above), so that the base to which the corporation tax rate is applied differs from the accounting net profit. Again, the tax is levied on capital profits ('chargeable gains') as well as trading profits and interest received, less paid ('income'), the two elements making up 'profits' within the meaning of the Income and Corporation Taxes Act, 1970 (the consolidating statute).

The amortization of expenditure on fixed assets creates some problems. All depreciation charged in the accounts must be disallowed, and 'capital allowances' substituted. These consist basically of a 'first-year allowance' on the cost of most tangible fixed assets (except ordinary motor cars and second-hand buildings) purchased during the accounting period, and a 'writing-down allowance' on the written-down value of those acquired earlier. For plant and machinery in general, the writing-down allowances take the form of reducing balance depreciation; for industrial buildings and structures, writing-down allowances are on a straight line basis. In the development areas and in Northern Ireland, and on ships, free depreciation is allowed, i.e. write-off of expenditure at the company's discretion—up to 100 per cent in the first year, if desired—and this has recently been extended to most plant elsewhere. There is, however, no depreciation allowance on non-industrial buildings in general.

From this rapid survey it is apparent that capital allowances can hardly ever be equal to the accounting depreciation which they replace. If the company is using straight line depreciation, the substitution of capital allowances will lead to more generous tax allowances in the earlier years of the assets' lives, and less generous ones later on. In other words, the company pays less tax in the earlier years, and more in the later years, than if it were permitted to apply its own depreciation charges. This deferment of tax complicates the accounting, as shown below. Nothing can be done about depreciation disallowed altogether, as on houses, shops, hotels, offices, etc.

The accounting methods described below are, in general, those set out in Statement of Standard Accounting Practice No. 8: *The treatment of taxation under the imputation system in the accounts of companies* (1974) (see also Chapter 14, sub-section **14.6.5**).

12.3.2 Accounting for corporation tax

The essence of corporation tax accounting consists in debiting the profit and loss account, and crediting a Corporation Tax Account, with an estimate of the year's liability, usually rounded upwards to, say, the nearest £1,000. The credit balance of the corporation tax account appears in the balance sheet as a provision for a deferred liability—below loan capital and above current liabilities—under the name of 'corporation tax—current year' or some similar caption. During the following year the assessment will normally be agreed, hopefully at a somewhat lower figure than that provided and, at the end of the second year, the excess provision will be written back to the credit of the profit and loss account. If the first year's corporation tax has not been paid by the end of the second (as will happen if the accounts of an 'old' company are made up to a date between 6 April and 31 December inclusive), the amended credit balance will appear on the balance sheet as a current liability, captioned as, e.g. 'corporation tax—previous year', while the current year's tax (passed through the second section of the profit and loss account) appears above as 'corporation tax—current year'. That, in its turn, will be adjusted to the actual amount assessed, and brought down to current liabilities, at the end of the third year—during which the first year's tax will be paid.

Under the imputation system (from 6 April 1973) it is necessary also to account for advance corporation tax (ACT). As explained in section **12.3**, payment of a dividend (not covered by franked investment income) during a quarter makes the company liable to pay to the Inland Revenue, within 14 days of the end of the quarter, a sum on account of corporation tax, equal to the tax credit on the dividend, plus (for 1974-75) a 50 per cent surcharge. This ACT (and surcharge) are credited to Bank and debited to Corporation Tax Account. In balancing the latter, ACT is set off against the tax liability for the accounting period *during which* the dividend was paid; normally this reduces the estimated liability for the current year, as shown in the year-end balance sheet—the residue (before deducting the surcharge) being known as *mainstream corporation tax*. In the case of the proposed final dividend on ordinary shares, the standard procedure is to credit the prospective ACT to ACT on Proposed Dividend Account, and debit it to ACT Recoverable Account; the first balance appears in the balance sheet as a current liability (after proposed dividend stated net of tax credit), and the second as a 'deferred asset', under a separate heading after current assets. When the ACT is paid in the next year, the sum is debited to ACT on Proposed Dividend (extinguishing the credit balance), while the debit balance on ACT Recoverable is transferred to the debit of Corporation Tax and offset against the *second* year's tax liability (where there is no deferred taxation account—see below). Where a dividend is paid before the year-end, and the ACT is payable after it, the ACT should be debited to corporation tax and credited to ACT Payable Account—the latter balance being included among the creditors.

Example 8 The accounts of Profit Ltd are made up to 31 December in each year, and its mainstream corporation tax is payable on 1 January next but one. At 1 January 19.3 the corporation tax account stands credited with the liabilities for the years ended 31 December 19.1 (mainstream actual), £25,000 and 31 December 19.2 (mainstream estimated), £36,000. ACT plus surcharge on the proposed dividend (£16,000) at 31 December 19.2 is £11,821 (i.e. 99/134th of £16,000). During 19.3 the tax for 19.1 is paid, and the mainstream assessment for 19.2 agreed at £35,000. The total liability for the year ended 31 December 19.3 is estimated at £52,000. Ordinary dividends for that year are: interim, £10,000 (paid in July); final, £20,000. There is no franked investment income. (Basic rate of income tax 33 per cent; ACT plus surcharge, 1½ times tax credit).

The relevant entries (with other figures assumed as necessary) are:

Corporation Tax

19.3		£	19.3		£
Jan 1	Bank		Jan 1	Balance b/d	
	Tax 31.12.19.1	25,000		Tax 31.12.19.1	25,000
Apr 14	ACT recoverable	11,821		Tax 31.12.19.2	36,000
Oct 14	Bank		Dec 31	Profit and loss a/c	
	ACT on interim dividend	7,389		Tax 31.12.19.3	52,000
Dec 31	Profit and loss a/c				
	Tax 31.12.19.2				
	(Adjustment)	1,000			
Dec 31	Balance c/d				
	Tax 31.12.19.2	35,000			
	Tax 31.12.19.3	32,790			
		£113,000			£113,000
			19.4		
			Jan 1	Balance b/d	
				Tax 31.12.19.2	35,000
				Tax 31.12.19.3	32,790

ACT on Proposed Dividend

19.3		£	19.2		£
Apr 14	Bank	11,821	Dec 31	ACT recoverable	11,821
			19.3		
			Dec 31	ACT recoverable	14,777

ACT Recoverable

19.2		£	19.3		£
Dec 31	ACT on proposed		Apr 14	Corporation Tax	11,821
	dividend	11,821			
19.3					
Dec 31	ACT on proposed				
	dividend	14,777			

Profit and Loss Account for the Year ended 31 December 19.3 (first section omitted)

	£	£		£
Corporation Tax		52,000	Net profit before taxation	100,000
Net profit after			Corporation tax provision for	
taxation		49,000	previous year no longer	
			required	1,000
		£101,000		£101,000
Dividends			Net profit after taxation	49,000
Ordinary			Balance brought forward from	
Paid	10,000		previous year	12,000
Proposed	20,000			
		30,000		
Balance carried forward				
to next year		31,000		
		£61,000		£61,000

	£	£		£	£
14% Debentures		100,000	Current Assets		
Corporation Tax—			Stock	190,000	
Current Year		32,790	Debtors	100,000	
			Bank & Cash	60,000	
Currient Liabilities					350,000
Creditors	80,000				
Corporation tax—			Deferred Asset		
previous year	35,000		ACT recoverable		14,777
Proposed dividend	20,000				
ACT on proposed					
dividend	14,777				
		149,777			

ACT is recoverable against corporation tax of the current year, only to the extent of (1974-75) 33 per cent of the taxable profit, plus the whole of the surcharge imposed in 1974—i.e. 33/52ths of the current year's tax, plus the surcharge. Any excess of the ACT proper may be offset against corporation tax for the two previous years, but in no case against tax arising before 1 April 1973. Any remaining excess unrecovered may be carried forward and added to recoverable ACT of future years; in the meantime it should be debited to ACT Recoverable Account. If any ACT is deemed to be irrecoverable (within the next tax-year) it should be written off to the debit of profit and loss account. Thus, in *Example 8* the maximum ACT (proper) recoverable against the tax for 19.3 was (£52,000 x 33/52) = £33,000; in fact, only £12,806 arose. Had dividends totalling £120,000 been paid in 19.3, related ACT would have been (£120,000 x 33/67) = £59,104. Only £33,000 could have been offset against 19.3's tax liability; the other £26,104 might have been recovered against tax for 19.2 and 19.1.

The picture is complicated, in practice, by the element of tax deferment arising from the divergence between accounting depreciation and capital allowances, as explained above. The accepted procedure today, as set forth in the ASSC's Exposure Draft 11: *Accounting for deferred taxation* (1973) (see Chapter 14, sub-section **14.6.6**), allows for this factor by the use of a Deferred Taxation Account. The debit to profit and loss account, for the current year's corporation tax, is computed by substituting, for the capital allowances, the corresponding depreciation charges (omitting any for which no capital allowances are granted at all), while the corporation tax account is credited with the estimated legal liability, computed by using the capital allowances. If capital allowances for the year are greater than depreciation charges the 'current' corporation tax, related as closely as possible to the accounting profit, is greater than the 'legal' tax, and the difference represents tax theoretically due for this year, but legally deferred until later. It is therefore credited to deferred taxation account, as a provision for a tax liability expected to arise in later years as a result of acquiring fixed assets in the recent past. The credit balance on deferred taxation account should appear on the balance sheet as a provision, between debentures and current corporation tax, since it is a liability remoter in time than the later.

If, in course of time, capital allowances for any year fall below depreciation charges, the current tax charge in profit and loss account will be less than the legal liability in corporation tax account, indicating that the deferred liability is being drawn upon. The difference is therefore debited to the deferred taxation account.

This process continues, theoretically, until the deferred taxation account balance is reduced to nil. In practice this is unlikely to happen, as drafts upon the account in respect of old assets are continually offset by fresh deferments of tax on new ones.

Changes in the corporation tax rate from time to time raise a problem, to which there are two alternative solutions. By the *deferral method,* tax is simply deferred at the rate ruling at the time, and written back at the same rate when the timing difference reverses itself. The balance of the deferred taxation account is not adjusted for intervening changes of tax rate—it is a mere total of past tax provisions in respect of unreversed timing differences or unrealized capital gains, and not necessarily an accurate statement of tax payable in the future. By the *liability method,* on the other hand, the deferred taxation account balance is adjusted proportionately whenever the tax rate changes (the benefit or burden of the adjustment falling upon the profit and loss account), and write-backs of deferred tax are made at the current rate. Thus the balance of the account represents the liability for future tax, on the assumption that the current rate remains in force. In neither case is any attempt made to discount the balance to its estimated net present value. The uncertainties inherent in the assumptions undermine the apparent precision of the liability method, and ED11 therefore recommends the use of the deferral method, as being simpler and as avoiding distortion of the results of intervening years.

Where ACT is irrecoverable from current or past corporation tax liabilities (see above), it may be offset against deferred taxation (up to, at present, 33/52ths thereof), to the extent that such deferred taxation stems from timing differences, and not from anticipated chargeable gains on revalued fixed assets. The same applies to ACT on proposed dividend, which may (subject to these limitations) be debited at the year-end to deferred taxation, instead of to ACT recoverable—thus eliminating, or reducing, the 'deferred asset' in the balance sheet. When the ACT is paid, though, the amount must be transferred from corporation tax (*Dr.*) back to deferred taxation (*Cr.*), thus clearing the relevant credit balance on the former account and reinstating the amount temporarily 'borrowed' from the latter.

Example 9 Assume the same figures as in *Example 8,* except that, if accounting depreciation is substituted for capital allowances, corporation tax of the year ended 31 December 19.3 becomes £53,500, and that the credit balance on deferred taxation account at 1 January 19.3 was £30,000 (all derived from timing differences). The entries then become:

Corporation Tax

19.3		£	19.3		£
Jan 1	Bank		Jan 1	Balance b/d	
	Tax 31.12.19.1	25,000		Tax 31.12.19.1	25,000
Apr 14	Deferred taxation			Tax 31.12.19.2	36,000
	ACT on final dividend		Dec 31	Profit and loss a/c	
	31.12.19.2	11,821		Tax 31.12.19.3	52,000
Oct 14	Bank				
	ACT on interim dividend	7,389			
Dec 31	Profit and loss a/c				
	Tax 31.12.19.2				
	(Adjustment)	1,000			
Dec 31	Balance c/d				
	Tax 31.12.19.2	35,000			
	Tax 31.12.19.3	32,790			
		£113,000			£113,000
			19.4		
			Jan 1	Balance b/d	
				Tax 31.12.19.2	35,000
				Tax 31.12.19.3	32,790

Deferred Taxation

19.3		£	19.3		£
Dec 31	ACT on proposed				
	dividend	14,777	Jan 1	Balance b/d	30,000
Dec 31	Balance c/d	28,544	Apr 14	Corporation Tax	
				ACT on final dividend	
				31.12.19.2	11,821
			Dec 31	Profit and loss a/c	
				Tax 31.12.19.3	1,500
		£43,321			£43,321
			19.4		
			Jan 1	Balance b/d	28,544

ACT on Proposed Dividend

19.3		£	19.2		£
Apr 14	Bank	11,821	Dec 31	Deferred taxation	11,821
			19.3		
			Dec 31	Deferred taxation	14,777

Profit and Loss Account for the Year ended 31 December 19.3 (first section omitted)

	£	£		£
Corporation tax		53,500	Net profit before taxation	100,000
Net profit after			Corporation tax provision for	
taxation		47,500	previous year no longer	
			required	1,000
		£101,000		£101,000
Dividends—			Net profit after taxation	47,500
Ordinary			previous year	12,000
Paid	10,000			
Proposed	20,000			
		30,000		
Balance carried forward				
to next year		29,500		
		£59,500		£59,000

Balance Sheet, 31 December 19.3 (extracts)

	£	£		£	£
14% Debentures		100,000	_Current Assets_		
Deferred Taxation		28,544	Stock	190,000	
			Debtors	100,000	
Corporation Tax			Bank & Cash	60,000	
Current Year		32,790			350,000
Current Liabilities					
Creditors	80,000				
Corporation tax—					
previous year	35,000				
Proposed dividend	20,000				
ACT on proposed					
dividend	14,777				
	149,777				

Franked investment income (see section 12.3) may rationally be treated in two ways. One is to credit it to profit and loss account at the actual amount received from the other company; but this distorts the net profit before taxation, or requires the FII to be added to net profit after taxation—both awkward expedients. For this reason SSAP No. 8 (see sub-section 12.3.1) requires FII to be shown as part of the taxable profit, at the amount received plus the underlying tax credit—the amount of the latter being shown separately on the debit side, as part of the tax charge. Thus, if a dividend of £67 is received this is augmented to £100 by adding the tax credit, £33, and the £100 included in net profit before taxation. In the tax charge is shown, separately, the tax credit, £33—thus adding a net £67 to the net profit after taxation. FII is therefore brought into account on a basis consistent with the company's other income.

A loss (for tax purposes) in any year means a nil assessment for the relevant accounting period, and a claim to present or future relief. The loss may be set off, in the first place, against the previous year's assessment (with adjustment if the two accounting periods are of different lengths). In the accounts this involves cancellation, in whole or in part, of any outstanding liability for the previous year by debiting corporation tax and crediting profit and loss account in the 'corporation tax' section. If the liability has already been met, relief may be obtained by repayment—the debit being made in the bank account, and the credit as above.

If the previous year's assessment is inadequate to cover the loss, the excess must be carried forward against future assessments on profits—or the whole loss may be so treated, if desired. No entry should be made in advance of obtaining such relief, since there is no legal claim against the Inland Revenue until then, but a note as to the position should be annexed to the published accounts. When profits arise, a normal provision for tax on them should be made by entries in the 'taxation' section of the profit and loss account, the corporation tax account, and the deferred taxation account. Tax in respect of the loss relieved should then be debited to corporation tax (affecting the deferred liability shown in the balance sheet) and credited to the appropriation section, as a prior year adjustment.

Most small private companies are 'close companies' (controlled by the directors, or by five or fewer 'participators', and with less than 35 per cent of the equity capital in the hands of the general public, and quoted on a stock exchange). Among other disadvantages, such a company is required to distribute its profits up to or beyond a somewhat arbitrary 'required standard distribution', or pay income tax at basic rate on any 'shortfall'. Tax on a shortfall should be debited to the appropriation section; any subsequent recovery, by offsetting the shortfall against a later distribution beyond the required standard, is credited to the section. Alternatively, the shortfall tax may be debited to Income Tax Account, and thus carried forward; when an offset occurs it is credited to income tax and debited to corporation tax.

Corporation tax on 'chargeable gains' should be debited to the accounts in which the gains are recognized, and credited to corporation tax account, only the post-tax amount of the gains being transferred to profit and loss account or capital reserve. Estimated corporation tax on *unrealized* gains recognised in the accounts (e.g. upward revaluations of assets not attracting capital allowances) should be debited to the capital reserve concerned, and credited to deferred taxation account. When the gains are realized, any tax assessed on them should be transferred from deferred taxation account to corporation tax account (the tax paid being debited thereto), while any difference between tax assessed and tax provided for in deferred taxation account should be set off against the book gain or loss, as compared with the amount of the revaluation.

A company with interests overseas will be taxed on profits earned there, by both the overseas and U.K. governments. In the U.K., however, the company will normally obtain *double taxation relief* by setting off the overseas tax against U.K. mainstream corporation tax on the same profits, up to the amount of the mainstream tax. The effect is thus, as a rule, to make the company bear in total the higher of the two rates of tax on the overseas profits. ACT on the company's own dividends (net of franked investment income) is set first against corporation tax on U.K. profits, and only if these are insufficient is ACT set against U.K. tax on the overseas profits—thus restricting the mainstream tax against which the overseas tax can be relieved. In the profit and loss account, the charge for U.K. tax is shown net of double taxation relief, while the overseas tax charge is shown in full; and similarly as to the respective liabilities in the balance sheet. Any part of the overseas tax charge which is unrelieved as the result of paying dividends (because of the offsetting of excess ACT) should be distinguished (see Chapter 14, sub-section **14.6.5**).

12.4 'Fictitious' assets

A company's general ledger commonly contains a number of debit balances representing, not assets in any real sense, but intangible items of cost, relating to the setting-up and financing of the enterprise, which it is not considered expedient to charge immediately to revenue. These are:

a preliminary expenses;
b expenses of issuing shares and debentures;
c commissions paid in respect of shares and debentures;
d discounts on debentures; and
e discounts on shares.

The first three represent money paid out; the other two, mere differences between capital moneys received and the nominal value of the relevant securities. In no case is there any realizable asset, and in financial analysis such items are treated as negative reserves. This appears, in fact, to be the essential nature of the first three, and there is a case for deducting them inset from the total of reserves, rather than showing them as 'other assets', after current assets. The normal practice is to write them off the share premium account (if any) immediately—a procedure specifically sanctioned by the 1948 Act, s. 56—or off revenue reserves over an arbitrarily short term of years, say three.

There are some theoretical objections to this. Preliminary expenses may be said to benefit the company over its whole existence, in that the considerable expense of forming it need never be incurred again, and this should be taken into account by a prospective purchaser of the business, or of a controlling shareholding; on this view the item should never be written off, except on liquidation. Issue expenses and commissions, similarly, benefit the company continuously, and ought in the case of debentures to be written off over their currency, and in the case of shares, only on liquidation. On the whole, though, it may be said that a write-off to share premium account or other capital surplus meets the objections, and serves to simplify the balance sheet; a write-off to revenue is more questionable, but the amounts involved are rarely significant.

12.4.1 Debenture and share discount

Discount on debentures is of a different nature. It is general today to issue debentures somewhat below par, so as to increase slightly the true rate of interest on the money advanced, and offer a small 'bonus' on redemption at par. Thus, if £100 debentures bearing interest at 10 per cent per annum nominal are issued for five years at 95, the running rate (before tax) is $(10 \times 100)/95$, or 10.526 per cent per annum. The yield to redemption, though, is the rate of interest at which the net present value of the relevant cash flows (assumed year-end) becomes zero (i.e. the internal rate of return, in DCF terms); for an investment of £95 in year 0, five receipts of £10 in years 1–5, and one of £100 at end-year 5, the rate of return is 11.365 per cent per annum before tax. Had the debentures been issued, and redeemed, at par for any term of years, the running and redemption yields would both have been 10 per cent per annum.

The common method of amortizing the discount in this situation is to write it off to revenue in equal annual instalments over the currency of the debentures, as being additional interest deferred to the end of the term. This equation of current and deferred interest, giving equal money charges in all years, is theoretically incorrect. To show the proper time-pattern of interest, the company must regard itself as paying the true rate (in the example, 11.365 per cent) on the money advanced, treating the actual interest payments (here, £10 per annum per £100 nominal) as being on account of this, and writing off discount so as to make up the annual charge to the true rate, allowing for the accumulation of 'true' interest underpaid. This means that the amount of discount written off must rise from year to year, instead of remaining constant. In the balance sheet, unamortized discount should be deducted inset from the nominal value of the debentures, the difference representing the amount advanced plus unpaid 'true' interest to date.

Example 10 On the facts above, the time-pattern of debenture discount amortization is as follows, for an issue of £100,000 nominal of debentures:

	1	2	3	4	5	6	7
Year	Nominal value of debentures (£100,000) less unamortized discount at beginning of year (column 5)	Column 1 x 1.11365 (1 + true rate of interest) (columns 1+3+6)	Annual interest paid	Nominal value of debentures (£100,000) less unamortized discount at end of year (column 7)	Unamortized discount at beginning of year	Discount amortized in year	Unamortized discount at end of year (columns 5—6)
	£	£	£	£	£	£	£
1	95,000	105,797	10,000	95,797	5,000	797	4,203
2	95,797	106,684	10,000	96,684	4,203	887	3,316
3	96,684	107,672	10,000	97,672	3,316	988	2,328
4	97,672	108,773	10,000	98,773	2,328	1,101	1,227
5	98,773	110,000	10,000	100,000	1,227	1,227	—

When debentures are redeemed by annual drawings, the conventional method of amortizing the discount is by the 'sum of years' digits' approach. Thus, for a five-year period, the sum of the digits is $5 + 4 + 3 + 2 + 1 = 15$; 5/15ths of the discount is written off in the first year, 4/15ths in the second, and so on—on the argument that the company has the use of 5/5ths of the money lent for the first year, 4/5ths for the second, etc. This procedure, again, is simplistic, in that it ignores the proper time-pattern of interest. The true (DCF) rate should be computed, and applied as above, taking account of the capital repayments as well as the (declining) interest payments.

Example 11 Suppose that £100,000 nominal of 10 per cent debentures are issued at 95, and redeemed at par by equal annual drawings over five years. The true rate of interest is 12.155 per cent per annum. The discount is amortized thus:

Year	1 Nominal value of debentures unredeemed less unamortized discount at beginning of year (column 6)	2 Column 1 x 1.12155 (1 + true rate of interest) (columns 1+3+7)	3 Annual interest paid	4 Nominal value of debentures redeemed in year	5 Nominal value of debentures unredeemed less unamortized discount at end of year (column 8)	6 Unamortized discount at beginning of year	7 Discount amortized in year	8 Unamortized discount at end of year (columns 6–7)
	£	£	£	£	£	£	£	£
1	95,000	106,547	10,000	20,000	76,547	5,000	1,547	3,453
2	76,547	85,852	8,000	20,000	57,852	3,453	1,305	2,148
3	57,852	64,884	6,000	20,000	38,884	2,148	1,032	1,116
4	38,884	43,610	4,000	20,000	19,610	1,116	726	390
5	19,610	22,000	2,000	20,000	–	390	390	–

Shares are very rarely, if ever, issued at a discount. Since they have no determinate life, the discount cannot be amortized in any scientific manner; it should theoretically be kept on the books indefinitely. In practice it would probably be written off immediately against share premium account, or against revenue over a short period of years by the straight line method. In the meantime it should appear in the balance sheet as a deduction from reserves.

13

Capital structure of a limited liability company

The legal requirements and customary terms of issue of different company securities have been summarized in Chapter 11. It is now necessary to look more closely at the practical problems of company finance, and at the accounting aspects of changes therein over time.

13.1 Planning a company's capital

In any company the overriding objective of the directors, in so far as they act rationally and in the interests of their ultimate 'masters', is to maximize the wealth of the equity shareholders within the constraints of law, morality, and public policy; and the said shareholders, if they in turn act rationally in their own best interests, will reward the directors according to the measure of success which they achieve, thus making their duty and interest coincide—*a fortiori* in small private companies, where the directors generally hold all or most of the shares. Many factors often prevent these ideals from being attained in practice, among them being bad judgement, excessive caution or rashness, pessimism or optimism, megalomania or desire for a quiet life, on the side of the directors; and apathy, lack of cohesion, failure of vigilance, or sheer inability to obtain vital information, on the part of the members. Yet the principles of good management are well established and financial objectives clear, though hard to gain.

Maximization of equity shareholders' wealth requires the achievement of two sub-objectives; 1 the obtaining of the maximum rate of return on the funds entrusted to the company; and 2 the raising of these funds at minimum cost, relative to existing equity shareholders' interests. The first is the province of management accounting, in the sphere of capital budgeting and project appraisal, and must, for the purposes of this book, be taken largely for granted. The second, however, is the principal concern of financial management, in relation to the design of the company's initial capital structure and its modification over time, and calls for some discussion, if the reader is to see any point in the extensive expositions of accounting mechanics which occupy so much space in the present text.

13.1.1 Design of the financial structure

The long-term and medium-term capital of a company may most usefully be divided for this purpose into three classes: i *loan or debt capital*; ii *preference capital*; and iii *equity capital.*

Classes i and ii are from many points of view best considered together, as *fixed-return capital,* in contrast to equity capital, which has no fixed dividend or guaranteed redemption value. Equity includes not only ordinary and (where applicable) deferred shares, but reserves and undistributed profits, since these represent additional investments by equity shareholders in the company, and would be paid out to them on liquidation. It also includes unrealized capital gains, less losses, whether or not shown on the face of the balance sheet—for the same reasons as before.

Loan capital (generally in the form of debentures) is clearly differentiated from the other classes, except in the case of convertible debentures, which are 'potential equity'. Normal preference shares, with a fixed dividend (usually cumulative) and a fixed capital payment on redemption or liquidation, also belong clearly to the fixed-return category, as do participating preference shares, as long as the participating rights are not operative. If they are, the shares become 'conditional equity', up to the point where the normal maximum dividend is reached, when they revert to their preferential status. Preference shares with a right to share in surplus assets on liquidation may generally be regarded as pure preference capital where no liquidation is in prospect, since the company's free reserves, after paying the preference dividend, are still wholly available for ordinary dividend. In the rather uncommon case where deferred shares are issued as well as ordinaries, the latter are the equity until their maximum or 'threshold' dividend is reached. Beyond that, either the ordinaries become preference capital and the deferred shares equity, or both become equity (if they share in surplus profits beyond the 'threshold'). The same considerations apply, *mutatis mutandis,* to preferred and deferred ordinary shares. In the following discussions, though, the three basic classes will be assumed separate and distinct unless otherwise stated.

13.1.2 Capital gearing (leverage)

The heart of the matter is the judicious use of *gearing* (in America, *leverage*) to lift the rate of return on equity above that on capital employed generally. Gearing may be defined as the raising of part of the capital in the form of fixed-return securities, at a rate lower than the average return on capital employed, so that the residual profits, or 'equity earnings', being expressed as a return to a smaller capital base, afford a higher rate of return to equity than the average; as in the following simple illustration.

Example 1 The capital structures of A Ltd, B Ltd, C Ltd, and D Ltd, are as follows, the total of loan, preference, and equity capital being £100,000 in each case. Below, also, are their profit and loss accounts for the same year (summarized); each company made a net trading profit, before taxation, of £20,000, and corporation tax was 52 per cent.

	A Ltd £	B Ltd £	C Ltd £	D Ltd £
Capital Structure				
15% Debentures	—	10,000	20,000	50,000
8% Preference shares	—	—	10,000	20,000
Ordinary shares of £1 each	50,000	50,000	40,000	20,000
Reserves (mean for year)	50,000	40,000	30,000	10,000
	£100,000	£100,000	£100,000	£100,000

Profit and Loss Account

Net trading profit before taxation	20,000	20,000	20,000	20,000
Debenture interest	–	1,500	3,000	7,500
Net profit before taxation	20,000	18,500	17,000	12,500
Corporation tax (52%)	10,400	9,620	8,840	6,500
Net profit after taxation	9,600	8,880	8,160	6,000
Preference dividend	–	–	800	1,600
Equity earnings after taxation	£9,600	£8,880	£7,360	£4,400
	% p.a.	% p.a.	% p.a.	% p.a.
Return on Book Value of Equity	9.60	9.87	10.51	14.67
Equity Earnings per £1 Share	19.2p	17.8p	18.4p	22.0p

For purposes of financial analysis and interfirm comparison, it is common to measure gearing G as the ratio of the *nominal* value of the fixed-return capital F to the book value of the equity capital E, i.e.

$$G = F/E.$$

This is a dubious procedure, since the latter figure is a purely conventional one, arising from the use of historical-cost accounting; however, on this basis the gearing ratios of the four companies in *Example 1* are:

A Ltd $G =$ 0/100,000 = 0.00
B Ltd $G =$ 10,000/ 90,000 = 0.11
C Ltd $G =$ 30,000/ 70,000 = 0.43
D Ltd $G =$ 70,000/ 30,000 = 2.33

The four companies are examples, respectively, of zero, low, medium, and high gearing. As the ratios rise, so does the return on the book value of equity—provided that the average return is higher than the weighted average return on the fixed-return capital. Thus, in the illustration, the companies all earn 20 per cent per annum before tax on a total employed capital (at book value) of £100,000. The weighted average return on the debentures and preference shares is computed as below, allowing for the fact that debenture interest is chargeable in arriving at the taxable profit, and preference dividend is not:

	A Ltd £	B Ltd £	C Ltd £	D Ltd £
Weighted Average Return on Fixed– Return Capital				
Before Taxation				
Debentures, 15% interest	–	1,500	3,000	7,500
Preference shares, 8% dividend x 100/48	–	–	1,667	3,333
	–	£1,500	£4,667	£10,833
Total nominal capital	–	10,000	30,000	70,000
	% p.a.	% p.a.	% p.a.	% p.a.
Average rate of return thereon	–	15.00	15.56	15.48
	£	£	£	£
After Taxation				
Debentures, 15% interest x 48/100	–	720	1,440	3,600
Preference shares, 8% dividend	–	–	800	1,600
	–	£720	£2,240	£5,200

306 Capital structure of a limited liability company

	A Ltd £	B Ltd £	C Ltd £	D Ltd £
Total nominal capital	–	10,000	30,000	70,000
	% p.a.	% p.a.	% p.a.	% p.a.
Average rate of return thereon	–	7.20	7.47	7.43

Suppose now that the net trading profit were £10,000 (i.e. 10 per cent gross) in all cases. The profit and loss accounts would then appear as:

	A Ltd £	B Ltd £	C Ltd £	D Ltd £
Profit and Loss Account				
Net trading profit before taxation	10,000	10,000	10,000	10,000
Debenture interest	–	1,500	3,000	7,500
Net profit before taxation	10,000	8,500	7,000	2,500
Corporation tax (52%)	5,200	4,420	3,640	1,300
Net profit after taxation	4,800	4,080	3,360	1,200
Preference dividend	–	–	800	1,600
Equity earnings after taxation	£4,800	£4,080	£2,560	(£400)
	% p.a.	% p.a.	% p.a.	% p.a.
Return on Book Value of Equity	4.80	4.53	3.66	(0.13)
Equity Earnings per £1 Share	9.6p	8.2p	6.4p	(2.0p)

It should be noted that in the cases of B Ltd, C Ltd and D Ltd the equity return is now below that on fixed-return capital.

The effect of reducing trading profit by £1,000 is to reduce equity earnings after tax by £480 in each case. With any gearing above zero, though, the change in earnings is more than proportionate to the change in profit. Thus, when profit falls by 50 per cent, the earnings of A Ltd fall by 50 per cent also, but those of B Ltd, C Ltd, and D Ltd fall by, respectively, 54.10 per cent, 65.18 per cent, and 100.89 per cent—and the same thing happens, in the opposite direction, with a 50 per cent rise in profit. Equity earnings per share move in the same manner, since the relevant fraction has a different set of numerators, though the same set of denominators.

An index (S_r) of the sensitivity of earnings to a change in net trading profit may therefore be defined as the number of percentage points by which the (post-tax) rate of return on equity changes, in response to a change of one percentage point in the (pre-tax) rate of return on capital employed. The formula is

$$S_r = C(1 - T)/E$$

where C = capital employed, at book value; E = equity, at book value; and T = rate of corporation tax.

For the companies in the illustration, the indices of sensitivity are

A Ltd	$S_r = 100,000(1 - 0.52)/100,000 = 0.48\%$
B Ltd	$S_r = 100,000(1 - 0.52)/\ 90,000 = 0.53\%$
C Ltd	$S_r = 100,000(1 - 0.52)/\ 70,000 = 0.68\%$
D Ltd	$S_r = 100,000(1 - 0.52)/\ 30,000 = 1.60\%$

For this purpose, as for that of the previous formula ($G = F/E$), the composition of the fixed-return capital, and the rates of return on it, are immaterial; indeed S_r may be calculated directly from G (if enough decimal places are taken) by using the relationship

$$S_r = G \times C(1 - T)/F$$

which will be found to hold good in all the examples given (except for A Ltd, where it becomes 0/0, which is of indeterminate value). For example, in C Ltd

$$S_r = 0.4286 \times 100,000(1 - 0.52)/30,000$$
$$= 0.6858 \text{ (to 4 places of decimals)}$$

The sensitivity S_e of equity earnings per share (in pence) to a change of one percentage point in the rate of return on capital employed may similarly be expressed by the formula

$$S_e = C(1 - T)/N$$

where N = nominal value of equity capital, in £1 shares. Thus, for the four imaginary companies

A Ltd $S_e = 100,000(1 - 0.52)/50,000 = 0.96\text{p}$
B Ltd $S_e = 100,000(1 - 0.52)/50,000 = 0.96\text{p}$
C Ltd $S_e = 100,000(1 - 0.52)/40,000 = 1.30\text{p}$
D Ltd $S_e = 100,000(1 - 0.52)/20,000 = 2.60\text{p}$

A measure of gearing more closely related to the actual capital structure lies in the degree of cover, at different levels of profit, for debenture interest and preference dividend. This may be applied to the foregoing example, at the two assumed profit levels, thus:

	A Ltd £	B Ltd £	C Ltd £	D Ltd £
Net Trading Profit before Taxation: £20,000				
Cover for debenture interest (P/I) (times)	–	13.33	6.67	2.67
Cover for preference dividend $\{P/(I+D)/(1-T)\}$ (times)	–	–	4.29	1.85
Net Trading Profit before Taxation: £10,000				
Cover for debenture interest (as above) (times)	–	6.67	3.33	1.33
Cover for preference dividend (as above) (times)	–	–	2.14	0.92

Here, P = net trading profit before tax; I = debenture interest; and D = preference dividend. In the computation D has to be grossed up, relative to corporation tax, in order to make it comparable with debenture interest, and with pre-tax profit. Note that, at each stage, all prior charges to that point are added together for comparison with profit.

13.1.3 Application to financial policy

All these measures are most useful to the board of directors in planning the company's capital structure, and changes in it from time to time, in combination with forecasts of the probable levels of profit and of ordinary dividends for the next few years. The techniques for making such forecasts are outside the scope of this book, but, taking the figures for granted, an illustration may be constructed, showing the considerations present to the directors' minds when deciding on how to raise new capital.

Example 2 Four companies–E Ltd, F Ltd, G Ltd, and H Ltd–all have, as at 1 January 19.1, issued share capital of £100,000 in £1 ordinary shares, and reserves £50,000. Profits to date, before taxation, have averaged £30,000 per annum, and average dividends of 10 per cent per annum (gross) have been paid on the shares. Each company now wishes, as at 1 January 19.1, to raise an additional £50,000 by some combination of ordinary shares, 8 per cent preference shares, and/or 15 per cent debentures. Corporation tax is 52 per cent. The existing ordinary shares all have a market value of £1.50, and it is considered that preference shares, and debentures, could be issued at par at the rates given above.

The four boards have made profit forecasts for the next five years as shown below, giving for each year the best possible, most probable, and worst possible outcomes, by the application of 'Bayesian' probabilities (assuming the investment of the additional £50,000 capital):

Years	19.1 £	19.2 £	19.3 £	19.4 £	19.5 £	Comment
E Ltd						
Best possible	40,000	45,000	50,000	55,000	60,000	Steady,
Most probable	30,000	35,000	40,000	45,000	50,000	predictable
Worst possible	20,000	25,000	30,000	35,000	40,000	growth
F Ltd						
Best possible	50,000	60,000	70,000	65,000	65,000	Cyclical
Most probable	35,000	45,000	50,000	45,000	40,000	fluctuation,
Worst possible	15,000	20,000	30,000	25,000	20,000	more risk
G Ltd						
Best possible	60,000	35,000	60,000	100,000	70,000	More
Most probable	40,000	20,000	30,000	60,000	40,000	speculative
Worst possible	10,000	−10,000	0	20,000	5,000	business
H Ltd						
Best possible	100,000	120,000	50,000	120,000	110,000	Extremely
Most probable	30,000	40,000	10,000	50,000	35,000	speculative
Worst possible	−40,000	−20,000	−50,000	−10,000	−30,000	business

All four companies have, initially, zero gearing, an average return on capital employed of 20 per cent per annum before tax, and 9.6 per cent after tax, equity earnings per share averaging 14.4p, and dividends 10.0p per share, covered 1.44 times. It is to be supposed that the directors, in all cases, will wish to maintain or improve this position vis-à-vis the existing ordinary shareholders.

E Ltd The injection of £50,000 (an immediate increase in capital employed of 33.33 per cent) into a business with good growth prospects and considerable stability of returns would appear to provide a sound basis for the issue of £50,000 debentures at 15 per cent. Net assets would be £200,000, and gross assets probably much more, giving ample security of capital. The gross interest of £7,500 per annum is not excessive in relation to the expected profits, though in the earliest years it might well depress the equity earnings per share, and compel the directors to reduce the cover for dividends, or even pay them out of reserves. The gearing, too, would initially be only 0.33 (£50,000/£150,000); this is moderate by British standards, and would tend to fall as retained earnings accumulated. At worst, too, the debenture interest would be covered 2 2/3rd times—probably four—and five times is considered a healthy minimum. Finally, 15 per cent debentures, costing only 7.2 per cent per annum net of tax, are cheaper than 8 per cent preference shares, costing the full 8 per cent, despite the greater flexibility of preference dividends, which can be passed in hard times.

On this basis, then, the most probable outcome is a fall in equity earnings in 19.1 to £10,800 (10.8 per share), allowing the 10 per cent dividend to be maintained without cutting into reserves. The initial position would be restored by 19.3, and by 19.5 earnings would be (£50,000 − £7,500 − £42,500 x 0.52) = £20,400, or 20.4p per share—a growth of 41.67 per cent in five years, allowing for a rise in dividend and (other things being equal) a corresponding increase in market value, even after placing some profits to a sinking fund to redeem the debentures in, say, 10 years, costing much less than £5,000 per annum.

The best possible outcome—a rise in equity earnings to £25,200 (25.2p per share) by 19.5—is contrasted with a worst possible outcome of growth to £15,600 (15.6p per share). This is still better than the 14.4p per share which would result from issuing 33,333 shares at 50p premium (£24,000/133,333), and the risk of a debenture issue is therefore acceptable.

F Ltd The pattern of projected results differs from that for E Ltd, in that growth is less steady and the 'spread' between the best and worst possible outcomes is wider. If the £50,000 is raised entirely in 15 per cent debentures the overall results, if the most probable outcome is achieved, will be even better than for E Ltd; on the best possible assumptions, equity earnings will rise as high as 30p per share. On the worst outcome, though, the cover for interest could be as low as two times, and equity earnings per share consistently lower than in the past. However, there still seems no danger of being unable to meet the interest, and reserves are adequate to maintain the present rate of ordinary dividend, even in a spell of bad trade. Thus, the conditionality of preference dividends does not compensate for the higher cost of such finance, and even that is cheaper than ordinary shares which, if issued at 50p premium, would still deprive existing holders of one-fourth of the total earnings—more, if larger numbers than 33,333 had to be issued at a lower price. For these reasons the directors would probably decide on debentures, though they might in the circumstances have to issue them at some discount.

G Ltd Profits here are much more variable and uncertain than in the two previous cases, and there is a risk that debenture interest might have to be paid out of reserves. A debenture issue is unlikely to be attractive to investors, but some institutions (investment trusts, unit trusts, insurance companies, pension funds, etc.) might take up preference shares, which are more attractive to them as corporation tax payers, since 15 per cent debentures would yield them only 7.2 per cent after tax, while 8 per cent preference dividends, as 'franked investment income', would yield the full 8 per cent. With cumulative dividends the average return on equity, on the 'most probable' basis, would be (£190,000 − £98,800 − £20,000)/5 x 100,000 = 14.25 per cent per annum—worse than now; while on the worst assumptions the preference dividends could not be fully met.

The directors may therefore decide to play safe by issuing, say £18,000 of 8 per cent cumulative preference shares and £24,000 nominal of ordinary shares at 33.3p premium. This would make the preference dividends £1,440 per annum, and ensure that they could be covered in the worst event; in the most probable, the average earnings per share would be (£19,000 − £98,000 − £7,200)/5 x 124,000 = 3.5p, or in the best possible outcome (£325,000 − £169,000 − 67,200)/5 x £124,000 = 24.0p—a proposition likely to attract the more venturesome investor.

H Ltd The wild fluctuations in profitability, and the possibilities both of massive gains and of crippling losses, perhaps leading to insolvency, make any fixed commitments to interest or dividends out of the question. The directors can only issue ordinary shares, at a premium appreciably below the present market figure—e.g. £40,000 nominal at £1.25. The most probable earnings per share would then average (£165,000−£85,800)/5 x 140,000 = 11.3p—scarcely enough to maintain the present dividend of 10p per share—but with an outside chance of making(£500,000 − £260,000)/5 x 140,000 = 34.3p.

Such, in these simplified situations, are the principles which influence decisions as to the capital structure of a limited company. More advanced expositions should be sought in specialized works on financial management.[1] The theoretical implications of capital gearing, as they affect the financial analyst, are discussed in Chapter 18, sub-section **18.2.2**.

13.2 Changes in capital structure

Besides straightforward issues of shares and debentures for cash, there are several ways in which the capital structure of a company may be altered, and some of these ways involve a change in the gearing ratio. The principal types of change are explained below.

13.2.1 Bonus or scrip issues

In Chapter 11, sub-section **11.3.1**, reference was made to the subdivision of shares into smaller units of nominal value. This is a useful device to employ when, owing to the continued prosperity of the company and its accumulation of large reserves out of profits, the ordinary dividend has risen to a large percentage on the nominal value of the shares, and this has made the market price of individual shares inconveniently 'heavy', thus rendering them less marketable. Splitting the shares reduces the unit price to more manageable proportions, but does not alter the disparity between nominal and market value, nor change the rate of dividend.

All three objectives are attained by the device of a *bonus,* or *scrip, issue* of ordinary shares. It is effected by permanently capitalizing reserves which either cannot be, or are most unlikely to be, distributed in dividend, because the law forbids it (as with the share premium account and capital redemption reserve fund), or it is financially unsound (as with the general capital reserve), or a large part of the revenue reserves have been invested in fixed assets and stocks, and there are no liquid assets out of which dividends of that magnitude could safely be paid. The book entries consist simply of transferring the amounts of the relevant reserves to the credit of ordinary share capital. Authorized capital must first be increased, if necessary, by ordinary resolution in general meeting, the capital clause of the memorandum of association altered, and additional duty and fees paid to the Registrar of Companies. After the issue, extra certificates for fully-paid shares are made out and distributed, free of charge, to existing shareholders, proportionately to their holdings. Any shares not so allotted, because of awkward fractions in some

[1] E.g. Samuels, J. M. and F. M. Wilkes, *Management of Company Finance,* 2nd edition, Nelson, 1975.

holdings, are sold by private placing through trustees, and the cash proceeds divided among the members who have not received their exact entitlement of shares.

Example 3 Affluent Ltd's balance sheet, as at 31 December 19.1, appears thus (summarized):

Affluent Ltd

Balance Sheet, 31 December 19.1

	£	£		£	£
Share Capital			*Fixed Assets*		
Authorized, Issued and Fully Paid			Sundries		200,000
20,000 8% cumulative preference shares			*Current Assets*		
of £1 each	20,000		Stocks	50,000	
50,000 ordinary			Debtors	60,000	
shares of £1 each	50,000		Bank balance	10,000	
		70,000			120,000
Reserves					
Share premium account	20,000				
General reserve	100,000				
Profit and loss a/c	40,000				
		160,000			
		230,000			
Corporation Tax —					
Current Year		30,000			
Current Liabilities					
Sundries		60,000			
		£320,000			£320,000

It is decided to capitalize all the reserves, except £10,000 of the profit and loss account, by means of a 3 for 1 bonus issue of ordinary shares, and this is done on 1 January 19.2. The authorized capital is increased as at that date to 20,000 8 per cent cumulative preference shares and 200,000 ordinary shares, all of £1 each; the duty, fees, and other costs of the issue are £800. The relevant book entries (except Bank) are:

Ordinary Share Capital

19.2		£	19.2		£
Jan 1	Balance c/d	200,000	Jan 1	Balance b/d	50,000
			Jan 1	Share premium a/c	20,000
			Jan 1	General reserve	100,000
			Jan 1	Profit and loss a/c	30,000
		£200,000			£200,000
			19.2		
			Jan 2	Balance b/d	200,000

Share Premium Account

19.2		£	19.2		£
Jan 1	Ordinary share capital	20,000	Jan 1	Balance b/d	20,000

General Reserve

19.2		£	19.2		£
Jan	1 Ordinary share capital	100,000	Jan	1 Balance b/d	100,000

Profit and Loss Account

19.2		£	19.2		£
Jan	1 Ordinary share capital	30,000	Jan	1 Balance b/d	40,000
Jan	1 Balance c/d	10,000			
		£40,000			£40,000
			19.2		
			Jan	2 Balance b/d	10,000

Share Issue Expenses

19.2		£
Jan	1 Bank	800

The balance sheet now appears thus:

Affluent Ltd

Balance Sheet, 1 January 19.2

	£	£		£	£
Share Capital,			*Fixed Assets*		
Authorized, Issued			Sundries		200,000
and Fully Paid			*Current Assets*		
20,000 8% cumulative			Stocks	50,000	
preference shares			Debtors	60,000	
of £1 each	20,000		Bank balance	9,200	
200,000 ordinary					119,200
shares of £1 each	200,000		*Other Assets*		
		220,000	Share issue expenses		800
Reserves					
Profit and loss a/c		10,000			
		230,000			
Corporation Tax—					
Current Year		30,000			
Current Liabilities					
Sundries		60,000			
		£320,000			£320,000

It is apparent that the total owners' equity remains unaltered, except that the share issue expenses fall to be written off it in due course; nor have the company's expectations as to future profits been changed in any way. The new 200,000 shares are worth, on that basis, just the same as the old 50,000 ones, and the stock market will react accordingly, by reducing the price to one-fourth of its old level. Each member's holding is thus unchanged in total value. Hence, the 'bonus' is illusory, and the term 'scrip issue' (not the same as a scrip dividend—see Chapter 12, sub-section 12.2.2) is more realistic.

This reasoning holds absolutely, provided that other things remain equal. In fact, where the scrip issue is moderate in proportion to the existing share capital, the company generally announces its intention of maintaining the rate of dividend unchanged on the expanded number of shares—thus, in effect, increasing the rate for the present holders, and so tending to maintain the old unit price, and to increase the holders' wealth. Even without this, the operation makes the shares of smaller unit value and thus more easily marketable, so that the price is unlikely to fall exactly in proportion to the issue. This effect is combined with a belief that a scrip issue is a sign of financial strength and growing profitability, and this feeling has itself a favourable effect on the price.

Successful companies, with large 'plough-backs' of profit over time, tend to make scrip issues every so often, and in financial analysis of time-series it is necessary to make allowance for this phenomenon.

Scrip issues are normally confined to equity capital. Such an issue to preference shareholders, at the same rate of dividend, would be a genuine bonus to them, at the expense of the ordinary shareholders, and it is almost impossible to imagine any circumstances in which it would be made. But it has been known occasionally for ordinary shareholders to be given a bonus in the form of preference shares, paid up out of reserves in the manner already indicated. Lastly, all 'bonus' shares must be fully paid on issue; partly-paid ones would impose on members a contingent liability to contribute to the company's capital beyond their original commitment, and this is illegal and void.

13.2.2 Rights issues

An established company, whose shares are widely held and quoted on the stock exchange, almost always raises new equity capital by means of a *rights issue*. No prospectus or offer for sale is issued (though a statement in lieu of prospectus must be filed with the Registrar); instead, the existing ordinary shareholders are furnished with 'rights certificates', authorizing them to take up, at a stated price, new shares in numbers proportionate to their existing holdings, or alternatively to sell these rights to others—since they cannot be compelled to subscribe fresh capital. This procedure is an inexpensive method of raising funds, enables the present membership to show its confidence in the company as a medium of investment, and minimizes the likelihood of a change in the balance of control.

The issue price is usually pitched somewhat below the current market price, as an inducement to existing shareholders to take up their rights in full. The cheapness of the new shares, however, is illusory, since, if other things remain equal, the market price after the issue will be adjusted to the weighted average of the old market price and the rights price to allow for the dilution of the equity, thus

$$P_n = (P_o C_o + P_r C_r)/C_n$$

where P_n, P_o, P_r = (respectively) the market prices after, and before, the issue and the rights price; and C_n, C_o, C_r = (respectively) the corresponding numbers of shares involved.

The market value of each holding after the rights are taken up will thus be equal to the original market value of the old shares plus the total amount of new money invested by the holder.

Example 4 A company's issued capital consists of 500,000 £1 ordinary shares, whose market price is £1.50. It makes a rights issue of 250,000 shares (1 for 2) at a price of £1.38. The price subsequent to the issue (*ceteris paribus*) will be

$$P_n = (£1.50 \times 500,000 + £1.38 \times 250,000)/750,000 = £1.46$$

If a holder renounces his rights by selling his rights certificate on the market, he will expect to receive (*ceteris paribus*) a price which will just compensate him for the drop in market value of the old shares which he retains, and thus leave him (theoretically) indifferent as between taking up his rights and renouncing them. This price is:

$$P_q = (P_o - P_n) S_o/S_r \ (or \ P_q = P_n - P_r)$$

where P_q = price obtained for each share comprised in the rights certificate; S_o = number of shares already held by the certificate-holder; and S_r = number of rights shares offered to him.

Thus, in *Example 4*, for every two shares held a member receives a rights certificate for one new share, and

$$P_q = (£1.50 - £1.46) \, 2/1 = £0.08 \ (or \ P_q = (£1.46 - 1.38) = £0.08$$

i.e. he receives 8p per rights share, compensating for a drop of 4p in the price of his two old shares. (He is, of course, at liberty to take up some of his rights and sell the others, but the market mechanism should always operate so as to render him indifferent as between the chosen course of action and any others open to him.)

From the side of the buyer of rights certificates, he is indifferent as between purchasing old shares and taking up the rights attached to them, and purchasing an equivalent number of rights certificates and then taking up the rights; i.e.

$$P_o S_o + P_r S_r = (P_q + P_r)(S_o + S_r)$$

Thus, in the case supposed, a buyer wishing to acquire three shares is indifferent as between

$$P_o S_o + P_r S_r = £1.50(2) + £1.38(1) = £4.38$$

and

$$(P_q + P_r)(S_o + S_r) = (£0.08 + £1.38)(2 + 1) = £4.38$$

P_q is therefore the price, per rights certificate for one share, which ensures this equilibrium in the market. In practice it would tend to be a little higher than as computed above, since the buyer of rights certificates saves the transfer stamp duty (1 per cent on the price) which he would have to pay on a purchase of an equivalent number of shares in the market; i.e. he should be indifferent as between

$$1.01(P_o S_o) + P_r S_r$$

and

$$(P_q + P_r)(S_o + S_r)$$

Equating the two expressions and solving for P_q, its value is found to be

$$P_q = \{1.01(P_o S_o) - P_r S_o\}/(S_o + S_r)$$

With the figures in *Example 4*, the rights certificate price per share becomes, theoretically

$$P_q = \{1.01(£1.50)(2) - (£1.38)(2)\}/(2 + 1) = £0.09$$

and the seller of the rights thus makes 1p profit per rights share, over and above what is needed to compensate for the fall in the value of the existing shares.

In essence, then, a rights issue is a combination of a bonus issue with a straight cash issue at the existing market price. As with a bonus issue, there may be no fall in price of the existing shares if the company declares its intention of maintaining the old dividend rate on the expanded capital, or a mitigated fall if the rights issue is thought to make a more active market in the shares, and/or to be a sign of financial health and vigour.

13.2.3 Capital reorganization

Sometimes a company, without raising any new money or repaying any capital in cash or kind, may wish to vary the rights of existing shareholders. Authority to do so must be given in the memorandum or articles of association, and the consent of the shareholders affected must be signified in the manner prescribed. (Table A, art. 4, requires the consent in writing of the holders of three-fourths in value of the issued shares of the class affected, or the passing of an extraordinary resolution (requiring a three-fourths majority of votes) at a separate general meeting of shareholders of that class).

Even if consent is so obtained, the holders of 15 per cent or more of the issued shares of the class concerned, being persons who did not consent to or vote in favour of the resolution for the variation, may, within 21 days of the consent or vote, apply to the High Court to have the variation cancelled. The variation may not take effect until the case has been settled. The High Court, after hearing the applicants and any other interested parties (including the company), may either confirm the variation, or disallow it on the ground that it would unfairly prejudice the shareholders of the class affected (Companies Act, 1948, s. 72).

The power to vary shareholders' rights has been most frequently invoked in recent years for the purpose of converting preference shares into debentures. Until 1964 a company paid income tax on its profits before charging either interest or dividends paid, but deducted tax from both at standard rate and retained it. Income tax was therefore borne only upon undistributed profits. The company also paid profits tax (finally, 15 per cent) on its profits *after* charging debenture interest (gross of income tax) but before charging preference dividend; this widened the rate-gap between the two classes (debentures were a little cheaper, because of the better security), but not always enough to offset the advantages of greater flexibility, in that preference dividends could be passed at need.

By the Finance Act, 1965, though, the present system of corporation tax was introduced as from about that year (the exact date of change-over depending upon the company's year-end). Corporation tax (initially 40 per cent) was imposed, like profits tax, upon profits after charging (gross) debenture interest but not preference dividend, while from the income tax year 1966–67 companies could no longer retain income tax deducted at source, but had to account for it monthly to the Inland Revenue. Debentures thus became a much cheaper source of finance than preference shares or (*a fortiori*) equity, and an incentive was suddenly offered to raise the capital gearing of British companies, then very low by international standards. There was a spate of debenture issues in 1965 and 1966 (despite historically high rates of interest), a dearth of equity issues, and virtually no preference ones—indeed, repayments outweighed new moneys. Many companies with irredeemable preference shares persuaded the holders to vote for conversion into debentures on advantageous terms, including current rates of interest which, though often higher that the dividend rates on old preference shares, were still cheaper for the company after allowance for corporation tax savings.

By 1970 this movement had largely spent itself. Most companies had raised their gearing to what they considered safe levels, and were issuing equity as well as debentures in order to expand further. Interest rates were higher than ever—10 per cent or more on sound debentures—but preference dividend rates were actually lower—8–9 per cent—and a modest number of such shares were being issued. The reason was that such securities were preferred by institutional investors; preference (and equity) dividends were exempt from corporation tax in their hands, as franked investment income, while tax had to be paid on all interest received. Institutional demand thus forced rates down to levels where the after-tax cost gap, as compared with debentures, was no longer penal, and companies could once more afford to raise capital in the form of preference shares.

13.2.4 Reduction of capital

The Companies Act, 1948, s. 66, confers on all limited companies having a share capital the power (rarely exercised today) to *reduce their share capital,* subject to authorization by the articles *and* to confirmation by the High Court. In particular, a company may:

1 extinguish or reduce the liability on any of its shares in respect of share capital not paid up; *or*
2 cancel any paid-up share capital which is lost or unrepresented by assets; *or*
3 pay off any paid-up share capital which is in excess of the company's wants.

The company must pass a special resolution to effect the reduction, and apply to the High Court for an order confirming it. The Court must, on a reduction under head 1 or 3, and may in any other case, settle a list of creditors (as complete as possible) of the company who are entitled to object to the proposed reduction. In the case of a type 1 or 3 scheme, however, the Court may exclude any class or classes of creditors from these provisions. If any creditor does object (normally on the ground that his security for payment is diminished by cancellation of the right to call up unpaid share capital, or by the return to shareholders of moneys otherwise available to creditors), the Court may dispense with his consent, on the company's securing payment of his claim by appropriating a sum equal to the full amount of the claim if it is certain and admitted, or such sum as the Court shall decide if the claim is disputed, contingent or unascertained (s. 67).

Once all creditors have consented, or their claims have been paid or satisfactorily secured, the Court may make an order confirming the scheme. It may, if it thinks fit, order the company to add to its name for a specified period the words 'and reduced'; and/or require the company, by a further order, to publish the reasons for the reduction, or such other information as the Court thinks expedient in the public interest, and, if it thinks fit, the causes which led to the reduction (s. 68). These powers have seldom or never been used in recent times.

Extinction or reduction of liability on capital not paid up involves no book entry. In the balance sheet it is necessary only to change the designation of the issued capital from (say) 'ordinary shares of £1 each, 75p paid' to 'ordinary shares of 75p each, fully paid', and to amend the authorized capital accordingly. If there is actual repayment of capital, the book entry is obvious—*Dr.* Ordinary Share Capital (say), *Cr.* Bank—with similar amendment as above to the balance sheet description of the share capital.

Cancellation of paid-up share capital which is lost or unrepresented by assets is much the most common form of reduction. Just as a successful company with a conservative dividend policy tends to accumulate large reserves, and capitalize them periodically by bonus issues of ordinary shares, so an unsuccessful one, by making large losses, dissipates any revenue reserves it may have had and throws its profit and loss account into debit. If the directors see no realistic hope of recovering prosperity without raising fresh capital, the existence of a debit balance on the profit and loss account will be a deterrent to investors, who will see no prospect of dividends as long as it is uncleared. The first step needed, therefore, is recognition of the position of writing off the loss against the capital reserves and equity capital, which would have to bear it on a liquidation. At the same time a general revaluation of assets and liabilities is made, and the net gain or loss thereon is also adjusted into the capital reserves/equity capital, through a Capital Reduction Account. The company can then start with a clean slate, as a result of what is effectively a 'reverse bonus issue'.

After writing down the equity capital, it is as well to consolidate the shares into a smaller number of the same denomination as before, and issue these proportionately to the original holders. The old authorized capital may then be left undisturbed, allowing of further issues free of capital duty.

Where the company's capital gearing is rather high, it may prove difficult to issue fresh ordinary shares, even after the reduction, unless something is done to lower the gearing. In particular, arrears of preference dividend may need to be eliminated, in return for some *quid pro quo* to the preference shareholders, such as the transfer to them of part of the equity—so giving them a stake in future prosperity, if any. It is not usually possible to persuade preference shareholders, much less debenture-holders or unsecured creditors, to accept any write-down of their capital or claims, or any reduction in the rate of dividend or interest—such would be a real sacrifice on their part, whereas a write-down of equity is not one for the ordinary shareholders, but merely a recognition of events which have already happened.

Example 5 The balance sheet of Nogo Ltd, as at 30 June 19.1, appears below.

Nogo Ltd

Balance Sheet, 30 June 19.1

	£	£		£	£
Share Capital,			*Fixed Assets*		
Authorized, Issued			Freehold property	40,000	
and Fully Paid			Plant	60,000	
20,000 8% cumulative					100,000
preference shares			Goodwill		10,000
of £1 each	20,000				
100,000 ordinary					110,000
shares of £1 each	100,000		*Current Assets*		
		120,000	Stocks	20,000	
Reserves			Debtors	30,000	
Share premium account		15,000			50,000
			Note: The 8% cumulative		
		135,000	preference dividends		
Less Profit and loss a/c			are three years in		
—Debit balance		50,000	arrear.		
		85,000			
10% Debentures		50,000			
Current Liabilities					
Bank overdraft	10,000				
Creditors	15,000				
		25,000			
		£160,000			£160,000

A capital reduction scheme takes effect on 1 July 19.1. The share premium is to be written off, the ordinary share capital written down as required, and the reduced shares consolidated into new ones of £1 each. The arrears of cumulative preference dividend are to be cancelled, and the holders are to have transferred to them one (new) ordinary share for every five preference shares held—the ordinary shareholders to bear this sacrifice proportionally to their holdings.

The assets are revalued thus: freehold property, £60,000; plant, £45,000; goodwill, nil; stocks, £15,000; and debtors, £25,000.

The Capital Reduction Account, and balance sheet as at 1 July 19.1, appear thus:

Capital Reduction Account

19.1		£	19.1		£
Jul	1 Profit and loss a/c	50,000	Jul	1 Ordinary share capital	100,000
do	1 Plant	15,000	do	1 Share premium a/c	15,000
do	1 Goodwill	10,000	do	1 Freehold property	20,000
do	1 Stocks	5,000			
do	1 Debtors	5,000			
do	1 New ordinary share capital	50,000			
		£135,000			£135,000

Nogo Ltd

Balance Sheet, 1 July 19.1

	£	£		£	£
Share Capital—			Fixed Assets		
Authorized			Freehold property	60,000	
20,000 8% cumulative			Plant	45,000	
preference shares					105,000
of £1 each	20,000		Current Assets		
100,000 new ordinary			Stocks	15,000	
shares of £1 each	100,000		Debtors	25,000	
					40,000
	£120,000				
Issued and Fully Paid					
20,000 8% cumulative					
preference shares					
of £1 each	20,000				
50,000 new ordinary					
shares of £1 each	50,000				
		70,000			
10% Debentures		50,000			
Current Liabilities					
Bank overdraft	10,000				
Creditors	15,000				
		25,000			
		£145,000			£145,000

13.2.5 Reconstruction of capital

As shown above, any scheme for the writing-off of capital which is lost or unrepresented by assets normally involves a measure of rearrangement of the capital structure. Where the scheme is very drastic, complex and far-reaching, with a major reorganization of the business as well, it is more convenient to liquidate the existing company and form a new one, with a similar name, to take over such assets and liabilities as are to continue as effective parts of the enterprise. Shares and debentures in the new company are issued to the shareholders and debenture-holders in the old one, in agreed proportions, in full satisfaction of their claims. Such a process is a *capital reconstruction,* properly so called. The accounting entries are on the lines of those in a normal liquidation, as set out in Chapter 17, followed by those for a new company, as shown in Chapter 11.

13.3 Shares of no par value

The insistence of British company law on shares of a fixed nominal value in all cases has led to much needless complexity in dealing and accounting, and to much misunderstanding, among the unsophisticated, of the nature of par value, and of dividends expressed as a percentage thereof. This would be avoided, to a considerable degree, by the authorization of *shares of no par value,* which have been legal in the U.S.A. and Canada for some 50 years. Such a change in the law was recommended by the majority in the Gedge Report on Shares of No Par Value (1954), and in the Jenkins Report (1962). A clause to that effect was inserted in the Companies Bill, 1967, but removed by the government during debate, with a promise to implement the change in the next Companies Act, when the complications relative to taxation had been dealt with.

13.3.1 Accounting for shares of no par value

The strongest objection to fixed nominal values is that they are largely meaningless. The par value of an ordinary share, especially, bears no logical relation to its market value, the book value of the underlying assets, their value in use or in exchange, or their break-up value on liquidation of the company; while the declaration of a dividend as a large percentage of the par value makes many ill-informed persons believe that the company is making exorbitant profits when the return on capital employed (including its massive reserves) may be quite modest. The cumbrous and much-misunderstood procedure of a bonus or scrip issue is necessary to correct the position from time to time. The need for a share premium account is another anomaly. When the market price is below par, the issue of fresh ordinary shares is in practice out of the question—no use appears to have been made of the permission to issue shares at a discount.

The majority of the Gedge Committee accordingly recommended that ordinary shares of no par value should be authorized. (The Trades Union Congress representative dissented, on the ground that it would be even more difficult than it was to explain company finance to the workingman!) A company should be allowed to have *either* shares with a fixed nominal value *or* shares of no par value, but not both, and to convert one into the other at will. The whole proceeds of a no par value issue should be credited to a Stated Capital Account, with the number of shares given as a note, and each share should represent merely an aliquot part of the total equity. No dividends would be payable out of the stated capital account, nor could any part of it be distributed without sanction of the High Court; but it could be debited with preliminary expenses, share issue expenses, and commissions on issue of shares—there being no share premium account. Reserves not required for distribution could be capitalized by transferring them to the stated capital account, with no need to issue bonus shares as at present. This operation would leave the market price of the shares unchanged, but if they became too 'heavy' they could simply be split into a larger number of units, whose market price would be automatically adjusted. Dividends would be expressed as so many pence per share, and a share split would reduce this figure also.

The Jenkins Committee substantially adopted the majority report of the Gedge Committee, but went further in two respects. First, they favoured the debiting to the stated capital account of discounts on shares and debentures, as at present with respect to the share premium account (a recommendation which, in relation to debenture discount, is unsound from the standpoint of accounting theory—see Chapter 12, sub-section 12.4.1). Secondly, they recommended legalization of *preference* shares of no par value. These could be issued with a fixed dividend—say 5p per share—at whatever price they would currently fetch, be it more or less than £1, and preference shares issued at different dates could form one class, ranking *pari passu*, with no need to have several classes with different rates of dividend. All such shares would have priority for £1 repayment on winding up—the only matter in which a par value is significant. And there the case rests.

14

The published accounts of limited liability companies

In recent years the published accounts of British limited companies have been subject to a degree of detailed regulation which has made them foremost in Europe in the amount of information disclosed. Even so, they lag behind the degree of disclosure required of American companies by the Securities and Exchange Commission, particularly with regard to the profit and loss account, and their use to investors and their professional advisers is still somewhat circumscribed.

14.1 Disclosure in company accounts

Published accounts in all countries suffer from failure to define clearly the intended readers, or the purposes for which they are expected to use the information. Are the accounts addressed primarily to existing shareholders? to prospective investors in the company? to financial experts (stockbrokers, investment analysts, etc.)? or to the world at large? Is their purpose merely to render an account of the directors' stewardship? to state the current position of the company? to enable the trend of its profits to be observed over time? to allow readers to compare the results with those of other undertakings? or to enable them to take a view of future prospects, as the basis of a decision to buy, hold or sell the company's securities? Should they be based on historical-cost, replacement-cost, or current purchasing power accounting principles? or on some combination of any or all of these? Until the interested parties—businessmen, investors, the stock exchanges, the accountancy institutions, the legal profession, government, etc.—are able to agree on more precise answers to all these questions than are now current, it is hard to see how any fundamental improvement can come about.

As it is, British published accounts have evolved in a gradual, piecemeal, and legalistic fashion, since the Companies (Consolidation) Act, 1908, first compelled public companies to file their annual balance sheets with the Registrar. After each new Act (about every twenty years) has laid down minimum disclosure requirements—thought to strike a fair balance between the desire to inform investors about the business and the fear that too much exposure will damage it by giving valuable information to competitors—the more enlightened and public-spirited undertakings begin to go beyond the letter of the law and produce further detail. After a time the stock exchanges demand this detail in annual accounts, as a condition of granting quotations to new or additional issues of securities. In due course a governmental Committee on Company Law is set up, and its recommendations, two or three years later, include new disclosure requirements, generally based on the stock exchange rules and on the present practice of the 'best' large companies. In a few more years a new Companies Act is passed, on the lines of the committee's report—and the process begins again.

Such was the sequence of events leading up to the 1929, 1948, and 1967 Acts, based on the Greene, Cohen, and Jenkins Reports of 1925, 1945, and 1962. The 1929 Act first required the filing of a profit and loss account by public companies, but said virtually nothing as to what it was to contain. The 1948 Act demanded much more detail in the balance sheet, and a more informative profit and loss account, as well as proper group accounts from holding companies (see Chapter 16), but, in particular, did not require the disclosure of turnover—a sop to the business lobby, who voiced their usual exaggerated fears that competitors would take unfair advantage. The Act of 1967 enacted most of the Jenkins Committee's recommendations on accounts—withdrawal of exemptions from filing them, disclosure of turnover, more information regarding revaluation of assets, etc.—but also added some demands seemingly prompted by partisan considerations, such as expanded details of directors' emoluments, and revelation of payments to political organizations. The Act was rather hastily passed to combat, in Part II, the pressing evils of unsound or fraudulent motor insurance companies, and there are some loopholes in Part I, relating to ordinary businesses—though nothing as ludicrous as s. 68(5), which provides for the *imprisonment* of an insurance company guilty of certain offences! Finally, although the European Communities Act, 1972, makes no reference to published accounts, it is expected that a future Directive of the European Commission will deal with the matter, and will have to be implemented eventually in the U.K. (see section **14.11**).

The heavy-footed legalistic policy of extracting a few more disclosures, every twenty years or so, from an over-secretive business community contrasts with the position in the U.S.A., where grave financial scandals and abuses, coming to light especially after the stock market crash of 1929, led to the setting up in 1934 of the Securities and Exchange Commission, a Federal agency to regulate the affairs of all quoted companies. The Commission requires annual accounts from all such corporations, and makes them available to inquirers, much as does the Department of Trade in Britain, but it is free to make its own rules as to the degree of disclosure, and they go well beyond even the Companies Act, 1967, demanding, for instance, particulars of the cost of goods sold, overheads under broad groupings, analysis of inventories (with statement of the basis of valuation), and a statement of source and application of funds as well as an 'income statement' and 'position statement'. Again, the ethos of American business sets more store by openness than by secrecy, on the ground that it is a prime function of 'financial statements' to guide investors (through their advisers) as to the relative merits of different stocks and bonds, and thus promote the proper working of the stock markets, and of the capitalist system in general. This is shown by the willingness of large corporations to vie with one another in presenting financial statements which go beyond the letter of the State laws on accounts—though some such policy is admittedly necessary with regard to widely-held stocks in a very large country without a uniform company law.

Such a body as the Securities and Exchange Commission is less needed in a unitary state with a single company code. It might, however, advance the cause of more rational and informative published accounts if Parliament, in some future Act, were to delegate to the Department of Trade the making of detailed rules as to their contents, with the advice and assistance of some statutory body representative of industry, commerce, finance, the stock exchange, accountancy, law, and other relevant interests. Such a scheme would give much-needed flexibility to the regulation of these matters, and enable government to respond far more quickly to changes in the climate of opinion in the business world.

14.2 Preparation of company accounts

The general provisions of the two Companies Acts with regard to accounts are now summarized, with the use of smaller type for matter relating to exceptional or uncommon circumstances.

14.2.1 Books of account

The Companies Act, 1948, s. 147, requires every company to keep *proper books of account* with respect to:

a all sums of money received and expended by the company and the matters in respect of which the receipt and expenditure take place;
b all sales and purchases of goods by the company; and
c the assets and liabilities of the company.

The books must be such as are necessary to give a true and fair view of the state of the company's affairs and to explain its transactions. The books shall be kept at the registered office or such other place as the directors think fit, and be at all times open to inspection by the directors.

If the books are kept outside Great Britain, there shall be sent to, and kept in, Great Britain, and be open at all times to inspection by the directors, accounts and returns sufficient to disclose with reasonable accuracy the financial position of the business at six-monthly intervals at longest, and enable the final accounts to be prepared in accordance with the Acts.

In addition, the 1948 Act, s. 331, imposes penalties on officers of the company if, on winding up, it is shown that proper books of account were not kept for at least two years before the commencement of the winding up (see Chapter 17, subsection **17.1.1**), or for the life of the company if shorter. The books must for this purpose must be such as are necessary to exhibit and explain the transactions and financial position of the business, including detailed entries from day to day of all cash received and paid, statements of the annual stocktakings (where goods have been dealt in), and (except in the case of goods sold by way of ordinary retail trade) statements of all goods sold and purchased, showing the goods, and their buyers and sellers, in sufficient detail to enable the goods, buyers and sellers to be identified.

Both sections are easily complied with if a regular double entry system, with proper and sufficient internal control and check, is installed and efficiently operated. The meaning of 'books of account' is not restricted to bound books, but includes any method of recording the matters in question (and similarly with registers, indexes, and minute books required by the Acts); but if bound books are not used, adequate precautions shall be taken for guarding against falsification and facilitating its discovery (1948 Act, s. 436). The point is particularly important in relation to an EDP system, where many detail entries are made by changes of state in the components of the computer, and never recorded in permanent form. This, too, does not violate the law, as long as there are effective controls on input, programming, computer operation, and output, and the external auditors are satisfied that they are working properly.

14.2.2 Publication of final accounts

The Companies Acts require every company to prepare final accounts as described below, and these must be:

1 laid before the company in general meeting
2 circulated before the meeting to all members and debenture-holders, and all other persons entitled to attend meetings of the company; and
3 filed with the Registrar of Companies, along with the annual return.

The 1948 Act, s. 148, requires the directors to lay before the company in general meeting, within 18 months of incorporation and subsequently once in each calendar year, a *profit and loss account* (or, in the case of a non-trading company, an income and expenditure account) made up to a date not earlier than the date of the meeting by more than nine months (or, in the case of a company carrying on business or having interests abroad, more that twelve months) and covering the period since incorporation or since the preceding account, as the case may be; together with a *balance sheet* as at the date to which the profit and loss account is made up. (The periods of nine, and twelve, months may be extended by the Department of Trade, if for any special reason they think fit so to do).

A holding company is required (s. 150) to lay *group accounts* before the meeting with the company's own accounts; these group accounts are discussed separately in Chapter 16. They are to be 'annexed' to the balance sheet with the profit and loss account, and the *auditor's report* (s. 156) and the *directors' report* (s. 157) are to be 'attached' to it—in practice, a distinction without a difference. The auditors' and directors' reports are compulsory for all companies, but require modification if group accounts are presented.

The 1948 Act, s. 158, as amended by the 1967 Act, s. 24, requires a copy of each of the documents above mentioned (profit and loss account, balance sheet, auditor's report, directors' report and, where applicable, group accounts) to be sent, at least 21 days before the meeting at which they are to be laid before the company, to every member and debenture-holder, and every other person entitled (by law or by the articles) to receive notices of general meetings. The accounts are in practice sent with the notice of meeting, which must also go out at least 21 days beforehand.

The company need not send copies to a member or debenture-holder who is not entitled to notices of general meetings, and of whose address the company is unaware; to more than one of joint share- or debenture-holders, none of whom are entitled to such notices; nor to non-entitled joint holders where other such holders are entitled. If the documents are sent out less than 21 days before the meeting, this informality may be overlooked if all members, entitled to attend and vote, so agree.

There is no rule that the aforesaid general meeting shall be the annual one, but such is the almost invariable usage.

In addition, any member or debenture-holder is entitled on demand, without charge, to a copy of the latest accounts.

The 1948 Act, s. 127, as amended by the 1967 Act, s. 2, requires every limited company to forward to the Registrar with its annual return (see Chapter 11, sub-section 11.4.2) a complete copy, certified by a director and by the company secretary to be a true copy, of each set of accounts laid before the company in general meeting in the period covered by the return.

Any document which is in a foreign language shall be accompanied by an English translation, certified as above to be a correct one. If any document did not comply with the law as at the date of the audit, regarding the form of the document, the copy submitted to the Registrar shall be amended as necessary to make it comply as aforesaid, and the fact that it has been amended shall be stated on the copy.

The Registrar's copy of the accounts is placed in the company's file at Companies House, 55–71 City Road, London EC1Y 1BB, or Exchequer Chambers, 102 George Street, Edinburgh EH2 3DJ (according to the situation of the registered office), and the file may be consulted by anyone for a fee of 5p. This is the only 'publication' which the law requires.

In addition, public companies often arrange for newspaper reproduction of the *chairman's statement,* commonly bound with the statutory accounts. This document is purely voluntary, and mentioned nowhere in any Act. It normally reviews, at some length, the trading results for the past year, assesses the prospects for the coming year, comments on the position shown by the accounts, and gives details of major capital expenditure or developments, and any other information of interest to the shareholders.

14.3 Content of published company accounts

By the Companies Act, 1948, s. 149, as amended by the 1967 Act, s. 9, every company's profit and loss account and balance sheet shall:

a give a true and fair view of, respectively, the profit or loss for the financial year, and the state of affairs as at the end thereof; and
b comply with Schedule 2 of the 1967 Act, so far as it is applicable.

The Department of Trade may, on the application or with the consent of a company's directors, modify any of the requirements of the Acts as to the matters to be stated in the profit and loss account or balance sheet, for the purpose of adapting them to the company's circumstances; except that it may not relieve the company of the obligation to give a *true and fair view.*

The components of this expression occur frequently, in similar contexts, in the accounting literature of the last century and more. They were brought together in the 1948 Act, superseding the earlier phrase 'true and *correct* view'. Today, 'true and fair view' has become a term of art. It is generally understood to mean a presentation of accounts, drawn up according to accepted accounting principles, using accurate figures as far as possible, and reasonable estimates otherwise; and arranging them so as to show, within the limits of current accounting practice, as objective a picture as possible, free from wilful bias, distortion, manipulation, or concealment of material facts. In other words the spirit, as well as the letter, of the law must be observed; and 1948, s. 149(3), makes it clear that the obligation to comply with 1967, Schedule 2, shall be without prejudice, either to the general requirement to show a true and fair view or to other requirements of the Acts. That is, literal observance of Schedule 2 may not be used as a cloak for an intention to distort or conceal the real position of the company—the accounts must go beyond the normal disclosure requirements, if need be.

14.3.1 Presentation of published accounts

Schedule 2 of the Companies Act, 1967, does not prescribe any *form* in which accounts are to be presented, but only requires them to give certain *information*—as do some sections of the Acts themselves, additional to the Schedule. Subject to the need to prepare a profit and loss account and balance sheet, the company's accountants are left free to present the information in as clear, logical, and imaginative a manner as they can contrive. Since the majority of shareholders in public companies are not businessmen, financiers, or accountants, it is a moral obligation of the company to produce its accounts in a form which laymen can understand, and to use any device which helps them to assimilate the important points with a minimum of toil and a maximum of interest. Thus, it is common to abandon or modify the traditional 'double entry' layout in favour of a single-sided or 'plus and minus' type of profit and loss statement (rather than account), in which net trading profit is progressively reduced to net profit after taxation and extraordinary items, and its disposal shown; together with a balance sheet showing working capital, instead of current liabilities and assets separately, and/or presenting the figures in two 'single-sided' blocks, exhibiting capital employed and the net assets in which it is invested. Amounts are rounded off to the nearest thousand, hundred thousand, or even million, pounds; current year and previous-year comparative figures are printed in contrasting colours, or displayed against differently coloured backgrounds; and the accounts proper are limited to showing important items, with subsidiary detail relegated to supporting notes, carefully cross-referenced to the accounts figures. Captions are in simple, everyday language, devoid of accounting jargon; or the 'legal' accounts are preceded by a simplified summary intended for the lay shareholder. In addition, they may be accompanied by graphs, diagrams, and picture-charts, presenting the information in visual terms; summaries (not as yet required by law) of salient figures—capital employed, book value of equity, turnover, equity earnings, dividend rates, etc.—for five, ten, or twenty years to date; and miscellaneous statistical information about the company and its various activities.

The design of published accounts has vastly improved in recent decades, as may be seen by comparing modern ones with those of even twenty-five years ago—often 'Victorian' in appearance, and in many cases still showing amounts in pounds, shillings, and pence! The annual awards by *The Accountant,* for the best two sets of accounts of British companies (one large and one small), have helped to raise standards in the past few years, but the average still seems markedly below that attained in North America, though comparing very favourably with that on the continent of Europe.

In the following expositions of the legal requirements relative to published accounts, the various provisions are rearranged in the order in which the items would normally occur in the profit and loss account, and balance sheet, of an ordinary industrial or commercial company without subsidiaries. The reader is recommended to refer constantly to the comprehensive illustration in section **14.12.**

14.4 The profit and loss account

This generally stands first among the accounts proper, as printed. There is no legal obligation to cover one year, though this is normal, unless the year-end has been changed, causing extension or curtailment of one period. Sometimes a 52-week reporting period is adopted, with occasional 53-week periods to keep in step with the calendar—the object being to synchronize the financial statements with internal management accounts based on 4-week, or 4/5-week, periods instead of months. The making-up of the accounts to arbitrary dates, such as 31 December (or the Saturday before it), is still far too common, and not much progress has been made in this country in persuading companies to adopt the 'natural business year' for the type of enterprise concerned.

14.4.1 Disclosure in the profit and loss account

The fragmentary nature of the disclosure requirements in the Acts—they do not even mention profit figures, or balances brought and carried forward—makes the typical published profit and loss account still a mere skeleton. No manufacturing or trading account is presented, nor any of their components except turnover (from 1967) and depreciation. Indeed, the selective character of the charges revealed demands the single-sided form of statement, avoiding the need to debit them against a meaningless credit figure, neither gross profit nor net. The contents of the modern type of profit and loss account are as follows (references are to 1967, Schedule 2, unless otherwise stated).

Turnover (or gross receipts) (para. 13A)

This must be given (except in so far as it is attributable to the business of banking or discounting, or such other business as the Department of Trade may prescribe), unless the company is neither a holding company nor a subsidiary of another body corporate, *and* the turnover (or gross receipts, in the case of a 'service' business) does not exceed £50,000 (increased, in 1972, to £250,000 by DTI Order)—a concession to the small family company, often in competition with unincorporated firms, which publish no accounts. The method by which turnover is arrived at must also be stated.

Turnover or gross receipts normally heads the profit and loss account, as a ruled-off figure. Alternatively, it may be included in the notes on the accounts—as is, almost invariably, the statement of the method by which it is arrived at. This is often no more informative than 'net sales as invoiced', or 'net sales less purchase tax', or some such formula, and the requirement does very little to make turnover comparable between one company and another, even in the same industry.

The next item is usually *net trading* (or *operating*) *profit,* preferably before charging interest payable, but after charging certain other costs, generally set out below it in a 'box' or unextended inset, or relegated to the notes. These costs are as follows.

Directors' remuneration (1948 Act, s. 196; 1967 Act, ss. 6, 7)

The rules for disclosing these are given in the body of each Act. 1948 Act, s. 196, is long, complex, and repetitious, but its essence is that the company must reveal separately, so far as they apply, the aggregate amounts of:

a   directors' *emoluments*—i.e. remuneration for current services, in the form of fees, salaries, bonuses, commissions, etc., including taxable expense allowances, the value of benefits in kind, and the company's contributions to superannuation schemes;

b   directors' or past directors' *pensions*—but excluding any paid out of a fund which is substantially maintained by the contributions paid into it; and

c   *compensation* to directors or past directors in respect of loss of office—but excluding any which is liable to be forfeited (under 1948, s.193) for nondisclosure in connection with a take-over bid (see Chapter 15, sub-section **15.4.4**).

There must be included all remuneration paid to the company's directors, by the company and its subsidiaries if any, and in the case of compensation by other persons, such as a new holding company which turns out the old directors. Where remuneration is paid otherwise than by the company, the figures must be shown in the notes; and this is the normal situation with a holding company (see Chapter 16, sub-section **16.2.4**)

Each of the aggregates under heads **a**, **b**, and **c** must be analysed as between amounts paid:

i in respect of services as directors (or past directors) of the company or its subsidiaries (e.g. directors' fees pure and simple); and

ii in respect of other services (e.g. salaries, etc., as managers, executives, technologists, etc.).

In addition, compensation must be further analysed as between amounts paid by:

1 the company;
2 its subsidiaries; and
3 any other person.

Thus, at a maximum, *nine* amounts may have to be distinguished; fortunately this seldom happens! If any of the requirements of s. 196 are not complied with in the accounts or notes, the auditors must include the missing particulars in their report, so far as they are reasonably able to do so.

As if this were not enough, the 1967 Act, s. 6, calls for further disclosures, relative to directors' *emoluments* only. Confusion is increased by the fact that these are defined differently from those in **a** above, in that they now exclude the company's contributions to superannuation schemes (which often cannot be apportioned to individual directors), and also *all* emoluments of directors whose duties were discharged wholly or mainly outside the U.K. There must be stated:

a the total emoluments of the *chairman* (or the total for two or more successive chairmen during the year);

b the total emoluments of the *highest paid director* (one man only), if he was not the chairman; and

c the *numbers* of directors (including the above-mentioned) whose emoluments were between nil and £2,500, between £2,501, and £5,000, and so on upwards in bands of £2,500 width.

Lastly, 1967, s. 7, requires a statement of:

a the number of directors who have *waived rights* to receive emoluments which would otherwise have been included in the total of emoluments (as defined by 1948, s. 196); and

b the aggregate amount of the emoluments waived.

If any of these requirements are not complied with, the auditors' duty is as before.

None of the information under 1967, ss. 6 and 7, need be given, however, if the company is neither a holding company nor a subsidiary of another body corporate, *and* the total directors' emoluments, as defined in 1948, s. 196, do not exceed £7,500 (increased, in 1972, to £15,000 by DTI Order)—a concession to the chairman and/or highest paid director of a small family company, who might be acutely embarrassed by the revelation of his income.

Emoluments of employees over £10,000 (1967 Act, s. 8)

There must be given in the notes the *numbers* of employees, other than directors, whose emoluments (calculated as for directors under s. 6) were between £10,001 and £12,500, between £12,501 and £15,000, and so on upwards in bands of £2,500 width. Employees who worked wholly or mainly outside the U.K. are excluded.

The auditors' duty in the event of non-disclosure is as above.

Auditors' remuneration (1967 Act, Schedule 2, para. 13)

The amount of this, including expenses paid by the company, shall be shown separately.

Hire of plant and machinery (para. 12(1)(gb))

The amount charged to revenue under this head is to be shown. Hire purchase payments are not included, since they consist partly of interest, and partly of instalments of cost, upon which depreciation is charged.

The 1967 Act failed to give effect to the Jenkins Committee's recommendation that *rents payable for land and buildings* should be disclosed—a strange anomaly, in view of the popularity of financing by sale and lease back of freehold properties.

Depreciation, etc., of fixed assets (paras. 12, 14)

There shall be shown the amount charged to revenue by way of provision for depreciation, renewals or diminution in value of fixed assets (para. 12(1)(g)). (In practice, the total is usually analysed between different classes of asset, on the same lines as in the balance sheet.)

If the same assets are subject, both to a depreciation provision *and* to a provision for renewals, both amounts shall be shown separately (para. 12(3)). If the amount charged to revenue for depreciation, etc., of fixed assets (other than investments) has been determined otherwise than by reference to the balance sheet values of the assets, that fact shall be stated (para. 12(4)). If depreciation or replacement of fixed assets is provided for by some method other than a depreciation charge or provision for renewals, or is not provided for, the method by which it is provided for, or the fact that it is not provided for, shall be stated (para. 14(2)).

To the net trading profit are added:

Income from investments (para. 12(1)(g))

Income from quoted, and unquoted, investments shall be distinguished. The amounts should be shown gross of income tax. (For modern practice with regard to income from investments in associated companies, see Chapter 16, section 16.7.)

Rents receivable from land (para. 12(1)(ga))

The amount thereof, net of ground-rents, rates, and other outgoings, shall be shown, if it forms a substantial part of the year's revenue.

From the total to this point is deducted:

Interest payable (para. 12(1)(b))

Distinction shall be made between interest on:

i bank loans and overdrafts;
ii other loans (whether or not secured by debentures) which are repayable within five years from the day after the year-end, or by instalments, the last of which falls due within that period; and
iii loans not repayable within five years as aforesaid, or repayable by instalments, some of which fall due after that period.

The sum now left in the profit and loss account is *net profit before taxation and extraordinary items*. It is reduced by:

Taxation (paras. 12, 14)

This consists of:

a the charge for U.K. *corporation tax* (estimated on the lines set out in Chapter 12, section 12.3);
b where double taxation relief has been obtained, the amount which would have been charged but for the relief (as a note); and
c the charge for *taxation imposed outside the U.K.* on profits, income, and capital gains (if these are credited to revenue).

There shall also be shown (in the appropriation section of a close company's account):

d the charge for U.K. *income tax* (on a shortfall in distributions) (para. 12(1)(c)),
since this is related to distributions, not profits.

There shall further be stated, by way of note, the basis on which the charge for U.K. corporation tax (and income tax, where applicable) is computed (para. 14(3)); also any special circumstances which affect liability in respect of taxation of profits, income, or capital gains, for the financial year or for succeeding financial years (para. 14(3A)).

Deduction of corporation tax, etc., and separate adjustment of the previous year's tax in the normal course, leaves *net profit after taxation and before extraordinary items. Extraordinary items*, including prior year adjustments of an 'extraordinary' nature (see below, and sub-section 14.6.3) are added or subtracted, leaving *profit for the year*, to which is added the *balance* of the profit and loss account, *brought forward* from the previous year. From the resulting sub-total are subtracted the *appropriations*, leaving at the end the *balance carried forward* to next year. Alternatively, the opening and closing balances may be omitted, as well as the transfers to and from other reserves, and the concluding figure then becomes the *retained profit* for the year. The total retentions to date may then be explained separately (see section 14.7).

The disclosure requirements for the above-mentioned items are as follows:

Extraordinary items (para. 14(6))

There shall be shown, by way of note or otherwise, any material respects in which any items shown in the profit and loss account are affected by:

a transactions of a sort not usually undertaken by the company or otherwise by circumstances of an exceptional or non-recurrent nature; or
b any change in the basis of accounting.

This is wide-ranging and somewhat permissive, and is discussed more fully in SSAP No. 6 (1974) of the Accounting Standards Steering Committee (see sub-section **14.6.3**).

Prior year adjustments (para. 12A)

The amount of any charge or credit arising in consequence of the occurrence of an event in a preceding financial year shall, if not included in a heading related to other matters, be stated under a separate heading. This is rather tautological and, again, decidedly permissive; more light is thrown on the question by SSAP No. 6.

Provisions (para. 12(1)(f))

There shall be disclosed:

a the amount, if material, set aside to provisions, other than for depreciation, renewals, or diminution in value of assets; or
b the amount, if material, withdrawn from such provisions and not applied for the purposes thereof.

Redemption of share capital and loans (para. 12(1)(d))

The respective amounts 'provided' for redemption of share capital (i.e. redeemable preference shares) and loans shall be disclosed. *Pace* the Act, these are transfers to reserves, not provisions.

Transfers to reserves (para. 12(1)(e))

There shall also be shown the amount, if material, set aside or proposed to be set aside to, or withdrawn from, reserves. Since the profit and loss account is itself a reserve, this may be taken as authority for the common practice (especially in the consolidated profit and loss account of a holding company) of omitting the actual transfers, and the balances brought and carried forward, and showing the concluding figure as 'retained profit for the year' or as 'amount added to reserves'. The transfers must still be shown, however, by way of note.

Dividends (para. 12(1)(h))

There shall be shown the aggregate amount (before deduction of income tax) of the dividends paid and proposed. In the case of 'free of tax' dividends the grossed-up amounts are given. (See Chapter 12, sub-section **12.2.2** re dividends paid after 5 April 1973).

Comparative figures (para. 14(5); 1967, s. 11)

There are required, finally, the corresponding amounts for the immediately preceding financial year for all items shown in the profit and loss account (except in the first year's accounts). They usually appear in a left-hand column, or in a right-hand column beside the current figures, and distinctively printed.

The Companies Act, 1967, s. 11, imposes similar requirements in respect of all figures relative to directors' remuneration/emoluments (including waivers), and emoluments of employees over £10,000.

14.5 The balance sheet

Published company balance sheets today take a number of forms, the main ones being:

1 the orthodox two-sided form, with all liabilities on the left;
2 a modification of (1), with current liabilities deducted from current assets on the right (or set out, unextended, on the left, with the total deducted on the right as aforesaid);
3 a two-block form, showing shareholders' funds in the first block, and in the second, fixed assets less debentures and deferred liabilities, and current assets less current liabilities; or
4 a two-block form, showing capital employed (share capital, reserves, debentures, and deferred liabilities) in one block, and employment of capital (fixed assets, and net current assets) in the other—with variable order and captioning.

Layout 4 is used in the illustration in section 14.12. The tendency is to produce as 'clean' a balance sheet as possible, with salient figures emphasized and statutory detail relegated to copious notes—where, too often, it remains unread. The argument is that such balance sheets are intended for lay shareholders, and the notes for the investment analyst or other expert; but there is something to be said for a moderately 'dirty' balance sheet, with more of the detail placed to catch the eye.

14.5.1 Disclosure in the balance sheet

The legal requirements are as below, arranged as far as is practicable in the order in which the items normally appear in a conventional two-sided balance sheet—beginning with the left-hand side, passing to the right-hand side, and ending with the notes. References are to the 1967 Act, Schedule 2, unless otherwise stated.

Signatures (1948, s. 155)

Every balance sheet shall be signed on behalf of the board by two directors, or by the sole director.

General layout (1967, Schedule 2, paras. 2, 4)

The authorized share capital, issued share capital, liabilities, and assets shall be summarized, with such particulars as are necessary to disclose the general nature of the assets and liabilities (para. 2). The reserves, provisions, liabilities, and assets shall be classified under heads appropriate to the company's business; but where the amount of any class is not material, it may be included under the same heading as some other class, and where assets of one class are not separable from assets of another class, both may be included under the same heading (para. 4(1)). Fixed assets, current assets, and assets which are neither fixed nor current shall be separately identified (para. 4(2)).

Share capital (2, 11(2),(3))

As stated above, the authorized and issued capital shall both be summarized.
Redeemable preference shares issued shall be separately specified, as well as the

earliest and latest dates on which the company has power to redeem them, whether redemption is compulsory or at the company's option, and whether any (and, if so, what) premium is payable on redemption (para. 2(*a*)).

There shall be separately specified any share capital on which *interest out of capital* has been paid during the financial year, and the rate thereof; so far as the information is not given in the profit and loss account (para. 2(*b*)).

There shall be stated, by way of note or otherwise, the number, description, and amount of any (unissued) shares for which any person has an *option to subscribe,* together with the period for which the option is exercisable, and the price payable for shares subscribed for under it (para. 11(2)).

There shall also be stated the amount of any *arrears of fixed cumulative dividends,* and the period or periods for which they are in arrear. The normal 'less tax' dividends shall be stated gross; 'free of tax' ones, though, shall be shown net of tax, and the fact stated (para. 11(3)). (Free of tax dividends are not to be grossed up, since the future dates of payment, and ruling rates of income tax, are not known.) (But see now the position re tax, in Chapter 12, sub-section 12.2.2.)

Reserves and provisions (paras. 2, 6, 7, 27; 1948, s. 58)

A *provision* means any amount written off or retained by way of providing for depreciation, renewals, or diminution in value of assets; or retained by way of providing for any known liability of which the amount cannot be determined with substantial accuracy. Any other credit balance of this nature which is not a liability determinable with substantial accuracy, or a sum set aside to be used to prevent undue fluctuations in taxation, is a *reserve.* But where any 'provision' as above defined is in excess of the amount which in the opinion of the directors is reasonably necessary for its purpose, the excess shall be treated as a reserve, not as a provision (para. 27).

The aggregate amounts respectively of reserves and provisions (other than provisions for depreciation, etc.) shall be stated under separate headings; but if the amount of either is not material, it need not be separately stated. The Department of Trade may direct that it shall not require a separate statement of the amount of provisions where they are satisfied that it is not required in the public interest and would prejudice the company—but subject to the condition that any heading stating an amount arrived at after taking into account a provision (other than for depreciation, etc.) shall be so framed or marked as to indicate that fact (para. 6).

The *share premium account* (para. 2(*c*)) and *capital redemption reserve fund* (1948, s. 58) shall be stated separately. In practice, other reserves, and provisions other than for depreciation, etc., are also shown under separate headings, if of material amount.

Unless it is shown in the profit and loss account, or the amount is not material, there shall be shown the source from which is derived any *increase* in the reserves, or the provisions (other than for depreciation, etc.), as compared with the amount at the end of the preceding year; and the application of the amount of any *decrease* in reserves as compared with the amount at the end of the preceding year, and of any such decrease in provisions (other than as above), not accounted for by application of amounts for the stated purposes. Where the total reserves or provisions are subdivided (as is usual), the movements on each separate reserve or provision shall be specified as aforesaid (para. 7).

Debentures (paras. 2, 8, 9, 10, 30)

There is, curiously, no specific requirement to disclose these, but there is an obligation to show under a separate heading the aggregate amount of *loans* made to the company (other than bank loans and overdrafts) which are repayable after the expiration of the period of five years beginning with the day next following the expiration of the financial year, or by instalments, any of which fall due for payment after the expiration of that period (para. 8(1)(*d*)). Nothing is said about 'non-bank' loans repayable within five years, but the overriding requirement to exhibit a 'true and fair view' would seem to preclude omission to state separately any debentures due for redemption within that time. All the same, it is a pity that the Act is not more clear on this point.

A loan, or instalment, shall be deemed to fall due for repayment, or payment, on the earliest date on which a lender could require it if he exercised all options and rights available to him (para. 30).

In relation to each loan mentioned above, there shall be stated, by way of note or otherwise, the *terms* on which it is repayable and the *rate of interest* payable. If, however, the number of loans is such that, in the opinion of the directors, compliance with this requirement would result in a statement of excessive length, it shall be sufficient to give a general indication of the terms of repayment, and rates of interest, applicable (para. 8(4)).

Where any liability of the company is *secured* otherwise than by operation of law on any assets of the company, the fact that the liability is so secured shall be stated, but it shall not be necessary to specify the assets on which the liability is secured (para. 9). This covers the case of debentures secured by a fixed or floating charge, or both.

There shall be specified particulars of any *redeemed debentures* which the company has power to re-issue (para. 2(*d*)); these will appear among the assets, while the nominal value will still be included as a liability. This extends to debentures (whether redeemed or not) held by a nominee of, or trustee for, the company; in which case the nominal amount of the debentures, and the amount at which they are stated in the company's books, shall be stated (para. 10).

Taxation (paras. 7A, 11(8A), (10))

If an amount is set aside to be used to *prevent undue fluctuations in charges for taxation* (i.e. a deferred taxation, or taxation equalization, account), it shall be stated (para. 7A). If any part of this sum has been used during the financial year for another purpose, there shall be stated the amount so diverted, and the fact that it has been so used (para. 11(8A)).

There shall also be stated the basis on which the amount, if any, set aside for U.K. corporation tax is computed (para. 11(10)). This is generally taken to apply to the 'current year' provision only.

Current liabilities (para. 8(1))

Two items under this head shall be disclosed separately:

a the aggregate amounts of *bank loans and overdrafts*; and
b the aggregate amount (before deduction of income tax) which is recommended for distribution by way of *dividend* (i.e. the proposed dividend) (para. 8(1)(*d*), (*e*)).

The legal requirements relative to *assets* are as follows:

Physical fixed assets (paras. 4(3), 5, 11(6A), (6B), (6C), 29, 31)

The method(s) used to arrive at the amount of the fixed assets under each heading shall be stated (para. 4(3)).

The normal method of arriving at the amount of any fixed asset shall be to take the difference between:

a its *cost* or, if it stands in the books at a *valuation*, the amount thereof; and
b the aggregate amount provided or written off since the date of acquisition or valuation, as the case may be, for *depreciation or diminution in value* (para. 5(1)).

Both amounts shall be shown for the assets under each head, as well as the net difference (para. 5(3)). This is commonly done by setting out the figures of cost, etc., accumulated depreciation, and net book value in three columns, and ruling off the totals of the first two (but see the illustration in section 14.12).

If the relevant figures, for assets on hand at the commencement of the 1948 Act (1 July 1948), cannot be obtained without unreasonable expense or delay, the net book value at that date may be treated as the amount of a valuation of those assets made at that date. The amount of any subsequent sales may be set off against the 1948 net book value, and the difference treated as if it were the amount of a valuation of the remaining assets (para. 5(1)).

The general rule does not apply to 'pre-1948' assets; to assets whose replacement is wholly or partly provided for by charging the cost of replacement against a provision for renewals, or direct to revenue (leaving the undepreciated cost of the original asset on the books); to quoted investments, or unquoted investments whose value as estimated by the directors is shown as the amount of the investments or by way of note; or to goodwill, patents or trade marks (para. 5(2)). As to assets whose cost of replacement is written off, there shall be stated:

a the *means* by which their replacement is provided for; and
b the aggregate amount (if any) of *unused provisions for renewals* (para. 5(4)).

The 1967 Act was the first to recognize specifically the common practice today of revaluing long-lived assets from time to time, and revising depreciation charges accordingly, where applicable. If any assets (other than unquoted investments) whose amount is stated on the 'cost-or-valuation less depreciation' basis have been *revalued,* there shall be stated the years (so far as known to the directors) in which the assets were severally valued and the several values, and, in the case of assets that have been valued during the *current* year, the names of the persons who valued them or particulars of their qualifications for doing so and (whichever is stated) the bases of valuation used by them (para. 11(6A)).

There shall further be stated, in the case of fixed assets other than investments, the aggregate amount of the assets *acquired* during the year, as determined for the purpose of making up the balance sheet; and the aggregate amount, as determined for the purpose of making up last year's balance sheet, of any such assets included in that balance sheet which have been *disposed of or destroyed* during the current year (para. 11(6B)). There is no obligation to state the proceeds of sale, or of insurance claims, relative to such assets.

Lastly, there shall be stated how much of the amount of the *land* included in fixed assets is ascribable to freehold tenure and how much to leasehold, and, of the latter, how much is ascribable to land held on long lease, and on short lease (para. 11(6C)). For this purpose, 'long lease' means one of which the unexpired term is not less than 50 years, and 'short lease' is defined accordingly; 'lease' includes an agreement for a lease (para. 29).

In Scotland, 'land of freehold tenure' means land in respect of which the company is proprietor of the *dominium utile*, or, in the case of land not held on feudal tenure, is the owner; 'land of leasehold tenure' means land of which the company is tenant under a lease; and the reference in para. 12(1)(*ga*) to ground rents, rates, and other outgoings includes a reference to feu-duty and ground annual (para. 31).

Goodwill, patents, and trade marks (para. 8)

There shall be shown separately, so far as it is not written off, the amount of *goodwill, patents and/or trade marks,* or such part of it as is shown as a separate item in the books of account, or is otherwise ascertainable from any contract for the sale or purchase of any property to be acquired by the company, or from any documents in its possession relating to stamp duty payable in respect of any such contract or the conveyance of any such property (para. 8(1)(*b*)). In other words, only purchased goodwill, etc., need be shown, at cost less any amounts written off to date. Para. 5(2)(*d*) makes it clear that there is no need to show the original cost if it has been written down; but the general rule still applies, that the method(s) used to arrive at the amount of any fixed assets shall be stated (para. 4(3)). There is no need to state the three amounts otherwise than as a single item (para. 8(2)).

Investments (paras. 5A, 8, 11(8), 28)

There shall be shown separately the aggregate amounts respectively of the company's *quoted investments* and *unquoted investments* (para. 8(1)(*a*)). The heading for quoted investments shall be subdivided, where necessary, to distinguish the investments which have, and have not, been granted a quotation on a *recognized stock exchange* (para. 8(3))—since a 'quoted investment' means an investment which has been granted a quotation or permission to deal on a recognized stock exchange (i.e. in Great Britain), or on any stock exchange of repute outside Great Britain (para. 28).

There shall also be shown the aggregate *market value* of the quoted investments, where it differs from the amount thereof as stated, and the *stock exchange value* also, if the market value is shown at a higher figure (para. 11(8)). Normally, the stock exchange value (i.e. the 'middle' value, as a rule) is taken as the market value; but sometimes the quoted price is regarded as unrealistically low—e.g. if the shares are seldom dealt in—and a higher estimate taken instead.

None of the above provisions overrides the general obligation to divide the company's investments between fixed, current and other assets, as the facts shall warrant.

Para. 5A demands additional information relative to *unquoted* investments in the *equity share capital* of other bodies corporate. 'Equity share capital' has the same meaning as it has in the 1948 Act, s. 154 (relative to the definition of a subsidiary company—see Chapter 16, sub-section **16.2.1**); that is, it includes all shares or stock *except* preference shares without participating rights and without the right to share in surplus assets on liquidation.

Such investments may be dealt with in two ways. *Either* their values as estimated by the directors (individually or collectively, or a mixture of both) shall be shown, as the balance sheet amount or by way of note, *or* certain objective information must be given, by way of note or otherwise, i.e:

a the aggregate amount of the company's income for the financial year that is ascribable to the investments;
b the amount of the company's share, before and after taxation, of the aggregate profits (less losses) of the bodies invested in, for the several periods covered by the accounts sent by the said bodies to the company during the financial year;
c the amount of the company's share of the aggregate undistributed profits (less losses) accumulated by the bodies concerned since the time when the investments were acquired; and
d the manner in which any losses incurred by the said bodies have been dealt with in the company's accounts.

Such information is valuable to an analyst, but the option of substituting a subjective valuation by the directors is rather too easy.

The special rules relating to investments in subsidiary companies, and to investments constituting over 10 per cent of another body's equity or over 10 per cent of the company's own assets, are given in Chapter 16, sub-section **16.2.2**.

Current assets (para. 11(7), (8B))

There shall be stated the manner in which the amount carried forward for *stock in trade or work in progress* has been computed, if it is material for the members' appreciation of the company's state of affairs or profit or loss for the financial year (para. 11(8B)). In practice, such particulars tend to be brief and rather uninformative. There is no obligation, for instance, to state whether the 'cost' figure for stock is calculated on a FIFO, LIFO, average cost, or other basis, or whether it does or does not include an allowance for manufacturing or other overheads—all vital points for appraisal of a company's reported profits or losses, and for comparing them from year to year.

If in the opinion of the directors any of the current assets have not a value, on realization in the ordinary course of the company's business, at least equal to the stated amount, the fact shall be stated (para. 11(7)).

Loans for the purpose of acquiring shares in the company (para 8)

By 1948, s. 54, a company is prohibited from giving financial assistance for the purchase of its own shares or those of its holding company, except for the following:

a a loan in the ordinary course of business, where the company's business includes the lending of money;
b the provision by a company in accordance with any scheme for the time being in force, of money for the purchase of, or subscription for, fully paid shares in the company or its holding company, by trustees of, or for, shares to be held by, or for the benefit of, employees of the company, including any director holding a salaried employment or office in the company; or
c the making by a company of loans to persons, other than directors, bona fide in the employment of the company, to enable them to purchase or subscribe for

fully paid shares in the company or its holding company, to be held by themselves by way of beneficial ownership.

The aggregate amount of any outstanding loans made under heads **b** and **c** above shall be shown separately (para. 8(1)(*c*)).

Loans to officers of the company (1948, s. 197)

The 1948 Act, s. 197, requires the accounts to contain particulars showing:

a the amount of any loans made during the financial year to
   i any officer of the company; or
   ii any person who, after the making of the loan, became during that year an officer of the company;
  by the company or a subsidiary thereof or by any other person under a guarantee from, or on a security provided by, the company or a subsidiary thereof (including any such loans which were repaid during that year); and
b the amount of any such loans made before the financial year and still outstanding at the end of it;

but *excluding* any loan made in the ordinary course of a business which includes the lending of money, and any loan made by the company or subsidiary to one of its own employees, not being over £2,000 *and* being certified by the relevant company's directors to have been made in accordance with any practice adopted, or about to be adopted, by the company or subsidiary with respect to loans to its employees—unless such loans are made by one company, and guaranteed or secured by another company, in the same group.

Expenses not written off (para. 3)

There shall be stated separately, so far as they are not written off:

a the preliminary expenses;
b any expenses incurred in connection with any issue of share capital or debentures;
c any sums paid by way of commission in respect of any shares or debentures;
d any sums allowed by way of discount in respect of any debentures; and
e the amount of the discount allowed on any issue of shares at a discount.

Comparative figures (para. 11(11))

There shall be shown (except in the first year's accounts) the corresponding amounts at the end of the immediately preceding financial year for all items shown in the balance sheet.

Sundry matters (paras. 11(4), (5), (6), (9))

There shall, finally, be shown by way of note or otherwise:

a particulars of any charge on the assets of the company to secure the liabilities of any other person, including where practicable the amount secured (para. 11(4));
b the general nature of any other contingent liabilities not provided for and, where

practicable, the aggregate amount or estimated amount of those liabilities, if it is material (para. 11(5));

c where practicable, the aggregate amounts or estimated amounts, if they are material, of

    i contracts for capital expenditure, so far as not provided for; and

    ii capital expenditure, authorized by the directors, which has not been contracted for (para. 11(6)); and

d the basis on which foreign currencies have been converted into sterling, where the amount of the assets or liabilities affected is material (para. 11(9)).

14.6   The Accounting Standards Steering Committee

The *Accounting Standards Steering Committee* was founded in 1970 by the three Institutes of Chartered Accountants (in England and Wales, of Scotland, and in Ireland); later the Association of Certified Accountants, and the Institute of Cost and Management Accountants, became members. The Chartered Institute of Public Finance and Accountancy (formerly the Institute of Municipal Treasurers and Accountants) remains outside the ASSC, since its own members are not generally concerned with business accounts.

The ASSC issues *Statements of Standard Accounting Practice* (SSAP), or 'accounting standards', which describe methods of accounting approved by the member bodies for application to all financial accounts intended to give a true and fair view of financial position and profit or loss (including the published accounts of limited liability companies). Significant departures in financial accounts from applicable accounting standards should be disclosed and explained. The financial effects should be estimated and disclosed unless this would be impracticable or mis-leading in the context of giving a true and fair view. If the financial effects of departures from standards are not disclosed, the reasons should be stated.

Before issuing a SSAP, the Committee circulates an *Exposure Draft* (ED) of the text for discussion and comment, in the light of which the final version is prepared. In the meantime the ED is of persuasive authority only, but it is often followed by many progressive companies.

Accountants who are members of the ASSC's constituent bodies, and who assume responsibilities in respect of financial accounts, are expected to observe accounting standards. As directors or other officers of companies the onus is on them to ensure that the other directors and officers fully understand the existence and purpose of standards, and to use their best endeavours to ensure that they are observed or, if not, that significant departures are disclosed and explained in the accounts and their effect, if material, disclosed. Where members act as auditors or reporting accountants the onus is on them, not only to ensure disclosure of significant departures from standards but also, to the extent that their con-currence is stated or implied, to justify them. Their own institution may inquire into apparent failures by members to observe these requirements.

Accounting standards are not intended to be a comprehensive code of rigid rules; such a code could not possibly cover every situation or case, or provide in advance for innovations in business and financial practice. There may also be situations in which standards are inapplicable because they are impracticable or, exceptionally, would be inappropriate or give a misleading view. In such cases modified or alternative treatments must be adopted, and departures from standard disclosed and explained. In exceptional or borderline cases regard must be paid to the spirit of the standards as well as to their precise terms, and the overriding need for a true and fair view must be borne in mind.

SAAPs are not intended to apply to accounts prepared and audited overseas for local purposes; but are intended to apply where accounts of overseas subsidiaries and associated companies are incorporated in U.K. group accounts.[1]

To date (June 1975) nine SSAPs have been issued, together with five EDs not yet finalized. They are:

Statements of Standard Accounting Practice

No. 1   *Accounting for the results of associated companies* (1971, revised 1974)
No. 2   *Disclosure of accounting policies* (1971)
No. 3   *Earnings per share* (1972, revised 1974)
No. 4   *The accounting treatment of government grants* (1974)
No. 5   *Accounting for value added tax* (1974)
No. 6   *Extraordinary items and prior year adjustments* (1974, revised 1975)
No. 7   *Accounting for changes in the purchasing power of money* (1974)
No. 8   *The treatment of taxation under the imputation system in the accounts*
No. 9   *Stocks and work in progress* (1975)

Exposure Drafts

No. 3   *Accounting for acquisitions and mergers* (1971) (out of print)
No. 11   *Accounting for deferred taxation* (1973)
No. 13   *Statements of source and application of funds* (1974)
No. 14   *Accounting for research and development* (1975) (see sub-section **6.4.2**)
No. 15   *Accounting for depreciation* (1975) (see sub-section **6.3.5**)

Consideration of SSAP No. 1, and of ED3, is deferred to Chapter 16, because of their close association with consolidated accounts. SAAPs Nos. 4 and 5, which are very short and deal with minor issues, have already been treated in Chapter 6, sub-sections **6.3.5** and **6.1.1** respectively. SSAP No. 9 (formerly ED6) is of more importance, but it, too, has been covered in Chapter 5, sub-section **5.3.5**.

14.6.1 Statement of Standard Accounting Practice No. 2 (1971): Disclosure of accounting policies

This document, while disclaiming any intention of developing a basic theory of accounting, finds it convenient to lay down four *fundamental accounting concepts,* to be taken as broad basic assumptions underlying the financial accounts of business enterprises. These are:

a the 'going concern' concept—the enterprise will continue in business for the foreseeable future;
b the 'accruals' concept—revenues and costs are recognized as they are earned or

---

[1]See: *Statements of Standard Accounting Practice: Explanatory Foreword,* Institute of Chartered Accountants in England and Wales, 1971.

incurred (irrespective of cash flows), matched with one another so far as their relationship can be established or justifiably assumed, and dealt with in the profit and loss account of the period to which they relate;

c the 'consistency' concept—like items are treated consistently within each accounting period and from one period to the next; and

d the concept of 'prudence'—revenues and profits are not anticipated, but recognized in the profit and loss account only when realized in the form of cash or of other assets, the ultimate cash realization of which can be assessed with reasonable certainty; and provision is made for all known liabilities, expenses, and losses, whether the amount of these is known with certainty or is a best estimate in the light of the information available. This concept overrides **b** where the two conflict.

It is clear from Chapter 1 that the author, for one, does not consider these four concepts as 'fundamental' in the true sense, nor as being of the same nature, or the same degree of inviolability. Such philosophical arguments, though, are beside the point here. Concepts **a** to **d** are generally accepted in business accounting; the fact that they have been followed in a particular set of accounts need not be stated, and observance is presumed in the absence of a contrary statement. If, however, accounts have been prepared on the basis of assumptions which differ in material respects from any of the four concepts, the fact should be explained.

SSAP No. 2 speaks further of accounting bases and accounting policies. *Accounting bases* are the methods developed for applying 'fundamental accounting concepts' to financial transactions and items with special reference to recognizing revenue and costs in particular accounting periods, and determining the balance sheet amounts of material items. *Accounting policies* are the specific accounting bases selected and consistently followed by a business enterprise as being, in the opinion of the management, appropriate to its circumstances and best suited to present fairly its results and financial position. The ASSC member bodies have especially in mind those items for which several alternative accounting bases are in common use, and which are often of such size that the choice of one base or another can have a material effect on reported results and financial position; such as depreciation of fixed assets, treatment and amortization of intangibles, stock and work in progress valuation, long-term contracts, and consolidation policies.

Accordingly, the second part of the Statement requires that the accounting policies followed for dealing with items judged material or critical in determining profit or loss for the year and in stating the financial position should be disclosed by way of note to the accounts. The explanations should be clear, fair, and as brief as possible.

This directive is, perhaps, the most important pronouncement so far of the ASSC. There are many matters upon which the Companies Acts are silent, but where some degree of disclosure is vital if an external analyst is to have any real idea how the profit or loss for the year has been arrived at—let alone how far one company's accounts are comparable with those of another, even in the same industry. It is in relation to the net trading profit that the analyst has been most in the dark hitherto, and the author submits that this is the figure to which a note on accounting policies is most suitably attached. (See also sub-section 14.7.1).

14.6.2 Statement of Standard Accounting Practice No. 3 (1972, revised 1974): Earnings per share

The original SSAP No. 3 was published in 1972, when the classical system of corporation tax was in force. The introduction of the imputation system necessitated a revision, and the new version appeared in 1974. Before its requirements are detailed, though, something needs to be said about the underlying concepts.

For several years financial analysts have made increasing use of a company's *price/earnings ratio* (or P/E ratio)–i.e. the current market price of the equity shares divided by the *earnings per share* (see Chapter 18, sub-section **18.2.3**). It is therefore imperative that earnings per share (EPS) should be calculated and disclosed on a comparable basis as between one company and another, and as between one financial period and another, so far as possible.

EPS are accordingly defined as the profit in pence attributable to each equity share, based on the (consolidated) profit of the period after tax and after deducting minority interests (where applicable) and preference dividends, but before taking into account extraordinary items, such profit being divided by the number of equity shares in issue and ranking for dividend in respect of the period. It should include the company's proportion of associated companies' earnings (see Chapter 16, sub-section **16.7.1**). Under the classical system of corporation tax this calculation was straightforward as regards the numerator of the fraction (total equity earnings for the year), but under the imputation system there are two alternative bases of computation.

On the *nil basis,* equity earnings are computed as though the company's distributions in respect of the period were nil. They thus consist of the pre-tax profit less a tax charge made up of the elements unaffected by distribution, and less preference dividends. On the *net basis,* however, the tax charge includes also those elements which arise because of the actual distributions, and which would be absent if they were nil. The aforesaid elements of the tax charge are:
Constant
a corporation tax on income;
b tax attributable to dividends received;
c overseas tax unrelieved because the rate of overseas tax exceeds the rate of U.K. corporation tax.
Variable
d irrecoverable ACT
e overseas tax unrelieved because dividend payments restrict the double tax credit available (see Chapter 12, sub-section **12.3.2**).
On the nil basis only elements a to c are included, while on the net basis d and e are included also. In the majority of cases d and e will be absent, and both bases will give the same answer; differences will arise only where the company has over-distributed its earnings since 5 April 1973, and/or where it has income taxed overseas, of which a significant proportion is distributed.

In either case, preference dividend is the amount declared and payable to the shareholder. With cumulative preference shares the normal dividend is taken into account, whether or not it has been earned or declared, and regardless of any arrears made up from past periods. With non-cumulative shares the actual dividend is taken. With participating preference shares the dividend to be deducted is the fixed element plus the appropriate proportion of the period earnings to arrive at the participating element—or the full dividend, if the participating element has a fixed ceiling.

Losses, or negative earnings, should be used as they stand to compute a *loss per share* (LPS). Where the tax charge is reduced by losses brought forward, the charge as it stands should be used to calculate EPS, but with an adequate explanation of the effects of tax relief on EPS for the current year and the preceding year. No deduction is required for transfers to a loan redemption reserve of sinking fund, since these do not affect total earnings.

Determination of the proper *number of equity shares issued* (the denominator of the fraction) is more complex. If one assumes in all cases that the relevant earnings for the year ended 31 December 19.1 were £200,000, and the number of (£1) ordinary shares in issue at the beginning of the year was 1,000,000, the EPS in various circumstances are computed as follows:

1 No change in issued capital during the year
   $EPS = £200,000/1,000,000 = 20.0$ p
2 500,000 shares issued for cash at full market price on 1 October 19.1 (use of weighted average number of shares)
   $EPS = £200,000/(1,000,000 \times 9/12 + 1,500,000 \times 3/12)$
   $= £200,000/(750,000 + 375,000) = 17.8$ p
   Note No adjustment of previous year's EPS.

3 1,000,000 bonus shares issued at any time during the year
   $EPS = £200,000/2,000,000 = 10.0$ p
   Note Previous year's EPS (if based on 1,000,000 shares) scaled down to $1,000,000/2,000,000 (=1/2)$ of sum reported in previous year's accounts.
4 Each share split into two of 50p each
   Proceed as in 3.
5 Additional shares issued during the year in exchange for a majority holding in another company
   Assume the shares to have been issued at the beginning of the first period from which the new subsidiary's earnings are included in the consolidated earnings of the group, and proceed as in 2. If the 'merger' method of consolidation is used (see Chapter 16), assume the shares to have been issued at the beginning of the *previous* year, and adjust the previous year's EPS accordingly.
6 Rights issue of 500,000 ordinary shares at 85p per share on 1 July 19.1 (market price on 30 June 19.1, 100p)
   500,000 shares at 85p produce £425,000 which, being averaged with 1,000,000 shares at 100p, gives a theoretical ex-rights price, after the issue of

   $ERP = (1,000,000 \times 100p + 500,000 \times 85p)/1,500,000 = 95p$

A similar effect would have resulted from a cash issue of 425,000 shares at the full cum-rights price of 100p, followed by a bonus issue of 75,000 shares, or 1 for 19 on 1,425,000 shares; causing the price to fall to 19/20ths of its old level, or from 100p to 95p. In computing the EPS, the transaction should be treated as a combination of the two elements. The weighted average of 1,000,000 shares for the first six months, and 1,425,000 for the second, is 1,212,500 shares. To this is applied the factor of 20/19 for the notional bonus issue, making the relevant number of shares 1,276,316.

The same result is attained by using the actual number of shares before and after the rights issue, but grossing up the pre-issue total—as though the 1 for 19 bonus issue had been based on 1,000,000 shares (making them 1,052,632), and new shares issued for full market price in the proportion of 425 new ones to 1,000

old (making 1,500,000). Thus
$$EPS = £200,000/(1,000,000 \times 20/19 \times 6/12 - 1,500,000 \times 6/12)$$
$$= £200,000/1,276,316 = 15.7p.$$

The 'bonus issue' factor is the same as the fraction
Cum-rights price/Ex-rights price—i.e. 100p/95p, or 20/19—
and this is conveniently used in such computations. Its reciprocal—Ex-rights price/Cum-rights price, or in this case 95p/100p—must be applied to the previous year's EPS, on the principle enunciated in **3** above, to deflate it for the bonus element in the rights issue.

The above calculations are made on the footing that all the equity shares rank for dividend in the current year. If there is more than one class of such shares, and/or different amounts are paid up on different shares, earnings will have to be apportioned over the various classes according to their rights, and/or the number of shares in a class weighted for the different paid-up amounts.

Where a company voluntarily publishes summaries of results, or key figures for several years to date, the basic EPS should be given for each year, but not for years before the company became liable to corporation tax. Retrospective adjustments should be made for bonus and rights issues, and in other circumstances where the corresponding amount for the previous year would be different from that originally published.

The SSAP proper was effective in its original form for accounting periods starting on or after 1 January 1972, the revision taking effect from 6 April 1973. It applies to companies having a listing on a recognized stock exchange for any class of equity, other than companies claiming exemption from disclosure requirements under Part III of Schedule 2 of the Companies Act, 1967 (see section **14.9**).

In the audited accounts, the earnings per share should be shown on the face of the profit and loss account on the net basis, both for the period under review and for the corresponding previous period. (It is desirable, but not mandatory, to show also the EPS on the nil basis, where the difference between the two figures is material). The basis of calculation should be disclosed in the profit and loss account or in a note thereto; in particular, the amount of the earnings and the number of equity shares used in the calculation should be shown. (In the Republic of Ireland, the tax charge will be the charge for corporation profits tax and income tax, and the EPS should be described as: 'Earnings per share after deducting corporation profits tax and income tax'.)

Where a company has at the balance sheet date contracted to issue further shares after the end of the period, or where it has already issued shares which will rank for dividend later, the effect may be to dilute future EPS. In addition, therefore, to the *basic earnings per share* (BEPS), as above, the *fully diluted earnings per share* (FDEPS) should also be shown on the face of the profit and loss account, where:

a the company has issued a separate class of equity shares which do not rank for dividend in the period under review, but will do so in the future;

b the company has issued debentures or loan stock (or preference shares) convertible into equity shares of the company; or

c the company has granted options or issued warrants to subscribe for equity shares of the company.

In each case:

i   the basis of calculation of FDEPS should be disclosed;

ii   the FDEPS need not be given unless the dilution is material – i.e. at least 5 per cent of the BEPS (nor should FDEPS be given if it is higher than BEPS);

iii   FDEPS for the corresponding previous period should not be shown unless the assumptions on which it was based still apply; and

iv   equal prominence should be given to BEPS and FDEPS, wherever both are disclosed.

(See section 14.12 for a practical illustration).

14.6.3   Statement of Standard Accounting Practice No. 6 (1974, **revised 1975**): Extraordinary items and prior year adjustments

SSAP No. 6 supersedes EDs 5 and 7. ED5 *Extraordinary items and prior year adjustments* (1971) was itself replaced by ED7 *Accounting for extraordinary items* (1972), which abandoned the distinctive treatment of prior year adjustments in ED5. The final SSAP, however, reverts to the position of ED5.

One current view of exceptional and non-recurring items is, that they should be excluded from the current year's profit and loss account and adjusted directly into reserves. SSAP No. 6 takes the opposing view–that all extraordinary items, and most prior year adjustments, should pass through the current year's profit and loss account, and be separately disclosed. The reasons given are that this enables the account to give a better view of a company's profitability and progress; that exclusion, being a matter of subjective judgement, could lead to variations and loss of comparability between companies' reported results; and that it could result in the relevant items' being overlooked in any consideration of results over a series of years.

Extraordinary items are defined as those items which derive from events or transactions outside the ordinary activities of the business and which are both material and expected not to recur frequently or regularly. They do not include items which, though exceptional on account of size and incidence (and which therefore may require separate disclosure), derive from the ordinary activities of the business. They do not include prior year items merely as such. For example, extraordinary items include profits or losses arising from discontinuance of a significant part of the business; sale of an investment not acquired with the intention of resale; writing off of intangibles, including goodwill, because of unusual events or developments during the period; and expropriation of assets. They do not include, for example, abnormal charges for bad debts, and write-offs of inventory and research and development expenditure; abnormal provisions for losses on long-term contracts; and most adjustments of prior year tax provisions.

Prior year adjustments are defined as those material adjustments applicable to prior years, arising from changes in accounting policies and from the correction of fundamental errors. They do not include the normal recurring corrections and adjustments of prior year accounting estimates. Changes in accounting policies should not be made except on the ground that the new policy will give a fairer presentation of the business's results and financial position; for example, the issue of a SSAP which creates a new accounting basis, or prefers a basis not in use in the company, is sufficient grounds for making a change. Fundamental accounting errors are those occurring in accounts already issued, of such significance as to destroy the true and fair view, and hence the validity, of those accounts and which would have led to their withdrawal had the errors been recognized at the time.

The Standard Practice therefore requires (in relation to accounting periods beginning on or after 1 January 1974) that the profit and loss account for the year should show a profit or loss after extraordinary items, reflecting all profits and losses recognized in the accounts of the year other than prior year adjustments and unrealized surpluses on revaluation of fixed assets, which should be credited direct to reserves. Items of an abnormal size and incidence, derived from the ordinary activities of the business, should be included in arriving at the profit for the year before taxation and extraordinary items, and their nature and size disclosed. Extraordinary items (less attributable taxation) should be shown separately in the profit and loss account after the results derived from ordinary activities, and their nature and size disclosed.

Prior year adjustments (less attributable taxation) should be accounted for by restating prior years, the opening balance of retained profits being adjusted accordingly. The effect of the change should be disclosed where practicable by showing separately in the restatement of the previous year the amount involved. Items which represent the normal recurring corrections and adjustments of accounting estimates made in prior years should be included in the profit and loss account for the year and, if material, their nature and size should be disclosed.

The profit and loss account for the year should, where applicable, include:

Profit before extraordinary items;
Extraordinary items (less taxation attributable thereto); and
Profit after extraordinary items.

A statement of retained profits/reserves, showing any prior year adjustments, should immediately follow the profit and loss account for the year.

14.6.4 Provisional Statement of Standard Accounting Practice No. 7 (1974): Accounting for changes in the purchasing power of money

The principles of this Statement have been discussed in Chapter 7, section 7.3, but its importance is such that some recapitulation is called for here.

Superseding ED8 (1973), it was issued as a Provisional Standard only, so as not to prejudice the conclusions of the Sandilands Committee of Inquiry on Inflation Accounting, set up by the then Department of Trade and Industry in 1973. This has not yet reported (June 1975), and in the meantime PSSAP No. 7 is not of binding effect, but persuasive only. Nevertheless the member bodies of the ASSC strongly recommend its adoption in accounts as soon as possible and preferably not later than the first accounting period beginning after 30 June 1974.

The standard applies to the published annual accounts of listed companies; but the method described is capable of application to every type of business, and its general adoption is recommended as good practice in the interests of more informattive reporting.

All accounts laid before the members of listed companies in general meeting should be supported by a supplementary statement showing, in terms of pounds of purchasing power at the end of the accounting year, the financial position at that date and the results for the year.

The supplementary statement should be prepared by converting the basic amounts by the application of a general index of prices, as described in Chapter 7, sub-section **7.3.1**. The statement need not give a converted figure for each item in the basic accounts but may be in reasonably summarized form. It should contain separate figures, if material, for depreciation and for the loss or gain on holding monetary items (i.e. the net loss or gain in purchasing power resulting from the effects of inflation on the company's net monetary assets or liabilities).

In the case of a listed holding company presenting group accounts in the form of consolidated accounts (see Chapter 16), the supplementary statement need deal only with the consolidated accounts. It should in any case contain a note outlining the method of conversion used, including the treatment of accounts originally prepared in foreign currencies. The auditors should report on the statement.

The index to be used in the conversion process should be:

a In the U.K.—

for periods up to end 1938, the Ministry of Labour cost-of-living index; for periods between end 1938 and end 1961, the consumers' expenditure deflator; for periods from 1962 onwards, the general index of retail prices based on January 1974 = 100;

b In the Republic of Ireland—

the official Consumer Price Index.

The figure for the index at the beginning and end of the accounting period and the date of the base of the index should be shown in a note to the supplementary statement.

In all the supplementary statements except the first, all corresponding amounts shown for the preceding year should be 'updated' so that they are restated in terms of the purchasing power of the pound at the end of the year under review. It is not necessary to provide corresponding amounts in the first statement, but this is recommended.

The above provisions are the substance of the PSSAP proper. The specimen company accounts in section **14.12** include a supplementary statement of current purchasing power accounts, modelled on the suggested format given in Appendix 2 to PSSAP No. 7.

14.6.5 Statement of Standard Accounting Practice No. 8 (1974): The treatment of taxation under the imputation system in the accounts of companies

This Statement is dealt with in principle in Chapter 12, sub-section **12.3.2**, but also requires some recapitulation. Like the first six SSAPs, it is fully binding on all qualified accountants who prepare, or report on, the published accounts of listed companies.

SSAP No. 8 supersedes ED12, except for its effects on earnings per share, dealt with in an amendment (1974) to SSAP No. 3 (see sub-section **14.6.2**). It is effective for accounting periods beginning on or after 1 January 1975, but does not apply to companies resident in the Republic of Ireland.

In the profit and loss account, the following items should be included in the taxation charge, and where material, should be separately disclosed:

a the amount of the U.K. corporation tax, specifying—

  i the charge for corporation tax on the income of the year (where such tax includes transfers between the deferred taxation account and the profit and loss account these should also be separately disclosed where material);

ii tax attributable to franked investment income;

iii irrecoverable ACT; and

iv the relief for overseas taxation; and

b the total overseas taxation relieved and unrelieved, specifying that part of the unrelieved overseas taxation which arises from the payment or proposed payment of dividends.

If the rate of corporation tax is not known for the whole or part of the accounting period, the latest known rate should be used and disclosed. Outgoing dividends should not include either related ACT or attributable tax credit; but incoming dividends from U.K. resident companies should be included at the amount of cash received or receivable plus tax credit.

In the balance sheet, dividends proposed (or declared and not yet payable) should be included in current liabilities, without the addition of the related ACT. The ACT on proposed dividends (whether recoverable or irrecoverable) should be included as a current tax liability. If such ACT is regarded as recoverable, it should be deducted from the deferred taxation account if such account is available for this purpose. Otherwise, ACT recoverable should be shown as a deferred asset. Where the title of a class of preference shares (or participating or preferred ordinary shares) issued before 6 April 1973 includes a fixed rate of dividend, the new rate should be incorporated in the description of the shares in the balance sheet.

Such is the substance of the standard accounting practice proper. The specimen accounts in section **14.12** illustrate the method of disclosure, in a complex case, suggested in Appendix 1 to SSAP No. 8.

14.6.6 Exposure draft 11 (1973): Accounting for deferred taxation

ED11 has yet to become a SSAP. Once again, the principles have been discussed in Chapter 12, sub-section **12.3.2** and only the actual recommendations regarding the published accounts are given here. (The provisions will require modification to adapt them to companies subject to taxation in the Republic of Ireland.)

Deferred taxation should be accounted for on all material timing differences, using the deferral method (i.e. making the deferral at the current rate of corporation tax, without adjusting the balance of the deferred taxation account for subsequent changes or rate). A choice may be made between calculating the taxation effect of each timing difference or of each similar group of timing differences, or effecting a single computation on the net change of all similar ones; whichever alternative is adopted, it should be applied consistently from year to year.

In the profit and loss account, the taxation effect of timing differences dealt with in that account should be shown separately as a component of the total taxation charge or credit, or by way of note to the accounts. To the extent that amounts of deferred taxation arise which relate to extraordinary items, these should be shown separately as part of such items.

In the balance sheet, deferred taxation account balances should be shown separately and described as 'deferred taxation'. They should not be shown as part of shareholders' funds, nor included under current assets or current liabilities. A note to the accounts should indicate the nature and amount of the major elements of which the net balance is composed and a description of the method of calculation adopted. Where amounts of deferred taxation arise which relate to movements on reserves (e.g. resulting from a revaluation of assets) the amounts transferred to or from deferred taxation account should be shown separately as part of such movements. Where the value of an asset is shown by way of note on the face of or annexed to the accounts, and that value differs from the book value, the note should also show, if material, the tax implications which would result from the realization of the asset at the balance sheet date at the stated value.

On introduction of the proposed standard, the opening balance on deferred taxation account, in respect of past timing differences which have not yet been reversed, should be established, or recalculated, by retroactive adjustment if necessary, using the deferral method. Where such a calculation would not be practicable the liability method should be used (i.e. applying the current rate of corporation tax to the net amount of timing differences), and thereafter the deferral method should be applied.

14.6.7 Exposure Draft 13 (1974): Statement of source and application of funds

The nature and construction of a statement of source and application of funds have been explained in Chapter 7, section 7.4. At present there is no legal requirement to include one in published accounts, but the practice has grown rapidly in Britain in the last few years. In 1972-73 the proportion of the 300 largest British companies which presented a funds statement was 39 per cent, compared with 20 per cent two years earlier.[2]

ED13 recommends that, as soon as possible, audited financial accounts should include a statement of source and application of funds, both for the period under review and for the corresponding previous period. The statement should show the profit or loss for the period together with the adjustments required for items which did not use (or provide) funds in the period. The following other sources and application of funds should, where material, also be shown:

a dividends paid and proposed;
b acquisitions and disposals of fixed and other non-current assets;
c funds raised by increasing, or expended in repaying or redeeming, medium-long-term loans or the issued capital of the company; and
d increase or decrease in working capital subdivided into its components, and movements in net liquid funds.

Where the accounts are those of a group, the funds statement should be so framed as to reflect the operations of the group.

In this connection, 'working capital' means stocks and debtors, less creditors; while 'net liquid funds' are defined as cash at bank and in hand and cash equivalents (e.g. investments held as current assets), less bank overdrafts and other short-term borrowings repayable within one year. The suggested format (adopted in the specimen accounts in section 14.12) shows source of funds, followed by application including changes in 'working capital', and the difference reconciled with 'movement in net liquid funds'. This mode of presentation is not, however, intended to be prescriptive, and a company will be at liberty to adopt another form if it prefers.

[2]*Survey of Published Accounts 1972-1973*, General Educational Trust of the Institute of Chartered Accountants in England and Wales, 1973.

A company with subsidiaries should base the funds statement on the group accounts. It should reflect the effects of any purchases or disposals of subsidiaries upon the separate assets and liabilities dealt with in the statement, so that acquisition of a subsidiary will be dealt with as an application of funds in acquiring its fixed assets (including goodwill), and as a change in working capital. It will generally be necessary also to summarize the effects of an acquisition or disposal in a footnote indicating, in the case of an acquisition, how much of the purchase price has been discharged in cash and how much by the issue of shares. (See also the specimen published group accounts in Chapter 18, section **18.3**)

14.6.8 Exposure Draft 14 (1975): Accounting for research and development

ED14 has been dealt with in sub-section **6.4.2**; here the proposed standard accounting practice itself is summarized.

Expenditure on research and development should be written off in the year of expenditure. The cost of fixed assets acquired or constructed to provide facilities for R & D activities should be capitalized and written off over their useful life.

The amount expended during the year on R & D should be separately disclosed in financial statements. On first introduction of the standard there should also be disclosed the amount written off in respect of balances of deferred expenditure brought forward; this item should be treated as a prior year adjustment (under SSAP No. 6) and charged against the opening balance of retained profits (see sub-section **14.6.3**).

14.6.9 Exposure Draft 15 (1975): Accounting for depreciation

ED15 has been dealt with in sub-section **6.3.5**; its treatment here is similar to that of ED14, above.

Provision for depreciation of fixed assets having a finite useful life should be made by allocating the cost less estimated residual values of the assets, as fairly as possible to the periods expected to benefit from their use. Where the useful life is revised, the unamortized cost should be charged over the revised remaining useful life. However, if at any time the unamortized cost is seen to be irrecoverable in full, it should be written down immediately to the estimated recoverable amount, and the latter charged over the remaining useful life.

Where there is a change from one method of depreciation to another, the unamortized cost of the asset should be written off over the remaining useful life on the new basis, commencing with the period in which the change is made. The effect, if material, should be disclosed in that year. Where assets are revalued in the accounts, the depreciation provision should be based on the revalued amount and current estimate of remaining useful life, with disclosure in the year of change of the effect of the revaluation, if material.

The method by which depreciation is calculated for each category of assets should be disclosed in the accounts, together with the effective useful lives assumed.

Where existing buildings are depreciated for the first time under the terms of the new standard, this will represent a change in accounting policy. Hence, the amount of depreciation relating to prior years should properly be treated as a prior year adjustment and charged against the opening balance of retained profits.

14.7 The International Accounting Standards Committee

The *International Accounting Standards Committee* (IASC) was formed in 1973, by agreement between the leading accountancy bodies of Australia, Canada, France, West Germany, Japan, Mexico, the Netherlands, the United Kingdom and the Republic of Ireland, and the United States. Accountancy bodies of other countries may become associate members. The IASC is part of the International Co-ordination Committee for the Accountancy Profession.

The objectives of the IASC are to formulate and publish, in the public interest, basic standards to be observed in the presentation of audited accounts and financial statements, and to promote their worldwide acceptance and observance. The member bodies are pledged to support these standards and to use their best endeavours to ensure that published accounts comply with them or disclose the extent of non-compliance; that auditors either satisfy themselves that accounts comply with the standards, or report the extent to which they do not; and that, as soon as practicable, appropriate action is taken in respect of auditors whose reports do not meet these requirements. The members also undertake to persuade governments, stock market authorities, and the industrial and business community that published accounts should comply with the standards.

In view of the wide diversity of accounting standards, policies and regulations in different countries, it is the IASC's intention to concentrate on basic standards. It will thus endeavour to confine its standards to essentials, and avoid complexities which would prevent effective worldwide application. There is no intention of overriding local regulations; either these are in harmony with the standards or they are not—in which case the accounts, and the auditor's report, should indicate the fact and extent of divergence.

Like the British/Irish Accounting Standards Steering Committee, the IASC issues *Exposure Drafts* for discussion, leading to the promulgation of *International Accounting Standards*. An Exposure Draft requires the approval of two-thirds of the nine member countries (the British/Irish accountancy profession being taken as one), and an IAS, of three-fourths of them—i.e. of six, and seven, members respectively. The definitive standard is published in English; member bodies are responsible for translations, where appropriate.[3]

The IASC has so far published one International Accounting Standard and two unfinalized Exposure Drafts. The first two items are summarized below, and E3 is dealt with in Chapter 16, section **16.8.**

14.7.1 IASI (1975): Disclosure of accounting policies

This is remarkably similar to the ASSC's SSAP No. 2, but its insight into accounting principles appears deeper. It sets out three 'fundamental accounting assumptions', namely:

    a going concern,

    b consistency, and

    c accrual.

[3]*Commentary on the Statements of International Accounting Standards,* International Accounting Standards Committee, 1974.

It also identifies three 'considerations governing the preparation of financial statements', viz.:

a prudence;

b substance over form (the need to present transactions and events in accordance with their substance and financial reality, and not merely with their legal form); and

c materiality (disclosure of all items material enough to affect evaluations or decisions).

The first four principles are parallel with the 'fundamental accounting concepts' of SSAP No. 2, but greater theoretical correctness is achieved by ranking prudence lower than the other three. Otherwise, IAS1 is on rather similar lines to the British/Irish Statement.

Financial statements should be prepared in conformity with fundamental accounting assumptions, the three set out above being at present so recognized. The three considerations, above, should also govern the preparation of financial statements. These should be prepared on a comparative basis, showing corresponding figures of the previous period. If a fundamental accounting assumption is not followed, that fact, and the reasons, should be disclosed.

Financial statements should include clear and concise disclosure of all significant accounting policies used in their preparation. Such disclosure should be an integral part of the statements, and the policies should normally be disclosed together. However, inappropriate treatment of items in financial statements is not rectified, either by disclosure of accounting policies or by way of explanatory notes. A change in an accounting policy that has a material effect in the current year, or may have one in subsequent years, should be disclosed together with the reasons. The effect of the change in the current year should, if material, be disclosed and quantified.

14.7.2 Exposure Draft 2 (1974): Valuation and presentation of inventories in the context of the historical cost system

E2 deals with ordinary manufacturing and merchanting inventories—raw materials, work in progress, and finished goods—and (unlike the ASSC's SSAP No. 9) excludes consideration of inventories accumulated under long-term construction and similar contracts. The historical cost basis of valuation is assumed throughout, as being the one most generally in use.

The 'Standard Method' of valuation of inventories is the lower of historical cost and net realizable value.

The historical cost of manufactured inventories should be based on absorption costing. Accordingly, it should include an allocation of those fixed production overheads and variable overhead costs that clearly contribute to putting the inventories in their present location and condition. In a period of low production, or with idle plant, allocation of fixed production overheads to conversion costs should be restricted on the basis that the denominator of the fraction used is related to capacity of the facilities and not to actual level of throughput (i.e. there will be under-absorption of overheads in such periods). Costs of exceptional amounts of wasted material, labour, or other expenses should not be included in inventory cost. Non-production overheads should be included only to the extent that they clearly contribute to putting inventories in their present location and condition.

Generally speaking, historical cost of inventories should be accounted for by using the FIFO, or an average cost, formula. Inventories of items not ordinarily interchangeable, or goods manufactured and segregated for specific projects, should be accounted for by using specific identification of their individual costs. The LIFO formula may, however, be used generally, provided there is disclosure of the difference between the balance sheet value of the inventories and their valuation at the lower of prices current at the balance sheet date (i.e. replacement cost) and net realizable value. The related taxation effects should also be disclosed. The base stock, NIFO, and latest purchase price formulae should not be used.

Inventories may be written down to net realizable value item by item, on an inventory class basis, or by class of business, the chosen method being consistently applied; they should not be so written down on an all-inclusive basis. Net realizable value of the quantity of inventory held to satisfy firm sales contracts should be based on the contract price; but if sales contracts are for less than the quantities held, net realizable value for the excess should be based on general market prices.

Techniques such as the standard cost method of valuing products, or the retail method of valuing merchandize (i.e. at selling price less mark-up), may be used for convenience if they approximate consistently the results which would be obtained by using the Standard Method. Normal quantities of raw materials and other supplies held for incorporation in the finished product should not be written down below historical cost if the relevant finished products are expected to be realized at or above historical cost. Nevertheless, a decline in the price of raw materials may indicate that the historical cost of finished products exceeds net realizable value, in which event a write-down of the inventories should be made.

The profit and loss account of the period should be charged with the cost of inventories sold or used (unless allocated to other asset accounts), and with the amount of any write-down below historical cost of inventories on hand at the balance sheet date.

In the balance sheet, or in notes to the financial statements, inventories should be classified in a manner appropriate to the business and so as to indicate the amounts held in each main category. Manufacturing inventories should be sub-classified at least into raw materials, work in progress, and finished goods. If items are shown under 'Inventories', other than goods held for sale in the ordinary course of business, or in process of production for sale, or to be consumed in normal production of goods or services, then their nature, amounts, and basis of valuation should be disclosed. If inventories have been written down below cost to net realizable value, this should be stated; terms such as 'market' and 'book value' are not clear and should not be used.

The accounting policies adopted and cost formula used for inventory valuation should be disclosed with precision and in reasonable detail. A change in such an accounting policy that has a material effect in the current year, or may have one in subsequent years, should be disclosed together with the reasons and quantified. If a practice used in inventory valuation or presentation does not comply with the Standard Method, the practice shall be described and the fact of non-compliance disclosed.

Such is the substance of E2. It follows similar lines regarding manufacturing and merchanting inventories to the British/Irish SSAP No. 9 but, being of international application, has to accommodate practices (such as LIFO valuation) which, although well-established and respectable in, for example, the United States, are here looked at askance by the accountancy profession and the tax laws. There is, however, nothing in E2 which would be infringed by strict application of SSAP No. 9 as it stands.

E3 (1974): *Consolidated financial statements and the equity method of consolidation* is dealt with in Chapter 16, section **16.8**, for reasons sufficiently indicated by the title. Two further drafts (E4 and E5 (1975), appeared too late for inclusion in this edition.

14.8 Auditors' and directors' reports

Included in every set of published accounts are the *auditors' report* and the *directors' report*, documents which are required by the 1948 Act, ss. 156 and 157, as amended by the 1967 Act, s. 24, respectively, to be 'attached to the balance sheet'. The 1967 Act considerably extended or modified the legal obligations as to their contents.

14.8.1 The Auditors' report

All companies are now required to have their accounts audited by independent persons holding accountancy qualifications acceptable to the Department of Trade, or otherwise having satisfied that body that they have acquired adequate skill and experience in the public practice of accountancy. The auditors are appointed by the company in general meeting, and automatically reappointed at each annual general meeting, as long as both they and the company agree, and as long as they remain qualified. The auditors are given valuable safeguards against arbitrary removal for improper reasons (1948, ss. 159 to 161; 1967, s. 13).

The auditors shall make a *report* to the members on the accounts examined by them, and on every balance sheet, profit and loss account, and set of group accounts laid before the company in general meeting during their tenure of office (1967, s. 14(1)). The report shall be read before the company in general meeting, and be open to inspection by any member (s. 14(2)). As already stated, it forms part of the published accounts for all purposes.

The report shall state whether in the auditors' opinion the company's balance sheet and profit and loss account and (where applicable) the group accounts have been properly prepared in accordance with the provisions of the Companies Acts, 1948 and 1967, and whether in their opinion a true and fair view is given:

i in the case of the balance sheet, of the state of the company's affairs as at the end of its financial year;

ii in the case of the profit and loss account (unless framed as a consolidated profit and loss account—see Chapter 16, sub-section **16.4.3**), of the company's profit or loss for the year; and

iii in the case of a holding company's group accounts, of the matters in i and ii relative to the company and its subsidiaries dealt with by the accounts, so far as concerns members of the holding company (s. 14(3)(*a*)).

In the case of a company which claims exemption from disclosing certain information, under Part III of the 1967 Act, Schedule 2 (see section **14.9**), the auditors are required merely to state whether in their opinion the balance sheet, etc., have been properly prepared in accordance with the Acts; nothing is said about a true and fair view (s. 14(3)(*b*)).

The auditors express no opinion on the directors' report, nor have they any statutory duty to validate the information given therein.

14.8.2 The directors' report

Under the 1948 Act, the directors' report was a short, formal document, adding little to the profit and loss account. The 1967 Act made it into an important supplement to the accounts, giving much additional information. The items which it must contain are as follows.

1 A report by the directors with respect to the state of the company's affairs (1948, s. 157(1)).
2 The amount, if any, which they recommend should be paid by way of dividend (*ibid.*).
3 The amount which they propose to carry to reserves (*ibid.*).
4 The names of the persons who, at any time during the financial year, were directors of the company (1967, s. 16(1)).
5 The principal activities of the company and of its subsidiaries (if any) in the course of that year, and any significant changes therein during the year (*ibid.*).
6 Particulars of significant changes during the year in the fixed assets of the company or of any of its subsidiaries (1967, s. 16(1)(*a*)).
7 In the case of fixed assets, as above, consisting of interests in land, an indication, with such degree of precision as is practicable, of any substantial difference between the market value as at the year-end and the balance sheet amount, if the difference is, in the directors' opinion, of such significance as to require that the attention of members or debenture-holders should be drawn to it (*ibid.*).
8 If any shares or debentures have been issued in the year, the reasons for making the issue, the classes of shares or debentures issued, and as respects each class, the number of shares, or amount of debentures, issued, and the consideration received by the company (s. 16(1)(*b*)).
9 As regards any contract with the company, either subsisting at the end of the year or having subsisted during it, in which a director of the company has, or had at any time during the year, in any way, whether directly or indirectly, an interest (the contract being, in the directors' opinion, of significance to the company's business, and one in which the director's interest is or was material):

   i the fact of the contract's subsisting or having subsisted;
   ii the name of the parties (other than the company);
   iii the name of the director (if not a party);
   iv an indication of the nature of the contract; and
   v an indication of the nature of the director's interest in the contract (s. 16(1)(*e*)).

   Particulars are not required, though, in respect of a director's contract of service, or of a contract between the company and another body corporate, in which the director has or had an interest by virtue only of his being a director of that other body (s. 16(3)).
10 As regards any arrangements, to which the company is or was a party, either subsisting at the end of the year or having subsisted during it, the objects of which include the enabling of directors of the company to acquire benefits by means of the acquisition of the shares or debentures of the company *or any other body corporate;* a statement explaining the effect of the arrangements and giving the names of the persons who at any time in the year were directors of the company and held, or whose nominees held, shares or debentures acquired in pursuance of the arrangements (s. 16(1)(*d*)).

11 In respect of each director as at the end of the year, a statement as to whether or not he was, at the year-end, interested in the shares or debentures of the company, or of its holding company, subsidiaries or fellow-subsidiaries, and if he was, of the number and amount of shares or debentures of *each* such body corporate in which he had an interest—with similar particulars of his interests at the beginning of the year, or at the date, if later, when he became a director. The information is to be derived from the statutory register of directors' interests in shares and debentures of the companies in the group, required by the 1967 Act (s.29) (see Chapter 11, sub-section **11.4.1**) (s.16(1)(*e*)). If a person became a director on more than one occasion, his interests shall be dealt with as at the time when he first became a director (s. 16(4).

12 Particulars of any matters, not otherwise required to be disclosed, so far as they are material for the appreciation of the state of the company's affairs by its members, being matters whose disclosure will not, in the directors' opinion, be harmful to the business of the company or of any of its subsidiaries (s. 16(1)(*f*)).

13 If the company is obliged to disclose its turnover or gross receipts for the year (under the 1967 Act, Schedule 2, para. 13A), and has during the year carried on two or more classes of business (other than banking or discounting, etc.) which, in the directors' opinion, differ substantially from each other, a statement of:

   a the proportions in which the turnover for the year, as stated, is divided amongst those classes (describing them); and

   b the extent or approximate extent (expressed in monetary terms) to which, in the directors' opinion, the carrying on of business of each class contributed to, or restricted, the profit or loss of the company for the year before taxation (s. 17(1)).

If the company has subsidiaries at the year-end and prepares group accounts in the form of consolidated accounts (see Chapter 16), similar information shall be given *instead* in respect of the division of *group* turnover, etc., among two or more substantially different classes of business carried on by the company and its subsidiaries covered by the accounts, and of the contribution, etc., of each class of business to the *group* profit or loss for the year before taxation (s. 17(2)).

14 A statement of:

   a the average number of persons employed by the company in each week of the financial year; and

   b the aggregate remuneration paid or payable for the year to the persons mentioned in **a** (s. 18(1)).

If at the end of the year the company has subsidiaries, similar information shall be given *instead* as to the average number of persons employed by the company and its subsidiaries *combined,* and as to the aggregate remuneration of them all (s. 18(2)). The number in **a** is to be computed as the arithmetic mean of the numbers on the payroll at the end of each week of the year for the company, or the company and its subsidiaries combined, as the case may be (s. 18(3)). The aggregate remuneration in **b** is to be the gross remuneration for the year, including bonuses, whether contractual or not (s. 18(4)). Employees working wholly or mainly outside the U.K. are to be disregarded (s. 18(6)).

A company is *exempt* from giving this information if the average number of employees, as computed, is less than 100; or if the company is a wholly-owned subsidiary of a company incorporated in Great Britain (s. 18(5)).

15 If a company has, in a financial year, given money for political or charitable purposes or both, in excess of £50, a statement of the amount of money so given and, in the case of political payments:

a the name of each person to whom money in excess of £50 has been given, and the amount given; and

b the identity of any political party to which more than £50 has been donated or subscribed, and the amount so given (s. 19(1)).

The wholly-owned subsidiary of a company incorporated in Great Britain is *exempt* from giving this information (*ibid.*). If a company (other than a wholly-owned subsidiary) has subsidiaries which have given money as above, similar particulars shall be given in respect of the total amounts given by the company and its subsidiaries, if the total exceeds £50 (s. 19(2)). A company is treated as giving money for political purposes if, directly or indirectly:

a it gives a donation or subscription to a political party of the U.K. or any part thereof; or

b it gives money as aforesaid to a person whose activities, or proposed activities, known to it, can at the time of the payment be reasonably regarded as likely to affect public support for a party as in a (s. 19(3)).

Money given for charitable purposes to a person who was at that time ordinarily resident outside the U.K. shall be disregarded (s. 19(4)).

16 If a company's business consists in, or includes, the supplying of goods, and its turnover (required to be disclosed under the 1967 Act, Schedule 2, para. 13A) exceeds (now) £250,000 for the financial year, a statement of the value of goods exported by the company from the U.K., or a statement that no goods have been so exported (s. 20(1)).

If the company has subsidiaries at the year-end, and the business of any of these companies consists in, or includes, the supplying of goods, and the turnover, as disclosed in the group accounts, exceeds (now) £250,000, a similar statement to the above shall be produced, distinguishing the values of the goods exported by each company in the group (s. 20(2)).

Goods exported by the company as the agent of another person shall be disregarded (s. 20(3)). The information specified above need not be given if the directors satisfy the Department of Trade that it is in the national interest that the information should not be disclosed (s. 20(4)).

Finally, if any item is shown in the directors' report instead of in the accounts (as permitted by the 1948 Act, s. 163) the report shall show also the corresponding amount for the previous year.

14.9 Exemptions from disclosure in special cases

Part III (paras. 23 to 26) of the Companies Act, 1967, Schedule 2, exempts special classes of company from disclosing in their published accounts certain items normally required.

14.9.1 Banking and discount companies

Any company which satisfies the Department of Trade that it ought to be treated as a banking or discount company is entitled to a wide range of exemptions from disclosure (1967 Act, Schedule 2, para. 23(3)). These are allegedly designed to avoid revealing temporarily adverse circumstances (such as falls in the market prices of investments) which might conceivably alarm depositors and lead to panic withdrawals of funds. Today it is unlikely that many depositors are so naive, especially since, beginning with the calendar year 1969, the London clearing banks, and the Bank of England, have agreed to waive all their exemptions and publish full commercial accounts. Other banks, and discount houses, however, still claim the immunities, as follows:

Profit and loss account

The only items which need to be disclosed are:

1 directors' remuneration, analysis of their emoluments, and particulars of waivers;
2 analysis of emoluments of employees over £10,000;
3 auditors' remuneration;
4 rents from land (less outgoings), if material;
5 prior year adjustments (if not included under another heading);
6 dividends paid and proposed; and
7 corresponding amounts of 1 to 6 for the previous year (1967 Act, Schedule 2, para. 23(1)(*b*)).

In addition, the profit and loss account shall indicate by appropriate words the manner in which the stated profit or loss has been arrived at (para. 23(1)). This is normally the net profit or loss after taxation and extraordinary items, and after making undisclosed transfers to and from provisions and reserves. It is thus impossible to discover the genuine profit or loss, or the equity earnings; nor can the earnings per share, or the price/earnings ratio, be computed.

Balance sheet

Here it is more convenient to list the omissions, as compared with normal company accounts. They are:

1 distinction between reserves, provisions and liabilities (except that the share premium account and the capital redemption reserve fund must be shown separately); but any heading stating an amount arrived at after taking into account a reserve or provision shall be so framed or marked as to indicate that fact;
2 movements on reserves and provisions during the year;
3 amount set aside to prevent undue fluctuations in charges for taxation, and movements thereon;
4 particulars of loans not repayable within five years;
5 bank loans and overdrafts;
6 detailed methods of arriving at the amount of fixed assets, including historical cost or valuation, and accumulated depreciation, or provisions for renewals;
7 particulars of fixed asset revaluations;
8 movements on fixed assets during the year;
9 particulars of interests in land;
10 the market value of quoted investments; and
11 detailed particulars of unquoted investments in the equity of other bodies corporate (including directors' valuations) (para. 23(1)(*a*)).

The effect is to make it impossible to discover the book amount of owners' equity, or of net capital employed, or to compute the rate of return on either of these; nor can the values of the fixed assets be appraised in any intelligent fashion.

14.9.2 Insurance companies

These are governed by the *Insurance Companies Act,* 1974, and the provisions of the Companies Acts have little relevance in framing their published accounts. Where an insurance company is entitled to the exemptions stated below, then any wholly-owned subsidiary shall also be so entitled if its business is entirely complementary to insurance business of the classes carried on by the insurance company (para. 24(2)). If, however, an insurance company carries on, to a substantial extent, non-insurance business, the Department of Trade may withdraw or restrict the exemptions (para. 24(1), proviso).

Profit and loss account

This need not disclose:

1 any particulars of charges to revenue by way of provision for depreciation, renewals or diminution in value of fixed assets;
2 charges for hire of plant and machinery;
3 income from investments;
4 rents of land; or
5 transfers to or from provisions or reserves (except reserves for redemption of share or loan capital) (para. 24(1)(*b*)).

The profit and loss account shall indicate by appropriate words the manner in which the stated profit or loss has been arrived at (para. 24(1)).

Balance sheet

This need not disclose:

1 the distinction between reserves, provisions and liabilities (except that the share premium account and the capital redemption reserve fund must be shown separately); but any heading stating an amount arrived at after taking into account a reserve or provision shall be so framed or marked as to indicate that fact;
2 movements on reserves and provisions during the year;
3 the distinction between fixed, current, and other assets;
4 anything of the methods used to arrive at the amount of the physical fixed assets;
5 particulars of fixed asset revaluations;
6 movements on fixed assets during the year;
7 particulars of interests in land;
8 the distinction between quoted and unquoted investments;
9 the market value of quoted investments;
10 detailed particulars of unquoted investments in the equity of other bodies corporate (including directors' valuations);
11 the directors' opinion that any current assets have not a realizable value at least equal to the stated amount;
12 particulars of charges on the company's assets to secure the liabilities of other persons; or
13 the nature and amount of the contingent liabilities (para. 24(1)(*a*)).

14.9.3 Shipping companies

A shipping company is defined as one which, or a subsidiary of which, owns ships or includes among its activities the management or operation of ships; being a company which satisfies the Department of Trade that, in the national interest, it ought to be granted the relevant exemptions from disclosure in its accounts (para. 25(3)).

Profit and loss account

This need not disclose:

1 turnover or gross receipts, or the method by which it is arrived at;
2 any particulars of charges to revenue by way of provision for depreciation, renewals or diminution in value of fixed assets; or
3 transfers to or from provisions or reserves (except reserves for redemption of share or loan capital) (para. 25(1)(*b*)).

Balance sheet

This need not disclose:

1 the distinction between reserves, provisions and liabilities (except that the share premium account and the capital redemption reserve fund must be shown separately);
2 movements on reserves and provisions during the year;
3 detailed methods of arriving at the amount of fixed assets, including historical cost or valuation, and accumulated depreciation, or provisions for renewals;
4 particulars of fixed asset revaluations; or
5 movements on fixed assets during the year (para. 25(1)(*a*)).

These exemptions are intended to strengthen the British shipping industry against unfair competition from foreign shipowners, making use of building or operating subsidies, flag discrimination, flags of convenience, and/or low taxation of profits—none of them available to British owners. By keeping foreign competitors in the dark about gross revenue, cash flow, profits, and financial strength, the British shipowner (it is argued) avoids being placed at a disadvantage in a rate war, intended to drive him off the seas. The Jenkins Committee thought these arguments weak, and recommended withdrawal of the somewhat similar exemptions in the 1948 Act; but Parliament chose instead to modify them.

In relation to *holding companies* entitled to the benefit of any of the foregoing three sets of exemptions, the relevant provisions are extended to the consolidated accounts (para. 26).

As regards the *directors' report,* all three classes of company are exempted from requirements 6 and 7 in sub-section 14.8.2 (1967 Act, s. 16(2)). They are also exempted, by implication, from requirements 13 and 16, since they do not have to disclose their turnover or gross receipts.

14.10 Stock Exchange requirements

The additional requirements of the Federation of Stock Exchanges in Great Britain and Ireland, imposed upon all companies which seek a quotation on any of the member exchanges (including London), are now contained in the *Listing Agreement—Companies,* introduced in June 1972 in place of the old General Agreement, and revised in March 1973. The obligations relative to published accounts are as follows:

1 To notify the Quotations Department (or its provincial equivalent) of an explanation for the delay in any case where no annual report and accounts have been issued by the company within the six months following the year-end, at the same time indicating when publication is expected.

2 To prepare a half-yearly or interim report which must be sent to the investors or inserted as paid advertisements in two leading daily newspapers not later than six months from the date of the notice convening the annual general meeting of the company.

3 To circulate with the annual report of the directors:

a a statement by the directors as to the reasons for adopting an alternative basis of accounting in any case where the auditors have stated that the accounts are not drawn up in accordance with the standard accounting practices approved by the accountancy bodies;

b a geographical analysis of turnover and of contribution to trading results of those trading operations carried on by the company (or group) outside the U.K.;

c the name of the principal country in which each subsidiary operates (see Chapter 16);

d the following particulars regarding each company in which the group interest in the equity capital amounts to 20 per cent or more:

  i the principal country of operation;

  ii particulars of its issued share and loan capital and, except where the group's interest therein is dealt with in the consolidated balance sheet as an associated company, the total amount of its reserves;

  iii the percentage of each class of loan capital attributable to the company's interest (direct or indirect) (see Chapter 16, sub-section 16.2.2);

e a statement as at the end of the financial year showing the interests of each director in the share capital of the company appearing in the register maintained under the provisions of the Companies Act, 1967, distinguishing between beneficial and non-beneficial interests; such statement should include by way of note any change in those interests occurring between the end of the financial year and a date not more than one month prior to the date of the notice of meeting or, if there has been no such change, disclosure of that fact;

f a statement showing particulars as at a date not more than one month prior to the date of the notice of meeting of an interest of any person, other than a director, in any substantial part of the share capital of the company and the amount of the interest in question or, where appropriate, a negative statement;

g i a statement showing whether or not, so far as the directors are aware, the close company provisions of the Income and Corporation Taxes Act, 1970 (and of any amendments thereto) apply to the company and whether there has been any change in that respect since the end of the financial year;

  ii in the case of an investment trust a statement showing the status of the company under the provisions of the Income and Corporation Taxes Act, 1970 and of any amendments thereto (i.e. whether or not the company pays capital gains tax of 30 per cent, instead of full corporation tax on such gains), and of any change in that status since the end of the financial year:

h particulars of any contract subsisting during or at the end of the financial year in which a director of the company is or was materially interested and which is or was significant in relation to the company's business;

i particulars of any arrangement under which a director has waived or agreed to waive any emoluments; and

j particulars of any arrangement under which a shareholder has waived or agreed to waive any dividends.

The minimum information to be contained in the half-yearly or interim report in 2 above is as follows:

1 Company (or group) turnover.
2 Company (or group) profit (or loss) after all charges including taxation.
3 U.K. and, where material, overseas taxation charged in arriving at 2.
4 (Where relevant) amount of 2 attributable to members of holding company, i.e. after deduction of outside interests.
5 If material, extent to which 2 has been affected by special credits (including transfers from reserves) and/or debits.
6 Rates of dividend(s) of (holding) company paid and proposed and amounts absorbed thereby.
7 In respect of any year or other full accounting period, earnings per share expressed as pence per share.
8 Comparative figures of 1 to 7 inclusive for the corresponding previous period.
9 Any supplementary information which, in the opinion of the directors, is necessary for a reasonable appreciation of the results of the year or of other material changes in the aggregate of the balances on profit and loss account and other reserves (of the group).

14.11 European Economic Community: proposed Fourth Directive of the Council (1974)

Since entering the European Economic Community on 1 January 1973 the United Kingdom and the Republic of Ireland have been subject to the *Directives* of the Council of the EEC, as drafted by the EEC Commission in Brussels. These Directives, having been ratified by the Council, are notified to the governments of the nine Member States, which must within 18 months incorporate them in their own legal systems, and within 30 months bring them into force in their own countries. Thus the European Communities Act, 1972, was passed to incorporate in our law the Directives then in force; but it had no bearing upon published company accounts.

Now, the proposed *Fourth Directive* provides for co-ordination of national legislation regarding the annual accounts of limited liability companies. Since the entry of the U.K., Ireland and Denmark the draft has been considerably revised, and the latest version appeared in February 1974. The revision bears many marks of British/Irish influence, with its emphasis upon meaningful disclosure to investors, the presentation of a 'true and fair view'—a phrase now incorporated in the draft— and the need for consolidated accounts in groups of companies. Despite this, however, the fundamental concepts are still those of Continental accounting, seen primarily as a source of micro-economic data for administrative purposes, rather than as information for investors in particular firms; hence the final Directive is unlikely to please professional opinion in the British Isles.

A detailed discussion of the proposed Fourth Directive is impracticable here on grounds of length. The main objectives are to impose a standard form of balance sheet and profit and loss account upon all companies in the EEC, and to lay down rules for determining the figures to be presented. Two alternative layouts are shown, for both balance sheet and profit and loss account, and companies are to be free to choose one or the other; both are far more minutely analytical than any normal British set of accounts, and would be hard to fit into the present scheme of the Companies Acts. (It has even been suggested that a British company might have to publish two sets of accounts, to meet British *and* EEC requirements; and the Institute of Chartered Accountants in England and Wales has published (July 1974) its own alternative layout.) Some relaxations, however, are proposed for companies whose balance sheet totals do not exceed 1,000,000 units of account (i.e. U.S. dollars).

The imposition by Directive of rules as to accounting *methods* is, to the Anglo-Irish world, fraught with even graver objections. As will be clear to any reader thus far, there is no general agreement even as to the objectives of published accounts, still less as to the best ways of producing and presenting the information in them. If this is true of one country, and legal system, how much greater are the problems across nine countries! In fact, the rules in the proposed Fourth Directive are largely those of conventional historical-cost accounting, though replacement-cost methods are permitted as an alternative—doubtless as a concession to the Dutch. British/Irish influence is also evident, as in the requirement to use absorption cost as the basis of valuing industrial inventories. Even so, there are rules which seem eccentric or arbitrary, such as the injunction to write off company formation expenses in a maximum of five years (why?). As a means of raising standards in countries (such as Italy) where the accountancy profession is underdeveloped, the Directive would be of some value; but in the U.K. or Ireland the imposition of accounting rules by the fiat of bureaucrats trained in a quite different, and more authoritarian, tradition would mean not progress, but regress. It is fervently to be hoped that the EEC Commission will study the question further before making final recommendations to the Council.

14.12 Specimen published company accounts

Below are the complete published accounts of an imaginary company without subsidiaries or associates, but with overseas investments. The modern single-sided form has been adopted throughout, and extensive use made of supporting notes, properly 'keyed' to the items in the accounts themselves, where applicable. The latest requirements of the Federated Stock Exchanges are also complied with, as well as those of Standard Accounting Practices Nos. 2 to 9, and the recommendations of Exposure Drafts 11, and 13 to 15. Regard is also paid to the IASC's IAS1 and E2.

Modern Motor Supplies Ltd

Profit and Loss Account for the 52 weeks ended 26 July 1975

	52 weeks ended 26 July 1975		52 weeks ended 27 July 1974	
	£000	£000	£000	£000
Turnover (see Note 1)		10,000		9,200
Net trading profit (see Note 2)		1,000		900
after charging the items below—				
Directors' remuneration (see Notes 3 and 4)	52		81	
Auditors' fees and expenses	3		3	
Hire of plant and machinery	30		27	
Depreciation of fixed assets and amortization of intangibles (see Note 15)	630		410	
Provision for loss through insolvency of major customer (see Note 6)	200		—	
Income from investments				
From quoted securities	31		40	
From unquoted securities (see Note 19)	32		28	
		63		68
Rents receivable from land (net of outgoings)		20		10
Net profit before interest, taxation and extraordinary items		1,083		978
Interest payable				
On bank overdraft	2		6	
On debentures wholly repayable after 31 July 1979 (see Note 13)	68		70	
		70		76
Net profit before taxation and extraordinary items		1,013		902
Taxation based on the profits for the current accounting period				
United Kingdom corporation tax on income at 52 per cent (including £250,000 (1973/74, £200,000) transferred to deferred taxation account)	500		440	
Less relief for overseas taxation	60		50	
	440		390	
Overseas taxation	65		53	
Tax credit on United Kingdom dividends received	10		13	
	515		456	
Less Adjustment of United Kingdom corporation tax charge for the previous year	20		10	
		495		446

Net profit after taxation and before extraordinary items		518		456
Extraordinary items (adjusted for taxation in respect thereof)—				
Profit on sale of quoted investments held as fixed assets		30		—
Compensation payable for infringement of patent (see Note 7)		(24)		—
Loss on devaluation of Ruritanian dinar		—		(7)
Net profit for the accounting period		524		449
Unappropriated profit brought forward from the previous accounting period		172		16
Amount available for appropriation		696		465
Transfers to reserves (see Note 12)—				
10 per cent (now 7 per cent plus tax credit) redeemable cumulative preference shares redemption reserve	35		33	
General reserve	250		200	
		285		233
		411		232
Dividends, paid and proposed (see Note 8)—				
Preference	35		35	
Ordinary	308		140	
		343		175
Unappropriated profits		68		57
Effect of a change in the basis of valuation of work in progress and finished goods stocks as at 27 July 1974 (see Note 9)		—		115
Unappropriated profits carried forward to the next accounting period		68		172
Basic earnings per ordinary share of 25p (see Note 10)		5.6p		6.1p
Fully-diluted earnings per ordinary share of 25p (see note 11)		3.9p		

Modern Motor Supplies Ltd

Balance Sheet as at 26 July 1975

Net funds employed by the Company	26 July 1975 £000	£000	27 July 1974 £000	£000
Authorized share capital				
500,000 10 per cent (now 7 per cent plus tax credit) redeemable cumulative preference shares of £1 each	500		500	
12,000,000 ordinary shares of 25p each	3,000		3,000	
	3,500		3,500	
Issued share capital				
10,400,000 (27 July 1974, 4,000,000) ordinary shares of 25p each, fully paid		2,600		1,000
Reserves (see Note 12)				
Share premium account	—		150	
Fixed assets revaluation reserve	—		120	
10 per cent (now 7 per cent plus tax credit) redeemable cumulative preference shares redemption reserve	335		300	
General reserve	214		300	
Profit and loss account (unappropriated profits)	68		172	
		617		1,042
Total equity shareholders' funds		3,217		2,042
Issued preference share capital				
500,000 10 per cent (now 7 per cent plus tax credit) redeemable cumulative preference shares of £1 each, fully paid (see Note 13)		500		500
Total shareholders' funds		3,717		2,542
Loan capital				
9,000 (27 July 1974, 10,000) 7 per cent convertible debentures of £100 each (see Note 14)	900		1,000	
Less Discount thereon, less amounts written off	10		14	
		890		986
Deferred taxation (see Note 15)				
Amount set aside to prevent undue fluctuations in taxation charges		596		250
Liabilities for taxation levied on the current period's profits				
United Kingdom corporation tax	39		236	
Overseas taxation	65		53	
		104		289
		5,307		4,067

Net assets in which the Company's funds are invested	26 July 1975 £000	£000	27 July 1974 £000	£000
Fixed assets (see Notes 16 and 17)				
Freehold land	500		400	
Freehold buildings	500		125	
Leasehold land and buildings (see Note 18)	300		320	
Plant, fixtures, vehicles, loose tools and office equipment	1,500		800	
		2,800		1,645
Goodwill, patents and trade marks		100		110
		2,900		1,755
Long-term investments, at cost				
In quoted securities	300		350	
(market value £350,000; at 27 July 1974. £600,000)				
In unquoted securities (see Note 19)	200		200	
		500		550
Current assets (see Note 20)				
Inventory (see Note 2)—				
Raw materials and bought out parts	372		347	
Work in progress	619		565	
Finished goods	1,094		948	
	2,085		1,860	
Loans to officers of the company (see Note 21)	10		8	
Accounts receivable, less provisions for bad and doubtful debts, for discounts, and for loss through insolvency of a major customer (see Note 5), and prepaid expenditure	1,507		1,600	
Bills of exchange receivable, less provision for discounts	200		170	
Bank balances and cash in hand	226		5	
	4,028		3,643	
Less Current Liabilities				
Bank overdraft	—		156	
Accounts payable and accrued expenditure	1,541		1,362	
Bills of exchange payable	50		40	
United Kingdom corporation tax for the previous period	216		200	
Proposed dividend on ordinary share capital (see Note 8)	208		70	
Advance corporation tax on proposed dividend	112		52	
	2,127		1,880	
Net Current assets		1,901		1,763
Share and debenture issue expenses, less amounts written off		2		1
Difference on conversion to sterling of amounts in foreign currency (see Note 22)		4		(2)
		5,307		4,067

Signed: William Crankcase, Chairman
S.G. Piston, Managing Director.

Modern Motor Supplies Ltd

Summary of Results and Financial Position Adjusted for the Effects of Inflation (see Note A)

	Historical basis		Current purchasing power basis	
	52 weeks ended 27 July 1974 £000 £000	52 weeks ended 26 July 1975 £000 £000	52 weeks ended 26 July 1975 £000 £000	52 weeks ended 27 July 1974 £000 £000
Results for Accounting Period				
Turnover	9,200	10,000	11,300	12,740
Net profit before taxation and extraordinary items (see Note B)	902	1,013	1,068	1,185
Taxation	446	495	495	558
Net profit after taxation and before extraordinary items	456	518	573	627
Extraordinary items (adjusted for taxation)	(7)	6	7	(10)
Net profit for accounting period	449	524	580	617
Dividends	175	343	358	228
Retained profit for accounting period	274	181	222	389
Financial Position at End of Accounting Period				
Net current assets	1,763	1,901	1,942	2,250
Long-term investments	550	500	743	800
Fixed assets less depreciation	1,755	2,900	3,540	3,270
	4,068	5,301	6,225	6,320
Less Preference share capital	500	500	500	625
Loan capital	1,000	900	900	1,250
Deferred taxation	250	596	744	400
Current taxation	289	104	104	361
	2,039	2,100	2,248	2,636
Total equity interest	2,029	3,201	3,977	3,684
Ratios				
Basic earnings per share (p) (based on 8,556,790 (1974, 6,913,580) ordinary shares of 25p in issue during period	6.1	5.6	6.3	8.4
Dividend cover (times)	2.8	1.6	1.7	6.1
Return on total equity interest (%)	20.4	15.3	13.7	15.5
Net assets per share (p) (based on 10,400,000 (1974, 6,913,580) ordinary shares of 25p (or equivalent) in issue at end of period	29.3	30.8	38.2	53.3

Notes

A The figures in the current purchasing power basis columns were arrived at by converting the corresponding figures in the historical basis columns by reference to the changes in a general price index between the dates of the original transactions and

26 July 1975. The current purchasing power basis figures for both this and last accounting periods are measured in pounds of purchasing power at 26 July 1975. The general price index used was that specified in Provisional Statement of Standard Accounting Practice No. 7. The Retail Price Index at 26 July 1975 was 137.1 and at 27 July 1974 was 109.7. Both figures are based on January 1974 = 100.

As the Inland Revenue do not at present accept CPP basis accounting, taxation liabilities are calculated by reference to profits on the historical basis and no adjustment therefore is made to the tax charge in the CPP basis column.

B *Net profit before taxation and extraordinary items*
How the difference between profit on a historical basis and on a current purchasing power basis is made up.

	52 weeks ended 26 July 1975		52 weeks ended 27 July 1974	
	£000	£000	£000	£000
Net Profit Before Taxation and Extraordinary Items (historical basis	1,013		902	
Adjustment to convert to current purchasing power basis:				
Stocks and Work in Progress Additional charge based on restating the cost of stocks and work in progress at the beginning and end of the accounting period in pounds of current purchasing power, thus taking the inflationary element out of the profit on the sale of stocks	(429)		(238)	
Depreciation and Amortization Additional depreciation, etc., based on cost, measured in pounds of current purchasing power, of fixed and intangible assets	(109)		(60)	
Monetary Items Net gain in purchasing power resulting from the effects of inflation on the Company's net monetary liabilities and preference share capital	409		236	
Sales, Purchases and All Other Costs These are increased by the change in the index between the average date at which they occurred and the end of the accounting period. This adjustment increases profit as sales exceed the costs included in this heading	184		108	
		55		46
Net Profit Before Taxation and Extraordinary Items (current purchaisng power basis at end of accounting period under review)	1,068		948	
Adjustment required to update last period's profit from pounds of 27 July 1974 purchaisng power to pounds of 26 July 1975 purchasing power	–		237	
Net Profit Before Taxation and Extraordinary Items (current purchasing power basis at 26 July 1975)	1,068		1,185	

C The loan capital and preference share capital at 28 July 1974 amounted to £1,500,000. £1,500,000 at 28 July 1974 is equivalent in purchasing power to £1,875,000 at 26 July 1975 (because) inflation has been 25.0 per cent during the period). As the Company's liability to the providers of loan capital, and the nominal value of the preference shares, are fixed in money terms this liability, and nominal value, have declined during the period in real terms from £1,875,000 to £1,400,000 (after allowing for conversions of £100,000 of debentures into ordinary shares during the period). On this basis there has been a reduction of £363,000 in the Company's obligations in terms of current purchasing power, and this is included in the net gain on monetary items of £409,000 shown in Note B.

Modern Motor Supplies Ltd

Statement of Source and Application of Funds for the 52 weeks ended 26 July 1975

	52 weeks ended 26 July 1975 £000	£000	52 weeks ended 27 July 1974 £000	£000
Source of Funds				
Net profit after taxation and extraordinary items		524		449
Adjustment for items not involving the movement of funds—				
Depreciation and amortization of fixed and intangible assets	630		410	
Discount on debentures written off	4		3	
Profit on disposal of fixed assets	(10)		(4)	
Profit on sale of long-term investments	(30)		—	
Increase (Decrease) in taxation liabilities—				
Deferred (on profits only)	190		200	
Current	(185)	599	40	649
Total generated from operations		1,123		1,098
Funds from other sources				
Issue of ordinary shares for cash—				
Nominal value	500		—	
Premium	250		—	
	750		—	
Issue of ordinary shares on converstion of 7 per cent debentures—				
Nominal value	60		—	
Premium	40		—	
	850		—	
Proceeds of sale of long-term investments	80		—	
		930		—
		2,053		1,098
Application of Funds				
Dividends paid and proposed		343		175
Redemption of 7 per cent debentures, by conversion into ordinary shares		100		—
Purchases of fixed assets	1,500		520	
Less Proceeds of sale	35		24	
		1,465		496
Increase in stocks and work in progress		225		104
Increase (Decrease) in receivables and sundries		(84)		40
Decrease (Increase) in payables		(393)		(80)
		1,656		735
Movement in Net Liquid Funds				
Increase in bank and cash balances	377		353	
Increase in bills receivable, less payable	20		10	
		397		363

Notes on the accounts

1 Turnover

This is defined, for both accounting periods, as total sales to external customers before charging purchase tax, and net of goods returned to the Company and allowances to customers.

2 Net trading profit: accounting policies followed in computing this amount

Certain major accounting items, entering into the computation of the net trading profit, are susceptible of different modes of calculation which, while not affecting the total profit or loss of the Company in the long run, may make an appreciable difference to the allocation of profit or loss to particular accounting years, and to the values placed upon the assets and/or liabilities as at the ends of such years. In relation to such matters the Company has during the 52 weeks ended 26 July 1975 followed the accounting policies outlined below and, except where otherwise indicated, the same policies were followed in the 52 weeks ended 27 July 1974.

a *Valuation of stocks and work in progress*

Raw materials and bought-out parts have been charged to production, and the year-end stocks valued at cost, on the 'first in, first out' (FIFO) basis, in which it is assumed that materials enter into production in the same order as that in which they were delivered.

Work in progress and finished goods have been similarly valued on the FIFO basis as regards cost, but reduced to net realizable value where lower than cost for any item. Up to and including the 52 weeks ended 27 July 1974, work in progress and finished goods were valued on the basis of raw material and direct labour cost only, but as from 28 July 1974, cost has included an allowance for manufacturing overheads, on the basis of normal levels of operation (see also Note 8).

b *Repairs and renewals*

All items of expenditure on fixed assets, up to £50, are written off to revenue. Items over £50 are either written off or capitalized, according to their nature.

c *Depreciation of fixed assets*

All tangible fixed assets, except freehold land, are depreciated on the 'straight line' basis (by equal annual instalments of cost or later valuation), at rates designed to amortize the cost (or later valuation) over the estimated working lives of the assets, assumed as follows:

Freehold buildings	30 years
Leasehold land and buildings	15 to 25 years
Plant, fixtures, vehicles, loose tools and office equipment	1 to 10 years

d *Treatment of intangible assets*

Research and development expenditure is written off against revenue in the year in which it is incurred. Expenditure on patents is amortized by equal instalments over 16 years, or the shorter remaining life of purchased patents; purchased goodwill and trade marks are not amortized, unless it is considered that their value has declined.

3 Directors' remuneration

This is analysed as follows:

	52 weeks ended 26 July 1975 £	52 weeks ended 27 July 1974 £
a Directors' emoluments for current services to the Company (including the Company's contributions to their superannuation scheme, and benefits in kind):		
i for services as directors;	5,000	4,000
ii for services in a managerial, executive or technological capacity	47,000	39,000
	£52,000	£43,000
b Director's compensation for loss of office:		
i for services as a director;	—	8,000
ii for services in a managerial capacity	—	30,000
	—	£38,000
Total remuneration	£52,000	£81,000

The whole of the compensation for loss of office was paid by the Company.

4 Directors' emoluments

For this purpose the emoluments exclude the Company's contributions to superannuation schemes for the Directors, all of whom discharged their duties wholly or mainly within the United Kingdom.

	52 weeks ended 26 July 1975	52 weeks ended 27 July 1974
The emoluments of the Chairman (Sir William Crankcase) were	£12,500	£10,000
The emoluments of the highest paid director were	£15,000	£12,000
The numbers of directors (including the above) whose emoluments fell into the under-mentioned categories were—		
Not over £2,500	—	—
Over £2,500 but not over £5,000	—	—
Over £5,000 but not over £7,500	1	1
Over £7,500 but not over £10,000	2	2
Over £10,000 but not over £12,500	1	1
Over £12,500 but not over £15,000	1	—
	5	4

No Directors have waived, or agreed to waive, their rights to any emoluments in either of the accounting periods.

5 Employees' emoluments over £10,000

The emoluments (defined as in Note 3) of Employees (other than Directors) who worked wholly or mainly within the United Kingdom and earned over £10,000, fell into the under-mentioned category:

	52 weeks ended 26 July 1975	52 weeks ended 27 July 1974
Over £10,000 but not over £12,500	4	2

6 Provision for loss through insolvency of major customer

This refers to the whole amount receivable from Bowles Boyes Ltd as at 23 June 1975, the date of that company's liquidation. The amount of the provision has been deducted in computing the total of Accounts Receivable, etc., in the Balance Sheet.

7 Compensation payable for infringement of patent

In May 1975, the Company agreed with Ovoid Ball Bearings Ltd to pay the latter company compensation for infringement of one of its patents, as from 1 April 1972. £50,000 has accordingly been paid to Ovoid Ball Bearings Ltd in respect of infringements occurring between 1 April 1969 and 26 July 1975. Corporation tax at 52 per cent (£26,000) has been deducted, leaving £24,000.

The dispute with Ovoid Ball Bearings Ltd was noted among the contingent liabilities as at 27 July 1974, but no provision was made in respect of it (see Note 23).

8 Dividends, paid and proposed

These have been computed as follows:

	52 weeks ended 26 July 1975		52 weeks ended 27 July 1974	
	per cent	£	per cent	£
Redeemable cumulative preference shares of £1 each, fully paid				
Paid during period (half-yearly on 1 January and 1 July)	7.0	35,000	7.0	35,000
Ordinary shares of 25p each, fully paid				
Interim dividend paid during period on 4,000,000 shares (nominal value £1,000,000) in issue throughout both periods	10.0	100,000	7.0	70,000
Final dividend proposed on 10,400,000 shares (nominal value £2,600,000) (at 27 July 1974, 4,000,000 shares, nominal value £1,000,000) in issue at end of period	8.0	208,000	7.0	70,000
		£308,000		£140,000

No shareholder has waived, or agreed to waive, any dividends.

9 Effect of a change in the basis of valuation of work in progress and finished goods stocks as at 27 July 1974

As from 27 July 1974 the method of computing the cost of Work in Progress and Stocks of Finished Goods was changed from the prime cost basis (in which no allowance is included for overhead expenses incurred in manufacturing) to the absorption cost basis (in which such an allowance is included). It is estimated that if this change had not been made, the net trading profit would have been greater by £80,000, and that, after deducting corporation tax at 52 per cent (£41,600), the net profit after taxation would have been greater by £38,400.

No adjustment has been made to the corresponding figures in the Profit and Loss Account for the 52 weeks ended 27 July 1974, but it is estimated that on the new basis the total stocks at that date would have been increased to £1,860,000. The amount of the increase, £240,000, has therefore been added to the opening balance of the Profit and Loss Account for the 52 weeks ended 26 July 1975, and the corresponding figure of stocks has been adjusted in the Balance Sheet as at that date.

10 Basic Earnings per ordinary share of 25p

The basic earnings per ordinary share of 25p are calculated on earnings of £483,000 (52 weeks ended 27 July 1974, £421,000), and on the weighted average (adjusted for the rights issue, debenture conversion, and bonus issue, of which details are given in the Directors' Report at paragraph 6) of 8,556,790 shares ranking for dividend during the 52 weeks ended 26 July 1975 (52 weeks ended 27 July 1974, adjusted as above, 6,913,580 shares).

Earnings of £483,000 are computed on the net basis, after charging taxation as determined by the actual distributions to ordinary shareholders during the period. On the nil basis (as though the distributions were nil) the taxation charge, and the earnings, would be unaltered.

11 Fully-diluted earnings per ordinary share of 25p

The fully-diluted earnings per ordinary share of 25p are based on adjusted earnings of £516,000 after adding back interest (net of corporation tax) on the 7 per cent Convertible Debentures. £100,000 of these were converted on 1 May 1975 into 2,400,000 new Ordinary Shares of 25p, leaving £900,000 of the Debentures outstanding. The maximum number of shares into which the remaining Debentures are convertible as at 1 May 1976 is 3,000,000, making a total of 13,400,000 Ordinary Shares issued and issuable as at 26 July 1975.

12 Reserves and movements thereon

Movements on the reserves during the 52 weeks ended 26 July 1975 were as follows:

	Share Premium account £000	Fixed assets revaluation reserve £000	10 per cent (now 7 per cent plus tax credit) redeemable cumulative preference shares redemption reserve £000	General reserve £000	Profit and loss account £000
s at 27 July 1974	150	120	300	300	172
etained earnings (net)	–	–	–	–	181
ights issue of ordinary shares	250	–	–	–	–
onversion of 7 per cent debentures into ordinary shares	40	–	–	–	–
evaluation of fixed assets (*less* deferred corporation tax)	–	300	–	–	–
	–	(156)	–	–	–
ransfers from profit and loss account	–	–	35	250	(285)
onus issue of ordinary shares	(440)	(264)	–	(336)	–
s at 26 July 1975	–	–	335	214	68

13 10 per cent (now 7 per cent plus tax credit) redeemable cumulative preference shares

These must be redeemed by the Company between 1 January 1977 and 31 December 1979 (both dates inclusive) at a premium of 2 per cent.

14 7 per cent convertible debentures

These were issued at £98 per £100 nominal on 1 May 1972 and, if not converted as described below, are to be redeemed at par on 1 May 1982. They are secured by a floating charge on the general assets of the Company.

Each £100 Debenture is convertible, at the option of the holder, into Ordinary Shares of the Company of 25p each, fully paid, on the following terms (subject to proportionate adjustment for any bonus issue made subsequent to the issue of the debentures):

On conversion at 1 May 1975–240 shares (now, 400)
On conversion at 1 May 1976–200 shares (now, 333-1/3)
On conversion at 1 May 1977–160 shares (now, 266-2/3)
On conversion at 1 May 1978–120 shares (now, 200)
On conversion at 1 May 1979–100 shares (now, 166-2/3)

Debentures to a nominal, and book, value of £20,000 were held, at 26 July 1975 (27 July 1974, £20,000), by the Trustees of the Company's Superannuation Fund.

15 Deferred taxation

This represents Corporation Tax deferred to later years:
a by the application of capital allowances in excess of depreciation charged in the accounts—the deferred tax becoming payable in later years when capital allowances on the relevant fixed assets fall below depreciation charged in the accounts; and
b by the upward revaluation of fixed assets, at whose disposal tax is expected to be payable on capital gains then arising.

Advance corporation tax provided for on the proposed dividend at the end of the accounting period is offset against deferred taxation in respect of **a** above; when the ACT is paid the amount thereof is transferred from corporation tax (for the accounting period when payment occurs) to deferred taxation, thus cancelling the previous offset.

16 Valuation of fixed assets, and movements thereon

Movements on the Fixed Assets (other than Investments) during the 52 weeks ended 26 July 1975 were as follows:

	As at 27 July 1974 £000	Revaluation during period £000	Acquisitions during period at cost £000	Disposals during period at cost or valuation £000	As at 26 July 1975 £000
Cost or valuation					
Freehold land	400	—	100	—	500
Freehold buildings	350	—	400	—	750
Leasehold land and buildings	400	—	—	—	400
Plant, fixtures, vehicles, loose tools and office equipment	1,500	550	1,000	(50)	3,000
	2,650	550	1,500	(50)	4,650

	As at 26 July 1975 £000	Revaluations during period £000	Depreciation provided during period £000	Depreciation eliminated during period £000	As at 26 July 1974 £000
Accumulated depreciation					
Freehold land	—	—	—	—	—
Freehold buildings	225	—	25	—	250
Leasehold land and buildings	80	—	20	—	100
Plant, fixtures, vehicles, loose tools and office equipment	700	250	575	(25)	1,500
	1,005	250	620	(25)	1,850

	As at 27 July 1974 £000	Acquisitions during period at cost £000	Disposals during period at cost £000	Amount written off during period £000	As at 26 July 1975 £000
Cost less amounts written off					
Goodwill, patents and trade marks	110	—	—	10	100

17 Revaluations of fixed assets

Details of revaluations of existing Fixed Assets are as follows:

As at 1 August 1971:	Freehold land valued at	£250,000
	Freehold buildings	£150,000
As at 28 July 1974:	Plant, fixtures, vehicles, loose tools and office equipment valued at	£1,100,000

The valuation of Plant, etc., in the current accounting period was made by professional valuers, assisted by the Chief Accountant and Chief Engineer of the Company, and was based on current replacement prices, less an allowance for depreciation to date.

18 Leasehold land and buildings

The leases concerned had all less than 50 years to run, as at 26 July 1975, and the position was similar as at 27 July 1974.

19 Long-term investments—unquoted securities

These are all investments in the equity share capital of other bodies corporate, in no case amounting to more than 10 per cent of the issued share capital, of any class, of the other body concerned. Particulars of these Investments are as follows:

	52 weeks ended 26 July 1975 £000	52 weeks ended 27 July 1974 £000
Aggregate amount of the company's income ascribable to the said investments	32	28
Amount of the company's share of the aggregate profits (less losses) of the bodies concerned, for the several periods covered by their accounts, as sent to the company during the accounting period—		
Before taxation	107	100
After taxation	63	60
Amount of the company's share of the aggregate undistributed profits (less losses) accumulated by the bodies concerned since acquisition of the investments	128	97

No provision for losses incurred by the said bodies corporate has been made at any time in the Company's accounts.

20 Current assets

In the opinion of the Directors, none of the current assets has a value, on realization in the ordinary course of business, less than the amount stated in the Balance Sheet.

21 Loans to officers of the company

Movements on these during the 52 weeks ended 26 July 1975 were as follows:

	£000
Loans outstanding at 27 July 1974	8
Less: Repayments during the 52 weeks ended 26 July 1975	2
	6
Advances during the above period	4
Loans outstanding at 26 July 1975	10

22 Difference on conversion to sterling of amounts in foreign currency

Amounts in the books of overseas branches have been covered to sterling on the following bases:

a fixed assets and depreciation thereon—at rates of exchange ruling when the assets were acquired;

b current assets and liabilities—at the rates of exchange ruling on the last day of the accounting period; and

c remittances—at the net amounts realized in sterling.

23 Contingent liabilities

The estimated amounts of contingent liabilities, not provided for in the Accounts, were:

	26 July 1975 £000	27 July 1974 £000
In respect of dispute with Ovoid Ball Bearings Ltd, over alleged infringement of one of their patents (see Note 7)	–	45
As drawer or indorser of bills of exchange receivable discounted during the accounting period, but not yet due at the end thereof	30	26
In respect of costs of an action pending against a newspaper company for libel on this company	10	–
	40	71

24 Capital expenditure commitments

The estimated amounts of commitments to capital expenditure, not provided for in the Accounts, were:

	26 July 1975 £000	27 July 1974 £000
Amount of contracts placed for capital expenditure	475	110
Amount of capital expenditure authorized by the directors but not yet contracted for	25	35

Report of the auditors to the members of Modern Motor Supplies Ltd

In our opinion, the Accounts set out on pages 00 to 00 give a true and fair view of the state of the Company's affairs at 26 July 1975 and of the profit for the 52 weeks ended on that date and comply with the Companies Acts, 1948 and 1967, and with all the requirements and recommendations of the Accounting Standards Steering Committee as at the date of preparation of the Accounts.

Signed: CHECK, VOUCH & VERIFY
Chartered Accountants,
10 December 1975.

Report of the directors to the members of Modern Motor Supplies Ltd

The Board of Directors hereby presents its report on the affairs of the Company for the 52 weeks ended 26 July 1975.

1 The Company's principal activities are the manufacture of motor vehicle components, spares, and accessories, and their sale to motor vehicle manufacturers and others at home and overseas.

In September 1974 the Company acquired a chain of shops in the North of England, dealing in motor and pedal cycles, accessories therefor, and allied goods, manufactured by the Company and others.

2 The principal change in the fixed assets of the Company during the period, apart from the purchase of the shops mentioned in paragraph 1, was the completion and bringing into production of the new factory at Coketown.

3 The Directors are of the opinion, based on advice from professional valuers, that the market value of the Company's interests in land, both freehold and leasehold, exceeds the total of the amounts stated in the Balance Sheet by at least £300,000, and that sale of the properties at such prices would attract an additional liability for corporation tax, amounting to at least £156,000.

4 The different classes of business carried on by the Company, the proportions in which the Company's turnover for the 52 weeks ended 26 July 1975 was divided amongst them, and the extent to which they contributed to the Company's profit before taxation, were as follows:

	Proportions of turnover £000	Per cent	Contributions to net profit before taxation £000
Sales of motor vehicle components, spares, and accessories:			
To U.K. motor vehicle manufacturers	6,289	62.9	684
To U.K. wholesalers and retailers	1,986	19.9	379
To overseas customers	1,200	12.0	125
Operation of chain of motor cycle and pedal cycle and accessories shops	525	5.3	60
	10,000		1,248
Less Expenses not allocable to particular activities			235
Net profit before taxation and extraordinary items			1,013

5 The Company's total exports from the United Kingdom during the 52 weeks ended 26 July 1975 were £129,000.

6 The following securities were issued by the Company during the 52 weeks ended 26 July 1975, for the consideration, and for the reasons, stated:

31 January 1975: 2,000,000 Ordinary Shares of 25p each, fully paid. Rights issue for cash, of one share for each two held, at 37½p per share (market price immediately prior to issue, 42p per share). To finance building of new factory, and for additional working capital.

1 May 1975: 240,000 Ordinary Shares of 25p each, fully paid. Conversion of £100,000 of 7 per cent Convertible Debentures at the rate of 240 shares per £100 nominal of debentures.

26 July 1975: 4,160,000 Ordinary Shares of 25p each, fully paid. Bonus issue of two shares for each three held. To capitalize certain reserves, as stated in Note 12 on the Accounts.

7 The Board of Directors recommend the declaration at the Annual General Meeting of the Company on Thursday, 8 January 1976, of the following dividends for the 52 weeks ended 26 July 1975:

On the 500,000 10% (now 7% plus tax credit) Redeemable Cumulative Preference Shares of £1 each, fully paid: 7 per cent, or £35,000, of which 3½%, or £17,500, was paid on 1 January 1975, and 3½ per cent, or £17,500, on 1 July 1975.

On the 4,000,000 Ordinary Shares of 25p each, fully paid, in issue at 12 January 1975: 10 per cent (2½p per share), or £100,000, paid on that date as an interim dividend.

On the 10,400,000 Ordinary Shares of 25p each, fully paid, in issue at 26 July 1975: 8 per cent (2p per share), or £208,000, as a final dividend.

8 The Board of Directors propose to carry the following amounts to reserves:

	£000
To 10% (now 7% plus tax credit) redeemable cumulative preference share redemption reserve	35
To general reserves	250
To profit and loss account—unappropriated for the 52 weeks ended 26 July 1975	68
	353

9 The following amounts have been donated or subscribed by the Company during the 52 weeks ended 26 July 1975:

	£
For charitable purposes	1,000
For political purposes	420
Payments in excess of £50 for political purposes were made to:	
The Conservative and Unionist Party of Great Britain	200
Coketown Conservative and Unionist Association	100

10 The average number of persons employed by the Company as at the end of each of the 52 weeks ended 26 July 1975 (excluding persons working wholly or mainly outside the U.K.) was 1,711.

The aggregate remuneration of those persons for the 52 weeks ended 26 July 1975 was £4,792,000.

11 The names of the Directors of the Company during the 52 weeks ended 26 July 1975, and the securities of the Company in which they, or their wives, or their children under 18, were in any way interested, were as follows:

	Interests as at 27 July 1974, or later appointment to board		Interests as at 26 July 1975	
	Beneficial	Other	Beneficial	Other
Sir William Crankcase (Chairman)—				
10% (now 7% + tax credit) redeemable cumulative preference shares of £1 each, fully paid	50,000 shares £50,000	10,000 shares £10,000	50,000 shares £50,000	10,000 shares £10,000
Ordinary shares of 25p each, fully paid	100,000 shares £25,000	20,000 shares £5,000	300,000 shares £75,000	60,000 shares £15,000
7 per cent convertible debentures	£50,000	—	—	—
Mr S. C. Piston (Managing Director)—				
Ordinary shares of 25p each, fully paid	50,000 shares £12,500	5,000 shares £1,250	125,000 shares £31,250	10,000 shares £2,500
7 per cent convertible debentures	£10,000	—	£10,000	—
Mr L. M. Bearing (Director)—				
Ordinary shares of 25p each, fully paid	20,000 shares £5,000	—	50,000 shares £12,500	—
Mr T. B. Gasket (Director)—				
Ordinary shares of 25p each, fully paid	10,000 shares £2,500	—	25,000 shares £6,250	—
Mr R. J. Tappet (Director from 1 January 1975)—				
Ordinary shares of 25p each, fully paid	1,000 shares £250	—	2,500 shares £625	—

No changes in the above particulars occurred between 26 July and 30 November 975.

12 The names of persons, other than Directors, who held substantial interests (i.e. 10 per cent or more) in any class of the Company's issued share capital, and the amounts of those interests, as at 26 July 1975 were as follows:

	Interests	
	Beneficial	*Other*
Surefire Insurance Company Ltd		
10% (now 7% plus tax credit) redeemable cumulative preference shares of £1 each, fully paid	100,000 shares £100,000	–
Ordinary shares of 25p each, fully paid	1,250,000 shares £312,500	–
Messrs B. Careful and L. K. Out (Trustees of the Estate of T. N. Flywheel, deceased)—		
Ordinary shares of 25p each, fully paid		1,500,000 shares £375,000

13 Sir William Crankcase and Mr S. C. Piston, being respectively Chairman and Managing Director of the Company, have an interest in a contract made on 30 June 1975, between the Company and the Foursquare Construction Company Ltd, for the erection of a new warehouse for the Company at Bruddersford, in that they each hold substantial numbers of ordinary shares in the Foursquare Construction Company Ltd.

14 There were no arrangements in force during the 52 weeks ended 26 July 1975, whereby the Directors of the Company, or any of them, were enabled to acquire benefits by means of the acquisition of shares or debentures in the Company or in any other body corporate.

15 So far as the Directors are aware, the close company provisions of the Income and Corporation Taxes Act, 1970 (and of any amendments thereto) do not apply to the Company for the 52 weeks ended 26 July 1975, and have not become applicable to it at any time since that date.

16 There are no matters, not otherwise disclosed, which in the opinion of the Directors are material for the appreciation by the members of the state of the Company's affairs.

By order of the Board
W. R. Camshaft.

14.12.1 Computation of earnings per share

In the accounts of Modern Motor Supplies Ltd, the *basic earnings per ordinary share of 25p* (BEPS) are computed as follows:

	52 weeks ended 26 July 1975 £000	*53 weeks ended 27 July 1974 £000*
Net Equity Earnings		
Net profit after taxation and before extraordinary items	518	456
Less Preference dividend	35	35
	483	421

Equivalent number of ordinary shares

This takes into account, for the current period:

a the total shares in issue at 27 July 1974, adjusted for the bonus element in the rights issue of 31 January 1975;
b the rights issue as aforesaid–i.e. 6 months after the beginning of the period;
c the debenture conversion of 1 May 1975–i.e. 9 months after the beginning of the period–treated as a new issue at the full market price, on the assumption that the past proceeds of the debenture issue represented the 'going rate' for the terms offered; and
d the two-for-three bonus issue of 26 July 1975–i.e. the last day of the period–in the light of which the previous figures are all adjusted by the factor 5/3.

A one-for-two rights issue at a price of 37½p, with a cum-rights price, immediately beforehand, of 42p, gives a theoretical ex-rights price of:

$$\{(2 \times 42p) + (1 \times 37\frac{1}{2}p)\}/3 = 40\frac{1}{2}p$$

and the factor (Cum-rights price/Ex-rights price) becomes 42/40½. The computation proceeds (see sub-section **14.6.2**):

			Shares
a	4,000,000 × 6/12 × 42/40½	=	2,074,074
b	6,000,000 × 3/12	=	1,500,000
c	6,240,000 × 3/12	=	1,560,000
			5,134,074
d	Equivalent number of ordinary shares = 5,134,074 × 5/3	=	8,556,790

Basic earnings per ordinary share of 25p

This is NEE/ENS = £483,000/8,556,790 = 5.6p

For the 52 weeks ended 27 July 1974 the original **BEPS** was £421,000/4,000,000 = 10.5p. For a true comparison with the current period, this must be adjusted, both for the rights issue and the later bonus issue, thus:

$$BEPS = 10.5p \times 40\frac{1}{2}/42 \times 3/5 = 6.1p$$

(In the accounts, the denominator is adjusted: 4,000,000 × 42/40½ × 5/3 = 6,913,580 shares).

The fully-diluted earnings per ordinary share of 25p (FDEPS) apply to the current period only. The figure is computed on the assumption that all the convertible debentures outstanding at the end of the period (here, £900,000) had been converted, at the *beginning* of the period, at the *highest* rate still available after the *end* of it (here, 333-1/3–originally 200–shares per £100 nominal of debentures). This gives a maximum addition to ordinary share capital of 3,000,000 shares of 25p. This, being added to the *actual* number of shares in issue at 26 July 1975 (10,400,000), gives a total of 13,400,000 shares issued and issuable.

The net equity earnings for the current period are also adjusted on the assumption that all the debentures were converted at the beginning of the period—by adding back the debenture interest notionally saved, less an allowance for the resulting increase in the amount of corporation tax payable. Thus, in the case supposed:

	£000	£000
Net Equity Earnings		
As previously computed		483
Add Debenture interest	68	
Less Corporation tax thereon (52 per cent)	35	
	—	33
		516

Thus—
FDEPS = £516,000/13,400,000 = 3.9p

15

Accounting for business combinations

Thus far, company accounting has been considered in relation to single enterprises. It is now necessary to examine the methods used to account for combinations of two or more businesses under common control.

15.1 Motives for combination of businesses

In modern times the rapid growth of many organizations, from modest firms of mainly local importance to gigantic, nationally-known corporations whose assets total tens, or hundreds, of millions of pounds and whose annual profits reach seven or eight figures, has been one of the most significant of economic phenomena. Some of this growth has resulted from expansion of the original businesses; but much more has been due to the acquisition of existing enterprises as going concerns, followed by reorganization, rationalization, and (if the directors' judgement was sound) increased profitability.

The haphazard acquisition of unrelated businesses is not calculated to improve the return on the acquiring company's capital employed, or equity capital. The combination of two or more firms, whatever legal and financial machinery is utilized, must above all make business sense, in the context of some consistent policy for long-term development, designed to strengthen the group's competitive power and enable it to evolve to meet the challenges of a swiftly changing environment. The possible strategies are many, and some discussion of them is desirable before considering their implications for financial accounts.

15.1.1 Vertical integration

One approach to the problem of enlarging the undertaking is *vertical integration* —the acquisition of a manufacturing company's main supplier(s) (backward integration), or of its main customer(s) (forward integration), or both. The effect, in the first case, is to gain control of the supply of raw materials, bought-out parts and/or fuel to the main business, to organize their delivery to it with more assurance, and to deny them to competitors—especially where materials or fuel are bulky in relation to their market value (and thus need to be drawn from a source fairly near at hand, if transport costs are to be kept down), or when purchased parts are highly specialized. In the second, the company's main wholesale and/or retail outlets are taken over, so that its products are more aggressively sold to retailers or consumers, and competing products excluded while complementary ones may be retained. In either case the profits made by the formerly independent suppliers or customers are (hopefully) captured by the manufacturer, and increased by rationalization, including the elimination of unnecessary variety of products.

The main difficulties of vertical integration lie in the need to manage businesses of a different nature from the original one. Linked with them is the problem of finding objective measures of efficiency and profitability for companies supplying goods within the group, where transfer prices are necessarily artificial, and of providing incentives to their managements to improve their performance in the absence of market competition. The determination of transfer prices has already been discussed in Chapter 8, sub-section **8.4.2**, in relation to divisional accounting, and the arguments apply whether the divisions are or are not separate legal entities. Whatever solution is adopted, it is clear that profits and return on capital make little sense in relation to any constituent company, but only as regards the whole group; transfer prices, and internal profits, being significant mainly in setting objectives for divisional managements, against which their performance can be measured.

15.1.2 Horizontal integration

A strategy more favoured in the retail trades is *horizontal integration*—the acquisition of businesses of a similar nature, with the objects of enlarging the scale of one's own operations, and (in many cases) of transcending its current geographical limitations. The obvious example is that of a multiple shop company which buys a chain of stores in a different area from that of the original chain, and thus not directly competitive with it.

In manufacturing, horizontal integration often takes the form of acquiring businesses whose products are complementary to those of the first one, or which compete with it in several lines—one company having an advantage in some lines, and the other in others. It is then possible to rationalize production, each company concentrating on the products which it is best equipped to make, and both reaping the benefits of economies of scale and of longer runs. Alternatively, makes of product which are directly competitive may be brought within the same group, thus increasing monopolistic power and allowing of economies in marketing effort, in eliminating competition among selling agents, and so on—as in the British motor industry. It is also possible for a retail group, where supplying manufacturers are relatively small, numerous and ill-organized, to offer them such advantages by the growth of its market demand that it is able to dictate prices and product specifications—as, notably, in the case of Marks & Spencer Ltd., which does no manufacturing but induces several hundred garment makers, legally independent, to sink their identities in its 'St Michael' brand name.

Enlargement of an undertaking in this manner brings increased problems of co-ordination and product planning, as well as the traumas of employee redundancy in the earlier stages. Accounting difficulties are less, in theory, than with vertical integration, since all prices are external, and fixed by market competition or the exertion of monopolistic (or monopsonic) power. Problems of control, however, are if any greater as regards both supervision to prevent waste, inefficiency, and dishonesty, and managerial control to secure consistency and coherence in business policy and rational utilization of resources. These are primarily matters for the management accountant; but the financial accountant, as such, is concerned with the calculations which lead up to the decision to acquire a new subsidiary whose business is competitive with or complementary to that of the parent.

15.1.3 Diversification

Lastly, a company may adopt a policy of *diversification* into fields of enterprise whose connection with the existing business is more or less tenuous. Usually the motive is to spread risks rather than invest shareholders' funds entirely in a single industry—particularly one which is stagnating or declining through foreign competition, loss of markets, or product obsolescence. The tendency is then to acquire businesses of a type allied to the original one—e.g. a motor-cycle manufacturer may take over firms making motor-car components—so that much of the technical and managerial know-how obtained in the first industry can be utilized in the second. It is more hazardous to seek entry into a new and growing industry with little or no connection with the original trade—e.g. to diversify out of household electrical appliances into computers. A policy of taking control of any and every company which promises an above-average return on the investment—producing a *conglomerate* group, generally dominated by one class of firm—is more questionable still, since it can lead to serious fragmentation of managerial effort, grave errors of judgement through lack of knowledge in certain fields, and heavy losses through reluctance to discard subsidiaries which turn out to be unprofitable, or incompatible with the rest of the group. There is a danger, too, especially in groups dominated by one man of strong personality, of megalomania and financial gigantism, often ending in major disaster and the break-up of the organization.

The above three approaches to combination—vertical and horizontal integration, and diversification—may in practice be used concurrently in the same group, in various proportions. The financial accountant, however, is more immediately concerned with the legal forms employed, and with the terms on which an acquisition is effected.

15.2 Forms of business combination

There are essentially two forms of business combination, as regards the relationship between the undertakings concerned—absorption and amalgamation; and this holds true, whether or not the businesses, or either of them, lose their separate legal identities. There are likewise two methods of satisfying the consideration for either an absorption or an amalgamation—by cash payment, or an issue of debt capital or preference shares, on the one hand, and by an issue of equity shares, on the other.

15.2.1 Absorption

When a relatively small undertaking is acquired by a much larger organization, so that the original proprietors are displaced, or compensated by a small share in the enlarged equity, there is said to be *absorption* of the smaller firm by the larger. In simple cases, such as the purchase of a single shop by a chain store company, the absorbed business is bought outright, for cash, debentures and/or shares. The old firm goes out of existence (particularly if it is unincorporated), and its assets are added to those of the main company. As a rule, in order to save stamp duty on the contract of sale, only the physical assets—land and buildings, plant, fixtures, etc., and stocks—are taken over. The vendors are left with the cash; they collect the moneys owing by debtors and pay off the creditors; then they wind up the firm and share out the final cash balance, and the securities, if any, issued by the purchasing company.

In the vendor's books, the entities are similar to those set out in Chapter 10, section **10.5** for dissolution of a partnership—a Realization Account being debited with the book values of the assets disposed of, credited with the amount of the sale consideration, and adjusted for any losses or gains on collection of book debts and payment of creditors; after which the net book gain or loss is transferred to the partners' capital accounts in profit-sharing ratio, If the consideration consists wholly or partly of debentures or shares they should be brought in at market value, known or estimated.

In the acquiring company's books, if the absorbed business is purchased for cash, the amount is credited to Bank and debited to the asset accounts affected. The acquired assets are valued, normally, at current replacement price less an allowance for depreciation to date—the so-called 'then value'—or at market price (estimated) in the case of freehold land. If, as is usual, the total imputed value of the physical assets amounts to less than the purchase consideration, the excess is deemed to be the cost of the *goodwill* acquired (see Chapter 6, sub-section **6.4.2**), and this sum is debited to a new, or existing, Goodwill Account, thus completing the double entry.

Where the consideration is wholly or partly satisfied by the issue of debentures, these should be taken at middle market price (the best estimate of the value of the consideration), where they are uniform with existing quoted debentures; otherwise at an estimate of the market value, based on the present value of future interest payments and payments for redemption of capital, discounted at the average rate of return on similar debentures. In the company's books the nominal value of the debentures will be credited to the appropriate account and the excess thereof over the market, or 'surrogate market', price debited to debenture account.

Where shares (preference or ordinary) are employed, the middle market price, or some substitute where the shares are unquoted, is again the significant value—the nominal amount being credited to the share capital account, and the difference between it and the market value credited to share premium account. The underlying assumption is, that the issue involves no dilution of future earnings, and therefore will have no tendency to lower the market price of all shares of the class concerned. This assumption may prove right or wrong in the event; at the time it is the only rational one, provided that the acquisition price is based on a genuine pre-estimate of future incremental earnings from the acquisition (see section **15.3**).

Example 1 Northern Groceries Ltd purchases the undertaking of Brown & Johnson, grocers (exclusive of their cash, debtors, and creditors) on 1 January 19.1, in return for the issue to them of 20,000 ordinary shares of 50p each (market price on 1 January 19.1, 93–97p), and £5,000 nominal of 9 per cent debentures (market price at 1 January 19.1, 92–93p), and the payment of £3,000 in cash. The tangible assets acquired are valued as follows: leasehold shop, £10,000; fixtures, £2,000; motor vans, £3,000, and stocks, £5,000. The relevant journal entry is:

		Dr. £	Cr. £
Jan 1	Leasehold land and buildings	10,000	
	Fixtures	2,000	
	Motor vehicles	3,000	
	Stocks	5,000	
	Discount on 9 per cent debentures	375	
	Goodwill	6,625	
	Ordinary share capital		10,000
	Share premium account		9,000
	9 per cent debentures		5,000
	Bank		3,000
		£27,000	£27,000

Acquisition of business of M/s Brown & Johnson, for consideration of 20,000 Ordinary shares of 50p each, fully paid, at a price of 95p; £5,000 of 9 per cent debentures at a price of 92½; and £3,000 in cash—a total of £26,625 for tangible assets valued at £20,000 and Goodwill £6,625.

Where both businesses concerned are limited companies, and the smaller one is of appreciable size, the latter usually retains its separate identity as the other's *subsidiary*. The larger company may acquire all its ordinary shares, or merely a majority of them—thus gaining control through holding a majority of votes at general meetings, and being able to appoint and remove directors at will. The *holding company* then has the absolute disposition of the subsidiary's assets (subject to the claims of creditors), and runs its business as part of its own organization, without much reference to the wishes of the minority shareholders (if any). They are mere providers of additional equity capital, entitled to a proportionate share in the earnings and to the same rates of dividend as are paid to the holding company, but disfranchised and powerless. If the holding company owns 75 per cent or more of the equity it is, as a rule, completely dominant, since it is able to guarantee the passing of extraordinary or special resolutions, and thus to alter the articles of association, or even put the subsidiary into voluntary liquidation, if its directors think fit. In a vertically-integrated group, or otherwise where one company sells goods to the other, transfer prices may be deliberately manipulated so as to increase the profits of the holding company or its wholly-owned subsidiaries at the expense of those of partly-owned ones, and thus perpetrate what amounts to legalized fraud upon the minority shareholders. The Companies Act, 1948, s. 210, contains provisions designed to combat this and other forms of 'oppression', but they have not proved very effective to date.

Acquisition of another company is generally followed by reorganization of the business in general, and of the higher management in particular—the holding company turning out all or most of the old directors and replacing them with members of its own board, and/or promotees from the ranks of its senior executives. Control is thus further cemented and common policies enforced throughout the group. The device of a holding company and subsidiaries is eminently adapted to the operation of a decentralized managerial structure, where each subsidiary can reasonably be treated as a managerial unit and the whole group becomes a financial unit of more nearly optimal size, able to raise capital on better terms than any of the constituent companies could do in isolation.

Acquisition of a subsidiary involves, from an accounting point of view, the taking on to the holding company's books of a block of the subsidiary's shares, valued in the first instance at cost. The methods for determining this, whether the purchase consideration consists of cash, debentures, shares, or any combination of these, do not differ in principle from those which apply to an outright purchase of a business, as explained above. In all cases the subsidiary's shares are valued at the amount imputed to the consideration which, in the case of the holding company's debentures or shares, is the current market value, with the resulting discount or premium allowed for in the books. No entries at all are made in the subsidiary's books of account in respect of the actual acquisition, but it is the practice to make a general revaluation of its assets, adjusting the physical ones to replacement price (with allowance for depreciation to date, where applicable) or realizable value (of land), and (sometimes) writing the value of goodwill up or down by such sum as is needed to bring the book amount of the equity of ordinary shareholders to the value placed on the subsidiary's shares in the holding company's books—or, where the whole of the ordinary shares are not acquired, to the value which would have resulted if they had been. Such a procedure is now recommended by the Accounting Standards Steering Committe (see Chapter 16, sub-section **16.4.2**).

Example 2 Achilles Motors Ltd acquires 80 per cent of the 200,000 £1 ordinary shares of Patroclus Engineering Ltd., for a consideration of three £1 ordinary shares in Achilles for every four in Patroclus. At the date of acquisition (1 July 19.1) the price of the Achilles shares stood at £2.18–£2.22. Patroclus's reserves, as at 30 June 19.1, totalled £50,000, but a revaluation of its tangible assets as at 1 July 19.1 increased their book amounts by a total of £35,000 net.

Achilles issues 120,000 new £1 ordinary shares in exchange for 160,000 £1 ordinary shares in Patroclus. These are valued in Achilles's books at (120,000 x £2.20 =) £264,000; £120,000 is credited to Ordinary Share Capital and £144,000 to Share Premium Account.

On this basis, the market value of Patroclus's total share capital is (£264,000 x 200,000/160,000 =) £330,000, and its equity should be revalued to this amount; i.e. the reserves should become £130,000. Revaluation of tangible assets having increased the reserves to £285,000, the goodwill should be valued at £45,000 (or any existing balance on Goodwill Account increased by as much), in order to bring the reserves up to £130,000.

15.2.2 Amalgamation

When two or more businesses, not greatly disparate in size, agree to merge their identities in a new and larger undertaking, then *amalgamation* occurs. In the case of limited companies there are two possible procedures. One is to form a new company, and sell to it the entire undertakings of the old ones, which receive shares in the new one as the whole of the purchase consideration, since the new company has nothing else to give, at that stage. The shares are then distributed among the shareholders of the old companies, which go into liquidation and cease to exist.

This method is really appropriate only if the companies are relatively small and simply organized. When large and complex groups of companies decide to join forces, on a footing of something like equality and with no partner clearly dominant over the other(s), it is more usual to form a new company as above, but to make it a holding company for the merging companies (or the parent companies of the merging groups), which continue in existence as its immediate subsidiaries.

There is no obvious difference in the eyes of the shareholders concerned—in either case they surrender their shares in the old companies and receive in exchange shares in the new one. The difference lies in the fact that in a simple merger the new company directly owns the assets of the old businesses, but in an exchange-of-shares merger it acquires only their shares, and treats the old companies as subsidiaries.

The accounting for an amalgamation does not differ in principle from that employed in a simple absorption, by either of the corresponding methods, and the book entries are the same, except that three or more companies are involved instead of two. Whichever amalgamation procedure is used, the assets should be revalued as at the date of the merger, since there has been a major change in the ownership of the equity and a major reorganization of the underlying businesses. The real difficulties, as in the case of absorption, arise in determining the consideration, and these are now examined.

15.3 Financial aspects of combination

Nothing has been said so far of the process by which the amount of cash, or number of debentures or shares, offered in exchange for another company's undertaking or shares is arrived at; in the illustrations figures have simply been assumed, and the accounts balanced by bringing in residual goodwill. In practice, of course, businessmen do not just 'think of a number', but bargain hard and carefully, with the aid of merchant bankers, accountants, lawyers and other experts on both sides. A bid is made for the shares of another company; it is considered insufficient by the directors, who advise their shareholders to reject it. A higher offer is then made and considered by the company's directors—and the process continues until it is thought that no better terms are likely to be forthcoming, and the biddee's directors either break off negotiations or advise acceptance, which usually follows. In a prospective amalgamation the haggling is fiercer still, between the boards of the companies concerned, before they can thrash out a plan, which then needs to be submitted for acceptance to all their members, who must, as a rule, approve it by a three-fourths majority in value in each company.

15.3.1 Terms of an acquisition

The actual terms on which the shares of the biddee are acquired result from the bargaining process. There are, however, certain lower and upper limits between which the final price can normally be expected to settle.

The absolute rock-bottom price from which bargaining for an acquisition can commence is the current market price of the biddee's shares—as it stands if cash is offered, or relative to the market price of the bidder's debentures or shares, if these are offered in exchange. In practice, though, bidding commences at a price, or its equivalent, some 20 per cent higher than the theoretical minimum, in order to arouse some interest on the biddee's shareholders' part.

Example 3 National Ltd makes an offer for the 500,000 £1 ordinary shares of Provincial Ltd, at a time when National's 2,000,000 £1 ordinary shares stand at a middle market price of £2.50 and Provincial's £1 ordinary shares at £1.50. National will normally begin by offering, say, £1.80 per Provincial share in cash, or 18 National shares for 25 Provincial ones (both are worth £45, or £1.80

per Provincial), or some mixture of equivalent total value. (The theoretical minimum offer is £1.50 per Provincial share, or three Nationals for five Provincials, both being worth £7.50.)

The (unrevealed) maximum offer, below which the bidder must, if its directors are rational men, keep its actual bids, is the level at which, in their judgement, the probable rate of return on the investment in the biddee becomes unacceptably low. The upper limit of a cash offer is, theoretically, that at which

$$C_0 = \sum_{j=1}^{t} [D_j/(1+r)^j] + Vt/(1+r)^t$$

where
C_0 = cost of shares in subsidiary at end of year 0;
D_j = maximum possible dividend at end of any year j;
V_t = value of subsidiary's shares at the end of year t;
t = number of years over which it is considered realistic to make a projection; and
r = company's annual cost of capital (per cent/100).

That is, the maximum offer is the price equal to the present value of the expected maximum dividends per share up to a chosen 'time-horizon', plus the expected value of each share in the subsidiary at that horizon, discounted at the company's cost of capital (cf. Chapter 6). The calculation follows the same lines where an offer of debentures is to be made; C_0 then becomes the present value of the relevant interest payments (adjusted for corporation tax savings) and terminal redemption payment of the debentures, discounted at the cost of capital.

In both cases the company commits itself to pay out cash, in a single sum or in a stream of payments over time, and this cash must have an actual cost (if it is to be raised from outside the company, now or later) or an opportunity cost (if it is available within the business, but must be diverted from other profitable investment opportunities). In fact, the actual cost is the significant one, since, even if the money is on hand now, use of it for acquisition of another company will increase the *eventual* demand for outside finance. Hence the cost of capital (a rather nebulous concept, as Chapter 6 explains) is the correct discounting rate to be applied to the expected stream of cash receipts from the acquisition, assuming that the new subsidiary were to distribute all its earnings after retaining enough to provide for replacement of capital assets at current prices—i.e. its earnings after providing realistic rates of depreciation based on replacement costs. If the present value of this hypothetical stream of dividends, plus that of the estimated market value of the investment at the end of the forecasting period, is greater than the present value of the cash invested or financial obligations assumed by a debenture issue, then in accordance with discounted cash flow analysis the investment is probably profitable, as tending to increase the earnings per share of the existing equity shareholders. Bidding for another company's shares should not, therefore, be allowed to rise to a level where there is much danger of an inadequate rate of return, and therefore of a dilution of existing equity earnings per share, if the forecast earnings of the biddee (after reorganization by the bidder's directors) are found to have been even moderately overestimated.

Where the bid takes the form of an exchange of shares, the theoretical maximum offer is that at which the accession of distributable earnings from the subsidiary is precisely balanced by the dilution of the *combined* distributable earnings, resulting from the issue of additional shares in exchange for those of the subsidiary. The distributable earnings of both companies must be forecast for a reasonable number of years, the terminal market value of the shares estimated (as a surrogate for more extended earnings forecasts), and the two streams discounted at the holding company's cost of capital. The resulting present values are then compared, and the ratio which the present value of the subsidiary's total equity bears to that of the holding company denotes the maximum extent to which the latter's issued ordinary share capital may be expanded without diluting its expected earnings per existing ordinary share.

   Example 4 In the circumstances of Example 3, National Ltd, whose cost of capital is estimated at 15 per cent per annum, forecasts its own distributable earnings for the next five years, and the terminal market value of its equity, as

Year	1	2	3	4	5
£	340,000	380,000	400,000	400,000	420,000 + 6,300,000

The corresponding figures, as computed by National Ltd for Provincial Ltd, on the assumption that the latter is reorganized by the former, are:

Year	1	2	3	4	5
£	50,000	70,000	80,000	90,000	100,000 + 1,500,000

The present values of the two streams, discounted at 15 per cent per annum, are: National, £4,415,724; Provincial, £995,951. The theoretical maximum number of ordinary shares which National can issue without dilution of the combined earnings per share is

$$2,000,000 \times 995,951/4,415,724 = 451,093$$

and the best offer to Provincial's existing shareholders is therefore 451,093 National shares for 500,000 Provincial ones, or (say) nine Nationals for ten Provincials.

15.3.2 Terms of a merger

All true mergers of two or more companies involve, directly or indirectly, the exchange of the new company's shares for those held by shareholders in the old companies. What matters most, however, is not the actual number of shares issued to each set of old shareholders, but the relative proportions in which the various groups participate in the equity of the merged businesses.

  To begin with, projections need to be made of future distributable earnings of each constituent company for a period of years, and of the market value of its equity at the end thereof, on the assumption that no merger takes place. The projected figures are then discounted at each company's cost of capital to give the present value of each earnings-stream. A similar projection is then made of the distributable earnings, etc., of the new undertaking, on the assumption that the merger does take place, and this earnings-stream is discounted at the expected cost of capital of the new company or, if this cannot be agreed, at (say) the weighted average cost of capital of the existing companies. The second figure should be appreciably larger than the total of the other figures, or there is no point in proceeding with the merger; but the question then arises as to the most equitable distribution of the expected surplus among the shareholders of the various constituent companies, by way of the allocation of shares in the new one.

At a minimum, each board will insist on having at least as many shares as will give its company a proportion of the estimated present value of the new undertaking's earnings, numerically equal to the estimated present value of the company's earnings if there is no amalgamation. Beyond that, relative bargaining power, and relative anxiety for the merger, will determine the actual division of the new shares between the companies. Apart from this, the scheme most likely to be approved by the shareholders of all companies is one which allocates new shares in proportion to the present value of the old companies' expected earnings—which will usually mean different rates of exchange between new and old shares.

Example 5 North Ltd, Midland Ltd, and South Ltd agree to merge by forming a common holding company, England Ltd, as on 1 January 19.1. Their equity capital consists respectively of 500,000, 300,000, and 200,000 £1 ordinary shares. The present values of their forecast future distributable earnings are respectively (in round figures) £1,000,000, £750,000, and £250,000, and the corresponding estimate for England Ltd is £3,000,000.

The present values of the unmerged companies' earnings are in the proportions 0.5 : 0.375 : 0.125. If each company is to obtain earnings from the merger equal to those expected from continuing the existing arrangements, then North will require a minimum of £1,000,000, or 0.333 of £3,000,000, and Midland and South will need at least £750,000 (0.25), and £250,000 (0.083). Beyond that the position is open, but if it is agreed to allocate England's shares proportionately to present values of earnings, and to fix its initial capital at 12,000,000 ordinary shares of 25p each, or £3,000,000 nominal (equal to the present value of earnings); then North's shareholders will receive 6,000,000 new shares for 500,000 old ones (or 12 for 1), Midland's, 4,500,000 for 300,000 (15 for 1), and South's, 1,500,000 for 200,000 (7½ for 1). In drawing up the opening balance sheet of England Ltd, physical assets will be revalued and goodwill brought in to make up the net assets to £3,000,000.

These figures are artifically simple, and the arithmetic would seldom be so convenient. Even so, it helps in practice to round off the present value estimates to, at least, the nearest £1,000, since the last three digits are hardly significant. Opportunity may also be taken, as in the example, to issue new shares of smaller denomination than the old, so as to make them 'lighter' for dealing purposes, and to create more of them, thus simplifying the numbers in the exchanges, and avoiding fractions if possible; if not, holdings will have to be rounded off to the nearest whole share.

15.3.3 Miscellaneous points on combinations

The techniques of forecasting future distributable earnings are more complex than the illustrations imply, and some of the difficulties have been dealt with in Chapter 6. In particular, projections need to be made of turnover, variable, and fixed costs, capital expenditure, and taxation rates. A view must also be taken on future rates of price inflation, and how to allow for them; and Bayesian methods are utilized to adjust for uncertainty in the estimates.

The orthodox limits of a take-over bid may be exceeded if there is competitive bidding for the same company's shares by two rival groups. Each may be more eager to secure a strategic advantage over the other than to obtain directly a realistic rate of return on the investment, and one may end by paying a quite 'fancy' price for its new subsidiary. Again, a group which is short of liquid funds may issue shares to acquire a company which, though of mediocre profitability, has excess cash which may then be lent to other companies in the group—at low, or even nil, rates of interest. Sometimes, too, the real object of a take-over is to gain control of valuable properties which are under-utilized by the present owners and undervalued in their books, and sell them at a handsome profit ('asset stripping'). This type of deal, though, is harder to achieve now than in former years, when managements were less financially sophisticated; the normal reaction of the biddee's directors today would be to have the assets revalued, and advise their members to reject a bid which plainly looked like an attempt to acquire the properties below their market value—however generous the offer might seem in relation to the current price of the biddee's shares.

15.4 Take-over bids

It remains to discuss the legal and institutional constraints upon the making of offers by a company to acquire all, or a controlling holding, of the voting shares of another company, such offers being commonly known as *take-over bids*. Proposals for a merger of two or more companies by the creation of a new company, made jointly by the boards of the merging companies, are also covered, subject to suitable modifications of the general rules.

15.4.1 Legal restrictions on the making of offers

The Companies Act, 1967, says nothing about take-overs or mergers as such, and the 1948 Act contains only two or three special sets of rules, to be discussed in due course. In law anyone, company or individual, is at liberty to make an offer to acquire a company's shares, or any of them, on such lawful terms as the present holders may be induced to accept. In public companies, though, this involves at some stage the circularization of shareholders with the terms of the offer, and this is governed: **i** by the *Prevention of Fraud (Investments) Act*, 1958; and **ii** by the voluntary, but powerfully supported, *City Code on Take-overs and Mergers*, dating in its present form from 1974.

S. 14 of the Prevention of Fraud (Investments) Act, 1958, confines to specified classes of persons the right to distribute circulars containing offers (by anyone) to sell or purchase securities, not being prospectuses within the meaning of the Companies Act, 1948. Take-over circulars thus fall within the ambit of the 1958 Act. The classes of person permitted to distribute such circulars are the classes permitted to deal in securities under the Act, and these include, in particular:

a members of recognized stock exchanges;
b 'exempted' dealers in securities (i.e. bankers, discount houses, issuing and other financial houses, who deal in securities only as a sideline, and in all cases operate through stockbrokers);
c recognized associations of dealers; and
d 'licensed' dealers in securities (i.e. small brokers, not members of **c** above—a very small class).

Other persons may distribute take-over circulars only with express permission of the Department of Trade.

Thus, while the Companies Act, 1948, allows anyone to distribute a prospectus offering newly-issued shares for subscription, but rigorously specifies the minimum information to be given by it, with severe penalties for making false or misleading statements; the Prevention of Fraud (Investments) Act, 1958, prefers to limit the right to distribute take-over circulars, without specifying the information to be given in them. Circulars issued by licensed dealers are, however, governed as to terms by the *Licensed Dealers (Conduct of Business) Rules, 1960,* made by the (then) Board of Trade under powers conferred by s. 7 of the 1958 Act. Despite their restricted application, these rules were generally followed voluntarily by the stock exchanges, and by other dealers in securities.[1]

The Jenkins Report (1962) recommended that the Board of Trade be given regulatory powers, under a new Companies Act, to protect offeree shareholders. The 1967 Act contained no such provisions, in part because, following a number of widely publicized scandals, the financial community of the City of London had already signified its desire to set up machinery of its own, more flexible and more swift in operation than any statutory authority was likely to be, and thus calculated to be more effective in preventing or minimizing loss to investors through unfair or unethical practices, and in penalizing those who engage in them.

15.4.2 The City Code on Take-overs and Mergers

In 1967 the Governor of the Bank of England reconvened the City Working Party, a voluntary body representative of the main financial institutions including the Stock Exchange, to draw up the City Code on Take-overs and Mergers. The same institutions, at the same time, set up a Panel on Take-overs and Mergers to enforce the Code. The first version was issued in 1968, but was found to lack adequate 'teeth'; its main sanction, suspension of dealings in an offeree's securities, proved too blunt an instrument. An amended Code was therefore issued in 1969, and was found to work quite well. A third edition came out in 1972, a fourth in 1974; the following exposition is based on the latter.

The 1974 Code consists of 12 *General Principles* and 39 *Rules*. It is impracticable to summarize them directly without substantially repeating them, and the reader is strongly recommended to obtain a copy.[2] General Principle 1 is, however, worth quoting in full:

It is considered to be impracticable to devise rules in such detail as to cover all the various circumstances which arise in take-over or merger transactions. **Accordingly, persons engaged in such transactions should be aware that the spirit as well as the precise wording of these General Principles and of the ensuing Rules must be observed.** Moreover, it must be accepted that the General Principles and the spirit of the Code will apply in areas or circumstances not explicitly covered by any Rule.

The main objects of both Principles and Rules are apparently to ensure that:

i an offer for the whole, or a controlling amount, of a company's capital is made through the proper channels;

ii the offeree's shareholders are given the fullest and most reliable information without delay;

iii the shareholders are given adequate opportunity to make up their minds whether or not to accept the offer;

[1] See: Briston, R. J. *The Stock Exchange and Investment Analysis,* George Allen & Unwin, 2nd edition, 1973.

[2] *The City Code on Take-overs and Mergers,* obtainable from The Secretary, Issuing Houses Association, Roman Wall House, 1-2 Crutched Friars, London EC3N 2NJ.

iv all shareholders of a class are treated equally and fairly;

v no false market in the shares of either offeree or offeror (if a company) is created, nor any opportunity given to anyone to make dishonest gains by abuse of confidential information; and

vi the offeree company's directors will act bona fide, and in the best interests, as they see them, of their own shareholders, doing nothing without consulting them, which is calculated to alter the position materially, or to frustrate the offer.

Each object is now considered in turn.

i *Offer through the proper channels*

An offer must always go first to the offeree company's directors, who are entitled to be satisfied that the offeror is or will be able to implement the offer in full. The identity of the offeror must be disclosed at the outset, if he acts through an agent. As soon as the offeree's directors are notified of a possible serious offer they must issue a press notice without delay, promptly followed by a copy thereof, or a separate circular, to their shareholders—irrespective of whether the board favours the offer or not (Rules 1, 2, 3, 5).

ii *Duty to inform offeree's shareholders without delay*

Shareholders must be given all facts necessary for an informed judgement of the merits and demerits of an offer, accurately and fairly presented, and early enough to enable a decision to be made in good time. An offeror company's obligations towards the offeree company's shareholders are no less than towards its own members. In particular, information should be given about the offeror (including the names of its directors); its intentions regarding continuance of the offeree's business, major changes therein (including redeployment of its fixed assets), and continued employment of its employees; and the long-term commercial justification for the proposed offer (Rule 15).

Any document or advertisement addressed to the offeree's shareholders must be treated with as much care as a prospectus or offer for sale, and must state that the directors of the offeror and/or offeree, as appropriate, have taken all reasonable care to ensure that the facts stated and opinions expressed therein are fair and accurate and, where appropriate, that no material factors or considerations have been omitted. It must also state that all directors jointly and severally accept responsibility accordingly; if any director has not done so, this must be formally stated in the document or advertisement. A copy of the board's authority for issue of the document must be lodged with the Panel on Take-overs and Mergers (Rule 14).

When an offer is announced the identity of the offeror must be disclosed, and the offeror must also disclose any existing holding in the offeree company which it owns or controls, directly or indirectly. Any conditions to which the offer is subject (including the normal ones relating to acceptances, quotation and increase of capital) must be stated in the formal announcement. In particular, if an offer is liable to be referred to the Monopolies and Mergers Commission, there must be a condition that it will be withdrawn in that event. All conditions must be fulfilled or the offer must lapse within 21 days of the first closing date, or later date of becoming or being declared unconditional as to acceptances, If an offeror which has announced its intention to make an offer does not proceed with it within a reasonable time, it must be prepared to justify the circumstances to the Panel. An announced offer may be withdrawn only with the Panel's consent—granted only in exceptional circumstances (Rules, 8, 9).

The offer document must state: i the offeror's shareholdings in the offeree company; ii the shareholdings in the offeror (in the case of a share exchange only) and in the offeree in which the offeror's directors are interested; iii the shareholdings, as in ii, which are owned or controlled by any persons (naming them) who are acting in concert with the offeror; and iv those owned or controlled by any persons (naming them) who, prior to posting of the offer document, have irrevocably committed themselves to accept the offer. If the offer is made wholly or partly for cash, the offer document must include confirmation by the offeror's financial adviser, or other independent party, that the offeror has resources available to satisfy a full acceptance of the offer. It must also state (except in the case of a cash offer) whether the emoluments of the offeror's directors will be affected by acquisition of the offeree (Rules 17, 18, 19).

The document of the offeree company, advising its shareholders whether to accept or reject the offer, must state: i the offeree's shareholdings in the offeror; ii the shareholdings in both companies in which the offeree's directors are interested; and iii whether the offeree's directors intend, in respect of their own beneficial shareholdings, to accept or reject the offer. Details (including dates and prices) must be given of any dealings by the persons mentioned, in this and the previous paragraph, in the shares in question, between 12 months before the announcement of the offer and the latest practicable date before posting of the offer document. Shareholdings include holdings of securities convertible into equity. Particulars must also be given of all service contracts of directors with the offeree company or any of its subsidiaries, having more than 12 months to run, and in the case of those entered into or amended within 6 months before the date of the offer document, particulars of the contracts amended or replaced (Rules 17, 19).

Copies of all public announcements, and all documents bearing on a take-over or merger transaction, must be lodged with the Panel as they are made or despatched (Rule 20). The requirements of the Code regarding profit forecasts and asset valuations are dealt with at length in sub-section 15.4.3.

iii *Opportunity to decide whether to accept or reject the offer*

An offer document must incorporate the following conditions (Rule 26):

1 If voting control of the offeree company is sought, the offer shall not become or be declared unconditional (i.e. bind the offeror to take any of the offeree's shares concerned in exchange for the purchase consideration offered) unless the offeror has acquired, or agreed to acquire, by the close of the offer, shares carrying over 50 per cent of the equity voting rights. No offer need be made for non-equity capital. No offer for equity may be declared unconditional unless, in addition to the above, the offeror has acquired over 50 per cent of the voting power at general meetings of the offeree company (excluding votes exercisable only in restricted circumstances, such as preference dividends in arrear). Equitable treatment must be accorded to different classes of equity capital, and as between voting and non-voting capital. (This rule does not apply to offers

covered by Rule 34—see **iv**) (Rule 21).

2 An offer must be open for at least 21 days after posting. If revised, it must remain open for at least 14 days after posting of the revision notice. An acceptor shall be entitled to withdraw his acceptance after the expiry of 21 days from the original closing date, if the offer has not thereby become unconditional; the right to withdraw continues until the offer becomes or is declared unconditional. An offer must become cr be declared unconditional by, at latest, 3.30 p.m. on the 60th day after posting; if it is not unconditional by then, it may not be replaced by a new offer without the permission of the Panel. If, however, a competing offer is made during the 60 days, the original offer may be extended beyond that time with the Panel's permission (Rule 22).

3 After an offer has become or is declared unconditional, it must remain open for at least 14 days; unless it was to become unconditional at an expiry date, and the offeror has notified the offeree company's shareholders in writing, at least 10 days beforehand, that the offer will not be open for acceptance after the expiry date. Such notice shall not be enforceable in a competitive situation (Rule 23).

4 By 9.30 a.m. on the dealing day following the expiry date of the offer, or the day on which it becomes unconditional, the offeror shall announce, and simultaneously inform the Stock Exchange, that the offer has lapsed, been extended, closed, or become unconditional. It shall also state the total number of shares for which acceptances have been received, of those held before the offer period, and of those acquired or agreed to be acquired during it (Rule 24).

5 If an offeror fails to comply with any of the requirements of Rule 24 within the time-limit, the Stock Exchange will consider suspension of dealings in the offeree's shares and, where appropriate, in the offeror's, until the information is given. If the offeror, having declared an offer unconditional, fails by 3.30 p.m. on the day mentioned above to give the information concerning numbers of shares, then any acceptor shall be entitled to withdraw his acceptance, but (subject to the 60-day rule in 2 above) belated compliance with the rules allows an offeror to declare the offer unconditional once more—but not within 8 days of the original default. (The new declaration then becomes the commencing date for the 14-day period mentioned in 3 above (Rule 25).)

iv *All shareholders of a class treated equally and fairly*

Offers for less than 100 per cent of an offeree's voting rights not already held by the offeror raise special problems; if the offeror considers such an offer justified, the Panel's consent must be obtained in advance. Offers designed to give the offeror and persons acting in concert between 30 and 50 per cent of voting rights at the end (i.e. to make the offeree an 'associated company'—see Chapter 16, section **16.7**) are in general undesirable, and will be permitted only in special circumstances. The precise number of shares offered for should be stated, and the offer may not be declared unconditional unless acceptances are received for at least that number. Offers designed to obtain over 50, but less than 100, per cent of voting rights (i.e. to make the offeree a partly-owned subsidiary) will not normally be permitted unless the offeree's board agrees *and* the offer requires approval by holders of at least 50 per cent of voting rights not already owned by the offeror and persons acting in concert. Partial offers must be made to all shareholders of the class, and arrangements made for all willing shareholders to accept in full for the relevant percentage of their holdings. Where a company has more than one class of equity share capital a comparable offer must be made for each class (Rule 27).

Separate offers must be made for two or more classes of share, and the offeror company should state its intention of resorting to powers under s. 209 of the Companies Act, 1948 (to buy out compulsorily a minority of 10 per cent or less—see sub-section **15.4.4**) only in respect of each class separately. Arrangements must be made to safeguard the interests of holders of conversion or subscription rights, or options, to ensure that their rights are not prejudiced (Rules 28, 29).

If the offeror or any person acting in concert with him/it purchases shares, in the market or otherwise, during the offer period at more than the (current) offer price, then the offer price shall be increased to not less than the highest price (excluding stamp duty and commission) paid for the said shares. If the offer involves a further issue of already quoted securities, their value for the purpose of ascertaining the increased minimum price shall be calculated by reference to the quotation of the existing securities on the day on which the transaction at the 'highest price' was effected. If securities not already quoted are to be issued, the value shall be based on a reasonable estimate of what the price would have been had they been quoted. If the market in the offeror's securities is restricted, or the new issue is large in relation to the amount already quoted, the Panel may require justification of prices used to determine the value of the offer. The offeree's shareholders must be notified in writing of the increased price payable for their shares, at least 14 days before the offer closes (Rule 32).

If the offeror and any persons acting in concert with him/it purchase for cash, through the market or otherwise, during the offer period and within 12 months prior to its commencement, more than 15 per cent of the shares of any class under offer, or the Panel considers it necessary otherwise in the interests of fairness, then, in general, the offer for that class shall be in cash (or accompanied by a cash alternative) at not less than the highest price (excluding stamp duty and commission) paid for such shares during the period aforesaid. If the offeror considers this inequitable for any reason, he should ask the Panel to use its discretion to agree an adjusted price (Rule 33).

Except with the Panel's consent, where any person acquires (with persons acting in concert, if any) shares carrying 30 per cent of a company's voting rights; or, being the holder (as above) of between 30 and 50 per cent of such rights, acquires in any 12-month period additional shares which increase his percentage of the voting rights by more than 1 per cent; such person shall within a reasonable period of time extend an offer to the remaining shareholders of the same class(es), and a comparable offer to the holders of any other class of equity shares, voting or otherwise. Such offer shall be conditional upon the receipt of enough acceptances to raise the voting power of the offeror and persons acting in concert to more than 50 per cent of the voting rights, but no other condition shall be imposed. (If the offeror, etc., already has/have over 50 per cent the offer shall be unconditional.) All such offers shall be in cash, or be accompanied by a cash alternative, at not less than the highest price (excluding stamp duty and commission) paid by the offeror, etc., for similar shares within the preceding 12 months—the Panel being consulted if shares have been acquired other than for cash, and/or as to the offer for any shares of which none have been acquired during the said 12 months, or where more than one class is involved. A person who considers that the 'highest price' should not apply in his case should consult the Panel, which has a discretion as in Rule 33. (Any acquisition liable to give rise to an offer under this rule must not be made if implementation of such offer would or might depend on a resolution of the offeror's shareholders, or other consents or arrangements) (Rule 34).

Except with the Panel's consent, where an offer has been made but has not become unconditional, the offeror and persons acting in concert may not, within 12 months from the date of lapse of the offer, acquire any further shares of the offeree if that would oblige them to make an offer under Rule 34 (Rule 35).

The offeror or persons acting in concert with him/it may not arrange to deal in, or make purchases or sales of, shares of the offeree company, during an offer or when one is reasonably in contemplation, if these transactions involve special favourable conditions not capable of being extended to all shareholders (Rule 36).

v Avoidance of a false market and of opportunity for dishonest gains

In negotiations for an offer to acquire shares, an announcement should be made (preferably a joint one by offeror and offeree company) as soon as the two sides are agreed on the basic terms and reasonably confident of a successful outcome to the negotiations. There must be absolute secrecy before an announcement is made (Rules 5, 6, 7).

In any situation which might lead to an offer's being made, the market should be closely watched. In the event of an untoward movement in share prices an immediate announcement should be made, with such comment as may be appropriate (Rule 5).

No person who is privy to preliminary discussions, or to an intention to make an offer for shares, may deal in any way in the shares of the offeror or offeree companies, between the making of an initial approach (or the time when there is reason to expect an approach or offer) and the making of an announcement; unless, in the case of the offeror's shares, the proposed offer is not deemed price sensitive in relation to them (Rule 30).

Generally, it is considered undesirable to fetter the market. Thus, all parties to a take-over or merger transaction (other than a partial bid) and their associates are free to deal at arm's length without discrimination between sellers, subject to daily disclosure (by 12 noon of the following dealing day) to the Stock Exchange, the Panel and the press, of the total of all shares of either company acquired or sold for their own account on any day during the offer period, and the average price. (Dealings by associates on behalf of clients need not be reported to the press.) In the case of a partial offer, the offeror and his/its associates may not purchase shares in the offeree company during the offer period; if a controlling interest is not to be acquired, the prohibition is extended to a period of 12 months after the offer closes (Rule 31).

Since dealings by an associate with a commercial interest in the outcome of an offer may result in frustration of a bona fide offer or affect its outcome, he should consult the Panel in advance and be prepared to justify his proposed action, as not being prejudicial to the interests of shareholders as a whole (Rule 37).

The directors and officials of an offeree company should see that during a take-over or merger transaction share transfers are promptly registered, so that all members are able freely to exercise their voting and other rights; provisions in articles of association for a qualifying period, during which a newly-registered holder cannot vote, are highly undesirable (Rule 39).

vi *Directors to act bona fide, in shareholders' interests*

Directors must always act in the interests of the shareholders taken as a whole. Where the directors effectively control the company, the attitude of the board to any offer will be decisive. If such a board should reject an offer, or prefer a lower one, it must very carefully examine its motive for so doing, and be prepared to justify its good faith; competent outside advice must be taken (Rule 10).

Except with the Panel's consent, no shares held by directors, their close relatives, or related trusts may be sold nor, before an offer is formally submitted to shareholders, may an irrevocable commitment to accept it be entered into, if the shares in question, aggregated with those already held by the purchaser or the beneficiary of the commitment (and persons acting in concert with him) carry 30 per cent or more of the voting rights. If the Panel does consent to a sale in such circumstances, the directors must require, as a condition, that the purchaser fulfils his obligation under Rule 34 (see under iv) (Rule 11).

Any information given to a preferred suitor should on request be furnished equally and as promptly to a less welcome but bona fide potential offeror (Rule 12).

It is essential that after an offer has been announced the offer document and a letter setting out the views of the offeree's board should be circulated as soon as practicable (Rule 13).

Where an offer is not at arm's length (as where a parent company makes an offer for minority shares in a subsidiary), competent outside advice is essential, so that the interests of the offerees are protected and seen to be protected (Rule 4).

Finally, when an offer has been made or is believed to be imminent, the offeree's board must not (except in pursuance of an existing contract), without the approval of a general meeting, issue fresh shares, or issue or grant options on unissued shares, or create or issue, or permit the creation and issue of, securities carrying rights of conversion into or subscription for shares, or deal in, or agree to deal in, assets of material amount, or enter into contracts otherwise than in the ordinary course of business. The Panel must be consulted, and its consent obtained, as to the fulfilling of an obligation not arising from a formal contract (Rule 38).

Such, though not in the original order, are the main provisions of the City Code. The functions of the Panel on Take-overs and Mergers are set out in the (unchanged) Introduction to the 1972 version. They are to give advice and rulings on points of doubt and difficulty, to settle disputes between parties who refer them to the Panel, and to impose sanctions upon individuals or companies violating the Code. These sanctions include private reprimand or public censure, or in more flagrant cases further action designed to exclude the offender, temporarily or permanently, from access to the facilities of the securities markets. The alleged offender will in all cases be given the opportunity to answer the allegation and bring witnesses, and may appeal to the Appeal Committee of the Panel. Proceedings are all informal, and no legal representation is permitted.

15.4.3 Profit forecasts and asset valuations

The practising accountant is most particularly concerned with reporting on *profit forecasts* made in connection with a take-over bid or merger proposals. Rule 16 of the City Code (1974) governs his duty in•this regard, and may be summarized as follows.

Despite the obvious hazards, any profit forecasts must be compiled with the greatest care by the directors whose sole responsibility they are. In any document addressed to shareholders the assumptions, including the commercial assumptions, upon which the directors have based their profit forecasts must appear in the document. The accounting bases and calculations for the forecasts must be examined and reported on by the auditors or consultant accountants, while any financial adviser mentioned in the document must also report on the forecasts. Both reports must be contained in the document and accompanied by statements that the accountants, and adviser, have given and not withdrawn their consent to publication. Profit forecasts relating to a period in which trading has already commenced must be supported by the latest available unaudited profit figures for the period to date, with comparative figures for the preceding year—or a statement made that no such figures are available. When revaluations of assets appear in connection with an offer, the board should be supported by the opinion of a named independent professional expert and the basis of valuation clearly stated. The document should also state that the expert has given and not withdrawn his consent to the publication of his name therein.

Contemporaneously with the second edition of the City Code (1969), the Institute of Chartered Accountants in England and Wales published *Statement S15*, 'Accountants' reports on profit forecasts'. It emphasizes that profit forecasts necessarily depend on subjective judgements, and are subject to inherent uncertainties, which increase, the further forward the forecasts stretch in time. Hence they cannot be confirmed or verified in the same way as financial statements relating to past events, and certainly cannot be audited, even though the reporting accountants may also be the company's auditors. Accountants must in their reports avoid giving any impression that they are confirming, underwriting, guaranteeing, or otherwise accepting responsibility for the ultimate accuracy or reliability of forecasts. Their functions are to review, critically and objectively, the accounting bases and calculations for the forecasts, and verify that the latter have been properly computed from the underlying assumptions and data, and are prepared on a consistent basis.

In accepting instructions from the directors the reporting accountants should make the above points quite clear. They should further insist upon adequate time in which to obtain sufficient information on which to exercise their professional judgement, and, in view of the increasing uncertainty of profit forecasts the further they reach into the future, the accountants should not normally undertake to review and report on forecasts for more than the current accounting period and, provided a sufficiently significant part of the current year has elapsed, the next following year. They will also wish to establish the purpose for which the forecasts have been prepared and for which the accountants' report is required, to be assured that the directors will assume the responsibilities laid upon them by Rule 15 of the City Code, and to know the identities of the company's merchant bankers, advisers, or other independent professional experts who are to report on other aspects of the matter, and with whom the accountants should consult and keep in touch.

Reporting accountants will direct their main attention to the following matters:

a the nature and background of the company's business;

b the accounting practices normally followed by the company, to ensure that acceptable accounting principles have been followed in financial statements, and consistently applied in preparing interim accounts and profit forecasts. Particular attention will be paid to such crucial areas as stock and work in progress valuation, computation of profits and losses on long-term contracts, bases for calculating depreciation, and the treatment of research and development expenditure, exceptional items, and taxation;

c the assumptions on which the forecasts are based. The accountants are not responsible for these, but must assure themselves that the forecasts are consistent with them; and

d the procedures followed by the company for preparing forecasts—whether they are regularly prepared for management's use, or specially for the immediate purpose; if regularly, how reliable they have proved in the past, and how frequently and thoroughly they are revised; whether the forecasts represent management's best estimates of what is likely to be achieved, as distinct from targets set as desirable; how far the forecast results for expired periods are supported by reliable interim accounts; the extent to which the forecasts are built up from more detailed ones relating to particular activities of the business, distinguishing between more, and less, predictable elements in the estimates; the treatment of material exceptional items; the making of adequate provision for foreseeable losses and contingencies; the adequacy of working capital, as evidenced by proper cash flow forecasts, and the making of proper arrangements for obtaining short-term finance as necessary; and whether the forecasts have been prepared and presented on acceptable bases consistent with the accounting principles and practices of previous years; or if not, whether the fact and effects of any material change of basis are made clear.

Subject to all this, the matters on which the accountants are expected to satisfy themselves are indicated in the specimen form of unqualified report, set out in *Statement S15*, as follows:

To the directors of X Ltd.

We have reviewed the accounting bases and calculations for the profit forecasts of X Ltd (for which the directors are solely responsible) for the periods . . . set out on pages ** of this circular. The forecasts include results shown by unaudited interim accounts for the period. . . . In our opinion the forecasts, so far as the accounting bases and calculations are concerned, have been properly compiled on the footing of the assumptions made by the Board set out on page ** of this circular and are presented on a basis consistent with the accounting practices normally adopted by the company.

The report must be qualified if the accountants are unable to satisfy themselves that any one or more of the above statements can be conscientiously made.

Finally, before giving written consent to publication of the report (required by Rule 16), the accountants should require to see the whole text of the circular, and satisfy themselves that it is appropriate, and not misleading, for their report to appear in the form and context in which it is included.

15.4.4 Legal provisions on take-overs and mergers

The few provisions of the Companies Act, 1948, relative to take-overs and mergers, may be summarized quite shortly.

In such a transaction there are often arrangements to pay *compensation for loss of office* to directors of an offeree company who will or may be displaced if the bid succeeds. This applies particularly to 'family' directors who have no formal contracts of service, but rely on their large shareholdings to keep them in office. Hence, if they sell out, they will be unable to sue the company for damages if they are dismissed. In order to induce them to agree to the bid, and/or recommend the other shareholders to accept it, the offeror company often undertakes to pay ex gratia compensation to a considerable amount. Such payments are governed by ss. 191 to 194 of the 1948 Act.

A company may not pay compensation for loss of office, or as consideration for or in connection with his retirement, to any director without disclosure of the proposed payments (including the amount thereof) to members, and approval of the proposal by the company (s. 191). The same applies to such payments in connection with the transfer of the whole or any part of the undertaking or property of a company, with the addition that, if any such payment is made illegally, the director must hold the money in trust for the company (s. 192). Where compensation as above is proposed in connection with the transfer to any person of all or any of a company's shares, resulting from an offer to shareholders in general, or a take-over bid by another body corporate, or an offer by an individual to acquire one-third or more of the voting power at general meetings, or any other offer conditional on acceptance to a given extent, then it is the duty of any director concerned to see to it that particulars of the proposed payment (including the amount) are included in or sent with any notice of the offer made for their shares which is given to any shareholders. If this is not done, the director or other person responsible for the default may be fined up to £25 and compelled, in effect, to distribute any moneys so received, at his own expense, among those shareholders who have sold their shares as a result of the offer. The second procedure, but not the fine, also applies if the proposed payment of compensation is not, before the transfer of any shares in pursuance of the offer, approved by a special meeting of the holders of all classes of shares affected by the offer (s. 193). Ss. 192 and 193 apply, unless the contrary is shown, to any payment as above, made in pursuance of any arrangement entered into as part of the agreement for the transfer, or within one year before or two years after the agreement or offer, where the company or any transferee was privy to the arrangement. Compensation includes any excess price paid for a director's shares, above what could have been obtained at the time by other holders of similar shares, or any valuable consideration given to a director; but it does not include (for the purpose of ss. 191 to 193) any bona fide damages for breach of contract, or any pension or superannuation payment (s. 194).

Lastly, s. 209 contains provisions for acquiring compulsorily the shares of an obstinate minority (of 10 per cent or less) who reject an offer accepted as fair by the holders of the other 90 per cent or more of the shares involved—and countervailing provisions whereby a '10 per cent' minority may compel the offeror company to acquire their shares, if it is unwilling to do so. Briefly, if under any scheme or contract whereby a 'transferor' company's shares are transferred to a 'transferee' company, the terms have been accepted, within four months of the offer, by the holders of at least 90 per cent of the shares involved (*excluding* those held at the date of the offer by the transferee or its subsidiaries or their respective nominees); then the transferee may, within a further two months, give notice to dissenting shareholders of intention to acquire their shares, and this binds the transferee company to give them the same terms as the majority have accepted— unless, within one month of the notice, the dissentients apply to the High Court to intervene. These rules do not apply, however, where the transferee company initially held more than 10 per cent of the class of shares concerned, *unless* the same terms are offered to all the remaining shareholders of that class, *and* the accepting shareholders constitute a majority of at least 90 per cent in value and 75 per cent in number, of the holders of the 'outstanding' shares at the offer date. Subject to any order by the High Court (on application as above), the transferee shall, after one month from giving notice to dissentients, arrange with the transferor company for transfer to itself of the dissentients' shares, and send the consideration to the transferor company for distribution to the dissentients.

If, on the other hand, 90 per cent or more of the shares of a class (*including* those held at the outset by or on behalf of the transferee company) have been transferred, then within one month of the date of the transfer the transferee company shall give notice of the fact to the holders of the remaining shares. Within three months of that notice any dissentient shareholder may require the transferee company to acquire his shares on the same terms as have been accepted by the majority, or on such other terms as may be agreed, or as the High Court may order on application by either party.

16

Published accounts of groups of companies

Chapter 14 was concerned with the legal requirements for disclosure in the published accounts of single companies. Today, though, the great majority of quoted companies are the parent companies of extensive groups, consisting of holding company, subsidiaries and/or associates. Under the Companies Acts, 1948 and 1967, each company must publish final accounts as prescribed, but these individually, or even all of them together, cannot tell the whole story. The law therefore imposes upon the parent or holding company the further obligation to publish *group accounts*.

16.1 The nature of group accounts

Group accounts are intended to provide management, investors, analysts, and other interested parties with a synoptic view of the year's results, and year-end position, of the group as a 'super-entity' (see Chapter 1, sub-section 1.2.1) made up of the separate entities of the companies concerned. Each one has its own accounting system, whose 'end-product' for each year is the set of final accounts—profit and loss account and balance sheet. The group as a whole has no accounting system, but produces group accounts by combining the final accounts of all its components in such manner as to exhibit the year's results, and year-end position, of the group as though it were a single company.

The device of a holding company with subsidiaries is admirably suited for linking together a number of decentralized managerial units, of something like optimal size, into a single financial unit, whose optimal size is generally much larger. Since only a majority holding of ordinary shares is normally needed to secure control, additional equity finance can be obtained from minority shareholders in subsidiaries without giving them any effective say in the management, and this possibility can be extended to the setting-up of two or more tiers of subsidiaries, sub-subsidiaries, etc., each having a minority, thus disfranchized. Again, it is possible for the holding company, or a subsidiary, to hold a large proportion—but not more than half—of the shares of an 'associated' company, either as the only large shareholder (the others being weak and unorganized), or as one of two or more large corporate shareholders who become, in effect, partners in the associated business; so that the holding company secures a considerable measure of control thereover, without making it legally a subsidiary. Super-entities of the kind described became common in America from the 1920s, and in Britain from the 1930s, but effective accounting disclosure was not enforced for some years. Indeed it was all too easy for a holding company, conducting its main businesses through subsidiaries, to publish a profit and loss account whose net profit consisted of dividends from subsidiaries less the holding company's own expenses, and a balance sheet whose principal asset was 'shares in subsidiary companies', at historical cost—thus hiding most of the essential facts.

In the U.S.A. the Securities and Exchange Commission began, from 1934, to compel the filing of more informative accounts from quoted companies, including proper group accounts where applicable. In Britain reform was effected by the Companies Act, 1948, which prevented public companies' subsidiaries, registered as private companies, from gaining exemption from filing their accounts. The Act goes on to impose additional disclosure requirements upon holding companies and subsidiaries, and to compel holding companies to publish group accounts; and the Companies Act, 1967, extends these provisions.

16.2 Legal requirements for disclosure in the accounts of holding companies and subsidiaries

There follows a summary of the additional disclosure provisions of the Companies Acts, 1948 and 1967, relative to group companies. Legislation relating to exceptional circumstances is summarized in smaller type.

16.2.1 Definition of holding company and subsidiary

The Companies Act, 1948, ss. 150 to 153, requires the publication of group accounts by a holding company. S.154 defines a 'subsidiary' as a company of which another body corporate (its 'holding company') *either* i is a member of it and controls the composition of its board of directors, *or* ii holds more than half in nominal value of its equity share capital; or is a company which is a subsidiary of the holding company's subsidiary.

A company controls the composition of another's board of directors if it is able, without the consent or concurrence of any other person, to appoint or remove all the directors or a majority of them. This includes need for action by the holding company to obtain the appointment of any other person; the automatic appointment of a director of the holding company to the subsidiary's board; and the holding of a directorship by the holding company itself or another subsidiary. As to the holding of equity share capital, shares held by a nominee, or by a subsidiary or *its* nominee, are included; but shares held by the holding company, or a nominee, etc., in a fiduciary capacity, or to secure an issue of debentures by the subsidiary, or as security for money lent in the ordinary course of business, are disregarded (and similarly with any power, so exercisable, to appoint or remove directors). 'Equity share capital' is defined as issued share capital, *other than* share capital whose rights to dividend and to capital repayment are both limited to a certain amount; that is, it includes not only ordinary and deferred shares, but participating preference shares, and preference shares with the right to share in surplus assets on liquidation.

The Act does not mention control by holding a majority of votes at general meetings. The substance of control lies in domination of the management through power to appoint directors, prevent their appointment, or remove them from office—thus ensuring that they follow only policies approved by their 'masters'. The power resides in a majority of ordinary shareholders, on the normal basis of one vote per share, and becomes much more real when the majority is in the hands of one corporate body. There are, however, other ways of dominating the board—contractual rights to appoint the chairman and/or a majority of members, family solidarity, gentlemen's agreements, etc.—and a too-restrictive definition of holding company status would have encouraged evasion of the extended disclosure rules.

The alternative test, of a majority holding of 'equity', adds little to the law. The Jenkins Committee considered the provision redundant, and suggested control of the board as the only criterion; but no change was made by the 1967 Act.

16.2.2 Additional disclosure in the accounts of holding companies

By the Companies Act, 1967, s. 3, any company having subsidiaries at the end of its financial year must state in its accounts, or in a note on or statement annexed to them, in respect of each subsidiary:

a its name;

b its country of incorporation, if different from that of the holding company (including Scotland, where the holding company is incorporated in England, and vice versa); and

c the identity, and proportion of issued shares held, of each class of the subsidiary's shares held.

As regards c, only those shares are to be included which would be treated as held by the company for the purposes of the 1948 Act, s. 154; and a distinction must be made between shares held by the company or its nominees, and those held by subsidiaries or their nominees.

The above information may be withheld in respect of any subsidiary incorporated outside the U.K., or incorporated in the U.K. and carrying on business outside it, if, in the opinion of the holding company's directors, disclosure would be harmful to the business of the company or of any of its subsidiaries, and the Department of Trade agrees that the information need not be disclosed.

If, in the opinion of the holding company's directors, the number of subsidiaries is so large that full particulars of them all would be excessively long, information need be given only about those whose business results, in the directors' opinion, principally affected the amount of profit or loss, or of assets, of the group. It must be made clear, however, that the information is so restricted; and particulars of all the subsidiaries must be sent to the Registrar of Companies with the next annual return.

By the 1967 Act, s. 4, moreover, any company holding, at the end of its financial year, more than 10 per cent in nominal value of any class of 'equity' shares of another body corporate, not being its subsidiary, must state in its accounts etc.:

a the name of the other body corporate;

b its country of incorporation, if different from that of the company (including Scotland, where the company is incorporated in England, and vice versa);

c the identity, and proportion of issued shares held, of the class concerned; and

d similar particulars of shares of any other class held in the body corporate (whether equity or not).

Any company holding, at the end of its financial year, *any* shares in another body corporate, not being its subsidiary, whose value for the purposes of its accounts exceeds 10 per cent of the total value of its assets for those purposes, must state in its accounts, etc., particulars similar to a, b and c above.

Only those shares shall be taken into consideration, under either head, which would be treated as held by the company under the 1948 Act, s. 154, but with the omission of reference to shares held by a subsidiary or its nominee. In other words, '10 per cent' shareholdings through subsidiaries are not covered by the 1967 Act, s. 4, and a holding company can easily escape disclosure by transferring such shares to subsidiaries, or letting them acquire the shares in the first place.

Exemptions, similar to those in s. 3, apply to shares in bodies incorporated, or carrying on business, outside the U.K., and to 'excessively long' particulars thereof.

By the 1967 Act, Schedule 2, para. 15(2) and (3), a holding company (even if itself a subsidiary of another body corporate) must, in addition to the general requirements of the 1967 Act, disclose separately in its balance sheet the aggregate amounts of:

a assets consisting of shares in its subsidiaries;
b indebtedness from subsidiaries; and
c indebtedness to subsidiaries.

Investments in subsidiaries are exempt from the requirements of 1967, Schedule 2, as regards investments in general, and from those relating to fixed asset valuation, except the obligation to disclose the method or methods used to arrive at the investments' value. This means that they may be stated as being valued at cost, or on some other basis, without need to disclose their market value, or particulars of earnings, dividends, etc.

A note must also be made, on the balance sheet or annexed to it, of the number, description, and amount of shares and debentures of the holding company held by its subsidiaries or their nominees; but excluding those shares or debentures held by the subsidiary, merely as personal representative of a deceased member, etc., or as trustee of a trust in which neither the holding company nor any subsidiary has a beneficial interest (other than by way of security for a loan made in the ordinary course of its business) (see sub-section **16.6.4**).

In addition, the 1972 *Listing Agreement–Companies* (revised 1973), of the Federated Stock Exchanges requires every quoted holding company to state in its directors' report the name of the principal country in which each subsidiary operates (see Chapter 14, section **14.9**.)

16.2.3 Additional disclosure in the accounts of subsidiaries

By the 1967 Companies Act, s. 5, any company which at the end of its financial year is a subsidiary of another body corporate must state in its accounts, etc., the name of the body corporate regarded by the directors as being the company's ultimate holding company and, if known to them, its country of incorporation.

This information may be withheld by a subsidiary carrying on business outside the U.K. if, in the directors' opinion, disclosure would be harmful to the business of the ultimate holding company, or of that or any other subsidiary, and the Department of Trade agrees that the information need not be disclosed.

By 1967, Schedule 2, para. 16, a subsidiary must disclose separately in its balance sheet the aggregate amounts of:

a its debentures held by its holding company or fellow-subsidiaries;
b other indebtedness to its holding company or fellow-subsidiaries;
c debentures held by it in its holding company or fellow-subsidiaries;

d other indebtedness to it from its holding company or fellow-subsidiaries; and
e assets consisting of shares in fellow-subsidiaries.

There is no requirement to disclose the aggregate amount of shares held in the holding company (see sub-section **16.6.4**). A company is defined as a 'fellow-subsidiary' of another body corporate if both are subsidiaries of the same body corporate but neither is the other's.

16.2.4 Presentation of group accounts

As already stated, the core of the legislation on group accounts lies in the 1948 Companies Act, ss. 150 to 154, of which s. 154, the definition clause, has already been dealt with.

S. 150 requires a holding company to lay group accounts before the company in general meeting, with the company's own accounts; while s. 156 requires group accounts to be annexed to the balance sheet for all purposes, including circulation to members, etc., and filing with the Registrar. There is exemption for any company which is itself a wholly-owned subsidiary, at the end of its financial year, of another body incorporated in Great Britain, since all accounting information about the company and its own subsidiaries will be included in the group accounts of the other body. A wholly-owned subsidiary is a body corporate which has no members other than its holding company and the latter's wholly-owned subsidiaries, and its and their nominees.

A company which does publish group accounts may omit from them any subsidiary if the company's directors are of opinion that:

i inclusion is impracticable, or would be of no real value to members of the company in view of the insignificant amounts involved, or would involve expense or delay out of proportion to the value to members of the company; or

ii the result would be misleading, or harmful to the business of the company or any of its subsidiaries; or

iii the business of the holding company and that of the subsidiary are so different that they cannot reasonably be treated as a single undertaking.

If the directors are of such an opinion about every subsidiary, then group accounts are not required. Omission of a subsidiary on ground i is at the directors' discretion; omission on grounds ii and iii requires the approval of the Department of Trade.

When no group accounts are prepared, then the 1967 Act, Schedule 2, para. 15(4) applies. A statement must be annexed to the balance sheet, showing:

a the reasons why subsidiaries are not dealt with in group accounts;

b the net aggregate amount, so far as it concerns members of the holding company and is not dealt with in the company's accounts, of the subsidiaries' profits, less losses (or vice versa)—

  i for their financial years ending with or during that of the holding company; and

  ii for their previous financial years since they respectively became its subsidiaries;

c the net aggregate amount of the subsidiaries' profits, less losses, distinguished as in b(i) and (ii), so far as profits are dealt with, or losses provided for, in the holding company's accounts; and

d any qualifications in auditors' reports on the subsidiaries' accounts for the current year(s), and any note or saving in those accounts, calling attention to a matter which would otherwise have been properly referred to in a qualification; insofar as the matter concerned is not covered by the holding company's accounts and is material from the point of view of its members;

or, if any of this information is not available, a statement to that effect.

The Department of Trade may, on application from the holding company's directors or with their consent, direct that, in relation to any subsidiary, requirements a to d shall not apply, or shall apply only to the extent stated in the direction.

By para. 15(5), b and c above apply only to subsidiaries' profits and losses, properly regarded as revenue profits or losses in the holding company's accounts. Profits and losses arising before acquisition of a subsidiary's shares by the holding company or any of its subsidiaries are to be omitted, except, in a proper case, where the company is itself a subsidiary of another body corporate, and the shares were acquired from it or from another of its subsidiaries. For purposes of apportioning profits or losses, accrual from day to day within an accounting period may be assumed where the facts do not allow more accurate calculations to be made.

When group accounts are prepared but some subsidiaries are excluded from them, 1967, Schedule 2, para. 21, requires particulars of shareholdings in the excluded subsidiaries, indebtedness from and to them, and holding company's shares and debentures held by them, to be disclosed in accordance with para. 15(2) and (3), as though the group accounts were the accounts of an actual company of which the excluded companies were subsidiaries; while a statement of the excluded subsidiaries' aggregate profits, less losses, etc., must be annexed to the accounts, as detailed in para. 15(4).

By the 1948 Act, s. 151, *consolidated accounts* are prescribed as the normal format for group accounts. They are to consist of:

a a *consolidated balance sheet* dealing with the state of affairs of the company and all relevant subsidiaries; and

b a *consolidated profit and loss account* dealing with the profit or loss of the company and these subsidiaries.

The directors are, however, at liberty to use any other form if they are of the opinion that it is better for the purpose of presenting the same or equivalent information, so that it may be readily appreciated by the holding company's members. In particular, they may use two or more sets of consolidated accounts for different groups of subsidiaries (including the holding company in one set); separate accounts for each subsidiary; statements expanding the information about the subsidiaries in the company's own accounts; or any combination of these. The group accounts may be wholly or partly incorporated in the company's own balance sheet and profit and loss account.

By s. 152(1) and (3), the group accounts must give a true and fair view of the state of affairs and profit or loss of the company and the subsidiaries dealt with thereby as a whole, so far as concerns members of the holding company. If prepared as consolidated accounts, they must comply with the requirements of the 1967 Act, Schedule 2, as far as applicable thereto, and if not so prepared, must give the same or equivalent information; except that the Department of Trade may, on application by the directors or with their consent, modify the requirements of Schedule 2 for the purposes of adapting them to the company's circumstances.

By the 1967 Act, Schedule 2, paras. 17 to 19, the consolidated balance sheet and profit and loss account shall combine the information contained in the separate balance sheets and profit and loss accounts of the companies involved, but with such adjustments (if any) as the holding company's directors think necessary. The consolidated accounts shall comply as far as practicable with the requirements of the two Companies Acts as if they were the accounts of an actual company. They are not, however, required to comply with 1948, ss.196 (directors' remuneration) and 197 (loans to officers), nor with 1967, ss.4 ('10 per cent' holdings) and 6 to 8 (further particulars of directors' and senior employees emoluments), though these items of information must still be given in relation to the holding company's own accounts.

Finally, by the 1948 Act, s. 153, a holding company's directors must cause the financial year of each subsidiary to coincide with that of the holding company, except where in their opinion there are good reasons against it. The Department of Trade has power, where it appears desirable to extend a subsidiary's financial year to secure such coincidence and to postpone submission of the accounts to a general meeting from one calendar year to the next, to grant the subsidiary's directors, on application, a dispensation from submitting accounts as aforesaid, holding an annual general meeting, or making an annual return, in respect of the first calendar year involved.

Where a subsidiary's financial year does not coincide with that of the holding company, 1948, s. 152(2), requires the group accounts to incorporate the subsidiary's accounts for the financial year ending with or last before that of the holding company, unless the Department of Trade, on the application or with the consent of the holding company's directors, shall direct otherwise. Where all the years do not end together, the 1967 Act, Schedule 2, para. 22, requires a statement to be annexed to the balance sheet, showing:

a the reasons why the company's directors consider that the subsidiaries' financial years should not end with that of the company, and
b the dates on which the subsidiaries' financial years, ending last before that of the company, respectively ended, or the earliest and latest of those dates.

A similar statement is required where group accounts are not submitted (para. 15(6)).

16.3 Group accounts and the accountancy profession

Group accounts in Britain are largely creatures of statute law, of which an attempt has been made to summarize the prolix and unwieldy mass, complicated by Parliament's determination to provide for all manner of exceptional cases. Remarkably little of this legislation concerns the holding company's accountant in the normal, straightforward case of consolidated accounts, covering the whole group, with all the financial years coinciding; and the rest of the chapter will be mainly devoted to standard practice in this situation.

The Companies Acts say next to nothing about the mechanics of consolidation. In the Anglo-Saxon world two approaches are widely used:

1 the *acquisition* method (called the 'purchase method' in America), in which a subsidiary is treated as a subordinate part of the holding company's organization; and
2 the *merger* method ('pooling of interests method' in America), in which all subsidiaries are regarded as partners in the group, with the holding company as a co-ordinating body.

American corporations in the 1930s and 1940s generally adopted the 'purchase' method. When, in 1948, group accounts were made compulsory in Britain, the

Institute of Chartered Accountants in England and Wales followed current American practice in its Notes, *Group Accounts in the form of Consolidated Accounts* (1949), describing the workings of the acquisition (purchase) method. No Recommendation on Accounting Principles was ever issued, but the 1949 Notes became the basis of British practice until about 1970. By then, however, American companies had largely changed over to the 'pooling of interests' (merger) method, and a few British groups had begun to use it. In 1971 the Accounting Standards Steering Committee published its Exposure Draft 3, *Accounting for acquisitions and mergers,* in which both practices were considered, and approval given to the merger method in certain circumstances (see section 16.5). This has caused much controversy, at a time when the Accounting Principles Board of the American Institute of Certified Public Accountants has had serious difficulty in arriving at any consensus on the proper rôle of the latter technique, on which strong attacks have been made by some leaders of the profession in the U.S.A. ED3 is now (1975) out of print, and is thought to have been tacitly abandoned; but in the absence of definite information it has been thought best to let the present text stand.

On accounting for *associated companies* English law is still silent. In America, in the 1960s, discussion developed as to whether a company should take into account its share of the earnings of an associate, irrespective of their distribution, instead of merely bringing into its books the dividends received. The earnings method (see section 16.7) is now accepted practice in the United States, and in England the Institute of Chartered Accountants enjoins its use in its Statement of Standard Accounting Practice No. 1, *Accounting for the results of associated companies* (1971).

16.4 Acquisition method of consolidation

The remainder of this chapter is largely concerned with the established treatment of consolidated subsidiaries, as having been acquired by the holding company. Before going into details, it is necessary to delimit the respective spheres of the two accepted methods.

16.4.1 Acquisition and merger methods distinguished

The 1971 Exposure Draft 3, *Accounting for acquisitions and mergers,* proposes four tests for determining whether a combination of two or more companies should be regarded as an acquisition or a merger. Any combination which passes all the tests should be treated as a merger, any which does not, as an acquisition. If in a group of three or more companies some satisfy the 'merger' test, but others do not, a mixture of the two methods should be used.

The tests proposed for a merger are that:

a the substance of the main business of the constituent companies continues in the amalgamated undertaking;

b the equity shareholders of any one constituent company do not obtain voting rights in the amalgamated undertaking, in excess of three times those given to the equity shareholders of any other company;

c the amalgamation results from an offer to equity voting shareholders, and 90 per cent at least of the consideration is in the form of equity capital with the same voting rights as attach to the shares given up (convertible loan stock, or voting equity convertible into cash through an underwriting agreement, is not to count); and

d the offer is approved by the offeror company's voting shareholders, and accepted by at least 90 per cent in value of the offeree company's equity shareholders, voting or non-voting.

The essential distinction is between the linking together of two or more businesses not grossly disparate in size, so that no set of investors in the constituent companies is dominant over the rest, the existing businesses are substantially retained, and there is a genuine pooling of profits among the old investors; and the addition to a larger organization of a smaller undertaking, whose shareholders are either bought out or given only a small stake in the group, whose business is reorganized or loses its separate existence, and whose profits go wholly or mainly to existing members of the holding company. The suggested three-to-one maximum ratio of voting rights, as between the largest and smallest companies in a merger, is arbitrary, but offers a working rule for deciding whether or not there is a gross disparity in size. The 90 per cent criteria in **c** and **d** are also arbitrary, but intended as assurances that there has been substantial continuity of ownership, without considerable buying-out of old shareholders.

It is now necessary to explain the acquisition method in some detail, and then the modifications required for the merger situation.

16.4.2 Acquisition method of balance sheet consolidation

The object of either mode of consolidation is to replace the 'paper' asset 'shares in subsidiary company' in the holding company's published balance sheet with the underlying 'tangible' assets, and their countervailing liabilities, in the published balance sheet of the subsidiary, while cancelling out inter-company shareholdings and indebtedness. These items do not always cancel out as they stand, and certain adjustments are needed to complete the balance sheet of the group. The difference between acquisition and merger accounting lies in the character of these adjustments.

The two methods are identical in the simplest case of all—the acquisition of the subsidiary's entire equity capital, by a cash purchase at par value or a one-for-one exchange of shares valued at par, at a time when the subsidiary's reserves were precisely zero. This is unrealistic, unless the subsidiary was set up by the holding company's management in the first place, but is a useful starting-point for an exposition in which the assumptions will be relaxed one by one. The first example will be used to illustrate the standard method of attacking the problem; later ones will be more briefly summarized.

Example 1 Wholly owned subsidiary, equity capital acquired at par, no pre-acquisition reserves.

Great Ltd, on 1 January 19.1, acquired all the £1 ordinary shares of Small Ltd, (reserves at that date, *nil*) for cash at £1 per share. The two companies' balance sheets (simplified) as at 31 December 19.1 were as follows:

Great Ltd

Balance Sheet, 31 December 19.1

	£	£		Cost £	Depreciation £	Net £
Share Capital			**Fixed Assets**			
Ordinary shares		50,000	Freehold property	34,000	4,000	30,00
			Plant	61,000	29,000	32,00
Reserves				£95,000	£33,000	62,00
Share premium account	8,000					
Profit and loss account	2,000					
		10,000	**Shares in Subsidiary Company,**			
			at cost			10,00
		60,000				
			Current Assets			
Debentures		20,000	Stock		11,000	
			Debtors		15,500	
Corporation Tax—			Subsidiary company—			
Current Year		6,000	current account		1,000	
			Bank balance		500	
						28,0
Current Liabilities			**Deferred Asset**			
Creditors	4,000		ACT recoverable			3,6
Corporation tax—						
previous year	5,000					
Proposed dividend	5,000					
ACT on proposed dividend	3,694					
		17,694				
		£103,694				£103,6

Small Ltd

Balance Sheet, 31 December 19.1

	£	£		Cost £	Depreciation £	Net £
Share Capital			**Fixed Assets**			
Ordinary shares		10,000	Plant	£14,000	£4,000	10,00
Reserves						
Profit and loss account		1,000	**Current Assets**			
			Stock		2,500	
		11,000	Debtors		3,000	
						5,50
Corporation Tax—						
Current Year		1,000	**Deferred Asset**			
Current Liabilities			ACT recoverable			73
Bank overdraft	300					
Creditors	500					
Holding company—						
current account	800					
Corporation tax—						
previous year	900					
Proposed dividend	1,000					
ACT on proposed dividend	739					
		4,239				
		£16,239				£16,239

The task of consolidation, especially in a complex case with a large number of subsidiaries, is best performed by means of a work-sheet, as shown below. Its layout is fairly obvious, and the adjustments are explained in the notes.

The method consists, firstly, in adding together all physical and financial assets, and external liabilities, of the group, class by class, and eliminating inter-company indebtedness. Note the complication caused by the difference in the two (opposite) current account balances, resulting from the dispatch of £200 from Small Ltd to Great Ltd just before the year-end. (In practice, Great Ltd would transfer £200 in its own books: *Dr.* Cash in Transit, *Cr.* Small Ltd, Current Account.) Note also that the holding company's bank balance and the subsidiary's overdraft are not offset; the bank's only legal recourse is against the assets of Small Ltd, and it is best to recognize the two opposite claims. (It would be otherwise if Great Ltd had guaranteed the overdraft, and offsetting would then be the proper procedure.)

Next, the whole of the subsidiary's share capital must *always* cancel out in consolidation, leaving only the holding company's shares in the consolidated balance sheet; the latter is prepared from the standpoint of the holding company's shareholders, to show their net interest in the group and the assets, less liabilities, by which it is represented—all at book amounts. Finally, the subsidiary's reserves, in this simple case, are consolidated with those of the holding company; note, however, that any proposed dividend in a subsidiary's accounts must *always* be added back to its profit and loss account (of which it is, legally, a detached part), so that only the holding company's proposed dividend appears in the consolidated balance sheet—again, in order to reflect the position vis-à-vis the holding company's shareholders. In the subsidiary's balance sheet, the ACT on proposed dividend is cancelled out against the deferred asset, ACT recoverable, or added back to deferred taxation (as the case may be), and consolidation performed on that basis.

ʳeat Ltd and its Subsidiary

ʳlance Sheet Consolidation Work-Sheet, 31 December 19.1

	Great Ltd £	Small Ltd £	Sub-Total £	Adjustments Debit £		Adjustments Credit £	Consolidated Balance Sheet £
ˣed Assets							
Freehold Property							
Cost	34,000	–	34,000				34,000
Depreciation	(4,000)	–	(4,000)				(4,000)
Plant							
Cost	61,000	14,000	75,000				75,000
Depreciation	(29,000)	(4,000)	(33,000)				(33,000)
ʳares in Subsidiary							
Company	10,000	–	10,000	(1)		10,000	–
ʳrrent Assets							
Stock	11,000	2,500	13,500				13,500
Debtors	15,500	3,000	18,500				18,500
Subsidiary company							
current account	1,000	–	1,000	(2)		200)	–
				(3)		800)	
Bank balance	500	–	500				500
Cash in transit	–	–	–	(2)	200		200
ʳerred Asset							
ACT recoverable	3,694	739	4,433	(5)		739	3,694
	£103,694	£16,239	£119,933				£108,394

Share Capital							
Ordinary shares	50,000	10,000	60,000 (1)	10,000			50,00
Reserves							
Share premium account	8,000	–	8,000				8,00
Profit and loss account	2,000	1,000	3,000	(4)	1,000		4,00
Debentures	20,000	–	20,000				20,00
Corporation Tax–							
Current Year	6,000	1,000	7,000				7,00
Current Liabilities							
Bank overdraft	–	300	300				30
Creditors	4,000	500	4,500				4,50
Holding company–							
current account	–	800	800 (3)	800			–
Corporation tax–							
previous year	5,000	900	5,900				5,90
Proposed dividend	5,000	1,000	6,000 (4)	1,000			5,00
ACT on proposed dividend	3,694	739	4,433 (5)	739			3,69
	£103,694	£16,239	£119,933	£12,933	£12,739		£108,39

Notes on adjustments

1 Holding company's investment in subsidiary set off against the latter's share capital.

2 Cash in transit from subsidiary to holding company at year-end, adjusted on current account as shown in the holding company's books.

3 Two current account balances, now equal and opposite, cancelled out.

4 Subsidiary's proposed dividend added back to its profit and loss account balance.

5 Subsidiary's ACT on proposed dividend cancelled against its ACT recoverable.

Great Ltd and its Subsidiary

Consolidated Balance Sheet, 31 December 19.1

	£	£		Cost £	Depreciation £	Net £
Share Capital of			Fixed Assets			
Great Ltd			Freehold property	34,000	4,000	30,000
Ordinary shares		50,000	Plant	75,000	33,000	42,000
Reserves						
Share premium				£109,000	£37,000	72,000
account	8,000					
Profit and loss						
account	4,000		Current Assets			
		12,000	Stock		13,500	
			Debtors		18,500	
		62,000	Bank balance		500	
			Cash in transit		200	
Debentures		20,000				32,700
Corporation tax–			Deferred Asset			
Current Year		7,000	ACT recoverable			3,694
Current Liabilities						
Bank overdraft	300					
Creditors	4,500					
Corporation tax–						
previous year	5,900					
Proposed dividend						
of Great Ltd	5,000					
ACT on proposed						
dividend	3,694					
		19,394				
		£108,394				£108,394

Example 2 Wholly-owned subsidiary, equity capital acquired at a cost above par, pre-acquisition reserves.

Master Ltd, on 1 January 19.1, acquired all the 40,000 £1 ordinary shares of Servant Ltd in exchange for 50,000 of its own £1 ordinary shares, market value £62,000. Servant Ltd's reserves at that date (including proposed dividend, £2,000) were £17,000. The balance sheets (abbreviated) as at 31 December 19.1 were as follows:

Master Ltd

Balance Sheet, 31 December 19.1

	£	£		£
Share Capital			Fixed Assets	90,000
Ordinary shares		150,000		
			Shares in Subsidiary Company,	
Reserves			at cost less dividend out of subsidiary	
Share premium			company's pre-acquisition profits	60,000
account	12,000			
Profit and loss				
account	18,000		Current Assets	100,000
		30,000		
			Deferred Asset	11,082
		180,000		
Corporation Tax—				
Current Year		25,000		
Current Liabilities				
General	30,000			
Proposed dividend	15,000			
ACT on proposed				
dividend	11,082			
		56,082		
		£261,082		£261,082

Servant Ltd

Balance Sheet, 31 December 19.1

	£	£		£
Share Capital			Fixed Assets	55,000
Ordinary shares		40,000		
			Current Assets	30,000
Reserves				
Profit and loss			Deferred Asset	2,955
account		20,000		
		60,000		
Corporation Tax—				
Current Year		10,000		
Current Liabilities				
General	11,000			
Proposed dividend	4,000			
ACT on proposed				
dividend	2,955			
		17,955		
		£87,955		£87,955

When an acquisition is effected by an exchange of shares, those acquired from the subsidiary's former shareholders are valued in the holding company's books at the *market value* of the shares issued in exchange (i.e. the nominal value plus a premium, the share premium account being credited). This market value is not necessarily the market *capitalization* (number of shares x stock exchange price), since the quoted price is fixed on the assumption that only a small number of shares will be traded at once, and is subject to short-term influences. The acquisition market value should be assessed on the long-term prospects of the acquirer, having regard to all relevant factors. Should part of the acquisition price be paid in cash, the amount thereof should be added to the market value of the shares issued, and similarly if securities other than equity are issued, the present value being used in the case of debentures or other loan stock.

In consolidation at any future date, the balance sheet valuation of the investment in the subsidiary is compared with the valuation of the shares, according to the subsidiary's books, as at the date of acquisition—i.e. the book value of assets, less liabilities, since this is deemed to be the value of the tangible part of the consideration. This in turn is found by adding together the subsidiary's share capital and reserves (including proposed dividend) at the date of acquisition. Thus, in *Example 2,* a cost of £62,000 is compared with a net amount in the subsidiary's books of (£40,000 + £17,000 =) £57,000, giving a difference of £5,000.

Such a difference is normal, since the take-over price bears no close relationship to book amounts. After acquisition the subsidiary's tangible assets should be revalued in its books, and a capital reserve credited with any net appreciation. This will form part of the *pre-acquisition reserves,* and thus reduce the excess of investment cost over net book value. (A deficiency should be debited to any available capital reserves, or failing these to revenue reserves.) It is advisable to revalue the holding company's assets at the same time, so that in consolidation like is added to like.

If any dividend is paid to the holding company out of the subsidiary's pre-acquisition reserves, it must be credited in the former's books to Shares in Subsidiary Company, as being a partial refund of the cost (as in *Example 2*). The pre-acquisition reserves must also be considered as reduced by the same amount.

If, after any revaluation, 'shares in subsidiary company' still exceed the subsidiary's share capital plus pre-acquisition reserves (both adjusted, if necessary, as described in the previous paragraph), the difference will not cancel out in consolidation. It must be regarded as the price paid for the subsidiary's undisclosed *goodwill,* and brought into the consolidated balance sheet as an asset, so described—being either included with any goodwill already on the books, or (better) disclosed separately. British companies tend to retain goodwill, so arising, indefinitely in successive accounts. In America, though it is considered better to write it off, either against consolidated earnings over a period of years (as representing a purchase of future super-profits, needing to be amortized as they materialize), or immediately, in one sum, against reserves (as representing the present value of future expectations of income, paid for out of the holding company's equity). These three treatments reflect different views on the nature of goodwill, as discussed in Chapter 6, sub-section **6.4.2.** The order in which they are given corresponds to the author's ascending order of preference; but the accountancy profession has yet to make up its mind—indeed, the English branch of it scarcely seems aware that a problem exists.

The acquisition method treats pre-acquisition reserves as quasi-capital reserves from the standpoint of the group. Only 'post-acquisition' reserves are consolidated with those of the holding company; where control was acquired during a financial year, the equity earnings will need to be apportioned (on a time basis if greater accuracy is impracticable) between the periods before and after acquisition. Any distributions by the subsidiary to the holding company are deemed to come first out of the post-acquisition reserves, unless the contrary is made clear; but if these are exhausted the excess must be regarded as coming out of pre-acquisition reserves, and thus as constituting a partial return of the purchase price (see earlier).

The work-sheet and (simplified) consolidated balance sheet are now illustrated for *Example 2*.

Master Ltd and its Subsidiary

Balance Sheet Consolidation Work-Sheet, 31 December 19.1

	Master Ltd £	Servant Ltd £	Sub-total £	Adjustments		Consolidated balance sheet £
				Debit £	Credit £	
Fixed Assets	90,000	55,000	145,000			145,000
Goodwill Arising on Consolidation	—	—	—	(3) 5,000		5,000
Shares in Subsidiary Company	60,000	—	60,000		(1) 40,000 ⎫ (2) 15,000 ⎬ (3) 5,000 ⎭	—
Current Assets	100,000	30,000	130,000			130,000
Deferred Asset	11,082	2,955	14,037		(5) 2,955	11,082
	£261,082	£87,955	£349,037			£291,082
Share Capital Ordinary shares	150,000	40,000	190,000	(1) 40,000		150,000
Reserves Share premium account	12,000	—	12,000			12,000
Profit and loss account	18,000	20,000	38,000	(2) 15,000	(4) 4,000	27,000
Corporation Tax— Current Year	25,000	10,000	35,000			35,000
Current Liabilities General	30,000	11,000	41,000			41,000
Proposed dividend	15,000	4,000	19,000	(4) 4,000		15,000
ACT on proposed dividend	11,082	2,955	14,037	(5) 2,955		11,082
	£261,082	£87,955	£349,037	£66,955	£66,955	£291,082

Notes on adjustments

1 Subsidiary's ordinary share capital set off against holding company's investment (reduced by amount of 'pre-acquisition' dividend from subsidiary).
2 Subsidiary's pre-acquisition reserves (so reduced) set off as in 1.
3 Remaining balance of holding company's investment ascribed to unrecorded goodwill of subsidiary.
4 Subsidiary's proposed dividend added back to its profit and loss account (post-acquisition).
5 Subsidiary's ACT on proposed dividend cancelled against its ACT recoverable.

Master Ltd and its Subsidiary

Consolidated Balance Sheet, 31 December 19.1

	£	£		£
Share Capital of Master Ltd		150,000	Fixed Assets General	145,000
			Goodwill arising on consolidation[1]	5,000
Reserves				150,000
Share premium account	12,000			
Profit and loss account	27,000	39,000	Current Assets	130,000
		189,000	Deferred Asset	11,082
Corporation Tax— Current Year		35,000		
Current Liabilities				
General	41,000			
Proposed dividend of Master Ltd	15,000			
ACT on proposed dividend of Master Ltd.	11,082	67,082		
		£291,082		£291,082

[1] Or better, perhaps, Net premium arising on consolidation; see below.

Example 3 Wholly-owned subsidiary, equity capital acquired at a cost less than its nominal value plus pre-acquisition reserves.

Suppose the same figures as in *Example 2,* except that Servant Ltd's pre-acquisition reserves (excluding its proposed dividend) were £21,000.

On consolidation, shares in subsidiary company, £60,000, are set against the subsidiary's total share capital and pre-acquisition reserves, £61,000, leaving £1,000 of the latter uncancelled. This item appears in the consolidated balance sheet as a capital reserve, which may be described as 'arising on consolidation', since it is undistributable by the holding company, and since any distribution of it by the subsidiary to its parent would result in a countervailing reduction of the latter's investment.

When the amount is thought of thus, rather than as a 'negative goodwill' or 'badwill' (as in some explanations), it is easy to expose the fallacy of those American accountants (once supported by an Opinion of the Accounting Principles Board, now withdrawn) who contended for the writing-off of a consolidation reserve to the credit of revenue over a period of years—as though pre-acquisition reserves became distributable merely by lapse of time. British accountants have never subscribed to this heresy; but they still consider it legitimate to offset a capital reserve in respect of one subsidiary against a goodwill in respect of another—which, if the capital reserve is indeed such, appears questionable. It becomes justifiable, however, if goodwill is regarded rather as a contra capital reserve, to be written off on acquisition against capital surplus, and then, if necessary, against revenue—in which case, residual goodwill ought not to be left on the consolidated balance sheet! English thinking and practice seem sadly muddled, and authoritative guidance, based on proper research, is long overdue. A reasonable interim compromise might be to avoid the terms 'goodwill' and 'capital reserve', and describe the items as, e.g. 'excess of cost of shares in subsidiaries over the book amount of the net assets of those companies at the date of acquisition'—and vice versa.

In the consolidated balance sheet of Master Ltd and its subsidiary, as modified, there will be no goodwill. The share capital and reserves will appear as below (with Profit and Loss Account £6,000 less), and the other figures (except the grand totals) will be the same as in *Example 2*.

	£	£
Share Capital of		
Master Ltd		
Ordinary shares		150,000
Reserves		
Share premium account	12,000	
Capital reserve arising		
on consolidation	1,000	
Profit and loss account	21,000	
		34,000
		184,000

Example 4 Partly-owned subsidiary, with pre-acquisition reserves and a 'goodwill' element.

Capital Ltd acquired in 19.0 for £51,000 75 per cent of the ordinary shares of Country Ltd, whose reserves at the time were £4,000. The two balance sheets (simplified) as at 31 December 19.1 were as follows:

Capital Ltd

Balance Sheet, 31 December 19.1

	£	£		£
Share Capital			*Fixed Assets*	60,000
Ordinary shares		100,000		
			Shares in Subsidiary	
			Company,	
Reserves			at cost	51,000
Share premium account	10,000			
Profit and loss account	15,000		*Current Assets*	59,000
		25,000		
			Deferred Asset	5,910
		125,000		
Corporation Tax—				
Current Year		16,000		
Current Liabilities				
General	21,000			
Proposed dividend	8,000			
ACT on proposed				
dividend	5,910			
		34,910		
		£175,910		£175,910

Country Ltd

Balance Sheet, 31 December 19.1

	£	£		£
Share Capital			**Fixed Assets**	58,000
Ordinary shares		60,000		
			Current Assets	42,000
Reserves				
Profit and loss account		12,000	**Deferred Asset**	4,433
		72,000		
Corporation Tax—				
Current Year		9,000		
Current Liabilities				
General	13,000			
Proposed dividend	6,000			
ACT on proposed dividend	4,433			
		23,433		
		£104,433		£104,433

With a partly-owned subsidiary, all true assets and liabilities are consolidated as for a wholly-owned company, since they are all controlled, and owned, by the group, and elimination of inter-company indebtedness is effected in the same manner as before. The additional complexities arise from the need to segregate the book value of the *minority interest*; to set off the holding company's investment against the relevant portion only, instead of the whole, of the subsidiary's share capital and pre-acquisition reserves; and to bring into group reserves only the relevant portion of the post-acquisition element.

The accepted method of dealing with the subsidiary's share capital, reserves, and proposed dividend is first to assign to the minority its rateable proportion of these items—the distinction between pre-acquisition and post-acquisition reserves is irrelevant here. The remainder (holding company's interest) is then analysed as before, and a goodwill or capital reserve found by subtraction of the cost of the shares, thus (for the companies in *Example 4*):

	Holding company, 75 per cent		Minority interest, 25 per cent
	Pre-Acquisition £	Post-Acquisition £	£
Country Limited			
Share Capital			
Ordinary shares	45,000	–	15,000
Reserves			
Profit and loss account	3,000	6,000	3,000
Proposed Dividend	–	4,500	1,500
	48,000	£10,500	£19,500
Capital Limited			
Shares in Subsidiary			
Company	51,000		
Goodwill	£3,000		

This table provides the less obvious figures for the work-sheet, not illustrated. The (simplified) consolidated balance sheet appears thus:

Capital Ltd and its Subsidiary

Consolidated Balance Sheet, 31 December 19.1

	£	£		£
Share Capital of Capital Ltd		100,000	*Fixed Assets* General	118,000
			Goodwill arising on consolidation	3,000
Reserves				
Share premium account	10,000			121,000
Profit and loss account	25,500			
		35,500		
			Current Assets	101,000
		135,500		
Minority Interest in Share Capital and Reserves of Subsidiary		19,500	*Deferred Asset*	5,910
Corporation Tax — Current Year		25,000		
Current Liabilities				
General	34,000			
Proposed dividend of Capital Ltd	8,000			
ACT on proposed dividend of Capital Ltd	5,910			
		47,910		
		£227,910		£227,910

Note that the minority interest is placed immediately after the sub-total of the holding company's share capital and attributable reserves, as being an additional source of equity to the group.

The conventional English treatment of goodwill (or capital reserve) in the case of a partly-owned subsidiary has little to commend it on logical grounds. If the amount really represents the subsidiary's goodwill (or badwill), why is only the holding company's proportion taken into account? Surely, if 75 per cent of Country Ltd's goodwill is £3,000, then the total is (100/75 × £3,000 =) £4,000; this should be the valuation in the consolidated balance sheet, and the minority interest should be increased by £1,000. (A capital reserve should similarly be increased to its full amount, and the minority interest reduced *pro tanto*.) If, on the other hand, the £3,000 is a contra capital reserve, it should not be increased, since it affects only the holding company, but ought to be written off capital surplus, or failing that off revenue reserves, either in one sum or by instalments over several years, as suggested earlier for a wholly-owned subsidiary.

16.4.3 Acquisition method of profit and loss account consolidation

The Companies Acts require a consolidated profit and loss account as well as a balance sheet, and the 'acquisition' method of preparing it is now considered. But whereas the consolidated balance sheet is additional to the separate balance sheet of the holding company, the consolidated profit and loss account normally *displaces* the holding company's account, which need not be published if the consolidated one 'shows how much of the consolidated profit or loss for the financial year is dealt with in the accounts of the [holding] company' (1948 Act, s. 149(5)). The common mode of compliance is illustrated below.

A consolidated profit and loss account is prepared by combining the information contained in the notional published profit and loss account of the holding company, and the actual ones of the subsidiaries. In a straightforward case the figures of turnover, net trading profit, charges disclosed inset (except for directors' remuneration, which is disclosed for the holding company's directors only, in the notes on the accounts), miscellaneous income from outside the group, and corporation tax (including write-backs) are simply aggregated, while inter-company dividends and subventions (i.e. subsidies from profitable to unprofitable companies) are omitted, and adjustments made for inter-company loan interest. Group net profit, before and after taxation, is arrived at by subtraction. Thus the first part of the consolidated account is prepared from the standpoint of the whole group, regardless of any minority interests in subsidiaries.

The second part, however, reveals the position from the standpoint of the holding company's shareholders. It begins with the net profit, after taxation, attributable to such shareholders—i.e. the group net profit less minority interests in it. The total amount of these may be deducted overtly from the group figure, or the latter may be ruled off and the account recommenced with the holding company's proportion (as shown below). The holding company's dividends and other distributions are then deducted from the sub-total; the subsidiaries' distributions to their minorities have already been eliminated with the underlying earnings. The closing figure represents the amount added to the group reserves by the trading operations for the year, and will enter into the statement of movements on reserves, in the notes on the accounts.

Finally, in order to comply with the 1948 Act, s. 149(5), and so avoid publishing the holding company's profit and loss account, a note is made of the amount of consolidated profit (or loss) 'dealt with in the accounts of the [holding] company'. This is the net profit after taxation, as shown in that company's unpublished profit and loss account—i.e. its own profit/loss, plus/minus dividends received from subsidiaries.

Example 5 Below are exhibited the work-sheet for consolidating the profit and loss accounts of National Ltd and its 75 per cent owned subsidiary, Provincial Ltd (with notes on the adjustments), and the consolidated account (simplified). National Ltd holds 20 per cent of Provincial Ltd's debentures.

National Ltd and its Subsidiary

Profit and Loss Account Consolidation Work-Sheet for the Year ended 31 December 19.1

	National Ltd £	Provincial Ltd £	Sub-total £	Adjustments Debit £	Adjustments Credit £	Consolidated Profit and Loss A/c £
Turnover	£500,000	£200,000	£700,000			£700,000
Vet Trading Profit after charging	50,000	22,000	72,000		(1) 1,000	73,000
Auditors' remuneration	3,000	2,000	5,000			5,000
Depreciation	20,000	10,000	30,000			30,000
Debenture interest	8,000	5,000	13,000		(1) 1,000	12,000
Dividend from subsidiary company	6,000	—	6,000 (2)	6,000		—
Income from investments—						
Quoted	4,000	1,000	5,000			5,000
Unquoted	1,000	—	1,000 (1)	1,000		—
Net Profit before Taxation	61,000	23,000	84,000	7,000	1,000	78,000
Corporation tax	28,000	12,000	40,000			40,000
Less Overprovision in previous year	(2,000)	(1,000)	(3,000)			(3,000)
Net Profit after Taxation	£35,000	£12,000	£47,000	£7,000	£1,000	£41,000
Attributable to Company's Shareholders	35,000	12,000	47,000	(3) 7,000 3,000	1,000	38,000
Dividends						
Paid	10,000	8,000	18,000		(4) 8,000	10,000
Proposed	15,000	2,000	17,000		(5) 2,000	15,000
Amount Added to Reserves	£10,000	£2,000	£12,000	£10,000	£11,000	£13,000

Notes on adjustments

1 20 per cent of subsidiary's debenture interest (£5,000) received by holding company; added back to subsidiary's net trading profit and deducted from holding company's income from unquoted investments.
2 Inter-company dividend paid, eliminated.
3 Minority interest (25 per cent) in subsidiary's net profit after taxation, eliminated.
4, 5 Subsidiary's dividends eliminated.

Note The debit and credit adjustment columns do not 'balance', as the profit and loss accounts are not complete, and some adjustments appear once only. The sub-totals and grand totals account, at each stage, for the difference between the third and sixth columns.

National Ltd and its Subsidiary

Consolidated Profit and Loss Account for the Year ended 31 December 19.1

	£	£
Turnover		£700,000
Net Trading Profit,		73,000
after charging the items below:		
Auditors' remuneration	5,000	
Depreciation	30,000	
Debenture interest	12,000	
Income from Investments		
Quoted		5,000
Net Profit before Taxation		78,000
Corporation tax	40,000	
Less Overprovision in previous year	3,000	
		37,000
Net Profit after Taxation		£41,000
Attributable to Shareholders in National Ltd		38,000
(of which £35,000 is dealt with in the accounts of that company)		
Dividends of National Ltd		
Paid	10,000	
Proposed	15,000	
		25,000
Amount Added to Reserves of Group		£13,000

Such are the main principles of consolidation by the acquisition method. The modifications required for the merger method now call for exposition.

16.5 Merger method of consolidation

In sub-section **16.4.1** it was explained that, in the opinion of the Accounting Standards Steering Committee, the merger method should be used to consolidate the accounts of a group which was formed by bringing together two or more companies whose businesses were substantially continued, wholly or mainly by an exchange of voting equity shares, such that no constituent company's shareholders obtain more than three times as many votes in the merged undertaking as those of any other such company, and with no minority interest in any subsidiary, greater than 10 per cent of the total share capital. The practical treatment of balance sheet and profit and loss account items follows standard American lines, as described below.

16.5.1 Details of the merger method

Aggregation of balance sheet assets and liabilities, class by class, and offsetting of inter-company indebtedness, are as already stated. Minority interests in subsidiaries are computed in the same manner, by taking the relevant proportions of share capital, reserves, and proposed dividends. The treatment of shares in subsidiaries, and of the corresponding share capital and reserves, etc., is different.

Holdings in a subsidiary are regarded as having been acquired for the nominal value of the holding company's shares issued in exchange, plus any cash payment. The market value of the shares is ignored, and no credit is made to the share premium account. In consolidation, all the subsidiary's reserves (apart from any minority interest) are simply added, class by class, to those of the holding company and, insofar as they are distributable by the subsidiary, are considered free for distribution through the holding company's profit and loss account. There is no distinction between pre-acquisition and post-acquisition elements.

The holding company's asset 'shares in subsidiary company' is then offset against the relevant proportion of the subsidiary's share capital. If the latter amount is larger, so that it does not fully cancel out, the difference is entered on the consolidated balance sheet as a 'capital reserve arising on consolidation'. If 'shares in subsidiary company' is the larger amount, the excess is regarded as a 'contra capital reserve', and deducted from any capital surplus which has otherwise arisen—e.g. from similar differences the other way, or from revaluation of tangible assets by any of the companies. If the capital surplus is insufficient or non-existent, the balance of the contra reserve must be deducted from revenue reserves of the group (*not* from share premium account or capital redemption reserve fund, as they cannot legally be applied in this manner).

Consolidation of the profit and loss accounts is effected as for an acquisition, except in the year when the merger takes place. The merged companies' accounts are consolidated as they stand, as though the merger had been in force throughout the year, and the corresponding amounts for the previous year are adjusted to the same basis, as though the merger had been in force then—thus emphasizing the continuity of the businesses. In a year of acquisition, on the other hand, the pre-acquisition element in the new subsidiary's profit/loss is excluded, and the corresponding amounts are taken from the previous year's consolidated accounts, without retrospective adjustment.

Finally, ED3 recommends that in the year of the merger the group accounts should disclose:

a the fact that a merger has taken place, accounted for as above;
b the names of the constituent companies;
c particulars of securities issued in respect of the merger; and
d details of significant accounting adjustments amongst the constituent companies to achieve consistency of accounting bases, and of the financial effects of such changes.

In subsequent years it should always be made clear that the merger method has been employed.

Example 6 Brother Ltd and Sister Ltd are merged on 1 January 19.1, by the formation of a new holding company, Siblings Ltd, with which they make an exchange of shares. Siblings Ltd issues 100,000 voting ordinary shares of £1 each to the members of Brother Ltd, and 50,000 to those of Sister Ltd, at par, in exchange for the entire equity capital of the two companies. On 1 July 19.1, Siblings Ltd issues 35,000 voting ordinary shares at par in return for 90 per cent of those of Stranger Ltd. The existing businesses of the three subsidiaries are continued.

The four balance sheets (summarized) as at 31 December 19.1 were as follows:

Siblings Ltd and its Subsidiaries

Balance Sheets (summarized), 31 December 19.1

	Siblings Ltd £	Brother Ltd £	Sister Ltd £	Stranger Ltd £
Sundry Assets	27,000	168,000	85,500	74,500
Shares in Subsidiary Companies, at nominal value of ordinary shares of Siblings Ltd issued in exchange	185,000	–	–	–
Deferred Asset	13,668	7,388	3,325	1,847
	£225,668	£175,388	£88,825	£76,347
Share Capital				
Ordinary shares	185,000	100,000	45,000	50,000
Reserves				
Share premium account	–	20,000	15,000	–
Revaluation surplus	–	10,000	5,000	–
Profit and loss account	5,000	8,000	6,000	10,000
	190,000	138,000	71,000	60,000
Sundry Liabilities	3,500	20,000	10,000	12,000
Proposed Dividend	18,500	10,000	4,500	2,500
ACT on Proposed Dividend	13,668	7,388	3,325	1,847
	£225,668	£175,388	£88,825	£76,347

The group as a whole qualifies for treatment as a merger (voting rights 20: 10: 7), and the share capital of the subsidiaries is dealt with thus:

	Total £	Brother Ltd £	Sister Ltd £	Stranger Ltd £
Share Capital				
Ordinary shares	195,000	100,000	45,000	50,000
Less Minority interest	5,000	–	–	5,000
	190,000	100,000	45,000	45,000
Siblings Ltd–				
Shares in subsidiary companies	185,000	100,000	50,000	35,000
Capital Reserve/(Contra Capital Reserve)	£5,000	–	(£5,000)	£10,000

A net capital reserve of £5,000 thus results, and the consolidated balance sheet (simplified) is as below. Had Siblings Ltd issued 45,000 shares in exchange for Stranger Ltd's shares, there would have been a net contra capital reserve of £5,000, which would have been deducted from the revaluation surplus, reducing it, in total, to £10,000.

Siblings Ltd and its Subsidiaries

Consolidated Balance Sheet, 31 December 19.1

	£	£		£
Share Capital of Siblings Ltd			*Sundry Assets*	355,000
Ordinary shares		185,000		
Reserves			*Deferred Asset*	13,668
Share premium account	35,000			
Capital reserve arising on				
consolidation	5,000			
Revaluation surplus	15,000			
Profit and loss account	44,750			
		99,750		
		284,750		
Minority Interest in Share				
Capital and Reserves of				
Subsidiary		6,250		
Sundry Liabilities		45,500		
Proposed Dividend of Siblings				
Ltd		18,500		
ACT on Proposed Dividend of				
Siblings Ltd		13,668		
		£368,668		£368,668

Had Siblings Ltd issued only 30,000 shares in exchange for those of Stranger Ltd, the latter would have had to be treated as an 'acquired' company, since the voting disparity with Brother Ltd would have been 10: 3, or more than three to one. It would have been necessary to consolidate Siblings, Brother, and Sister by the merger method, and treat the resulting 'super-entity' as a holding company, with which Stranger would have then to be consolidated by the acquisition method. (The reader may find this an instructive exercise, on the assumptions that the pre-acquisition reserves of Stranger Ltd were £8,000, and that Siblings Ltd valued its 'acquisition' share issue at £54,000.)

16.5.2 Acquisition and merger methods compared

The essential difference between the two methods lies in the treatment of the subsidiaries' pre-acquisition reserves. The acquisition approach regards the relevant proportion of these as capitalized from the standpoint of the holding company's shareholders, so that any distribution of the said reserves to the holding company must be reckoned as a partial return of the purchase consideration, which is based on a realistic assessment of the market value of the shares issued in exchange. The merger method, on the other hand, rests on a conception of the group as a mere framework uniting a number of enterprises, previously independent, which have now joined forces voluntarily, and whose entire revenue reserves are still available for distribution to the united body of investors, represented by the shareholders of the holding company—which is not an outside purchaser, but a mere co-ordinating agency created by the constituent companies themselves. Valuation of the consideration shares at par is a mere book-keeping device to ensure elimination of the subsidiaries' share capital in consolidation—any difference between the two sets of par values being adjusted into the group reserves, so that the consolidated equity is always equal to the total equities of the subsidiaries (after adding back 'internal' proposed dividends and eliminating minority interests), plus the holding company's reserves, themselves derived from 'internal' distributions by subsidiaries. Thus, in

Example 6, the group equity, £284,750, is equal to the sum of the subsidiaries' equities, as adjusted, minus the 10 per cent minority interest in Stranger Ltd, and plus the reserves of Siblings Ltd:

$$£148,000 + £75,500 + (£62,500 - £6,250) + £5,000 = £284,750.$$

(In North American mergers, where shares of no par value are exchanged, those issued by the holding company are valued at the book amounts, excluding reserves, of the subsidiaries' shares taken in return, so that inter-company holdings cancel out precisely.)

An acquisition normally involves a revaluation of the new subsidiary's assets, in order to establish a realistic figure of goodwill or capital reserve. In a merger there is often no revaluation, so that consolidation of assets tends to produce aggregates of imperfectly-additive values within classes, and thus to compound the theoretical anomalies arising from summation of physical, financial, and intangible assets. This has given further ammunition to those who assert that the merger method is unsound in principle; but such practices are not inherent in the method, and a general revaluation at the time of amalgamation should always be made.

Some critics contend that the merger method is illegal in Great Britain. The Companies Act, 1948 s. 56(1), states that where a company issues shares at a premium, whether for cash or otherwise, a sum equal to the aggregate amount or value of the premium *shall* be transferred to the share premium account. Further the Companies Act, 1967, Schedule 2, para. 15(5), says that, where subsidiaries' aggregate profits or losses are stated in lieu of including them in group accounts, pre-acquisition profits/losses are to be omitted (see sub-section **16.2.4**). This might be held to indicate a Parliamentary intention that such profits/losses should be excluded generally from group accounts, and thus compel the courts to rule against a technique which does not make the distinction. As already stated, the ASSC seems to have had serious doubts on the whole question, and ED3 appears to have been quietly dropped.

16.6 Further points on consolidation

Thus far attention has been concentrated, for the sake of clarity, upon the crucial relationships between the holding company's investment and the subsidiaries' share capital and reserves, while asset consolidation has been taken for granted, as well as the precise determination of pre-acquisition reserves, where applicable. These and other matters now call for consideration.

16.6.1 Inter-company sales and stocks

It is common, especially in vertically integrated groups, for goods to be sold, or services rendered, by one group company to another. In the consolidated profit and loss account such inter-company transactions should be eliminated, at their gross amounts, from group turnover or gross receipts, and a note made to this effect. Turnover, etc., will then represent only sales, etc., to persons outside the group.

Inter-company services, as distinct from sales, require no further adjustment, since any profit made by one company merely reduces the profit of the other, and the two, being aggregated, produce a correct total profit for the group. The same applies to inter-company sales of goods, where the selling company acquires or manufactures them, and the buying company resells them to outsiders, both within the same accounting year. The costs of purchase or manufacture, and the ultimate proceeds of sale, both enter into the group net profit for the year, and costs and revenues are matched in consolidation.

Complications arise, however, when the inter-company sale and the outside sale take place in different years. The goods will then be taken into stock at the year-end by the purchasing company, at a price which includes a profit to the selling company. This is realized from the standpoint of the latter, and properly included in its net profit for the year; but it is unrealized from the standpoint of the group, and needs to be eliminated from the consolidated accounts for the current year, and included in those of the following year, when it is realized by a sale out of the group.

In the consolidated balance sheet, 'inter-company' stock must be reduced to its cost, as calculated by the supplying company—whether on a FIFO, LIFO, average-cost or other basis, or in the case of goods manufactured within the group, on a full-cost, variable-cost or relevant-cost basis, as appropriate. The eliminated profit, where there is no minority interest in the supplying company, is deducted from the consolidated balance of profit and loss account.

Where there are minority shareholders in the supplying company, the inter-company profit is realized from their point of view, and it is argued by many accountants that the minority interest should be shown in the consolidated balance sheet at its full amount, including the minority's proportion of the inter-company profit in stock. The entire sum should be charged to group profit and loss account, and thus the whole burden of the adjustment will fall upon the holding company's shareholders. Other accountants consider this unfair to the latter class, and prefer to apportion the burden of the adjustment *pro rata* between group reserves and minority interest; the last-named amount is regarded as a balancing figure only, of no practical interest to any actual minority shareholder, who will ascertain the book value of his interest from the accounts of his own company. This seems to the author to be the soundest opinion, and is followed in the ensuing illustration. (Yet other practices are, to eliminate from stock, and from group profit and loss account, only the holding company's proportion of the profit—thus stating correctly both group and minority interests, but valuing the stock unrealistically; or to do this, but analyse the stock figure, inset, between its 'pure' cost and the minority's proportion of the inter-company profit, added back as representing a cost arising from omission to acquire 100 per cent ownership of the subsidiary.)

In the consolidated profit and loss account, the net trading profit and the net profit before taxation are both reduced by the full amount of profit eliminated from year-end stock, irrespective of any minority interest. They are also increased by the amount which was eliminated at the end of the previous year, since the goods have been sold in the current year, and the inter-company profit in them has now been realized. These adjustments are performed on the work-sheet, only the amended figures appearing in the published accounts.

Where the amounts involved are material, the corporation tax charge should be adjusted also. The current year's liability, as shown in the consolidated balance sheet, is computed without regard to the carrying-forward procedure just described, and any net difference between the two consolidated figures will have to be adjusted into the (consolidated) deferred taxation account balance. This credit balance is reduced by the tax on the amount of profit deferred to next year, but taxed in this year, and increased by the tax on the amount of profit brought forward from last year (thus reversing last year's adjustment); and the net change is adjusted, in the opposite direction, into the group profit and loss account balance, to make it consistent with the consolidated profit and loss account.

On the latter, when the minority interest is deducted to arrive at the holding company's share of the group net profit after taxation, any (pre-tax) inter-company profit adjusted into the minority interest on the consolidated balance sheet must be added back to the holding company's amount—the calculation being, again, performed on the work-sheet.

Example 7 Sun Ltd has an 80 per cent subsidiary, Planet Ltd, and their consolidation work-sheets are shown below for the year ended 31 December 19.1. Planet's shares were acquired by Sun at par, when Planet had no reserves. Planet sold to Sun during the year, for £50,000, goods which had cost £40,000. Of these, Sun had £25,000 in stock at the year-end (cost to Planet, £20,000). The corresponding figures for the previous year-end were £10,000 and £8,000. Corporation tax in both years, 52 per cent.

Sun Ltd and its Subsidiary

Balance Sheet Consolidation Work-Sheet, 31 December 19.1

	Sun Ltd £	Planet Ltd £	Sub-total £	Adjustments Debit £	Credit £	Consolidated Balance Sheet £
Sundry Assets	200,000	150,000	350,000			350,000
Shares in Subsidiary Company	80,000	—	80,000		(1) 80,000	—
Stock	120,000	60,000	180,000		(2) 4,000	175,000
					(3) 1,000	
	£400,000	£210,000	£610,000			£525,000
Share Capital						
Ordinary shares	250,000	100,000	350,000	(1) 80,000		250,000
				(2) 20,000		
Reserves						
Profit and loss a/c	30,000	50,000	80,000	(6) 11,000	(5) 5,000	71,560
				(2) 4,000	(7) 1,560	
	280,000	150,000	430,000			321,560
Minority Interest	—	—	—	(3) 1,000	(4) 20,000	30,000
					(6) 11,000	
Deferred Taxation	5,224	3,306	8,530	(7) 1,560	(8) 3,694	10,664
Corporation Tax—						
Current Year	17,836	9,918	27,754			27,754
Current Liabilities						
General	62,164	38,082	100,246			100,246
Proposed dividend	20,000	5,000	25,000	(5) 5,000		20,000
ACT on proposed dividend	14,776	3,694	18,470	(8) 3,694		14,776
	£400,000	£210,000	£610,000	£126,254	£126,254	£525,000

Notes on adjustments

1 Elimination of inter-company shareholding.
2 80 per cent of inter-company profit in stock, £5,000, set off against group reserves.

3 Remaining 20 per cent set off against minority interest.
4 20 per cent of subsidiary's share capital transferred to minority interest.
5 Subsidiary's proposed dividend added back to profit and loss account.
6 20 per cent of subsidiary's adjusted profit and loss account balance transferred to minority interest.
7 Tax on excess (£3,000) of 19.1 inter-company profit in closing stock (£5,000) over that of 19.0 (£2,000), at 52 per cent (£1,650), transferred from deferred taxation to profit and loss account.
8 Subsidiary's ACT on proposed dividend transferred back to deferred taxation, to which it was previously debited (no deferred asset).

Sun Ltd and its Subsidiary

Profit and Loss Account Consolidation Work-Sheet for the Year ended 31 December 19.1

	Sun Ltd £	Planet Ltd £	Sub-Total £	Adjustments Debit £	Adjustments Credit £	Consolidated Profit and Loss A/c £
Turnover	£800,000	£400,000	£1,200,000(1)	£50,000	–	£1,150,000
Net Trading Profit	80,000	40,000	120,000 (2)	5,000 (3)	2,000	117,000
Dividend from subsidiary company	8,000	–	8,000 (4)	8,000		–
Net Profit Before Taxation	88,000	40,000	128,000	13,000	2,000	117,000
Corporation Tax	40,000	21,000	61,000		(5) 1,560	59,440
Net Profit After Taxation	£48,000	£19,000	£67,000	£13,000	£3,560	£57,560
Attributable to Company's Shareholders	48,000	19,000	67,000	13,000 (6) 3,800	3,560) (7) 1,000)	54,760
Dividends—						
Paid	10,000	10,000	20,000		(8)10,000	10,000
Proposed	20,000	5,000	25,000		(9) 5,000	20,000
Amount Added to Reserves	£18,000	£4,000	£22,000	£16,800	£19,560	£24,760

Notes on adjustments

1 Inter-company sales eliminated.
2 Inter-company profit in closing stock carried forward to next year.
3 Inter-company profit in opening stock brought forward from last year.
4 Inter-company dividend eliminated.
5 See Note 7 on balance sheet consolidation (*Dr.* Deferred Taxation Account).
6 Minority interest (20 per cent) in subsidiary's net profit after taxation, eliminated.
7 See Note 3 on balance sheet consolidation.
8,9 Subsidiary's dividends eliminated.

16.6.2 Fixed assets

When physical fixed assets are transferred from one group company to another, any profit or loss on the sale requires adjustment on the same lines as for inter-company stocks. The depreciation charge in the profit and loss account will also need adjusting (*Dr.* Fixed Assets, *Cr.* Profit and Loss Account, for a reduction—vice versa for an increase).

When the acquisition method of consolidation is used, the written down value of the subsidiary's fixed assets at the date of take-over is usually treated as their cost for purposes of the consolidated balance sheet (as long as those assets remain on the books), and accumulated depreciation is shown only for the period since the company joined the group. The amount of the 'pre-acquisition' depreciation is deducted from cost, etc., and from accumulated depreciation, leaving the net book value unchanged. This adjustment is omitted when the merger method is used, since continuity of business, before and after amalgamation, is assumed.

16.6.3 Determination of pre-acquisition reserves

In acquisition accounting, the precise date at which a new subsidiary joins the group is not always obvious, even when a controlling holding is purchased in one block, by negotiations with the other company. Normally the operative date is that on which the consideration passes, but the contract may specify an earlier date. The opinion of the ASSC (Exposure Draft 3, 1971) is, that the date of acquisition should be no earlier than the date when substantial agreement was reached on terms, or that from which the subsidiary's income accrued to the holding company; in no circumstances should it be earlier than the date of the subsidiary's last audited balance sheet. If profits are deemed to accrue before consideration in cash or loan stock is paid or issued, an interest adjustment is necessary, in the subsidiary's favour.

Where control is acquired by means of a series of purchases in the open market, until a majority holding is amassed, the subsidiary's pre-acquisition reserves are those on hand at the point in time when control was acquired (with apportionment of the year's profits, as necessary). If, however, a number of large blocks of shares are purchased over time (e.g. 30 per cent, 30 per cent, 40 per cent), then control is acquired when, e.g. 60 per cent has been bought. In such a case it is best to assign to each block, retrospectively, its due proportion of the reserves as at the date of purchase, and take the total allocation as the pre-acquisition reserves.

16.6.4 Cross-holdings between subsidiary and holding company

The Companies Act, 1948, s. 27, forbids a subsidiary, or its nominee, to acquire shares from its holding company; except where the subsidiary, etc., is interested only as personal representative, or as trustee (unless either company is beneficially interested under the trust, and not merely by way of security for money lent in the ordinary course of business). Subsidiaries which held shares in their holding companies before the Act was passed are allowed to retain them, but not to vote at meetings in respect of them. The same exception apparently extends to companies which held shares in each other, at the date when one company acquired control of the other.

In the consolidated balance sheet the nominal amount of the subsidiary's holding is deducted, inset, from the holding company's total issued capital, leaving only outside shareholders' holdings. Where the subsidiary is wholly owned no further adjustment is needed, since the whole undertaking of both companies is effectively owned by the holding company's outside shareholders—except that cross-payments of, and provisions for, dividends will have to be cancelled out.

Where a partly-owned subsidiary is in question, however, the position is more complex. Any distribution by the holding company goes partly to the subsidiary, and the latter's minority shareholders gain an interest in part of it, the rest going back to the holding company! The possible number of circular distributions of this kind is theoretically infinite; each time round there is a dividend to the minority, and the amount distributed grows rapidly smaller.

Example 8 High Ltd owns 80 per cent of the equity of Low Ltd, which in turn owns 10 per cent of High Ltd's equity. Their share capitals at 31 December 19.1 were respectively £100,000 and £50,000, and their reserves (including proposed dividends) were £20,000, and £10,000.

The best approach is to compute the minority interest in the total reserves, and find the group interest by subtraction. If a series of successive total distributions is assumed, then the minority's proportions thereof are found thus:

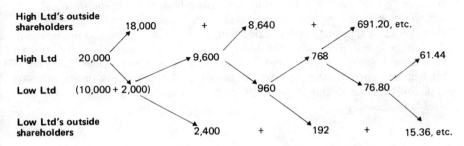

The minority's hypothetical dividends become very small after the third round, and the total tends towards a limit of £2,608.69. If the 20 per cent shareholding in Low Ltd is added (£10,000), the minority interest is found to be £12,609 (to the nearest £).

The minority's share of the reserves can be computed directly by the formula

$$M = \frac{r_1(S + r_2 H)}{1 - r_2(1 - r_1)}$$

where M = the minority interest in the group reserves;
H = the holding company's reserves;
S = the subsidiary's reserves;
r_1 = the minority interest in the subsidiary; and
r_2 = the subsidiary's interest in the holding company.

In the case supposed, substitution into the formula gives:

$$M = \frac{0.2\{£10,000 + 0.1\,(£20,000)\}}{1 - 0.1(1 - 0.2)}$$

$$= \frac{£2,400}{0.92}$$

$$= £2,609 \text{ (to the nearest £)}$$

From the solution, it is apparent that the formula simplifies to

$$\frac{D}{1-r_2 r_3}$$

where D = the subsidiary's hypothetical 'dividend' at the first round; and

r_3 = the holding company's interest in the subsidiary.

This simpler form is the recommended one for use in computation.

Some accountants reject the concept of distributions *ad infinitum,* and merely 'go once round', obtaining, in *Example 8,* £2,400 as the value of the minority interest in reserves. Since the formula is available, though, it seems a weakness not to use it. In either case, the basis adopted should be disclosed.

Cross-holdings between subsidiaries may cause further complications in a few cases; solutions can be found with the techniques just described.

16.6.5 Multiple consolidations

Where a group has two or more tiers of subsidiaries, sub-subsidiaries, etc., consolidation should be performed in stages. Each company on the next-to-lowest level should be separately consolidated with its own subsidiaries, and the figures in the last columns of its work-sheets incorporated in the work-sheets of its own immediate holding company—and so on upwards, until the parent company is reached, and consolidated accounts can be prepared from *its* work-sheets. Interests in fellow-subsidiaries should be dealt with according to the facts, on the lines already indicated.

16.6.6 Group companies' accounts made up to different dates

While it is obviously desirable, in the interests of coherence and consistency, to cause all companies in a group to make up their accounts to the same date each year, this is not always practicable, particularly where some of the subsidiaries are incorporated abroad. In such cases the best that can be done is to consolidate the accounts for the year ended next before the holding company's year-end. Where any inter-company items fail to cancel out because of non-coincidence of dates a balancing figure will have to be inserted, with a caption describing its nature. Full provision should be made for any loss incurred by the subsidiary between its accounting date and that of the holding company.

16.6.7 Consolidation of overseas subsidiaries' accounts

The published accounts of subsidiaries incorporated abroad will be prepared according to the laws of the countries concerned, and often will not contain all the information required in British company accounts. The subsidiaries should therefore furnish the parent company with confidential accounts drawn up to British specifications.

The second problem arises from the use of currencies other than sterling. The figures in the accounts will require conversion on appropriate bases, as described in

Chapter 8, section 8.2, with the insertion in the consolidated balance sheet of a 'difference arising on conversion of foreign currencies', where applicable.

16.7 Accounting for associated companies

The threefold, and overlapping, requirements of the Companies Act, 1967, with regard to information about non-subsidiary shareholdings—quoted/unquoted securities, unquoted equity holdings, 10 per cent holdings—make no mention of associated companies as such; i.e. those which, though not subsidiaries, are to some extent dominated by the parent company. Standard practice in the United States now requires partial consolidation of their annual results with those of the holding company, and it was in the light of this that Statement of Standard Accounting Practice No. 1: *Accounting for the results of associated companies* was issued in 1971. It was slightly revised in 1974.

16.7.1 Statement of Standard Accounting Practice No. 1 (1971, revised 1974): Accounting for the results of associated companies

It is accepted practice for a company not to take credit in its (unconsolidated) profit and loss account for undistributed profits of other companies, since they are separate legal entities, and investment income should not normally be taken into account before it is received or receivable. Where, however, the company conducts an important part of its business through other companies, the mere disclosure, or inclusion, of dividend income alone is unlikely to give shareholders adequate information regarding the sources of their income and the manner in which their funds are being employed. As regards subsidiaries, the Companies Act, 1948 already requires the publication of group accounts.

In recent years some companies have developed the practice of conducting parts of their business through other companies (frequently consortia or joint venture companies) in which they have a substantial but not a controlling interest. At the same time investors have come to attach importance to earnings as distinct from dividends, and hence to the price/earnings (P/E) ratio, and to earnings per share. Thus, in order to provide a total of earnings from which the most meaningful ratios of this kind can be calculated, it is considered necessary to extend the coverage of consolidated accounts to include the company's share of earnings of so-called 'associated companies'.

The Statement defines an *associated company* as a non-subsidiary company, such that:

a the investing group or company's interest in the associated company is effectively that of a partner in a joint venture or consortium; or
b the said interest is for the long term and is substantial (i.e. not less than 20 per cent of the equity voting rights) and, having regard to the disposition of the other shareholdings, the investing group or company is in a position to exercise a significant influence over the associated company.

In both cases it is essential that the investing group or company participates (usually through representation on the board) in commercial and financial policy decisions of the associated company, including the distribution of profits.

SSAP No. 1 accordingly requires (in relation to accounting periods commencing on or after 1 January 1971) that income from investments by a company or its subsidiaries in associated companies should be brought into account on the following bases:

a In the investing company's own accounts—
    i dividends received up to the investing company's accounting date; and
    ii dividends receivable in respect of accounting periods ending on or before that date and declared before the accounts are approved by the directors.
b In the investing group's consolidated accounts—
    the investing group's share of profits less losses of associated companies.

A company without subsidiaries, or one which, for any other reason, does not prepare group accounts, must incorporate the information in b in its ordinary profit and loss account. Where the associated company is itself a holding company, the profits or losses to be dealt with under b are those of the group of which the associated company is parent.

The accounts used for this purpose should be audited accounts, either coterminous with those of the investing company or made up to a date not more than six months before, or shortly after, that of the investing group's own accounts. In the absence of such audited accounts (for which there should be justifiable cause) unaudited accounts may be used, provided the group is satisfied as to their reliability. In the case of associated companies listed on a recognised stock exchange, only published financial information should be used. Before incorporating results of an associated company based on accounts issued some appreciable time before the completion of the investing company's accounts, care should be taken to ensure that later information has not materially affected the view shown by the associated company's accounts. If accounts not coterminous with those of the investing company, or unaudited accounts, are used, the facts and the dates of year-ends should be disclosed.

The investing group should include its share of all material results of associated companies, whether profits or losses. Such results should be omitted only on the same grounds as would permit group accounts not to deal with a subsidiary (see sub-section **16.2.4**), and the reason for omission should be stated. Where the effect is material, adjustments similar to those used in consolidation should be made, to exclude from the investing group's consolidated accounts such items as unrealized profits on 'inter-company' stocks (see sub-section **16.6.1**), and to achieve reasonable consistency with the group's own accounting practices.

In the consolidated profit and loss account, the investing group should treat the main items in a manner consistent with the principles enunciated above. The group's share of associated companies' pre-tax profits, less losses, should be shown in one figure, suitably captioned, and included in the group's results before tax. The taxation charge should include the tax attributed to the said share of associated companies' profits, separately disclosed as a component of the total charge. The group's share of associated companies' extraordinary items should be included in the 'extraordinary items' figure in the consolidated profit and loss account; unless the amount is material in the context of the group's results, when it should be separately disclosed. The group's share of aggregate net profits, less losses, retained by associated companies should be shown separately. On the other hand, such items as turnover and depreciation of associated companies should not be included in the group accounts; but if the results of one or more such companied are of such significance in the context of the group's accounts that more detailed information about them would assist in giving a true and fair view, then separate disclosure should be made of the totals of the said companies' turnover, depreciation charge, profits, less losses, before taxation, and the amounts of such profits attributable to the group.

In the consolidated balance sheet, the group's total interest in associated companies should (unless shown at a valuation) be stated at:

a the cost of the investments less any amounts written off; *plus*

b the group's share of the associated companies' post-acquisition retained profits and reserves.

If for any reason there is no consolidated balance sheet, the investing company's share of b should be shown as a note to the ordinary balance sheet. Information regarding associated companies' tangible and intangible assets, and liabilities, should be given if materially relevant for appreciation by the investing company's members of the nature of their investment. In stating the group reserves in the consolidated balance sheet, distinction should be made between profits retained by the group, and by associated companies. If retained profits of overseas associated companies would be subject to further tax on distribution, this should be made clear. It will also be necessary to take account of, and disclose, movements on associated companies' other reserves, e.g. surplus on revaluation of fixed assets.

The investing group should give particulars of the names of, and interests in, companies treated as associated companies, and also of any other companies in which it holds not less than 20 per cent of the equity voting rights, but which are not treated as associated companies. Finally, on first introduction of the method of accounting required by SSAP No. 1, the corresponding amounts for the preceding period should be appropriately stated on a comparable basis.

16.7.2 Practical accounting for interests in associated companies

SSAP No. 1 requires the substitution on the consolidated profit and loss account of the holding company's share of the associated company's *net profit before taxation* for its dividends received from that company, and the addition to the group corporation tax charge of the same proportion of the charge in the associated company's accounts. The effect is to incorporate the relevant proportion of the associated company's *net profit after taxation* in the corresponding figure for the group. Adjustment must then be made 'below the line' for the group's proportion of the associated company's extraordinary items and of its preference dividends (not mentioned in SSAP No. 1, but requiring deduction, where they exist, so as to leave the group's share of the associated company's *earnings*.) Where there are two or more associated companies the relevant amounts at each stage must be added algebraically. Finally, the *amount added to group reserves* must be analysed between retained earnings of the holding company, subsidiaries, and associated companies— the last amount being found by aggregating the group's proportions of the figures in the associated companies' profit and loss accounts, so that inter-company dividends are included in retentions of the holding company and/or subsidiaries.

In the consolidated balance sheet, the *group's proportion of associated companies' total retentions since acquisition* will appear separately among the group reserves, while inter-company dividends since acquisition will be included in the group profit and loss account balance. In order to equalize the two sides of the consolidated balance sheet, it is necessary to add the sum shown as associated companies' retentions to the cost of the investments in the said companies' equity. The parent company balance sheet is not adjusted, the investments appearing at book amounts (cost or below).

A company with associated companies but no subsidiaries will make the adjustments in its ordinary profit and loss account, but not in its balance sheet. The company's share of associated companies' retained earnings since acquisition will appear only in a note to the balance sheet. (The logic of this differential treatment is not clear, since the relationship between the investing company and associated companies is the same, whether the former has subsidiaries or not; but the information is made available nevertheless.)

Example 9 Multiplex Ltd, a holding company whose year-end is 31 December 19.2, owns 40 per cent of the voting equity share capital of Dependant Ltd, and has a seat on its board of directors. The investment is shown in the books at cost, £400,000. Dependant's accounts for the year ended 30 September 19.2 show pre-tax profits of £200,000, corporation tax £100,000, post-tax profits £100,000, extraordinary items after tax (*Dr.*) £20,000, preference dividends £10,000, and ordinary dividends £40,000. Retained earnings between 1 January 19.0 (when Multiplex acquired its holdings) and 30 September 19.1 were £60,000. During the year ended 31 December 19.2 Multiplex received ordinary dividends from Dependent of £16,000. The consolidated profit and loss account of Multiplex Ltd (with other figures assumed as necessary) for the year ended 31 December 19.2, in the format suggested in SSAP No. 1, might appear thus:

Multiplex Ltd and its Subsidiaries

Consolidated Profit and Loss Account for the Year ended 31 December 19.2

	£	£
Turnover [of investing company and subsidiaries]		£3,000,000
Net Trading Profit [as aforesaid] after charging the items below:		300,000
Auditors' remuneration	15,000	
Depreciation	150,000	
Debenture interest	45,000	
Share of Profits of Associated Company		80,000
Net Profit Before Taxation		380,000
Corporation Tax		
On the profits of Multiplex Ltd and its Subsidiaries	156,000	
On the profits of the Associated Company	40,000	
		196,000
Net Profit After Taxation		£184,000
Attributable to Shareholders in Multiplex Ltd		175,000
(of which £150,000 is dealt with in the accounts of that Company)		
Extraordinary Items [specified] —Group's proportion after		
taxation, after deducting minority interests and including share		
of Associated Company's items	10,000	
Preference Dividends of Subsidiaries and Associated Company—		
Group's proportion after deducting minority interests and		
including share of those of Associated Company	5,000	
		15,000
Profit Attributable to Shareholders in Multiplex Ltd		160,000
Dividends of Multiplex Ltd—		
Paid	40,000	
Proposed	80,000	
		120,000
Amounts Added to Reserves of—		
Multiplex Ltd	20,000	
Subsidiaries	8,000	
Associated Company	12,000	
		£40,000

Amounts relative to the associated company (shown separately or included in other items) are:

	Total	Group's Share 40%
Net profit before taxation	£200,000	£ 80,000
Corporation tax	(100,000)	(40,000)
Net profit after taxation	100,000	40,000
Extraordinary items (after taxation)	(20,000)	(8,000)
Preference dividends	(10,000)	(4,000)
Equity earnings	70,000	28,000
Ordinary dividends	(40,000)	(16,000)
Retained earnings	£30,000	£12,000

The value placed upon the investment in Dependent Ltd in Mutliplex Ltd's consolidated balance sheet is:

Historical cost			£400,000
Share of retained earnings of Dependant Ltd—			
1.1.19.0 to 30.9.19.1	(40 per cent of £60,000)	£24,000	
1.10.19.1 to 30.9.19.2	(40 per cent of £30,000)	12,000	
			36,000
			£436,000

The share of retained earnings, £36,000, will appear separately among the group reserves, suitably captioned.

Finally, the *Listing Agreement—Companies* (revised 1973) of the Federated Stock Exchanges requires (as stated in Chapter 14, section **14.10**) a statement in the directors' report, in respect of every company in which the group holds 20 per cent or more of the equity, of:

i the principal country of operation;

ii particulars of issued share and loan capital and (except where the company is treated as an associate) total reserves; and

iii the percentage of each class of loan capital attributable to the holding company's interest (direct or indirect).

16.8 IASC Exposure Draft 3 (1974): Consolidated financial statements and the equity method of accounting

As explained in section **14.7**, the standards of the International Accounting Standards Committee are binding upon the British/Irish accountancy bodies. The IASC's latest proposals, in E3, constitute (except for the ASSC's SSAP No. 1 and ED3) the first authoritative recommendations on group accounting to be received in the U.K. or the Republic of Ireland. E3 was published while this edition was in the press, and it was thus impracticable to integrate the recommendations fully with the rest of the text, or to provide numerical examples; nor has any notice been taken of them in the comprehensive illustration in Chapter 18.

Preliminary discussion is brief and general, and substantially incorporated in the proposed IAS itself. More interesting are the definitions of certain key terms. A *parent company* is one which directly or indirectly controls a *subsidiary*. *Control* exists if the parent either:

a owns directly or indirectly more than half of the voting power in the subsidiary; or

b has the power to control, by statute or by agreement, the subsidiary's financial and operating policies—e.g. by power to nominate a majority of its board of directors, by management contract, or by court decree.

An *associated company* is an *investee* (a company in which another company is an *investor*), such that:

a it is not a subsidiary;

b the investor's interest in the investee's voting power is 'substantial' (not further defined, but see below) *and* the investor has the power to exercise 'significant influence' (see below) over the investee's financial and operating policies; and

c the investor intends to retain its interest as a long-term investment.

Significant influence is participation in the financial and operating policy decisions of the associated company, but not control, as above defined. It may be exercised, e.g., by representation on the board of directors, participation in policy-making processes, material inter-company transactions, interchange of management personnel, or dependency on technical information. If, however, the investor holds less than 20 per cent of the voting power it should be presumed that it cannot exercise significant influence, unless the contrary can be clearly demonstrated.

It is instructive to compare these definitions with those in the Companies Acts, 1948 and 1967 (subsidiaries) and SSAP No. 1 (associated companies). In both sets of prescriptions the emphasis is on substance rather than form, and in practice it does not seem likely that there will be any serious conflict between them in this country.

The proposed IAS is long and complex, but its requirements are fairly clear. A parent company should issue 'consolidated financial statements' (profit and loss account, and balance sheet), and generally consolidate all subsidiaries, domestic and foreign; but it need not produce such statements if it is itself a wholly-owned subsidiary. A subsidiary should be excluded from consolidation only if:

a   control is likely to be temporary; or

b   the subsidiary operates under conditions in which severe long-term restrictions on the transfer of funds jeopardize control by the parent over the subsidiary's assets or operations.

The reasons for not consolidating a subsidiary should be stated.

Associated companies, and non-consolidated subsidiaries, should be included in the consolidated financial statements on the *equity method* of accounting— under which the investor's investment account and income statement are adjusted periodically for the change in the investor's share of net assets, and for its share in net earnings, of the investee (as under SSAP No. 1).

If an investee company ceases to be a subsidiary but the parent retains significant influence over it, the investment should be accounted for as an associated company. If the parent loses both control and significant influence over a subsidiary, or significant influence over an associated company (as when the other company is placed under the control of a court, or when liquidation or similar proceedings are instituted against it), or a subsidiary ceases to be consolidated; then the investment in any such company should be stated in the consolidated balance sheet at the carrying value under the equity method, as at that date, and the investor should cease making adjustments for its share of the investee's subsequent earnings or losses. Should the carrying value of an investment under the equity method exceed its current fair value (other than temporarily), the carrying amount should be written down to the current fair value (undefined).

Consolidation of the accounts of parent and subsidiaries should be effected on a 'line by line' basis, by adding together like items of assets, liabilities, revenue, and expenses. Inter-company balances and transactions (including inter-company sales, charges and dividends) should be eliminated, and the cost of the parent's investment in each subsidiary should be eliminated against the parent's portion of the subsidiary's share capital, reserves, and pre-acquisition profits or losses (except where the 'merger' or 'pooling of interests' method is used—see section **16.5**). Unrealized profits from inter-company transactions should be eliminated from asset values and (after adjustment for minority interests) from the profit and loss account. Tax on such eliminated profits should be carried forward until the profits are realized by the group (i.e. by adjustment of the deferred taxation account). A difference at the date of acquisition between the cost of an investment and the investor's share in the recorded net assets of a subsidiary should be allocated in consolidation, if possible, to identifiable assets and liabilities on the basis of their fair values at that date; the remainder should be shown in the consolidated balance sheet, appropriately described (except where the merger method is used). Taxes payable (in some countries) on the distribution of earnings from subsidiary to parent should be accrued, if it is reasonable to assume that such earnings will eventually be distributed; otherwise there should be disclosure of the cumulative amount of undistributed earnings on which no distribution tax has been provided, and of the parent's intention to undertake long-term reinvestment of such earnings.

The minority interest in subsidiaries' equity should appear as a separate item in the consolidated balance sheet, and not be included in shareholders' equity. The minority interest in subsidiaries' earnings or losses should be shown as a separate item in the consolidated income statement.

The parent and subsidiaries should have a common financial reporting period; if not, the dates to which the subsidiaries' accounts are made up, and the reasons for the difference, should be disclosed. The difference in balance sheet dates should be consistent from period to period. If financial statements on divergent dates are consolidated, significant transactions or events in the interim period should be recognized through adjustments or disclosure, to avoid making the statements misleading.

Earnings of a subsidiary for the reporting period in which it is acquired should be consolidated only from the date of acquisition, and its retained earnings should be included in group retained earnings only from that date (except where the merger method is used).

Uniform accounting policies should preferably be followed by companies within a group. If different policies are adopted for assets or liabilities grouped within a single balance sheet classification, the proportion of assets or liabilities carried on each accounting basis should be stated, when complying with IAS 1.

Should the losses applicable to the minority interest in a subsidiary exceed the minority interest in shareholders' equity of the subsidiary (before the losses arise), then the excess should be charged against the majority interest (unless the minority has an obligation to make good the losses). If the subsidiary later reports earnings, these should be all be credited to the majority interest, until the losses previously absorbed by it have been recovered. If a subsidiary has outstanding cumulative preferred shares, the parent should compute its share of earnings or losses after deducting the preferred dividends, whether declared or not.

Many of the procedures appropriate for the application of the equity method of accounting for associated companies are similar to those used in consolidating subsidiaries. Thus, the group's share of earnings or losses should be adjusted so as to eliminate unrealized inter-company profits; differences in balance sheet dates between associated company and investor (the associated company's date being always earlier) should be disclosed, with consistency from period to period and proper treatment of significant transactions or events in the interim period; taxes payable on distribution of the associated company's undistributed earnings should be accrued; and adjustment should be made for the investee's cumulative preferred dividends, whether declared or not. (It is hard to see the point of a recommendation that a difference on acquisition between the cost of an investment and the investor's share in the investee's recorded net assets should be allocated, if possible, to identifiable assets or liabilities of the investee, since such items are not brought into the investor's consolidated balance sheet.)

Apart from all this, an investment dealt with under the equity method should appear in the consolidated balance sheet at cost, plus/minus the parent's share of the associated company's post-acquisition earnings/losses, minus dividends received from the latter. In the consolidated income statement, the parent's share of earnings or losses of associated companies and unconsolidated subsidiaries should be separately classified, with extraordinary or unusual items shown separately in accordance with the parent's accounting policies (cf. SSAP No. 6). A gain or loss on sale of shares in an investee by an investor should be recognized in the latter's consolidated income statement, at an amount equal to the difference between proceeds of sale and carrying amount of the shares sold.

If the investor's share of an investee's losses equals or exceeds the carrying value of the investment plus any advances to the investee by the investor, then the investor should cease applying the equity method—providing for further losses only if it has guaranteed them, or is otherwise committed to provide further financial support. If the investee subsequently reports net income, the investor should use its share thereof to extinguish its share of losses not recognized while the equity method was suspended, and only then resume use of that method. Should an investment be written down from its normal carrying value to its (lower) fair current value, the write-down should be disclosed as a charge to consolidated income, and as a deduction in the balance sheet from the carrying amount. The amount of write-down should be reviewed at each balance sheet date; any adjustment should be disclosed in the consolidated income statement, and the related investment should be identified.

All the foregoing procedures should be used consistently from one period to another.

Apart from the disclosures already indicated, the following ones should be made:

a the consolidation policies adopted, describing the bases on which subsidiaries have been consolidated and associated companies dealt with by the equity method;

b for each subsidiary and associated company of significant size, its name, nature of business, and proportion of voting power held; and where a subsidiary qualified as one otherwise than through a majority holding of voting power, the nature of the relationship with the parent;

c analysis of the significant balance sheet captions of the group, by major geographical areas, by continent, or by country; and

d analysis of group retained earnings between those of the parent company, consolidated subsidiaries, unconsolidated subsidiaries, and associated companies, respectively (all post-acquisition, except for the parent), together with any restrictions on the distribution of such retained earnings.

For investments in non-consolidated subsidiaries (other than those excluded because control is likely to be temporary), and in companies which are neither subsidiaries nor associated companies, the following additional disclosures should be made for each company:

i share of the group in its net assets;

ii carrying value of the investment in the consolidated balance sheet;

iii dividends received by the group during the period; and

vi earnings or losses for the period, with separate disclosure of extraordinary or unusual items.

Finally, it should be apparent from the foregoing that E3 covers only the general principles of group accounts prepared by the 'acquisition' or 'purchase' method, together with those of the 'equity' method of accounting for associated companies. It does not deal with the 'merger' or 'pooling of interests' method of consolidation (much used in North America), nor enter into the vexed question of accounting for goodwill or capital reserves. Neither does it deal with specialized matters, such as the treatment of accounts in foreign currencies, or of cross-holdings between companies in a group. For all that, E3 is much more comprehensive than any statement so far issued by the ASSC, and seems likely to have considerable influence on consolidation practice in the U.K. and the Republic of Ireland.

16.9   General illustration of published group accounts

The reader is referred to the set of group accounts used to illustrate the principles of accounting analysis, in Chapter 18, section **18.3**.

17

Accounting for company liquidation and receivership

A limited liability company is a more permanent form of business undertaking than a partnership, in that its corporate status remains unaltered by any number of changes in the identities of its shareholders. Yet even a company is not immortal; though it usually has no determinate life-span, there are circumstances in which the management may find it impracticable to continue the business, or desirable to bring it to an end, or to merge it in a larger entity. A body corporate cannot die, nor can it be made bankrupt, like an individual; but the Companies Act, 1948, provides procedures by which an unsuccessful company, or one which has served its purpose, may be put into liquidation, or wound up. The *liquidation* or *winding up* is the corporate equivalent of death, often preceded by that of bankruptcy. Whereas for an individual bankruptcy is a means whereby he is saved from the worst consequences of financial failure and enabled, as far as justice to his creditors permits, to make a fresh start unencumbered by his old debts, the winding up of a company, with payment of its creditors as far as possible and distribution to the shareholders of any remaining assets, is usually a prelude to extinction as a corporate body, and not to financial resurrection.

17.1 Legal procedure in a winding up

The statute law on liquidation is contained in Part V of the 1948 Act (ss. 211 to 365), supplemented by the *Companies (Winding-Up) Rules,* 1949, made under s. 365 of the Act. There is nothing about winding up in the Companies Act, 1967, though the Jenkins Committee made a number of recommendations for amendment. Only a small part of this mass of law need be referred to here.

S. 211 of the 1948 Act lays down three modes of winding up: a by the court; b voluntary; or c subject to the supervision of the court. These are considered in turn.

17.1.1 Procedure in a winding up by the court

The High Court (Chancery Division) has jurisdiction to wind up any company registered in England; the Chancery Courts of the Counties Palatine of Lancaster and Durham have concurrent jurisdiction within their areas. If the company's paid-up capital does not exceed £10,000, the winding up may be conducted by the local County Court having bankruptcy jurisdiction (s.218). Companies registered in Scotland are wound up by the Court of Session, or by the local Sheriff Court if the paid up capital does not exceed £10,000 (s.220).

There are six grounds on which a company may be wound up by the Court, namely that:

a the company has passed a special resolution to that effect;

b default has been made in delivering the statutory report to the Registrar, or in holding the statutory meeting;

c the company has not commenced business within one year of incorporation, or has suspended its business for a whole year;

d the number of members is below the legal minimum of two for a private, or seven for a public, company;

e the company is unable to pay its debts; or

f the court is of opinion that it is just and equitable that the company should be wound up (s. 222).

e is by far the commonest reason; **f** is invoked only in special situations, and **a** to **d** very seldom arise.

A company is deemed to be unable to pay its debts if a creditor for more than £50 has served on the company, at its registered office, a signed demand for payment, and the company has not paid, secured, or compounded for the sum to the creditor's reasonable satisfaction within three weeks; if execution or similar process against the company on a judgement debt has been returned unsatisfied in whole or in part; or (most commonly) if it is proved to the satisfaction of the court that the company is unable to pay its debts—its contingent and prospective liabilities being taken into account (s. 223).

Winding-up proceedings commence with the presentation to the court of a *petition,* generally by one or more creditors (occasionally by the company itself or, in special circumstances, by one or more 'contributories'–i.e., in a company limited by shares, the shareholders, since they are liable at need to contribute towards the company's debts to the extent of the amounts, if any, unpaid on their shares) (s. 224). If convinced by the petitioners' allegations, the court makes a *winding-up order* (s. 225), whose effect is to stay all proceedings against the company (s. 231), and to appoint the court's Official Receiver in Bankruptcy as provisional liquidator (s. 239). An important date for most legal purposes is the *commencement of winding up.* This is the date of presentation of the successful petition, unless the company was already in voluntary liquidation, when winding up commences from the date of the resolution to wind up voluntarily (s. 229).

There follows the submission to the Official Receiver (or to any other person whom the court may appoint in his stead as provisional liquidator) of a *statement as to the affairs of the company,* in the form prescribed by the Companies (Winding-Up) Rules, 1949. This shows the state of the company's affairs at the 'relevant date' (see below), with its assets valued at the estimated realizable amounts, full particulars of all creditors and their securities if any, and other information as described in sub-section 17.2.2. The statement of affairs must be submitted and verified by one or more directors and by the secretary of the company, or by certain other persons if the Official Receiver so requires, within 14 days of the relevant date or within such extended time as may be specially granted. The relevant date is that of the winding-up order, unless a provisional liquidator has been appointed earlier, in which case the date of his appointment is taken (s. 235). As soon as practicable after receipt of the statements the Official Receiver shall submit a *preliminary report* to the court, as to the amount of capital issued, subscribed, and paid up, and the estimated amount of assets and liabilities; as to the causes of the company's failure, if applicable; and whether in his opinion further inquiry is desirable as to any matter relating to its promotion, formation, or failure, or the conduct of its business. He may also, if he thinks fit, make a further report or reports as to the manner in which the company was formed, whether in his opinion fraud has been committed at any stage by any promoter or officer, and any other matter which he considers desirable to bring to the court's notice (s. 236).

One of the Official Receiver's (or provisional liquidator's) first duties is to summon separate meetings of creditors and contributories, to decide whether they shall apply to the court for the appointment of a permanent *liquidator* in place of the Official Receiver, etc., and of a *committee of inspection* to act with him, and if so (as is usual), to submit names (ss. 239, 252). The court then appoints the liquidator (normally a chartered or certified accountant) and the committee of inspection (consisting of creditors and contributories or their agents), as requested; if no committee is appointed, the liquidator will discharge its functions (ss. 239, 253, 254). Before commencing to act, the liquidator must notify his appointment to the Registrar of Companies, and give security for due performance of his duties, as required by the Department of Trade (s.240).

The liquidator's functions are to realize the company's assets in the most advantageous manner, and to distribute the proceeds, first to the creditors in legal order of priority and then, if there is any money left, to the shareholders in the order of priority established by the articles of association or the terms of issue. He is accordingly given wide powers, enabling him to take control of the company's undertaking and property, to sell the assets by auction or otherwise, to carry on the business so far as may be necessary for beneficial realization, to raise temporary finance, to deal with interested parties, to employ agents to do any business which he is not qualified to do himself, and to do all other things necessary to wind up the company's affairs and distribute its assets. Some of these powers he exercises on his own authority (subject to appeal to the court by any creditor or contributory), others require the sanction of the court or (more usually) the committee of inspection (s. 245). The latter body meets once a month or oftener (s. 253), and exercises supervision over the liquidator on behalf of the creditors and contributories; but major policy decisions generally require the approval of meetings of the whole body of creditors or contributories, or both, and resolutions of such meetings override the directions of the committee (s. 246).

The liquidator is also subject to general oversight by the Department of Trade, to which he renders accounts and returns as described in sub-section 17.2.5, and which has power to inquire into his conduct of the winding up, and in extreme cases to remove him from office and/or take proceedings against him (s.250). When he has realized all the company's property (or so much as in his opinion can be realized without needlessly protracting the liquidation), distributed a final dividend to the creditors, adjusted the rights of the contributories among themselves, and made a final return (if any) to them; or if he has resigned or been removed from office; the DoT shall, on the liquidator's application, cause a report on his accounts to be prepared and, if all is in order, grant him his release—thus terminating his office and (except in case of fraud or concealment of material facts) his liability for all acts or defaults as liquidators (s.251). Finally, the court may, on the liquidator's application, make an order dissolving the company as a body corporate; a copy must be sent to the Registrar of Companies within 14 days (s.274).

17.1.2 Procedure in a voluntary winding up

Sometimes the shareholders take the initiative in bringing a company's business to an end, particularly where it is still solvent, but does not appear to have much future; or where the business has been sold as a going concern and the shareholders wish to distribute the proceeds, or another company has acquired all the shares and wishes to dissolve the new subsidiary as a separate entity. The company may then pass a *resolution for voluntary winding up.* This may be:

a an ordinary resolution (passed by a simple majority), if the articles provide for winding up at the end of a fixed period which has expired, or on the occurrence of a certain event which has occurred;

b a special resolution (by a three-fourths majority, after 21 days' notice to members); or

c an extraordinary resolution (by a three-fourths majority, without notice) to the effect that the company cannot by reason of its liabilities continue its business, and that it is advisable to wind up voluntarily (s. 278).

A resolution for voluntary winding up shall, within 14 days, be advertized in the *London Gazette* (or the *Edinburgh Gazette,* as the case may be) (s. 279). A voluntary winding up is deemed to commence at the time of passing of the resolution (s. 280), and thereupon the company shall cease to carry on its business, except so far as may be required for beneficial realization (s. 281), and any subsequent transfer of shares (except to, or with the sanction of, the liquidator), and any alteration in the members' status, shall be void (s. 282).

Before this stage is reached the directors (or the majority of them, if there are more than two) may make a statutory *declaration of solvency,* to the effect that they have made a full inquiry into the company's affairs, and formed the opinion that the company will be able to pay its debts in full within twelve months from the commencement of the winding up (or such shorter period as may be specified). The declaration shall be made at a directors' meeting within five weeks before the passing of the resolution to wind up, and delivered to the Registrar of Companies for registration before that event. It shall also embody a statement of the company's assets and liabilities as at the latest practicable date before the making of the declaration. The making of a declaration of solvency, without reasonable grounds for the opinion that the company is solvent as above defined, renders the directors who made it liable to imprisonment not exceeding six months and/or a fine not exceeding £500; and there is a presumption of guilt (until the contrary is shown) if the company is in fact unable to pay its debts in full within the stated period. If the declaration is duly made the subsequent proceedings are conducted as a members' voluntary winding up; if it is not, as a creditors' voluntary winding up (s. 283).

In a *member's voluntary winding up,* one or more liquidators are appointed by the company in general meeting, and all the directors' powers cease unless it is otherwise resolved, or permitted by the liquidator (s. 285). The winding up is conducted without consulting the creditors, who are normally paid in full, and the residual assets distributed to the shareholders. In particular, a special resolution may authorize the liquidator to sell the business or property, or any part of it, to another company in return for securities of, or interests in, the other for distribution among the members of the company in liquidation; but any member who did not vote for the special resolution may, within seven days after its passing, serve his written dissent upon the liquidator at the registered office, and either restrain the liquidator from carrying out the resolution, or compel him to purchase his (the member's) interest at a price agreed, or fixed by arbitration (s. 287). If the winding up lasts for more than one year the liquidator shall call a general meeting at the end of each year from the commencement of winding up, and lay before it an account of his acts and dealings and of the conduct of the liquidation during the year (s. 289). When the affairs of the company are fully wound up he shall call a final general meeting (giving at least one month's notice in the *Gazette*), lay his account before it as aforesaid and, within one week, send to the Registrar of Companies a copy of his account, and a return of the holding of the meeting (or of the fact that it was not held, because there was no quorum present). After another three months the Registrar shall dissolve the company (s. 290).

In a *creditors' voluntary winding up,* a creditors' meeting must be summoned when the general meeting is summoned, at which the resolution to wind up voluntarily is to be proposed. The creditors' meeting must be advertised in the *Gazette* and in two local newspapers, and held on the same day as the other meeting, or the day after it. One of the directors shall take the chair, and a full statement of the company's position, with a list of creditors and the estimated amount of their claims, shall be laid before the meeting (s. 293). The two meetings may nominate a liquidator; if they nominate different persons the creditors' choice shall prevail, unless the court, on application within seven days, orders otherwise (s. 294). The creditors' meeting may also appoint up to five persons to a committee of inspection, and the company meeting, or a subsequent one, may then appoint up to five other persons—with a right of veto by the creditors, unless the court overrules the objections (s. 295).

Apart from this, a creditors' voluntary winding up proceeds much as a members' winding up, except that the liquidator's powers must be exercised with the sanction of the committee of inspection, and that the annual, and final, general meetings must be paralleled by creditors' meetings, and a return thereof in the case of the final one (ss. 298 to 300). Such meetings must be summoned in the case of a *members'* winding up, if the liquidator is at any time of opinion that the company's debts will not be paid in full, as promised in the declaration of solvency (ss. 288, 291); but there is no provision for the appointment of a committee of insepction.

17.1.3 Winding up subject to the supervision of the court; informal liquidation

Ss. 311 to 315 of the Companies Act, 1948, empower the court to order that a voluntary winding up, already in progress, shall continue subject to the supervision of the court. The procedure is seldom or never invoked today, and the Jenkins Committee recommended its abolition.

Lastly, many small private companies are not formally wound up at all. The director-shareholders simply go out of business, sell off the assets, pay the creditors, divide the remaining cash, and disperse. In due course the Registrar, receiving no accounts or returns from the company, writes to inquire whether it is carrying on business or in operation. If there is no reply within one month, after another 14 days a registered letter is sent, to the effect that if there is no answer this time within one month, a notice will be published in the *Gazette* with a view to striking the company off the register. If there is still no answer, a notice is published in the *Gazette,* and sent to the company, that in three months' time the Registrar intends to strike the company off the register and dissolve it. This is normally done, and notice thereof published in the *Gazette* (s. 353). In the meantime, however (and it may be over a year before the Registrar takes any action), the company remains in being as a corporate 'shell', without assets, liabilities, or issued capital, but still capable of being taken over and resuscitated to carry on any business permitted by the memorandum of association. There are at any time hundreds of such 'dormant' companies in existence, some with valuable tax losses which may be carried forward against the profits of any business having any similarity to, and continuity with, the original one; and 'company brokers' can usually find a client a private company to suit his requirements, and so save him the trouble and expense of registering a new one—apart from the possible tax savings.

17.2 Accounting aspects of winding up

In the bankruptcy of an individual the assets available for creditors are legally vested by the receiving order in the Official Receiver, and passed on to the trustee in bankruptcy when appointed. The trustee keeps his own set of accounts, using the debtor's statement of affairs as the starting-point. If the bankrupt has a business the trustee continues its books, linking them to his own by means of the bankrupt's capital account—a credit balance in the firm's books, and an equal and opposite debit balance (asset) in the trustee's, or vice versa; or, if the business is closed down, bringing its assets and liabilities into the trustee's books.

A company in liquidation, on the other hand, remains the legal owner of its assets and ower of its liabilities. The liquidator is a quasi-officer of the company, as well as being in a fiduciary position towards the creditors and shareholders; hence he continues the company's books of account, while keeping certain memorandum records of his own for legal purposes.

17.2.1 Company accounts prior to liquidation

The first question when liquidation supervenes (whether compulsory or voluntary) is that of preparing accounts for the period since the last accounting date—a necessity in any case, in order to prepare the statement of affairs. If there is an interval of some months between the last year-end and the winding-up order or resolution, then the profit and loss account should be drawn up on a normal commercial basis, the assets separately revalued to estimated realizable value and liabilities amended (to include, for instance, prospective damages for breach of contract because of the company's failure), and the reserves adjusted accordingly. The normal continuity assumption is thus abandoned, and the probability of loss on forced realization explicitly recognized.

The 1948 Act says nothing about publication of accounts of a company in liquidation, and the ordinary law therefore applies—i.e. accounts up to the winding-up order or resolution must be published, if no others have been published in that calendar year; if they have, circulation and filing would appear to be optional. A problem may arise if liquidation supervenes while the regular accounts are being prepared: should they, or should they not, be amended with hindsight of a disaster which may not have been clearly foreseeable at the accounting date? At present there is no generally agreed solution. Possibilities range from preparing the accounts as though in ignorance of what was coming, but with a note as to subsequent events—through preparing a normal profit and loss account, but making large provisions for losses in the balance sheet—to extending the accounting period to the date of the winding-up order, etc., and drawing up accounts in the light of expected realizable values. Even if delay is ccaused, this is surely the lesser evil; the extension of time economizes the expense of preparing accounts, and avoids the publication of unrealistic ones as at the normal year-end.

17.2.2 The statement of affairs; creditors

As to the liquidation itself, the starting-point in a winding up by the court is the statement of affairs, which must be presented in the form prescribed by the 1949 Rules, and available at any law stationer's. The main statement is illustrated below; in practice it is supported by Lists 'A' to 'H', referred to in the statement, but only List 'H'—the Deficiency or Surplus Account—calls for illustration. It explains how the deficiency, or surplus (the final figure on the statement) has arisen over the previous three years or more. The normal practice is to go back to the balance sheet next before the date three years before that of the statement, and to annex a copy of it to the account.

In a creditors' voluntary winding up the 1949 Rules require the preparation and submission to creditors and shareholders, of a statement of affairs in similar form to that exhibited below. In a members' voluntary winding up a simpler form is prescribed, in which no order of priority is imposed on the liabilities, since they are assumed to be all payable in full, leaving a surplus for shareholders.

Example 1 The (imaginary) Statement of Affairs, and List 'H', of the N.B.G. Co. Ltd, ordered to be wound up on 1 April 1975, are shown on pp. 458-468.

Schedule of Estimated Losses now written off	£
Adjustment of assets to estimated realizable value:	
Freehold property	(2,500)
Leasehold property	500
Plant and machinery	12,134
Furniture, fittings, utensils, etc.	95
Patents, trade marks, etc.	180
Stock in trade	5,946
Work in progress	1,883
Trade debtors	1,237
	19,475
Provision for contingent liability:	
Damages and costs in pending litigation against the company	5,000
	£24,475

The statement of affairs is the 'liquidation' balance sheet of the company, with the items classified and arranged so as to show the estimated amounts available to meet the claims of each class of creditor, and the final deficiency as regards the members (i.e. the debit balance on profit and loss account, less any capital reserves). List 'H' summarizes the changes in reserves over the period covered. The items are mostly self-explanatory, but some call for further comment.

17.2.3 Creditors

Preferential creditors are those whose claims rank ahead of all others, except those of mortgagees, debenture-holders with fixed charges, and other holders of specific securities. All preferential debts rank equally among themselves and, if the assets are insufficient to pay them in full, are proportionately abated—a rule which applies to any class of creditors with respect to whom a deficiency first appears, so that subsequent classes receive nothing. The preferential debts are listed in s. 319 of the 1948 Act, as follows (allowing for later modifications in the law):

1 local rates becoming due and payable within twelve months before the relevant date (see sub-section **17.1.1**);
2 corporation tax assessed on the company up to the 5 April before the relevant date, and not exceeding one year's assessment (in practice, the highest outstanding assessment is taken);
3 value added tax due within twelve months before the relevant date;
4 wages, salaries, and commissions of employees (but *not* directors or officers), earned within the previous four months, up to a maximum of £200 for any one person;
5 accrued holiday remuneration due to employees (as above), or in respect of deceased ones, on termination of their employment by, or before, the winding-up order or resolution;
6 (except in a voluntary winding up merely for the purpose of reconstruction, or amalgamation with another company), all national insurance contributions due from the company during the twelve months before the relevant date.

Other items mentioned in s. 319 are no longer applicable. In the case of **4** and **5**, any person advancing money to pay employees any sums due from the company becomes a preferential creditor to the same extent as the employees would otherwise have been.

Certain liabilities, though not legally preferential or shown as such in the statement of affairs, are in practice often paid before the general body of unsecured debts. The liquidator, if he finds it necessary to remain in occupation of the company's premises for a time, is compelled to pay outstanding accounts for rent, and for continuing services such as electricity, gas, water, and telephone, in order to avoid eviction or disconnection. It is unlikely that the arrears will be very large, and in the circumstances such payments are not regarded in law as fraudulent preferences. Where, however, the business is a very large consumer of continuing services, the liquidator may be in a strong enough position to compel the suppliers to accept payment in due order, with the other ordinary creditors.

Debentures secured by a floating charge rank after preferential creditors, but before unsecured ones (s. 94). If, however, a floating charge was created within twelve months before the commencement of winding up, it shall be invalid (except as regards any cash paid to the company at the time or later, and in consideration of the charge, plus interest at the rate of 5 per cent per annum) unless it is proved that the company was solvent immediately after the creation of the charge (s. 322). Otherwise, *all* debenture holders are entitled to full interest up to the date of actual repayment of the principal.

All claims in liquidation must be formally 'proved' by affidavit. Under the 1949 Rules a creditor whose claim did not originally bear interest may include in his proof interest (at a maximum rate of 4 per cent per annum up to the commencement of winding up) if his debt was payable at a certain date by virtue of a written instrument; or if he has made a written demand for payment, giving notice that he will claim interest in future until he is paid. A debt payable at a future date may be proved in full, but interest at 5 per cent per annum must be deducted from any dividend paid in advance of the due date. S. 317 of the 1948 Act applies the general laws of bankruptcy to creditors. One rule is, that if the assets are sufficient to meet all creditors' claims in full, the creditors shall be entitled, before any distribution is made to shareholders, to interest at the rate of

4 per cent per annum on their claims, from the commencement of winding up to the actual dates of payment.

17.2.4 Proceedings of the liquidator

The liquidator's principal duties are to realize the assets as advantageously as possible and, as substantial sums in cash accumulate, to apply them in dividends to the creditors in due order of priority. The physical assets, other than land and buildings, are usually sold by auction; land and buildings by auction or by private treaty; quoted investments on the stock exchange; and unquoted ones by such means as may be appropriate. Anyone selling property on behalf of the liquidator must hand over the gross proceeds to him; but the auctioneer's or other agent's costs and charges (after 'taxing' by the court) are a first charge upon the proceeds. They must then be applied, in order, to pay:

1 the costs of the winding-up petition (including those of any person appearing on the petition whose costs are allowed by the court;
2 the remuneration of a special manager (if any) appointed to assist the Offical Receiver;
3 the costs of any person who makes, or concurs in making, the statement of affairs;
4 the charges of any shorthand writer appointed to take an examination;
5 the liquidator's disbursements (other than the costs of getting in and preserving the assets, already allowed for);
6 the costs of any person properly employed by the liquidator;
7 the liquidator's remuneration;
8 the out-of-pocket expenses of members of the committee of inspection (if approved by the DoT).

All these costs must be taxed by the Taxing Officer of the court. Only after paying them is cash available for dividends to creditors (1949 Rules).

In the case of a winding up by the court in England, the liquidator shall pay all moneys coming into his hanss into the *Companies Liquidation Account,* kept by the Department of Trade at the Bank of England, unless the committee of inspection satisfy the Department that it is more advantageous that the liquidator should have an account at another bank. The liquidator shall not, without good cause shown, retain any sum of more than £50 for more than ten days; if he does, he shall pay interest on the money improperly retained, at 20 per cent per annum, and is liable to disallowance of all or part of his remuneration, and to removal from office, by the Department, as well as to pay any expenses occasioned by his default. In no circumstances may he pay liquidation moneys into his private bank account (s. 248). Under Rules made by the then Board of Trade in 1958 the liquidator must bank all moneys received at least once a week, or forthwith if £200 or more is received. In a voluntary winding up banking arrangements are at the discretion of the committee of inspection, if any. Under the Companies (Winding-Up) Rules, 1949, surplus cash balances may be temporarily invested, and the investments later realized, by the liquidator at the request of the committee, if the Department of Trade approves (or carries out the transactions, where the moneys are in the Companies Liquidation Account).

The liquidator's remuneration is fixed, in a winding up by the court, by the court itself (s. 242). The terms are those recommended by the committee of

STATEMENT as to the affairs o

on the 1 April 1975, the date ___of the Winding-up Order___ showing assets at
~~directed by the Official Receiver~~

estimated realizable values and liabilities expected to rank.

	Estimated Realizable Values £
Assets not Specifically Pledged (as per List 'A')	
Balance at Bank	—
Cash in Hand	10
Marketable Securities	—
Bills Receivable	—
Trade Debtors	20,350
Loans and Advances	—
Unpaid Calls	—
Stock in Trade	15,000
Work in Progress	2,000
....	
....	
Freehold Property	—
Leasehold Property	5,000
Plant and Machinery	18,000
Furniture, Fittings, Utensils, etc.	200
Patents, Trade Marks, etc.	500
Investments other than marketable securities	—
Other property, viz.:—	
....	
....	
....	
	61,060

Assets Specifically Pledged (as per List 'B')	(a) Estimated Realizable Values £	(b) Due to Secured Creditors £	(c) Deficiency ranking as Unsecured (see next page) £	Surplus carried to last column £
Freehold Property	22,500	20,500	—	2,000
....				
....				
....				
	£22,500	£20,500	—	£2,000

	Estimated Realizable Values £
Estimated surplus from Assets specifically pledged	2,000
Estimated Total Assets available for Preferential Creditors, Debenture-holders secured by a Floating Charge, and Unsecured Creditors* (carried forward to next page) £	63,060

Summary of Gross Assets	(d) £
Gross realizable value of assets specifically pledged	22,500
Other Assets	61,060
Gross Assets	£83,560

THE N.B.G. COMPANY Limited

			£
	Estimated Total Assets available for Preferential Creditors, Debenture-holders secured by a Floating Charge, and Unsecured Creditors* (brought forward from preceding page)		63,060

(e) Gross Liabilities £	*Liabilities* (to be deducted from surplus or added to deficiency as the case may be)		
20,500	*Secured Creditors* (as per List 'B') to extent to which claims are estimated to be covered by Assets specifically pledged (item (a) or (b) on preceding page, whichever is the less) [Insert in 'Gross Liabilities' column only.]		—
1,540	*Preferential Creditors* (as per List 'C')		1,540
	Estimated Balance of assets available for Debenture-holders secured by a floating charge, and Unsecured Creditors*	£	61,520
55,000	*Debenture-holders* secured by a floating charge (as per List 'D')		55,000
	Estimated Surplus/Deficiency as regards Debenture-holders*	£	6,520
	Unsecured Creditors (as per List 'E'):—	£	
	Estimated unsecured balance of claims of Creditors partly secured on specific assets, brought from preceding page (c)	—	
11,765	Trade Accounts	11,765	
—	Bills Payable	—	
350	Outstanding Expenses	350	
53	Bank Overdraft	53	
	....		
	....		
	Contingent Liabilities (state nature):— Damages and Costs in pending Litigation		
5,000	against the Company	5,000	
			17,168
	Estimated Surplus/Deficiency as regards Creditors* being difference between:	£	
	Gross Assets brought from preceding page (d) and	83,560	
	Gross Liabilities as per column (e)	94,208	
£94,208			10,648
	Issued and Called-up Capital	£	
	10,000 preference shares of £1 each £1 called-up (as per List 'F')	10,000	
	50,000 ordinary shares of £1 each £1 called-up (as per List 'G')	50,000	
	....		
	....		60,000
	Estimated Surplus/Deficiency as regards Members* (as per List 'H')	£	70,648

* These figures must be read subject to the following notes:—
  (1) (f) There is no unpaid capital liable to be called up *or*
    ~~(g) The nominal amount of unpaid capital liable to be called up is £~~   Strike out
    ~~estimated to produce £   which is/is not charged in favour of~~   (f) *or* (g)
    ~~Debenture-holders.~~

  (2) The estimates are subject to costs of the winding-up and to any surplus or deficiency on trading pending realization of the Assets

(Lists A—G are not reproduced.)

List 'H'—Deficiency or Surplus Account

The period covered by this Account must commence on a date not less than three years before the date of the winding-up order (or the date directed by the official receiver) or, if the company has not been incorporated for the whole of that period, the date of formation of the company, unless the official receiver otherwise agrees.

Items Contributing to Deficiency (or ~~Reducing Surplus~~):		£
1. Excess (if any) of Capital and Liabilities over Assets on the 31 December 1971 as shown by Balance Sheet (copy annexed)		–
2. Net dividends and bonuses declared during the period from 31 December 1971 to the date of the Statement		9,600
3. Net trading losses (after charging items shown in note below) for the same period		47,684
4. Losses other than trading losses written off or for which provision has been made in the books during the same period (give particulars or annex achedule)		–
5. Estimated losses now written off or for which provision has been made for the purpose of preparing the Statement (give particulars or or annex schedule) See annexed Schedule		24,475
6. Other items contributing to Deficiency or reducing Surplus: None		–
		81,759

Items Reducing Deficiency (or ~~Contributing to Surplus~~):	£	
7. Excess (if any) of Assets over Capital and Liabilities on the 31 December 1971 as shown on the Balance Sheet (copy annexed)	11,044	
8. Net trading profits (after charging items shown in note below) for the period from the 31 December 1971 to the date of the Statement	–	
9. Profits and income other than trading profits during the same period (give particulars or annex schedule) Profit on sale of Investments	67	
10. Other items reducing Deficiency or contributing to Surplus: None	–	11,111
Deficiency/~~Surplus~~ as shown by Statement	£	70,648

Note as to Net Trading Profits and Losses:	£	
Particulars are to be inserted here (so far as applicable) of the items mentioned below, which are to be taken into account in arriving at the amount of net trading profits or losses shown in this Account:—		
Provisions for depreciation, renewals, or diminution in value of fixed assets	10,700	
Charges for United Kingdom income tax and other United Kingdom taxation on profits	–	
Interest on debentures and other fixed loans	18,500	
Payments to directors made by the company and required by law to be disclosed in the accounts	32,000	
Exceptional or non-recurring expenditure: None	–	
	61,200	
Less:—Exceptional or non-recurring receipts:— None	–	
	61,200	
Balance, being other trading profits ~~or losses~~	13,516	
Net trading ~~profits or~~ losses as shown in Deficiency or Surplus Account above	£ 47,684	

Signature U. N. LUCKY, Director   Dated 15 April 1975

inspection, and must take the form of: **a** a percentage on (gross) amounts realized, *less* payments to secured creditors (other than debenture-holders) out of the proceeds of their securities; and **b** a percentage on amounts distributed in dividend—i.e. to unsecured creditors (1949 Rules). In a members' or creditors', voluntary winding up the liquidator's remuneration is fixed, respectively, by the company in general meeting (s. 285), or by the committee of inspection, or the general body of creditors if there is no committee (s. 296). There is no obligation to follow the 1949 Rules in a voluntary winding up, but this is the normal practice.

17.2.5 The liquidator's accounts and returns

By the Companies Act, 1948, s. 247, every liquidator in a winding up by the court in England shall keep, in manner prescribed, proper books containing entries or minutes of proceedings at meetings, and of such other matters as may be prescribed; and such books shall be open to inspection by any creditor or contributory or his agent.

The Companies (Winding Up) Rules, 1949, prescribe two books:

a a *record book,* in which the liquidator is to enter all minutes, proceedings, and resolutions of meetings of creditors or contributories, or of the committee of inspection, and all such matters as are necessary to give a correct view of his administration, except that documents of a confidential nature are not to be entered; and

b a *cash book,* in which he is to enter his receipts and payments daily. The prescribed form provides several analysis columns on both debit and credit sides, with stereotyped headings, including columns for moneys drawn from and paid into the bank—i.e. it is a memorandum record, primarily designed to enable the liquidator's receipts and payments to be easily understood and audited, by persons often without professional accounting knowledge.

The record book and cash book, with any other books, documents, and vouchers needed to support them, shall be submitted to the committee of inspection when required, and at least once every three months. The committee is to audit the cash book at least once every three months.

In a voluntary winding up there are no rules as to books to be kept by the liquidator, or audit by the committee of inspection.

Where the liquidator carries on the company's business for the purpose of beneficial realization, the Rules require him to keep a *'distinct account of the trading',* and to incorporate the weekly totals of receipts and payments in the cash book. No form is prescribed, but the usual practice is to draw up a 'trading account' in cash only—i.e. a mere statement of receipts from sales of goods, etc., and of payments for wages, rent, electricity, etc., totalled weekly, with no allowance for accruals, prepayments, depreciation, etc. The trading account shall be verified, at least once a month, by affidavit and submitted to the committee of inspection, or some member designated for the purpose, who are/is to examine and certify the account.

S.249 of the 1948 Act requires the liquidator to send to the Department of Trade, at least twice a year, an *account of his receipts and payments,* in prescribed form, in duplicate, and verified by a statutory declaration. He shall also send such vouchers and information as the DoT shall require, to enable it to have the account audited—one certified copy being placed in the file at Companies

House, and the other sent to the court. The liquidator shall then post a printed copy of the account, or a summary thereof, to every creditor or contributory, unless the DoT grants a dispensation.

The 1949 Rules require the account to take the form of a copy of the cash book, rendered every six months from the date of the winding-up order, with a final account when the assets are fully realized and distributed. All accounts are to be in duplicate, and accompanied by vouchers and copies of the committee of inspection's audit certificates, a report in prescribed form upon the position of the liquidation and, in the case of the first account only, a summary of the company's statement of affairs, showing the amounts realized and explaining why any assets are still unrealized. All accounts shall be verified by affidavit—or an *affidavit of no receipts or payments* sent, where there have been none since the last audit.

S. 342 of the 1948 Act requires, in the case of *any* winding up not concluded within one year after its commencement, a *statement by the liquidator to the Registrar of Companies,* in prescribed form and containing prescribed particulars with respect to the proceedings in and position of the liquidation. The form is set out in the 1949 Rules; in the case of a voluntary or supervision winding up the first statement must cover the first twelve months from commencement, and be rendered within 30 days of expiry of that period, with subsequent statements every six months for as long as the winding up continues. If it appears, from any statement or otherwise, that the liquidator has in his hands or under his control any unclaimed or undistributed moneys or dividends six months after receipt, he shall pay the moneys into the Companies Liquidation Account—from which the claimants may withdraw them on application to the DoT, which will require the liquidator's certificate before paying out (s. 343).

17.2.6   The accounts of a company in liquidation

Besides keeping his own memorandum books, the Official Receiver, and his successor the liquidator, will continue the company's books as from the date of the statement of affairs. The separate creditors' balances are replaced by one Creditors Account for each priority class enumerated in the statement, including the bank overdraft, if any, under its appropriate head; while individual claims are listed on memorandum sheets, with additional columns for dividends, and for a final deficiency, or payment of statutory interest, as the case may be. The balance(s) of the Preference Share Capital Account(s), together with the provision(s) for cumulative dividend(s) up to the commencement of winding up (if any), are transferred to the credit of a Preference Members Account, and the balance(s) of the Ordinary and/or Deferred Share Capital Account(s) to the credit of (an) Ordinary Members and/or Deferred Members Account(s)—all supported by lists of contributories. If the net balance of the adjusted reserves (including share premium account) is debit, they should all be transferred to a Deficiency Account; if credit, to a Surplus Account—the opening balance agreeing with the ending figure of the statement of affairs, since all the assets except cash will have been revalued in accordance with the latter.

As assets are realized piecemeal, the gross proceeds are credited to the relevant accounts and the associated costs and charges debited thereto. When each class of assets is fully realized, the balance of the account (deficiency or surplus as compared with the estimated realizable value) is transferred to a Realization Account. The final balance of the realization account is transferred to the deficiency (or surplus) account, as are all general expenses, including the liquidator's remuneration.

The proceeds of asset realization, after payment of the expenses of realization, are first applied in paying, in order, the costs and charges listed in sub-section 17.2.4, with provision for any not paid immediately. The rest of the cash is used, from time to time, to pay dividends (of so many p in the £) to the various classes of creditors in order of priority—each Creditors Account being debited until its balance is reduced to nil, or until there are no more assets. In the former case each creditor, not otherwise entitled to interest, is paid 4 per cent per annum on the amount of his original claim, computed from the commencement of winding up to the several dates of payment (with debits to deficiency or surplus account); in the latter, the uncleared credit balance(s) on the creditors account(s), and that (those) of the members account(s), are written off against the deficiency account debit balance. Should there be any cash left for the members it will go, first to preference members (if any) and then to ordinary and/or deferred members, according to the articles of association; with a final write-off of the deficiency or surplus account balance, first to ordinary (or deferred) members, and so on upwards as appropriate. The books are then closed.

The liquidator's remuneration, as it is earned, is provided for by debiting Remuneration of Liquidator and crediting Liquidator—with actual payments debited to the latter account, and a final transfer of the former's balance to deficiency account. Of the two parts of the remuneration, the percentage on gross proceeds of realization of assets is provided as the proceeds are received, while the percentage on dividends to unsecured creditors is provided when a dividend is paid, but taken into account in computing it. It should be noted that the second percentage is on the amount *paid out*, so that if the percentage is, say, 2 per cent, then in order to pay a dividend to creditors of £1,000, £1,020 must be in hand; generally, with remuneration of x per cent, a dividend of $£D$ needs $£D\{(100+x)/100\}$ to finance it.

Example 2 In the situation envisaged in *Example 1*, the liquidator's principal ledger accounts (with some detail omitted) might appear as below, on the assumption that his remuneration was fixed at 3 per cent on realizations (less payments to secured creditors out of the proceeds of their securities) and 2 per cent on dividends. The assets produced the sums indicated, and all creditors proved for the amounts shown in the statement of affairs (including claims for electricity, gas, water, and telephone, £300). 'Secured creditors' consisted of a mortgage of £20,000 at interest of 9 per cent per annum, and the floating charge related to debentures of £50,000 at 10 per cent per annum; with, in both cases, interest accrued to the commencement of winding up (date of presentation of the petition), 29 February 1975.

N.B.G. Company Ltd

(In Compulsory Liquidation)

Cash

1975		£	1975		£
Apr 1	Balance b/d	10		Costs of realization—	
	Proceeds of realization—		Apr 28	Plant & machinery.	
Apr 28	Plant & machinery,			furniture, fittings,	
	furniture, fittings,			utensils, etc.	400
	utensils, etc.	17,600	Jun 23	Freehold property	500
Jun 23	Freehold property	24,000	Jun 30	Leasehold property	100
Jun 30	Leasehold property	6,000	Jul 21	Patents, trade marks, etc.	50
Jun 30	Work in progress	1,300	Oct 31	Trade debtors	30
Jul 21	Patents, trade marks,		Apr 1 ⎫	Costs of winding-up	
	etc.	1,000	to ⎬	petition & statement	
Apr 1 ⎫	Stock in trade	20,000	Nov 30 ⎭	of affairs	80
to ⎬	Trade debtors	21,700		Liquidator's disbursements	750
Oct 1 ⎭				Expenses of committee of	
				inspection	40
			Apr 30	Unsecured creditors –	
				Electricity, gas, water	
				& telephone	300
			Jun 30	Secured creditor	21,100
			Jun 30	Preferential creditors	1,540
			Aug 31	Debenture-holders	
				(floating charge)	57,500
			Nov 30	Unsecured creditors –	
				1st & final dividend,	
				41.26p in £	6,966
			Nov 30	Liquidator	2,254
		£91,610			£91,610

Freehold Property

1975		£	1975		£
Apr 1	Balance b/d	22,500	Jun 23	Cash (proceeds)	24,000
Jun 23	Cash (costs)	500			
Jun 23	Realization a/c	1,000			
		£24,000			£24,000

[Other Assets similarly—not shown]

Realization Account

1975		£	1975		£
Apr 28	Plant & machinery,		Jun 23	Freehold property	1,000
	furniture, fittings,		Jun 30	Leasehold property	900
	utensils, etc.	1,000	Jul 21	Patents, trade marks, etc.	450
Jun 30	Work in progress	700	Apr 1 ⎫	Stock in trade	5,000
Nov 30	Deficiency a/c	6,970	to ⎬	Trade debtors	1,320
			Nov 30 ⎭		
		£8,670			£8,670

[Sundry expenses accounts not shown]

Remuneration of Liquidator

1975		£	1975		£
Apr 1 to Nov 30	Liquidator— Percentage on realizations (3 per cent on £91,600 less £21,100)	2,115	Nov 30	Deficiency a/c	2,254
Nov 30	Percentage on dividend (2 per cent on £6,966)	139			
		£2,254			£2,254

Liquidator

1975		£	1975		£
Nov 30	Cash	2,254	Apr 1 to Nov 30	Remuneration of liquidator— Percentage on realizations	2,115
			Nov 30	Percentage on dividend	139
		£2,254			£2,254

Secured Creditor

1975		£	1975		£
Jun 30	Cash	21,100	Apr 1	Balance b/d— Principal	20,000
				Interest, 9 per cent p.a. to 28 Feb 1975	500
			Jun 30	Interest, 9 per cent p.a. to 30 Jun 1975	600
		£21,100			£21,100

Preferential Creditors

1975		£	1975		£
Jun 30	Cash	1,540	Apr 1	Balance b/d	1,540

Debenture-Holders (Floating Charge)

1975		£	1975		£
Aug 31	Cash	57,500	Apr 1	Balance b/d— Principal	50 000
				Interest, 10 per cent p.a. to 28 Feb 1975	5,000
			Aug 31	Interest, 10 per cent p.a. to 31 Aug 1975	2,500
		£57,500			£57,500

Unsecured Creditors

1975		£	1975		£
Apr 30	Cash — Electricity, gas, water and telephone	300	Apr 1	Balance b/d	17,168
Nov 30	Cash — 1st & final dividend, 41.26p in £	6,966			
Nov 30	Deficiency a/c	9,902			
		£17,168			£17,168

Preference Members

1975		£	1975		£
Nov 30	Deficiency a/c	£10,000	Apr 1	Balance b/d	£10,000

Ordinary Members

1975		£	1975		£
Nov 30	Deficiency a/c	£50,000	Apr 1	Balance b/d	£50,000

Deficiency Account

1975		£	1975		£
Apr 1	Balance b/d	70,648	Nov 30	Realization a/c	6,970
Nov 30	Costs of winding up petition & statement of affairs	80	Nov 30	Ordinary members	50,000
			Nov 30	Preference members	10,000
Nov 30	Liquidator's disbursements	750	Nov 30	Unsecured creditors	9,902
Nov 30	Expenses of committee of inspection	40			
Nov 30	Interest—secured creditor	600			
Nov 30	Interest—debenture- holders	2,500			
Nov 30	Remuneration of liquidator	2,254			
		£76,872			£76,872

Notes

1 The liquidator's 3 per cent on realizations is computed on the gross proceeds of all assets turned into money, excluding the opening cash balance, but subject to deduction of the total amount paid to the secured creditor out of the proceeds of his security—i.e. the liquidator is paid for the amount which he realizes *for the creditors without fixed securities,* before deducting any costs of the winding up.

2 Before paying the final dividend to unsecured creditors, the liquidator had £7,105 in hand to meet claims (after paying the 'quasi-preferential' ones) of £16,868. He therefore provided for remuneration of 2/102ths of this amount, or £139, which was 2 per cent of the balance, £6,966. The latter was 6,966/16,868 of the claims, or (approximately) 41.26p in the pound. There was, of course, nothing left for the members, whose balances, and the unsatisfied claims of the unsecured creditors, were written off against the deficiency account balance—thus closing the books.

17.2.7 Calls on contributories

As soon as may be after making a winding-up order, the court shall settle a list of contributories, and rectify the register of members as needed; unless it appears to the court that it will not be necessary to make calls on contributories or adjust their rights. In settling the list of contributories (if any) the court shall distinguish between contributories in their own right, and contributories as representatives of, or liable for the debts of, others (s. 257).

The court has, further, a general power to make calls on contributories for payment of any money considered necessary to satisfy the debts and liabilities of the company, and the costs, charges and expenses of winding up, and for the adjustment of the rights of the contributories among themselves; taking into consideration the probability that some contributories may partly or wholly fail to pay the call (s. 260). The above powers, and others, may be delegated to the liquidator as an officer of the court (s. 273), and usually are.

The power to make calls is normally valueless in the winding up of a company limited by shares, as it is unusual for shares to remain partly paid for any length of time. In a company limited by guarantee the maximum call on any contributory is the amount guaranteed by the memorandum of association. In an unlimited company there is no restriction, and the members can be compelled to meet the entire deficiency as regards creditors.

In a limited company, a full call is made if the maximum proceeds are clearly short of the amount needed to pay prior claimants 100p in the pound. The whole proceeds of the call (less the liquidator's percentage on the dividend) are distributed to the creditors and/or preference shareholders, and the shareholders who paid the call receive nothing. If the proceeds of a full call would be excessive, and necessitate a return of cash to the same shareholders, then only part of the outstanding amount should be called—with generous allowance for default, since a small excess to be refunded is less inconvenient than a small deficit to be made up by a further call. In the unlikely situation of having two or more classes of partly-paid shares and a deficiency as regards unsecured creditors (or fully paid shares of a prior class), the shares of lowest priority should be called to the extent needed to pay creditors and repay the fully- or partly-paid shares of higher priority; then, if necessary, resort should be had to the next class of shares above, and so on.

17.3 The accounts of receivers and managers

When debentures are issued which are secured by a floating charge, or when a bank loan or overdraft is secured by a single debenture of no fixed amount with a floating charge, the articles of association or terms of issue provide a remedy in the event of default in paying interest or repaying the principal, or of any act or default of the company which jeopardizes the debenture-holders' or bank's security. This remedy is the appointment of a *receiver*, whose functions are to take possession of the company's assets covered by the floating charge, and realize sufficient of them to repay the debenture-holders or bank, principal and interest, and to pay all liabilities ranking in priority to the debenture(s), together with the costs and charges of the receivership, and the receiver's remuneration. If (as is common) the receiver is granted powers to manage the company's business for the limited purpose of beneficial realization, he becomes a *receiver and manager*.

17.3.1 Proceedings and accounts of the receiver (and manager)

The appointment of a receiver for the debenture-holders commonly accompanies, or precedes, the winding up of the company by the court. In that case the Official Receiver, or provisional liquidator, is normally appointed as receiver also, and in the case of the Official Receiver relinquishes the office to the liquidator in due course. If, however, the receiver's appointment precedes the making of the winding up order, or the previous appointment of a provisional liquidator, or passing of a resolution to wind up voluntarily; then, for the purposes of s. 319 of the 1948 Act (computation of the claims of preferential creditors—see sub-section **17.2.3**), the 'relevant date' becomes the date of the receiver's appointment (s. 94).

A receiver or manager of the whole or substantially the whole of the property of an English company, appointed on behalf of the holders of debentures secured by a floating charge, shall forthwith send to the company notice of his appointment, and within 14 days (or such longer time as may be allowed by the receiver or the court (if any) which appointed him) one or more directors, and the secretary, of the company (or certain other persons, if required) shall make out, verify by affidavit, and submit to the receiver a *statement of affairs,* in the prescribed form as illustrated in connection with winding up by the court. Within two months after receiving the statement the receiver shall send copies of it, with any comments he sees fit to make thereon, to the Registrar of Companies and to the court (or to the DoT, if he has been appointed under the powers contained in any instrument) and, to the Registrar only, a summary of the statement, and of his comments if any. He shall also send to the company a copy of his comments, or a notice that he does not see fit to make any; and to the trustees for the debenture-holders and (as far as he is aware of their addresses) the debenture-holders themselves, a copy of the aforesaid summary. If the receiver becomes liquidator (or vice versa) the same provisions apply, with any necessary modifications (ss. 372, 373). Every invoice, order for goods, or business letter issued by or on behalf of the company, in or on which the company's name appears, shall contain a statement that a receiver or manager has been appointed (s. 370).

The said receiver or manager shall, as at the end of every twelve months from the date of his appointment and as at the date of his ceasing to act, send within two months (or such extended time as the court (or DoT) may grant) to the Registrar of Companies, the trustees for the debenture-holders, the company, and (as far as he is aware of their addresses) the debenture-holders, an *abstract of his receipts and payments,* in prescribed form, for the period since his appointment or since the date of the previous abstract, with the aggregate amounts of his receipts and payments for all previous periods (s. 372).

Where the previous paragraph does not apply, every receiver or manager appointed under the powers contained in any instrument shall, as at the end of every six months from the date of his appointment and as at the date of his ceasing to act, send within one month (or such extended time as the Registrar may grant) to the Registrar of Companies an abstract of his receipts and payments, in prescribed form, for the period since his appointment or since the date of the previous abstract, with the aggregate amounts of his receipts and payments for all previous periods (s. 374).

17.3.2 The accounts of a company in receivership

As far as concerns the accounts of the company, a receivership which does not lead to a winding up should be treated as a partial liquidation. Final accounts should be made up to the date of appointment of the receiver; but, since the assets are not all to be realized, there is no case for adjusting the assets and liabilities to the amounts shown in the statement of affairs, except to the extent that particular assets are expected to be realized. Realization proceeds only to the point at which the receiver has funds to repay the debenture-holders or the bank, after paying creditors with fixed securities, preferential and 'quasi-preferential' creditors, expenses of running the company (if he is a receiver and manager), costs and charges of the receivership, and his own remuneration. No distribution is made to unsecured creditors, whose claims are 'frozen' until the receiver ceases to act. The accounts for share capital and reserves are not affected (except by partial revaluations, and/or profits or losses on realization), and there is no deficiency or surplus account. In a word, the receiver interferes with the company's books of account no more than is strictly necessary, and always assumes that the business will be handed back to the directors when he has finished with it.

If a receiver is appointed, and then becomes liquidator, it is, perhaps, best to proceed as above in the first place, and then change over to a 'liquidation' basis of accounting as at the date of the winding up order. It is extremely improbable, in a normal case, that the court would appoint any other person as liquidator; if it did, the change-over in accounting bases would occur at the date of the receiver's ceasing to act, when it would become the duty of the liquidator to realize and distribute any assets left for the unsecured creditors and shareholders.

The remuneration of the receiver is fixed by the instrument under which he is appointed, and normally takes the form of a percentage on amounts realized, less payments to creditors with fixed securities out of the proceeds thereof. A receiver and manager may also be awarded an annual salary, accruing from day to day, in his capacity as manager. If a liquidator is appointed, he may apply to the court to fix, by order, the amount of any receiver's or manager's remuneration. Such order may have retrospective effect and, if it reduces the receiver's or manager's remuneration, require him to refund excess payments; but such refunds shall not be required as to any period before the making of the order, unless in the opinion of the court there are special circumstances making it proper for this power to be exercised (s. 371).

18

Analysis and criticism of published accounts

After an extensive and intensive examination of the financial and legal aspects of company accounting, it is now necessary to return to the theme of *Part I*— accountancy as a system for recording, analysing, and summarizing micro-economic data, and presenting the resulting information in a manner calculated to motivate to appropriate action the persons to whom that information is addressed. It is the province of management accounting to determine what information is presented, and how, to those involved in the day to day management and operation of the business. In this chapter attention is focussed rather upon the problems of communicating financial information to persons outside the management hierarchy, through the medium of the published final accounts.

18.1 Utility of published accounts

Of all the documents about a company which are available to persons other than its directors and senior managers, the annual accounts are by far the most detailed, the most rigorously drawn up, the most carefully and solemnly attested, the most regularly produced, the most widely circulated, and the most highly publicized. They are also the ones in which most faith is ordinarily reposed by the public, and the ones most likely to be accepted by the unsophisticated as embodying unimpeachable truth. In a normal situation they are taken as the best evidence for forecasting the level of dividends in the near future, which empirical research suggests as the main determinant of the market price of the shares; as the only basis for computing the price/earnings ratio, which is the principal indicator of the rationality of that price; and as the only real clue to the solvency, stability, liquidity, and profitability of the business.

As the reader will have gathered already, such implicit faith is scarcely justified, and is not shared by knowledgeable perusers of the accounts. The principles upon which they are compiled are to a large extent arbitrary, and increasingly suspect the farther one departs from short-term cash flows. Even within the context of conventional practice, the choice of bases for dealing with many items—stocks, depreciation, intangibles, extraordinary items, prior year adjustments, etc.—is a wide one, and combinations of these allow reported profits, and the book amount of equity, to take almost any desired values within a considerable range; indeed, it has been estimated (by R. J. Chambers) that, in a complex set of group accounts, over thirty million different combinations of figures may be permissible—and that there is no one set of values which could not be reported by *some* competent auditors as giving a true and fair view, without qualification! The accountancy profession, particularly in Britain, is only just beginning to put its house in order and restrict the inordinate diversity of practices; and until the publication of Statement of Standard Accounting Practice No. 2, in 1971, there was no requirement even to disclose what bases had been used in most areas of the accounts.

These objections apply within the context of historical-cost accounting, and are compounded, in the vast majority of quoted companies' financial statements, by consolidation of parent and subsidiary companies' accounts, and of the earnings of associates. The problems become worse when it is sought to assess the results of the same company or group over a number of years, and virtually insoluble when inter-firm comparison is attempted, even within the same industry—especially in view of the conglomerate character of so many modern groups. Further complications are caused by the incidence of chronic price inflation, making conventional accounts of limited utility even for a single year, and aggravated, if anything, by piecemeal attempts to correct for it, as by occasional revaluations of fixed assets. Finally, published accounts relate to past results and are of limited value as indicators of future trends, upon which the market value of securities should most rationally be based.

Much of this chaos springs from failure, by management, the law, and the accountancy profession, to define even the purposes for which final accounts are prepared, the uses to which consumers may be expected to put them, or the kinds of action to which the accounts are to motivate them—much less the types of data needed to attain optimal results. Legal regulation has been the main factor in promoting disclosure, and it has been financial institutions and lawyers, rather than accountants, who have demanded more and more detail, without any overall assessment of its value and purpose. The shortcomings of accountants have lain in complacent acceptance of the situation, and in a fatalistic belief that financial statements are bound to remain a mystery to the ordinary investor, and that this is all right as long as there are experts available to analyse them. Detailed disclosure is supposed to serve the expert rather than the layman but little attention has been paid to the quality, as distinct from the quantity, of information compulsorily made accessible, and without any real idea of the objects of publishing accounts it is hard to see how any genuine improvement can come about.

18.1.1 Uses of published accounts to different readers

As it is, the one set of annual accounts has *faute de mieux* to meet the needs of many different inquirers, and no single document can meet them all equally well. It is thus not surprising that the accounts serve some purposes better than others, or that they seem hardly suitable at all for some of the most important.

The first class to be considered are the company's *trade creditors*. They are principally concerned about security for payment of their claims, and wish to be assured that the company is solvent and likely to continue in business, and that it has adequate cash resources to pay its debts promptly as they fall due. For them the published accounts are of limited value, since they come out only once a year, and are several weeks or months out of date by then. Hence, trade suppliers rely mainly on their own estimates of the company's credit-worthiness, supplemented by reports from credit protection agencies. Once a company has become a regular customer, its credit rating can be assessed by the supplier's experience as to its promptitude or otherwise in paying on the due dates and in taking cash discount, if any. Even so, the published accounts of important customers should be scanned to see that the current assets and liquidity ratios appear healthy, and that the break-up value of the assets seems sufficient, on the most pessimistic estimates, to cover both secured and unsecured creditors with a margin for shareholders.

Bankers (usually secured by a floating charge) are more concerned about early liquidation of an overdraft by regular cash flows than about formal security, unless the company's position becomes desperate. In negotiations for borrowing facilities full managerial accounts and cash flow projections are demanded, as well as ample security. Annual accounts can then be used to monitor the security position in a general way, with special reference to profit levels, major investment projects, and the creation of charges ranking prior to or *pari passu* with the bank loan (insofar as this is permitted). Actual cash flows can be plotted in detail from the bank's own accounting records, and the peaks and troughs of the overdraft noted, together with any rising or falling trends.

The *Inland Revenue* have little or no interest in the published accounts. The local inspector of taxes always receives a full set of managerial accounts and supplementary schedules in support of the corporation tax return and draft computation, and uses them to validate the latter. He is thus able to observe the soundness or otherwise of the financial position, and hence the security for the Inland Revenue's (partly preferential) claims, without waiting for the public accounts and reports.

Debenture-holders and other long- and medium-term lenders, who generally receive from the company only their half-yearly interest payments, must rely much more upon the accounts for assurances that their security is not in jeopardy, despite the fact that the financial statements are sometimes a year or more out of date. When the accounts are still fairly fresh, though, it is useful to see whether the interest is well covered by profits (before interest and taxation), or alternatively whether there are large revenue reserves; and whether the assets charged as security are likely to realize at least the amount of the loan on a forced sale.

Preference shareholders are in a similar situation to debenture-holders, except that, having no formal security, they will look at the accounts to see whether reduction of the asset values to break-up level is likely to eliminate entirely the reserves and ordinary share capital, their only cushion against liquidation losses. They also wish to observe whether the preference dividend is well covered by the net profit after taxation, and appears in no danger of being passed. A potential investor in preference shares (today, almost certainly a financial institution, able to claim tax exemption for the dividends) will tend rather to analyse the trend of profits over several years to date, and to extrapolate it into the future on such evidence as is available, including any profit forecasts in the prospectus or offer for sale of a new issue.

It is the *ordinary (or deferred) shareholder* to whom the final accounts as published are of most equivocal value, and who finds the greatest difficulty in rationally interpreting them as a guide to whether he should sell his shares, hold them, or buy more. It is to him, too, that most investment advice, both professional and journalistic, is addressed. For him the question of security of capital is largely irrelevant; he knows that any catastrophe leading to liquidation is likely to deprive him of all or a great part of his investment, and that the value of his shares depends on the successful continuance of the business (or its acquisition by some other company on terms advantageous to the present equity shareholders). In other words, the equity shareholder's wealth is a function of the efficiency, acumen, foresight, determination, and luck of the company's senior management, as measured by its success in maximizing the earnings per (existing) share, in paying commensurate dividends, and in arousing and fulfilling market expectations of increasing earnings and dividends to come.

Few private shareholders are competent to form any judgement of a company's long-term performance from its published accounts. Most rely on hunches, on the opinions of financial journalists, or on professional advice from bankers or stockbrokers. The latter, and the large investing institutions, such as unit trusts, investment trusts, insurance companies and pension funds, employ investment analysts to assess all the determinants of the market price of each security in which they are interested, to take a view of the probable course of such price, and of the rate of return to be expected on the shares, and to give opinions which will guide the analyst's principal in taking investment decisions or giving advice to clients. The analyst uses many sources of evidence as to the performance of any given shares, and of the underlying business—announcements to shareholders and to the press, newspaper reports of major developments, inside information, rumours and the expectation that they will be widely believed, assessments of the likely effects of current events on particular industries or firms, sophisticated statistical analysis of past movements of earnings, dividends, and share prices with extrapolation of observed trends into the future (techniques commonly known as 'chartism'), and much else. His main source of information, however, about past events must always be the published accounts, and the parameters which he is able to extract from them. Yet it is here, in his attempts to assess what are fundamentally the results of successful or unsuccessful management, that the investment analyst is most frustrated by the inherent defects, contradictions and inconsistencies of present-day accounting practice.

18.2 Ratio analysis of published accounts

When analysing published accounts in any depth it is necessary to compute a good many *ratios,* or arithmetical relationships between sundry pairs of figures within the accounts. The total number of such relationships which it is possible to extract, even from the abbreviated statements furnished under the Companies Act, 1967, is very large; but relatively few are really significant, and not all of these are independent, in the sense that they could not be logically derived from other ratios without further reference to the original figures. Indeed, it is mathematically demonstrable that the number of fully independent ratios derivable from a set of accounts is always two, or one, less than the number of items, according to whether the governing totals are, or are not, completely analysed. Such reasoning says nothing about the usefulness of the ratios, but does convey a warning against 'overkill' through computing parameters which must vary directly or inversely as other parameters, and so add little to the analysis. For example, when $A + B = C$, there is little point in calculating A/C, B/C, and A/B (and/or their reciprocals), since either of the first two ratios can be found by subtraction of the other from 1, and the third is the product of the first and of the reciprocal of the second; and similarly for all their reciprocals. This illustrates the rule above enunciated, since with three figures as stated any *one* ratio suffices for analysis. If three components add to a total, it is necessary only to relate two of the components to the total; and so on for any number of items.

Accounting figures may be compared to instrument readings, relative to a scientific experiment or an industrial process. The company is a 'black box' whose inner workings are unknown, but certain aspects of its operation are susceptible of measurement at regular intervals. The measurements, taken together and judiciously interpreted, allow an opinion to be formed as to whether the business is healthy in a financial sense, and as to how well it is achieving its financial objectives, whatever they are considered to be; for this purpose they are (rather heroically) assumed to be the maximization of profit, and of the return to equity shareholders. As Chapter 4 should have made clear, it is open to serious doubt whether business managers really have this, or any other single objective, consistently in view; but the investor is deemed, insofar as he acts rationally, to seek the maximization of his wealth commensurately with the risks involved, or at any rate a return on his investment which at least compensates for those risks, and to judge the company's performance accordingly.

The analogy with instrument readings breaks down, in that the instruments of the research scientist, the engineer, or the industrial chemist are deliberately designed to measure, as accurately as possible, the physical phenomena in which they are interested for purposes of verification or control. The 'instruments' read by the financial analyst, on the other hand, have been installed by those whose activities he is monitoring, without consulting him, on principles of which he does not always approve, often with no clear idea of what is to be measured, and sometimes with no particular desire that he should be accurately informed; and are generally subject to large and unquantifiable biases or propensities to error. However meticulously he takes his readings (calculates his ratios), and however careful he is to interpret them consistently, the analyst can only regard them as giving a general indication of the state of the company's affairs as at a past point in time, and of its progress over a period already ended. Confusion is worse confounded when an attempt is made to appraise the company's performance over a number of years, for some of the 'instruments' may have been 'recalibrated' from time to time, and a whole battery of them may have been installed only recently—as when a new Companies Act is passed. Finally, each set of ratios is valid, even within the above limitations, for the one company or group only, and comparisons with other businesses are usually fallacious; whereas a thermometer or a pressure gauge gives readings of equal reliability wherever it is installed, and whoever uses it.

Ratios may be classified, in the first place, according to their nature, as:

a balance sheet, point-of-time, or quantity, ratios—comparisons of two 'static' figures derived from the balance sheet of a company at a given date, and/or from its supporting notes or statements;

b profit and loss account, period, or flow, ratios—comparisons of two 'dynamic' figures derived from the profit and loss account, etc.; and

c inter-statement, period/point, or flow/quantity, ratios—comparisons of a figure from the profit and loss account with one from the balance sheet.

These all relate to the same set of annual accounts. In addition, ratios (in the form of percentages or index numbers) may be computed as between corresponding figures for the same company or group at several different balancing dates or over several different periods, as compared with the same figure for a base date or period. Corresponding figures may also be compared as between two or more companies or groups for (as nearly as possible) the same date or period (inter-firm comparison). Such comparisons are performed more scientifically by the *Centre for Inter-Firm Comparison Ltd*, which obtains confidentially from subscribers a large amount of managerial accounting information, computes a battery of ratios, and reports these to the subscriber concerned, together with the ratios for the 'best' and 'worst' subscriber in each respect, and the averages for them all, within the industry concerned. The external analyst, however, is confined to published accounts, which are in many respects not truly comparable.

For the purposes of this discussion, though, it is more helpful to classify accounting ratios according to the aspects of business which they are designed to illuminate. These may be identified as:

i financial soundness and stability, short-term and long-term;
ii efficiency, profitability, and return on equity; and
iii potentiality for future growth, or its actual achievement.

18.2.1 Measures of financial soundness and stability

The first priority of any business is survival, and this cannot be assured, even in the short run, unless the company remains both liquid and solvent—i.e. able to pay its debts as they fall due, both immediately and in the foreseeable future. To begin with, then, attention is directed to the

> 1 *Liquidity, quick assets,* or *'acid test' ratio*
> Liquid (or quick) assets/immediate (or quick) liabilities *or*
> liquid (or quick) assets/current liabilities

'Liquid (or quick) assets' are defined as cash, and assets capable of being turned into cash, in the ordinary course of business and without substantial loss or inconvenience, within the time allowed for payment of the 'immediate (or quick) liabilities'. Liquid assets thus consist normally of cash and bank balances, bills of exchange receivable, quoted securities held as current assets, and trade debtors; while immediate liabilities comprise trade creditors, accrued expenses, and sometimes corporation tax for the previous year and/or proposed dividends. 'Current liabilities' bear their usual meaning, and include bank overdraft if any.

This ratio is taken from the current balance sheet, and measures the ability of the company to match its obligations with cash in the immediate future—say, within one month at most. The rule, as commonly stated, is that the ratio—preferably with current liabilities as the denominator—should equal 1 or slightly more, if the company is to be considered safe in the short term.

This rule holds rigorously for an industrial or commercial business, buying and selling on credit terms of approximately equal length for receivables and payables, and making no use of overdraft facilities. In fact, the liquidity ratio would need to be rather more than 1, since wages, at least, have to be paid weekly. The 'crude' form of the ratio is misleading, though, if the periods of credit given, and received, differ considerably in length; if a large part of the sales are for cash; or if the company's overdraft is appreciably below the (unknown) limit agreed with the bank. The analyst seldom has accurate information about the third point. The second he may guess from the nature of the business (a multiple shop company can operate with a formal liquidity ratio somewhat below 1, since its cash sales for a week far exceed its wages bill). The first may be tested by reducing debtors to (say) one-twelfth of the turnover and recomputing the ratio. On the whole, though, it is best to take the 'crude' ratio for a few years back and see whether the current figure is consistent with the series; the old values must, prima facie, have been adequate, since the firm has survived!

2 Current assets, or working capital, ratio
Current assets/current liabilities

This differs from (1) chiefly by including stocks and work in progress (if any), and prepayments, in the numerator, and cash received in advance in the denominator, as well as bank overdraft. The ratio is regarded as an index of the adequacy of the working capital, and is conventionally required to be between 2 and 3.

No good reason for fixing on these numbers seems ever to have been given, beyond the observed fact that the majority of industrial and commercial balance sheets produce current assets ratios in this range. Again, the companies have survived and the figures must be about right—especially since it is also observed that companies whose current assets ratios fall much below 2 often find themselves in difficulties quite soon. The latter phenomenon usually goes, though, with inadequate liquidity, and there may be some confusion between cause and effect. It is recognized, too, that a margin of net current assets much beyond that needed for survival represents idle capital (generally in the form of excessive stocks and/or cash balances) and consequent impairment of the overall rate of return.

As Chapter 5 makes clear, the determinants of an optimum level of working capital are much more complex than the above simplistic calculation suggests. Few of the factors involved are accessible to an external analyst, and he can, at best, compute the

3 Working capital to turnover ratio
(Current assets − current liabilities)/turnover

either as a decimal or (multiplying it by 12) as the number of months' sales represented by the net current assets, and compare it with the corresponding figures for past years—once more, on the assumption that, if it has not fallen markedly, it should be adequate. Even so there is no proof that it is optimal, or that the period arrived at by the second method bears any close relation to the length of the cash cycle. Nor does such a procedure remove distortion caused by inability to keep expenditure on fixed assets precisely in phase with accumulations of depreciation provided; while an issue of shares or debentures during the year, with no time to spend much of the proceeds before the year-end, may produce a quite atypical level of cash, and hence inflate ratios (1) to (3) out of all proportion. These objections do not apply to the

4 Stock to turnover ratio
Stocks and work in progress/turnover, and

5 Debtors to turnover ratio
Debtors/turnover

Both (4) and (5) may be computed either as decimals or as so many months' sales. The latter is more valid for (5), since debtors are more truly a function of sales than are stocks; these are really related to cost of sales, but published accounts do not normally show this. Comparisons are, again, made with previous years, to see whether the ratios show any propensity to rise, suggesting failure to exercise proper control over stock levels, and the granting of longer credit to customers, respectively, with increasing likelihood of losses through stock obsolescence and/or bad debts.

These five parameters are in many cases rendered less significant than they might be, through failure to make the financial year coincide, even approximately, with the natural business year ending at or near the time of minimum stocks and debtors, and maximum liquidity. British businessmen, unlike Americans, have proved stubborn in clinging to traditional dates such as 31 December and 31 March, regardless of their relation to the annual cycle of production and sales though from an analytical point of view the harm is minimized as long as consistency is observed.

After short-term survival the next priority is long-term financial stability, with adequate security for the payment of all liabilities. This means, firstly, that shareholders' funds must be large enough to provide a 'cushion' for unsecured creditors, against loss through forced realization of assets on liquidation. The basis test is the size of the

> **6** *Proprietary ratio*
> Shareholders' funds/total assets,

calculated in both cases after deduction of the book amounts of goodwill, or other intangible assets expected to lose all or most of their value on liquidation of the company. The resulting figure is the proportion of the total book amounts of the tangible assets which must be lost on forced realization, before the position of unsecured creditors is jeopardized; it should never be less than 0.5. (Alternatively, but less satisfactorily, the ratio may be computed as

> Shareholders' funds/total liabilities

with a crucial minimum of 1.)

The position of secured and preferential creditors is assessed more directly, by comparing the amounts due to them with the book values of the assets on which they are secured, by contract or by law. The relevant ratios are—

> **7** *Cover for debentures secured by a floating charge*
> (Total assets – creditors with fixed securities – preferential creditors)/debentures secured by a floating charge;

> **8** *Cover for preferential creditors*
> (Total assets – creditors with fixed securities)/preferential creditors; and

> **9** *Cover for creditors with fixed securities*
> Assets specifically charged/creditors with fixed securities

A bank overdraft secured by a floating charge should be included in the denominator of (7). Preferential creditors cannot be directly calculated from a published balance sheet, but the larger of the two corporation tax liabilities should be taken, plus (say) 5 per cent of the total payroll for the year (from the directors' report), as a rational estimate of the amounts likely to be preferential on a sudden liquidation. None of these ratios should be less than 2, for the reason given in connection with (6).

> **10** *Cover for preference shares* (or *equity ratio*)
> Equity funds/total assets

indicates, on the lines of (6), the proportion of the book value of assets which must be lost before the preference capital (if any) is endangered. (More rigorously, goodwill, etc., should be deducted from both numerator and denominator.) It also shows how easily the ordinary shares could become worthless on liquidation, whether there is any preference capital or not.

Measures of capital gearing are more logically dealt with in connection with the rate of return on equity funds, in the next section.

18.2.2 Measures of efficiency, profitability, and return on equity

There is not much that a financial analyst can do to measure a company's efficiency from its published accounts. Most of the necessary information is lacking, and the few ratios that can be computed are crude and over-generalized; nor can most of them be applied to accounts earlier than 1967. They are—

11 *Turnover of fixed and current assets*
Turnover/(fixed assets + current assets)

12 *Turnover of fixed assets*
Turnover/fixed assets

13 *Turnover of capital employed*
Turnover/total assets (*or* turnover/(total assets − current liabilities))

'Turnover' means sales or gross receipts for the current year. 'Fixed assets' exclude long-term investments, which do not contribute to turnover. The balance sheet items may be taken at the end of the current year, or (more reasonably) at the beginning of it, or (better still) as a mean between the opening and closing figures; it is normally impracticable to weight them for specific additions or disposals at definite points in time. Goodwill may be included or excluded.

Ratios (11) to (13) are measures of utilization of assets to generate turnover, and (13) is also connected with ratios (18) and (19) below. All suffer from a common defect of calculations based on depreciated historical cost of tangible assets—the fact that these give misleading results in a time of changing price levels, the further the date of acquisition recedes into the past. Since turnover is more directly and immediately affected by inflation than are asset values, such ratios will tend to rise (improve) year by year, even if there is no real gain in efficiency, and to fall sharply after a major acquisition, or revaluation, of assets. The norms, as far as there are any, also vary from industry to industry, and from firm to firm within an industry—much more between groups with interests in more than one industry—and are thus truly comparable only for the same firm over a short period of years, and preferably only for two successive years. Where there are several different activities the directors' report will generally analyse turnover between them, but there is usually no corresponding analysis of assets.

In addition, the publication in the directors' report of the total payroll and average number of employees for the year allows of the computation of

14 *Average remuneration per employee*
Payroll/average number of employees;

15 *Turnover per employee*
Turnover/average number of employees; and

16 *Net profit per employee*
Net profit before interest and taxation/average number of employees

Again, these figures all rise over time, merely through the effects of inflation. They are more significant for inter-firm comparison within an industry, over about the same periods of time, as indications of relative efficiency.

More relevant, but still needing to be used with caution, are the standard measures of profitability, i.e.—

17 *Net trading profit to turnover (per cent)*
Net trading profit x 100/turnover;

18 *Pre-tax return on capital employed (per cent per annum)*
Net profit before interest and taxation x 100/capital employed; and

19 *Post-tax return on capital employed (per cent per annum)*
(Net profit after taxation + interest net of corporation tax) x 100/capital employed

Ideally, one should compute the gross profit as a percentage of turnover, but the necessary data are normally unavailable to outsiders. Ratio (17) is a surrogate, designed to measure the success of management in extracting profit from the manufacturing and/or trading operations, undistorted by investment income and rents receivable, and by interest payable and taxation. Turnover, however, may be arrived at in more than one way (e.g. gross or net of purchase tax or excise duty—preferably net), and the calculation of trading profit is affected by different methods of valuing stocks and work in progress, allowing for profit on uncompleted long-term contracts, computing depreciation, and accounting for intangibles, such as research and development expenditure. There is also no distinction between fixed and variable costs, so that, other things being equal, the net profit margin is bound to rise and fall with turnover, as the fixed element in costs becomes a smaller or larger proportion of the sales revenue; besides which, inflation affects turnover and variable costs more immediately than fixed costs, producing further exaggeration of the percentage, while any revaluation of fixed assets increases depreciation charges and reduces the net profit. Comparability over time is thus limited within the same company, and almost non-existent between firms, even in the same industry. It follows that no particular norms can be laid down, except perhaps as industry averages, and that appraisal of movements in the ratio can only be tentative, and subject to numerous caveats.

Return on capital employed is regarded as the obvious indicator of success or failure in managing the business, irrespective of its financial structure—hence the use in the numerator of net profit before charging interest, i.e. what the profit, pre-tax or post-tax, would have been if the debenture capital had been raised by a share issue instead. (In the pre-tax calculation, dividends—not interest—from other companies should be grossed up with reference to the underlying rate of corporation tax, as is now recommended for the post-1973 tax structure—see Chapter 12, section 12.5). The objections in the previous paragraph, with respect to calculation of the net trading profit, apply here with equal force; and there are further problems, as to whether any adjustment should be made for 'below the line' amounts of extraordinary gains or losses, and/or retrospectively for prior year items. In general, if the company has followed the criteria laid down in SSAP No. 6 of the Accounting Standards Steering Committee (see Chapter 14, sub-section 14.6.3), there should be no need to adjust for truly extraordinary items; prior year adjustments, if 'extraordinary' in that sense, can be ascribed to the correct years. If, however, the principles of SSAP No. 6 have not been adhered to in any respect (particularly in older accounts), then judicious changes may have to be made in arriving at a representative figure of net profit before interest, whether before or after tax.

As to the denominator of the ratio, 'capital employed', it may be defined, either as total funds or assets (including or excluding goodwill and the like), or as total funds other than current liabilities (or total assets, as above, less current liabilities). It may further be computed at the end or the beginning of the year, or as a weighted mean of funds (on either of the above two bases) made available during it. (If bank overdraft is included, then interest thereon charged in the profit and loss account will have to be added back, gross or net of corporation tax, in calculating the numerator of the ratio.) Once again the historical-cost basis of valuation partly vitiates the computation in a period of changing price levels. Indeed there is double distortion, in that under inflationary conditions the numerator is exaggerated by the charging of unrealistically low depreciation on older fixed assets, while the denominator is understated in terms of replacement prices—the two errors thus reinforcing one another in overstating the rate of return.

All these factors, with other shortcomings of conventional accounting, make the ratio of very dubious value for inter-firm comparison, especially as between firms with old, and new, plant—the former may show the higher return on capital, although it is the less efficient of the two. The ratio is more valid for assessment of the progress of one company or group over time, since the inherent defects apply continuously, and should, at least partially, cancel out in inter-year comparison, though occasional revaluations of fixed assets, and other changes in accounting bases, will break the series.

Some accountants and analysts regard the return on capital employed (on whatever basis) as the product of two other ratios, namely:

Net profit before interest x 100/turnover; and
Turnover/capital employed

The latter has already been considered, as number (13) above. The former ratio, though, is definitely artificial (insofar as it differs from net trading profit x 100/turnover), since it includes items, such as investment income, not related to turnover. It also infringes the canons of independence laid down in section 18.2, in that it can be derived directly from ratios (13), and (18) or (19). All the same, such decomposition of the rate of return does emphasize an important truth: that success in maximizing the rate is attainable by two strategies—maximizing turnover of a given amount of assets, and maximizing the rate of profit on sales.

Of most immediate interest to ordinary shareholders are—

20 *Pre-tax return on equity funds (per cent per annum)*
(Net profit before taxation – minority interest grossed up for corporation tax – preference dividend similarly grossed up) x 100/(equity share capital + reserves); and

21 *Post-tax return on equity funds (per cent per annum):*
(Net profit after taxation – minority interest – preference dividend) x 100/(equity share capital + reserves)

The significant portion of the numerator in both cases is the equity earnings (before and after tax); the grossing-up factor in (20) is

$$100/(100 - T)$$

where T = the rate of corporation tax.

Ratios (20) and (21) express equity earnings as a rate of return upon the funds invested by the equity shareholders, as capital moneys contributed and as retained profits; the distinction is very often blurred or effaced by the making of bonus or rights issues from time to time. The amount of the denominator, in either case, is thus determined by the values imputed to the underlying assets, and the ratio in both forms suffers from the same theoretical limitations as (18) and (19). It bears no close relationship to the rate of return obtainable by purchasing the company's shares in the open market (see sub-section **18.2.3**).

The 'book' rate of return on equity, however computed, is normally higher than the rate of return on capital employed (net of current liabilities), even with zero capital gearing, since the denominator of the second ratio includes the deferred corporation tax liability, for the current year and beyond. Positive gearing widens the gap between the two rates and, as Chapter 13 explains, the judicious use of fixed-interest finance is one of management's principal strategies for increasing the wealth of the ordinary shareholders. Thus the equity rate of return is a function (though not a simple one) of return on capital employed and

22 *Capital gearing ratio*
(Debentures + preference shares)/(equity share capital + reserves)

The 'book' gearing should be computed for comparative purposes—the optimum for industrial and commercial companies in Britain is commonly thought to be about 0.5—but the ratio is more meaningful, in both theory and practice, if related to the market values of the securities (see sub-section **18.2.3**). Even so, the conventional figure is useful as a first indication as to whether the company's financial policy is prudent or the reverse.

Lastly, the analyst should compute the cover for remuneration of the various classes of capital—another aspect of financial gearing. The ratios are—

23 *Cover for interest (of parent company)*
(Net profit before interest and taxation − minority interest grossed up for corporation tax)/interest;

24 *Cover for preference dividend (of parent company)*
(Net profit before interest and taxation − minority interest grossed up for corporation tax)/(interest + preference dividend grossed up for corporation tax; and

25 *Cover for equity dividend (of parent company)*
(Net profit before interest and taxation − minority interest grossed up for corporation tax)/(interest + preference dividend grossed up for corporation tax + equity dividend similarly grossed up)

Debenture interest is taken as it stands, since it is paid out of pre-tax profits. Dividends (gross of income tax) are paid out of post-tax profits, and need to be grossed up (by the factor $100/(100 - T)$) to render them comparable with the pre-tax figure (after interest). This is a more reliable procedure than comparison of the simple dividends with post-tax net profit or equity earnings, as it avoids the distortion arising from estimation of the corporation tax charge in advance of assessment. Extraordinary items should be omitted when cover ratios are calculated for a single year, but ratios (23) to (25) should also be computed as an average for five or more previous years (if accounts are available for so far back), and in that case some of the excluded items may be brought in at the analyst's discretion, as they are not necessarily abnormal for the period as a whole. One last parameter in this section is the

26 *Pay-out ratio*
Equity dividend/(net profit after taxation – minority interest ± extraordinary items – preference dividend)

This supplements (25), and indicates the proportion distributed, of the total net amount available to equity shareholders for the current year. (In the past this ratio has not always been precisely calculable, owing to lack of consistency in accounting for 'below the line' items.)

The accepted minimum cover for both debenture interest and preference dividend is approximately 5, since the measure is one of security of income, complementing the ratios in sub-section **18.2.1** relative to security of capital. For the minority holder of equity shares, too, the dividend cover is a measure of income security, supplementing the earnings rate of return; the expected cover is about 1.5, and the pay-out ratio, though not its precise reciprocal, should be about 0.6–0.7 at most. For majority shareholders the dividend cover and pay-out ratio are of little interest, since control of the company enables them to manipulate dividend payments themselves, particularly in private companies.

18.2.3 Measures of achieved or potential growth

After analysing the published accounts by means of standard ratios, it is necessary to relate them to the market price of the equity shares as at the date of the analysis, which is naturally some time after the date of the accounts. It is then the task of the analyst to form an opinion as to the shares' potential for further growth in the market price, viewed as the market's collective estimate at any time of the present value of expected future cash flows from holding the shares. The first step is to compute the

27 *Book value of net assets per equity share*
(Equity share capital + reserves)/number of equity shares

for comparison with the market price per share. The latter will normally exceed (27) by a considerable margin, unless the company has lately had a poor earnings record and reduced or passed its dividends. In any case the book value of the shares is no guide to their break-up value on liquidation, which may well be nil. Somewhat more relevant is the company's

28 *Capital gearing based on market capitalization*
(Total market value of debentures + total market value of preference shares)/total market value of equity shares; *or*

(total market value of debentures + total market value of preference shares)/total market value of all company's securities

In modern financial theory this ratio (particularly in its second form) is more significant than the 'book' gearing ((22) above), as an indicator of the extent to which the management has been successful in maximizing the market value of the total securities of the company, and thus minimizing its cost of capital (and especially of equity) for the purposes of discounted cash flow appraisal of internal investment projects (see Chapter 7). This is achieved by using such a proportion of, in particular, loan capital (giving tax relief on the interest) as serves to lever up the equity earnings per share, without so reducing cover for the principal and interest of the debentures that they become unduly risky. If this process of gearing up is carried to excess, the cost of debenture capital rises (the market demands a higher rate of return to compensate for the risk), while equity earnings become too volatile in response to movements in net profit, and the price of the shares is depressed (thus increasing the cost of equity capital). Excessive gearing thus defeats the object of maximizing the company's total market capitalization, while unduly low gearing fails to secure the full advantages of tax relief on debenture interest. In relatively slow-growing economies such as those of the U.S.A. and U.K. the optimum gearing ratio in this context is thought to be about 0.5 by the first formula, or 0.33 by the second (one part of debt capital to two parts of equity); but more dynamic economies allow of higher gearings as long as expansion is expected to continue at its current rate—in Japan, market gearings of 3 to 4, or 0.75 to 0.80, respectively, are not uncommon.

The last group of ratios connect the company's reported earnings more directly with its share prices. They are—

29 *Earnings per share*
Equity earnings after taxation/number of equity shares;

30 *Price/earnings ratio*
Market price per equity share/earnings per share;

31 *Earnings yield (per cent per annum)*
Earnings per share x 100/market price per share; and

32 *Dividend yield*
Dividend per share x 100/market price per share

As explained in Chapter 14, sub-section **14.6.2**, the Accounting Standards Steering Committee has enjoined in its Statement of Standard Accounting Practice No. 3 that all quoted companies should compute the earnings per share figure and publish it in the accounts; but the analyst will generally have to do this for himself, with accounts earlier than 1971.

The EPS provide, from the issue of one set of accounts to the issue of the next, a 'standing' denominator to which the market price for any day may be applied as numerator, producing the price/earnings (or P/E) ratio for the day. It is properly applicable only in connection with the 'classic' (American and 'old' British) system of corporation tax (a single charge on distributed and undistributed profits, with a further charge on distributions in the shareholders' hands), and with the 'imputation' (French and 'new' British) system (as before, but with income tax on distributions reduced by relief for underlying corporation tax). It is inappropriate to the 'two-rate' (West German) system, in which distributed profits bear a lower rate of corporation tax and are taxed again in the shareholders' hands, so that corporation tax and EPS vary with the level of distributions.

The P/E ratio is conceived as the number of years' purchase of the latest known earnings, represented by the share price at any given time. In this sense it is, perhaps, best understood as the reciprocal, multiplied by 100, of the earnings yield (the EPS expressed as a rate of return on the market price). The higher the P/E ratio, the lower the earnings yield—e.g. a P/E ratio of 10 corresponds to an earnings yield of 10 per cent per annum, but a P/E ratio of 20 answers to a yield of 5 per cent per annum. Thus a high P/E ratio is the result of the market's bidding up the price beyond what the latest reported annual earnings would appear to justify, in the expectation that future earnings will rise and enable larger dividends to be paid, giving a (DCF) rate of return on the shares higher than the current dividend yield. It can be demonstrated that, given a certain current dividend yield and the expectation that dividends will increase exponentially by some other rate per cent per annum (the market price being also expected to grow exponentially at the same rate), the expected DCF rate of return to an investor over any period of time is the sum of the dividend yield and the growth rate; e.g. for an investment of £100, an initial yield of 5 per cent per annum (before income tax), a growth rate of 3 per cent per annum, and sale of the shares at the end of five years, the cash flows will be

Year	0	1	2	3	4	5
	−100	5	5.15	5.3045	5.463635	5.627544 + 115.927407*

* I.e. $100(1.03)^5$.

and the internal rate of return will be exactly 8 per cent per annum, i.e. $(5 + 3)$ per cent per annum. It follows that, if an 8 per cent rate of return is regarded as acceptable for that class of investment, the shares (supposing the dividend pattern is accurately foreseen) are correctly priced, and that, if dividends are twice covered by equity earnings (giving a 10 per cent earnings rate of return), a P/E ratio of 10 is also correct.

The analyst cannot, of course, predict the future dividends and market prices in relation to any shares at any time. What he can do is to find the dividend rate of return and compare it with the rate of return, in DCF terms and adjusted for inflation, currently regarded as reasonable compensation for the risks of investing in such a security as the one under review. The difference between the two rates, if like is compared with like, is the expected exponential growth rate implied by the current P/E ratio, and the analyst must then form an opinion as to whether such an expectation is rational. If in his opinion it is not, then the price of the shares is excessive and may be expected to fall, and the client, if he holds any, is advised to sell them. Alternatively, the analyst may consider that the projected growth rate, and the share price, are about right (the client should hold his shares for the present), or too conservative (the price is likely to rise, and the client should buy now).

The full range of techniques for forming such opinions is outside the scope of this book.[1] Enough should have been said, though, to indicate the important part played by scientific analysis of the company's published accounts, and the inadequacy of a mechanistic approach. All the ratios need to be taken together, supplemented by all other available information, quantitative and otherwise, and the analyst's judgement applied to them, before he can draw up his report.

[1] For further information, see, e.g., Samuels, J. M., and Wilkes, S. T., *Management of Company Finance* (2nd edition, Nelson, 1975).

18.3 Ratio analysis—a comprehensive illustration

There follows a set of accounts of the parent company of a manufacturing and trading group, with abridged particulars of relevant items outside the consolidated profit and loss account, and the consolidated, and parent company's, balance sheets; and the accounting ratios computed therefrom, as set out in section **18.2**. These accounts serve also as an illustration of the published accounts of a holding company (see Chapter 16, section **16.8**).

Excelsior Ltd and its Subsidiaries

Consolidated Profit and Loss Account for the Year ended 31 December 19.1

	Year ended 31. 12. 19.1		Year ended 31. 12. 19.0	
	£000	£000	£000	£000
Turnover (see Note 1)		5,000		4,000
Net Trading Profit (see Note 2)		411		300
after charging the items below (see also Notes 3, 4 and 5)—				
Auditors' remuneration and expenses	6		5	
Hire of plant and machinery	32		28	
Depreciation of fixed assets (see Note 11)	364		291	
Amortization of patents	1		1	
Group's Share of Profits (Less Losses) of Associated Companies		30		25
Income from investments (other than in subsidiary and associated companies)				
Quoted investments	3		—	
Unquoted investments	4		5	
		7		5
Net Profit Before Interest and Taxation		448		330
Interest payable				
On bank overdrafts	1		—	
On mortgage (repayable within 5 years)	10		—	
On debentures (redeemable after more than 5 years)	100		100	
		111		100
Net Profit Before Taxation		337		230
Corporation tax based on current year's profits				
Of Excelsior Ltd and its subsidiaries at 52 per cent (including £30,000 (19.0, £20,000) transferred to deferred taxation account)	155		105	
Of associated companies	15		12	
	170		117	
Tax credit on United Kingdom dividends received	1		—	
	171		117	
Less Adjustment for previous year's tax overprovided	5		4	
		166		113
Net Profit After Taxation		171		117

Attributable to Shareholders in Excelsior Ltd (of which £130,000 (19.0, £85,000) is dealt with in that company's accounts)		150	100
Extraordinary items (group's proportion after taxation and after deducting minority interests, and including the group's share of associated companies' items) (see Note 6)		(15)	(3)
Profit Attributable to Shareholders in Excelsior Ltd		135	97
Dividends of Excelsior Ltd			
Preference—paid	7		7
Ordinary—paid	40		32
—proposed	40		32
		87	71
Amounts Added to Reserves of			
Excelsior Ltd	37		14
Subsidiaries (Excelsior Ltd's proportion)	5		7
Associated companies (Excelsior Ltd's proportion)	6		5
		48	26
Earnings per Share (see Note 7)		8.0p	5.8p

Excelsior Ltd and its Subsidiaries

Consolidated Balance Sheet, 31 December 19.1

	31. 12. 19.1		31. 12. 19.0	
Net Funds employed by the Group	*£000*	*£000*	*£000*	*£000*
Share Capital of Excelsior Ltd—Authorized, Issued and Fully Paid				
100,000 10 per cent (now 7 per cent plus tax credit) cumulative preference shares of £1 each.	100		100	
2,000,000 (19.0, 1,600,000) ordinary shares of 50p each	1,000		800	
		1,100		900
Reserves (see Note 8)				
Share premium account	250		200	
Fixed assets revaluation reserve	61		–	
10 per cent debenture redemption reserve fund	155		75	
General reserve	20		20	
Profit and loss account	1		34	
Retained profits of associated companies (group's proportion)	72		66	
		559		395
Total Funds of Excelsior Ltd's Shareholders		1,659		1,295
Interest of Minority Shareholders in Subsidiaries		93		92
10 Per Cent Debentures (see Note 9)	1,000		1,000	
Less Discount not yet written off	40		45	
		960		955
Mortgage on Freehold Property (see Note 10)		200		–
Deferred Taxation (see Note 11)		120		30
Corporation Tax—Current Year		53		21
		3,085		2,393

H. R. ENTERPRISE, Chairman
N. B. DRIVE, Managing Director

Net Assets in which Company Funds are invested	31. 12. 19.1		31. 12. 19.0	
	£000	£000	£000	£000
Fixed Assets (see Notes 11 and 14)				
Freehold land	550		500	
Freehold buildings	252		240	
Leasehold land and buildings (see Note 13)	63		70	
Plant, machinery, vehicles, fixtures and loose tools	977		782	
		1,842		1,592
Goodwill (being excess of cost of investments in subsidiaries over net tangible assets thereof at date of acquisition), patents and trade marks (see also Note 2)		52		38
		1,894		1,630
Investments (Unquoted) in Associated Companies at cost plus the group's share of retained earnings to the dates of the latest accounts of the said companies (see Note 15)		259		253
Investments (Unquoted) in Other Companies at cost (see Note 16)		80		80
Investments (Quoted) in Respect of 10 Per Cent Debenture Redemption Reserve Fund at cost (market value £152,000 (19.0, £76,000))		155		75
Current Assets				
Inventory (see Note 2)—				
Raw materials and components	156		120	
Work in progress	56		44	
Finished goods	223		188	
	435		352	
Trade debtors and prepaid expenditure	620		510	
Short-term investments (quoted) (market value £68,000 (19.0, nil))	70		–	
Bank balances and cash in hand and in transit	192		11	
	1,317		873	
Less Current Liabilities				
Bank overdrafts (see Note 17)	16		4	
Trade creditors and accrued expenditure	518		444	
Corporation tax—previous year	16		14	
Proposed dividend of Excelsior Ltd	40		32	
ACT and surcharge on proposed dividend	30		24	
	620		518	
Net Current Assets		697		355
		3,085		2,393

Excelsior Ltd

Balance Sheet, 31 December 19.1

Net Funds employed by the Company	31. 12. 19.1 £000	31. 12. 19.1 £000	31. 12. 19.0 £000	31. 12. 19.0 £000
Equity Share Capital—Authorized, Issued and Fully Paid				
2,000,000 (19.0, 1,600,000) ordinary shares of 50p each		1,000		800
Reserves (see Note 18)				
Share premium account	250		200	
Fixed assets revaluation reserve	35		—	
10 per cent debenture redemption reserve fund	155		75	
General reserve	20		20	
Profit and loss account	(5)		33	
		455		328
Total Equity Shareholders' Funds		1,455		1,128
Preference Share Capital—Authorized, Issued and Fully Paid				
100,000 10 per cent (now 7 per cent plus tax credit) cumulative preference shares of £1 each		100		100
Total Shareholders' Funds		1,555		1,228
10 Per Cent Debentures (see Note 9)	1,000		1,000	
Less Discount not yet written off	40		45	
		960		955
Mortgage on Freehold Property (see Note 10)		200		—
Deferred Taxation (see Note 11)		100		16
Corporation Tax—Current Year		44		15
		2,859		2,214

H. R. ENTERPRISE, Chairman
N. B. DRIVE, Managing Director

Net Assets in which Company Funds are invested	31. 12. 19.1		31. 12. 19.0	
	£000	£000	£000	£000
Fixed Assets (see Notes 19 and 20)				
Freehold land	309		276	
Freehold buildings	168		160	
Plant, machinery, vehicles, fixtures and loose tools	605		541	
		1,082		977
Patents and trade marks (see also Note 2)		9		10
		1,091		987
Shares in Subsidiary Companies at cost (see Note 21)		939		689
Investments (*Unquoted*) in Associated Companies at cost (see Note 22)		187		187
Investments (*Quoted*) in Respect of 10 Per Cent debenture redemption reserve fund at cost (market value £152,000 (19.0, £76, £76,000))		155		75
Current Assets				
Inventory (see Note 2)—				
Raw materials and components	122		85	
Work in progress	41		30	
Finished goods	152		136	
	315		251	
Amounts owed by subsidiary companies	28		116	
Trade debtors and prepaid expenditure	387		322	
Short-term investments (quoted) (market value £68,000 (19.0, nil))	70		—	
Bank balance and cash in hand	149		7	
	949		696	
Less Current Liabilities				
Amounts owing to subsidiary companies	10		40	
Trade creditors and accrued expenditure	374		318	
Corporation tax—previous year	8		6	
Proposed dividend	40		32	
ACT and surcharge on proposed dividend	30		24	
	462		420	
		487		276
Net Current Assets		2,859		2,214

Excelsior Ltd and its Subsidiaries

Summary of Group Results and Financial Position Adjusted for the Effects of Inflation (see Note A)

	Historical basis		Current purchasing power basis	
	Year ended 31.12.19.0 £000 £000	Year ended 31.12.19.1 £000 £000	Year ended 31.12.19.1 £000 £000	Year ended 31.12.19.0 £000 £000
Group Results for Year				
Turnover	4,000	5,000	5,556	5,455
Net profit before taxation	230	337	554	460
Taxation	113	166	166	141
Net profit after taxation	117	171	388	319
Minority interest	17	21	26	24
Net profit after taxation attributable to shareholders in Excelsior Ltd	100	150	362	295
Extraordinary items attributable to those shareholders	(3)	(15)	(17)	(4)
Profit attributable to shareholders in Excelsior Ltd	97	135	345	291
Dividends of Excelsior Ltd	71	87	92	93
Retained profits of Group	26	48	253	198
Group Financial Position at End of Year				
Net current assets	355	697	732	455
Investments—				
On debenture redemption reserve fund	75	155	155	94
In non-group companies	80	80	120	120
In associated companies	253	259	407	400
	408	494	682	614
Fixed assets less depreciation	1,592	1,842	2,077	1,960
Intangible assets	38	52	72	55
	2,393	3,085	3,563	3,084
Less Preference share capital	100	100	100	125
Minority interest	92	93	132	130
Loan capital	1,000	1,000	1,000	1,250
Mortgage on freehold property)	—	200	200	—
Deferred taxation	30	120	200	45
Current taxation	21	53	53	26
	1,243	1,566	1,685	1,576
Total equity interest	1,150	1,519	1,878	1,508
Ratios				
Earnings per share (p) (based on 1,800,000 (19.0, 1,600,000) ordinary shares of 50p in issue during year)	5.8	8.0	19.7	17.8
Equity dividend cover (times)	1.4	1.6	4.0	3.4
Return on total equity interest (%)	8.1	9.4	18.8	18.9
Net assets per share (p) (based on 2,000,000 (19.0, 1,600,000) ordinary shares of 50p in issue at end of year)	71.9	76.0	93.9	94.3

Notes

A the figures in the current purchasing power basis columns were arrived at by converting the corresponding figures in the historical basis columns by reference to the changes in a general price index between the dates of the original transactions and 31 December 19.1. The current purchasing power basis figures for both this and last years are measured in pounds of purchasing power at 31 December 19.1. The general price index used was that specified in Provisional Statement of Standard Accounting Practice No. 7. The Retail Price Index at 31 December 19.1 was 150.0 and at 31 December 19.0 was 120.0. Both figures are based on January 1974 = 100.

As the Inland Revenue do not at present accept CPP basis accounting, taxation liabilities are calculated by reference to profits on the historical basics and no adjustment therefore is made to the tax charge in the CPP basis column.

B *Group net profit before taxation.*

How the difference between profit on a historical basis and on a current purchasing power basis is made up.

	Year ended 31.12.19.1		Year ended 31.12.19.0	
	£000	£000	£000	£000
Group Net Profit Before Taxation (historical basis)		337		230
Adjustment to convert to current purchasing power basis:				
Stocks and Work in Progress Additional charge based on restating the cost of stocks and work in progress at the beginning and end of the year in pounds of current purchasing power, thus taking the inflationary element out of the profit on the sale of stocks	(65)		(37)	
Depreciation and Amortization Additional depreciation, etc., based on cost, measured in pounds of current purchasing power, of fixed and intangible assets	(47)		(32)	
Monetary Items Net gain in purchasing power resulting from the effects of inflation on the Group's net monetary liabilities and preference share capital	242		137	
Sales, Purchases and All Other Costs These are increased by the change in the index between the average date at which they occurred and the end of the year. This adjustment increases profit as sales exceed the costs including in this heading	87	217	70	138
Group Net Profit Before Taxation (current purchasing power basis at end of year under review)		554		368
Adjustment required to update last year's profit from pounds of 31 December 19.0 purchasing power to pounds of 31 December 19.1 purchasing power		–		92
Group Net Profit Before Taxation (current purchasing power basis at 31 December 19.1)		554		460

C The loan capital, mortgage and preference share capital at 1 January 19.1 amounted to £1,100,000. £1,100,000 at 1 January 19.1 is equivalent in purchasing power to £1,375,000 at 31 December 19.1 (because inflation has been 25.0 per cent during the year). As the Group's liabilities to the providers of loan capital and to the mortgagee, and the nominal value of the preference shares, are fixed in money terms these liabilities, and nominal value, have declined during the year in real terms from £1,375,000 to £1,300,000 (after allowing for the raising of a mortgage of £200,000 on freehold property during the year—current purchasing power equivalent £222,000). On this basis there has been a reduction of £297,000 in the Group's obligations in terms of current purchasing power, and this is included in the net gain on monetary items of £242,000, shown in Note B.

Excelsior Ltd and its Subsidiaries

Statement of Source and Application of Funds for the Year ended 31 December 19.1 (based on the Accounts of the Group)

	Year ended 31.12.19.1		Year ended 31.12.19.0	
	£000	£000	£000	£000
Source of Funds				
Profit attributable to shareholders in Excelsior Ltd		150		100
Extraordinary items (Group's proportion)		(15)		(3)
		135		97
Adjustments for items not involving the movement of funds—				
Minority interest in Group profits	21		17	
Depreciation and amortization of fixed and intangible assets	365		292	
Discount on debentures written off	5		5	
Profits retained in associated companies	(6)		(5)	
Profit on disposal of fixed assets	(10)		(6)	
Increase in taxation liabilities—				
Deferred (on profits only)	24		10	
Current	32		20	
		431		333
Total generated from operations		566		430
Funds from other sources				
Ordinary shares issued in consideration of the acquisition of a subsidiary—				
Nominal value	200		—	
Premium	50		—	
	250		—	
Mortgage assumed on freehold property	200		—	
Interest on investments in respect of debenture redemption reserve fund	5		—	
		455		—
		1,021		430

Application of Funds
Dividends, paid and proposed—

Of Excelsior Ltd.	87		71	
Of Subsidiaries (minority's proportion)	20		15	
		107		86
Purchase of fixed assets*	587		350	
Less Proceeds of sale	110		70	
		477		280
Purchase of goodwill on acquisition of a subsidiary*		15		—
Increase in investments in respect of debenture redemption reserve fund		80		75
Increase in stocks and work in progress*		83		40
Increase in receivables*		110		66
(Increase) in payables*		(90)		(47)
		782		500

Movement in Net Liquid Funds

Increase (Decrease) in bank and cash balances*	169		(70)	
Increase in short-term investments (quoted)	70		—	
		239		(70)

*Summary of the effects of the acquisition of Midland Motor Components Ltd:

Net Assets Acquired

Fixed Assets	173
Goodwill	15
Stocks and work in progress	53
Receivables	71
Payables	(72)
Bank and cash balances	10
	250

Discharged By
Ordinary shares issued—

Nominal value	200	
Premium	50	
		250

Notes on the accounts
Consolidated profit and loss account

1 Turnover consists of sales to customers outside the Group, net of returns inward but before deducting cash discounts.
2 The Group has for several years consistently followed the accounting policies described below, in relation to certain items materially affecting the calculation of the net trading profit from one year to another:

a *Stocks and work in progress*
Raw materials and components purchased are priced out to production, and the year-end stocks valued, by the 'first in, first out' (FIFO) method. Work in progress and stocks of finished goods are valued at standard cost, adjusted for changes in prices and wages since the standards were set, and including a percentage on total labour content, as an allowance for manufacturing overheads. Items are reduced to net realizable value if lower than standard cost.

b *Research and development expenditure*
This is wholly written off in the year when it is incurred.

c *Depreciation of fixed assets*
All tangible fixed assets, except freehold land and loose tools, are depreciated by equal annual instalments of the historical cost or later revaluation, over their estimated economic lives, as follows:

Freehold buildings	25 years
Leasehold land and buildings	15 to 25 years
Plant, machinery, vehicles and fixtures	3 to 10 years

No depreciation is charged on freehold land. Loose tools are revalued by appraisal at each year-end, and depreciation written off accordingly.

Patents are amortized by equal annual instalments over 16 years, or the shorter remaining lives of purchased patents. There is no systematic amortization of goodwill or trade marks.

d *Repairs and renewals*
All items of expenditure on existing plant, etc., not exceeding £100, are charged to revenue as repairs or renewals. Items exceeding £100 are apportioned to repairs and renewals, or capitalized as additions to fixed assets, according to their nature.

e *Hire of plant and machinery*
All hire or rental charges are charged to revenue as they accrue, and no account of such items is taken in the Consolidated Balance Sheet or in the Balance Sheet of Excelsior Ltd.

f *Consolidation policies*
The annual accounts of Excelsior Ltd and all its subsidiaries are consolidated by the 'acquisition' (or 'purchase') method, in which each subsidiary's share capital and reserves, as at the date of acquisition (so far as concerns the holding company), are offset against the cost of the subsidiary's shares and the difference imputed to goodwill (or, if negative, to capital reserve). Inter-company sales and indebtedness are eliminated, as is any element of inter-company profit in year-end stocks of raw materials, components or finished goods, acquired by one Group company from another. The proportion of such inter-company profit attributable to minority shareholders in subsidiaries is eliminated in computing their interests in profits and net assets of the Group.

3 The total emoluments of the Directors of Excelsior Ltd from all sources within the Group (including superannuation contributions from Group companies) were:

	Year ended 31. 12. 19.1	Year ended 31. 12. 19.0
As directors of group companies	6,000	5,500
In other capacities	76,000	71,000
	£82,000	£76,500

4 The total emoluments (excluding superannuation contributions from Group companies) of the Chairman (and highest paid Director) of Excelsior Ltd, and of the numbers of Directors (including the Chairman) whose emoluments (as above) fell within the ranges indicated, were:

	Year ended 31. 12. 19.1	Year ended 31. 12. 19.0
Chairman's emoluments	£14,000	£12,000
Numbers with emoluments in ranges		
£0 to £2,500	—	—
£2,501 to £5,000	2	2
£5,001 to £7,500	4	5
£7,501 to £10,000	3	3
£10,001 to £12,500	2	1
£12,501 to £15,000	1	—

No Director has waived, or agreed to waive, any emoluments in either year.

5 The numbers of employees (other than Directors) whose emoluments (defined as in Note 4) fell within the ranges indicated, were:

	Year ended 31. 12. 19.1	Year ended 31. 12. 19.0
£10,001 to £12,500	2	2
£12,501 to £15,000	1	—

6 Extraordinary items were as follows:

	Year ended 31. 12. 19.1 £000	Year ended 31. 12. 19.0 £000
Group Companies		
Loss through fraud by agent	(22)	—
Associated Companies (Group's share)		
Damages recovered for libel on company	7	—
Costs against company in unsuccessful action for infringement of a patent	—	(3)
	(15)	(3)

7 Earnings Per Share are computed on the basis of weighted average numbers of ordinary shares in Excelsior Ltd: 1,800,000 shares of 50p each, fully paid, for the year ended 31 December 19.1, and 1,600,000 such shares for the year ended 31 December 19.0; and equity earnings after taxation of £143,000, and £93,000, respectively.

Consolidated balance sheet

8 Movements on Group reserves during the year ended 31 December 19.1 were as follows:

	Share premium account £000	Fixed assets revaluation reserve £000	10 per cent debenture redemption reserve fund £000	General reserve £000	Profit and loss account £000	Retained funds of Associated Companies (Group's proportion) £000
Balances at 31 December 19.0	200	–	75	20	34	66
Premium on ordinary shares issued by Excelsior Ltd	50	–	–	–	–	–
Revaluation of fixed assets (see Note 14)	–	127	–	–	–	–
Transfer to deferred taxation	–	(66)	–	–	–	–
Retained earnings	–	–	–	–	42	6
Appropriation thereof for redemption of 10 per cent debentures	–	–	75	–	(75)	–
Investment income received in respect of 10 per cent debenture redemption reserve fund (less corporation tax)	–	–	5	–	–	–
Balances at 31 December 19.1	250	61	155	20	1	72

9 The £1,000,000 10 per cent Debentures were issued by Excelsior Ltd on 1 January 19.0 at 95, and are redeemable at par on 31 December 19.9. They are secured by a floating charge on the general assets of the Company.

10 The £200,000 Mortgage was raised by Excelsior Ltd on 1 July 19.1, at interest of 10 per cent per annum, and is repayable on 30 June 19.6. It is secured on the whole of the Company's freehold land and buildings.

11 Deferred Taxation represents corporation tax deferred to later years: a by the excess to date of capital allowances on existing fixed assets, over depreciation charged in the Accounts; and b in relation to expected capital gains on disposal of fixed assets which have been revalued. Adjustments are made in respect of advance corporation tax (ACT) provided for on proposed dividends at the end of the year, and (in the case of the Consolidated Balance Sheet) for inter-company profits, treated in the Accounts as unrealized but subjected to corporation tax as for the current year.

12 Details of Fixed Assets, and of movements thereon during the year ended 31 December 19.1, were as follows:

Cost or other Valuation

	Balance at 31 December 19.0 £000	Revaluation during year £000	Additions during year, at cost £000	Disposals during year, at cost £000	Balance at 31 December 19.1 £000
Freehold land	500	50	—	—	550
Freehold buildings	300	30	—	—	330
Leasehold land and buildings	140	—	—	—	140
Plant, machinery, vehicles, fixtures and loose tools	1,500	100	587	(300)	1,887
	2,440	180	587	(300)	2,907

Accumulated Depreciation

	Balance at 31 December 19.0 £000	Revaluation during year £000	Provided during year £000	Re Disposals during year £000	Balance at 31 December 19.1 £000
Freehold buildings	60	6	12	—	78
Leasehold land and buildings	70	—	7	—	77
Plant, machinery, vehicles, fixtures and loose tools	718	47	345	(200)	910
	848	53	364	(200)	1,065

Intangible Assets

	Balance at 31 December 19.0 (cost less amounts written off) £000	Additions during year at cost £000	Disposals during year, at cost less amounts written off £000	Amounts written off during year £000	Balance at 31 December 19.1 (cost less amounts written off) £000
Goodwill, patents, and trade marks	38	15	—	(1)	52

13 All leases of land and buildings had less than 50 years to run as at 31 December 19.1.

14 Certain fixed assets of the Group were revalued on 1 July 19.1, as follows:

Freehold land	£550,000
Freehold buildings	£264,000
Plant, machinery, vehicles, fixtures and loose tools	£835,000

The valuations were carried out by professional valuers, on the basis of current realizable values in the case of freehold land, and of current replacement prices in the case of freehold buildings, plant, machinery, vehicles, fixtures and loose tools.

15 The Unquoted Investments in Associated Companies are holdings, of not less than 20 per cent nor more than 50 per cent, in the issued equity share capital of certain companies, by companies within the Group. (See also Note 22.)

16 The Unquoted Investments in Other Companies are holdings, of not more than 10 per cent, in the issued equity and other share capital of certain companies, by companies within the Group.

The Group's shares of the profits, distributions and retained earnings of the companies mentioned in this and the preceding Note were as follows:

	Year ended 31. 12. 19.1 £000	Year ended 31. 12. 19.0 £000
Net profits (less losses) before taxation	50	40
Net profits (less losses) after taxation	30	27
Distributions	16	15
Retained earnings (since acquisition of the shares by Group companies)	86	72

The losses of associated companies (so far as they concern Group companies) have been provided for in the Consolidated Balance Sheet, but no provision has been made for the losses of other companies outside the Group.

17 The bank overdrafts are secured by floating charges on the general assets of the respective companies in the Group which have borrowed the moneys.

Balance sheet of Excelsior Ltd

18 Movements on the Company's reserves during the year ended 31 December 19.1 were as follows:

	Share premium account £000	Fixed assets revaluation reserve £000	10 per cent debenture redemption reserve fund £000	General reserve £000	Profit and loss account £000
Balances at 31 December 19.0	200	–	75	20	33
Premium on ordinary shares issued	50	–	–	–	–
Revaluation of fixed assets (see Note 20)	–	72	–	–	–
Transfer to deferred taxation	–	(37)	–	–	–
Retained earnings	–	–	–	–	37
Appropriation thereof for redemption of 10 per cent debentures	–	–	75	–	(75)
Investment income received in respect of 10 per cent debenture redemption reserve fund (less corporation tax)	–	–	5	–	–
Balances at 31 December 19.1	250	35	155	20	(5)

19 Details of fixed assets, and of movements thereon during the year ended 31 December 19.1, were as follows:

Cost or other Valuation

	Balance at 31 December 19.0 £000	Revaluation during year £000	Additions during year, at cost £000	Disposals during year, at cost £000	Balance at 31 December 19.1 £000
Freehold land	276	33	—	—	309
Freehold buildings	200	20	—	—	220
Plant, machinery, vehicles, fixtures and loose tools	1,051	52	336	(225)	1,214
	1,527	105	336	(225)	1,743

Accumulated Depreciation

	Balance at 31 December 19.0 £000	Revaluation during year £000	Provided during year £000	Re Disposals during year £000	Balance at 31 December 19.1 £000
Freehold buildings	40	4	8	—	52
Plant, machinery, vehicles, fixtures and loose tools	510	32	212	(145)	609
	550	36	220	(145)	661

Intangible Assets

	Balance at 31 December 19.0 (cost less amounts written off) £000	Additions during year, at cost £000	Disposals during year, at cost less amounts written off £000	Amounts written off during year £000	Balance at 31 December 19.1 (cost less amounts written off) £000
Patents and trade marks	10	—	—	(1)	9

20 Certain fixed assets of the Company were revalued on 1 July 19.1, as follows:

Freehold land	£309,000
Freehold buildings	£176,000
Plant, machinery, vehicles, fixtures and loose tools	£561,000

The valuations were carried out by professional valuers, on the basis of current realizable values in the case of freehold land, and of current replacement prices in the case of freehold buildings, plant, machinery, vehicles, fixtures, and loose tools.

21 Excelsior Ltd's Subsidiary Companies as at 31 December 19.1 (all registered in England, unless otherwise stated), with the proportion held of the nominal value of the issued capital of each class, were:

Aspirant Engineering Company Ltd	100 per cent of 8 per cent preference shares 100 per cent of ordinary shares
Excelsior (Scotland) Ltd (registered in Scotland)	80 per cent of ordinary shares
Midland Motor Components Ltd (acquired 1 July 19.1)	100 per cent of ordinary shares

All shares were owned directly by Excelsior Ltd or its nominees.

22 The Unquoted Investments in Associated Companies held by Excelsior Ltd (defined as in Note 16) consisted of holdings in the issued equity share capital of the following companies:

Thompson Holdings Ltd	35 per cent of ordinary shares
Browning Manufacturing Company Ltd	25 per cent of ordinary shares

Excelsior Ltd's proportions of the profits, distributions and retained earnings of the above-mentioned companies were as follows:

	Year ended 31. 12. 19.1 £000	Year ended 31. 12. 19.0 £000
Net profits (less losses) before taxation	30	25
Net profits (less losses) after taxation	15	13
Distributions	9	8
Retained earnings (since acquisition of the shares by Excelsior Ltd)	72	66

No provision for the losses of these companies has been made in Excelsior Ltd's Balance Sheet.

General

23 One Subsidiary Company had a contingent liability, as at 31 December 19.1, in respect of costs in litigation pending against a company outside the Group, estimated at £3,000 (31 December 19.0, nil).

24 Contracts placed for capital expenditure, not provided for in the Accounts, amounted to:

	31. 12. 19.1 £000	31. 12. 19.0 £000
Excelsior Ltd	247	225
Subsidiary Companies	75	127

In addition, capital expenditure authorized by the relevant Boards of Directors, but in respect of which no orders had been placed, amounted to:

	31. 12. 19.1 £000	31. 12. 19.0 £000
Excelsior Ltd	25	12
Subsidiary companies	5	6

Auditor's report to the members of Excelsior Ltd

In our opinion, the Accounts set out on pp. 00 to 00 together give, as far as concerns members of Excelsior Ltd, a true and fair view of the state of affairs at 31 December 19.1 and of the profit for the year ended on that date and comply with the Companies Acts, 1948 and 1967, and with all the requirements and recommendations of the Accounting Standards Steering Committee as at the date of preparation of the Accounts. The accounts of one subsidiary company have been audited by by other accountants.

B.E. Prudent & Co.

16 March 19.2   Chartered Accountants

(Points from the directors' report)

a Analysis of Group turnover, and contributions to profit:

	Turnover £000	Contribution £000
General engineering	4,750	470
Motor component manufacture (from 1 July 19.1)	250	30
	5,000	500
Unallocated overheads		89
Group net trading profit		411

b Geographical analysis of Group turnover, and contributions to profit, from trading operations carried on outside the U.K.:

	Turnover £000	Contribution £000
North America	315	34
West Germany	136	9
	451	43

c Particulars of Subsidiary and Associated Companies (in whose equity Excelsior Ltd holds an interest of 20 per cent or more) as at 31 December 19.1:

	Principal country of operation	Particulars of issued share and loan capital
Subsidiary Companies		
Aspirant Engineering Company Ltd	U.K.	50,000 8 per cent Preference Shares of £1 250,000 Ordinary Shares of £1 £150,000 9 per cent Debentures (none held by Excelsior Ltd)
Excelsior (Scotland) Ltd	U.K.	300,000 Ordinary Shares of £1
Midland Motor Components Ltd.	U.K.	400,000 Ordinary Shares of 50p £100,000 10 per cent Debentures (none held by Excelsior Ltd)
Associated Companies		
Thompson Holdings Ltd	U.K.	200,000 Ordinary Shares of £1
Browning Manufacturing Company Ltd	U.K.	500,000 Ordinary Shares of 50p £100,000 7 per cent Debentures (none held by Excelsior Ltd)

d Share issue during year ended 31 December 19.1:

Excelsior Ltd—400,000 Ordinary Shares of 50p each, fully paid, on 1 July 19.1 (market value £250,000), in return for the acquisition of the entire Ordinary Share Capital of Midland Motor Components Ltd.

e Recommended dividends of Excelsior Ltd for the year ended 31 December 19.1:

Preference— 7 per cent on £100,000, or £7,000
Ordinary — 8 per cent on £1,000,000, or £80,000

f Proposed transfers to (from) reserves of Excelsior Ltd for the year ended 31 December 19.1:

10 per cent debenture redemption reserve fund	£75,000
Withdrawn from unallocated balance of profit and loss account as at 31 December 19.0	(38,000)
	£37,000

g The market value of Excelsior Ltd's land at at 31 December 19.1 was not, in the Directors' opinion, substantially in excess of the amounts shown in the Company's Balance Sheet.

h The average weekly number of employees of the Group for the year ended 31 December 19.1 was 1,200 (all employed wholly or mainly within the U.K.).

i The aggregate remuneration of the above-mentioned employees for the year as aforesaid was £3,000,000.

j Total contributions by Group companies for political, and charitable, purposes during the year as aforesaid were respectively £1,000, and £3,000.

k The total value of goods exported during the year as aforesaid, by Group companies, was £600,000.

18.3.1 Ratio analysis of the accounts of Excelsior Ltd

Below are the standard accounting ratios calculable for the years ended 31 December 19.0, and 19.1, in respect of the Excelsior Group and, as far as is practicable and relevant, of Excelsior Ltd separately. The complications arising from group accounting, and the derivation of certain figures (marked*) assumed to be available in the 19.0 accounts, are explained in the notes which follow the computations.

Measures of Financial Soundness and Stability

	Year ended 31. 12. 19.1		Year ended 31. 12. 19.0	
1a Liquidity ratio (Group):	$\{1,317-435-(70-68)\}/604$	1.46	$(873-352)/514$	1.01
	or		*or*	
	$\{1,317-435-(70-68)\}/620$	1.42	$(873-352)/518$	1.01
1b Liquidity ratio (Parent):	$\{949-315-(70-68)\}/462$	1.37	$(696-251)/420$	1.06
2a Current assets ratio (Group):	1,317/620	2.12	873/518	1.69
2b Current assets ratio (Parent):	949/462	2.05	696/420	1.66
3 Working capital to turnover ratio (Group):	$(1,317-620)/5,000$	0.14	$(873-518)/4,000$	0.09

		Year ended 31.12.19.1		Year ended 31.12.19.0	
4	Stock to turnover ratio (Group):	435/5,000	0.09	352/4,000	0.09
5	Debtors to turnover ratio (Group):	620/5,000	0.12	510/4,000	0.13
6a	Proprietary ratio (Group):	(1,659 + 93—52 —40)/(3,085 + 620 —52)	0.45	(1,295 + 92—38 —45)/(2,393 + 518 —38)	0.45
		or		or	
		(1,659 + 93)/(3,085 —1,752 + 40 + 620)	0.88	(1,295 + 92)/(2,393 —1,387 + 45 + 518)	0.88
6b	Proprietary ratio (Parent):	(1,555—9—40)/ (2,859 + 462—9)	0.47	(1,228—10—45)/ (2,214 + 420—10)	0.45
		or		or	
		1,555/(2,859—1,555 + 40 + 462)	0.86	1,228/(2,214—1,228 + 45 + 420)	0.85
7	Cover for debentures secured by a floating charge (Parent only):	{2,859 + 462—200 —44—0.05(3,000)} / 1,000	2.73	{2,214 + 420—0 —15—0.05(2,400*)} / 1,000	2.50
8	Cover for preferential creditors (Parent only):	(2,859 + 462—200) {44 + 0.05(3,000)}	16.09	(2,214 + 420—0)/ {15 + 0.05(2,400*)}	19.51
9	Cover for creditors fixed securities (Parent only):	477/200	2.39	Not applicable	—
10a	Cover for preference shares(or equity ratio) (Group):	(1,559 + 93—52—40)/ (3,085 + 620—52)	0.43	(1,195 + 92—38—45)/ (2,393 + 518 — 38)	0.42
10b	Cover for preference shares (or equity ratio) (Parent):	(1,455—40)/ (2,859 + 462)	0.43	(1,128 — 45)/ (2,214 + 420)	0.41

Measures of Efficiency, Profitability, and Return on Equity
(all Group only, unless otherwise stated)

		Year ended 31. 12. 19.1		Year ended 31. 12. 19.0	
11	Turnover of fixed and current assets:	5,000/(1,894 + 1,317)	1.56	4,000/(1,630 + 873)	1.60
		or		or	
		5,000/(1,630 + 873)	2.00	4,000/(1,600 + 850*)	1.63
		or		or	
		5,000/(1,762 + 1,095)	1.75	4,000/(1,615 + 862)	1.61
12	Turnover of fixed assets:	5,000/1,894	2.64	4,000/1,630	2.45
		or		or	
		5,000/1,630	3.07	4,000/1,600	2.50
		or		or	
		5,000/1,762	2.84	4,000/1,615	2.48
13a	Turnover of gross capital employed:	5,000/(3,085 + 620)	1.35	4,000/(2,393 + 518)	1.37
		or		or	
		5,000/(2,393 + 518)	1.72	4,000/(2,378 + 400)*	1.44
		or		or	
		5,000/(2,739 + 569)	1.51	4,000/(2,386 + 459)	1.41
13b	Turnover of net capital employed:	5,000/3,085	1.62	4,000/2,393	1.67
		or		or	
		5,000/2,393	2.09	4,000/2,378*	1.68
		or		or	
		5,000/2,739	1.83	4,000/2,386	1.68
14	Average remuneration per employee:	£3,000,000/1,200	£2,500	£2,400,000*/1,100*	£2,182
15	Turnover per employee:	£5,000,000/1,200	£4,167	£4,000,000*/1,100*	£3,637
16	Net profit per employee:	£448,000/1,200	£373	£330,000/1,100*	£300
17	Net trading profit to turnover:	411 x 100/5,000	8.22 (per cent)	330 x 100/4,000	7.50 (per cent)

18a	Pre-tax return on gross capital employed:	448 × 100/(3,085 + 620)	12.09 (% p.a.)	330 × 100/(2,393 + 518)	11.35 (% p.a.)
		or		*or*	
		448 × 100/(2,393 + 518)	15.39 (% p.a.)	330 × 100 / (2,378 + 400)*	11.88 (% p.a.)
		or		*or*	
		448 × 100/(2,739 + 569)	13.54 (% p.a.)	330 × 100/(2,386 + 459)	11.60 (% p.a.)
18b	Pre-tax return on net capital employed:	(448−1) × 100/ 3,085	14.49 (% p.a.)	(330−0) × 100/ 2,393	13.79 (% p.a.)
		or		*or*	
		(448−1) × 100/ 2,393	18.68 (% p.a.)	(330−0) × 100/ 2,378	13.88 (% p.a.)
		or		*or*	
		(448−1) × 100/ 2,739	16.32 (% p.a.)	(330−0) × 100/ 2,386	13.83 (% p.a.)
19a	Post-tax return on gross capital employed:	$\{171 + 0.48(111)\}$ × 100/ (3,085 + 620)	6.05 (% p.a.)	$\{117 + 0.48(100)\}$ × 100/(2,393 + 518)	5.67 (% p.a.)
		or		*or*	
		$\{171 + 0.48(111)\}$ × 100/(2,393 + 518)	7.70 (% p.a.)	$\{117 + 0.48(100)\}$ × 100/(2,378 + 400)	5.94 (% p.a.)
		or		*or*	
		$\{171 + 0.48(111)\}$ × 100/(2,739 + 569)	6.78 (% p.a.)	$\{117 + 0.48(100)\}$ × 100/(2,386 + 459)	5.80 (% p.a.)
19b	Post-tax return on net capital employed:	$\{171 + 0.48(110)\}$ × 100/3,085	7.25 (% p.a.)	$\{117 + 0.48(100)\}$ × 100/2,393	6.90 (% p.a.)
		or		*or*	
		$\{171 + 0.48(110)\}$ × 100/2,393	9.35 (% p.a.)	$\{117 + 0.48(100)\}$ × 100/2,378	6.94 (% p.a.)
		or		*or*	
		$\{171 + 0.48(110)\}$ × 100/2,739	8.17 (% p.a.)	$\{117 + 0.48(100)\}$ × 100/2,386	6.92 (% p.a.)
20	Pre-tax return on equity funds:	$\{337 − (21/0.48) − (7/0.48)\}$ × 100/ (1,000 + 559 − 40)	18.35 (% p.a.)	$\{230 − (17/0.48) − (7/0.48)\}$ × 100/ (800 + 395 − 45)	15.65 (% p.a.)
		or		*or*	
		$\{337 − (21/0.48) − (7/0.48)\}$ × 100/ (800 + 395 − 45)	24.23 (% p.a.)	$\{230 − (17/0.48) − (7/0.48)\}$ × 100/ (800 + 356* − 50*)	16.27 (% p.a.)
		or		*or*	
		$\{337 − (21/0.48) − (7/0.48)\}$ × 100/ (900 + 477 − 43)	20.89 (% p.a.)	$\{230 − (17/0.48) − (7/0.48)\}$ × 100/ (800 + 376 − 48)	15.96 (% p.a.)
21	Post-tax return on equity funds:	(171−21−7)/ (1,000 + 559−40)	9.41 (% p.a.)	(117−17−7)/ (800 + 395 − 45)	8.09 (% p.a.)
		or		*or*	
		(171−21−7)/ (800 + 395 − 45)	12.43 (% p.a.)	(117−17−7)/ (800 + 356−50)	8.41 (% p.a.)
		or		*or*	
		(171−21−7)/ (900 + 477−43)	10.72 (% p.a.)	(117−117−7)/ (800 + 376−48)	8.24 (% p.a.)
22a	Capital gearing ratio (Group):	(1,000 + 200 + 100)/(1,000 + 559 + 93 − 40)	0.81	(1,000 + 0 + 100)/(800 + 395 + 92 − 45)	0.89
22b	Capital gearing ratio (Parent)	(1,000 + 200 + 100)/(1,000 + 455 − 40)	0.92	(1,000 + 0 + 100)/(800 + 328 − 45)	1.02
23	Cover for interest (Parent):	$\{448 − 1 − 21/(0.48)\}/110$	3.67 (times)	$\{330 − 0 − 17/(0.48)\}/100$	2.95 (times)
24	Cover for preference dividend (Parent):	$\{448 − 1 − 21/(0.48)\}/\{110 + 7/(0.48)\}$	3.24 (times)	$\{330 − 0 − 17/(0.48)\}/\{100 + 7/(0.48)\}$	2.57 (times)
25	Cover for equity dividend (Parent):	$\{448 − 1 − 21/(0.48)\}/\{110 + 7/(0.48) + 80/(0.48)\}$	1.38 (times)	$\{330 − 0 − 17/(0.48)\}/\{100 + 7/(0.48) + 64/(0.48)\}$	1.19 (times)
26	Pay-out ratio (Parent):	80/(171−21−15 −7)	0.63	64/(117−17−3 −7)	0.71

Measures of achieved or potential growth
(Parent Company's Shares)

It is assumed that on 31 March 19.2 (the date on which the analysis is made) the debentures and preference shares stand at par on the stock exchange, and the 50p ordinary shares at £0.80. All computations are based on the 19.1 consolidated accounts.

27 Book value of net assets per equity share:
$(£1,000,000 + £559,000 - £40,000)/2,000,000$ 76.0p
28 Capital gearing based on market capitalization (assuming a par value for
the mortgage):
$(£1,000,000 + £200,000 + £100,000)/ £1,600,000$ 0.81
or
$(£1,000,000 + £200,000 + £100,000)/(£1,000,000 + £200,000 + £100,000$
$+ £1,600,000)$ 0.45
29 Earnings per share:
$(£150,000 - £7,000)/\{(1,600,000 \times 6/12) + (2,000,000 \times 6/12)\}$ 8.0p
30 Price/earnings ratio:
80p/8.0p   10.00
31 Earnings yield:
$8.0p \times 100/80p$ 10.00% p.a.
32 Dividend yield:
$4p \times 100/80p$.   5.00% p.a.

Notes on certain ratios

(6a), (6b): The minority interest, and the group's share of the associated companies' retentions, are included in the 'group' numerator, and the intangible and 'fictitious' assets deducted in computing both numerator and denominator. The 'parent' ratio leaves out of account the associates' retentions.

(7) to (9): These apply to the parent only, as it is the only company whose various classes of creditors can be distinguished from those of other group companies. Such calculations on the consolidated figures are invalid, since each company's creditors can legally claim only against that company's assets—though in an extreme case the parent company would probably accept liability. Preferential creditors are deemed to be the higher of the two corporation tax liabilities plus (say) 5 per cent of total remuneration of employees (from the directors' report). Intangibles are not excluded, since they contain no purchased goodwill, and patents and trade marks may be assumed to be as likely as physical assets to realize at least their book values at need.

(11) to (21): These all utilize figures from the consolidated profit and loss account, or the directors' report; there are no separate figures for the parent company. Where three alternative calculations are given, the denominators are derived respectively from the closing, and opening, consolidated balance sheets, and from the mean of the two sets of figures. The assumed opening consolidated balance sheet figures for 19.0 are:

Net Funds Employed

	£000	£000
Share capital of Excelsior Ltd—		
Preference	100	
Ordinary	800	
		900
Reserves:		
Share premium account	200	
General reserve	20	
Profit and loss account	75	
Retained profits of associated companies (group's proportion)	61	
		356
Total funds of Excelsior Ltd's shareholders		1,256
Interest of minority shareholders in subsidiaries		88
10 per cent debentures	1,000	
Less Discount not yet written off	50	
		950
Deferred taxation account		15
Corporation tax—current year		69
		2,378

Net Assets in which Funds are Employed

	£000	£000
Fixed assets:		
Tangible	1,561	
Intangible	39	
		1,600
Investments in associated companies		248
Investments in other companies		80
Current assets	850	
Less Current liabilities	400	
		450
		2,378

(18b):Note the deduction of bank interest, since the bank overdraft does not form part of the *net* capital employed.

(19a), (19b): Similarly, the bank interest, less tax, is added back in computing the post-tax return on the gross, but not the net, capital employed.

(20), (21): Equity earnings are calculated by deducting minority interest and preference dividend (both grossed up in (20)), while equity funds include associates' retentions (but not minority interest) and are reduced by unamortized debenture discount.

(22a), (22b): Capital gearing is more significant for the group, since the underlying assets are more realistically valued in arriving at the amount of equity funds.

(23) to (26): Like (7) to (9), and for similar reasons, these ratios are valid for the parent company only; (23) can be computed only in respect of the parent's debenture interest, where (as usual) it can be separately identified. (If interest on subsidiaries' externally-held debentures were included in the consolidated profit and loss account, a further adjustment would be needed.)

18.3.2 Current purchasing power accounts of Excelsior Ltd

Since the directors of Excelsior Ltd have elected to comply with Provisional Statement of Standard Accounting Practice No. 7 and produce supplementary summaries on a current purchasing power basis, the analyst is able to calculate from these a further set of ratios. These are designed below as, e.g., 6.C, and are thus keyed to the corresponding 'historical' ratios.

There cannot be a CPP ratio for each historical one. Some of the CPP figures are in insufficient detail, or the same figures are used in both sets, and some theoretical ratios would be irrelevant or misleading. The ones worth computing are, in the author's judgement, those which follow. They include those recommended for publication by PSSAP No. 7 (as shown on the published accounts of Excelsior Ltd), and relate to the group accounts only.

Financial Ratios on a Current Purchasing Power Basis

	Year ended 31.12.19.1		Year ended 31.12.19.0	
6.C Proprietary ratio:	(1,878 + 100 + 132 − 72)/(3,563 + 620 −72)	0.50	(1,508 + 125 + 130 − 55)/(3,084 + 1.25(518)−55 }	0.46
	or		*or*	
	(1,878 + 100 + 132)/ (1,685−232 + 620)	1.02	(1,508 + 125 + 130)/ {1,576−255 + 1.25(518)}	1.00
11.C Turnover of fixed and current assets:	5,556/(2,077 + 72 + 732 + 620)	1.59	5,455/{(1,960 + 55 + 455 + 1.25(518)}	1.75
	or			
	5,556/{1,960 + 55 + 455 + 1.25(518)}	1.78		
	or			
	5,556/(2,019 + 64 + 594 + 634)	1.68		
12.C Turnover of fixed assets:	5,556/(2,077 + 72)	2.59	5,455/(1,960 + 55)	2.71
	or			
	5,556/(1,960 + 55)	2.76		
	or			
	5,556/(2,019 + 64)	2.67		
13a.C Turnover of gross capital employed:	5,556/(3,563 + 620)	1.33	5,455/{3,084 + 1.25(518) }	1.46
	or			
	5,556/ {3,084 + 1.25(518)}	1.49		
	or			
	5,556/(3,324 + 634)	1.40		
13b.C Turnover of net capital employed:	5,556/3,563	1.56	5,455/3,084	1.77
	or			
	5,556/3,084	1.80		
	or			
	5,556/3,324	1.67		
15.C Turnover per employee:	£5,556,000/1,200	£4,633	£5,455,000/1,100*	£4,959
21.C Post-tax return on equity funds:	(362−8) × 100/ 1,878	18.84 (% p.a.)	(295−10) × 100/ 1,508	18.90 (% p.a.)
	or			
	(362−8) × 100/ 1,508	23.47 (% p.a.)		
	or			
	(362−8) × 100/ 1,693	20.95 (% p.a.)		

26.C Pay-out ratio(equity dividend cover):	(345–8)/(92–8)	4.01 (times)	(291–10)/(93–10)	3.39 (times)
27.C Value of net assets per equity share:	£1,878,000/ 2,000,000	93.9p	£1,508,000/ 1,600,000	94.3p
29.C Earnings per share:	(£362,000–£8,000)/ {(1,600,000 x 6/12) + (2,000,000 x 6/12)}	19.7p	(£295,000–£10,000)/ 1,600,000	17.8p
30.C Price/earnings ratio:	80p/19.7p	4.06		
31.C Earnings yield	19.7p x 100/80p	24.63 (% p.a.)		

It will be noted that not all forms of all ratios are calculated for the previous year. Some computations would involve taking end-of-year figures from two years back, and updating them by two years' inflation; and this is a dubious process in view of its inherent errors. As it is, certain ratios utilize figures not shown on the face of the CPP accounts, but obtained from the historical ones—notably the (monetary) current liabilities, used as they stand for 31 December 19.1 but 'inflated' 25.0 per cent for 31 December 19.0. The CPP preference dividends, not shown separately, are taken from the historical accounts and adjusted for estimated inflation; in practice the analyst would have to make his own estimates, from published index numbers.

18.3.3 Statement of source and application of funds of Excelsior Ltd

Like Modern Motor Supplies Ltd, Excelsior Ltd has had sufficient public spirit to comply with Exposure Draft 13, though it is not yet mandatory. ED13 does not seem very controversial, and may well be finalized before this edition appears. Where a company does not present a funds statement, it is generally possible for the analyst to construct a fairly accurate one of his own, using figures from the published profit and loss account, balance sheet and notes.[2]

The funds statement of Excelsior Ltd, while showing the net change in cash resources as the balancing item, nevertheless exhibits also all movements of funds which are of long-term financial significance, whether or not involving movements in cash. Thus it includes the issue of ordinary shares to acquire a subsidiary, and discloses in a note the assets and liabilities of the company taken over. It does not, however, take notice of fixed assets revaluation, as this is not a movement of funds in any sense, and has no effect on future flows of cash.

Publication of two years' figures (not by any means universal, among those British companies which publish a funds statement at all) gives the analyst some idea of any change which has occurred in the company's fortunes since last year. What is really needed, though, is a summary of funds flows for at least five years back, with cumulative totals, item by item, up to 31 December 19.1. The analyst will then be able to form an opinion of Excelsior's general financial policies over that period. In particular, he should compare, year by year and in total: a 'funds generated from operations', minus depreciation, amortization, and profit/loss on fixed assets disposed of, with increases in working capital and cash resources; and b 'funds from other sources', plus depreciation, etc., with increases in fixed

[2] See: Lee, G.A., Modern Financial Accounting, 1st edition, Thomas Nelson & Sons Ltd, 1973 (at Chapter 18, section 18.4).

and intangible assets. In other words, he should compare each broad category of sources with its 'normal' application category, and note the (equal and opposite) under- and over-applications. Thus, in the year ended 31 December 19.1 category a reveals 'operations' sources (adjusted as above) £211,000, and 'working capital and cash' applications £529,000 (over-application £318,000), while category b shows 'other' sources (adjusted as above in the opposite direction) £810,000, and 'fixed asset' applications £492,000 (under-application £318,000). In the year ended 31 December 19.0 the position in a was sources (adjusted) £143,000, application £150,000, over-application £7,000; and in b. sources (adjusted) £287,000, applications £280,000, under-application £7,000. In a five-year (or longer period) summary these wide fluctuations would tend to cancel out, and one would expect rough equality of 'revenue' and 'capital' sources (adjusted for depreciation and kindred items) with their respective applications. If this does not happen, an opinion may be formed: either that the company is using retained profits as its main source of finance, with minimal resort to the capital market and hence probable failure to optimize its gearing (consistent under-application of 'revenue' sources and over-application of 'capital' ones), or that it is deliberately distributing profits up to the hilt and having to borrow frequently, or issue shares for cash, in order to fund its chronic overdrafts from time to time (the reverse position as to funds flows). It is difficult to devise meaningful parameters here; the analyst must rely mainly on subjective judgement.

18.3.4 Appraisal of the accounts of Excelsior Ltd

The *measures of financial soundness and stability* ((1) to (10)) show some commendable improvement over the year ended 31 December 19.1. At the beginning of the year the group, and the parent company, appeared definitely under-capitalized. The liquidity ratios, nominally just above 1, were below that crucial level if one-third of the debtors were excluded on the ground that these represented about 1½ months' credit taken on average, so that only about two-thirds would be collectible within the 1 month's credit term which suppliers could be expected to allow. The current assets ratios were below 2—another sign of over-trading, as was the fact that working capital equalled only some 32 days' sales. The proprietary ratios were also below optimum levels—0.5, or 1.00, according to the mode of calculation—suggesting rather excessive reliance on debt finance. The capital gearing ratios ((22a) and (22b)) were also definitely on the high side. The assets cover was adequate for secured and preferential creditors, but a loss on liquidation of 50 per cent of asset values would have wiped out all share capital and caused loss to unsecured creditors.

The position at 31 December 19.1 was appreciably better, thanks in the main to the borrowing of £200,000 on mortgage half-way through the year. The liquidity and current assets ratios became adequate, even after allowance for the debtors' period of credit, and working capital became equal to some 51 days' sales—still on the low side, and certain to prove insufficient if the then level of activity was maintained. The proprietary ratios, though, were not improved, and the capital gearing was still ominously above the recommended 0.5 level, while cover for preference shares (and protection for unsecured creditors) was not yet satisfactory, even after a revaluation of fixed assets which made the figures more realistic. The analyst examining the accounts three months later would consider it imperative for Excelsior Ltd to make a substantial issue of ordinary shares for cash in the near future—probably in the form of a rights issue—and to increase the authorized capital accordingly. (Capital expenditure commitments at the year-end amount to about 1 year's depreciation charge—much the same as one year previously—and these, too, call for more long-term funds.)

As to the *measures of efficiency, profitability, and return on equity* ((11) to (26)), the various 'turnover' ratios, calculated on the most realistic bases, all show improvement over the year, though even so none of them is outstandingly good for an industrial group; (13b), for example, ought not to be less than 2 in its third form, especially where (as here) some plant is hired or rented. Again, though, revaluation of the fixed assets confuses the issue and partly destroys comparability from one year to the next—without, however, invalidating the preceding assessment. The 'employee' ratios, also, exhibit increases over the previous year; but these are partly due to inflation, and the take-over of Midland Motor Components Ltd during the year masks the nature of the change in the number of employees.

The 'profit' ratios are most encouraging, and all have improved since the previous year. Expansion (or contraction) of turnover is commonly accompanied by a rise (or fall) in the rate of net trading profit thereon, since the fixed elements of total cost do not rise (or fall) proportionately, at least over a considerable range. Acceleration of turnover of capital employed, as here, magnifies the effect on the return on capital employed (however defined), producing the handsome return (on average capital net of current liabilities) of some 16 per cent per annum before tax, and 8 per cent per annum after tax—comparing favourably with the cost of loan capital, some 10 per cent, and 5 per cent, per annum before, and after, tax. The rather high capital gearing serves to screw up the return on (average) equity funds to over 21 per cent per annum before tax, and nearly 11 per cent after it—gains of some 4, and 2½, percentage points as compared with 19.0, from a change of less than 0.75 of a point in the net trading profit on turnover, and that despite a revaluation of fixed assets. But the danger of such a financial policy is highlighted by the low rates of cover for interest and preference dividends. A fall of more than one-fourth in the net trading profit would make it impossible to maintain the ordinary dividend without dipping into reserves—despite the moderate pay-out ratio of less than two-thirds.

With regard to *measures of achieved or potential growth* ((27) to (32)), the market price of the ordinary shares is little above the book value of net assets per share (based on the consolidated balance sheet). On the basis of market prices (even when a par value is imputed to the unquoted loan on mortgage), the capital gearing is not excessive, despite the appearance of the consolidated balance sheet—based on historical cost or later revaluations of specific assets, and excluding any allowance for non-purchased goodwill. The price/earnings ratio is moderate also, and the earnings and dividend yields not too low by modern standards. If an acceptable long-term rate of return on the shares (in money terms) is 15 per cent per annum net of tax credit, then with a dividend yield of 5.00 per cent per annum dividends (hence, earnings) and share prices must grow by 10.00 per cent per annum—which, with gearing, needs a somewhat lower rate of growth of profits. In fact, with after-tax earnings of £143,000 for 19.1, an increase of (£143,000 x 10.00/100) = £14,300 would require a rise in net profit before interest and tax of £14,300 x 100/48) = £29,792. This is 6.65 per cent on £448,000, and seems reasonably achievable, given a continuance of good trading conditions and the maintenance of current profit margins on turnover.

If the current purchasing power ratios are examined, and the CPP valuations of non-monetary assets are accepted as surrogates for their replacement costs or their realizable values, the picture is somewhat modified. The proprietary ratio now looks just adequate, since inflation affects physical assets, but not liabilities, in the accounts. The turnover of assets is not much changed, nor is that of capital employed; but, contrary to the impression given by the historical ratios, there seems if anything to have been a slight worsening since 19.0. The CPP turnover per employee is also down, instead of up, as compared with last year. On the other hand the post-tax return on equity, and the earnings per share, come out much higher—twice or better—than with the historical figures, as does the earnings yield, which is nearly 25 per cent per annum, compared with 10. Scrutiny of Notes B and C to the CPP summaries, however, reveals that the whole, and more than the whole, of the inflation gain in earnings comes from the gain on long-term liabilities—an effect of the parent company's capital gearing, and not of the group's operating efficiency. Such a gain can hardly have been designed, or even foreseen, by the management, much less by the debenture-holders, who may well regard themselves as the victims of a legalized confidence trick. This case, though imaginary, is thoroughly typical of many real situations, and it is easy to see why the U.K. capital market is in such disarray at present (June 1975). Failing a spectacular easing of the rate of inflation, it would seem that only indexed bonds (with the capital repayment and/or rate of interest tied to the Retail Price Index) can hope to attract sophisticated lenders of long-term funds.

As to the statement of source and application of funds, in historical pounds, it is seen that, though there has been an increase of £239,000 in cash-type assets over the year, £200,000 of it has come from the raising of a mortgage, and that the acquisition of a new subsidiary by a share exchange made little obvious difference in this respect. The flow of funds from operations, though appreciably better than last year, has been more than absorbed by additions to fixed assets, stocks and reserve fund investments, and only £20,000 net has been added to receivables, less payables. Inflation is evidently having its effects on liquidity, and a cash issue of ordinary shares seems unavoidable if the group is not to run into trouble quite soon.

Subject, then, to any favourable or adverse factors or trends external to the group, and not revealing themselves in its accounts, and with reservations about the need for more equity capital to be raised in cash in the near future (perhaps causing some dilution of earnings per share in the short run), the analyst would regard the 50p ordinary shares of Excelsior Ltd as a sound investment at the current price of £0.80.

18.4 Conclusion

The interpretation of published accounts is not, and cannot be, an exact science. Whatever improvements in accounting methods may come in the future, experience and judgement must always have their parts to play. Enough has been said about the shortcomings of present-day accounting techniques to make this clear.

For the immediate future, no very radical reforms are to be looked for. The leading accountancy bodies, through their Accounting Standards Steering Committee, will continue the work of tightening up conventional practice and reducing the number of alternative treatments in controversial areas. More meaningful and relevant figures, within the present framework, will emerge through the adoption of supplementary financial statements, adjusted to current price levels by application of a general inded of purchasing power, or to replacement price levels by the use of specialized indices. A more revolutionary change would be the abandonment of historical accounting altogether, or its supplementation by forecasts of profits, or cash flows (perhaps on a DCF basis) for the coming year—with a review of the current year's forecast in the light of the achieved results. In 1973 the U.K. entered the European Economic Community (whose accounting standards, except in West Germany, the Netherlands, Denmark, and Ireland are markedly lower than ours), and considerable amendment will be needed in due course to our company and tax legislation, with, no doubt, a new Companies Act during the 'seventies. Accounting theory and practice are in a state of flux, and some of this book may well be out of date before it is published. Yet the canons of good accounting, so painfully worked out in seven centuries of experience since the days of the Italian bankers and merchants of the high Middle Ages, and which have proved so adaptable to the vastly more complex and sophisticated economy of to-day, will surely stand every test, and undergo whatever further evolution is necessary to meet the challenges of an ever-developing world.

Appendix:
Essay topics and exercises

Part 1: Accounting principles and practice
Chapter 1: Nature, methodology and development of accounting

1 Old fashioned expositions of double entry book-keeping began with the books of account and worked forward to the final accounts, while modern teaching tends to reverse the process. What advantages and disadvantages do you, as a student, see in the second approach?

2 Accounting, it is said, is a purely practical activity. What do you consider is gained by endeavouring to set out, in structured form, the principles upon which it is allegedly based?

3 Accounting appears to have developed historically as a series of responses to the growing needs of businessmen for more and more information relevant to the processes of management. Illustrate this contention by reference to *either* the evolution of double entry book-keeping in Italy up to the time of Luca Pacioli, *or* the history of accounting in Anglo-Saxon countries in the last hundred years.

4 The accepted principles of accounting are to some extent rationalizations of traditional practice. Illustrate, with particular reference to the common methods of recording changes in the imputed values of i current assets, and ii fixed assets.

5 Joe carries on the business of a self-employed ice cream vendor. The business is seasonal and all the sales are made from a van. Joe has his accounts of the business prepared each year to 31 December.

Joe has a contract with Mario's Ice Cream Ltd whereby he buys all his goods for resale from them at selling price less $33\frac{1}{3}$ per cent and less $2\frac{1}{2}$ per cent for monthly settlement. Joe always takes the $2\frac{1}{2}$ per cent. He also receives, at the end of the season, a rebate of 1 per cent of the cost of his purchases before cash discount if his sales for the season, which runs from 1 April to 30 October, exceed £5,000. In the year under review, he received £60.

The balances on Joe's books at 31 December 1969 were:

	£	£
Capital account		1,134
Van at cost	1,600	
Depreciation of van		800
Capital instalments due H.P company on van		520
Equipment at cost	350	
Depreciation of equipment		280
Garage rent due		5
Garages rates in advance	9	
Accountancy		60
Balance at bank	840	
	2,799	2,799

You obtain the following information of his transactions for the year to 31 December 1970:

1 From cheque books, paying in books and bank statements:

	£		£
Mario goods for resale	5,350	Rebate from Mario's Ice Cream Ltd	
Wages	280	(referred to above)	60
Van expenses	300	H.P. instalments on new van 7 @ £64	448
Laundry	104	Part deposit new van	240
Garage rent (52 weeks)	52	Refund H.P. instalment old van	50
Garage rates (two half years)	40	Sundry business expenses	110
Accountancy	60	Private payments	320
H.P. instalments on van 6 @ £50		Cash banked ex takings	7,574
(Capital £36 interest £14)	300	Balance at bank 31 December 1970	920

2 There is no record of takings and some goods for resale have apparently been paid for out of takings. The only cash payments recorded were:

	£
Petrol and oil	27
Casual wages	130
Sundry expenses	19

Any cash not accounted for is to be treated as drawings.

3 The old van was traded in for £700, and after settlement of the outstanding hire purchase by the garage, the balance of £360 together with a cheque for £240 was used as a deposit on a new van costing £1,800. The balance due on the new van of £1,200 was put on hire purchase with 24 monthly repayments of £64 per month.

4 Due to a power supply failure stock with a resale value of £30 was damaged and had to be destroyed.

5 Depreciation is to be provided on a straight line basis at 25 per cent on the van and 10 per cent on the equipment, the new van to be depreciated as if in use on 1 January 1970.

6 Hire purchase charges are to be written off by equal instalments over the life of the contract.

7 £60 is to be provided for accountancy.

You are required to prepare, for the year ended 31 December 1970, Joe's:

a Trading and Profit and Loss Account; and

b Balance Sheet as on that date.

(Institute of Chartered Accountants in England and Wales, Final Examination, Part I, May 1971—Advanced Accounting I)

6 Green trades as Fair Travel Agency, effecting sales of tickets for Tour Operators Ltd, Air Lines and British Rail. The commissions earned thereon are at the rates of 10 per cent, $7\frac{1}{2}$ per cent and 7 per cent respectively.

The accounts are made up to 31 October in each year.

The balances as on 31 October 1968 were as follows:

	£	£
Capital		5,100
Deposits from customers re Tour Operators Ltd		2,000
P.A.Y.E.		250
Accountancy		150
Advertising		100
Rates		100
Fixtures and fittings	1,000	
Motor car	900	
Debtors for rail tickets	500	
Debtors for air tickets	100	
Rent in advance	125	
Bank balance	5,075	
	7,700	7,700

You obtained the following information:

1 From bank statements, returned cheques and the paying-in slips for the year ended 31 October 1969:

	£		£
Bankings (cheques and cash)	82,000	Electricity	90
Payments for tickets—		Rates	300
Tour Operators Ltd	62,000	Accountancy	150
Air Lines	6,500	P.A.Y.E.	910
British Rail	7,000	Advertising	625
Rent (4 quarters)	500	Bank balance on 31 October 1969	9,000

2 Weekly expenditure (52 weeks) defrayed from cash takings before banking: staff wages £40 (net)   petty expenses £1   drawings £20 per week

3 From audit statements the following liabilities at 31 October 1969 were disclosed:

	£		£
Rates	110	Tour Operators Ltd	550
Advertising	50	Air Lines	160
British Rail	1,370	Accountancy	150

4 Customers' deposits on 31 October 1969, all re Tour Operators Ltd, were £1,000 and debtors for rail tickets were £100,

5 Depreciation of car and fixtures is calculated at 25 per cent p.a. and 10 per cent p.a. of the reducing balances respectively, and

6 Green agrees that any cash difference should be transferred to his Drawings Account.

You are required to prepare:

a Profit and Loss Account for the year ended on 31 October 1969 showing separately the commission from each class of ticket sold, and

b Balance Sheet as on 31 October 1969.

Ignore taxation.

(Institute of Chartered Accountants in England and Wales, Final Examination, Part I, May 1970—Advanced Accounting I)

7 The accounting records of the Ultimate Laundry Ltd are in a state of confusion. The Directors do not consider the business large enough to warrant the employment of skilled accounting staff, but prefer the cheaper alternative of an unqualified book-keeper in charge of an office staffed by part-timers. The book-keeper has, on medical advice, retired to a nursing home and is unable to receive visitors. Meanwhile the books of the Company have not been kept up to date, and the Directors have requested you as their Financial Adviser to produce a Trading Account and Profit and Loss Account for the Year ended 31 October 1970, and a Balance Sheet as at that date.

The information at your disposal is as follows:

1 Balance Sheet as at 31 October 1969

	£	Fixed assets	Cost £	Deprecia-tion £	Net £
Capital—Ordinary shares	8,000	Plant	31,600	15,400	16,200
General reserve	10,000	Vans	7,500	4,000	3,500
		Furniture and fittings	2,800	1,400	1,400
			41,900	20,800	21,100
Current liabilities		*Current assets*			
Trade creditors		Stock of raw material		4,800	
(materials)	20,460	Debtors (laundry bills)		15,120	
Accrued expenses	850	Prepayments		520	
Overdraft	2,280	Cash in hand		50	
					20,490
	£41,590				£41,590

2 A summarized Extract from the Bank Statement for the year.

Receipts	£	Payments	£
Received from debtors	180,718	Opening balance	2,280
		Payments to suppliers	114,243
		Expenses paid	15,970
		Factory wages	35,120
		Van drivers wages	4,160
		Managing director's salary	2,000
		Purchase of a van	1,100
		Closing balance	5,845
	£180,718		£180,718

3 Investigation reveals the following facts:

a The outstanding balances on the washing ledger total £18,423, whilst creditors for materials are owed £23,918, as at 31 October 1970.

b Accrued expenses are Rent £440, Audit and Accountancy £50, Electricity £89, and Gas £54, whilst rates have been paid in advance £140 and Insurance £173.

c The payment for the van was net after a trade-in allowance of £150 on an old van. This van originally cost £750 and stood in the books at £100 when sold.

d The Managing Director regularly drew £10 per week from the cash float held by the book-keeper, except during his annual holiday of two weeks. This money was to cover incidental expenses.

    e The percentage of Gross Profit to sales after charging factory wages has remained reasonably static in recent years at 20 per cent.

    f Depreciation is to be provided as follows:
Plant 15 per cent on written down value
Vans 20 per cent on original cost
Furniture and Fittings 10 per cent on original cost.

    g The vanmen collect the laundry money from customers. Before the cash was banked by the book-keeper, office salaries of £1,600 and miscellaneous expenses of £150 were paid from it.

    h Bad Debts of £490 have been written off during the year. They all related to a previous accounting period.

    i During the year a vanman was prosecuted for the theft of cash amounting to £810, which he had collected from customers.

    j Cheques drawn in payment for goods supplied, but not yet presented to the Bank at the year end totalled £470.

    k £640 have been retained from factory wages under the Christmas Savings Club operated by the Company, during the year. The vanmen have saved £418 through the club in the same period.

    l Cash on hand at 31 October was £94. There is no reason to suspect any dishonesty on the part of the book-keeper.

N.B. All workings should be shown.

(**Association of Certified and Corporate Accountants, Examination Section IV, December 1970—Advanced Accounting**)

8 The RST Learned Society arranges study conferences and lectures for its members, and publishes a monthly Magazine. Members pay separate subscriptions for general membership and for the Magazine. The following accounts were produced by the treasurer for the year 1970.

Receipts and Payments Account 1970

	£		£
Bank balance, January 1	578	Cost of producing magazine	1,025
Annual subscriptions	1,845	Lecture fees	228
Investment income	308	Postages and stationery	286
Magazine advertising receipts	435	Sundry expenses	389
Magazine subscriptions	948	New office equipment	68
		Rent and rates	305
		Wages and salaries	975
		Bank balance, December 31	838
	£4,114		£4,114

The following additional information is available:

1 £118 of the cost of postages and stationery was spent on distribution of the Magazine.

2 Wages and salaries amounting to £85 were outstanding at the beginning of the year and £80 at the end of the year.

3 Amounts owing to the Society for magazine advertisements were £70 at the beginning of the year and £108 at the end of the year.

4 Amounts owing to the printers of the Magazine were £248 at the beginning of the year and £288 at the end of the year.

5 Subscriptions for 1970 issues of the magazine received in 1969 were £218, and subscriptions for 1971 issues received in 1970 were £195.

6 The assets of the Society at the beginning of the year included Office Equipment of £850 (cost) and Investments of £4,380 (cost).

7 Equipment at the end of the year was valued at £875.

8 Annual Subscriptions received included £38 for 1969, and £224 for 1971.

You are required to prepare a Profit Statement for the magazine for 1970, and a General Income and Expenditure Account for the same year. Balance Sheets should also be provided to show the position at the beginning, and at the end of 1970.

(**Association of Certified Accountants, Examination Section IV, June 1971—Advanced Accounting**)

9 Rainbow Limited manufactures a patent soap powder. In order to promote sales, free vouchers were issued to the public, each voucher enabling its recipient to claim a reduction of 3d on each small packet of powder purchased. 60,000 vouchers were issued each month during the period from 1 July to 31 December 1969, and they were valid for the two calendar months following the month of issue. Retailers were charged the normal wholesale prices, but the company guaranteed to refund to them 4d for each voucher, provided claims were lodged within four calendar months of the month of issue.

During the three months ended 31 October 1969, Rainbow also operated a gift token scheme. Each large packet of powder contained a token entitling the buyer, on surrendering a certain number of tokens to the company, to choose a gift. Each token represented, on the average, the equivalent of 6d of the cost of the gifts purchased by the company. The number of packets issued containing tokens was 240,000. There was no time limit for surrender of tokens. The balances on the books as at 31 December 1969 included the following:

	Dr.	Cr.
Stocks—1 January 1969: Raw materials	5,000	
Cartons	1,750	
Work in progress	1,500	
Finished goods	12,000	
Purchases—Raw materials	97,000	
Cartons	26,250	
Production wages	22,500	
Overhead expenses—Factory	14,500	
Administration	9,600	
Sales		200,000
Advertising	6,500	

Advertising account has been debited with the cost of gifts purchased—£4,000.

All claims received up to 31 December 1969, from retailers, in respect of free vouchers, had been debited to sales account as follows:

Vouchers dated	£
July	800
August	850
September	700
October	650
November	550
December	300

Stocks at 31 December 1969 were:

	£
Raw materials	8,000
Cartons	3,000
Work in progress	700
Finished goods	20,000
Gifts	500

The directors require that the charge for advertising, shown in the annual profit and loss account, be analysed to indicate the total cost of each sales promotion scheme.
You are required to prepare:
    a the Advertising Account for the year ended 31 December 1969; and
    b a Manufacturing, Trading and Profit and Loss Account for the same period.
(Show all workings)

(Association of Certified Accountants, Examination Section V, December 1970—Advanced Accounting)

10 Stores Ltd, which runs a boutique, makes up its accounts annually to 31 January, and a summarized Trading and Profit and Loss Account for the year ended 31 January 1970 was as follows:

	£	£
Sales		216,000
Less: Cost of sales (after discount received)	93,840	
Workroom wages	48,000	
		141,840
Gross profit		74,160
Less: Fixed charges including shop assistants' wages		54,160
Net profit		20,000

On 1 October 1970, a fire seriously damaged the premises and no trading was possible until 1 February 1971, on which date half the shop was reopened for business, with the other half reopening on 1 April 1971.

The Consequential Loss Policy insured:

a The gross profit, including discounts received (defined as sales less variable charges).

b The workroom wages.

c Accountancy charges at £500 or 2 per cent of the amount of any claim before such charges, whichever is the greater.

The following points were agreed with the insurers:

1 Turnover increases by 15 per cent p.a.

2 Workroom wages increased by 10 per cent p.a.

3 The period 1 October to 31 December accounts for one-half of the annual turnover.

4 The remainder of the turnover is considered to arise equally over the other 9 months.

5 Fixed charges and all wages occur evenly throughout the year.

6 The rate of gross profit is constant.

7 Discounts received are assumed throughout to be equal to 1 per cent of turnover.

8 Both the amount of cover and the period of indemnity are adequate.

You are required to compute the Consequential Loss Claim for the period during which trading was affected by the fire.

(Institute of Chartered Accountants in England and Wales, Final Examination, Part II, November 1971—Advanced Accounting II)

Chapter 2: Accounting: its utility to management

1 Explain the principles on which a linked, and b integrated, financial and cost accounting records are constructed and operated, and illustrate with specimen entries.

2 Appraise the roles of i financial accounting, ii cost accounting, and iii budgetary control, in the management of a business enterprise, and show how all figures in ii and iii are derived from, or related to, those in i.

3 Assess the usefulness of a standard costing system to the financial accountant (as distinct from the cost accountant) of a company which manufactures several related products.

4 Variances may arise under three main headings, namely, a volume, b value and c efficiency.

You are required to write short notes to explain the different types of variance included under each of these three headings, their significance to management and their limitations.

(Institute of Chartered Accountants in England and Wales, Final Examination, Part II, November 1970—Advanced Accounting III)

5 C is in business manufacturing one product only which is sold from his warehouse. Separate operating accounts are maintained for the factory and the warehouse. Manufactured goods are delivered to the warehouse on proforma invoices. There are subsequently adjusted to factory cost plus 10 per cent. Stocks of manufactured goods both in the factory and the warehouse also are valued at factory cost plus 10 per cent in the departmental accounts. The excess over actual cost is adjusted in the general profit and loss account.

The manager of the warehouse receives a salary of £750 per annum and commission of 20 per cent of the profit as shown in the operating account of the warehouse after charging the salary.

The following information covers the transactions in 1967 but nothing has been charged to the warehouse relating to the manager's salary and commission.

Factory:	Units	£	Factory:	Units	£
Stocks:			Faulty goods returned by		
Raw materials:			warehouse scrapped,		
At 1 January		17,600	manufactured in 1967	100	
at 31 December		12,400	*Warehouse:*		
Manufactured:			Stock of manufactured		
At 1 January	210	6,930	goods 1 January, at		
at 31 December	196		departmental value	150	4,950
Purchases of raw materials		88,420	Sales	2,790	209,250
Wages		26,400	Returns to factory	100	
Manufacturing expenses		31,780	Shortages revealed at		
Deliveries to warehouse,			year-end inventory	20	
including all manufactured			Selling expenses		44,500
goods in stock 1 January 3,050			*General:*		
			Administration expenses		14,825

80 per cent of the actual loss arising from goods scrapped was to be borne by the factory and 20 per cent by the warehouse. The loss was not to be regarded as part of the manufacturing cost in 1967.

You are required to prepare for the year ended 31 December 1967: a factory operating account; b warehouse operating account; c profit and loss account.

(Institute of Cost and Works Accountants, Part III Examination, May 1968—Financial Accountancy (Second Paper))

6 Giles, a farmer, plans to erect additional farm buildings at a cost of £1,800, payment to be made in November 1970. He realizes that he will need to apply for more bank borrowing facilities than usual, and in December 1969 makes reasonable estimates of his likely transactions during 1970.

He makes the following assumptions:

1 Balance at bank on 1 January 1970 will be £750.
2 Monthly outgoings for wages and normal farm expenses will be £200.
3 The quarterly rent of £100 will be paid on the usual quarter days.
4 The main crop, barley, will be sold for cash in August for 22/6 per cwt. The estimated crop will be 4,000 cwts. The cost of seed, fertilizers and planting is estimated at £600, payable in April, and in addition harvesting expenses of £200 will be paid in August.
5 Subsidiary income is estimated as £700 from sale of fatstock in April and £100 from sale of hay in June.
6 The 1969/70 taxation liability has been agreed at £400 and will be paid on the due dates.
7 Personal drawings are estimated at £100 per month, with an additional amount of £200 in February to pay for a winter holiday.
8 It is not proposed to incur any capital expenditure during 1970 other than that relating to the additional farm buildings and the total provision for depreciation on all fixed assets for the year is to be £200. Sundry creditors in respect of farm expenses will be £125 more at the end of the year than at the beginning.

You are required to prepare:
a a budget statement showing the anticipated bank balance at the end of each month during 1970, for presentation to the bank, and
b a statement of the budgeted profit or loss for the year, showing how this is derived from the figures in the budget.

(Institute of Chartered Accountants in England and Wales, Final Examination, Part II, November 1969—Advanced Accounting II)

Chapter 3: Data processing systems

1 Internal control has been defined as comprising the plan of organization and all of the coordinate methods and measures adopted within a business to safeguard its assets, check the accuracy and reliability of its accounting data, promote operational efficiency, and encourage adherence to prescribed managerial policies.

As management accountant, you are requested to produce a check-list for the internal control system in your company.

(Institute of Cost and Management Accountants, Part IV Examination, May 1972—Management Accountancy 1)

2 Distinguish carefully the roles of internal check, internal audit and professional audit. Illustrate by reference to the handling of cash in a departmental store, in which a central cashier takes charge of all moneys received from customers.

3 As chief accountant of a medium-sized manufacturing company, you are considering the conversion of the sales ledgers from loose-leaf, hand-written form to cards, written up on keyboard machines. Set out the main points to which you should give attention, in deciding whether, and if so how, to make the change.

4 In relation to a large multiple shop company, keeping its records by means of punched-card equipment, devise a sequence of operations for recording all aspects of the procurement of goods for resale, and their reception into the central warehouse.

5 In what ways is a computerized system of management information different from one maintained by less sophisticated means? What opportunities, and what problems, does the installation of a computer create?

6 You are helping a client to improve his accounting and control systems with a view to the introduction of standard costing. The following decisions have been reached:

1 Work in progress will be costed on the basis only of raw materials and direct labour

valued at standard prices. All other expenditures, including the cost of consumable materials, will be treated as period costs.

2 Separate expense budgets will be prepared for the managers of each manufacturing cost centre and for the sales manager, the chief accountant and the general works manager and expenditures must be analysed accordingly.

3 Each manufacturing process will be a cost centre with its own work in progress account.

You find, however, that the client is still experiencing considerable difficulty in identifying the manager responsible for the various elements of cost and expense and in reliably recording the following documentation:

    i invoices for raw materials in the appropriate stock accounts;

    ii invoices for consumable materials in the appropriate stock accounts;

    iii vouchers for: raw material issues from stock; labour cost incurred; and work in progress transferred;

    iv expense invoices; and vouchers for consumable material issues.

You are told that the solution lies in preparing and introducing a suitable code of accounts.

You are required, in the circumstances explained, to:

    a illustrate the structure or groupings of the code which you would adopt;

    b give two reasons each for i the number of digits chosen and ii the arrangement of the structure adopted;

    c explain in a few lines how you would ensure reliable application of the code to solve each of the problems described under i to iv above.

(Institute of Chartered Accountants in England and Wales, Final Examination, Part II, May 1969—Advanced Accounting III)

7 Discuss, in relation to the Debtors Ledger, in what ways and in what circumstances a company can help management to improve both its understanding and its financial control of a business.

(Institute of Chartered Accountants in England and Wales, Final Examination, Part II, November 1971—Advanced Accounting III)

8 You are required to:

    a specify five of the basic tasks involved in clerical operations;

    b set out briefly under at least six heads the pros and cons of mechanizing a monthly payroll;

    c specify the five main units in a simple computer system and relate their functions to the basic tasks involved in clerical operations; and

    d differentiate in cost terms between mechanizing a monthly payroll by computer and by mechanical book-keeping machines, identifying three important cost implications for management. (You may assume that the volumes of data to be processed permit either course.)

(Institute of Chartered Accountants in England and Wales, Final Examination, Part II, May 1970—Advanced Accounting III)

9 Garish Ltd stocks and manufactures dyestuffs. About 100 orders a day are received in the company's post room, chiefly from food and cosmetic manufacturers. The orders are opened in the post room and passed to the manager of the sales administration department, who passes them to a validation clerk. The validation clerk checks that the goods which the customer has ordered are correctly described. Those where the goods are incorrectly described are passed to a technical sales team who clarify the descriptions with the customer over the telephone and return the orders to sales administration, on average within 24 hours.

Valid orders are passed to a pricing clerk who prices the goods ordered from files of product price cards and customer discount cards. Another clerk uses an adding calculating machine to extend the quantities and prices on the customer's order and total the extended values. The orders are then passed to a typist who types an order master stencil. A junior employee then uses a spirit duplicator to prepare multipart stationery from the stencil.

One stencilled copy of the order is passed to the accountant's department where it is compared as a credit check with the most recent weekly sales ledger print out from a computer bureau and returned to sales administration. Another stencilled copy of the order without prices and extensions is sent to the stockroom in the production department, where it is marked as to availability by the storekeeper after reference to a daily free stock balances print out from a computer bureau, and returned to sales administration.

Provided both checks are returned as satisfactory another stencil copy of the order is sent to the customer as an acknowledgement and the remaining documentation for effecting delivery and invoice of the order is released. Credit checks are nearly always satisfactory. On the other hand the storekeeper fairly frequently reports that stock is unavailable.

You are required to write a short report to the board:

a indicating to what extent and why the present order processing system is unnecessarily time consuming;

b indicating how it could be speeded by reallocating departmental responsibilities and copy records, and rearranging the sequence in which tasks are performed;

c charting your recommended sequence of tasks.

(Institute of Chartered Accountants in England and Wales, Final Examination, Part II, November 1970—Advancing Accounting III)

10 Snappits Ltd manufactures and sells photographic equipment. The whole of the factory's output is sent to and stored in one or other of the company's three depots from which all the company's retail shops are supplied. There are 60 of these shops. The company also buys equipment from other manufacturers and these goods, like the company's own products, are stored in the depots.

Of total shop sales, goods produced in the factory account for 30 per cent and bought-in goods for the remaining 70 per cent. Fifty per cent of the factory's total output is eventually sold through the company's own shops and 50 per cent to other retailers.

The company's own shop managers and other retailers are all charged at delivered-to-depot cost plus 20 per cent.

The company employs 50 shop managers of whom 10 run two shops each and the other 40 one shop each. Some of the shops are owned by the company and some rented on leases of varying length.

Although the company sets recommended retail prices, each manager is allowed some discretion to vary them. He is also allowed to sell on hire purchase or credit although the terms on which he may do so are fixed by the company. He is required to collect customers' debts and any bad debts which are incurred are taken into account in assessing his managerial performance.

The company is installing a computer to control its operations and improve its inadequate management information system.

You are required, as the newly appointed management accountant reporting directly to the managing director, to describe the accounting or other reports for the financial control of operations which you require from the computer.

Your answer should take the form of a brief memorandum, setting out the main contents of each of the financial reports, the frequency with which each is to be produced, the method of collecting the source data for each, and the means of transferring these data in each case to a form suitable for computer input. You may assume that the computer is capable of accepting input in any of the standard ways.

(Institute of Chartered Accountants in England and Wales, Final Examination, Part II, November 1969—Advanced Accounting III)

Chapter 4: Modern accounting thought

1 If accounting is a practical discipline, making sense only in the context of transactions in money or money's worth, why is it considered necessary to investigate its theoretical foundations? What kinds of practical improvement are to be looked for as a result of such investigation?

2 'Accounting is to be seen as a process of *measurement* and *communication*.' Elucidate this statement in terms of what accounting is supposed to measure and to communicate, and attempt an assessment of its current effectiveness in both respects.

3 Distinguish, in relation to accounting, between objectivity and reliability, and appraise *three* types of figure, commonly found in company balance sheets, in the light of your observations.

4 What difficulties are likely to be encountered by research workers, in any attempt to assess the effectiveness of accounting as a means of communicating financial information to the investing public? What kinds of improvement in accounting techniques may be expected to flow from such research, if it is successful?

5 What are the likely advantages, and shortcomings, as compared with conventional accounting, of a 'cash flow' accounting, and b 'present value' accounting?

6 Do you think that double entry book-keeping, in any recognizable form, is ever likely to be abandoned? Give reasons.

Chapter 5: Asset valuation and income measurement: historical-cost accounting (1)

1 Attempt a reasoned defence of historical-cost accounting against the attacks which are commonly made upon it today.

2 To what extent do you consider it necessary or advisable to apply time-discounting to short-term monetary items in the year-end balance sheet? Give reasons.

3 In accounting for hire purchase transactions, it is sometimes suggested that implicit interest should be written off to revenue on a 'straight line' basis, proportionately to the number of instalments received or paid during a period. What are the advantages and disadvantages of this procedure, as compared with theoretically more correct methods?

4 Comment on the difficulties involved in valuing the stock and work-in-progress of a manufacturing company with particular reference to current practice and recent recommendations.

How would you suggest that a partly manufactured desk should be valued, based on the following information?:

    1. Raw material used   £2.70

    2. Direct labour costs   £1.50

    3. Extract from current year's budget records when 100 desks are
       expected to be sold:

	£
Raw materials	300
Director labour costs	150
Production costs	100
Administration costs	75
Selling and distribution costs	50
Sundry costs	25
Total costs	700
Sales	1,080
Trading Profit	£380

(Association of Certified Accountants, Examination Section IV, December 1973—Advanced Accounting)

5 The exposure draft ED6 issued by the Accounting Standards Steering Committee on Stock and Work in progress referred to the special problems of "long term contract work in progress". A British construction company has agreed to build a dam in Africa for a fixed price of £12 million. They started work on 1 January 1971 and expect to complete by 30 November 1972. When preparing the accounts for the year ended 31 December, 1971 the following information was available:

Costs incurred up to 31 December 1971	£6 million
Estimated costs to complete the contract	£4 million
Value of work certified to 31 December 1971	£7 million
Cash received by 31 December 1971	£4 million

You are required to:

    a discuss the special problems which arise in these circumstances,

    b calculate the figures to be included in the accounts of the British construction company at 31 December 1971, and

    c illustrate how these matters would appear in the accounts of the mining company for whom the dam was being built, if they were drawn up as at 31 December, 1971.

(Association of Certified Accountants, Examination Section V, December 1972—Advanced Accounting)

6 From the information given below you are required to:

    a prepare the account of Q Limited as it would appear in the creditors' ledger of A Limited;

    b reconcile the account prepared in answer to a with the monthly statement which Q Limited has sent to A Limited;

    c state the amount of the remittance A Limited would send to Q Limited in settlement of the amount due; invoices not on the ledger are omitted from the settlement.

The summarized statement received from Q Limited was as follows:

	£
Balance brought forward at the beginning of the month	7,789
Invoices for goods supplied	4,456
Cash and discount received	4,727
Credit notes	581
Journal entry 1 ⎫	27
Journal entry 2 ⎬ see note 2 below	200
Journal entry 3 ⎭	369

Further information is given below:

1 The balance brought forward at the beginning of the month on the statement includes the following:

    i invoices totalling £1,898, and in abeyance at the end of last month, have been credited to the ledger this month;

    ii invoices totalling £725, and in abeyance at the end of last month, remained in abeyance;

    iii cash and discount of £4,727, the final payment for last month, has been entered by Q Limited on the statement this month;

    iv debit notes amounting to £87, posted in the ledger of A Limited last month, but not credited by Q Limited until this month.

2 Additional details concerning the statement are:

    i journal entry 1 for £27 corrects an error on the statement of the previous month where £3,363 was brought forward as £3,336;

    ii journal entry 2 for £200 corrects an error in the opening balance of the statement and relates to an overcharge on an invoice which was corrected by A Limited before being posted to the ledger;

    iii a contra of £179 for goods purchased from A Limited and debited in the ledger last month has been included in journal entry 3 of Q Limited for £369 this month.

3 Of the current month's invoices £1,347 have not yet been entered in the ledger.

4 There are debit notes totalling £52 in the ledger but not on the statement.

5 A cash and discount payment of £2,534 this month has not been shown on Q Limited's statement.

6 Credit notes on the statement of £581 includes an item of £26 not yet in the ledger of A Limited.

7 Contra items for the current month amounting to £253 have been posted to Q Limited's account in the creditors' ledger from the debtors' ledger.

(Institute of Cost and Works Accountants, Part III Examination, December 1971— Accountancy 3)

7 Finance Ltd began trading as a hire purchase finance company on 1 April 1971. The books of account are well kept but neither directors nor staff have any knowledge of the preparation of final accounts.

    The trial balance on 31 March 1972 was:

	£	£
20,000 ordinary shares of £1 each		20,000
Office expenses	2,000	
Formation expenses	300	
Directors' salaries	500	
Office equipment (at cost)	1,200	
Sundry trade debtors	300	
Sundry trade creditors		1,500
H.P. charges		12,600
Options to purchase		198
H.P. charges remitted on early redemption	17	
Options to purchase remitted on early redemptions	2	
Commission paid	3,150	
Short term loan interest paid (to 31 December 1971)	450	
Auditor's remuneration	500	
Short term loans at 8 per cent p.a.		25,000
Balance at bank	6,253	
Balance due from H.P. customers	44,626	
	59,298	59,298

You ascertain that:

1 all H.P. contracts are for 24 months and repaid by direct debit to customers bank accounts, the first instalment being due the month following the date of the contract;

2 the first 23 instalments are equal, the 24th is £2 greater than its predecessors as it includes the £2 option to purchase;

3 a commission of 25 per cent of the H.P. charges is paid to brokers who introduce the business and arrange the contracts with the hirers;

4 the summary of the contracts entered into during the year to 31 March 1972 from the contract book is:

Month	Cash price £	Deposit £	H.P. charges £	Option to purchase £	Charged to customers £	Commission paid £
April	3,000	1,000	600	10	2,610	150
May	3,000	1,000	600	8	2,608	150
June	3,000	1,000	600	10	2,610	150
July	4,500	1,500	900	14	3,914	225
August	4,500	1,500	900	16	3,916	225
September	4,500	1,500	900	14	3,914	225
October	6,000	2,000	1,200	20	5,220	300
November	6,000	2,000	1,200	18	5,218	300
December	6,000	2,000	1,200	18	5,218	300
January	7,500	2,500	1,500	24	6,524	375
February	7,500	2,500	1,500	22	6,522	375
March	7,500	2,500	1,500	24	6,524	375
	63,000	21,000	12,600	198	54,798	3,150

5 the H.P. charges and option to purchase remitted, relate to a contract entered into in July, the total H.P. charges on the contract being £60;

6 all instalments have been paid on the due dates;

7 there have been no changes in the short term loans since 31 December 1971;

8 formation expenses are to be written off;

9 office equipment is to be depreciated by 15 per cent.

You are required to prepare for the consideration of the directors drafts of:

    a the Trading and Profit and Loss account for the year ended 31 March 1972, and

    b the Balance Sheet as on 31 March 1972.

Ignore taxation.

All calculations to be made to nearest pound.

(Institute of Chartered Accountants in England and Wales, Final Examination, Part I, May 1972—Advanced Accounting I)

8 Your client, Mr Trapp, has expressed considerable doubt about the accuracy of accounts prepared for the six months to 31 March 1969 after a physical stocktaking at that date. He maintains that his estimated monthly statements show that the profit should be much higher. These statements, summarized below, show for each month the number of units put into work in progress, the number of units finished, the 'margin' (i.e. selling price less cost of materials and selling expenses) on the units finished, the actual wages and actual overhead, and the resultant estimated profit. In previous periods these statements have always agreed reasonably well with the financial accounts, also summarized below. You have been satisfied with the reliability of the financial records and of the physical stocktakings over the periods concerned, and ascertain, or are aware of, the other information set out below.

The summary of Mr Trapp's monthly statements reads:

Month	Units put into work in progress (thousands)	Units finished (thousands)	Margin 45s. per unit £	Actual wages £	Actual overhead £	Profit £
1968 October	44	43	96,750	53,000	34,000	9,750
November	40	42	94,500	51,000	34,000	9,500
December	46	45	101,250	55,000	36,000	10,250
1969 January	32	38	85,500	46,000	31,000	8,500
February	36	40	90,000	49,000	34,000	7,000
March	40	42	94,500	50,000	35,000	9,500
Totals	238	250	562,500	304,000	204,000	54,500

Target wages and overhead per unit 24s. 16s.
= 300,000 = 200,000

Overspent 4,000 4,000

Target profit 250,000 units at 5s. 62,500
Less: Overspent 8,000

54,500

The following is a summary of the financial accounts for the period under review and the two preceding periods:

Six months ended—	31 March 1968	30 September 1968	31 March 1969
Sales—units	200,000	220,000	245,000
	£	£	£
Sales—value	770,000	847,000	943,250
Add: Increase in finished stock 5,000 units at 68s.	—	—	17,000
	770,000	847,000	960,250
Opening work in progress	180,200	185,500	190,800
Materials	282,800	310,800	333,200
Labour	243,000	267,000	304,000
Overhead	162,000	178,000	204,000
	868,000	941,300	1,032,000
Less: Closing work in progress	185,500	190,800	159,000
	682,500	750,500	873,000
Selling expenses	40,000	44,000	49,000
Total costs	722,500	794,500	922,000
Profit	47,500	52,500	38,250

The following other information is, or may be, relevant:

a raw material stocks remain almost constant and may be ignored.

b other stocks are valued either as 'work in progress' or as 'finished'; intermediate stages can be ignored.

c the material element of stock is all incorporated prior to the work in progress stage and is valued at 28s. per unit. 15s. per unit is allowed for labour to the work in progress stage with a further 9s. per unit to finish. Overhead is calculated at $66\frac{2}{3}$ per cent of labour, and selling expenses average 4s. per unit, leaving a target profit of 5s. on each unit.

d wastage can be ignored.

Draft a letter to Mr Trapp indicating which set of figures for the six months to 31 March 1969 you consider to be correct, showing what real error, if any, has occurred, and suggesting how such differences or errors could be avoided in the future.

(Institute of Chartered Accountants of Scotland, Examination Part V, April 1969—Advanced Accounting II)

9 Sweetipies Ltd uses large quantities of a sweetening material for its products. The following figures relate to this material during the calendar year 1968:

Quarter ended:	Purchases Tons	Invoice cost per ton £	Consumption Tons
31 March	1,000	62	600
30 June	2,100	63	1,200
30 September	700	64	1,500
31 December	1,200	67	1,350
Market replacement cost:			
31 December 1968		66	
31 December 1967		61	

The stock of material on 31 December 1967 was 1,000 tons valued for accounting purposes at cost of £60 a ton. Delivery of goods to the factory is made on the first day of each quarter.

You are required:

  a to compute the value of the stock of material as on 31 December 1968, applying i L.I.F.O., and ii F.I.F.O., and

  b for internal accounting purposes to compare the effects, on the 1968 profits, of adopting each of the foregoing valuation methods in place of valuations based wholly on market replacement cost.

(Institute of Chartered Accountants in England and Wales, Final Examination, Part I, November 1969—Advanced Accounting I)

10 From the following information extracted from the books of Works Contractors Ltd you are required:

  a to prepare the general contract trading account for the year ended 31 December 1971;

  b to show how the various balances relating to assets and liabilities would appear in the balance sheet at 31 December 1971 to be submitted to the directors of the company.

	£	£
Cash received in respect of contracts (see note 1)		
On measurements		450,000
Retention moneys		43,000
Costs incurred on contracts for wages, materials, etc.		425,000
Payments to sub-contractors (see note 1)		
On measurements		36,000
Retention moneys		5,000
Plant account—		
Net book amount 1 January 1971 (cost £200,000)	120,000	
New plant purchased	18,000	
New plant on hire purchase (see note 2)		
Initial payment	2,000	
Instalments—9 at £500	4,500	
	144,500	
Less: Sales (cost £9,200—net book amount £4,000)	3,500	
		141,000

	Contracts £	Sub-contracts £
Retention moneys outstanding at 31 December 1970	45,000	4,000
Work in progress valuations (see note 3)		
As at 31 December 1970	15,000	2,000
As at 31 December 1971	19,000	3,000

Notes

  1 The company receives payment for work done on contracts under deduction of 10 per cent retention money. The retention money is received when the contract is satisfactorily completed but it is the company's normal practice to take credit in the trading account for the full amount of measurements. Payments are made to sub-contractors under similar arrangements.

  At 31 December 1970 there were no sums due on measurements of contracts or due to sub-contractors on measurements. It is ascertained, however, that, at 31 December 1971, no payment had been received in respect of a measurement of £38,000, gross, made on 15 December 1971. No sums were due to sub-contractors at 31 December 1971 for measurements made prior to that date.

2 The cash price of the new plant acquired under a hire-purchase contract was £10,000 and the total number of instalments is 18 of £500.

It is ascertained that certain special new plant costing £15,000 required for a particular contract has, in accordance with normal policy, been charged direct to the contract under the heading 'wages, materials, etc.'

Plant is depreciated by the straight line method at 10 per cent per annum on net cost.

3 Work in progress valuations represent work done but unmeasured.

(Institute of Chartered Accountants of Scotland, Examination Part III, September 1969—Advanced Accounting I (adapted))

Chapter 6: Asset valuation and income measurement: historical-cost accounting (2)

1 Define carefully the term 'provision' as used in modern accounting, and attempt a classification of the circumstances in which the device is applied in practice.

2 Long-term investments are conventionally accounted for on a historical-cost basis. What other bases of valuation are feasible, and what advantages and disadvantages have they? State, with reasons, whether you consider any of them likely to displace the conventional basis.

3 '. . . The word "Depreciation" has been grossly overworked, it has been and is currently used in varying senses and with different connotations. . . .'

(Professor Goldberg reprinted in *Studies in Accounting Theory* by Baxter and Davidson.)

Explain the different meanings of the word 'depreciation' when applied in common parlance to long lived assets.

(Association of Certified Accountants, Examination Section V, June 1971—Advanced Accounting)

4 What problems arise in accounting for intangible assets, separable from the business? How successful do you consider the orthodox solutions, and how far consistent with the revenue/cost matching concept?

5 Outline and evaluate the accepted methods of valuing goodwill for accounting purposes.

6 The Super Coach Co. Ltd has been in business for many years hiring out luxury coaches. It had been the company's experience that a new coach had a life of 4 years or 200,000 miles, when it had to be replaced, but some years ago it was found that the life could be extended by another 4 years or 100,000 miles by using the coaches as school buses and a number of coaches had been retained for this purpose.

The company has been providing for depreciation at the rate of 25 per cent p.a. on the reducing balance but when the 4-year-old coaches were sold, usually for £1,000, or the 8-year-old coaches were sold, usually for £200, a book loss had to be written off.

Before finalizing the accounts for the year ended 30 June 1971 the directors decided to review the depreciation provision for coaches.

All the coaches were brought into use on 1 July in the year of purchase and the details of each coach, all being purchased new, are as follows:

No. of coach	Year of purchase	Cost £	Depreciation to 30 June 1971 £	Net book amount £	Total mileage (000's) 30 June 1971	1970
1	1965	4,000	3,287	713	280	250
2	1966	4,000	3,050	950	280	220
3	1968	4,000	2,312	1,688	140	90
4	1969	5,000	2,187	2,813	90	60
5	1969	5,000	2,187	2,813	110	50
6	1970	5,000	1,250	3,750	40	—

You are required to write a concise letter to the directors setting out:

a the matters to be taken into consideration in deciding on a method of depreciation for the coaches;

b the method which you recommend the company to use, with brief reasons; and

c a draft of the entries in respect of coaches and depreciation which would appear in the Accounts to 30 June 1971 after putting into effect your recommendation.

Ignore Investment Grants and assume maintenance costs are evenly distributed over the life of the coaches.

(Institute of Chartered Accountants in England and Wales, Final Examination, Part I, November 1971—Advanced Accounting I)

7 The company of which you are the management accountant has obtained a contract to supply 200,000 metal fittings at £5 each.

To undertake this work a special purpose machine has been purchased for £22,000 which at the end of the contract will have a residual value of £2,000.

Estimated production costs are:

Direct material, per unit	£1.50	Fixed production overhead,	
Direct labour, per unit	£1.00	excluding depreciation, for	
Variable production overhead, of		the contract	£40,000
direct labour costs	60%	Variable selling overhead, per unit	£0.30
		Fixed selling overhead, for the	
		contract	£80,000

Although the contract has not yet started a second machine of more advanced design has been offered to the company for £36,000. This machine will produce 25 per cent more units per operator hour but will use 5 per cent more material. The machine will have no residual value at the end of the contract. The makers are prepared to buy back the first machine for £5,000.

The works manager has in the circumstances asked if the second machine should be purchased. You are required to advise the works manager of the action to be taken. Support your answer with a statement of the alternative total costs of the contract.

(Institute of Cost and Works Accountants, Part IV Examination, December 1971—Management Accountancy I)

8 You have received the following information relating to Engineering Manufacturers Limited which makes up its accounts to 31 December each year:

1 Two hydraulic presses were purchased, the first on 1 March 1969 for £9,000 and the second on 15 July 1969 for £12,000. Both these machines were bought under agreements providing for payment by instalments whereby a deposit of 20 per cent was payable on purchase and the balance of the price over two years in equal monthly instalments, commencing one month after the date of purchase. Interest under the agreements is 5 per cent over bank rate payable quarterly in arrear on the outstanding balance of principal at the beginning of each quarter.

2 Two lorries were purchased, the first on 1 April 1969 for £2,000 and the second on 1 July 1969 for £2,400. Both lorries were bought under hire-purchase agreements with a 25 per cent deposit on purchase and hiring charges of 7 per cent per annum on the balance which, together with the charges, is payable monthly over two years.

The first lorry was damaged beyond repair in an accident on 1 December 1969 and £1,700 was received from the insurance company in full settlement on 15 January 1970. The relative hire-purchase agreement was settled by a final payment of £1,100 on 24 December 1969.

3 The company's expenditure on plant and machinery qualifies for investment grants at 40 per cent and the method of accounting is that the grants receivable are deducted from the asset account, depreciation being calculated on the net cost.

4 The company charges depreciation by the straight line method at 15 per cent per annum on plant and 25 per cent per annum on vehicles, a full year's depreciation being charged in the year of purchase.

5 Bank rate remained at 8 per cent throughout 1969.

6 All payments under the respective agreements were made on the due dates.

Required: Show, in respect of these transactions, the entries which would appear in the balance sheet at 31 December 1969 and the profit and loss account for the year ended that date.

(Institute of Chartered Accountants of Scotland, Examination Part III, April 1970—Advanced Accounting I)

9. The Hairy Car Co. Ltd was incorporated on 1 January 1967, with a paid up capital of £8,000,000, to design, develop and manufacture a revolutionary sports car. During 1967 the company built up its organization, leased premises, purchased plant and recruited a development team. An amount of £3,000,000 was spent on plant and machinery, whilst the cost of materials, labour and overhead expenses recorded in the books amounted to £500,000 during the year.

In 1968, development work on a prototype continued, while the company prepared production facilities against the day when development would be complete. Expenditure of £1,000,000 on tooling costs was capitalized, a further £500,000 was spent on an advertising campaign, and the cost of materials used, labour and overhead expenses amounted to £1,000,000. When the company was incorporated the Board discussed depreciation of fixed assets and settled on a rate of 5 per cent on cost during the development years, and 10 per cent on cost thereafter.

At 31 December 1968, stocks of raw materials were valued at £200,000. There was no income of any sort during 1967 or 1968, and the board decided to charge the development costs to a 'development and experimental expense account' which appeared in the balance sheet at 31 December 1968 as deferred revenue expenditure.

On 1 January 1969, development of the prototype was satisfactorily completed and it was decided to retain the vehicle as a demonstration model. At this time the factory was prepared to produce cars at the rate of 400 per year to be sold direct to the consumer for cash at £2,500 each. However, teething troubles at the factory reduced production for the year to 80 vehicles, of which only 40 were sold. Rigorous economy in the face of this situation reduced labour costs to £50,000 for the year, whilst materials purchased cost £45,000. Advertising and other overhead costs amounted to £450,000. The stock of raw materials on 31 December 1969 was £95,000, there was no stock of work in progress, and closing stocks of finished goods were valued at direct cost. The board decided to charge the loss for 1969 to the development and experimental expense account.

During 1970 320 vehicles were produced, and 200 vehicles sold. Direct costs were reduced to £2,000 per vehicle, whilst advertising and overhead expenses were held at £450,000 for the year. Stocks of raw material remained at the same level throughout the year, and stocks of finished goods were accounted for on a F.I.F.O. basis. The board proposed once more to charge the loss to the development and experimental expense account, arguing that whilst prototype development was completed in 1968, their market had developed at a slower rate than was anticipated. They hope that expanding sales in the future will make it possible to set off development expenditure against revenue in later years when the project has matured.

You are required to:
    a draft balance sheets for the company as at 31 December 1968, 1969 and 1970, and
    b comment on the manner in which the circumstances outlined above have been treated in
       the accounts for the last three years, and suggest a course of future action.

(Association of Certified Accountants, Examination Section V, June 1971—Advanced Accounting)

10 A company in the oil business covers the activities associated with exploration, development, production and sale of crude. It operates in four geographical areas. Data relating to expenditure, sales and reserves for the first three years are shown below:

Year 1

	Area A	B	C	D	Total
Costs £'000					
Exploration	1,000	1,000	—	—	2,000
Development	2,000	—	—	—	2,000
Production	500	—	—	—	500
Output & Sales—units	500	—	—	—	500
£'000	2,500	—	—	—	2,500
Estimated reserves at year end—units	2,500	1,000	—	—	3,500

Year 2

	Area A	B	C	D	Total
Costs £'000					
Exploration		1,000	3,000	—	4,000
Development	500	1,000	—	—	1,500
Production	2,000	—	—	—	2,000
Output & Sales—units	2,000	—	—	—	2,000
£'000	10,000	—	—	—	10,000
Estimated reserves at year end—units	2,000	3,000	1,000	—	6,000

Year 3

Costs £'000

Exploration	–	7,000	–	2,000	9,000
Development	–	2,000	4,000	500	6,500
Production	1,500	3,000	1,000	–	5,500
Output & Sales—units	2,000	2,000	1,000	–	5,000
£'000	10,000	10,000	10,000	–	30,000
Estimated reserves at year end—units	–	4,000	–	2,000	6,000

There are at least three recognized methods of accounting for exploration and development expenditure:

1. Current expense, in which all expenditure is written off in the year it is incurred.

2. Conventional, one variation of which writes off in the year of incurrence all expenditure which is not likely to be recovered from production in the particular area. A maximum amount of £2,000 per unit is carried forward for recovery from future production and sale.

3. Full cost, or total cost, which assumes that all exploration and development costs contribute towards the discovery of reserves irrespective of the particular area in which they are spent. Again a maximum amount of £2,000 per unit would be carried forward for recovery from future production and sale.

You are required:

a. to calculate and present in a comparative form the reported profit for each year using the three methods, and

b. to comment on the relevance of the alternative methods for internal and external reporting.

(Institute of Chartered Accountants in England and Wales, Final Examination, Part II, May 1974—Advanced Accounting II)

Chapter 7: Accounting for price level changes; funds flow and cash flow

1 One criticism often made of conventional accounting methods is that they allow a competent professional auditor to report, as giving a 'true and fair view', any one of millions of possible combinations of figures, relative to the performance of a particular company for a particular period of time. How far do you think that the adoption of inflation-adjusted accounting would reduce such diversity in reported results for the same business over the same period?

2 In the 1960s replacement-cost accounting was advocated as a solution to the problems of reporting company financial performance in an age of inflation, in the 1970s, current purchasing power accounting is the fashionable remedy. Suggest reasons for the change of emphasis, in the light of differences in the aims and methods of the two systems.

3 Discuss the shortcomings of annual accounts of companies prepared on a historical cost basis. State any alternatives which you would put forward as an accountant, to give a more realistic indication of their performance and financial position.

(Institute of Municipal Treasurers and Accountants, Final Examination, Part 2, May 1973—Accountancy 4)

4 The managing director of a medium-sized manufacturing company, of which you are auditor, has written to you regarding reports he has read in the financial press on the growing interest in 'current price level accounting'.

REQUIRED:

Draft a reply explaining what is meant by 'current price level accounting' [i.e. current purchasing power accounting], stating what it sets out to achieve, and adding a brief note on the steps which would be necessary to set up such a system.

(Institute of Chartered Accountants of Scotland, Part II Examination, April 1974—Interpretation of Accounts (adapted)).

5 a What do you understand by the term depreciation? Do you feel that one of the objectives of depreciation should be to provide funds for replacement purposes?

b Several U.K. organizations provide for additional depreciation to reflect changes in the purchasing power of money. The managing director of C. Limited is considering the adoption of this policy in the accounts for the year ended 31 December 1972.

Present a reasoned report commenting in detail on the feasibility of this suggestion using the following information regarding fixed asset purchases, and showing how you would treat the charge for depreciation in the accounts.

Date of Acquisition	Fixed Asset Costs £	Average Index of Consumer Prices for the Year
1968	8,500	160
1969	11,500	170
1971	20,000	180
1972	30,000	192
	£70,000	

The Index of Consumer Prices at the end of 1972 stood at 200. Depreciation is normally provided for at 20 per cent of cost.

(Association of Certified Accountants, Examination Section IV, June 1973—Advanced Accounting)

6 One method which it has been suggested would improve the accounting for stewardship purposes of the annual accounts, is known as Current Purchasing Power Accounts.

A conventional balance sheet at 31 August 1972 in summary form is reproduced below:

	£	£		£	£
Share Capital			*Fixed Assets*		
Ordinary shares		100,000	Cost	250,000	
			Depreciation	80,000	
					170,000
Reserves					
Profit and Loss account		50,000			
5% Debentures			*Current Assets*		
			Stock	60,000	
Current Liabilities			Debtors	30,000	
Creditors	40,000		Cash and Bank balance	40,000	
Corporation Tax	10,000				
		50,000			130,000
		£300,000			£300,000

The share capital was issued at par on 31 August 1960. The Debentures were issued at par on 31 August 1972, and they are redeemable at par on 31 August 1982. The creditors are payable on 30 September 1972; the Corporation Tax on 1 January 1973. Fixed Assets were required on 1 September, in the following years, 1966 £50,000; 1969 £150,000; 1971 £50,000 and have been depreciated on a straight line basis of 10 per cent per annum. The replacement cost of similar plant was £400,000 on 31 August 1972. Stock was acquired evenly during June, July and August 1972 and if purchased on 31 August 1972 would have cost £70,000.

The conversion factors, based on an index of current purchasing power which it has been agreed should be used, have the following values:

Conversion factors

31 August	1960	150	1 September	1970	107
"	1962	140	"	1971	105
1 September	1966	125	Average for year to 31 August	1972	104
"	1967	122	Average for 3 months to 31 August	1972	101
"	1968	116	31 August	1972	100
"	1969	110			

You are required to:
  a prepare a Balance Sheet at 31 August in terms of 31 August 1972 purchasing power (show all your workings) and
  b comment on the usefulness of the current purchasing power balance sheet to share-holders.

(Association of Certified Accountants, Examination Section V, December 1972—Advanced Accounting)

7 Assess the value of the additional information provided to management by a (historical) flow of funds statement.

8 The summarized balance sheet at 30 June 1972 and the summarized profit and loss account for the year ended on that date, of John Jones Limited, were as follows:—

Balance Sheet at 30 June 1972

1971 £	1971 £		£	£
		Capital and Reserves		
		Issued capital:		
		400,000 ordinary shares of £1 each		
400,000		fully paid	400,000	
		100,000 6% redeemable preference		
100,000	500,000	shares of £1 each, fully paid	—	400,000
		Capital Reserve—the capital		
		redemption reserve fund		100,000
		Revenue Reserves		
150,000		General Reserve	170,000	
		Less transfer to capital redemption		
		reserve fund	100,000	
			70,000	
34,400	184,400	Unappropriated profits	41,750	111,750
	£684,400	Shareholders' interest		£611,750
		Represented by:—		
		Fixed Assets:		
	105,000	Fixed property—at cost		64,000
		Mortgaged per contra.		
85,000		Machinery, vehicles and office equip-		
		ment—at cost	87,000	
17,000		Less: accumulated depreciation	24,900	
	68,000			62,100
	21,000	Trade investments—at cost		29,500
	194,000	Total fixed assets		155,600
		Current Assets:		
341,200		Stock on hand and in transit	543,000	
		Sundry debtors—less provision for		
		doubtful debts £15,000		
383,000		(1971 £10,000)	517,100	
724,200			1,061,000	
		Less		
		Current liabilities:		
185,400		Sundry creditors	321,000	
48,000		Taxation	71,500	
400		Bank overdraft	122,350	
233,800	490,000		514,850	546,150
	684,400			701,750
		Less		
		Loan—secured by mortgage over		
—		land and buildings		90,000
	£684,400			£611,750

Profit and loss account for the year ended 30 June 1972

1971 £		£	. £
87,700	Trading profit		107,200
	Less: dpereciation written off		
7,600	Fixed assets	8,900	
−	Loss on sale of fixed property	8,000	
−	Interest on fixed loan	500	
2,100	Interest on bank overdraft	3,200	
9,700			20,600
78,000			86,600
	Profit on sale of machinery:		
−	Proceeds	600	
(100)	Net book value	350	
			250
77,900			86,850
22,200	Deduct: taxation		31,500
55,700	Net profit after tax		55,350
	Unappropriated profit at end of		
24,700	previous year		34,400
80,400			89,750
6,000	Preference dividend	3,000	
20,000	Ordinary dividend	20,000	
	Premium on redemption of preference		
−	shares	5,000	
20,000	Transfer to general reserves	20,000	
46,000			48,000
£34,400	Balance as per balance sheet		£41,750

You are required to prepare a statement of source and application of funds for the year ended 30 June 1972.

(Institute of Chartered Accountants in Ireland, Examination Part IV, Winter 1972—Advanced Accounting 1)

Chapter 8: Accounting for sub-entities; foreign exchange transactions

1 Following a policy decision to open up two provincial retail selling branches of the company, your Chairman requests your recommendations as to a suitable system of accounting to be adopted to serve the needs of both the head office and the proposed branches.

Write to him in concise tabulated report form, not exceeding 350 words, noting alternatives and advantages and disadvantages of each, but ignoring aspects of mechanization and computerization.

(Association of Certified and Corporate Accountants Examination Section IV, June 1969— Advanced Accounting)

2 Two alternative bases are in general use, for converting to sterling the figures in the accounts of overseas branches or subsidiaries, expressed in foreign currency. Compare and contrast these two bases, and state, with reasons, which you would adopt if you were chief accountant of a large group of companies with extensive international interests.

3 In what ways do the aims and methods of branch accounting, and of departmental accounting, resemble, and differ from, one another? Illustrate with simple numerical examples.

4 There arises frequently in the group company situation the problem of the pricing of intra-group company transfers, where the policy adopted can be vital to the profitability shown by the individual companies.

a Suggest the objectives to be borne in mind in transfer pricing.

b Detail three separate pricing methods and discuss the benefits and limitations of each.

(Institute of Cost and Management Accountants, Part IV Examination, May 1972—Management Accountancy 2)

5 With It Jane Ltd carries on business as a retailer of clothes through a head office and three branches in Bristol, Bath and Swindon.

All the purchases are made by head office and all the sales are made at the branches. Goods are invoiced to branches at selling price, being cost plus $33\frac{1}{3}$ per cent. The branches are allowed to sell for cash or on 30 days credit terms. The branch managers are paid a basic salary and a commission of $2\frac{1}{2}$ per cent of the gross profit of the branch out of which the manager must make good any stock losses at selling price and bad debts. The commission is paid quarterly.

Cash received by the branches is banked daily for the credit of head office and Debtors Ledgers are maintained at the branches to record transactions with credit customers but otherwise all branch accounting is dealt with by head office.

The branch transactions during the quarter ended 31 December 1970 and the opening balances at 1 October 1970 were:

	Bristol £	Bath £	Swindon £
Goods invoiced by head office	11,200	11,600	9,400
Goods returned to head office	—	900	300
Cash sales	4,530	5,200	4,870
Credit sales	5,820	7,390	4,760
Goods returned by credit customers	240	90	120
Cash received from credit customers	5,760	7,410	4,720
Stock 1 October 1970	5,700	8,300	4,200
Debtors 1 October 1970	990	760	570
Stock 31 December 1970	6,300	5,840	4,700
Debtors 31 December 1970 after writing off bad debts	810	640	485
Goods transferred at selling prices to Swindon Branch	(400)	(560)	960
Allowance by head office for goods sold at special prices	70	80	50

You are required to write up, in columnar form, in the books of head office, the appropriate Branch Accounts (including Branch Adjustment Accounts) recording these transactions and Branch Managers' Commission Accounts showing the commission due to each manager, for the quarter ended 31 December 1970.

(Institute of Chartered Accountants in England and Wales, Final Examination, Part I, May 1971—Advanced Accounting I)

6 *R* Limited operates a retail branch at Croydon, a town just outside London. All purchases are made by the Head Office in London, goods for the branch being delivered to it direct and charged out at selling price, which is cost price plus 50 per cent. All cash received by the branch is remitted to London. Branch expenses are paid by the branch out of an imprest account which is reimbursed monthly by London.

The branch keeps a sales ledger and certain essential subisidary books, but otherwise all branch transactions are recorded in the books of the London Office.

On 1 January 1970, stock-in-trade at the branch, at selling price, amounted to £4,896 and debtors to £645.

During the year ended 31 December 1970, the following transactions took place at the branch:

	£		£
Goods received by the branch, at selling price	15,330	Authorized reductions in selling prices	497
Cash sales	6,425	Cash received from debtors	3,266
Credit sales	3,228	Debtors written off as irrecoverable	165
Goods returned to branch by credit customers	90	Cash discounts allowed to debtors	212
Goods returned to London, at selling price	156		

The expenses relating to the branch for the year ended 31 December 1970 amounted to £1,029.

On 31 December 1970, physical stock-in-trade at the branch at selling price amounted to £8,340.

You are required to:

a write up the Branch Stock Account, and the Branch Total Debtors Account maintained in the London books. The Stock Account may be in two column form or combined with an adjustment account, b prepare the Trading and Profit and Loss Account of the branch for the year ended 31 December 1970, and

c comment on the branch results for 1970.

(Association of Certified Accountants, Examination Section IV, December 1971—Advanced Accounting)

7 Stakes Limited have their head office in Dublin and a branch in Rio. Goods are involved to the branch at cost plus 20 per cent. Goods are also purchased locally by the branch. The local currency in Rio is rotes and the exchange is 6 rotes to the £.

The following trial balance was prepared in the head office books on the 1 January 1972:

	Dublin		Rio	
	£	£	£	£
Premises	150,000		6,000	
Fittings	10,000		4,000	
Stock: cost price	4,400		600	
invoiced price			120	
Goods in transit to branch				
(invoiced price)	600			
Cash at bank	2,400		480	
Trade creditors		9,800		2,900
Cash in transit to head office	200			
Trade debtors	2,000		1,000	
Branch current account	9,300			
Head office current account				9,300
Provision for unrealized				
profit on stock		120		
Profit and loss account		3,980		
Issued capital		165,000		
	178,900	178,900	12,200	12,200

The following transactions were recorded during 1972:

	Dublin	Rio
	£	Rotes
Goods sent to Rio (invoiced price)	12,100	
Goods received from Dublin (1)		70,800
Cash sent to Dublin		96,000
Cash received from Rio (1)	15,600	
Purchases	60,000	18,000
Sales	120,000	144,000
Wages	25,000	30,000
General expenses	42,000	36,000
Freight charges on goods from Dublin		15,000
Cash received (2)		3,600

Notes—:

1 These amounts include cash and goods in transit on 1 January 1972.

2 Goods received from Dublin were destroyed in a fire in a Rio warehouse. The insurance company paid compensation for the cost price of the goods, plus freight charges indurred of 600 rotes. An adjustment is to be made between head office and branch, eliminating the mark up charged by the head office on these goods.

Otherwise any other adjustment required is to be made in the branch books.

3 Balances as on 31 December 1972:

		Dublin	Rio
		£	Rotes
Stocks on hand:	cost price	6,500	1,200
	invoiced price		2,880
Trade creditors		7,900	3,300
Trade debtors		3,500	8,400

4 Charge depreciation of fittings as follows: Dublin, £1,000; Rio, 2,400 rotes.

5 There was no discount allowed or received during the year. No expenses were prepaid or accrued on the 31 December 1972.

6 Goods and cash were in transit on the 31 December 1972.

You are required to prepare, in the head office books, in columnar form,

  a trading and profit and loss accounts for the head office, branch and combined group for the year ended 31 December 1972, and

  b balance sheets as on that date.

  N.B.: Workings are to be shown.

(Institute of Chartered Accountants in Ireland, Examination Part IV, Summer 1973— Advanced Accounting II).

---

8 From the details given for the month of April you are required to:

  a prepare journal entries to close the books as at 30 April 1973 in preparation for a separate profit and loss account for each department and an overall profit and loss account;

  b compile a comparative departmental profit and loss statement in columnar form showing results departmentally and in total.

  c determine four informative operating ratios, and write brief notes commenting on the buisness operations.

  d criticize the cost distribution bases suggesting alternatives where appropriate.

Data:

A retail establishment has three main selling departments A, B and C. The individual operations of each department are recorded on purpose designed stationery, e.g. sales tickets and purchase orders, so that management may appraise trading results departmentally.

The following debit balances are extracted from the general ledger at 30 April:

	£
Salaries and commissions	5,000
National Insurance	150
Purchasing costs	3,450
General office costs	2,400
Consumable stores	88
Rent	240
Rates	220
Fire insurance	44
Advertising	1,750
Bad debts	440
Transport costs—delivery	1,000
Telephone charges	88
Depreciation of fixtures and fittings	60

The following tabulation summarizes results for the period:

	Departments			
	A	B	C	TOTAL
	£	£	£	£
Stock: 1 April	7,500	10,000	2,500	20,000
Purchases	30,000	35,000	4,000	69,000
Stock: 30 April	11,500	12,000	500	24,000
Sales	41,000	40,000	7,000	88,000

The departmental distribution of apportioned costs is achieved on the following bases

Apportioned costs	Basis
Purchasing costs	Purchases
General office costs	Equally between departments
Fire insurance and rates	Average value of stock
Consumable stores, bad debts and telephone charges	Sales
National insurance	Salaries and commissions

Special surveys have been made to assess departmental benefits for other costs, as follow

Costs	Departments		
	A	B	C
	%	%	%
Advertising	60	30	10
Transport cost—delivery	20	45	35
Rent	40	35	25
Depreciation of fixtures and fittings	50	20	30
Salaries and commissions	50	30	20

(Institute of Cost and Management Accountants, Part IV Examination, May 1973—Management Accountancy 2)

9 A company has two divisions. Eastern Division manufactures a unique timing device. It is never sold outside the company and it cannot be obtained from any other source. Western Division incorporates this device in a finished product which it sells. One device is used for each unit of product. Most of Eastern Division's costs are fixed and for any output up to 1,000 units its total costs are £600. Thereafter total costs increase at the rate of £100 for every additional 1,000 units made. In the hope of optimizing his division's results, Eastern Division's manager has set a transfer price of 50p per unit.

Western Division costs in assembling the timing device in the finished product and selling it are, in addition to the transfer price of the timing device, £1,200 for any output up to 1,000 units and £200 for every 1,000 units thereafter. Western Division finds that it can only increase its sales by spending more on promotion or reducing selling prices. Western Division's sales forecast is

Sales in units	Net sales revenue per thousand units
	£
1,000	1,900
2,000	1,700
3,000	1,500
4,000	1,250
5,000	960
6,000	770

All costs, output rates and sales are per working day.

You are required on the same basis:

a to prepare a schedule of Western Division's costs (including purchases from Eastern Division), sales revenue and net income at the indicated sales levels,

b to state what level of sales maximizes Western Division's net income and calculate Eastern Division's net income and the net income of the company at that level,

c to assume that the company's divisional structure and transfer pricing is abandoned and prepare a further schedule of costs, sales, and net income for the company as a whole, at the indicated sales levels,

d to state what level of sales maximizes the company's net income and explain why it differs from that calculated under a divisional organization, and

e to state what transfer pricing policy will maximize the company's net income under the divisional organization.

(Institute of Chartered Accountants in England and Wales, Final Examination, Part II, May 1974—Advanced Accounting III)

10 A.B. Ltd. is a holding company with five operating subsidiaries. During the year to 31 March 1974 the parent company has charged to its subsidiaries loan interest totalling £77,000, based on a rate of 10 per cent per annum, on the average loan to or from the parent company during the year. A.B. Ltd. incurred bank overdraft interest of £45,000 during the year. A summary of the subsidiary company's draft balance sheets as at 31 March 1974 is—

	£000's				
	C.	D.	E.	F.	G.
Fixed assets	250	200	100	70	260
Net current assets	100	550	470	80	50
	350	750	570	150	310
Deduct:—Bank overdraft	20	160	50	–	40
	330	590	520	150	270
Representing:—					
Share capital and reserves	600	350	120	50	10
Parent company loans	(270)	240	400	100	260
	330	590	520	150	270
Other information—					
Profit for the year before interest	90	70	70	30	10
Loan interest payable/(receivable)	(28)	22	45	8	30
Bank overdraft interesr	1	19	7	—	4

Because of the widely differing capital structure of each company within the group, it has been recommended that each subsidiary should bear a total interest charge for the year based on its average capital employed during the year. Because a major part of the group's finances is provided by bank overdrafts and inter-company loans, these are considered part of capital employed. The average rate of bank interest throughout the year was 12½ per cent. Profits before interest accrued evenly throughout the year. The total loan interest receivable by A.B. Ltd. from its subsidiaries should be limited to £45,000.

REQUIRED:

1 Prepare a statement showing the revised allocation to the subsidiaries of loan interest chargeable by the parent company to the nearest £100.

2 Compare the profits of each company in the group before and after the revision of all interest charges, ignoring any other income or management expenses of A.B. Ltd.

Note:

Ignore taxation.

(Institute of Chartered Accountants of Scotland, Part II Examination, April 1974—Management Accounting)

Part II: Financial accounting in modern Britain
Chapter 9: Accounting for unincorporated businesses (1)

1 Appraise the conventional methods of partnership accounting, relative to capital contribution, sharing of profits and losses, and partners' drawings, and suggest ways in which their application might be improved.

2 State, with reasons, whether you consider the rules laid down in Partnership Act 1890, s. 24, to be satisfactory insofar as they affect the accounts of a firm, and suggest ways in which a partnership agreement should be drawn up so as to mitigate their drawbacks.

3 What difficulties arise in practice, relative to the division of profits and losses among partners, through the operation of the U.K. system of personal taxation? How can these difficulties be overcome?

4 E owned a wholesale business which was managed for him by an employee until 31 August 1968, at which date the employee left. On 1 September he brought into the business as his partner F, who introduced £500 as capital and agreed to manage the business. Profits were to be shared equally and there was to be no interest paid on capital.

F subsequently discovered that cash had been misappropriated by the previous manager With your assistance the following figures were extracted from the records for the year 1 January to 31 December 1968:

	1968		
	At 1 January	At 31 August	At 31 December
Balances:	£	£	£
Debtors	2,500	2,700	3,300
Creditors	2,400	2,800	3,100
Stock		2,600	2,200
Balance at bank	1,750		6,900
Cash in hand	150	80	
Capital account, E	5,000		

For the year:	£
Purchases on credit	28,000
Cheques drawn for wages	4,900
Cash and cheques received from debtors and cash sales	40,000

For the period from January to August inclusive:	
Cash purchases from cash received	700
Drawings from cash, E	900

For the period from September to December inclusive:	
Sales	11,000
Cheques drawn for payment of ledger accounts	6,800
Drawings from bank: E	400
F	400

On 1 September the cash in hand was banked, cash sales were stopped and all subsequent payments were made by cheque. The wages paid above included £900 to the previous manager and £100 to an additional employee who commenced on 1 October; the remainder accrued evenly over the year.

You are required to prepare:
a a profit and loss account for the year, showing clearly how the profit is to be shared (after the cash shortage has been charged to E);
b a balance sheet as at 31 December 1968.
Attention should be paid to the presentation of workings.

(Institute of Cost and Works Accountants, Part III Examination, June 1969—Financial Accountancy (First Paper))

5 CD Limited entered into partnership with Z as from 1 January 1970 for the manufacture and sale of goods made under a new patent developed and financed by Z.

From the information provided you are to reflect the effect of the partnership in the books of CD Limited by preparing:
a a statement showing the adjustments to the balance on the profit and loss account of CD Limited;
b the journal entries to record the acquisition of the assets of the partnership, together with any terminal adjustments;
c the balance sheet of CD Limited as at 31 December 1970 after all the necessary adjustments have been made.

You are informed that:
1 The partnership deed provided that as from 1 January 1970:
  i capital be contributed equally and profits and losses to be shared equally;
  ii the partnership to acquire the patent from Z for the sum of £10,000;
  iii Z be allowed drawings at the rate of £50 per week.
2 The trial balances of CD Limited and the Partnership at 31 December 1970 were as under:

	CD Limited		Partnership	
	£	£	£	£
Share capital:				
Authorized and issued:				
30,000 ordinary shares of £1 each		30,000		
Capital account:				
CD Limited				5,000
Z				5,000
Capital reserve, 1 January 1970		25,000		
Profit and loss account:				
Balance, 1 January 1970		8,300		
Profit for year, before depreciation		26,200	3,800	
Creditors: Trade		18,000		7,500
CD Limited				27,500
Plant and vehicles, at cost	29,300		2,600	
Depreciation on plant and vehicles		7,200		
Patents, at cost	3,000		10,000	
Investment in partnership	5,000			
Debtors: Trade	21,700		18,100	
Partnership	28,000			
Balance at bank	3,200		1,500	
Stocks	24,500		6,400	
Drawings by Z			2,600	
	£114,700	£114,700	£45,000	£45,000

Adjustments at 31 December 1970 are required in respect of:
   i a bill of exchange for £8,500 drawn by the partnership on a debtor but not recorded in the partnership's books;
   ii the writing down to nil value of the partnership's stock including goods in transit to the value of £500 which had been invoiced by CD Limited to the partnership but not recorded in the books of the latter;
   iii making a provision to cover a claim by one of the partnership's customers for defective goods supplied which had been agreed at £5,000;
   iv a vehicle standing in the books of CD Limited at £500 against an original cost of £800 was sold to the partnership on 1 December 1970 for the sum of £100, but the transaction had not been recorded in either set of books.
   v depreciation of £2,700 to be provided on plant and vehicles by CD Limited and at 20 per cent of the balance sheet value by the partnership.

3 In view of the loss sustained it was decided to dissolve the partnership at 31 December 1970 on the following terms:
   i CD Limited to take over the patent, the other assets of the partnership after making the adjustments set out above, and all liabilities of the partnership other than to Z;
   ii Z to be released from all partnership liabilities and surrender his interest in the partnership and the patent on consideration of receiving the sum of £600.
4 CD Limited revalued all its patents at £9,000 and wrote off against capital reserve the amount written off the patents and the partnership loss attributable to Z.

(Institute of Cost and Works Accountants, Part III Examination, December 1971— Accountancy 2)

6 On 1 January 1971 Jones and Brown commenced business in partnership as hoteliers. Jones owned the building, which was valued at £35,000 as at 1 January 1971, and it was agreed that this should represent part of his capital in the business. Jones also paid into the partnership bank account a cheque for £5,000 to provide some working capital. Brown paid in a cheque for £20,000 and this, together with his contribution of some general furnishings and kitchen equipment valued at £4,000 and a motor-car valued at £1,000, formed the basis of his capital. It was agreed that Jones and Brown would receive salaries of £1,000 and £500 per annum respectively from 1 April 1971, and that any remaining profits would be divided equally.

From the formation of the partnership until 31 March 1971 no trading took place, but the following receipts and payments occurred and were reflected in the partnership's bank account:

Receipts	£
Mar 1 Loan to partnership from J. Smith Ltd to bear interest at 7 per cent per annum payable annually in arrears	6,000

Payments	£
Jan 27 Plumbers Ltd—to replacing all plumbing in the building and fitting new guttering to the exterior of the building	4,000
Feb 4 Joiners Ltd—to building fitted chests and wardrobes in all bedrooms	6,000
Feb 27 Carpets Ltd—to supplying carpets for all rooms in the hotel	14,000
Mar 16 Spirits Ltd—to supplying miscellaneous beverages to stock the hotel bars	4,000
Mar 30 Grocers Ltd—to supplying miscellaneous foodstuffs for restaurant	500

On 1 April 1971 trading commenced and the following is a summary of the cash book for the nine months ended 31 December 1971. All payments were by cheque and all receipts were lodged in the bank:

Receipts	£
Restaurant drawings	10,428
Bar drawings	22,489
Letting of rooms	22,000

Payments	£
Wages (including partners' salaries)	14,726
Electricity	419
Gas	892
Rates and insurance	2,450
Groceries, meat and other consumables for restaurant	5,163
Spirits and beers	14,626
Cleaning materials	376
Miscellaneous	215

The partners have supplied the following additional information:

1 A 10 per cent 'service charge' is included in the totals of all restaurant and room-letting bills rendered during the year. This had not been paid to the staff at 31 December 1971, but the partners intended to pay over the entire amount to the staff in February 1972.

2 The following accounts or invoices have been received after 31 December 1971:

	£
Electricity account for the quarter to 31 January 1972	246
Sundry accounts for bar stocks supplied in December 1971	722
Insurance for year to 31 December 1972	412
Sundry accounts for groceries supplied in December 1971	156

3 The stocks in hand at 31 December 1971 were valued as follows:

	£
Wines, spirits and beers	3,160
Groceries	500

4 During the year cash was drawn on account of profits by the partners as follows:

	£
Jones	1,250
Brown	1,100

5 Depreciation is to be provided at 20 per cent straight line on all fixed assets at 31 December 1971, except for the building which is not to be depreciated.

REQUIRED:

Prepare:

1 The profit and loss account for the year ended 31 December 1971.

2 The balance sheet as at 31 December 1971.

(Institute of Chartered Accountants of Scotland, Examination Part III, April 1972—Advanced Accounting I)

7 Pixey and Jinks were in partnership and made up their accounts to 31 December each year. It was agreed that Lane, an employee of many years standing, be admitted as a partner from 1 January 1973 without requiring him to introduce any capital.

The new partnership deed stated inter-alia that:

  1 There was to be no adjustment made for goodwill.

  2 Partners were to receive 5 per cent on the balance of their Capital Accounts at 1 January each year as interest on capital.

  3 Pixey was to receive a salary of £1,500 and Jinks a salary of £2,700.

  4 Lane's share of the profits was to be the greater of:

    (a) a salary of £2,100 plus one-tenth of the profits after charging interest on capital and all the partners' salaries, or

    (b) one-sixth of the profits after charging interest on capital.

  5 The profits, after charging interest on capital, their own salaries and Lane's share of the profits were to be divided between Pixey and Jinks in the ratio of 2:1 except that any increase in Lane's share of the profits due to opting for method (b) instead of method (a) was to be charged against Pixey's share.

You ascertain that:

  1 Pixey and Jinks Capital Accounts on 1 January 1973 were £20,400 and £16,200 respectively.

  2 During the year to 31 December 1973 the following sums had been debited to partners' Capital Accounts on account of salaries and profits, Pixey £4,000, Jinks £3,000 and Lane £2,000.

  3 The profit for the year ended 31 December 1973 before charging interest on capital or partners's salaries was £25,200.

You are required to prepare in columnar form the partners' Capital Accounts for the year ended 31 December 1973.

Ignore taxation.

(Institute of Chartered Accountants in England and Wales, Final Examination, Part I, May 1974—Advanced Accounting I)

8 Fraser and Ross are in partnership as proprietors of the 'Highland Trading Post' general store. The firm's balance sheet at 31 March 1973 was :—

Assets	£	£
Cash at bank		740
Stock		7,425
Trade debtors (*less* bad debt provision of £55)		5,435
Motor vehicles at cost	2,470	
Less: Aggregate depreciation	1,050	
		1,420
Furniture and fittings at cost	567	
Less: Aggregate depreciation	304	
		263
Prepayments—Rates and insurance		68
		15,351

Liabilities:	£	£
Trade creditors		5,390
Fraser—Capital account	5,000	
Current account	1,241	
		6,241
Ross—Capital account	2,000	
Current account	573	
		2,573
Accrued charges—Heat and light	53	
Motor expenses	152	
		205
Provision for income tax 1972/73, second instalment		642
Stocking loans from suppliers		300
		15,351

The cash book for the year ended 31 March 1974 is summarized as follows:—

	£		£
Cash sales	51,653	Purchase ledger payments	55,148
Cash from debtors	26,734	Wages, national insurance, etc.	9,420
Capital paid in by Ross	750	V.A.T. remitted	1,250
		Rates and insurance	893
		Heat and light	426
		Motor expenses	596
		General expenses	212
		Income tax	1,550
		Purchase of car	750
		V.A.T. on expenses	60
Bank lodged	79,137	Bank drawn	70,305
Discount allowed	£672	Discount received	£1,028

Additional information:—

1 In terms of the partnership agreement interest at 5 per cent is allowed on the balance at credit of each partner's capital account at the beginning of the year and all profits and losses are divisible in the ratio Fraser three-fifths and Ross two-fifths.
2 Fraser owns the shop property and the annual rent of £250 is adjusted on his current account.
3 At 31 March 1974 stock at cost amounted to £6,732. Of this, stock costing £170 is considered obsolete and is to be written down to nil.
4 Trade creditors at 31 March 1974 amounted to £5,116 and trade debtors to £4,973. Bad debts of £75 are to be written off but no general provision is required.
5 Interest of 5 per cent per annum on the stocking loan is invoiced annually by the supplier on 31 March, and the amount for the year to 31 March 1974 is included in trade creditors.
6 Wages and national insruance includes drawings for fifty-two weeks of £20 per week by Fraser and £15 per week by Ross.
7 The cost of a Morris car purchasing during the year was £1,100 from which was deducted an allowance of £350 on the trade-in of an Austin. The Austin cost £840 in 1971 and its written down value at 31st March 1973 was £472.
8 Motor vehicles and furniture and fittings are depreciated by the reducing balance method, the former at 25 per cent and the latter at 20 per cent.
9 The 1973/74 income tax liability has been agreed at £1,816 (Fraser £1,056; Ross £760) and the first instalment of £908 has been paid, as has the second instalment, of the 1972/73 liability. Provision should be made in the firm's accounts for the second instalment of the 1973/74 liability.
10 The value added tax liability at 31 March 1974 is calculated as follows:—

	£	£
Output tax for year		5,615
Less: Allowable input tax for year—		
On expenses	60	
On goods for resale	3,972	
		4,032
		1,583
Less: Remitted during year		1,250
V.A.T. due at 31 March 1974		333

Only part of the firm's sales is subject to value added tax at the standard rate.

11 At 31 March 1974 rates and insurance were prepaid by £75 and heat and light and motor expenses accrued at £45 and £123 respectively.

REQUIRED:

Prepare

    1 the trading and profit and loss account of Highland Trading Post for the year ended 31 March 1974;

    2 the balance sheet as that date; and

    3 the partner's capital and current accounts in detail for that year.

(Institute of Chartered Accountants of Scotland, Part I Examination, May 1974—Financial Accounting)

Chapter 10: Accounting for unincorporated businesses (1)

1 Why is it important, when any change occurs in the identitites of the partners in a firm, or in the profit-sharing ratio, to provide for a revaluation of assets? How do alternative methods of dealing with goodwill (without general revaluation) fit into the situation?

2 What advantages are sought by partners who assure one another's lives for the benefit of the firm? Outline the accounting alternatives available.

3 What problems, affecting the accounts, are likely to arise when an unincorporated firm is dissolved, and how should they be dealt with by the accountant?

4 When an unincorporated firm is converted to a private limited company, what problems may arise in dividing up the share capital in the latter, and how might they be resolved? Illustrate with imaginary figures.

5 You have been asked by the Slipshod Shoe Company to prepare a trading and profit and loss account for the year ended 31 March 1969, the first year of the firm's trading as shoe retailers, and the balance sheet as at that date.

It has been ascertained that the partners, Smith and Jones, verbally agreed to commence business on 1 April 1968 and that profits and losses should be shared equally. The capital introduced on that date consisted of £9,000 cash from Smith, which was lodged in bank, and from Jones, shop fittings valued at £800 and stocks of shoes valued at £5,000. On 1 April 1968 they purchased shop premises which cost £7,000.

On 30 June 1968 further shop fittings were purchased for £2,400, the cash being provided by means of a loan from Green with interest at 8 per cent per annum. Subsequently on 1 October 1968 it was decided to assume Green as a partner on the basis that £400 of his loan account should be treated as goodwill and credited equally to Smith and Jones. The remainder of Green's loan is to be credited to his capital account. Green is to receive one-fifth share of the profits and Smith and Jones two-fifths each. Goodwill is not to appear in the balance sheet.

Inadequate records of transactions have been kept but the following summaries of cheque and cash payments are available:

	Cheque payments £	Cash payments £
Purchase of premises	7,000	
Purchase of goods for resale	8,575	975
General expenses	650	350
Local rates from 1 April 1968 to 15 May 1969	270	
Feuduty	40	
Electricity	105	
P.A.Y.E. and graduated pensions	350	
National insurance stamps—staff		325
Purchase of shop fittings	2,400	
Loan interest to Green (less tax, £20)	28	
Stationery and telephone	85	35
Cheques drawn for wages	200	

Examination of the wages book showed that net staff wages of £1,250 had been paid in cash and that the partners had each drawn cash at the agreed rate of £10 per week. The partners paid their national insurance contributions personally. It was also ascertained that after making cash payments the net cash available from sales was lodged in bank. Credit sales were recorded in a day book, the entries being crossed out on payment. The unpaid debts at 31 March 1969 amounted to £1,850, of which £75 was thought to be irrecoverable.

On 31 March 1969 the stock of goods for resale was valued at £6,500, stationery on hand at £20, the balance at credit of the bank account was £782 and cash in the till amounted to £30. There were outstanding creditors of £1,400 for goods, £45 for general expenses and £15 for telephone.

Depreciation on shop fittings should be taken at the rate of 10 per cent per annum.

(Institute of Chartered Accountants of Scotland, Examination Part III September 1969—Advanced Accounting I)

6 The following balances appear at 30 September 1972 in the accounts of Bumble and Corney, the elderly partners in an old established firm dealing in foodstuffs.

	£
Land and buildings (at cost)	12,750
Debtors	8,945
Equipment (at cost)	6,860
Stock	21,375
Depreciation Account (equipment)	5,140
Bad debts reserve	620
Creditors	13,235
Cash	415
Capital Account—Bumble	7,450
—Corney	22,350
Current Account—Bumble	750
—Corney	800

The partners share profits in proportion to their respective capital accounts which have been unchanged since 1965. The business has been managed by Oliver Twist since his appointment in October 1970 at an annual salary of £3,500. Since the appointment of Twist, Bumble and Corney have taken little active part in the business.

Profits available for distribution between the partners have recently been as follows:

		£
Year ended 30 September	1968	3,900
	1969	4,200
	1970	4,900
	1971	1,900
	1972	2,500

The return on capital employed in this type of business is customarily around 15 per cent.

Twist wishes to expand the business and has secured additional outlets for the firm's products which are estimated to increase by £23,000 profits available for distribution, or for meeting financing expenses, but this necessitates investment in a new warehouse. The development envisaged is estimated to cost £100,000 and vehicles will be purchased costing £6,000. This warehouse will, however, provide capacity in excess of business available from these new outlets.

After agreeing the following adjustments with Twist:

a Land and Buildings are to be revalued at £19,750;

b Provision for depreciation of equipment is to be increased by £720

c Bad debts totalling £1,000 are to be written off.

Bumble and Corney have offered Twist the following terms:

either

    i   Twist will be admitted as a partner if he contributes £12,000 cash of which £2,000 is to be a premium to be retained in the business. Bumble, Corney and Twist will share profits and losses in the ratio 1:3:6 recognizing that Twist will be the working partner, but he will not receive a salary;

or ii   Twist may purchase the business and take responsibility for all debtors (as revalued) and creditors in return for £45,000 consideration.

Twist has capital amounting to £15,000 which he is prepared to invest in the business.

A loan from Fagin and Dodger Limited of £100,000 carrying interest at 10 per cent and repayable by equal annual instalments in arrears over 10 years is available to the partnership to finance the development.

Alternatively, Twist can raise from Sykes £150,000 at 12½ per cent interest, repayable by equal annual instalments in arrears over 20 years, provided that he decides to purchase the business and undertake the development.

You are required to:

    i   Prepare estimated balance sheets to reflect the situations if Twist accepts either offer and assuming in each case that the development has taken place.

    ii   State what advice should be given to Twist in respect of each of the offers, giving reasons.

iii State what further information is required in order to advise Twist.

Ignore taxation.

(Institute of Municipal Treasurers and Accountants, Final Examination Part 2, November 1972 —Accountancy 4)

7 Oak, Ash and Beeche were trading in partnership sharing profits and losses 4 : 3 : 3 respectively. The accounts of the firm were made up to 31 December each year.

On 30 June 1969 Oak died.

The partnership deed provided that:

1 Interest was to be credited on capital accounts at 5 per cent p.a. on the balance at the beginning of the year,

2 no interest was to be charged on drawings accounts, and

3. on the death of a partner:

   i goodwill was to be valued at three years' purchase of the average profits of the three years up to the date of death, after deducting interest on capital employed at 8 per cent and a fair remuneration for each of the partners,

   ii the amount due to the deceased partner's estate was to receive interest at 6 per cent p.a. from the date of death until paid,

   iii land and buildings and fixtures and fittings were to be valued by an independent valuer, all the other assets and liabilities to be taken at book value, and

   iv accounts were not to be drawn up to the date of death but the profit or loss of the year in which a partner died was to be apportioned on a time basis.

The balances on the books of the firm at 31 December 1969, subject to final adjustment were:

	£	£
Capital and drawings accounts		
Oak	1,600	10,000
Ash	2,400	5,000
Beeche	2,400	6,000
Land and buildings	8,000	
Fixtures and fittings	1,500	
Stock	12,500	
Debtors	2,000	
Bank	4,000	
Creditors		3,000
Profit of year before charging interest		10,400
	34,400	34,400

You ascertain that:

1 the profits for the earlier years, before charging partners' interest, were:

	£
1966	11,200
1967	12,600
1968	12,000

2 the independent valuations at the date of death were:

	£
Land and buildings	10,000
Fixtures and fittings	1,000

3 any adjustment for goodwill was to be made in the capital accounts, but goodwill was not to be shown as an asset of the firm at 31 December 1969,

4 the land and buildings and fixtures and fittings were to be shown at the valuation figures,

5 Ash and Beeche would share profits equally from the date of death of Oak, and

6 it was agreed that a fair remuneration for the work done by the partners would be £2,500 per annum each and that the capital employed in the business was to be taken as £26,000.

You are required to prepare:

 a Partners' Capital Accounts in columnar form for the year ended 31 December 1969, and

 b Balance Sheet of the firm as on 31 December 1969.

Ignore taxation.

(Institute of Chartered Accountants in England and Wales, Final Examination, Part I, May 1970—Advanced Accounting I)

8 Tap, Die, Nut, Bolt and Screw were trading in partnership sharing profits in the ratio of 3 : 3 : 2 : 1 : 1 respectively.

The firm manufactured specialized components for a big manufacturer and also had a small reconditioning department with a number of customers.

The partnership deed which excluded the rule in Garner *v.* Murray provided *inter alia* that partners were to receive interest on their capital accounts at the rate of 6 per cent p.a., but that no interest was to be paid on current accounts.

Early in 1971 their main customer had a receiver appointed and by mid-March it was obvious that their main business had collapsed. The partners, therefore, agreed to dissolve the partnership on 31 March 1971. It was also agreed that as realization of the assets would take some time the cash available at the end of each month, after paying creditors, should be distributed to the partners in such a way as to ensure that no partner would be called on to repay any part of a distribution he had received.

The trial balance of the firm at 31 March 1971 after ascertaining the net profit for the 9 months ended on that date, but before making any transfers to partners, was:

	£	£
Capital accounts as on 30 June 1970		
Tap		8,000
Die		10,000
Nut		6,000
Bolt		3,000
Screw		5,000
Current accounts		
Tap	3,010	
Die	2,260	
Nut	2,365	
Bolt	1,505	
Screw	1,500	
Freehold land and buildings	8,000	
Plant and machinery	8,500	
Vehicles	2,000	
Loose tools	3,200	
Furniture, fixtures and fittings	2,100	
Stocks, raw materials	6,000	
Stocks, finished goods	2,500	
Debtors	18,000	
Balance at bank	3,380	
Creditors		11,830
Profit for the period		20,490
	64,320	64,320

The following realizations were made and on the last day of each month the cash available for the partners was distributed.

April 1971   Bolt agreed to purchase the reconditioning department for £7,800 made up as follows:

	Price £	Book amount £
Plant and machinery	1,500	1,000
Stocks raw materials	1,000	1,000
Loose tools	1,000	1,200
Furniture, fixtures and fittings	300	200
Vehicles	1,000	700
Goodwill	3,000	—

Bolt paid £4,000 by cheque and it was agreed that the balance was to be treated as a realized debtor in a separate account, to be cleared by set off against distributions due to him in the course of the realization.

Appendix **549**

£3,950 was received from debtors.

£1,600 was received on the sale of the balance of the vehicles.

May 1971 £450 was received from debtors.

£1,000 was received for the remainder of the loose tools.

£4,500 was received for the remainder of the plant and machinery.

£6,200 was received for the remainder of furniture, fixtures, fittings and stocks sold at auction.

£12,500 was received on the completion of the sale of the freehold land and buildings.

You are required to prepare:

a the realization account for the 2 months to 31 May 1971;

b the partners' capital accounts (in columnar form) for the 11 months to 31 May 1971; and

c the computation of the make up of the distributions to partners (in columnar form).

Ignore all forms of taxation and the costs of realization.

(Institute of Chartered Accountants in England and Wales, Final Examination, Part I, November 1971—Advanced Accounting I)

9 Moore, Gate and Place were trading in partnership, sharing profits and losses in the ratio 5, 4 and 3 respectively.

On 31 March 1970 they formed a limited company with an authorized capital of £20,000 in shares of £1 each (to be divided into different classes) to take over the business of the partnership.

The trial balance of the partnership, subject to charging interest on partners' capital accounts, on 31 March 1970 was:

	£	£
Capital accounts as on 31 March 1969		
Moore		6,300
Gate		4,200
Place		2,100
Drawings		
Moore	2,000	
Gate	2,000	
Place	1,500	
Plant and machinery at cost	8,500	
Depreciation of plant and machinery		2,500
Stocks and work in progress	6,420	
Debtors	6,650	
Creditors		8,470
Bank balance	8,830	
Trading profit for the year		12,330
	35,900	35,900

The partnership deed provided for interest to be paid on partners' capital accounts at the rate of 5 per cent p.a. on the balance at the beginning of the year.

You ascertain that:

1 Plant and machinery is to be transferred at its written down value for income tax, which is £6,600.

2 To avoid having to value goodwill, shares in the company are to be issued to the partners, at par, in such numbers and such classes as will give the partners, by reason of their shareholdings alone, the same rights as regards interest on capital and the sharing of profits and losses as they had in the partnership.

3 Before transferring the business the partners wish to draw from the partnership their profits to such an extent that the bank balance is reduced to £5,000. For this purpose sufficient profits of the year are to be retained in profit sharing ratio.

4 All assets and liabilities, except plant and machinery and the bank balance, are to be transferred at their value in the books of the partnership as on 31 March 1970.

You are required to prepare:

a the Profit and Loss Appropriation Account of the partnership for the year ended 31 March 1970,

b the Capital Accounts (in columnar form), showing all the adjustments required to dissolve the partnership,

c your computation of the number of shares of each class to be issued by the company to each of the partners and details of the rights attaching to those shares, and

d the Balance Sheet of the company immediately after acquiring the business of the partnership and issuing the shares.

(Institute of Chartered Accountants in England and Wales, Final Examination, Part I, November 1970—Advanced Accounting I)

10 A, B, and C were partners in Green & Co. sharing capital and profits in the proportions of 2 : 2 : 1. D and E were partners in Land & Co. sharing capital and profits in the proportions of 3 : 2.

On 1 January 1971, the partners of both firms agreed to amalgamate on the following terms:

1 A would retire, and any payments due to him would be made personally by B and C in accordance with their partnership agreement. Similarly any adjustments between B and C would be made personally outside the partnership.

2 The name of the new firm would be Greenland, and the initial capital of £20,000, and the profits/losses would be shared in the ratios: B, C, D and E 3 : 2 : 3 : 2.

3 The partnership to continue for a term of five years, but in the event of the death of any partner, his estate would be entitled to an immediate payment of capital to the extent of £1,000 or any other larger amount which the surviving partners chose to make. The balance of capital to be repaid over five years with interest at 6 per cent p.a. The current account balance to be paid at the end of one year after the date of death.

The balance sheets at 31 December 1970 of Green & Co. and Land & Co. were as follows:

		Green & Co.			Land & Co.	
		£	£		£	£
Capital accounts			10,000			6,000
Current accounts	A	900		D	600	
	B	500		E	400	
	C	100			—	
		—				1,000
			1,500			
			11,500			7,000
Represented by:						
Goodwill			1,000			600
Furniture, etc. at book value			1,000			100
Work in progress			1,000			100
Debtors			8,000			6,000
Cash			1,200			600
			12,200			7,400
Less Accrued expenses			700			400
			11,500			7,000

The following points are relevant:

1 Goodwill in the new firm is to be valued at £5,000.

2 Furniture, etc. is to be taken over at £500 from each of the old firms.

3 Debtors are taken over at agreed figures of £7,000 and £5,000 respectively and work in progress is to be valued at 15 per cent of the debtors taken over. The accrued expenses are taken over in full.

4 Any balance of capital is to be provided in cash.

5 Interest on capital is to be 6 per cent p.a.

6 Out of profits, there is to be a prior charge for salaries at the rate of £3,000 per annum for each partner.

7 Each partner drew against his share of the profit £200 on the last day of each month and an amount equal to 10 per cent of his capital in two equal instalments on 30 June and 31 December. No other cash drawings were made.

8 D died suddenly on 1 July 1971. No capital adjustments were made between the surviving partners and profits were shared in the original ratios. A capital payment of £2,500 was made immediately to his widow, but no other amounts were paid in 1971.

9 Due to a personal misfortune, C applied to the firm for a loan of £4,000 on 1 April 1971. This was agreed to with interest at 8 per cent p.a. and the loan was repaid on 30 September 1971. In addition he was to receive no credit for interest on his capital

during the period of the loan.

10 Profits of Greenland for the year 1971 were £19,640.

You are required to prepare:

a the balance sheet of Greenland on 1 January 1971, and

b the detailed current accounts of the partners in Greenland at 31 December 1971.

(Institute of Chartered Accountants in England and Wales, Final Examination, Part II, May 1972—Advanced Accounting II)

Chapter 11: Accounting for limited liability companies (1)

1 Analyse the advantages and disadvantages of converting a partnership to a private limited company. How satisfactory are the alternative courses of action open to the partners in the original firm?

2 Write a short explanation of each of the following methods by which a company may obtain a Stock Exchange quotation, setting out any material advantages or disadvantages in each case:

i exchange of shares for shares in a quoted company.

ii a Stock Exchange placing.

iii an issue to the public.

iv an offer for sale.

v an offer for sale by tender.

vi an introduction.

(Institute of Chartered Accountants of Scotland, Examination Part V, April 1969—Advanced Accounting II)

3 'Messrs Old & Wise are arranging a placing of 500,000 ordinary shares of 10p each in Newcoma Ltd at 40p a share.'

'Polo Securities Ltd offer for sale by tender 1,275,000 ordinary shares of 25p each in Chukka Ltd at a minimum price of 80p a share.'

REQUIRED:

In connection with the two press extracts, state:

1 What you understand by the term 'placing'.

2 What you consider to be the business of Messrs Old & Wise.

3 What you understand by the term 'tender'.

4 What you understand by the term 'striking price' and how it is fixed.

(Institute of Chartered Accountants of Scotland, Examination Part V, September 1971—Advanced Accounting II)

4 Trace the connection between limited liability and the variety of securities which a limited company is able to issue, as compared with an unincorporated business. Illustrate by reference to *four* of the types of company security commonly issued.

5 A. Penalty, I. Fowell and A. Header have been in partnership for a number of years as garage proprietors, trading under the title of Fairdeal Autos. Profits have been shared as follows:

Penalty	two fifths
Fowell	two fifths
Header	one fifth

No interest was allowed on capital.

The balance sheet of the firm as at 30 June 1971 was as follows:

	Cost £	Depreciation £	Net £
Heritable property	20,000	–	20,000
Plant and machinery	6,000	1,400	4,600
Motor vehicles	6,000	4,000	2,000
	32,000	5,400	26,600
Current assets		34,000	
Less: Current liabilities		29,000	
			5,000
			31,600
Representing—			
Capital accounts			
Penalty		14,000	
Fowell		9,600	
Header		8,000	
			31,600

On 1 January 1972 a limited company, Fairdeal Autos Ltd., was formed with authorized share capital of £40,000 in shares of £1 each. On the same date the whole business of the partnership, including all assets less liabilities, was transferred to the limited company. Fixed assets were transferred at the following values:

	£
Heritable property	30,000
Plant and machinery	2,500
Motor vehicles	1,600

Current assets and current liabilities were transferred at book values.

Each partner was allotted 10,000 shares in the limited company at par, the calls being charged against their capital accounts. A further 5,000 shares were issued for cash at £1.10 per share to Mr. A Gunn, who had been car sales manager with the firm for a number of years. The accounts of the limited company are to be made up as at 30 June each year. No accounts were made up at the date of transfer of the business.

The three partners of the original firm together with Mr Gunn were appointed directors of the limited company. Their annual salaries from 1 January 1972 were as follows:

	£
Penalty	5,000
Fowell	5,000
Header	4,000
Gunn	2,000

In addition, Mr. Gunn is to receive commission from 1 January 1972 of 10 per cent on the net profits after charging all expenses except taxation and commission. It is also agreed that Messrs. Penalty, Fowell and Header are to receive interest at 10 per cent per annum on the balances due to them after the transfer of the business, these accounts remaining as loans to the company.

All transactions from 1 July 1971 were continued in the same general ledger and a summarized trial balance of the ledger at 30th June 1972 was as follows:

	£	£
Heritable property at cost (note 2)	20,000	
Plant and machinery at ner book value (notes 1 and 2)	6,000	
Motor vehicles at net book value (note 2)	2,000	
Current assets	49,500	
Current liabilities		18,000
Gunn (notes 3 and 5)		5,800
Penalty ⎫		12,000
Fowell ⎬ (notes 4 and 5)		8,000
Header ⎭		5,700
Profit and loss accounts (notes 6 and 7)		28,000
	77,500	77,500

Notes:

1 *Plant and machinery:* New equipment costing £1,400 was purchased on 1 February 1972. A piece of equipment included in the 31 December 1971 valuation at £600 was sold to Mr Gunn on 1 April 1972 for £500, the proceeds being credited to Mr Gunn's account in the ledger.

2 *Depreciation:* From 1 January 1972 depreciation on fixed assets is to be computed on the straight line basis in each month, no charge being made in respect of new assets in the month of purchase. It is to be calculated at the following annual rates:

Heritable property	nil
Plant and machinery	10%
Motor vehicles	25%

3 *Gunn:* This balance represents the cash received on the issue of the shares and sale of the equipment, less company formation expenses of £200.

4 *Penalty; Fowell; Header:* These balances represent the partners' capital accounts, less drawings up to 31 December 1971.

5 *Gunn; Penalty; Fowell; Header:* The directors have not drawn any part of their salaries, interest or commission.

6 *Profit and loss account:* This balance represents the trading profit for the year to 30 June 1972 before charging depreciation (including loss on sale of fixed assets), loan interest, commission or director's remuneration. The trading profit is deemed to accrue evenly over the year.

7 *Dividend:* You are informed that the directors propose a dividend of 10 per cent actual in respect of the six months trading, for which no provision has yet been made.

REQUIRED:

Prepare—

1 A statement showing the balances due at 31 December 1971 to Penalty, Fowell and Header.

2 The draft balance sheet of the limited company as at 30 June 1972.

NOTE:

All calculations should be made to the nearest £. Ignore taxation.

(Institute of Chartered Accountants of Scotland, Part III Examination, September 1973—Advanced Accounting I).

6 Jupiter Ltd, resolved to raise further capital by an issue to the public of 300,000 ordinary shares of £1 each. The issue price was 25/-, payable as to 15/- on application on 31 July 1970, and the balance on 31 October 1970.

Mars Ltd, a finance company agreed to underwrite 50 per cent of the issue. The underwriting contract provided for a commission of 5 per cent, and an overriding commission of 1 per cent. Mars Ltd made an agreement with Pluto Ltd, another finance company, for the latter to sub-underwrite 5 per cent of the whole issue at a commission of 5 per cent.

The public subscribed for, and were allotted, 200,000 shares. Mars Ltd paid over to Jupiter Ltd the application moneys due on the shares it had taken up under the underwriting agreement and Pluto Ltd settled its indebtedness to Mars Ltd for the shares sub-underwritten.

All transactions including payment and receipt of all commissions were completed by 31 August 1970. The first and final call was paid on the relevant date.

Mars Ltd had further dealings in the shares of Jupiter Ltd, as follows:
1970
September 1 Purchased and paid for 20,000 shares at 15/- per share.
September 20 Sold and received payment for 40,000 shares at 16/- per share.
November 1 Granted a call option on 25,000 shares to Venus Ltd, at 22/- per share on or before 31 January 1971, in consideration of a commission of 1 per cent.

The market value of the shares in Jupiter Ltd was £1 each as at 30 November 1970, being the date when Mars Ltd closed its books for the year. Expenses incurred by Mars Ltd in buying and selling shares in Jupiter amounts to £450 at the year end. Ignore brokerage charges.

You are required to record the foregoing transactions in the Underwriting and Investment Account re shares in Jupiter Ltd, in the books of Mars Ltd, separating the account for the month of August from the account for the other three months.

(Association of Certified and Corporate Accountants, Examination Section IV, December 1970—Advanced Accounting)

7 H Company Limited had an authorized capital of 10,000 ordinary shares of £1 each. Its balance sheet as at 31 December 1967 was as follows:

H Company Limited

	£		£
Issued capital	10,000	Freehold buildings	30,000
Reserves	90,000	Plant and equipment	63,000
Creditors	23,000	Stock	31,000
Bank overdraft	35,000	Debtors	34,000
	£158,000		£158,000

In order that finance for expansion could be obtained more readily, the management decided to obtain a stock exchange quotation and make a share offer to the public. To achieve this the following steps were taken:
1 The freehold buildings were revalued at £50,000.
2 The authorized share capital was increased to £200,000 and classified into ordinary shares with a nominal value of five shillings each.
3 Existing members' shareholdings were sub-divided in accordance with the above. A bonus issue of 13 shares for every two shares already held was then made.
4 In exchange for the issue of 16,000 ordinary shares and £20,000 7 per cent debentures, the following assets and liabilities of P Limited were acquired:

	£	£
Freehold buildings	5,000	
Plant and equipment	22,000	
Stock	9,000	
Debtors	13,000	
Creditors		7,000
Bank overdraft		15,000

5 Two hundred thousand shares were offered to the public by tender. The minimum price to be offered was ten shillings per share and the full amount was due on application.
Applications were received for the following:

60,000 shares at 10s. each
120,000 shares at 12s. each
60,000 shares at 14s. each
60,000 shares at 15s. each

It was decided to fix the allotment price at 12s. per share and allotments were made to those tendering at or above this price on the basis of five shares for every six shares applied for. Surplus application money was returned.
6 The costs incurred amounted to £20,000.
You are required to show:
a the journal entries, including those for cash, covering all of these transactions;
b the final balance sheet as it appeared after the completion of the allotment and refund of surplus moneys.

(Trading items are to be assumed to remain unchanged.)
(Institute of Cost and Works Accountants, Part III Examination, December 1968—Financial Accountancy (First Paper)

8 You have been asked to act as reporting accountant for the purposes of a prospectus in connection with an issue of shares by a company of which you are not the auditor.

State how you would deal with the following matters which have arisen in the course of your investigation and give your reasons for the action you recommend:

    i the auditors of the company were not satisfied that the value attributed to work in progress, amounting to £69,000 at 31 December 1964, was correct. They, therefore, qualified their audit reports to the extent that they were unable to express an opinion as to whether the balance sheet at 31 December 1964, or the profit and loss accounts for the calendar years 1964 and 1965 showed a true and fair view respectively of the company's state of affairs and profits.

    ii the present directors all have contracts of service with the company and their remuneration amounting to £18,000, which has not changed for the last two years, will continue at the same figure in future.

    iii within the period covered by your report, members of the family controlling the company deposited money with the company from time to time in order that the company should not exceed the overdraft limit fixed by the bank. In certain cases these deposits have borne interest at 1 per cent above bank rate and in other cases have been interest free. The bank has recently raised the overdraft limit in order that the company should have sufficient working capital available.

    iv it has not been the company's policy to take credit in the accounts for investment grants receivable, but only to include them when actually received. The amounts of the estimated investment grants receivable have been noted on the accounts for the years ended 31 December 1967 and 1968 at £9,700 and £14,100 respectively.

    v a plant register has been maintained throughout the life of the company. Up to and including the year ended 31 December 1966, plant was depreciated by the reducing balance method. In respect of the year ended 31 December 1967, it was decided that this basis was not realistic and that in future plant would be depreciated by the straight line method over five years, as the plant had only a nominal scrap value after that time. In the year to 31 December 1967, additional depreciation was provided to reduce all existing plant to a net book value calculated on the new basis.

(Institute of Chartered Accountants of Scotland, Examination Part V, September 1969—Advanced Accounting II)

9 Arrangements are being made for Machine Ltd, a public company which commenced trading on 1 January 1966, to make a further issue of shares to the public, for cash. A firm of chartered accountants, Parts & Co., have been instructed to carry out the necessary investigation and to submit the accountants' report for inclusion in the prospectus.

The following information was obtained by the accountants:

    1 The audited accounts disclosed:

Year ended 31 December	Turnover £	Profit before depreciation and taxation £	Depreciation £	Issued share capital £	Dividend rate per cent %
1966	1,700,000	160,000	28,000	800,000	8
1967	2,200,000	269,000	37,000	800,000	10
1968	3,100,000	397,000	42,000	800,000	14
1969	3,300,000	381,000	44,000	800,000	14
1970	3,800,000	440,000	55,000	800,000	16

The summarized balance sheet as on 31 December 1970 showed:

	£	£
Fixed assets:		
Freehold land and buildings, at cost		200,000
Plant and machinery, at cost	300,000	
Less aggregate depreciation	130,000	
		170,000
		370,000
Current assets:		
Stock (at the lower of cost or net realizable value)	380,000	
Debtors	540,000	
Quoted investments, at cost (market value, £120,000)	80,000	
Balance at bank	40,000	
	1,040,000	
Less Current liabilities	110,000	
		930,000
		1,300,000
		£
Financed by:		
Share capital: 800,000 ordinary shares of £1 each		800,000
Reserves		400,000
		1,200,000
6% Debenture (redeemable 1 February 1971)		100,000
		1,300,000

2 The stock sheets for 1966 and 1967 had been destroyed, but an assurance was received from the auditors that stocks had always been properly taken and consistently valued. However, owing to errors occurring in the cost records, the stock at 31 December 1970 was valued at 5 per cent less than its true value, and furthermore the stock at 31 December 1969 (£441,000) at 5 per cent more than its true value.

3 The depreciation charge in 1967 included an exceptional write off of £5,000 in respect of the anticipated obsolescence of some process plant, which obsolescence in the event did not occur. This exceptional write off was not subsequently written back. Otherwise, depreciation on plant and machinery was provided throughout at 10 per cent per annum, on cost, which is considered reasonable in the light of the information available about the estimated useful life of the plant.

4 In 1968 the company closed down its wholesaling department which had previously 'broken even', suffering a loss on closure of £15,000. The turnover of this department amounted to £80,000 in 1966, £90,000 in 1967 and £40,000 in 1968. No fixed assets were employed in this department.

5 On 31 December 1970, the freehold land and buildings were professionally valued at £325,000.

6 On 1 February 1971 the debentures, which had been issued on the inception of the company, were redeemed, from the sale of one of the investments. Based on its sale price, this investment had given a dividend yield of 4 per cent in 1970 and 3 per cent in every earlier year.

7 The directors' emoluments were calculated on the basis of 10 per cent of the profits before taxation as shown by the audited accounts, after deducting therefrom the emoluments.

As from 1 January 1971 it had been agreed that in addition a director's fee of £1,000 would be paid to each of the four directors, but that these fees should not be deducted in arriving at the basic emoluments.

8 Turnover is the net aggregate amount receivable for goods supplied and services rendered.
You are required to prepare the accountants' report to be included in the prospectus.

Marks will be awarded for the presentation and form of the answer.

Ignore taxation.

(Institute of Chartered Accountants in England and Wales, Final Examination, Part II, November 1971—Advanced Accounting II)

10 You have been appointed to act as joint reporting accountant, with the company's auditors, in connection with the public flotation of Alpha Ltd. The last audited accounts of the company were drawn up to 31 March 1974 and you have obtained the following information about the company.

1 Information extracted from the audited accounts:

Years ended 31 March	1970 £000's	1971 £000's	1972 £000's	1973 £000's	1974 £000's
Turnover	1,350	1,456	1,863	2,251	2,930
Cost of sales	1,319	1,392	1,734	2,064	2,614
Profit before taxation	31	64	129	187	316
Cost of sales above includes the following:					
Depreciation	19	25	25	28	30
Interest on bank overdraft	13	13	12	10	4
Interest on long term loans	20	21	24	20	15
Investment grant release/(credit)	(3)	(5)	(5)	(6)	(7)
Loss/(profit) on sale of fixed assets	1	(2)	(20)	—	—
Directors' remuneration	10	10	11	12	13
Compensation paid to director for loss of office	—	15	—	—	—

2 Turnover represents the sales value of goods delivered to customers during the year.

3 Adequate records of stock and work in progress have been retained to enable you to satisfy yourself about the verification and valuation at each accounting date throughout the period under review. The basis was said to be the lower of cost and net realizable value. At 31 March 1974 'cost' consisted of all direct material and labour, together with the relevant factory overheads incurred in bringing the goods to their current state under normal operating conditions. However at accounting dates prior to 31 March 1974 'cost' consisted of only direct material and labour. The value of the stock and work in progress, calculated on the basis used at 31 March 1974, as compared with the value used in the audited accounts, is set out in the table below:

At 31 March	1969 £000's	1970 £000's	1971 £000's	1972 £000's	1973 £000's	1974 £000's
Value on basis used at 31 March 1974	120	125	145	170	200	250
Value in audited accounts	110	113	130	154	178	250

4 Depreciation is calculated on the straight line method to write off the book value of the fixed assets over their expected useful lives. The main rates are as follows:

Freehold buildings	2%
Service plant	7½%
Production plant	10%
Motor vehicles	20%

In the year ended 31 March 1967 production plant costing £150,000 was purchased and the cost was written off against the profit on a sale of a building in the same year. This plant is expected to last for the normal life of such plant of 10 years.

5 Investment grants are credited to the profit and loss account over the expected useful lives of the relevant assets.

6 Freehold land and buildings have been revalued at 31 March 1974 by X & Co., chartered surveyors, at £850,000, which amount was incorporated in the accounts at 31 March 1974. The property, which was purchased in 1967, was previously stated in the accounts at its cost of £350,000. The depreciation charge in future years will be increased by about £5,000.

7 Under new service agreements the total remuneration of the directors of the company in the year ending 31 March 1975 will be £17,000

8 At 31 March 1974 quoted investments, which had a market value at that date of £67,000, were shown in the balance sheet as cost of £52,000. These investments have subsequently been sold for £68,000.

9 No dividends have been paid during the five years ended 31 March 1974.

REQUIRED:

Prepare, for inclusion in the prospectus, the introductory paragraphs of the accountant's report, together with those sections dealing with the accounting policies and profits.

NOTE:

1 To reduce the amount of your calculations, information has not been given on the taxation of the company, but the draft should make appropriate provision for the relevant figures and comments to be included at a later stage.

2 The solution should show clearly how the figures in the report have been calculated.

(Institute of Chartered Accountants of Scotland, Part II Examination, April 1974—Interpretation of Accounts)

Chapter 12: Accounting for limited liability companies (2)

1 Explain the importance of distinguishing accurately between reserves and provisions in the accounts of a limited company. For what purposes should provisions be made, and what limits are normally set to the recognition in this way of items of the relevant genres?

2 In the Balance Sheet of B. Keen Ltd on 31 December 1971, the following item appears:

	£
Deferred taxation	93,000

A note on the **Balance Sheet** reads:

'Deferred taxation represents the deferred liability due to accelerated capital allowances.'

You are required to explain briefly the purpose of such an account, and the method of its computation. You may make any assumptions you think necessary for the purpose of illustration.

(Institute of Chartered Accountants in England and Wales, Final Examination, Part I, May 1972—Advanced Accounting I)

3 In deciding the dividend policy of a public company having a Stock Exchange quotation for its shares, outline the considerations which should be taken into account by the directors.

(Association of Certified and Corporate Accountants, Examination Section V, December 1970—Advanced Accounting)

4 Define (so-called) 'fictitious assets' in the accounts of a company, and outline the most rational methods of amortizing them (or not, as the case may be) in the years following the dates at which such items arise.

5 The summarized balance sheet of Amos Ltd. as on 30 June 1972 showed:

Share capital:	
8% Redeemable preference shares of £1 each	100,000
Ordinary shares of £1 each	150,000
8% Debentures	70,000
Revenue Reserves	400,000
	£720,000
represented by:	
Net assets	£720,000

The redeemable preference shares were due for redemption on 31 August 1972, and were duly paid off.

The company is permitted to redeem the debentures at any time at a premium of 10 per cent, and did so on 30 September 1972.

The company was in a reasonably liquid position, but to assist in providing funds for the redemption of the redeemable preference shares, a rights issue of ordinary shares was made. 20,000 ordinary shares were issued for cash at a premium of £2 per share, £1.25 payable on application on 15 July 1972 and the balance on allotment on 31 July 1972. All cash due was received on the due dates.

During the three months ended 30 September 1972, the company traded at a profit of £25,000.

You are required:

a To give the journal entries (including cash transactions) showing the relevant entries in respect of the above.

b To prepare a summarized balance sheet of Amos Ltd. as on 30 September 1972.

(Institute of Chartered Accountants in England and Wales, Final Examination, Part II, November 1972—Advanced Accounting II)

6 A. Miller is a sole trader and his summarized Balance Sheet on 31 December 1969 is as follows:

	£		£	£
Capital account	620	Lease of premises		1,000
Loan from brother	1,000	Furniture, at cost	1,000	
Creditors	3,200	*Less* depreciation	750	
Bank overdraft	900			250
		Stocks		4,000
		Debtors		420
		Cash in hand		50
	5,720			5,720

On 1 January 1970 a company A. Miller Ltd was incorporated to take over the business of A. Miller on that date on the following terms:

1 The company to take over all the assets of the business at book values, subject to adjustments set out below and to assume responsibility for the bank overdraft.

2 A. Miller to settle personally all loans and creditors.

3 It was decided that excessive depreciation had been provided on furniture and that the value should be taken as 50 per cent of cost.

4 It was decided that stocks should be written down by $12\frac{1}{2}$ per cent and that debtors included bad debts totalling £70.

5 A. Miller to have the consideration due to him settled by the issue of 1,000 ordinary shares of £1 each at par (out of a nominal capital of 2,000 ordinary shares of £1 each) and the balance paid to him in cash.

6 Formation expenses of the company amounted to £100 and had not been paid by 1 January 1970.

Friends of A. Miller agreed to subscribe for the remainder of the shares of the company and to provide a further £4,000 capital, secured by the issue to them of an equivalent amount of 8 per cent Redeemable Debentures 1980/84. All these monies were received and the amount due to A. Miller was paid to him on 1 January 1970.

You are required:

    a to show the opening journal entries of A. Miller Ltd, and

    b to prepare a summarized balance sheet of the company as on 1 January 1970.

(Institute of Chartered Accountants in England and Wales, Final Examination, Part II, May 1970—Advanced Accounting II)

7 S Ltd. is a manufacturing company. At the 31 December 1971, the following items were included in the Trial Balance:

	£
Sales	739
Purchases of raw materials	365
Carriage outwards	8
Wages and salaries (A)	243
Rates and insurance (A)	18
Sundry expenses (A)	46
Stock, 1 January 1971:	
Raw materials at cost	69
Finished goods	30
Motor vehicle expenses (A)	24
Fixed assets (all at cost)	
Factory Premises	200
Plant and Machinery	50
Motor vehicles (A)	12
Provision for depreciation, 1 January 1971:	
Factory Premises	28
Plant and Machinery	18
Motor vehicles (A)	5
Provision for doubtful debts	3
Provision for damages	15
Taxation payable 1 January 1972	40
Undistributed profits 1 January 1971	35

The following additional information is available:

1 Stock at 31 December 1971 was as follows:

	£
Raw materials at cost	82
Finished goods	35

2 Provision is to be made for depreciation on the plant and machinery and motor vehicles at 10 per cent and 25 per cent respectively, based on cost. No depreciation is to be provided for on the factory premises.

3 Items with A shown in brackets after the amount involved relate two-thirds to the factory, and one-third to administration.

4 The provision for doubtful debts is to be increased to £6.

5 The amount for wages and salaries includes the following salaries in respect of directors:

	£
T (Managing Director)	15
P (Chairman)	6
F (Sales Director)	8
G (Financial Director)	6

No fees are paid to directors.

6 The provision for damages relates to an amount awarded to a workman in respect of industrial injuries. The company has appealed against the award, but the matter has not yet been settled.

7 Sundry expenses include:

	£
Consultancy report on business	2
Auditor's fee and expenses	1
Hire of plant	3
Legal expenses—proposed acquisition of new premises	1

8 A valuation of the factory premises showed a current value of £240. This increase in value is to be incorporated into the accounts. No depreciation is to be written off in future.

9 Taxation payable on the current year's profits is estimated at £13.

10 Proposed dividends are £3 for preference shares, and £20 for ordinary shares. (Net amount for Irish candidates. Gross amount for all other candidates.)

11 All figures provided in the question are in thousands of pounds.

You are required to prepare in vertical statement form:

a The Manufacturing, Trading and Profit and Loss Accounts (including appropriation section) for the year ended 31 December 1971.

b The Published Profit and Loss Account for the same period.

Note: Particular attention should be paid to layout and presentation.

(Association of Certified Accountants, Examination Section IV, December 1972—Advanced Accounting)

8 On 1 April 1971 Col View Limited was formed, with an authorized share capital of 75,000 ordinary shares of £1 each, to take over and expand the activities of JX and Sons, a television retail business.

Using the information given you are required to prepare:

a the journal entries, including cash transactions, relating to the formation of the company;

b the provision for maintenance costs account;

c a statement of closing stock valuation;

d the operating results of the company for the eighteen months ended 30 September 1972, analysed under cash sales, hire-purchase sales and rental;

e the balance sheet of the company as at 30 September 1972.

The assets taken over from JX and Sons consisted of:

100 new television sets which had cost £150 each, 30 of which still had to be paid for, three freehold shops valued at £25,000;

fixtures and fittings valued at £2,000; and

outstanding debts for cash sales to account customers of £800.

Payment for these assets and liabilities was made partly by the issue of 30,000 ordinary shares at par, and the balance out of £50,000 cash raised by the issue of ordinary shares to friends of JX at a premium of £1.50 per share. These shares were duly allotted and paid for on 2 April 1971.

Company formation costs amounted to £3,000.

During the first eighteen months of the company's trading ended 30 September 1972, the following transactions took place, all of which related to the same model of set as originally taken over, with the purchase price remaining at £150 each.

1   500 sets were sold on a cash sale basis, the selling price being fixed to give a gross profit of 25 per cent on selling price.

2   1,500 sets were sold under hire-purchase agreements, the terms of which were an initial deposit of 20 per cent of the hire-purchase sales price, followed by four equal half-yearly instalments, the first being due six months after the payment of the deposit.

The hire-purchase sales price consisted of the sales cash price plus a finance charge of 20 per cent of the original cost price.

All instalments were received on the dates they became due.

The number of instalments received were for six months ended:

31 March 1972	300
30 September 1972	700

In calculating profits on hire-purchase sales the following policy was adopted:

i   credit for the gross profit, as related to the cash sales price, taken in the proportion that cash received bears to total hire-purchase sales price;

ii   credit for the financing charge taken on receipt of:

first instalment	8%
second instalment	5%
third instalment	4%
fourth instalment	3%
	20% of original cost price

3   On 1 July 1971, 300 sets were rented to the owner of a block of flats on a four year rental agreement at an annual rent of £150 each for the first year, reducing to £100 for the second year and £75 for each of the last two years. Rental payments were due quarterly in arrear and were received on time. It was estimated that over the four year period the cost of maintaining each set, including a replacement service, would average £50 per set and that at the end of the agreement the sets would have no value. During the period payments for maintenance costs amounted to £420. It was agreed that sets were to be depreciated evenly over the four year period and that credit be taken for rents as they became due.

4   On 30 September 1972 there were 40 sets in stock. Five of these had been used as temporary replacements and were valued at £125 each instead of the cost price of £150 each.

5   The following payments had been made during the period:

	£
Supplier of television sets	315,000
Salaries	6,600
Administration and delivery costs	2,700

There were no accruals of overhead costs.

(Institute of Cost and Management Accountants, Part III Examination, November 1972—Accountancy 3)

9 Orange Grove (Estates) Ltd was formed in London in 1965, and purchased freehold land on a Mediterranean shore for the purpose of creating a highly developed holiday centre and retirement estate. The area of land purchased consisted of 4,000 acres, out of which a plot of 20 acres was allocated as a sports and entertainment arena, whilst the remaining land was to be offered for sale at £500 an acre for luxury bungalow development.

At 30 April 1969, the position of the company was as follows:

	£	£		£	£
Authorized capital		1,300,000	Fixed assets: Entertainment Area including land and fittings		
Issued and fully paid £1 shares			at cost	1,511,000	
9% Redeemable preference shares		150,000	*Less* depreciation	25,000	
Ordinary shares		900,000			1,486,000
		1,050,000	Debenture redemption		
Balance of unappro-priated profit b/f	•	320,000	fund investments, at cost (Market value £250,000)		230,000
		1,370,000	Current assets:		
7% Debentures		600,000	Freehold land (2,000 acres) unsold, at		
Debenture redemption fund		230,000	cost	400,000	
Current liabilities:			Arena stocks	25,000	
Trade creditors	6,000		Arena debtors	4,400	
Proposed ordinary dividend	90,000		Balance at bank	150,600	
		96,000			580,000
		£2,296,000			£2,296,000

The following transactions took place in the year to 30 April 1970:

1 On 1 July 1969, to be effective from 1 May 1969, the company sold the entertainment arena to Sunset Enterprises Ltd, for £2,100,000, together with the Arena stocks and debtors at the balance sheet figures. Cash settlement was made on 20 July 1969.

2 The preference shares were redeemed on 30 June 1969, within the terms of the original issue, at a premium of 10 per cent, to be in lieu of any accrued dividend. The premium on redemption is to be written off to capital reserve.

3 On 1 July 1969, the proposed ordinary dividend was paid.

4 On 31 October 1969, the 7 per cent debentures were redeemed at 104, together with six months accrued interest. The premium on redemption is to be written off to capital reserve. The debenture redemption fund had been created out of profits.

5 On 1 November 1969, the company made a bonus share issue to ordinary shareholders of one fully paid ordinary share for every three ordinary shares held on that date. The Capital Reserve arising from the realization of fixed assets was used for this purpose.

6 During the course of the year 400 acres of land were sold at £500 an acre.

7 During the year the trade creditors at 1 May 1969 were paid off, and administration expenses of £15,000 were incurred, of which £7,000 was unpaid at 30 April 1970.

8 Income from investments (Market Value—31 October 1969 £260,000) amounted to £9,000.

You are required to prepare, in respect of Orange Grove (Estates) Ltd, for the year to 30 April 1970:

  a a Bank Account,
  b a Profit and Loss and Appropriation Account, and
  c a Balance Sheet as on the above date.

Show all your workings. Ignore Taxation.

(Association of Certified and Corporate Accountants, Examination Section III, June 1970—Advanced Accounting)

10 Units Ltd produces and installs, to order, purpose-built fittings and furniture for ships, aircraft, etc. The company has prepared its draft accounts for the year 1969, and the following are these accounts in summarized form together with the comparative figures for 1968, taken from the final accounts for that year.

	£	£	£	£
Share capital:				
100,000 shares of £1		100,000		100,000
Profit and loss account		138,000		120,000
		238,000		220,000
Fixed assets:				
Freehold factory	80,000		80,000	
Plant and machinery	44,000		40,000	
Fixtures and fittings	36,000		30,000	
		160,000		150,000
Current assets:				
Stocks	33,000		22,000	
Work in progress	120,000		100,000	
Debtors	100,000		90,000	
	253,000		212,000	
Less Creditors	(75,000)		(72,000)	
Bank-overdrawn	(100,000)		(70,000)	
		78,000		70,000
		238,000		220,000

Manufacturing, Trading and Profit and Loss Accounts

	1969		1968	
	£	£	£	£
Sales		600,000		500,000
Purchases	174,000		150,000	
Factory and site labour	258,000		200,000	
Factory overheads	30,000		25,000	
Administrative costs (including depreciation of fixtures and fittings £4,000)	66,000		50,000	
Selling costs	42,000		20,000	
Financial costs	12,000		5,000	
		582,000		450,000
Net profit		18,000		50,000

N.B. Taxation has been ignored.

Soon after December 1969 a potential purchaser of the entire share capital caused an investigation to be carried out into the accounts. It was ascertained:

1 Work in progress had always been valued at selling price, being the proportion of the selling price of each order based on the completed part at the Balance Sheet date. The work in progress was carried forward on the sales account.

2 Stocks were valued at the purchase price with the addition of 10 per cent to allow for the overhead costs of the buying office.

3 No provision had been made for doubtful debts. It was considered that at both 31 December 1968 and 1969 10 per cent of the debtors were likely to prove to be irrecoverable.

4 Depreciation was written off on the reducing balance method on the balance at each December at the rate of $12\frac{1}{2}$ per cent for plant and machinery and 10 per cent for fixtures and fittings. It was further ascertained, with regard to fixtures and fittings, that those produced by the company itself were capitalized at a figure representing the notional selling price to an outside customer including an allowance for profit; an amount equivalent to that capitalized being credited to sales. Of the £30,000 shown in the balance sheet, as on December 1968, £20,000 represented items made by the company. The additions of £10,000 in 1969 were all company produced.

Following discussion, the directors agreed to redraft the 1969 accounts with the following changes in the bases of accounting:

1 Work in progress. Eliminating all overhead expenses except factory and selling costs (commission is paid only on orders received).

2 Stocks. Eliminating the buying on-cost.

3 Debtors. Providing for doubtful debts at the suggested rate.

4 Fixtures and fittings. Eliminating the allowances for profit, and selling and financial costs. It was agreed that the proportionate level of overheads shown by the accounts to 31 December 1968 were representative of the earlier years when these items had been capitalized.

It was also agreed, so that the 1969 accounts would show a true and fair view of the year's profits, that the effect of the agreed changes in accounting on the opening figures at 1 January 1969 would be shown as prior year adjustments to the reserves at that date.

You are required to re-draft the 1969 accounts, incorporating the agreed changes in the accounting bases.

N.B. Ignore taxation. Comparative figures are not required.

(Institute of Chartered Accountants in England and Wales, Final Examination, Part II, November 1970—Advanced Accounting II)

Chapter 13: Capital structure of a limited liability company

1 'When the amount of ordinary capital is small in relation to preference capital and long-term loans, the capital structure is said to be highly geared, and the effect of this is that the equity capital is acutely responsive to fluctuations in profits.'

(Certified Accountants Journal, July/August 1971)

You are required to

    a comment on the above statement with the aid of suitable illustrations, and

    b report on capital and income gearing of B Ltd, as shown below.

B Ltd. Capital Structure (all issued) 31 December 1971

	£
Ordinary Share Capital (£1 units)	50,000
Undistributed profits	100,000
5% Preference Share Capital (£1 units)	50,000
6% Debentures	80,000

Future profits before interest and taxation are expected to be in region of £50,000.

Note: Irish candidates should base their answers on their current system of company taxation. All other candidates should assume a corporation tax rate of [52%].

(Association of Certified Accountants, Examination Section IV, December 1972—Advanced Accounting) (adapted)

2 Preference shares are commonly thought to be outmoded as a method of corporate finance at the present time.

    You are required to:

    a state the reasons for this decline in favour; and

    b state the fiscal or other reasons which might sometimes justify raising finance by issues of this type of share by

      i a quoted public company; and   **ii** a director-controlled private company.

    Numerical illustrations should be given where appropriate.

(Association of Certified Accountants, Examination Section V, December 1971—Advanced Accounting)

3 You are required to explain to your client Mr D., in a letter in which examples should be given, the different circumstances which govern the selection of, and the main principles applied in arriving at, the following bases of valuing interests in the equity share capital of companies which also have prior ranking share capital:

    a assets basis.

    b dividend yield basis.

    c capitalization of earnings basis.

    d break-up basis.

(Institute of Chartered Accountants of Scotland, Examination Part V, April 1969—Advanced Accounting II)

4 A capital reconstruction may be carried out for a number of reasons and involves a variety of problems.

REQUIRED:

    1 State five major objectives to be achieved by capital reconstructions.

    2 State to what particular matters you would have regard in allocating a loss on reconstruction.

(Institute of Chartered Accountants of Scotland, Examination Part V, September 1970—Advanced Accounting II)

5 The Balance Sheet of Essfore Ltd, as at 30 April 1970, is set out below. The debentures were due for repayment at par on 1 May 1970. A term of the trust deed governing the debentures provides for conversion of the debentures to ordinary shares at the rate of 160 ordinary shares of 2/- each for every £20 debenture, on the redemption date, at the option of the debenture holder.

Debenture holders whose holdings represented 75 per cent of the total debentures, exercized this option on 1 May 1970.

You are required to:

a calculate the capital gearing ratio of Essfore Ltd, as at 30 April, and as at 1 May, after the transactions detailed above had taken place,

b show the liabilities side of the Balance Sheet of Essfore Ltd, as at 1 May, and

c make comments to a prospective investor on the capital gearing of Essfore Ltd, at 1 May.

Essfore Ltd

Balance Sheet as at 30 April 1970

	£	£
Share Capital—Authorized		
7,500,000 Ordinary shares of 2s. each		750,000
100,000 10% Preference shares of £1 each		100,000
		£850,000
Share Capital Issued		
4,000,000 Ordinary shares of 2s. each		400,000
80,000 10% Preference shares of £1 each		80,000
Reserves		
Capital redemption reserve fund		20,000
Share premium account		50,000
General reserve		200,000
Unappropriated profits c/f		15,745
		765,745
Long Term Liabilities		
8% Debentures (secured on freehold buildings—redeemable 1970)		200,000
9% Unsecured loan stock (repayable 1985)		50,000
Current Liabilities		
Trade creditors	108,410	
Current taxation	32,890	
Dividend payable	7,500	
		148,800
		£1,164,545

	Cost £	Depreciation £	Net £
Fixed Assets			
Freehold land and buildings	400,000	—	400,000
Plant and machinery	350,497	98,306	252,191
Vehicles	17,469	9,439	8,030
	767,966	107,745	660,221
Trade investments			95,000
Current Assets			
Stock		240,765	
Debtors	140,347		
Less Provision for doubtful debts	20,218		
		120,129	
Quoted investments		23,216	
Bank and cash in hand		25,214	
			409,324
			£1,164,545

(Association of Certified and Corporate Accountants, Examination Section IV, June 1970— Advanced Accounting)

6 A company's share capital consists of:

100,000 ordinary shares of £1 each;

100,000 7 per cent redeemable preference shares of £1 each fully paid redeemable at a premium of 2s. per share.

The company had a credit balance on the profit and loss account of £60,000 and a balance on General Reserve of £80,000.

The company resolved to:

1 make a bonus issue of one ordinary share for every two ordinary shares held by the existing shareholders from General Reserve;

2 redeem the preference shares;

3 make a rights issue of one ordinary share for every three shares held (after the bonus issue) at a price of 25s. per share to provide part of the funds for the redemption of the preference shares;

4 issue a £50,000 8 per cent debenture at a price of 98.

The resolutions were duly carried into effect.

You are required to show:

a the ledger accounts necessary to record the above transactions making maximum use of existing capital reserves;

b the share capital, debenture, and reserves of the company as they would appear in the balance sheet after their completion.

(Institute of Cost and Works Accountants, Part III Examination, December 1968—Financial Accountancy (Second Paper))

7 There is set out below a summarized balance sheet of a manufacturing company.

	£'000	£'000		£'000	£'000
Share capital:			Fixed assets:		
Ordinary shares of 25p			Property as revalued in		
each, fully paid	600		1968		1,500
Reserves	700		Plant and equipment		400
		1,300			1,900
8% Mortgage debenture			Current assets:		
secured on property		1,125	Stock	690	
Current liabilities:			Debtors and pre-		
Bank overdraft	760		payments	930	
Creditors, accrued					1,620
charges and taxation	335				
		1,095			
		3,520			3,520

Profits have been rising steadily and for the year ended at the date of the balance sheet amounted to £240,000 after debenture interest and tax. The directors are satisfied that turnover and profits can be increased provided that finance can be obtained. The company's bankers, however, have indicated that, although they will be happy to continue to provide temporary fluctuating finance, they are not prepared to continue that part of the overdraft which has, in effect, become permanent. Other factors which may be relevant are:

1 The company's stock exchange quotation gives it a P.E. ratio of 15.

2 The plant is of a specialized nature, not particularly attractive to hire purchase or leasing financiers.

3 The products have a low material content supplied only on prompt payment terms.

4 The bank overdraft fluctuates by about £150,000 above and below the balance sheet figure, and bears interest currently at an average rate of 10 per cent.

5 The debtor and stock levels are reasonable for its type of trade and cannot be greatly reduced.

6 Apart from the need to repay a large part of the bank overdraft, the directors wish to invest a further £300,000 in expansion of the business.

7 The directors expect earnings, before tax, of about 25 per cent on the funds to be invested in expansion of the business.

8 Some of the directors are of the opinion that the additional finance should be sought from the existing shareholders and they have asked for your comments on making a rights issue.

REQUIRED:

1 Having decided that the finance should be raised through a rights issue, draft a report to the directors indicating:

 a the amount to be raised, and the reasons for selecting a rights issue as the means;

 b the terms of the rights issue; and c the value of the rights.

2 Attach to your report an amended balance sheet as it would appear if your proposals were put into effect.

NOTE: You may ignore the expenses of the issue.

(Institute of Chartered Accountants of Scotland, Examination Part V, April 1971—Advanced Accounting II)

8 Tyler, Carpenter Ltd are in business as builders' merchants and the following balances appeared in the books at 31 March 1971.

	£		£
Land and buildings (at cost)	91,200	Interim dividend	15,000
Investments (at cost)	54,500	Sales expenses	24,800
Debtors	24,900	Sales	909,200
Loan to officer	500	Interest	3,400
Plant and machinery (at cost)	32,000	Profit and loss account 1 April	
Equipment (at cost)	12,000	1970	33,600
Purchases	543,800	Share capital £1 ordinary shares	100,000
Stock at 1 April 1970	89,400	Creditors	29,300
Delivery transport costs	43,000	Cash overdrawn	49,500
Wages	82,000	Depreciation account—	
Salaries	51,600	Plant and machinery	4,000
Administration expenses	66,300	Depreciation account—	
		Equipment	2,000

It is decided to transfer £24,000 to a General Reserve and to declare a final dividend which will give a year's distribution of 25 per cent.

The loan to the officer was £2,500 when made two years ago.

Plant and Machinery is to be depreciated by £4,000 and equipment by £2,000.

Stock has been valued at the end of this year at £94,200 and bank loan facilities are available up to £80,000 at 2 per cent above bank rate.

The investment is for a fixed term expiring on 1 October 1973.

The company wish to engage in a modernization programme over the next 12 months costing £150,000 to maintain their present performance and regard £90,000 as the necessary working capital for the firm.

You are required to:

 i prepare the final accounts for the year, ignoring taxation, and

 ii comment upon the cash requirements of the company and the alternatives open in the light of advice that loans cost 10 per cent, that £1 shares, of which 400,000 are unissued, could be offered at 133p and that yields from shares of similar companies are about 16 per cent. Because of losses brought forward, there is a nil tax assessment for 1970-71 and the liability for 1971-72 is estimated to be £25,000.

(Institute of Municipal Treasurers and Accountants, Final Examination Part 2, May 1971—Accountancy 4)

9 The summarized Balance Sheet of Reorg Ltd as on 31 March 1972 was as follows:

	£
Authorized capital	250,000

Issued Capital and Reserves

	£
50,000 ordinary shares of £1 each	50,000
20,000 6 per cent preference shares of £1 each	20,000
10,000 8 per cent redeemable preference shares of £1 each	10,000
Share premium account	5,000
General reserve	100,000
Profit and loss account	55,000
	240,000
6 per cent Debenture stock	25,000
	265,000

	£
Fixed assets	80,000
Investment, £5,000 6 per cent Debenture Stock Reorg Ltd, at cost	4,500
Net current assets	180,500
	265,000

The directors decided to reorganize and simplify the capital and loan structure of the company by means of the following scheme to be implemented on 30 April 1972:

1 Pay off and cancel the 6 per cent Debenture Stock;
2 Redeem the redeemable preference shares by the issue of 1 new ordinary share of 25p fully paid and 80p cash for each share;
3 Convert each 6 per cent preference share into 4 new ordinary shares of 25p fully paid;
4 Make a bonus issue of 3 for 1 in respect of the £1 ordinary shares;
5 Convert each £1 ordinary share into 4 ordinary shares of 25p each fully paid.

Each step is to be taken in the order shown above. You are to assume that all agreements, resolutions, and notices have been dealt with, and there is sufficient cash available.

You are required to write up the Ledger Accounts of Reorg Ltd to give effect to the scheme (the cash, dividend and interest accounts are not required).

(Institute of Chartered Accountants in England and Wales, Final Examination, Part I, May 1972—Advanced Accounting I)

10 The two members of Plank Ltd require valuations of their shareholdings. Plank Ltd trades as builders' merchants. The Balance Sheet of the company as on 31 March 1969 is summarized below:

	£	£	£
Fixed assets, at cost less depreciation:			
Freehold buildings		100,000	
Fixtures and equipment		15,000	
Delivery vans		5,000	
			120,000
Goodwill			50,000
Net current assets:			
Stocks		150,000	
Trade debtors		130,000	
Balance with bank		18,000	
		298,000	
Trade creditors	110,000		
Corporation tax	28,000		
Proposed dividend (gross)	30,000		
		168,000	
			130,000
			300,000
Represented by:			
Ordinary shares of £1 each:			
190,000 held by Large		190,000	
10,000 held by Small		10,000	
			200,000
Revenue reserves: Brought forward			88,000
Balance for year			12,000
			300,000

During the 5 years ended 31 March 1969 the trading profits and appropriations have been very consistent and are expected to continue at the present levels. Profits for the year ended 31 March 1969 were:

	£	£
Trading profit		90,000
Deduct: Directors' remuneration:		
Large	15,000	
Others	3,000	
Depreciation	2,000	
		20,000
		70,000
Corporation tax		28,000
		42,000
Dividend—gross		30,000
		12,000

You ascertain that:
1 the freehold buildings have been revalued at £160,000 and could command a rent of £16,000 p.a. for use in the company's trade,
2 a company engaged in a similar trade, but of much larger size, is shown in the issue of the 'Financial Times' dated 31 March 1969 as having a price/earnings ratio of 8 and a gross dividend yield of 9 per cent p.a.,
3 Large could be effectively replaced by a man earning £10,000 p.a.,
4 depreciation and profits shown in the accounts accord closely with the comparative figures in the tax computations, and
5 take-over proposals or public issues are not under discussion.

You are required to write a report, supported by figures, giving your opinion of the values, as on 31 March 1969, of the shares in Plank Ltd held by **a** Large and **b** Small. The two holdings are to be offered separately to independent buyers.

You can make whatever assumptions you consider relevant but you should ignore the possible impact on the valuations of income tax, estate duty and tax on capital gains. Assume the rate of corporation tax to be 40 per cent.

(Institute of Chartered Accountants in England and Wales, Final Examination, Part I, November 1969—Advanced Accounting I)

Chapter 14: Published accounts of limited liability companies

1 How far do you consider the present system of Parliamentary regulation of disclosure in published company accounts to be satisfactory? To what extent do the recommendations of the Accounting Standards Steering Committee suggest an alternative method of control for the future?

2 Sandra Ltd is a company limited by shares, with neither subsidiary nor holding company.

You are required to prepare a schedule for the company's accountant setting out the matters which he will have to extract from the books of account of the company for inclusion in the Directors' Report for the year ended 31 March 1972.

(Institute of Chartered Accountants in England and Wales, Final Examination, Part I, May 1972—Advanced Accounting I)

3 You are required to state briefly how the following matters are to be shown in the published accounts of a company limited by shares which is neither a holding nor a subsidiary company.

   a £3,000 being the balance not written off the cost of making an issue of debentures. The balance includes £1,000 in respect of commission.

   b £5,000 expended in purchasing £6,000 nominal of the company's own debentures on the Stock Exchange, the debentures so purchased not being cancelled but held as available for reissue.

   c £40,000 being the charge on the profits of the year for Corporation Tax.

   d A loss of £20,000 in the value of the opening stock arising from a stocktaking error.

   e £1,400 provided for payment to the company's auditors being audit fee £1,000, taxation fee £300 and audit expenses £100.

   f £3,200 paid to the company's bankers being commission £200 and interest on overdraft £3,000.

(Institute of Chartered Accountants in England and Wales, Final Examination, Part I, May 1973—Advanced Accounting 1)

4 In the Statement of Standard Accounting Practice No. 2 the following terms are discussed:

   i   Fundamental accounting concepts.

   ii Accounting bases.

   iii Accounting policies.

You are required to—

   a define any two of the above terms;

   b indicate three fundamental accounting concepts which are regarded as having a general acceptability; and

   c write a short note on each of the three.

(Institute of Chartered Accountants in Ireland, Examination Part IV, Winter 1973—Advanced Accounting II)

5 O'Higgins Ltd., a public company, was formed in 1950 with an issued share capital of £500,000 in 10 per cent cumulative preference shares of £1, and £1,000,000 in ordinary shares of 25p.

On 1 December 1972, the company issued £1,250,000 8 per cent convertible unsecured loan stock for cash at par. Each £100 of nominal stock will be convertible in 1976/79 into the numbers of ordinary shares set out below:

On 31 March 1976	124 shares
On 31 March 1977	120 shares
On 31 March 1978	115 shares
On 31 March 1979	110 shares

The trading results for the company were as follows:

	Year ended 31 March	
	1974	1973
	£	£
Profits before taxation	1,000,000	916,818
Taxation	450,000	412,568
	550,000	504,250

You are required to show the information which is required to be given in the accounts in accordance with the Statement of Standard Accounting Practice No. 3 entitled, 'Earnings per Share'.

(Institute of Chartered Accountants in Ireland, Examination Part V, Summer 1974—Advanced Accounting)

6 Maryhill Blenders Ltd makes up its accounts annually to 31 December. At 31 December 1968 the net assets per the balance sheet were £1,423,347. Included in these net assets are the book values of the company's investment in three distilling companies, all incorporated in Scotland—Dram Ltd, Peg Ltd and Nip Ltd—none of whose shares are quoted on a stock exchange. Details of these investments are as follows:

	Dram Ltd	Peg Ltd	Nip Ltd
Ordinary shares of £1 in issue	750,000	500,000	2,000,000
Number held by Maryhill Blenders	50,000	100,000	100,000
Book value (cost) of investment in ordinary shares	£75,000	£100,000	£150,000
5 per cent preference shares of £1 in issue			100,000
Number held by Maryhill Blenders			1,000
Book value (cost) of investment in preference shares			£1,200
Undistributed profit at time of purchase (all prior to 31 December 1967)	£400,000	Nil	£800,000
Undistributed profit per most recent accounts received	£610,000	£350,000	£1,400,000
Profit/(*Loss*) for year before taxation	(*£30,000*)	£75,000	£640,000
Profit/(*Loss*) for year after taxation	(*£30,000*)	£40,000	£370,000
Dividend received during year by Maryhill Blenders		£6,000	£15,000

One set of accounts was received from each company during 1968. On the basis that the directors of Maryhill Blenders Ltd do not wish to value these investments show the information which must appear in the accounts of that company at 31 December 1968.

(Institute of Chartered Accountants of Scotland, Examination Part III, September 1969—Advanced Accounting I)

7 Pitch Ltd carries on the businesses of retail stationers and manufacturers of cricket balls. Its summarized accounts as on 31 March 1969 show the following position:

Balance Sheet

	£		£
Issued capital:		Freehold premises	100,000
240,000 Shares of £1 each,		Plant and machinery	70,000
fully paid	240,000		
Reserves	80,000		170,000
		Current assets	210,000
	320,000		
Current liabilities	60,000		
	380,000		380,000

Profit and Loss Account for the year

	£		£
Taxation	25,000	Profit from:	
Dividends (gross)		Stationery	35,000
Interim 2½ per cent paid	6,000	Manufacturing	20,000
Final 7½ per cent proposed	18,000		
Added to reserves	6,000		
	55,000		55,000

The turnover for the year from stationery amounted to £280,000 and from manufacturing £200,000.

The directors, at the beginning of the financial year, were Mr Charles (Chairman), Mr Douglas, Mr Arthur and Mr Peters. Mr Peters retired on 30 September 1968 and Mr Roberts was appointed to fill the vacancy on 1 October 1968. The directors' shareholdings at the beginning of the financial year were:

Mr Charles	10,000
Mr Douglas	8,000
Mr Arthur	5,000
Mr Peters	2,000

Mr Roberts owned no shares on becoming a director, but purchased 3,000 shares on 1 January 1969.

On 30 June 1968, 40,000 new shares of £1 each were issued at par by way of rights to existing shareholders on the basis of one new share for every five held. Each director took up his entitlement under the terms of issue. The proceeds of the issue were used to purchase additional plant and machinery costing £36,000 for use in the manufacturing business.

During the year the directors were advised that the market value of the company's freehold premises amounted to £150,000.

You are required to prepare the Directors' Report for the year ended 31 March 1969 for submission to the members in compliance with the requirements of the Companies Acts, 1948 to 1967. Your answer should cover all aspects required by the Acts and assumptions will need to be made where the figures and narrative in the question appear to be insufficiently informative.

Marks will be awarded for a concise clear presentation.

(Institute of Chartered Accountants in England and Wales, Final Examination, Part I, November 1969—Advanced Accounting I)

8 An old-established family business of wholesale chemists, selling to the home market only, trades under the name of Thrifty & Co. Ltd.

The shareholders are the Chairman, Albert Sturdy (all the preference shares and 40 per cent of the ordinary shares) and his three sons, Bernard (30 per cent of the ordinary shares) Charles (20 per cent) and Donald (10 per cent).

The final trial balance of Thrifty & Co. Ltd as on 31 March 1969 was as follows:

	£	£
Ordinary shares of £1 each, fully paid		20,000
8 per cent Redeemable preference shares, fully paid		8,000
General reserve		60,000
Profit and loss account (balance 1 April 1968 £8,600)		85,212
Freehold property—cost in 1932	21,000	
Plant and machinery—cost £34,000	18,000	
Motor vehicles—cost £4,200	2,400	
Quoted investments, at cost	6,100	
Loan to company secretary	2,500	
Stock, at cost	42,800	
Debtors	28,000	
Creditors		12,000
Bank overdraft, secured by floating charge		5,400
Cash in hand	200	
Additional revenue items:		
Salaries and wages (64 employees)	53,000	
Directors' emoluments	14,500	
Auditors' remuneration	1,200	
Legal fees	120	
Political contribution	42	
Bank interest	400	
Dividends from investments		250
Corporation tax—under provision 1968	600	
	£190,862	£190,862

The following information is relevant:

1 The loan to the company secretary is interest free and was made during the year.

2 Depreciation has been provided at the rates of 10 per cent and 20 per cent per annum respectively on book values at the beginning of the year on plant and machinery and on motor vehicles respectively, no additions having been made during the year.

3 Directors' remuneration has been paid as follows:
Albert Sturdy, £2,000; Bernard, £7,000; Charles, £4,000; Donald, £1,500.

4 Corporation tax of £3,600 is to be provided on the profits of the year.

5 The preference dividend for the year and a 10 per cent ordinary dividend are to be provided.

6 A further £2,000 is to be transferred to general reserve.

You are required to prepare the Profit and Loss Account for the year ended 31 March 1969 and Balance Sheet as on that date, together with a draft Directors' Report, showing only the minimum information required by the Companies Acts.

Comparative figures need not be given and you are to make such assumptions as are necessary.

(Institute of Chartered Accountants in England and Wales, Final Examination, Part II, May 1969—Advanced Accounting II)

9 You are employed as the accountant of *AB* Limited, a small public company, which manufactures desks and chairs. The Managing Director has asked you to prepare the published accounts for the year ended 30 September 1970, in a vertical statement form which will be easily understood by all the shareholders. The minimum amount required by law should be shown. The trial balance at 30 September 1970 contains the following information:

	£000s
Share capital (authorized, issued, and fully paid):	
5 per cent Redeemable preference shares of £1 each	40
Ordinary shares of £1 each	90
Administration expenses	32
Debtors	18
Creditors	15
Purchases of raw materials	193
Manufacturing expenses (excluding machinery depreciation)	50
Stocks at 1 October 1969:	
Raw materials	18
Finished goods	20
Work in progress	9
Factory premises, at cost	48
Sales for the year, net of returns	420
Investment income (gross)	1
Quoted investments, at cost	30
Interim preference dividend (gross)	1
Profit and loss account balance, 1 October 1969 (cr.)	43
Factory wages	86
Factory machinery (cost)	87
Selling expenses	21
Accumulated depreciation on factory machinery	20
Corporation tax payable 1 January 1971	12
Cash at bank	28

The following additional matters should be taken into account:

1 On 30 September 1970, quoted investments which had cost £25,000 were sold for £35,000 in cash. The market value of the remaining investments was £9,000. No entries had been made in the books for these transactions.

2 Administration expenses include £8,000 for one year's rent of new showrooms, from 1 January 1970.

3 Provision of £23,000 for depreciation on Factory Machinery. The company has previously calculated depreciation at 20 per cent of cost, but the amount to be used this year is based on 20 per cent of current replacement value, i.e. £115,000.

4 Provision of £10,000 for Corporation Tax based on the profits for the year. This includes tax in respect of the profit made on the sale of quoted investments.

5 Stocks at 30 September 1970 were:
Raw materials £25,000.
Finished goods £15,000.
Work in progress £11,000.
The valuations have been based on the lower of cost and net realizable value. Cost of the latter two items is based on prime cost plus factory overheads.

6 Proposed dividends:
2½ per cent on preference shares (making 5 per cent for the year).
10 per cent on ordinary shares.

7 A customer is suing the company for breach of contract and is claiming £9,000 damages.

8 The factory premises are considered to be worth £60,000, but no adjustment is to be made in the books of the company. Premises have not been depreciated in the past.

9 Included in the total of Manufacturing expenses is £7,000 for hire of plant and machinery, and £3,000 in respect of an agreed part of the Works Director's salary. An order has been placed for repairs and improvements to the factory estimated at £12,000.

10 Included in the Administration expenses total is £3,000 for Auditors' remuneration and £14,000 for Directors' emoluments. The latter is made up of £3,000 paid to *A* (Chairman), £6,000 paid to *D* (Managing Director), £4,000 paid to *B* (Finance and Sales Director) and £1,000 paid to *C* (Works Director). No fees are paid to Directors.

(Association of Certified Accountants, Examination Part IV, December 1971—Advanced Accounting)

10 The draft balance sheet of Fabricators Ltd as on 31 December 1970 was as follows:

	1970 £	1969 £
Plant and machinery, at cost	30,000	25,000
Less: Depreciation	15,000	11,000
	15,000	14,000
Freehold property, at cost	110,000	10,000
Quoted investment, at cost (market value £30,000)	—	25,000
Stocks and work in progress	48,000	32,000
Debtors and prepayments	34,000	23,000
Bank balances and cash	1,000	2,000
	208,000	106,000
Share capital—Authorized, issued and fully paid in shares of £1 each	50,000	50,000
Surplus on sale of investments, less taxation thereon	4,000	—
Profit and loss account balance	34,000	18,000
8½ per cent Debenture stock 1985 (secured)	70,000	—
Bank overdraft	4,000	—
Trade creditors	31,000	26,000
Taxation—future	10,000	5,000
—current	5,000	2,000
Proposed dividend (gross)	—	5,000
	208,000	106,000

Notes:
1 The following adjustments are to be made to the draft accounts:
   i further specific provision of £2,000 in respect of doubtful debts;
   ii provision of £3,000 to reduce a contract included in work in progress to net realizable value; and
   iii provision for a dividend at the rate of 10 per cent per annum.
2 Stocks are valued at the lower of cost and net realizable value.
3 Capital commitments amount to £4,000 (1969—£90,000) and the directors have authorized further expenditure of £2,000 (1969—£5,000).
4 There were no disposals of fixed assets during the year.
5 The rate of corporation tax for the year is to be taken as 40 per cent, and tax on the year's profits is payable on 1 January 1972.
You are required to prepare:
   a the adjusted balance sheet as on 31 December 1970, together with notes thereon in a form suitable for publication (the reports of the directors and auditors and the profit and loss account are not required); and
   b a statement showing the sources and application of funds for the year ended 31 December 1970.

(Institute of Chartered Accountants in England and Wales, Final Examination, Part II, November 1971—Advanced Accounting II)

Chapter 15: Accounting for business combinations
1 What are the principal aims promoted by a policy of expanding a business by take-overs or mergers? Outline the main strategies by which such a policy may be implemented.
2 Although there is a certain amount of overlapping it is common to consider the methods of defence open to a company against take-over bids under two groupings:
   1 Defensive measures which may be adopted before there is any real threat of a take-over bid; and
   2 Defensive measures adopted in the face of a take-over bid.
REQUIRED:
Make a list of methods of defence under each of the two groupings and write short notes on three methods of defence in each group. Your short notes should include your opinion as to any advantages and disadvantages of the methods chosen.
(Institute of Chartered Accountants of Scotland, Examination Part V, September 1971—Advanced Accounting II)

3 The Panel on Take-overs and Mergers has issued a booklet entitled 'The City Code on Take-overs and Mergers'.

REQUIRED:

1 Name any three of the bodies represented in the panel.
2 State to what extent the city code is legally binding.
3 State to whom the city code applies.
4 Give any three of the 'General Principles' laid down in the city code.

(Institute of Chartered Accountants of Scotland, Examination Part V, April 1970—Advanced Accounting II)

4 Profits forecasts in respect of companies are frequently required for disclosure to the public in formal documents.

REQUIRED:

1 State what you understand to be the extent of the reporting accountant's responsibility in this connection and to whom he reports.
2 State briefly the main points to which the reporting accountant should direct his attention prior to making his report.

(Institute of Chartered Accountants of Scotland, Examination Part V, April 1970—Advanced Accounting II)

5 The following information relates to Major Ltd, a quoted company, engaged in manufacturing:

1 *Summarized Balance Sheet as on 31 December 1970*

	£000	£000		£000	£000
Share capital			Fixed assets at cost		30,000
Ordinary shares of £1		5,000	*Less* depreciation		12,000
Reserves		14,000			
Loan capital					18,000
5 per cent Debenture			Current assets		
1973		3,000	Stocks	12,000	
6 per cent Debenture			Debtors	·9,050	
1979		5,000			21,050
Current liabilities					
Sundry creditors	8,000				
Corporation tax	800				
Proposed dividends	750				
Overdraft at bank	2,500				
		12,050			
		39,050			39,050

2 The turnover, profits (after tax), dividends paid, and the range of quotation of the shares over recent years have been:

	Turnover	Profits (after tax)	Dividends	Range of quotation
	£000	£000		
1966	32,000	1,100	20%	275p-325p
1967	37,000	950	15%	175p-225p
1968	33,000	1,300	15%	200p-250p
1969	39,000	1,050	15%	187½p-237½p
1970	38,000	1,200	15%	200p-250p

Note: Quotation in May 1971—225p.

Major Ltd wishes to acquire the whole share capital of a private company engaged in the same trade as itself, Minor Ltd. It wishes to do this by means of an exchange of securities. The following information is available with regard to Minor Ltd:

1 Summarized Balance Sheet as on 31 December 1970

	£000	£000		£000	£000
Share capital			Fixed assets at cost		3,000
Ordinary shares of £1 each		200	Less depreciation		2,100
5 per cent Preference					
shares of £1 each		300			900
Reserves		1,000	Current assets		
Current liabilities			Stocks	800	
Sundry creditors	1,150		Debtors	700	
Corporation tax	250		Investments (repayable		
Proposed dividends	100		within 5 years)	500	
		1,500	Balance at bank	100	
					2,100
		3,000			3,000

2

	Turnover	Profits (after tax)	Dividends on ordinary shares
	£000	£000	
1966	3,000	100	5%
1967	5,000	200	15%
1968	4,000	175	15%
1969	6,000	250	20%
1970	8,000	275	25%

3 A majority of the ordinary shares are held by present or past directors and their families and trusts. There are no corporate holders of the preference shares. 200,000 preference are held by a charitable trust, which uses its income to the full, and also owns a substantial block of the ordinary shares.

You are required to set out, with reasons, the terms of an offer which could be acceptable to the shareholders of Minor Ltd.

(Institute of Chartered Accountants in England and Wales, Final Examination, Part II, May 1971—Advanced Accounting II)

6 The chairman of B Limited has asked for your comments, as the company's financial director, on a suggestion made to him by the chairman of A Limited that A Limited should acquire the whole issued share capital of B Limited. Both companies are in the shipping and transport industries and their shares are quoted on the Scottish Stock Exchange.

The net tangible assets attributable to the respective ordinary shareholders, based on the audited consolidated balance sheets at 31 December 1971, may be summarized briefly as follows:

	A Limited £m	B Limited £m
Fixed assets, including ships, containers, vehicles and property	331	23
Trade investments	29	1
Current assets, less current liabilities	45	2
	405	26
Less: Loans	103	3
	302	23
Less: 5% preference shares	5	—
6% preference shares	—	5
Net tangible assets attributable to ordinary shareholders	297	18

The group profits, based on the audited consolidated accounts of both companies, and the gross amounts of the ordinary dividends paid for each of the five years ended 31 December 1971 were as follows:

A Limited	Group profit before taxation £m	Group profit after taxation and prior years' adjustments £m	Gross amount of ordinary dividend £m
1967	8.2	6.5	8.0
1968	14.2	12.9	8.0
1969	18.9	16.9	9.6
1970	18.3	16.5	9.6
1971	15.6	14.0	9.6
B Limited			
1967	0.7	0.5	0.4
1968	0.5	0.4	0.4
1969	1.0	0.9	0.4
1970	1.3	1.2	0.4
1971	1.1	1.0	0.4

The charge to taxation during the five years ended 31 December 1971 in both companies has been reduced by the application of capital allowances and of tax losses brought forward. This situation is likely to prevail at least for the year to 31 December 1972 when it may be assumed that the charge to taxation and prior years' adjustments taken together, will be about 10 per cent of the group profit before taxation for both companies.

The directors of A Limited have announced that they expect that the group profits of A Limited before taxation and prior years' adjustments for the year to 31 December 1972 will be in the region of £19.0 million and that they will be able to recommend payment of a dividend of 12 per cent for the year.

The directors of B Limited estimate that the group profits of B Limited before taxation and prior years' adjustments for the year to 31 December 1972 will be in the region of £1.0 million.

The authorized and issued share capitals of the companies at 31 December 1971 were as follows:

	Authorized £m	Issued and fully paid £m
A Limited		
5% preference shares of £1	5	5
Ordinary shares of £1	120	96
	125	101
B Limited		
6% preference shares of £1	5	5
Ordinary shares of £1	6	5
	11	10

In January 1969, £16 million of reserves in A Limited were capitalized and applied in the issue of fully paid ordinary shares.

The middle market quotations based on the closing prices, on the evening prior to your review, for the respective classes of shares of both companies were as follows:

	A Limited	B Limited
5% preference share of £1	67p	
6% preference share of £1		72p
Ordinary share of £1	264p	160p

The directors of A Limited are satisfied that A Limited has adequate working capital not only for its present requirements but also to enable the purchase, for cash, of the preference shares, but not of the ordinary shares, of B Limited.

It may be assumed that revenue savings of £200,000 before tax will arise in the year to 31 December 1972 as a result of the acquisition.

REQUIRED:
Prepare a brief paper for your chairman setting out a possible scheme by which A Limited might acquire the whole issued share capital of B Limited. Show the benefits of the scheme for

the shareholders of B Limited and give such ratios as you think might be helpful to your chairman.

(Institute of Chartered Accountants of Scotland, Examination Part V, April 1972—Advanced Accounting II)

7 A Limited and B Limited decided to amalgamate and form a new company to be named C Limited.

You are required to prepare:
a the ledger accounts closing the books of A Limited;
b the journal entries for the formation of C Limited.

The trial balances at the amalgamation date of the original two companies and the agreed values for amalgamation were:

A Limited	Trial balance £	Agreed values for amalgamation £
Share capital in shares of £1 each	8,000	
Reserves	11,000	
Creditors	3,700	3,600
	£22,700	
Land and buildings	5,800	7,000
Plant and machinery	4,400	4,200
Investment in B Limited, at cost, consisting of 2,000 shares	3,500	
Investment in D Limited, at cost, 6,000 shares	2,000	
Stock	1,000	900
Debtors	4,800	4,500
Cash	1,200	1,200
	£22,700	

B Limited	£	£
Share capital in shares of £1 each	5,000	
Reserves	10,000	
Creditors	2,600	2,600
	£17,600	
Land and buildings	8,000	10,000
Plant and machinery	4,000	4,100
Investment in D Limited, at cost, 8,000 shares	1,500	
Stock	2,000	1,800
Debtors	1,000	900
Cash	1,100	1,100
	£17,600	

Under the terms of the amalgamation it was agreed that:
i the values as shown above shall be used to decide the respective interests in the new company, C Limited;
ii the share capital of C Limited shall consist of 13,000 ordinary shares of £1 each to be allotted to the shareholders of the existing companies on the basis of the new values agreed;
iii the investments in D Limited shall be allotted as a scrip issue to the respective shareholders of A Limited and B Limited before the amalgamation takes place.

Note: Any problem arising from fractions of shares is to be ignored.

(Institute of Cost and Management Accountants, Part III Examination, May 1972—Accountancy 3)

8 Rich Ltd and Poor Ltd decided to amalgamate their businesses with a view to a public share issue. A holding company, Mix Ltd, is to be incorporated on 31 May 1969 with an authorized capital of 600,000 £1 ordinary shares. This company will acquire the entire ordinary share capital of Rich Ltd and of Poor Ltd in exchange for an issue of its own shares.

The consideration for the acquisitions is to be ascertained by multiplying the estimated profits available to the ordinary shareholders by agreed 'price/earnings' ratios. The following figures are relevant:

	Rich Ltd	Poor Ltd
Issued share capital:		
Ordinary shares of £1 each	£300,000	£120,000
6% Cumulative preference shares of £1 each	—	£100,000
5% Debentures, redeemable in 1990	—	£80,000
Estimated annual maintainable profits, before deduction of debenture interest and taxation	£60,000	£24,000
Price/earnings ratios	15	10

The shares in the holding company are to be issued to members of the subsidiaries on 1 June 1969 at a premium of 5/- a share and thereafter these shares will be marketable on the Stock Exchange.

It is anticipated that the merger will achieve significant economies but will necessitate additional working capital. Accordingly, it is planned that on 31 December 1969, Mix Ltd will make a further issue of 60,000 ordinary shares to the public for cash at a premium of 7/6 a share. These shares will not rank for dividends until 31 December 1970.

In the period ending 31 December 1969, bank overdraft facilities will provide funds for the payment by Mix Ltd of preliminary expenses estimated at £5,000 and management etc. expenses estimated at £600.

It is further assumed that interim dividends on ordinary shares, relating to the period from 1 June to 31 December 1969, will be paid on 31 December 1969 by Mix Ltd at $3\frac{1}{2}$ per cent, by Rich Ltd at 5 per cent and by Poor Ltd at 2 per cent.

You are required to project, as on 31 December 1969 for Mix Ltd, **a** the Balance Sheet as it would appear immediately after the fully subscribed share issue, and **b** the Profit and Loss Account for the period ending 31 December 1969.

Assume the rate of corporation tax to be 40 per cent and ignore income tax. You can make any other assumptions you consider relevant.

Marks will be awarded for clear, concise presentation of supporting notes.

(Institute of Chartered Accountants in England and Wales, Final Examination, Part I, May 1969—Advanced Accounting I)

9 The directors of A Ltd and B Ltd, after preliminary discussions between themselves, have concluded that it would be beneficial if the two companies were to amalgamate. The shares in both companies are held by the directors and their families. The two companies have never paid a dividend and because of the requirements of the businesses have, so far, been able to obtain the agreement of the Inland Revenue to this policy.

The directors have asked you, as an independent accountant, to prepare a report and scheme of amalgamation for their consideration. They have stressed to you that, since both companies carry on complementary general engineering businesses which do not compete with one another in any way, and since the founders and their families are still very active in the management of both companies, it will probably be best if the two companies retain their separate identities and existing organizations. They are of the opinion, therefore, that the merger should be effected by the formation of a new holding company which would acquire, in exchange for issues of its own shares, the whole issued capital of the two companies. If the merger is a success and the two companies continue to grow as they have been doing in recent years, especially in 1972, then the directors anticipate that the holding company will be able, within a short time, to seek a Stock Exchange quotation for its shares.

The most recent accounts, those for the year ended 31 December 1972 of both companies, may be summarized as follows:

Balance Sheets at 31 December 1972

	A Ltd £000's	A Ltd £000's	B Ltd £000's	B Ltd £000's
Fixed assets, at cost less depreciation:				
Land and buildings		49		47
Plant and machinery		174		145
Office furniture and fittings		4		3
Motor vehicles		10		8
		237		203
Current assets:				
Stock and work-in-progress	130		101	
Debtors, less provisions for doubtful debts, and prepayments	172		114	
Cash	3		2	
	305		217	
Less: Current liabilities:				
Bank	149		95	
Creditros and accrued charges	66		42	
Corporation tax payable 1 January 1973	17		16	
	232		153	
Net current assets		73		64
		310		267
Less: Deferred taxation:				
Corporation tax payable 1 January 1974	24		21	
Taxation equalization account	14		12	
		38		33
		272		234
Less: Finance company loans		100		100
Net assets		172		134
Representing				
Share capital:				
Authorized, issued and fully paid:				
Ordinary shares of £1 each		40		30
Reserves		132		104
		172		134
Commitments for capital expenditure not provided in the accounts		30		27

Profit and Loss Accounts for the year ended 31 December 1972

	A Ltd £000's	A Ltd £000's	B Ltd £000's	B Ltd £000's
Sales		680		600
Profits before taxation		85		75
after charging				
Directors' remuneration	41		40	
Depreciation	31		27	
Interest: overdraft	8		6	
on loans	8		8	
Hiring charges	5		4	
Audit fees	2		1	
Taxation				
Corporation tax	24		21	
Transfer to taxation equilization account	10		9	
		34		30
Profit after taxation retained		51		45

You are, of course, provided with detailed trading and profit and loss accounts for the ten years ended 31 December 1972 of both companies and given full access to all the books and records. You obtain the following additional information:

1 The directors of both companies have little personal capital other than their interests in the companies, and in the event of the death of any of them, the executors might ahve difficulty in obtaining funds to meet estate duty.

2 The fixed assets have been well maintained. In the case of plant in particular, enthusiastic attention to maintenance in the past has meant that items of machinery have been kept going well after their normal life had expired. To meet competition, however, and to cope with the expansion in business which they have achieved in 1972, and expect to continue in 1973, both companies are finding it necessary to spend heavily on extending their factories and on purchasing new equipment.

3 For the purposes of the proposed amalgamation the directors have agreed that the fixed assets should be valued by an independent valuer on a 'going concern' basis and that these valuations should be incorporated in the accounts. You have obtained a copy of the valuer's reports and his values may be summarized as follows:

	A Ltd £000's	B Ltd £000's
Land and buildings	150	145
Plant and machinery	250	200
Office furniture and fittings	5	4
Motor vehicles	12	10
	417	359

4 Your review of the accounts for the last ten years shows that the capital and reserves of both companies are fully employed in the businesses. In both companies turnover and profits have fluctuated to some extent over the past ten years but showed a moderately rising trend until 1972 when they increased sharply.

5 The loans from the finance company are repayable half-yearly by equal instalments over the five years commencing 1 January 1975. Interest is charged in both cases at a fixed annual rate of 8 per cent. The loans are secured by floating charges over all the assets of the companies.

6 The directors expect the sales and the profits before taxation for the year to 31 December 1973 to be some 10 per cent higher than those of the previous year in both cases.

REQUIRED:

1 Draft the scheme of amalgamation.

2 Draw up the skeleton of your report to the directors showing the subjects with which you might deal and the titles of the relative supporting schedules, including in your answer the complete schedule showing a pro-forma consolidated balance sheet of the new holding company using the figures available at 31 December 1972.

3 Explain in detail your reasons for selecting the capital structure you have chosen.
(Institute of Chartered Accountants of Scotland, Part V Examination, April 1973—Advanced Accounting II)

10 The directors of Screws Limited, a quoted company, and Nuts Limited, a private company, agreed in principle to each company acquiring a 25 per cent interest in the other. New shares were to be created for this purpose, and after the respective values had been finally determined any difference was to be settled in cash.

As a basis for negotiations the undermentioned values of the assets of the companies and those of Screws Ltd's subsidiary, Bolts Ltd, were agreed. Firstly share values were to be considered on the basis of the value of the underlying assets and secondly on the basis of the market value of Screws Ltd shares on 30 September 1970, at £1.1 per share and a notional market price for Nuts Ltd shares assuming:

   i maintainable annual profits would be £18,000,
   ii a dividend yield of 8 per cent covered $1\frac{1}{2}$ times by earnings, and
   iii Nuts Ltd would distribute this proportion of the profits by way of dividend.

The summarized Balance Sheets as at 30 September 1970, were as follows:

	Screws Limited Book value £	Agreed value £	Nuts Limited Book value £	Agreed value £	Bolts Limited Book value £	Agreed value £
Freeholds	86,000	120,000	50,000	76,000	—	—
Other fixed assets	104,000	92,000	64,000	52,000	30,000	34,0
Goodwill	30,000	40,000	22,000	50,000	36,000	8,0
Current assets	112,000	110,236	110,000	132,000	78,000	66,0
60 shares in Bolts Ltd at cost	80,000	—	—	—	—	—
	£412,000		£246,000		£144,000	
Issued capital:						
£1 shares f.p.	198,000		120,000		70,000	
Revenue reserves	84,000		56,000		16,000	
Current liabilities	110,000		70,000		44,000	
Proposed dividend	20,000		—		14,000	
	£412,000		£246,000		£144,000	

No provision has been made in the accounts of Screws Limited for the dividend receivable from Bolts Limited.

Ignoring taxation and the effect on the values of the respective shares consequent on the acquisition of the reciprocal holdings, prepare:

   a a statement showing the value per share of the existing shares of each company on the basis of the agreed value of the underlying assets;
   b a computation of the notional market value of the existing shares of Nuts Ltd; and
   c statements showing the number of new shares to be issued by each company and what would be the amount of the adjusting cash payment on each basis.

(Association of Certified and Corporate Accountants, Examination Section V, December 1970—Advanced Accounting)

Chapter 16: Published accounts of groups of companies

1 State the reasons why, in your opinion, the law requires a holding company to publish group accounts, and assess their importance to shareholders and prospective investors.

2 Expansion Ltd whose ordinary shares of £1 are quoted on the Stock Exchange at £4 each has just made an offer for the whole of the ordinary share capital of Stagnant Ltd. This offer on the basis of 1 for 1 was accepted and completed on 31 December 1971.

At this date the summarized Balance Sheets of the two companies were:

	Expansion Ltd £	Stagnant Ltd £
2,000,000 ordinary shares of £1		2,000,000
3,000,000 ordinary shares of £1	3,000,000	
Reserves	4,000,000	2,000,000
Current liabilities	5,000,000	3,000,000
	£12,000,000	£7,000,000
Fixed assets at Net Book Value	6,000,000	1,000,000
Current assets	6,000,000	6,000,000
	£12,000,000	£7,000,000
Market value at 31 December 1971	£12,000,000	£5,000,000

You are required to:

a prepare a consolidated Balance Sheet on a 'merger' basis,

b prepare a consolidated Balance Sheet on an 'acquisition' basis, and

c comment on the alternative procedures for presenting the combined figures, currently accepted within the accountancy profession.

(Association of Certified Accountants, Examination Section V, June 1972—Advanced Accounting)

3 How does Statement of Standard Accounting Practice No. 1 improve the presentation of information about associated companies? How does it compare with the relevant requirements of the Companies Act 1967?

4 How far do you consider that the International Accounting Standards Committee's Exposure Draft 3, *Consolidated Financial Statements and the Equity Method of Accounting,* is an advance on the ASSC's SSAP No. 1 and ED3? Ought it to have dealt more directly with the merger (pooling of interests) method of consolidation? Give reasons.

5 In the course of preparation of the consolidated accounts of Holdings Ltd, the parent of a group of companies, for the year ended 31 December 1969 the following matters come to your notice:

1 Arc Ltd and Bar Ltd have been wholly owned subsidiary companies for a number of years. Arc Ltd sells a substantial proportion of its production to Bar Ltd at a mark up of 20 per cent on its cost of production. At 31 December 1968 and 31 December 1969 the following amounts are included in stock and work in progress of Bar Ltd in respect of goods purchased from Arc Ltd:

	1968 £	1969 £
Stock	12,654	16,180
Work in progress	26,820	25,908

These goods have been valued at cost to Bar Ltd with the exception of goods included in work in progress in 1969 at a figure of £6,120 which had been charged to a contract on which Bar Ltd anticipates it will incur a loss. To meet this loss all costs charged to the contract have been reduced by a provision of 10 per cent.

2 Zuc Ltd is a wholly owned subsidiary company registered in and trading in a foreign country. The balance of its undistributed profits, which are all post acquisition, is converted to sterling at £245,000. Dividends from Zuc Ltd suffer tax in the foreign country of 15 per cent and this tax is not relieved against United Kingdom taxes. Remittance of dividends is strictly controlled by the government of the foreign country whose prior permission must be sought.

3 On 1 January 1969 Holdings Ltd sold an item of plant, which had originally cost £5,000, to Arc Ltd at its written-down value of £4,000. Arc Ltd charged the purchase price to plant account and calculated depreciation for the year on this figure. Depreciation on plant is provided, throughout the group, at 10 per cent on a straight line basis.

4 On 31 March 1969 Holdings Ltd acquired 100,000 £1 ordinary shares in Pan Ltd, at a cost of £175,000. The issued share capital of Pan Ltd, which is not quoted on any stock exchange, consists of 225,000 ordinary shares.

The following information is abstracted from the accounts of Pan Ltd for the year ended 31 December 1969:

	£	£
Profit before taxation		110,000
Taxation		50,000
Profit after taxation		60,000
Dividend for year—		
Interim paid 31 August 1969: 10%	22,500	
Final proposed: 10%	22,500	
		45,000
		15,000
Unappropriated profits 31 December 1968		195,000
Unappropriated profits 31 December 1969		210,000

REQUIRED:

State, as appropriate, in each of the above cases:

    1 the adjustments which would fall to be made in the preparation of the consolidated accounts of the group and the principles governing these adjustments.

    2 the disclosures which would require to be made in the consolidated accounts.

(Institute of Chartered Accountants of Scotland, Examination Part III, September 1970—Advanced Accounting I)

6 The summarized balance sheet of Repairs Ltd at 28 February 1972 showed:

	£
Fixed assets	581,500
Investment in associated company at cost	220,000
Net current assets	623,500
	1,425,000
Share capital and reserves	1,425,000

The investment in the associated company consists of 120,000 ordinary shares of £1 each fully paid in Drydock Ltd. At the date of acquisition by Repairs Ltd the undistributed profits of Drydock Ltd amounted to £360,000.

Repairs Ltd participates in policy decisions of Drydock Ltd through having a representative on the board of directors and is in a position to influence the amount of dividends paid by Drydock Ltd.

The ordinary shares of Drydock Ltd are not quoted on any stock exchange and no recent valuation of these shares is available.

The following particulars have been obtained from the latest audited accounts of Drydock Ltd for the year ended 31 December 1971:

	£
Issued share capital: 500,000 ordinary shares of £1	500,000
Undistributed profits	680,000
	1,180,000
Profit before taxation	225,000
Taxation	100,000
	125,000
Dividend for year, gross, payable 20 February 1972	75,000
Profit retained	50,000

Both Repairs Ltd and Drydock Ltd are registered in Scotland.

REQUIRED:

Show how the above information relating to Drydock Ltd should be presented in the published balance sheet of Repairs Ltd as at 28 February 1972 and its profit and loss account for the year ended on that date.

(Institute of Chartered Accountants of Scotland, Examination Part III, April 1972—Advanced Accounting I)

7 In preparing the consolidated balance sheet of L Limited as at 31 December 1969 you are required to show clearly what amounts, if any, you would include in respect of W Limited with regard to:

a cost of control or capital reserve;   b profit or loss;   c minority interests; under each of the following assumptions:

i   48,000 of the shares then in issue of W Limited were acquired at a cost of £75,000 on 1 March 1967; L Limited participated in the proposed dividend of £8,000;

ii 40,000 of the shares then in issue of W Limited were acquired at a cost of £60,000 on 31 December 1967; L Limited participated in the bonus issue but not the proposed dividend of £9,000;

iii 60,000 of the shares then in issue of W Limited were acquired at a cost of £80,000 on 1 July 1969; L Limited did not participate in the proposed dividend of £6,000.

The balance sheet of W Limited at at 31 December 1969 showed:

Share capital, authorized and issued:	£
Ordinary shares of £1 each, fully paid	80,000
Undistributed profits	24,000
7% Debentures 1990-98	40,000

The profits appropriation account, for the years ended 31 December, was as follows:

	1966 £	1967 £	1968 £	1969 £
Balance at beginning of year	16,000	22,000	43,000	28,000
Bonus issue of one for four— 1 January 1968			16,000	
			27,000	
Profit for the year	14,000	30,000	7,000	Loss (4,000)
	30,000	52,000	34,000	24,000
Proposed dividends	8,000	9,000	6,000	Nil
Balance carried forward	£22,000	£43,000	£28,000	£24,000

The only increase in issued share capital during this period has been from the bonus issue on 1 January 1968.

(Institute of Cost and Works Accountants, Part III Examination, June 1971—Accountancy 3)

8 The summarized balance sheets of Field Ltd and its subsidiary companies, Mouse Ltd and Water Ltd, as on 31 December 1970, and of its subsidiary company Rat Ltd as on 30 September 1970, were as follows:

	Field Ltd £	Mouse Ltd £	Water Ltd £	Rat Ltd £
Share capital				
Ordinary shares of £1 each	80,000	30,000	20,000	1,000
5% Preference shares	20,000	—	—	—
6% Preference shares	—	10,000	—	—
Share premium account	40,000	—	20,000	—
Profit and loss account	65,000	16,000	10,000 (Dr.)	800
Inter-company balances	5,000	25,000	—	600
Creditors	30,000	22,000	12,000	400
Corporation tax	15,000	4,000	—	—
Dividends—proposed				
Ordinary	6,400	4,800	—	—
Preference	500	600	—	—
Overdraft at bank	—	5,000	—	—
	261,900	117,400	42,000	2,800
Plant, at cost	90,000	40,000	10,000	—
less depreciation	30,000	15,000	8,000	—
	60,000	25,000	2,000	—
Freehold premises, at cost	40,000	30,000	—	—
	100,000	55,000	2,000	—
Shares in subsidiary companies, at cost	80,510	—	—	—
Inter-company balances	2,600	6,000	24,000	—
Stocks, at cost	30,000	25,000	6,000	—
Debtors	44,000	31,400	4,000	1,700
Bank balance	4,790	—	6,000	1,100
	261,900	117,400	42,000	2,800

The following information is available:

1 The shares in the subsidiary companies were acquired by Field Ltd:

	Cost £
Mouse Ltd—15,000 ordinary on 1 January 1966	30,000
7,500 ordinary on 1 January 1968	16,500
4,000 6% preference on 1 January 1968	3,500
Water Ltd —18,000 ordinary on 1 January 1967	30,000
Rat Ltd — 510 ordinary on 1 January 1960	510

2 The profit and loss account of Mouse Ltd had a debit balance of £4,000 on 1 January 1966 and a credit balance of £10,000 on 1 January 1968. On 1 January 1967 the credit balance on the profit and loss account of Water Ltd was £10,000.
The credit balance on the profit and loss account of Rat Ltd on 1 January 1960 was £200.

3 A cheque for £500 sent by Water Ltd to Mouse Ltd was not received by Mouse Ltd until after 31 December 1970.

4 The stocks of Water Ltd included £5,000 of goods purchased from Field Ltd who sold them so as to earn a profit of 20 per cent.

5 During the year Mouse Ltd transferred a machine to Field Ltd at the book figure of £1,500. This machine originally cost £4,000. The transfer had been recorded in the books of Mouse Ltd but not in those of Field Ltd.

6 Rat Ltd is a small marketing company situated overseas, the profit earned in the year ended 30 September 1970 being £100. The accounts are prepared by the accountants of the 49 per cent shareholder, whose own year end is 30 September. The current account with Field Ltd at 31 December 1970 showed a balance of £600. The only income ever received from Rat Ltd was a dividend of £102 in 1967. In view of the small amounts involved the accounts of Rat Ltd are not to be included in the consolidation of the Field Ltd group.

You are required, using the information given above, to prepare the consolidated balance sheet of Field Ltd and its subsidiary companies as on 31 December 1970, together with the relevant notes.

(Institute of Chartered Accountants in England and Wales, Final Examination, Part II, May 1971—Advanced Accounting II)

9 On 1 July 1969 Smith Ltd, which had held 80 per cent of the issued ordinary share capital of Jones Ltd for many years (both companies being engaged in the distribution and repair work of fire extinguishers), acquired 90 per cent of the issued ordinary share capital of Robinson Ltd, another old established company specializing in the repainting of fire extinguishers and the sale of motor vehicles.

All three companies enjoyed an even pattern of sales throughout the year.

The share capital and reserves of the companies as on 31 December 1968 were as follows:

	Smith Ltd £	£	Jones Ltd £	£	Robinson Ltd £	£
Share capital:						
Ordinary shares issued and fully paid £1		10,000		4,000		2,000
Balance of profit and loss account 31 December 1968	5,000		Dr 1,000		10,000	
Less: Dividends (paid March 1969)	2,500				4,000	
		2,500				6,000

The profit and loss accounts of the three companies for the year ended 31 December 1969 were as follows:

	Smith Ltd £	Smith Ltd £	Jones Ltd £	Jones Ltd £	Robinson Ltd £	Robinson Ltd £
Sales		60,000		20,000		20,000
Cost of sales		40,000		10,000		20,000
Gross profit		20,000		10,000		—
Franked investment income		500		400		20
Dividend gross from Jones Ltd (payable 1.1.1970)		3,200				
		23,700		10,400		20
Depreciation	2,050		300		75	
Directors' remuneration	5,000		100		—	
Loan interest	500		—		—	
Bank interest	20		20		5	
Audit	450		250		200	
General expenditure	1,680		630		100	
		9,700		1,300		380
		14,000		9,100		Dr 360
Corporation tax at 45%		8,125		—		—
		5,875		9,100		Dr 360
Dividends declared		5,000	(payable	4,000	(payable	—
			28.2.70)		1.1.70)	
		875		5,100		Dr 360

The following information is relevant:
1 Robinson Ltd sold to Smith Ltd, on 2 July 1969, a motor vehicle for £2,500, purchased for £2,000. Other inter company sales comprised invoices rendered to Jones Ltd by Smith Ltd of £1,000 and those rendered by Smith Ltd to Jones Ltd of £5,000 for goods supplied, none of which were in stock at 31 December 1969.
2 All three companies charged depreciation on motor vehicles at 20 per cent.
3 Directors' remuneration in the case of Smith Ltd includes the payment of a pension amounting to £250 to a director, who was formerly an employee, and who became entitled to it in the capacity of an employee.
4 Interest on loan was in respect of a loan repayable on 31 January 1974.
5 Auditors' remuneration includes £50 in respect of taxation services and £25 for out-of-pocket expenses.
6 No group relief arrangements had been entered into but, at 1 January 1969, Jones Ltd was entitled to the benefit of tax losses brought forward of £9,400.
You are required to prepare in statutory form the consolidated Profit and Loss Account of the three companies for the year ended 31 December 1969, together with such notes as may be required.
(Institute of Chartered Accountants in England and Wales, Final Examination, Part II, November 1970—Advanced Accounting II)

10 On 1 January 1970 A Limited held £100,000 ordinary stock in B Limited and 80,000 ordinary 5s. shares in C Limited. The shares in B Limited were acquired on that company's incorporation. The shares in C Limited were acquired for £30,000 in 1968 when the balance on the profit and loss account of that company was £4,500. A further 10,000 ordinary shares in C Limited were acquired on 30 June 1970 at a cost of £10,000.

Summarized balance sheets at 31 December 1970 and profit and loss accounts for the year ended 31 December 1970 are as follows:

Balance sheets:	A Limited £	B Limited £	C Limited £
Share capital	250,000	100,000	25,000
Profit and loss account	45,000	3,000	12,000
Creditors	13,100	18,000	7,200
Taxation	27,000	–	3,500
Inter-company current account	–	3,000	4,600
Bank overdraft	–	12,000	–
Dividends payable	25,000	–	3,000
	360,100	136,000	55,300
Heritable property—cost	70,000	40,000	–
Plant—cost	60,000	35,000	30,000
Plant—aggregate depreciation	20,000	15,000	6,000
	40,000	20,000	24,000
Investment in subsidiaries	140,000	–	–
Stock	42,000	31,000	8,000
Debtors	35,300	45,000	10,000
Inter-company current account	7,600	–	2,000
Dividend receivable	2,700	–	–
Cash in bank	22,500	–	11,300
	360,100	136,000	55,300

Profit and loss accounts:	A Limited £	B Limited £	C Limited £
Profit/(loss) before taxation	56,000	(5,700)	8,500
Taxation/(tax credit)	26,500	(2,000)	3,500
Profit/(loss) after taxation	29,500	(3,700)	5,000
Dividend from subsidiary	2,700	–	–
	32,200	–	–
Proposed dividend for year	25,000	–	3,000
	7,200	(3,700)	2,000
Balance brought forward at 1 January 1970	37,800	6,700	10,000
Balance carried forward at 31 December 1970	45,000	3,000	12,000

On 29 December 1970 C Limited sold goods to B Limited for £2,000, but no entry was made in the books of B Limited until January 1971. All goods are sold by C Limited at a mark up of 25 per cent on cost of production.

Depreciation in C Limited is calculated on a reducing balance method whereas the other companies calculate depreciation on a straight line basis. It has been agreed that, to bring C Limited into line with group policy, additional depreciation of £2,000 is required of which £500 refers to the year to 31 December 1970, accrued evenly over the year. Of the profit, after tax, of £5,000 in C Limited, £2,200 was earned in the period to 30 June 1970.

A Limited banks with the Giant Bank. B and C Limited both bank with the Perth branch of the Large Bank.

REQUIRED:
Prepare the draft consolidated balance sheet at 31 December 1970 of A Limited and its subsidiaries and the draft consolidated profit and loss account for the year ended on that date.

NOTE:
The solution may be framed in the form of working schedules.

(Institute of Chartered Accountants of Scotland, Examination Part III, April 1971—Advanced Accounting I)

Chapter 17: Accounting for company liquidation and receivership

1 To what extent does liquidation of a company displace the normal assumptions of conventional accounting? How is effect given to this displacement in **a** the final accounts for the period immediately prior to liquidation, and **b** the accounts of the winding up itself?

2 In what respects does receivership of a company differ from winding up, and how do the effects on the accounts differ between the two situations?

3 A winding-up order has been issued against Misfortune Ltd.

The following information is obtained with regard to the assets and liabilities as on 30 June 1971, the latest practicable date:

	£
Freehold premises (book value £30,000) valued at	25,000
1st Mortgage of freehold premises	20,000
2nd Mortgage of freehold premises	7,500
£10,000 8% Debentures carrying a floating charge on the undertaking, interest due 1 September and 1 April, and paid on due dates	
Managing director's emoluments (6 months)	1,500
Staff salaries unpaid (3 weeks)	650
Staff holiday fund (9 months)	420
Trade debts—good	2,100
doubtful, estimated to produce 50p in the £	860
bad	4,850
Plant and machinery at book value—estimated to realize £11,600	16,500
Bank overdraft—No. 1 account—unsecured	3,450
Bank overdraft—No. 2 account—advanced to cover 2 weeks' salaries	425
Cash in hand	55
Stock at cost, which it is estimated can be sold by offering a 33⅓% discount on cost price	3,390
Issued capital:	
10,000 ordinary shares of £1 each fully called up	
Calls in arrear amount to £200 of which it is estimated 50% are collectable	
Unsecured trade creditors	18,550
Unsecured expense creditors	1,200
Contingent liability in respect of a legal claim for damages amounting to £2,500, which it is estimated will be settled for £1,200	
PAYE, 1971/72	180
Corporation tax—for year ended 30 June 1969	350
Corporation tax—for year ended 30 June 1970	85

The reserves of the company on 1 July 1968 amounted to £500. During the three years ended 30 June 1971 trading losses amounted to £21,255, after charging:

	£
Depreciation	4,200
Directors' remuneration	7,500
Debenture and mortgage interest	3,750
Corporation tax	435

and crediting £3,000, being the profit arising on the sale of a freehold property.

You are required to prepare in the manner prescribed in a compulsory winding up:

a the Statement of Affairs, and   b the Deficiency Account.

Ignore any taxation implications of the terminal loss.

(Institute of Chartered Accountants in England and Wales, Final Examination, Part II, May 1972—Advanced Accounting II)

4 Down Ltd makes up its accounts each year to 31 March and has been trading at a loss. On 31 March 1970 a resolution for a voluntary liquidation was passed and the Balance Sheet as on that date was as follows:

	£	£
Capital and liabilities		
Paid-up capital		
10,000 10% Cum. preference shares of £1 each fully paid		10,000
25,000 Ordinary shares of £1 each fully paid		25,000
10,000 Ordinary shares of £1 each 10/- paid		5,000
		40,000
5% Debentures—1975	20,000	
Interest accrued	1,000	
		21,000
Creditors	22,500	
Bank overdraft	7,500	
		30,000
		91,000
Represented by		
Freehold property		22,000
Plant and machinery		5,500
		27,500
Stock	17,500	
Debtors	26,750	
Cash	250	
		44,500
Deficit on profit and loss account		19,000
		91,000

You ascertain that:

1 The debentures are secured by a floating charge on the assets and undertaking of the company.

2 The bank overdraft is secured by a fixed charge on the company's freehold property.

3 The Preference shares carry a right to a fixed cumulative dividend of 10 per cent p.a., up to the date of liquidation and on liquidation a repayment of £1 per share and no more, in priority to all other classes of shares. No dividend has been paid on the Preference shares since the one paid for the half year ended on 31 March 1968.

4 The creditors include:

	£
Directors' fees for one year	2,000
Rates for 6 months to 31 March 1970	250
Manager's salary for March 1970	350
Wages for 4 employees for 1 week	100
P.A.Y.E. for 2 months	650

5 The assets realized the following amounts:

	£
Freehold property	25,000
Plant and machinery	4,000
Stock	12,500
Debtors	24,500

6 The expenses of liquidation amounted to £250 and the liquidator's remuneration is fixed at £1,000.

You are required to prepare the liquidator's statement of account showing, in the order of priority, the payments made and your calculation of any calls to be made. Ignore taxation.

(**Institute of Chartered Accountants in England and Wales, Final Examination, Part I, November 1970—Advanced Accounting I**)

5 Primarily due to shortage of satisfactory labour, the shareholders of Bodger Ltd decided that the company should be placed into voluntary liquidation. The relevant special resolution was passed on 31 December 1968 and the declaration of solvency, filed the previous day, contained the following information:

	Estimated to realize or rank for payment £	£
Assets:		
Cash in hand		60
Trade debtors (book value £7,400)		6,200
Stock		2,000
Plant		4,900
		13,160
Liabilities:		
Bank overdraft secured by floating charge	2,800	
Unsecured loan—capital	1,500	
interest (gross) 9 months	90	
Trade creditors	4,700	
Rent—3 months arrears	300	
Rates—6 months to 31 March 1969	250	
Salaries—full-time secretary, 6 months arrears	600	
office staff, 1 month arrears	80	
Wages—1 week arrears	65	
P.A.Y.E. tax	120	
Audit fee	105	
Corporation tax—year to 31 December 1968	1,250	
Liquidation costs, estimated	750	
		12,610
Estimated surplus		£550

1 The share capital consists of 3,000 7 per cent preference shares of £1 each, fully paid, 10,000 A ordinary shares of £1 each, fully paid, and 8,000 B ordinary shares of £1 each, 10/- paid. The Articles provide that on a liquidation the preference shareholders shall receive a return of capital at the rate of 23/- per share in priority to ordinary shareholders but shall have no other rights. The two classes of ordinary shares rank *pari passu.*

2 During January 1969, the liquidator collected debts totalling £5,000 and on 31 January 1969 he complied with statutory requirements concerning preferential creditors apart from corporation tax, which was in course of being agreed with the Inland Revenue, and repaid £2,500 of the secured overdraft.

3 During February 1969, he collected the remaining good debts totalling £1,345 and on 28 February 1969 cleared the bank overdraft, together with accrued interest amounting to £85, and paid the agreed corporation tax liability of £1,150.

4 On 31 March 1969 he completed the sale of the plant and stock to a firm for a consideration of £4,750 and £1,900 respectively. This firm had taken occupation of the Bodger Ltd premises on 1 January 1969 and, when paying the completion moneys, account was taken of the rent liability and rates in advance at 1 January 1969.

5 On 31 March 1969, the liquidator declared and paid a first dividend of 15/- in the £ to unsecured creditors. The unsecured loan creditor waived his interest from 30 September 1968 and trade creditors were finalized at £4,755.

6 Calls were made on the B ordinary shareholders in order to obtain necessary funds and, on 31 May 1969, these were paid and the liquidator made all outstanding payments, including final liquidation costs of £960.

You are required to show in detail how the above transactions would appear in the liquidator's cash book.

(Institute of Chartered Accountants in England and Wales, Final Examination, Part II, May 1969—Advanced Accounting II)

6 The summarized balance sheets of PQ Limited and XY Limited at 31 December 1968 were as follows:

	PQ Limited £	£	XY Limited £	£
Authorized capital:				
7% cumulative preference shares of £1		–		150,000
6% cumulative preference shares of £1		25,000		–
Ordinary shares of £0.25		150,000		200,000
Issued capital:				
7% cumulative preference shares of £1 fully paid		–		100,000
6% cumulative preference shares of £1 fully paid		25,000		–
Ordinary shares of £0.25		100,000		150,000
Profit and loss account balance		–		15,400
6% Debentures		40,000		–
Trade creditors		39,000		37,000
Bank overdraft (secured)		24,000		–
Provision for doubtful debts (including £3,000 for PQ Limited)		–		4,000
		£228,000		£306,400
Fixed assets at cost less depreciation:				
Buildings	54,000		61,000	
Plant and machinery	29,000		73,000	
		83,000		134,000
Goodwill		20,000		15,000
Investments:				
50,000 shares of £1 in MN Limited at cost		40,500		–
9,550 6% debentures in PQ Limited at cost		–		9,100
Current assets:				
Stocks	31,000		28,900	
Debtors	21,500		77,400	
Balance at bank	–		42,000	
		52,500		148,300
Profit and loss account balance		32,000		–
		£228,000		£306,400

PQ Limited owed XY Limited £9,000 on current trading and this is included in the debtors and creditors of the respective companies.

The necessary meetings of debenture holders, creditors and members having been held, it was agreed that PQ Limited should cease trading at 31 December and go into liquidation on 3 January 1969 and XY Limited should take over the assets and liabilities of PQ Limited on the following terms and taking into account the following factors:

1 On 2 January 1969 PQ Limited paid into its bank account the following sums:

	£
Collections from trade debtors	2,500
Bad debt recovered	300

2 MN Limited had gone into liquidation on 31 August 1968 and on 3 January 1969 a final repayment of £0.1 in the £ was paid which was paid to the purchasing company on 3 January.

3 The assets of PQ Limited were to be taken over at the following valuations:

	£
Buildings	60,000
Plant	15,000
Stock	19,000
Goodwill	100
Trade debtors	At book value

4 The bank overdraft as on 3 January 1969 was to be paid off by XY Limited.

5 The debentures of PQ Limited (other than those held by XY Limited which were to be cancelled) were to be satisfied by an issue of $7\frac{1}{2}$ per cent debentures in XY Limited which were to be issued at an agreed value of 102.

6 PQ Limited's debt of £9,000 to XY Limited was to be cancelled.

7 In settlement of each £1 of their claim the creditors of PQ Limited were to receive an immediate allotment of:

two ordinary shares of £0.25 fully paid in XY Limited, followed by £0.3 cash, the latter to be paid by XY Limited on 1 February 1969.

8 Preference shareholders in PQ Limited were to receive two 7 per cent cumulative preference shares in XY Limited for each five shares of their present holding.

9 Ordinary shareholders in PQ Limited were to receive one ordinary share in XY Limited for every 50 shares of their present holding.

You are required to prepare:

a   purchase of business account in the books of XY Limited;

b   balance sheet of XY Limited as at 3 January 1969.

It should be noted that a recurring decimal of £1 is given in note 7 above. Taxation to be ignored.

(Institute of Cost and Works Accountants, Part III Examination, June 1969—Financial Accountancy (Second Paper))

Chapter 18: Analysis and criticism of published accounts

1 On what lines is financial analysis of published company accounts normally undertaken? What do you conceive to be the objectives of such analysis, and how far do you consider that current techniques are calculated to attain them?

2 In recent years a dynamic view of accounting has moved the published profit and loss statement into a more central position of attention than that of the published balance sheet. Explain the reasons for this change of emphasis.

(Association of Certified and Corporate Accountants, Examination Section III, June 1970—Advanced Accounting)

3 The managing director of the company in which you are employed as chief accountant has noticed the following quotation in a professional journal: 'The existence of a sufficient amount of working capital is essential to the continued well-being of a company.'

You are required to write a report to the managing director setting out—

a   the principal factors which determine the optimum level of working capital;

b   the significance of the working capital ratio; and

c   the accountant's responsibilities in relation to the maintenance of adequate working capital.

(Institute of Chartered Accountants in Ireland, Examination Part V, Summer 1974—Advanced Accounting)

4 From the comments in the financial press on companies' results it seems clear that the price-earnings ratio is regarded as a much more important guide for investors than the dividend yield.

REQUIRED:

1   Define   a price-earnings ratio, and

b dividend yield.

2   Explain the arithmetical relationship between the price-earnings ratio and the dividend yield.

3   Comment on the relative importance of the price-earnings ratio and the dividend yield in valuing quoted and unquoted equity shares.

(Institute of Chartered Accountants of Scotland, Part V Examination, September 1972—Advanced Accounting II)

5 The summarized balance sheet and accounts of Steel Components Ltd for the year ended 31 December 1970 with corresponding figures for the previous year are as follows:

Balance Sheet at 31 December 1970

	1970 £	£	1969 £	£
Fixed assets				
(At cost less depreciation)				
Property	140,000		120,000	
Plant	410,000		320,000	
		550,000		440,000
Current assets				
Stock	285,000		210,000	
Trade debtors	260,000		190,000	
Other debtors	15,000		10,000	
Investments	—		30,000	
Bank	10,000		30,000	
		570,000		470,000
Total assets		1,120,000		910,000
Current liabilities				
Trade creditors	280,000		140,000	
Other creditors	25,000		20,000	
Current tax	40,000		30,000	
Corporation tax	50,000		40,000	
Final dividend—proposed	30,000		20,000	
		425,000		250,000
		695,000		660,000
Representing—				
Share capital—400,000 shares of £1				
each, fully paid		400,000		400,000
Revenue reserves		195,000		160,000
		595,000		560,000
Debenture		100,000		100,000
		695,000		660,000

Trading and Profit and Loss Account for the year ended 31 December 1970

	1970 £	1969 £
Sales (all credit)	1,500,000	1,200,000
Cost of sales	1,080,000	900,000
Gross profit	420,000	300,000
Overhead expenses	290,000	200,000
Net profit before tax	130,000	100,000
Taxation	55,000	42,000
	75,000	58,000
Dividends—paid and proposed	40,000	30,000
	35,000	28,000

Using accounting ratios, comment on the changes between the two years disclosed by the figures above.

(Institute of Chartered Accountants in England and Wales, Final Examination, Part I, May 1971—Advanced Accounting I)

6 The figures shown below give information required by the Companies Acts. How far are they of use to shareholders or prospective shareholders? Do you consider the ordinary shares to be a sound long term investment and what ratios would you use in your evaluation?

Trading and Profit and Loss Accounts

	1969 £	£	1970 £	£	1971 £	£
Sales		1,342,190		1,563,420		2,927,570
Less						
Directors' emoluments	70,000		70,000		70,000	
Auditors' fees, etc.	5,000		5,250		5,500	
Cost of hiring equipment	4,000		8,000		17,550	
Interest on debentures	27,000		27,000		27,000	
Banks & short term loans	9,100		16,235		12,545	
Depreciation of fixed assets	5,250		5,250		2,365	
Other trading expenses	1,109,140	1,229,490	1,426,135	1,557,870	2,707,460	2,842,420
Net trading profit		112,700		5,550		85,150
Add						
Net profit on sale of assets not otherwise applied		–		–		5,000
		112,700		5,550		90,150
Less Corporation tax		55,180		2,450		40,550
Balance available for appropriation		57,520		3,100		49,600
Add						
Balance from previous year		3,000		1,020		–
		60,520		4,120		49,600
Less						
Transfer to or from (cr) reserves		3,500		23,880 cr		6,000
Dividends on ordinary shares		56,000 8%		28,000 4%		42,000 6%
Balance unappropriated–c/fwd		1,020		–		1,600

Balance Sheets

	1969 £	1970 £	1971 £
Liabilities			
Capital–£1 ordinary shares fully paid	700,000	700,000	700,000
Reserves	94,200	65,790	325,830
Unappropriated profit	1,020	–	1,600
Loans–			
Debenture stock 1980/85	350,000	350,000	350,000
Bank loan	136,470	204,550	165,560
Current liabilities– trade creditors	610,660	620,990	631,160
	1,892,350	1,941,330	2,174,150
Assets			
Premises	457,660	455,060	344,350
Plant and equipment	109,440	103,750	82,225
Vehicles and loose plant	91,000	84,770	60,425
Debtors	556,360	598,290	813,370
Stocks	677,160	698,850	873,050
Cash in hand	730	610	730
	1,892,350	1,941,330	2,174,150

(Institute of Municipal Treasurers and Accountants, Final Examination Part 2, November 1971–Accountancy 3)

7 Oriental Enterprises Ltd has a subsidiary company, Confucian Ltd, of which it owns 55 per cent of the ordinary shares. Confucian Ltd has enjoyed a marked degree of autonomy in the past, but recently its managing director has retired suddenly because of ill health. As a preliminary to further investigation the chairman of Oriental Enterprises Ltd has asked you to report to him on the current situation of Confucian Ltd, as revealed by the information set out below:

Confucian Ltd

Balance Sheet as at 31 March

	1970 £	1971 £
Ordinary share capital	150,000	150,000
General reserve	35,000	40,000
Profit and loss a/c	4,880	5,240
Debentures (secured on land and buildings)	50,000	25,000
Trade creditors	32,790	58,520
Current taxation	8,000	10,000
Dividend payable	15,000	15,000
Bank overdraft	—	50,000
	£295,670	£353,760

	£	£
Land and buildings (revalued 1970)	75,000	75,000
Plant (cost less depreciation to date)	65,000	113,000
Vehicles	10,000	12,000
Stock	50,940	73,235
Debtors	49,730	60,525
Quoted investments	44,000	20,000
Cash	1,000	—
	£295,670	£353,760

Sales revenue for the year to 31 March 1971 was £240,000. Depreciation for the same period on plant was £9,750, and vans £4,000.

(Association of Certified Accountants, Examination Section V, June 1971—Advanced Accounting)

8 The following information relates to New Products Ltd, a private company in the United Kingdom.

Balance Sheet at 31 July 1972

	£		£	£
Share Capital Issued		**Fixed Assets**		
25,000 10% Preference shares	25,000	Land & Buildings at		
50,000 Ordinary shares of £1	50,000	cost		40,000
Reserves	60,000	Plant & Machinery at		
Current liabilities		cost	70,000	
Creditors	153,000	*Less* depreciation	40,000	
Taxation	7,000			30,000
				70,000
		Current Assets		
		Stock	130,000	
		Debtors	70,000	
		Cash	25,000	
				225,000
	£295,000			£295,000

Year ended 31 July	Profit before depreciation and tax	Depreciation	Tax provision	Net
	£	£	£	£
1968	10,000	2,000	2,000	6,000
1969	12,000	3,000	3,000	6,000
1970	20,000	8,000	4,000	8,000
1971	25,000	12,000	5,000	8,000
1972	35,000	12,000	7,000	16,000

The stock has been valued at the lower of cost or market value. Its current replacement cost would be £150,000. Land and Buildings have been revalued on a going concern basis at £60,000; or if sold as house building land for which planning permission has been obtained, at £120,000. No ordinary dividends have been paid in recent years but in future 50 per cent of the available profit will be distributed. The preference shares are cumulative and redeemable at the option of the company in 1975.

You are required to:
- a define Dividend Yield, Price/Earnings Ratio and Earnings Yield,
- b value a holding of 1,000 ordinary shares stating clearly any assumptions you make, and
- c advise a client on the amount he should pay for the whole of the share capital.

(Association of Certified Accountants, Examination Section V, December 1972—Advanced Accounting)

9 Statistics in respect of a quoted company include the following:

1 Net current assets: fixed assets ratio	0.7 : 1
2 Working capital ratio	1.6 : 1
3 Current ratio	1.1 : 1
4 Stock turnover ratio	6
5 Debtors' turnover ratio	4
6 Net equity income: equity capital employed percentage	10%
7 Ordinary dividend cover	1.1 times
8 Ordinary dividend yield	3.3%

The capital structure of the company is:

	£
5% Preference shares of £1 each	700,000
Ordinary shares of £1 each	1,200,000
Reserves	3,200,000
	5,100,000

REQUIRED:
Draft the balance sheet and trading and profit and loss account of the company in brief form, inserting as necessary balancing figures in the balance sheet for cash, and in the profit and loss account for a expenses other than purchases, and b taxation.

(Institute of Chartered Accountants of Scotland, Examination Part V, September 1970—Advanced Accounting II)

10 The following Consolidated Profit and Loss Account, Balance Sheet and notes thereon have been taken from the published accounts of a quoted company. The annual report did not include a source and application of funds statement.

You are required to:
- a prepare a source and application of funds statement for the year ended 30 September 1969.
- b show the additional information which would appear in a source and application of cash statement for the same period.
- c comment on the information revealed by your statement under a above.

Consolidated Profit and Loss Account — Year ended 30 September 1969

	Notes	£	£	1968 £	£
Trading profit for the year	2		58,989		38,963
Miscellaneous income	3		1,428		1,939
Profit before taxation			60,417		40,902
Taxation based on this profit					
Corporation tax	4	32,000		17,050	
Less Adjustment of previous year		1,674		1,573	
			30,326		15,477
Profit after taxation			30,091		25,425
Adjustment of furnace relining provision			—		31,000
Net profit of the group			£30,091		£56,425
Dealt with as follows:					
Dividends			—		56,000
Added to unappropriated profits (balance sheet Note 2)			30,091		425
			£30,091		£56,425

Notes forming part of the Consolidated Profit and Loss Account — Year ended 30 September 1969

1 Turnover

		1968
Total turnover	£4,317,247	£3,568,323

The turnover stated is the amount receivable in respect of the year for goods and services supplied.

2 Trading profit

	£	1968 £
This is after charging:		
Depreciation	53,607	61,048
Less Withdrawal from investment grants reserve	895	955
	£52,712	£60,093
Furnace relining provision	18,496	9,565
Hire of plant	3,432	1,705
Auditors' remuneration	1,450	1,250
Bank interest paid	8,906	1,350
Directors:		
Fees	500	500
Other emoluments	15,102	15,566

The Chairman's emoluments were £1,000 (1968, £1,000) and the highest paid Director received £7,811 (1968, £6,293).

	Number	1968 Number
Other Directors received: Between Nil and £2,500	1	—
£2,500 and £5,000	1	1
£5,000 and £7,500	—	1

3 Miscellaneous Income

	£	1968 £
Interest on tax reserve certificates	898	1,433
Rent received	530	506
	£1,428	£1,939

4 Taxation

Corporation tax payable 1 January 1971, has been provided at the rate of 45% (1968, $42\frac{1}{2}$%).

Consolidated Balance Sheet 30 September 1969

	Notes	£	£	1968 £	£
Issued capital					
Shares of 2/- each, fully paid			800,000		800,000
Capital reserve	1		17,031		18,142
Revenue reserve	2		285,038		254,947
Total funds employed			£1,102,069		£1,073,089
Fixed assets	3				
Freehold land and buildings		278,228		219,253	
Plant and machinery		527,757		565,102	
			805,985		784,355
Current assets					
Stock	5	363,916		226,292	
Debtors	6	736,223		584,563	
Tax reserve certificates		–		24,152	
Cash		441		263	
		1,100,580		835,270	
Less Current liabilities					
Bank overdraft		189,989		144,536	
Creditors		545,188		302,136	
Furnace relining provision		36,893		23,761	
Corporation tax payable:					
1 January 1970		22,303		33,380	
1 January 1971		32,000		32,600	
Proposed dividend		–		32,000	
		826,373		568,413	
Net current assets			274,207		266,857
Goodwill, arising on consolidation			21,877		21,877
}Directors					
Total net assets			£1,102,069		£1,073,089

Notes forming part of the Balance Sheet 30 September 1969

	Group £	£
1 Capital reserve		
General—		
At 30 September 1968		–
Investment grants—		
At 30 September 1968		18,142
Year to 30 September 1969		
Transfer in respect of Capital Expenditure, *less* adjustment of prior year		(216)
		17,926
Credited to profit and loss account		(895)
		£17,031
As Balance Sheet		£17,031

The basis of calculation for the withdrawal from Investment Grants Reserve ensures that the amount of the grants received in respect of the assets will be brought to the credit of Profit and Loss Account over their expected life.

2 Revenue Reserve—Unappropriated Profits		
At 30 September 1968		254,947
Increase this year: Parent	97,524	
Less losses of subsidiaries	(67,433)	
		30,091
		£285,038

Appendix **601**

3 Fixed Assets	Freehold land and buildings £	Plant and machinery £
Cost or valuation:		
At 30 September 1968		
Valuation—1958	94,830	158,275
Valuation—1967	35,000	18,275
Cost	125,065	698,386
Additions	68,741	30,314
Disposals and transfers	(5,375)	(32,948)
	£318,261	£872,302
Depreciation:		
At 30 September 1968	35,642	309,834
Charge for the year	5,869	47,738
Adjustment on disposals and transfers	(1,478)	(13,027)
	£40,033	£344,545
Net book value—as Balance Sheet:		
At 30 September 1969	£278,228	£527,757
At 30 September 1968	£219,253	£565,102

The depreciation charge for the year as shown above is calculated on a straight line basis on the full cost of the Assets and is not affected by Investment Grants, which are credited to Capital Reserve (see Note 1).

4 *Receipts* from disposals and transfers of fixed assets

	Group	
Freehold land and buildings £		Plant and machinery £
5,000		23,000

5 *Stock*

Stocks continue to be valued at cost or, if less, at realizable value; overheads applicable to work-in progress and finished goods are included in the valuation.

	Group	1968
6 *Debtors* include:		
Investment grants estimated receivable	£8,887	£13,218
7 *Capital expenditure*	£	£
Contracts placed up to 30 September 1969 not included in these Accounts	14,500	1,000
Board authorization up to 30 September 1969, not contracted for at that date	1,000	75,000
	£15,500	£76,000

(Association of Certified Accountants, Examination Section V, December 1971—Advanced Accounting)

N.B. As an additional exercise, the reader is recommended to analyse the above accounts on the lines set out in Chapter 18, and to write a short report on them.

Index

210; of partnership, 216; of company, 269, 270; in financial planning, 304, 305; earnings, 305-311, 343, 347 (*see also* Earnings per share); unquoted holding of, in other body corporate, in published accounts, 337, 338; number of equity shares, in EPS calculations, 344, 345; defined for legal purposes, 408, 409

Essay topics and exercises; 514-602

Etor, J.: 76n.

European Communities Act, 1972: 323

European Economic Community: entry of U.K. into, 104, 513; proposed Fourth Directive of Council, 363, 364

Ex div., quotation of shares: 111

Exchange Control Act, 1947: 267

Exchanges: and accounting, 28

Excise duty: 85, 104; licences, 105

'Exempted' dealers in securities: 395

Exemption, certificate of: 259

Exemptions, from disclosure in published accounts: 358-361

Exercises: *see* Essay topics and exercises

Exports: in directors' report, 358

Exposure Drafts (ED), of ASSC: principles, 97, 341; ED3, *Accounting for acquisitions and mergers,* (1971), 341, 414, 415, 429, 432, 437; ED5, *Extraordinary items and prior year adjustments* (1971--withdrawn), 346; ED6, *Stocks and work in progress* (1972), 84-87, 92, 97-101, 341; ED7, *Accounting for extraordinary items* (1972), 346; ED8, *Accounting for changes in the purchasing power of money* (1973), 138; ED11, *Accounting for deferred taxation* (1973), 296, 349, 350; ED13, *Statements of source and application of funds* (1974), 180, 350, 351; ED14, *Accounting for research and development* (1975), 130, 131, 351; ED15, *Accounting for depreciation* (1975), 126-128, 351, 352;

Exposure Drafts (E), of IASC: E2, *Valuation amd presentation of inventories in the context of the historical cost system* (1974), 353, 354; E3, *Consolidated financial statements and the equity method of accounting* (1974), 355, 444-448

Extraordinary items: in published accounts, 331, 332; in SSAP No. 6, 346, 347

Farm: valuation of inventory, 89, 90

Federation of Stock Exchanges in Great Britain and Ireland: *see* Stock Exchange(s)

Fellow-subsidiaries: interests in, 411, 438, 439

'Fictitious' assets: 301-303: in published accounts, 335

Filing of accounts, of company: 257, 273, 324-326

Finance Acts: 1933, 256; 1965, 291

Financial accounting: defined, 1

Financial Accounting Standards Board: 69

Financial policy, of company: 304-311

Financial year: coincidence of holding company's and subsidiaries', 413; non-coincidence, 439

Financial year, in corporation tax: 291, 292

Finished goods stock: valuation of, 85, 86; in replacement-cost accounting, 143

First in, first out (FIFO): in inventory valuation, 90-93; in ED6, 98

Fixed assets: not dealt with by Pacioli, 9; amortization rule, 16; valuation of, 102, 110, 135; in replacement-cost accounting, 143, 144; in current purchasing power accounting, 158; in published accounts, 333; changes in, in directors' report, 356; inter-company transfers of, in consolidated accounts, 436

Fixed-return capital: in financial planning, 304-311

Florence, accounting in: 8, 9, 212 and n.

Forecasting, forecasts: 13; in financial planning, 308-311; in take-overs and mergers, 392-394; in City Code on Take-overs and Mergers, 403, 404

Foreign currencies: conversion of, 81, 189-197; basis of conversion of, in published accounts, 340

Forfeiture and reissue of shares: 264-266

Foster v. New Trinidad Lake Asphalte Co. Ltd (1902): 290n.

France: imputation system of corporation tax in, 483

Franked investment income, and payments, in corporation tax: 292-299

Freehold property: valuation of, 111, 112, land and buildings should be separately stated, per ED15, 127; in published accounts, 336, 337

Friendly society: 4

Full cost: *see* Absorption costing

Fundamental accounting concepts, in SSAP No. 2: 341, 342

Funds flow accounting: 176-181

Futures: sealings in, 86

Gambling, T.: 2n., 69

Garner v. Murray (1904): rule in, 250-253

Gazette (London, or *Edinburgh): see London (or Edinburgh) Gazette*

Gearing (leverage): of company's capital, 305-311; in financial analysis, 481

Gedge Report on Shares of No Par Value (1954): 320, 321

General Agreement (London Stock Exchange): 361

General Index of Retail Prices (RPI): 156, 157

General ledger: 35-39

General partnership' 214

(pooling of interests) method of consolidation

Position statement: 5; *see also* Balance sheet

Postulates of accounting: 2-5

Pre-acquisition reserves: of subsidiary, 419-424, 437

Preference shares: characteristics of, 268, 269; in financial planning, 303, 305; as bonus issue, 314; of no par value, 321; in published accounts, 332-334 holders, and published accounts, 472

Preferential creditors (debts): in bankruptcy, 249, 250; in winding up, 455, 456

Preliminary expenses of company: 263, 276, 301; in published accounts, 339

Preliminary report, of Official Receiver, etc.: in winding up, 450

Premium: on redemption of redeemable preference shares, 277-279; in published accounts, 334; *see also* Share premium (account)

Prepayments: 16, 22, 82

Pre-preferential creditors (debts): in bankruptcy, 249

Present value (discounted): 77; in hire purchase contracts, 82; in long-term contracts, 106-109; in fixed asset replacement, 113, 114; in goodwill valuation, 134; in economic theory, 138, 139; in take-over and merger calculations, 392-394

Prevention of Fraud (Investments) Act, 1958: 395, 396

Price/earnings (P/E) ratio: and earnings per share, 343; in financial analysis, 483, 484

Principal activities of company: in directors' report, 356

Principles of accounting: 2-6, 13-17, 70

Prior year adjustments: in published accounts, 332; in SSAP No. 6, 346, 347

Private (limited) company: 257, 258; issue of shares by, 262, 263

Procedural rules, of double entry: 15

Proceeds of disposal: of fixed assets, 122

Profit (or loss, where applicable): historical development of concept, 8-10; and prudence, 16, ascertainment from incomplete records, 24-26; on long-term contracts, 87; on maturing stocks, 89, in ED6, 99, 100; economic, in sole trader's accounts, 209-211; in partnership, 216-221; in company, 274, 275; for corporation tax, 291; relief for loss, 299, 300

Profit forecasts, in take-overs and mergers: accountant's report on, 403, 404

Profit and loss account: historical development of, 8-10; of sole trader, 23, 30, 33; in replacement-cost accounting, 144, 151; in current purchasing power accounting, 163-166, 167; appropriation section (or account), of sole trader, 211; of partnership, 216; of company, 274, 275, 284-288;

published, 327-332; *see also* Consolidated accounts

Profit-sharing ratio, in partnership: 216-220; if partners fail to agree, 221, 222; changes in, re income tax, 224, 225; revaluation of assets on, 235

Projections of profit: 133, 134; *see also* Forecasting, forecasts

Proposed dividend: 288, 289; in published accounts, 332, 335; in consolidated accounts, 417

Prospectus: 257-262, 395, 396; statement in lieu of, 257-262

Provisional liquidator: 450, 451

Provisions: for indirect taxation, 103-105; for other liabilities and losses, 105-110; in company accounts, 275, 276; in published accounts, 332-334, 336

Prudence (conservatism): convention, 16, 17; concept of, in SSAP No. 2, 342; in IAS1, 353

Public (limited) company: 257-262

Published accounts, of company: 11; exemptions from filing, withdrawn, 257; of company without subsidiaries or associates, 322-384; of groups of companies, 407-448, 485-503; their utility, 470-473; ratio analysis of, 473-484; illustrated, 485-512; future of, 513

Punched-card accounting systems: 62-64

Purchase method: *see* Acquisition (purchase) method of consolidation

Purchasing power of money: accounting for changes in, 68, 69, 154-175, 513 and n.

Quasi-equity: defined, 4; in linked financial and cost accounts, 39; in branch accounting, 188; in divisional accounting, 201

Quotations Department, of London Stock Exchange: 259, 362

Quoted investments: short-term, 81; long-term, 110; in replacement-cost accounting, 153; in published accounts, 330, 337

Railway companies: and development of accounting, 10, 11

Rate of return: DFC, in goodwill valuation, 134; in economic theory, 138, 139; conventional, on capital employed, 305; on equity capital, 305-311; in financial analysis, 479-481, 483

Ratio analysis, of published accounts: general principles, 473-475; measures of financial soundness and stability, 475-478; of efficiency, profitability and return on equity, 475, 478-482; of achieved or potential growth, 475, 482-484; illustrated, 485-512

Raw material stock: valuation of, 85, 86; in replacement-cost accounting, 143, 144

Rayman, R. A.: 181n.